Antarctic Ecology

Antarctic Ecology

Volume Two

edited by

R. M. Laws

British Antarctic Survey,
Cambridge, England

1984

Academic Press
(Harcourt Brace Jovanovich, Publishers)
London · Orlando · San Diego · San Francisco · New York
Toronto · Montreal · Sydney · Tokyo · São Paulo

ACADEMIC PRESS INC. (LONDON) LTD
24/28 Oval Road, London NW1 7DX

United States Edition published by
ACADEMIC PRESS INC.
(Harcourt Brace Jovanovich, Inc.)
Orlando, Florida 32887

British Library Cataloguing in Publication Data
Antarctic ecology.
  Vol. 2
  1. Ecology—Antarctic
  I. Laws, R. M.
  574.5'0998'9   QH84.2 .A58 1984 V.2
  ISBN 0–12–439502–3
  LCCCN 83–72134   57,689

Printed in Great Britain at
The Pitman Press, Bath

Contributors

W. Block   British Antarctic Survey, Natural Environment Research Council, High Cross, Madingley Road, Cambridge CB3 0ET, U.K.

W. N. Bonner   British Antarctic Survey, Natural Environment Research Council, High Cross, Madingley Road, Cambridge CB3 0ET, U.K.

S. G. Brown   Sea Mammal Research Unit, c/o British Antarctic Survey, Natural Environment Research Council, High Cross, Madingley Road, Cambridge CB3 0ET, U.K.

J. P. Croxall   British Antarctic Survey, Natural Environment Research Council, High Cross, Madingley Road, Cambridge CB3 0ET, U.K.

I. Everson   British Antarctic Survey, Natural Environment Research Council, High Cross, Madingley Road, Cambridge CB3 0ET, U.K.

T. D. Foster   University of California, Division of Natural Sciences, Santa Cruz, California 95064, U.S.A.

R. B. Heywood   British Antarctic Survey, Natural Environment Research Council, High Cross, Madingley Road, Cambridge CB3 0ET, U.K.

R. M. Laws   British Antarctic Survey, Natural Environment Research Council, High Cross, Madingley Road, Cambridge CB3 0ET, U.K.

C. H. Lockyer   Sea Mammal Research Unit, c/o British Antarctic Survey, Natural Environment Research Council, High Cross, Madingley Road, Cambridge CB3 0ET, U.K.

R. I. Lewis Smith   British Antarctic Survey, Natural Environment Research Council, High Cross, Madingley Road, Cambridge CB3 0ET, U.K.

D. W. H. Walton British Antarctic Survey, Natural Environment Research Council, High Cross, Madingley Road, Cambridge CB3 0ET, U.K.

T. M. Whitaker British Antarctic Survey, Natural Environment Research Council, High Cross, Madingley Road, Cambridge CB3 0ET, U.K.

M. G. White British Antarctic Survey, Natural Environment Research Council, High Cross, Madingley Road, Cambridge CB3 0ET, U.K.

Preface

Ecology is a youthful science and nowhere so young as in the Antarctic, where understanding of ecosystem structure and dynamics and of ecological processes is growing rapidly. These volumes are intended to indicate something of the opportunities and challenges inherent in Antarctic ecology. I hope that they convey the message that there are exciting and important studies to be made in the Antarctic, both large- and small-scale. I hope too that they succeed in drawing attention to the uniqueness of Antarctic ecosystems and their essential vulnerability to human impacts, thus emphasizing the need for adequate safeguards.

The Antarctic, that is the region south of the Antarctic Convergence, comprises one-tenth of the Earth's land surface and one-tenth of the world's ocean area; add to this sub-Antarctic islands and oceans and clearly we are dealing with a very substantial region. Developments in the last decade, including growing awareness of resource potential, both living and mineral, has led to greater support for research designed to improve our knowledge and to provide information that can be used both for management and conservation of living resources and to provide a baseline against which the environmental impact of future commercial developments might be measured.

The origin of this book was a suggestion in 1977 from Academic Press that I should update M. W. Holdgate's "Antarctic Ecology", which eventually led to the proposal for the present volumes. "Antarctic Ecology" presented the results of the Second Symposium on Antarctic Biology organized in 1968 under the auspices of the Scientific Committee on Antarctic Research (SCAR) and published in 1970. It had been preceded in 1962 by the first SCAR Symposium on Antarctic Biology; a third such symposium was held in 1974 and a fourth took place in September 1983.

The Antarctic lands are the subject of an unusually comprehensive and wide-ranging agreement—negotiated under the Antarctic Treaty—the

Agreed Measures for the Conservation of Antarctic Flora and Fauna of 1964, which apply mainly to land areas south of 60°S. In the seas whales are the subject of the International Whaling Convention. Other agreements for conservation of marine resources were concluded outside the Antarctic Treaty itself and two unusual Conventions have entered into force. The first is the 1972 Convention for the Conservation of Antarctic Seals, which came into force in 1978 and is unique in providing conservation arrangements allowing for rational commercial utilization, well in advance of any industry. The second is the Convention for the Conservation of Antarctic Marine Living Resources which was signed in 1980 and came into force in 1982. It too allows for rational utilization before a large industry has developed and its articles invoke ecological principles not previously incorporated in such agreements. This progress was only possible because of the advances in ecological knowledge during the last two decades and the successful implementation of all these measures depends on continuing ecological research.

The last ten years has also seen the conception and implementation of the international programme of Biological Investigations of Marine Antarctic Systems and Stocks (BIOMASS) under the auspices of SCAR and sponsored by other international bodies. The formulation of this programme depended on the accumulated knowledge of the Antarctic marine ecosystems and will itself greatly advance our knowledge and provide information crucial to the successful implementation of the 1982 Convention.

It seemed timely therefore in the light of these significant developments, to attempt to summarize and synthesize the present state of knowledge of the ecology of this vast region (40–50 million km^2) at the turn of the decade. I invited a number of colleagues to contribute chapters covering all aspects of Antarctic ecology. Most of the contributors are members of the British Antarctic Survey, two are in the associated Sea Mammal Research Unit, and I was pleased that a distinguished United States oceanographer, Professor Ted Foster, agreed to contribute a chapter on the marine environment.

The earlier volumes reporting on the first three Antarctic biology symposia tended to lack a well defined theme and the balance was unplanned, largely depending on what contributions were offered. We have had the advantage of planning a more balanced account and I hope we have succeeded although inevitably much has had to be omitted, and to some extent the content reflects our interests.

The Antarctic is an isolated continent, surrounded by a wide, deep and stormy ocean. All but 2% of this continent is ice covered and so life is virtually confined to the isolated nunataks, some unusual dry valleys, the coastal fringes, and offlying islands. The first volume addresses the ecology of these regions. Life on land and in inland waters is mainly influenced by

climate, soils and minerals. D. W. H. Walton describes the terrestrial
environment, its origin and special features, the macroclimate, and the
microclimate influencing plants and animals; he reviews the periglacial
processes leading to formation of various soil types and their age and genesis
are discussed. This leads into R. I. Lewis Smith's chapter on the terrestrial plant life, both native and introduced, which provides a comprehensive synthesis of knowledge of the origins and history of the present flora,
the diversity of species and phytogeography. He describes the vegetation of
the different Antarctic biological regions, its succession, zonation and pattern, both environmental and morphological. Aspects of plant biology,
such as phenology, diaspore production, germination, growth, standing
crop and production are covered, as well as physiological aspects including
gas exchange, translocation, and water relations; decomposition and plant
chemistry also receive attention and there is a discussion of survival strategies or adaptations. The micro-organisms, the micro-algae, and the invertebrates and their role in the various ecosystems are reviewed by W.
Block. These organisms are small and inconspicuous and so first he gives an
inventory by taxonomic groupings from protozoa to arthropods. A separate
section is devoted to the chemical, physiological and behavioural aspects of
invertebrate cold-hardiness, and another summarizes knowledge of
Antarctic terrestrial ecosystems, including descriptions of some recent
models. A chapter on inland waters by R. B. Heywood essentially gives a
parallel treatment of the evolution of Antarctic lakes, the aquatic environment and the organisms found therein. There are proglacial, freshwater
lakes and some other unusual lakes—saline, epishelf and volcanic lakes,
and other lakes, located miles beneath the continental ice sheet, never seen
by man but detected by remote sensing (radio-echo sounding). Knowledge
is accumulating on their biogeography, their physical and chemical environments and the ecology of their flora, microflora and animals.

W. N. Bonner writes about the introduced mammals of the sub-Antarctic
islands (the plants are dealt with in Chapter 2), ranging from mice to
reindeer, and including cats, rats and rabbits. There are interesting
examples of introductions which illuminate general principles and some
have led to ecological studies of great importance in their own right, for
example the introduced reindeer on South Georgia.

The second volume is mainly concerned with the marine ecosystems,
their biota and processes. The scene is set by T. W. Foster's chapter on the
marine environment, which outlines such unusual components as sea ice,
ice shelves and icebergs, the main features of the oceanic circulation,
namely the Antarctic Circumpolar Current, the Coastal Current and the
gyres and eddies that develop. The properties of Antarctic Intermediate
Water, Antarctic Bottom Water and Antarctic Circumpolar Water and the

mixing processes are introduced. It seemed logical next for R. B. Heywood and T. M. Whitaker to take a look at the marine flora, including the species composition, distribution and ecology of the phytoplankton, the ice-associated flora and the benthic flora. Environmental factors that influence physiology, especially macro- and micro-nutrients, temperature, light and the stability of the water column receive attention and in turn their effect on primary production by the various plant components is considered. An estimate is given of total annual primary production. A chapter on the marine benthic animals by M. G. White reviews their abundance and diversity, their affinities, and the fauna inhabiting that very unusual habitat, the sea bed beneath the *c*. 250 m thick floating ice shelves. A discussion of ecological strategies, involving modifications of development, growth, adult size and metabolism, permits some conclusions on adaptations to the Antarctic environment to be drawn.

The fish fauna is not very large and knowledge of fish biology is reviewed by I. Everson. He presents information on species composition and distribution and deals also with aspects of their ecology such as size and growth, reproduction, food and annual cycles. Adaptations to the Antarctic environment include stenothermy, freezing avoidance, metabolic adaptation and white bloodedness. A discussion of biomass and production leads to a brief introduction to commercial exploitation, which has already led to overfishing of certain stocks.

So far, with the exception of Chapter 4 on the introduced mammals, the organisms under consideration have tended to be rather inconspicuous as individuals. The next three chapters cover three groups of larger and therefore more conspicuous and often beautiful animals to which the term wildlife is appropriately given—the seabirds, seals and whales. J. P. Croxall has reviewed seabird ecology in a wide ranging contribution, which reflects modern interests. Again, he necessarily begins by summarizing zoogeography, taxonomy and speciation. Breeding dispersion and habitat lead, through consideration of the timing of the breeding season to patterns of breeding biology, eggs and incubation, the chick, fledging period and growth, and breeding success. An area in which great advances have been and are still being made concerns food and feeding ecology, involving studies of feeding methods and foraging range which are in the forefront of all seabird research. Non-breeding season events include the moult, migration and movements. Finally, information on seabird population structure and dynamics is presented and species and population aspects of energetic studies are discussed.

The biology of the six species of Antarctic seals is covered by R. M. Laws, starting with the breeding and non-breeding geographic distributions, then numbers, densities and habitat preferences. The ice-breeding and land-breeding species exhibit a range of social organization and behaviour which provide material for a comparison of mating systems and lead to a discussion of terrestrial breeding and the associated evolution of polygyny, and the several ice-breeding systems. Food and feeding behaviour, predation on penguins and other seals, diving behaviour, food requirements and energetics are related subjects. The timing of the breeding season and the annual cycle including delayed implantation receive attention. Information on life histories, pup growth and later growth, age at sexual maturity and senility is synthesized. Lastly, knowledge of their population dynamics is reviewed, bringing in age structure, pregnancy rates, survival, production and energetics.

The great whales are an exceptionally interesting group of animals which have attracted widespread public attention, and concern for their survival, and the Antarctic is their last major stronghold. S. G. Brown and C. H. Lockyer have contributed a comprehensive account beginning with their zoogeography, annual cycle, distribution and migrations. Growth and age, including fetal and postnatal growth of the calf is covered; reliable methods of age determination are now well established and allow them to draw up growth curves for older animals. Reproduction is an important topic, including the timing of the breeding season, the annual reproductive cycle and social structure. Feeding, food preferences and ecological separation are also dealt with. C. H. Lockyer has been much involved in research on their bioenergetics, and the amounts eaten, seasonal fattening, growth energy requirements, metabolic energy expenditure and the special demands of female reproduction are presented. Because of the effects of commercial activities many attempts have been made to estimate whale population sizes and biomass. It seemed appropriate to summarize the varied methods of estimating their abundance and the results obtained leading to conclusions on past and present numbers and biomass. In contrast to our extensive knowledge of the large whales, very little is known of the biology of the smaller species.

Too often specialists concern themselves with their own group of animals and I felt that a chapter drawing attention to the interactions between the various components of the marine ecosystem should be included. This is a system which has been much perturbed by human activities, first sealing, then whaling and now fishing for krill and fish. Some appreciation of the interactions is necessary in order to devise and introduce appropriate and wise conservation measures (as described in the final chapter). I. Everson agreed to attempt such a synthesis and has taken a fresh look at these questions. He broadly summarizes the food chain relationships, describes current ecological models and then presents a new interpretation of earlier work in the region around South Georgia, combined with more recent studies. This encompasses water circulation, nutrients and phytoplankton and the interrelation of krill and hydrography, phytoplankton, whales and birds. The overall conclusions are novel and as well as contributing to ecological understanding are very relevant to resource management.

This brings me to the final chapter on conservation written by W. N. Bonner. He touches on the meaning and need for conservation, in the special circumstances of the Antarctic and describes the potential adverse impacts of human activities. The best known impacts were from fur sealing, elephant sealing and whaling and he reviews the course of these industries and their effects, but points out that scientific expeditions also have impacts due to observation and collection and the installation of bases producing local impacts of varying severity.

The book was planned in 1978 and the intervention of lengthy Antarctic field seasons and last year's events in the South Atlantic has meant that the book has been longer in preparation than I would have wished. However, I believe that the chapters represent a definitive statement of the extent of knowledge of the region at the beginning of the 1980s. A standard treatment has not been possible to achieve. Because the state of knowledge differs from subject to subject, there may appear to be more or less emphasis on taxonomy, physiology, ecological processes, behaviour and so on according to the group under consideration. Also, as the pursuit of knowledge of the region is in some subjects still at an exploratory stage, there are some inevitable gaps. For example: there is virtually no quantitative knowledge and very little qualitative information on the ecology and biology of the cephalopods although they clearly constitute a very important component of the marine food web; work on processes in the fellfield ecosystem is just beginning; the bioenergetics and trophodynamics of the marine ecosystem are just beginning to be studied in a quantitative way, especially through the international BIOMASS programme; and ecological models of Antarctic systems are still conceptual rather than predictive.

However, there have been substantial advances since 1968 and I believe that most, if not all, of the significant achievements are discussed in this book. But there is still a long way to go before our knowledge is comparable with that of less remote areas of our planet. Probably fewer than 2000 biologists have worked in the Antarctic and more than that number have worked in some English counties. As in other parts of the world, geographical discovery has been replaced by scientific discovery. The titles of the papers cited reflect this fact and these references are designed to provide a reasonably comprehensive and up to date bibliography. For the future it seems likely that there will be an accelerated rate of research and development, not least because of the increasing attention focussed on the region by the events in the South Atlantic which began in April 1982 with the invasion of the Falkland Islands and South Georgia. All scientists must have been saddened to see this last major unspoiled region of our planet become the scene of discord and we can only hope that the Antarctic Treaty is robust enough to survive, so that ecological investigations can proceed, and provide the knowledge on which wise management of the region's resources must be based. There is ample justification for further research, both for this reason and because, as a reading of any chapter will show, there are still many purely scientific questions to be answered.

We would like to acknowledge help from a large number of colleagues in the preparation of this work, and especially the following:

D. W. H. Walton (Chapter 1) is grateful to D. W. S. Limbert and Drs R. I. Lewis Smith, W. Block and P. W. G. Tanner for their comments.

Many botanists involved in Antarctic or sub-Antarctic research have contributed towards Chapter 2 by offering helpful comments, either in discussion or in correspondence, and by making available certain of their unpublished work. In particular R. I. Lewis Smith is indebted to Dr V. D. Aleksandrova, B. G. Bell, Dr T. V. Callaghan, Professor C. H. Gimingham, Dr N. J. M. Gremmen, Dr M. W. Holdgate, Dr J. F. Jenkin, Dr R. E. Longton, Dr R. D. Seppelt, V. R. Smith and Dr D. W. H. Walton. W. Block thanks his colleagues at the British Antarctic Survey for many helpful discussions and provision of information for Chapter 3. In particular he appreciates the generous assistance of Dr D. D. Wynn-Williams for the section on microorganisms, and thanks Drs R. C. Davis, D. D. Wynn-Williams, A. J. Burn and Messrs J. R. Caldwell and C. C. West for allowing him to quote from their unpublished data. He is grateful to Dr L. Sømme for his comments on the manuscript. Finally, he thanks his wife for her help and forbearance in typing the draft of the chapter.

Professor R. J. Berry, Drs P. Condy and R. van Aarde read the manuscript of Chapter 4 or made helpful comments, or both. Dr R. van Aarde very kindly provided notes from Gleeson's thesis, which W. N. Bonner was unable to consult personally. He is very grateful to these friends for their help.

T. D. Foster is indebted to his collaborators in Antarctic research for helping him to develop some of the ideas expressed in Chapter 6, although he alone is responsible for any that may prove to be erroneous. He would like to thank in particular Sir George Deacon, Dr E. C. Carmack and Dr J. H. Middleton. This work has been supported for a number of years by the Division of Polar Programs, National Science Foundation, most recently by Grant DPP78–07797.

J. P. Croxall (Chapter 11) thanks D. G. Ainley, A. Berruti, I. Hunter, S. Hunter, R. E. Ricklefs, W. R. Siegfried, G. Thomas, W. Trivelpiece, N. J. Volkman and A. J. Williams who kindly allowed him to see their papers prior to publication. He is grateful to A. Baird and E. D. Kirkwood for considerable assistance with data compilation and preparation of figures respectively. R. M. Laws, P. A. Prince and J. Warham made many helpful comments on the manuscript whose drafts wer typed by Mrs F. Prince and Mrs C. Romm. He is particularly indebted to P.A. Prince for providing unpublished results, extensive discussion and above all for his contribution to the planning and execution of the studies at South Georgia.

R. M. Laws is grateful to colleagues who have provided information on unpublished work for Chapter 12, especially W. N. Bonner, Drs J. P. Croxall, G. L. Kooyman and D. B. Siniff. Anna Baird carried out analyses with him of extensive unpublished data on crabeater seals.

W. N. Bonner would like to thank particularly Drs R. Gambell, J. A. Heap, M. W. Holdgate, R. I. Lewis Smith and D. W. H. Walton, who all made many helpful suggestions for Chapter 15; S. G. Brown generously supplied data for the section dealing with whaling.

I would like to thank Roger Farrand and Konrad Guettler of Academic Press for advice and encouragement. I am greatly indebted to Mrs Marjorie Hallatt whose unstinting help in the preparation of the typescript is much appreciated. Tony Sylvester drew most of the figures, often from very rough originals. Finally, I would like to thank the authors for their contributions, which I believe to represent the most definitive synthesis to date on the state of the art of Antarctic ecology. They have accepted delays imposed by my other commitments, at least outwardly, with patience.

Cambridge   **R. M. Laws**
October 1983

Contents of volume two

Contents of volume one

The marine environment

T. D. Foster

1. Introduction

Although the ocean surrounding Antarctica consists of parts of the Atlantic, Pacific and Indian Oceans, oceanographers have found it convenient to refer to this circumpolar ring of ocean as the Southern Ocean. Figure 1 shows the geographic setting of the Southern Ocean in relation to the principal continental land masses. It also shows the mean position of the Antarctic Convergence, which marks the transition between the cold Antarctic surface water and the warmer sub-Antarctic water. Since this transition can be considered as an oceanic front, it has been termed the Antarctic Polar Front by some oceanographers. The Antarctic Convergence is not, however, a simple stationary front, but as Mackintosh (1946) has pointed out forms twists and loops that may extend as much as 150 km north and south and possible even forms isolated rings, much like the Gulf Stream system. Thus, crossings of the Antarctic Convergence may reveal the appearance of a primary and secondary front. The mean position of this zone of surface and sub-surface fronts, however, seems to be fairly well established (Deacon, 1964). Although the processes that take place in this region are still poorly understood and are variable in both space and time, the net result of these processes is the formation of Antarctic Intermediate Water and the sinking of water. Therefore, the term Antarctic Convergence seems to be appropriate for this region. The Antarctic Convergence forms the boundary between Antarctic and sub-Antarctic waters, but the Antarctic Circumpolar Current (or West Wind Drift) extends further north. Thus it is convenient not to define the term Southern Ocean too rigidly and to allow it to include most of the ocean up to the coastal waters of South America, Africa and Australia.

ANTARCTIC ECOLOGY VOL. 2
ISBN 0 12-439502-3

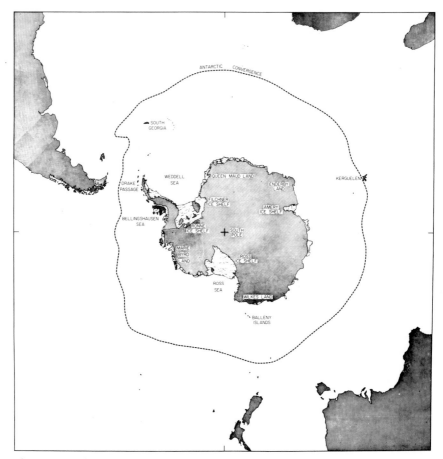

Fig. 1. Geographic setting of the Southern Ocean showing some of the principal features and the mean position of the Antarctic Convergence.

The bathymetry of the Southern Ocean is shown in Fig. 2. Three deep basins surround Antarctica: the Atlantic–Indian Basin, the Southern Indian Basin, and the South-east Pacific Basin. These basins are partially bounded on the north by the Scotia Ridge and Atlantic–Indian Ridge, the South-east Indian Ridge, and the Pacific–Antarctic Ridge respectively. These ridges and the Kerguelen Plateau tend to prevent the free flow of bottom waters and also even deflect the surface currents. The Drake Passage between South America and the Antarctic peninsula is the major constriction to the circulation around Antarctica and, as discussed later, has a profound influence on the oceanic circulation. The continental shelves of Antarctica are unusually deep compared to those of the other continents. In the Weddell and Ross Seas there are very broad shelves with depths ranging from 400 to 500 m. These deep shelves may have resulted from isostatic adjustment of Antarctica to its massive icecap, and from scouring by the Filchner Ice Shelf in the Weddell Sea and the Ross Ice Shelf in the Ross Sea, when their extent was much further north in the past. Thus the near-shore circulation can be expected to be quite different from that at lower latitudes.

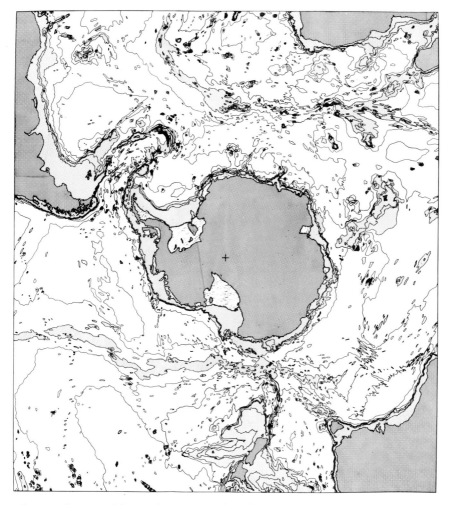

Fig. 2. Bathymetry of the Southern Ocean (after Glavnoe Upravlenie Geodezii i Kartolrafii, 1974). Depth contours every kilometre. Depths less than 3 km slightly stippled.

Environmental data for the Southern Ocean can be obtained from a variety of sources. Some of the most valuable sources are still the *Discovery Reports* published from 1929 to 1972 and in particular the report on the hydrography (Deacon, 1937). The Soviet *Atlas of the Antarctic* (1966), the U.S. Navy Hydrographic Office *Oceanographic Atlas of the Polar Seas: Antarctica* (1957), the U.S. National Center for Atmospheric Research *Climate of the Upper Air: Southern Hemisphere* (1969, 1971), and the American Geophysical Union *Antarctic Research* Series (1964–) are also useful sources. Physical and chemical oceanographic data from nearly all Antarctic expeditions can be obtained from the computer files maintained by the National Oceanographic Data Center (N.O.D.C.) (Washington, D.C.); satellite imagery, which is especially useful for determining seasonal sea ice cover, is obtainable from the National Oceanic and Atmospheric Administration, Satellite Data Services Branch (Washington, D.C.); and meteorological data from the computer files maintained by the various World Data Centers (e.g. National Climatic Center, Asheville, N.C.).

2. Ice Cover

Perhaps the greatest factor that distinguishes the Southern Ocean from the oceans in lower latitudes is the presence of ice. In the Antarctic glacial ice, mainly in the form of ice shelves and the large tabular icebergs, plays a much more important role in the marine environment than in the Arctic; however, sea ice is still the dominant influence.

2.1 Sea ice

The general distribution of sea ice in the Southern Ocean and its seasonal changes have been known for some time from scattered ship observations over many years. Through the use of microwave radiation measurements, that can penetrate the cloud cover to the sea surface, satellite imagery now provides nearly continuous year-round observation of the detailed changes that takes place in the pack ice. These observations have corroborated the previously obtained average ice distributions and have revealed many new details about the growth and decay of the sea ice field. Until very recently there has been little research into the dynamics of the Antarctic pack ice, which apparently behaves quite differently from the Arctic pack ice. Similarly, very little is known about the properties of the Antarctic pack ice within the ice field except for the observations made from ships that became beset and drifted with the pack over winter (*Belgica, Deutschland* and

Endurance). There have been, however, a fairly large number of observations near shore stations and at the seaward edge of the pack.

Our picture of sea ice in the Southern Ocean is thus rather incomplete; nevertheless certain general features have been ascertained. Figure 3 shows the changes in the sea ice coverage as determined by satellite for the period October 1973–August 1974. The general pattern of growth and decay has been similar in the years for which satellite imagery has been available, but there are considerable differences in the details. It is apparent that the ice does not grow and decay in a simple south–north progression and regression, but proceeds much more irregularly, especially in the Weddell and Ross Sea regions. In the Weddell Sea the pattern of growth and decay is evidently strongly influenced by both the atmospheric and oceanic circulation, which can be seen in the extension of the ice edge in the north, where

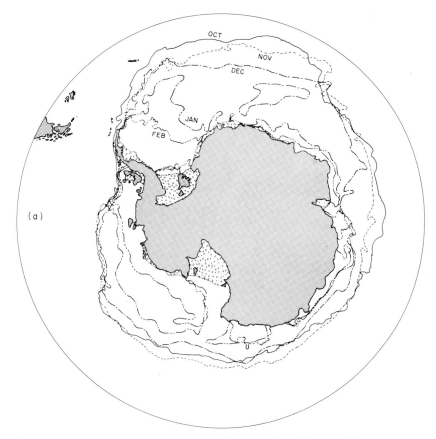

Fig. 3. (a) Decay of Antarctic sea ice cover from October 1973 to February 1974.

ice from the western Weddell Sea is carried around to the east, and in the rapid decay of ice in the south-east, where warmer surface water evidently enters the region.

Figure 4 shows the total area of sea ice coverage as a function of time for the period 1973–1980. The rapid growth of sea ice in the austral spring and the even more rapid decay in early austral summer can be seen. The variation of total ice coverage from a minimum in February–March to a maximum in August–October shows that from 75 to 80% of the sea ice must melt and freeze each year, and the percentage of the mass of ice that melts and freezes each year is probably even greater since the ice is quite probably thicker and more compact in winter than in summer. This is in sharp contrast to the Arctic where the variation of ice coverage is about 20–25%. Thus, while in the Arctic most of the ice remains for several seasons and becomes quite thick, of the order of 2–4 m, in the Antarctic multiyear ice is

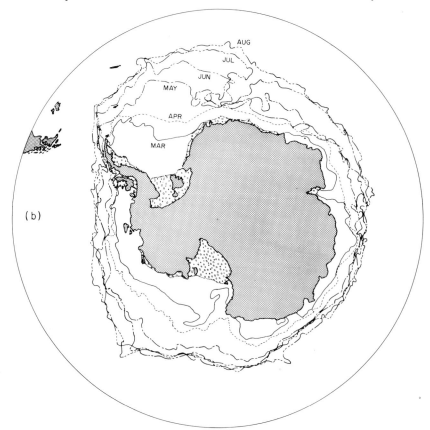

Fig. 3. (b) Growth of Antarctic sea ice cover from March 1974 to August 1974.

relatively rare and most of the ice is of the order of 1–2 m thick. The only areas in which multiyear ice is regularly found other than along the shoreline, are the western Weddell Sea and the Bellingshausen Sea. Wordie (1921) and Arctowski (1901) reported sea ice growth during the winter from 1 to 2 m during the drifts of *Endurance* and *Belgica*.

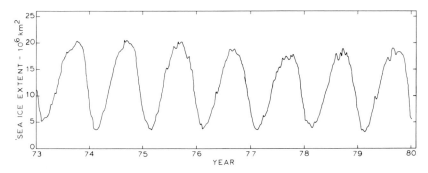

Fig. 4. Areal extent of sea ice from 1973 to 1980 (tick marks at 1 January).

Wordie also reported opening of leads during the winter months. In addition, satellite imagery has shown that large polynyas can occur. Some of the polynyas form from flaw leads along the coast of Antarctica when offshore winds are sufficiently strong and persistent. The katabatic winds blowing from the south-east off the continent (see Chapter 1) quite often result in the opening of a large flaw lead in the early austral spring in the south-east Weddell Sea. In some years the paths of cyclones in austral spring in the vicinity of the Antarctic Peninsula are far to the south of their usual path and the resulting offshore winds in the region to the east of the peninsula open a large flaw lead. This phenomenon allowed Captain Larsen to take the *Jason* to about 68°S just off the east coast of the Antarctic Peninsula in 1895. A very large polynya has been seen by satellite imagery in the region between about 20°W and 20°E and 62°S and 70°S, which remains nearly ice-free all winter long some years. It should be noted that once ice forms a relatively continuous layer, it acts like an insulator to retard the transfer of heat between the atmosphere and the ocean. Thus open leads and polynyas in the pack are loci for rapid heat transfer and ice formation, especially in winter.

The ice that crystallizes from sea water is pure although some salt is trapped in the ice as brine pockets. The salinity of sea ice is therefore much less, of the order of 6‰, than that of the sea-water from which it forms, of the order of 34‰. The actual salinity of sea ice depends upon the rate of freezing (the faster the freezing, the more salt is trapped) and upon its age (generally the older the sea ice, the less saline it is since the brine pockets tend to migrate). Thus the process of sea ice formation results in the increase of the salinity of the water just beneath the ice and a possibly unstable water column. Conversely, the melting of sea ice decreases the salinity of the surface water and stabilizes the water column. Over a year the processes of sea ice formation and melting largely counteract each other; however, since sea ice is advected away from the continent, some salt is left behind to accumulate, mainly over the continental shelves, and especially in the Weddell Sea region (Gill, 1973). Here rapid sea ice formation in open leads and polynyas causes haline convection throughout the entire water column on the shelf resulting in a very cold and saline water mass.

The edge of the pack ice is of particular interest since it is the habitat of marine mammals and birds. If the wind blows along the edge of the pack, the Ekman transport induced by the wind will tend to compact the pack ice if it is to the left of the wind and to loosen the pack if it is to the right of the wind. Thus, depending upon the wind strength and direction, the marginal ice zone may consist of a very sharp transition zone, of the order of a few hundreds of metres wide, from open ocean to close pack, or it may take the form of a very broad transition region, of the order of tens of kilometres wide, consisting of loose pack, which is easily traversed by ice-reinforced ships. Since the marginal ice zone is usually in a region of intermittent cyclones, the pack ice conditions are usually in a state of flux and can change in a few days. Ocean waves can propagate into the pack, but waves with short wavelengths are quickly attenuated. Waves with a longer wavelength penetrate further and can cause ice floes to crack and break up into smaller floes.

Sea ice cover not only inhibits the transfer of heat between the ocean and atmosphere but also almost entirely blocks the penetration of significant radiation into the water. The Antarctic sea ice is usually covered with a thick layer of snow which makes it even more opaque. Thus primary productivity in the water column may be delayed by the ice cover until quite late in the season, even when radiation is present at the surface.

2.2 Ice shelves and icebergs

Glacial ice in the Antarctic originates primarily from the extensive ice sheets which extrude from the continent. In the Ross and Weddell Seas the ice sheets float on the ocean forming the extensive Ross, Filchner and Ronne Ice Shelves. The layer of water under the Ross Ice Shelf varies from a few metres to several hundred metres thick and presents an unusual marine environment. The ice layer varies from about 200 m thick at the seaward edge except in the McMurdo Sound region, where it is less than 50 m thick, to over 800 m thick at the grounded edges. Thus, there is effectively no radiation to support primary production beneath the ice shelves. Phytoplankton can grow, however, in cracks in the ice shelf where water can rise to sea level and receive radiation. The temperature of the water under the ice shelves is near the *in situ* freezing point at the ice–water interface, but can be slightly warmer near the bottom. Due to the suppression of the freezing point by pressure, the temperatures of the sea-water under the ice shelves are usually colder than the freezing point at atmospheric pressure for the same salinity. Although the ocean beneath the ice shelves has only been sampled at one location under the Ross Ice Shelf (82°23'S, 168°38'W; Foster, 1978), the water along the seaward edge of the ice shelves has been sampled at many locations and has confirmed the existence of this very cold water.

The ice shelves are continually moving seaward at about 1 m a day due to the accumulation of snow on Antarctica. As the ice shelves extend into the open ocean, they are exposed to the action of long-period waves and eventually they crack and calve icebergs.

The large tabular icebergs, which can range from a few hundred metres up to about 100 km in horizontal extent, are usually about 200–300 m thick. It has been estimated (Radok *et al.*, 1975) that the total mass of icebergs is about one-third the mass of the sea ice at maximum extent. The average life of icebergs is about four years, but large ones have been tracked for many years (Swithinbank *et al.*, 1977). Many of the icebergs are transported northward into the Antarctic Circumpolar Current, and some are carried out of the Southern Ocean into the subtropical regions. The icebergs probably mostly melt in the northern reaches of the Southern Ocean (50–60°S) and here they exert a cooling and freshening influence on the surface waters. Due to their great draught they may exert a stirring action in the surface waters resulting in bringing nutrients to the surface in their wakes.

3. Oceanic Circulation

In general, the principal driving force for the currents of the Southern Ocean is the surface wind field although density differences can be important locally. The atmospheric pressure in the southern hemisphere is characterized by relatively high pressure over Antarctica, a belt of low pressure areas at about 65° and a belt of high pressure areas at about 30° (Fig. 5). The winds over the Southern Ocean are thus predominantly easterly near the continent and westerly north of about 60°S. There is, however, a great deal of variability, especially in the north where there is a continual succession of cyclones. The surface currents in the Southern Ocean largely reflect the predominant wind pattern, with westerly flowing water along the continent, the Antarctic Coastal Current (East Wind Drift), and easterly flowing water north of about 60°S, the Antarctic Circumpolar Current (West Wind Drift). Between these two relatively well-defined current regimes there is a series of irregular eddies. Figure 6 shows the general pattern of the surface currents in the Southern Ocean. Since the water column is weakly stratified south of the Antarctic Convergence, the ocean currents generally extend to the bottom of this region. Thus the deep circulation is quite similar to the surface circulation though the bottom waters may flow somewhat differently since they are more strongly influenced by the sea-floor topography.

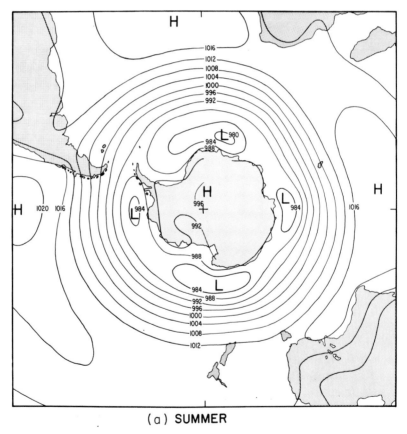

(a) SUMMER

Fig. 5. (a) Atmospheric pressure (mb) at sea level in summer (after Taljaard et al., 1969).

3.1 Antarctic Circumpolar Current

The Antarctic Circumpolar Current transports more water than any other current system (2–3 times that of the Gulf Stream), but this large transport is not due to high current speeds; rather it results mainly because the current extends to the bottom. Indeed, the maximum surface speeds are only of the order of 15–20 cm s^{-1} as compared to over 200 cm s^{-1} for the Gulf Stream. The Antarctic Circumpolar Current is unique in that it is the only zonal current and is almost unobstructed by continental land masses. The constriction at the Drake Passage is the only land obstacle. However, the Antarctic Circumpolar Current joins the great current gyres of the South Atlantic, South Indian and South Pacific Oceans, and thus the total current flowing from west to east in these regions is greater than that which

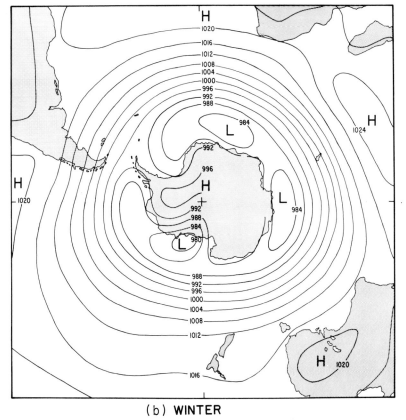

(b) WINTER

Fig. 5. (b) Atmospheric pressure (mb) at sea level in winter (after Taljaard *et al.*, 1969).

flows through the Drake Passage. In addition, the gyres and eddies south of 60°S will further add to the total eastward flow where they join with the Circumpolar Current. Short-term current measurements and geostrophic calculations have yielded wildly varying estimates of the transport of the Circumpolar Current. Recently, however, long-term measurements of the current through the Drake Passage (Bryden and Pillsbury, 1977) have allowed for the first time an accurate estimation of the average transport through the passage, as 139 ($\pm$36) $\times$ $10^6\,\mathrm{m}^3\,\mathrm{s}^{-1}$ to the east. The Circumpolar Current is very broad, varying from less than about 200 km wide south of Australia to over 1000 km wide in the Atlantic, and the boundaries are not

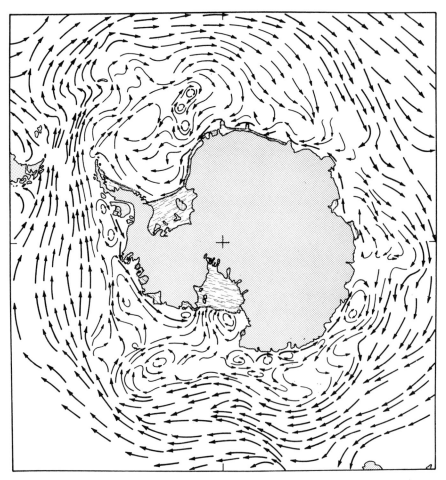

Fig. 6. Surface circulation of the Southern Ocean (after Treshnikov, 1964).

clearly defined. It is deflected where it passes over submarine ridges and has a strong northward component after it passes through the Drake Passage. There is also some evidence that there are meanders and even loops (Tchernia, 1974; Joyce and Patterson, 1977). The Antarctic Circumpolar Current is the subject of active investigation by physical oceanographers so we may expect that our ideas about this current may have to undergo revision as knowledge is gained.

3.2 Antarctic Coastal Current

The Antarctic Coastal Current has not been the subject of much research and thus is poorly known. Recent studies of iceberg drift using satellite tracked transmitters by Tchernia (1974) have shown that the average flow in the current is between 13 and 20 cm s^{-1}. but the current may not be continuous all along the coast. Rather, it seems likely that it is broken up into a series of gyres since icebergs have drifted north between 80 and 100°E away from the coast into the Circumpolar Current. In addition, it obviously flows northward when it reaches the Antarctic Peninsula. Hydrographic sections across the Coastal Current in the south-east Weddell Sea show that it may be up to 300 km wide, but that the main current is confined to just over the continental slope where it reaches speeds of the order of 20 cm s^{-1} (Carmack and Foster, 1975).

3.3 Gyres and eddies

The circulation between the two main Southern Ocean currents has also not been extensively studied. The large gyre in the Weddell Sea region seems to be well defined at least in the west from drifts of the *Endurance* and *Deutschland*, bottom photographs (Hollister and Elder, 1969), and two long-term current meter records (Foldvik and Kvinge, 1974; Middleton and Foster, 1977). The eastern extent of the gyre is not at all known except that it does not extend east of about 80°E and probably extends at least to 0°. Most likely the flow south is over a broad sector between these two meridians. The total transport in the Weddell Gyre may be quite large and Carmack and Foster (1975) have estimated it to be of the order of 100×10^6 m^3 s^{-1}. The other eddies shown in Fig. 6 can best be viewed as conjectural, since it seems likely that such small-scale features may be highly variable in time. The circulation of these gyres and eddies is of considerable importance to understanding the sea ice build-up and decay, and to understanding the distribution of biological species and their life histories.

The variability of the circulation in the vicinity of South Georgia may be

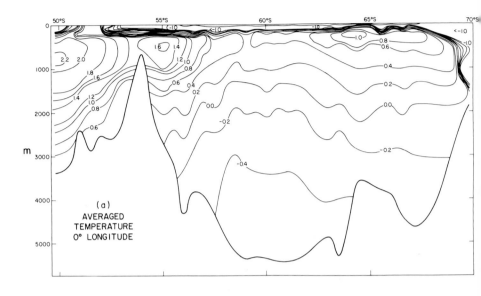

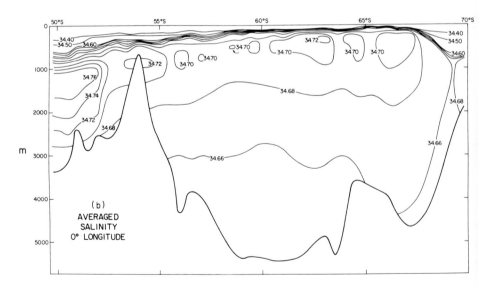

Fig. 7 (a) Averaged temperature (°C) section along 0° longitude in the Atlantic sector. Data from 5° on both sides of 0° were averaged for each 1/2° of latitude. (b) Averaged salinity (‰) section along 0° in the Atlantic sector.

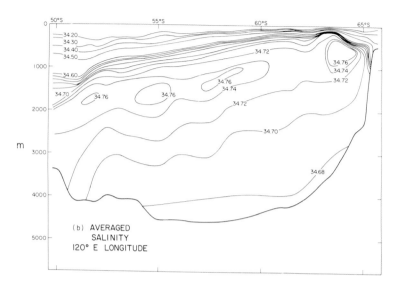

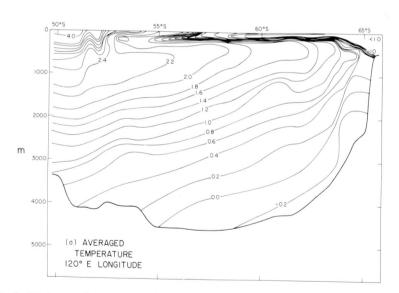

Fig. 8. (a) Averaged temperature (°C) section along 120°E in the Indian Ocean sector. (b) Averaged salinity section (‰) along 120°E in the Indian Ocean sector.

of particular interest to biologists due to the possible influence of the circulation on the abundance of krill in this region (Deacon, 1977). Owing to the proximity of the Drake Passage and the associated northward flow of the Antarctic Circumpolar Current as well as the flow of water from the Weddell Sea, the circulation near South Georgia is quite complex. The Antarctic Convergence becomes quite irregular east of the Drake Passage as evidenced by the current rings observed there (Joyce and Patterson, 1977). Similarly, the boundary between currents from the Weddell Sea and Drake Passage usually makes a northward loop near South Georgia, bringing cold waters from the Weddell Sea into the region. Our knowledge of these local circulations is, however, very incomplete at this time.

4. Distribution of Properties

The Southern Ocean can be divided into three principal hydrographic realms within which vertical profiles of hydrographic properties show the same general features: the area north of the Antarctic Convergence, the area south of the Antarctic Convergence, and the area on the continental shelf around Antarctica. Between these hydrographic realms are transition regions which are characterized by oceanic fronts. the averaged vertical sections of temperature and salinity for the Atlantic (Fig. 7), Indian (Fig. 8) and Pacific (Fig. 9) Oceans show the principal features of the hydrography in the Southern Ocean. Excluding the surface waters three water masses dominate the deep ocean: the Antarctic Intermediate Water found north of the Antarctic Convergence near the 1000 m level, the Antarctic Bottom Water near the bottom, and the Antarctic Circumpolar Water in between at various depths.

4.1 Antarctic Intermediate Water

The Antarctic Intermediate Water evidently forms by mixing across the fronts in the vicinity of the Antarctic Convergence although the exact mechanisms involved are still poorly understood. Possible mechanisms include the enhancement of mixing due to loops and rings in the convergence, deep wind mixing north of the convergence, and intrusions followed by double-diffusive convection (Joyce et al., 1978). Since the lines of constant density are steeply inclined in the vicinity of the convergence with the more dense water to the south, the mixtures will be more dense than the water to the north. Thus the net result is a sinking as the newly-formed Antarctic Intermediate Water moves northward until it reaches a quasi-equilibrium near the 1000 m level.

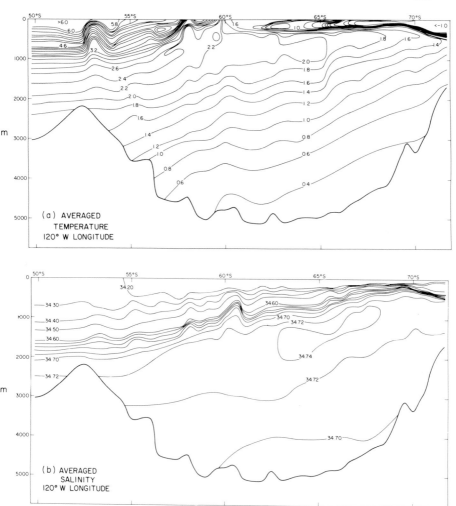

Fig. 9. (a) Averaged temperature (°C) section along 120°W in the Pacific sector. (b) Averaged salinity (‰) section along 120°W in the Pacific sector.

4.2 Antarctic Bottom Water

Antarctic Bottom Water is the other important water mass of the World Ocean that has its source in the Southern Ocean. The primary source region for this water mass has been known for a long time to be the Western Weddell Sea (Deacon, 1937). True bottom water of a somewhat saltier nature also forms in the Ross Sea, but the production rate is probably of an order of magnitude less than the Weddell Sea source (Carmack, 1977).

There are other source areas which probably contribute to what is commonly called Antarctic Bottom Water, but in general the water formed does not sink to the bottom. One such area is off the coast of Wilkes Land, where Carmack and Killworth (1978) have shown that water from the shelf probably sinks to about the 2000 m level. Another phenomenon that may be involved is deep convection in the open ocean similar to that observed in the Mediterranean in winter. One area where deep convection possibly occurs is in the northwest Weddell Sea (Deacon, 1937); another is the central Weddell Sea, where Gordon (1978) recently observed a possible remnant eddy of such a process. Brennecke (1921) proposed that Weddell Sea bottom water probably forms by a process in which very cold shelf water, which has had its salinity increased by sea ice formation, mixes with offshore intermediate water (Warm Deep Water) and flows down the continental shelf. Recent investigations have shown that this explanation is essentially correct, but that the offshore surface water (Winter Water) also makes up part of the sinking mixtures (Gill, 1973; Foster and Carmack, 1976a). It has been estimated by these investigators that about 2–$5 \times 10^6 \, \mathrm{m^3 \, s^{-1}}$ of newly-formed bottom water are produced on average in the Weddell Sea.

4.3 Antarctic Circumpolar Water

The Antarctic Circumpolar Water, which is usually called Warm Deep Water south of the Antarctic Convergence, is the most voluminous water mass in the Southern Ocean. This water mass acquires its characteristics from the North Atlantic Deep Water, which probably enters the Southern Ocean in the eastern South Atlantic and Indian Oceans, and by mixture with colder, fresher Antarctic waters possibly including the newly-discovered deep water that may form near the continent (see above) as well as surface and bottom waters. The Atlantic hydrographic section (Fig. 7) shows the entry of the North Atlantic Deep Water at depths between 1000 and 2000 m as a relatively warm, saline layer. It then rises over the Antarctic Bottom Water in the vicinity of the Antarctic Convergence to depths less than 500 m near Antarctica. One must keep in mind that the flow proceeds mainly perpendicular to the sections shown (Figs 7, 8, 9) and that the sub-surface flow closely follows the surface flow shown in Fig. 6.

4.4 Antarctic Surface Waters

The horizontal distributions of the properties of the surface waters are shown in Fig. 10a–f. All the data available on the N.O.D.C. computer tapes have been used and averaged for depths from 0 to 10 m by 5° squares. The surface waters south of the Antarctic Convergence are characterized by

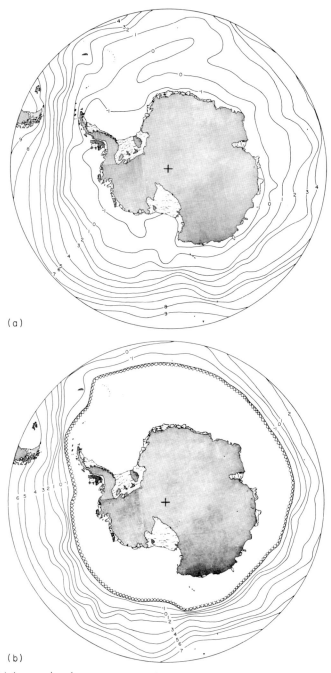

Fig. 10. (a) Averaged surface temperatures (°C) in summer. Data from 0 to 10 m depth were averaged by 5° squares. (b) Averaged surface temperatures (°C) in winter. Cross-hatched line shows average extent of sea ice in winter.

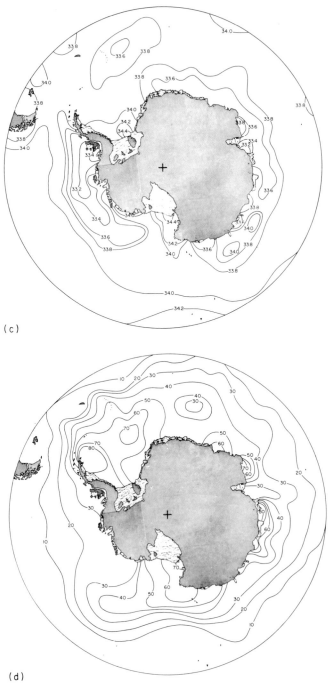

(c)

(d)

Fig. 10. (c) Averaged surface salinity (‰) in summer. (d) Averaged surface silicate (μg-at l^{-1}).

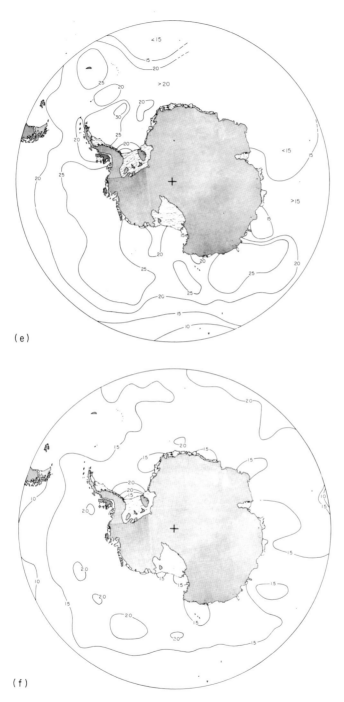

Fig. 10. (e) Averaged surface nitrate (μg-at l^{-1}). (f) Averaged surface phosphate (μg–at l^{-1}).

relatively low salinity and low temperatures. The surface layer is deepest near the convergence and the continental slope and shallowest in the region between the westerly and easterly winds where the Warm Deep Water rises to about 100 m below sea level, possibly because of a diverging surface flow (Foster and Carmack, 1976b). The Antarctic Surface Water shows considerable seasonal temperature variation, due to the great changes in radiative heating and salinity variation due to ice formation and melting. In winter the surface waters are near the freezing point and salt rejection during sea ice formation can cause convective mixing throughout the surface water layer, resulting in a nearly homogeneous layer with a salinity of less than about 34.51‰. Fofonoff (1956) has shown this salinity value cannot be exceeded in the open ocean because otherwise mixtures of surface water with the Warm Deep Water will be denser than the Warm Deep Water. In summer, the melting of sea ice and icebergs lowers the salinity in the top few metres and results in stably-stratified surface waters, which are usually several degrees above the freezing point at the sea surface in ice-free waters due to radiative heating. In the lower surface waters the temperatures are still near the freezing point and salinities approach 34.51‰. This remnant of winter convection is called Winter Water. Figure 11 shows the winter and summer profiles for temperature and salinity for stations in the central Weddell Sea which show these seasonal changes.

The surface waters on the continental shelves are quite similar to those over the deep ocean with the exception that there is no restriction on the salinity to values less than 34.51‰. Salinities up to about 35‰ are found on the continental shelves in the Weddell and Ross Seas, and this high salinity shelf water is an important precursor to bottom water formation. Temperatures on the shelves are probably near the freezing point by late winter. Close to Filchner and Ross Ice Shelves, water may be found that has been cooled by flowing under the ice shelves so that it is at temperatures below the surface freezing point, though not below the *in situ* freezing point, due to the pressure effect.

The concentrations of nutrients are lowest in the surface waters and greatest in the Warm Deep Water for nitrate and phosphate, and usually near the bottom for silicate. As can be seen in Fig. 10d–f the concentrations of nutrients in the surface waters south of the Antarctic Convergence are much higher than for oceanic surface waters in general. There does not seem to be a clear correlation between the surface distribution of nutrients and upwelling, although the Warm Deep Water probably is the source of the nutrients in the surface waters south of the convergence. Phosphate and nitrate appear to be regenerated in the Warm Deep Water layer, possibly by the sinking of phytoplankton (Deacon, 1963). The silicate distribution is more complicated since dissolution of siliceous diatom tests is apparently slower than the regeneration of the other nutrients. The result is that a

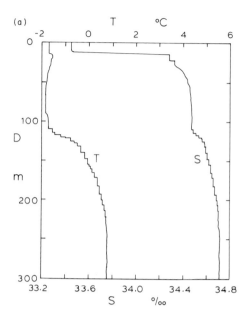

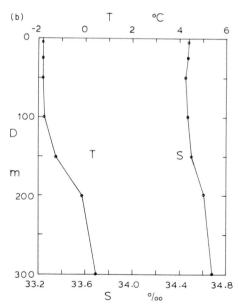

Fig. 11. (a) Vertical profiles of temperature and salinity for a station in the Weddell Sea in summer (*General San Martin* 3 February 1969, 68°55′S, 26°47′W). (b) Vertical profiles of temperature and salinity for a station in the Weddell Sea in winter (*Deutschland* 26 August 1912, 65°32′S, 43°00′W).

silicate maximum is found in the Warm Deep Water at a level lower than the core of this water mass in the Weddell Sea where the newly-formed bottom water shows a silicate minimum (Carmack, 1973); however, as the bottom water flows out of the Weddell Sea this silicate minimum quickly turns into a maximum as it dissolves silicate from the diatomaceous sediments. This latter silicate source probably does not have a direct effect on the silicate concentration of the Antarctic surface waters since the bottom water flows north of the convergence and out of the Southern Ocean. It may, however, diffuse upward into the North Atlantic Deep Water and ultimately renew the surface waters.

5. Mixing Processes

The stability of the water column and the wind stress on the sea surface are the two most important factors governing mixing in the ocean. Figure 12 shows a vertical profile of temperature, salinity and potential density for a summer station in the central Weddell Sea. We see that despite the large changes in temperature the water column has very nearly constant density due to compensating changes in salinity except in the surface layer down to about 150 m depth. In winter (see Fig. 11b) we would expect the surface layer to increase in salinity due to salt rejection during sea ice formation, and then the density would be nearly constant all the way to the surface in ice-covered areas. In the ice-free parts of the Southern Ocean the salinity of the surface layers will increase in winter due to lateral diffusion, but wind mixing will dominate. Thus south of the Antarctic Convergence we may expect a fairly stable ocean surface layer in summer (Fig. 12), with very little mixing, and a neutrally stable ocean surface layer in winter, with considerable deep mixing.

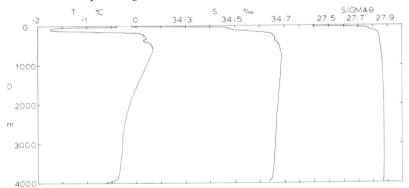

Fig. 12. Vertical profiles of temperature, salinity and potential density (sigmaθ = (potential density − 1) × 1000) for a station in the Weddell Sea in summer (*Glacier* 18 February 1976, 67°11′S, 45°38′W).

Other more subtle mixing processes take place between the Winter Water and Warm Deep Water, such as double-diffusive convection and the cabbeling instability (Foster and Carmack, 1976b). These processes probably help restore regenerated nutrients to the surface waters, especially in the region between the circumpolar and coastal currents. This region is characterized by a series of atmospheric lows (see Fig. 5), and thus the average wind field tends to produce an oceanic surface flow which is divergent (due to the deflection of the currents to the left by the Coriolis force, the Ekman transport). The result is a weak upwelling which in the Weddell Gyre has been estimated to be of the order of a metre per day (Foster and Carmack, 1976b); however, as the Warm Deep Water rises, it interacts with the Winter Water above, and thus probably reaches the surface only as a mixture with the Winter Water.

Another type of upwelling takes place at the edge of the continental shelf where a tongue of nutrient-rich water intrudes onto the shelf. this phenomenon has been observed in the southern Weddell Sea and in the Ross Sea, but its role in nutrient regeneration is not clear. Most of the intruded water apparently undergoes mixing with the shelf water and sinks down the continental slope to form bottom water, though it is also probable that some of this water mixes with the surface waters.

Regions of upwelling in the Antarctic are not clearly delineated, and though the mixing processes that are associated with upwelling probably serve to renew the nutrients in the surface waters, there does not seem to be any clear correlation between upwelling and biological productivity. Probably the direct mechanical effects of horizontal transport and vertical mixing are of more importance to the biosphere. The cycle of low stability near the surface during winter and high stability in summer can result in a cycle of enhanced turbulence in winter and suppressed turbulence in summer. The coupling of enhanced surface turbulence with greatly diminished solar radiation in winter and suppressed turbulence with greatly increased radiation in summer may have a major effect on both phyto- and zooplankton.

6. References

Arctowski, H. (1901). The Antarctic voyage of the "Belgica" during the years 1897, 1898 and 1899. *Geographical Journal* **18**, 353–394.
Brennecke, W. (1921). Die ozeanographischen Arbeiten den deutschen antarktischen Expedition 1911–1912. *Aus dem Arkiv der Deutschen Seewarte* **39** (1), 1–214.
Bryden, H. O. and Pillsbury, R. D. (1977). Variability of deep flow in the Drake Passage from year-long current measurements. *Journal of Physical Oceanography* **7**, 803–810.

Carmack, E. C. (1973). Silicate and potential temperature in the deep and bottom waters of the western Weddell Sea. *Deep-Sea Research* **20**, 927–932.

Carmack, E. C. (1977). Water characteristics of the Southern Ocean south of the Polar Front. *In* "A Voyage of Discovery" (M. Angel, ed.), pp. 15–41. Pergamon Press, Oxford.

Carmack, E. C. and Foster, T. D. (1975). On the flow of water out of the Weddell Sea. *Deep-Sea Research* **22**, 711–724.

Carmack, E. C. and Killworth, P. D. (1978). Formation and interleaving of abyssal water masses off Wilkes Land, Antarctica. *Deep-Sea Research* **25**, 357–369.

Deacon, G. E. R. (1937). The hydrography of the Southern Ocean. *Discovery Reports* **15**, 1–124.

Deacon, G. E. R. (1963). The Southern Ocean. *In* "The Sea" (M. N. Hill, ed.), Vol. II, pp. 281–296. Wiley Interscience, New York.

Deacon, G. E. R. (1964). A discussion on the physical and biological changes across the Antarctic Convergence. Introduction. *Proceedings of the Royal Society* Ser. **A281**, 1–6.

Deacon, G. E. R. (1977). Seasonal variations in the water temperature and salinity near South Georgia 1927–1937. *Institute of Oceanographic Sciences Report* No. 49, 1–30.

Fofonoff, N. P. (1956). Some properties of sea water influencing the formation of Antarctic bottom water. *Deep-Sea Research* **4**, 32–35.

Foster, T. D. (1978). Temperature and salinity fields under the Ross Ice Shelf. *Antarctic Journal of the United States* **13**, 81–82.

Foster, T. D. and Carmack, E. C. (1976a). Frontal zone mixing and Antarctic Bottom Water formation in the southern Weddell Sea. *Deep-Sea Research* **23**, 301–317.

Foster, T. D. and Carmack, E. C. (1976b). Temperature and salinity structure in the Weddell Sea. *Journal of Physical Oceanography* **6**, 36–44.

Gill, A. E. (1973). Circulation and bottom water formation in the Weddell sea. *Deep-Sea Research* **20**, 111–140.

Glavnoe Upravlenie Geodezii i Kartolrafii (1974). Bathymetricheskaya Karta Antarktiki, Moscow.

Gordon, A. L. (1978). Deep Antarctic convection west of Maud Rise. *Journal of Physical Ocenography* **8**, 600–612.

Hollister, C. D. and Elder, R. B. (1978). Contour Currents in the Weddell Sea. *Deep-Sea Research* **16**, 99–101.

Joyce, T. M. and Patterson, S. L. (1977). Cyclonic ring formation at the polar front in the Drake Passage. *Nature* **265** (5590). 131–133.

Joyce, T. M., Zenk, W. and Toole, J. M. (1978). The anatomy of the Antarctic Polar Front in the Drake Passage. *Journal of Geophysical Research* **83**, 6093–6113.

Middleton, J. M. and Foster, T. D. (1977). Tidal currents in the central Weddell Sea. *Deep-Sea Research* **24**, 1195–1202.

Radok, U., Streten, N. and Weller, G. E. (1975). Atmosphere and ice. *Oceanus* **18**, 16–27.

Swithinbank, C., McClain, P. and Little, P. (1977). Drift Tracks of Antarctic icebergs. *Polar Record* **18**, 495–501.

Taljaard, J. J., von Loon, H., Crutcher, H. L. and Jenne, R. L. (1969). *In* "Climate of the Upper Air: Southern Hemisphere", Temperature, dew points, and heights at selected pressure levels. Vol. 1. United States Department of Commerce, ESSA.

Tchernia, P. (1974). Étude de la derive antarctique Est-Quest au moyen d'icebergs suivi par le satellite. *Comptes Rendus, Academie des Sciences* (Paris) **278**, 667–670.

Treshnikov, A. F. (1964). Surface water circulation in the Antarctic Ocean. *Soviet Antarctic Expedition* **2** (45), 81–83. [English translation.]

Wordie, J. M. (1921). Shackelton Antarctic Expedition, 1914–1917: The natural history of pack-ice as observed in the Weddell Sea. *Transactions of the Royal Society of Edinburgh* **52**, 795–829.

The Antarctic marine flora

R. B. Heywood and T. M. Whitaker

1. Introduction

From the very beginning of Antarctic exploration collections of marine
plants have provided information on the taxonomy and distribution of the
flora of the Southern Ocean (Gaudichaud, 1826; Ehrenberg, 1844; Montagne, 1845, 1846; Hooker, 1847; and others). However, there was no investigation of plant ecology until the *Discovery* Investigations, 1925–1939.
The reports of Clowes (1934, 1938), Deacon (1933, 1937a,b), Hart (1934,
1937, 1942) and Hardy and Gunther (1935) are still an important source of
correlated oceanographic and phytoplankton data. Hart's work on phytoplankton distribution, areal and seasonal variation in biomass, and his
ideas on growth-limiting factors are of special importance.

Until the early 1960s there were only a few further assessments of phytoplankton standing stocks, although these were based on more accurate
sampling techniques, followed by cell counts and measurement of plant
pigments. Hasle (1969) has provided an excellent review of this work. The
development of radiocarbon uptake techniques by Steemann-Nielsen
(1952) provided a convenient and sensitive method of measuring the rate of
primary production, which has been used increasingly in the Southern
Ocean in systematic studies of plant physiology and production. Of particular significance have been the extensive cruises of U.S.N.S. *Eltanin* and
the Russian ship *Ob* during which integrated studies were carried out on
phytoplankton standing crop and productivity, nutrient chemistry and
hydrographic conditions. Reviews of this work are to be found in Balech *et
al.* (1968), El-Sayed (1970a,b, 1971a, 1973a, 1978) and Holm-Hansen *et al.*
(1977). Some work has recently been carried out on the physiology and
production of benthic plants (Delépine, 1976; Drew, 1977; Hastings, 1977).

However, although the Southern Ocean presents a paradox of consider-

ANTARCTIC ECOLOGY VOL. 2
ISBN 0 12–439502–3

able scientific and commercial interest—a hostile environment seemingly teeming with life—to date there has been relatively very little research on the life histories, physiology, behaviour and population dynamics of even the most common components of the marine ecosystem. This is particularly true of the marine flora which must survive low temperatures and, in the southernmost areas, long periods of darkness because of ice cover and the polar night.

2. Species, Distribution and Ecology

The Southern Ocean is generally considered to extend from the Antarctic continent to the Sub-tropical Convergence, and has an area of 36×10^6 km^2, approximately 10% of the total world ocean area. There are two main hydrographic zones: the Antarctic zone lying between the continent and the Antarctic Convergence, and the sub-Antarctic zone lying between the Antarctic Convergence and the Sub-tropical Convergence. The temperature of the surface water in the Antarctic zone increases from $-1.0°C$ near the continent to $3.5°C$ at its northern boundary in summer, and from -1.8 to $0.5°C$ in winter. At the Antarctic Convergence the temperature rises quickly by 2–3 degrees and in the sub-Antarctic zone the corresponding summer and winter temperatures are $5.5°C–14.0°C$ and $3.0°C–11.0°C$ respectively. The Sub-tropical Convergence is marked by a sudden temperature increase of about 4°C. Salinities increase from about 33.0 to 33.8‰ with decreasing latitude in the Antarctic zone, and from 34 to 34.5‰ in the sub-Antarctic zone. The Southern Ocean is a deep water environment; the continental shelf of Antarctica is deep (500 m) and narrow, and very deep basins extend from near the continent into the Atlantic, Indian and Pacific Oceans. A description of the bathymetry and hydrography of the Southern Ocean is given by Foster (Chapter 6).

The Antarctic marine flora consists entirely of algae. Phytoplankton dominate and ice associated forms are probably of considerable importance, because microalgal growth has been observed in the pack-ice and first year ice which cover up to 73% of the Southern Ocean by the end of the winter (18% of the ocean is permanently ice covered). The benthic flora is relatively unimportant although locally around sub-Antarctic islands it is sufficiently productive to have economic potential (Delépine, 1976; El-Sayed, 1977).

2.1 The phytoplankton

Over 100 species of diatom, 60 species of dinoflagellate and a few species of other algal classes have been identified from Antarctic phytoplankton samples. Diatoms, particularly *Chaetoceros, Corethron, Nitzschia* and *Thalassiosira* spp., dominate the plankton populations. Hart (1934, 1942) was able to show that the onset of the period of maximum production changed from early spring to late summer or early autumn with increasing latitude (Fig. 1); the period of maximum production decreased in duration with increasing latitude; different species were active at various times during the period of maximum production; and some species had secondary peaks of activity. Hart was also able to show that annual differences in hydrographic conditions could affect the timing and magnitude of these peaks and the species active during the period. Neritic species differed from oceanic species and because many neritic species were also associated with sea ice, which varied in extent and effect each year (Chapter 6), they could be found in considerable numbers in oceanic areas in certain years. Hart's results also indicated that the most important diatom taxa were circumpolar in distribution (Baker, 1954). Fryxell and Hasle (1979) present similar evidence for some *Thalassiosira* spp., and so far there is no evidence to suggest a different pattern for other taxa.

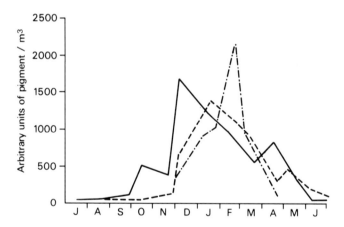

Fig. 1. Seasonal variation in plant pigment concentrations with latitude in the Southern Ocean (after Hart, 1942). ——, Northern zone, c. 50°.00′–55°.50′S and ————, Intermediate zone, c. 55°.50′–66°.00′S (both varying with the position of the Antarctic Convergence); —·—·—·—, Southern zone, above 66°.00′S.

Consequently, results from the various areas of this vast ocean can be compared if due allowance is made for the phenomena outlined above. This has not always been easy. Most expeditions have been of very brief duration. Sampling has often been outside the period of maximum production, or during only part of it, giving rise to unrepresentative measurements. Further diffculties have arisen from the different techniques used. Net samples have not necessarily included the small species, or have retained them in disproportionately small amounts which have not reflected their true importance. Water bottle samples have often been of too small a volume to include any but the most abundant species. Samples have often been examined years after collection, by which time the more delicate diatoms and the dinoflagellates had disintegrated and become unrecognizable. Finally, there have been the almost inevitable differences of opinion on identity.

Hart drew attention to these problems in 1942 when he reviewed the phytoplankton of the Antarctic zone. He divided the zone into three main biogeographical regions—northern, intermediate and southern—with some designated special areas where the neritic and ice-associated influence was especially high (i.e. South Georgia, Scotia Sea, Weddell Sea, north of Ross Sea, western coastal waters of the Antarctic Peninsula and certain islands). He also separately arranged the diatom species into four groups of oceanic species distinguished by size, form and period of maximum production, and one group of neritic and ice-associated forms. Other schemes based on water types, zones or latitude have been put forward by Hustedt (1958), Beklemishev (1958, 1960), Fukase (1962), Kozlova, (1962, 1964) and Cassie (1963).

Hasle (1969), after analysing phytoplankton from the Pacific region of the Southern Ocean (*Brategg* Expedition, 1947–1948), presented a review in which taxonomic and distribution differences were discussed in detail and the relative and absolute accuracies of various sampling methods were described. The nannoplankton was numerically the most important group, but if cell volume was the measure of standing stock the less abundant medium-sized, and occasionally the larger species, were dominant. Hasle questioned the value of Hart's classification of the oceanic diatoms according to periods of maximum production, because it had little general validity in the Southern Ocean, where the timing varied so much from year to year and from zone to zone with changing hydrographic conditions. Grouping of species according to geographical distribution has more general applicability, according to Hasle, especially if the more recent knowledge and theory is used to determine which species are accidental or occasional introductions to a particular zone (exogenetic or allogenetic species, Wimpenny, 1966), and which species are characteristic and able to reproduce there (endogenetic or autogenetic species).

Guided mainly by the *Brategg* material, but with reference to Atlantic and Indian Ocean phytoplankton, Hasle (1969) presented a scheme in which the phytoplankton was arranged in six fairly distinct groups according to their distribution over sub-Antarctic, northern Antarctic and southern Antarctic zones. However, one of two groups of species occurring in all three zones was subdivided according to the observed period of "maximum standing stock". Hart's timing of the periods of maximum production was deliberately confined, one suspects, to the loose terms of "early spring", "mid-summer", "early autumn", etc. because of his observations of the yearly variation. Hasle's criticism is therefore groundless and her scheme may be considered a modified version of Hart's 1942 plan. The special areas and the "intermediate Antarctic zone" of Hart were not used, but many of the species Hart thought characteristic of them are now known to have a more widespread distribution (Beklemishev, 1960). Many controversial points remain but few modern studies describe the phytoplankton biomass in terms of species.

A list of the more important species is given in Table I in a form based upon the scheme of Hasle (1969) with reference to Hart (1934, 1942), Hardy and Gunther (1935), Hendey (1937), Beklemishev (1958, 1960), Hasle (1968), El-Sayed (1971b, 1973b), Vladimirskaya *et al.* (1976), Holm-Hansen *et al.* (1977) and others. Species printed in bold italics have frequently been observed as dominant members of a community (see Tables III and IV).

2.2 Ice-associated (sympagic) flora

The association of plants with sea ice has been known since Hooker (1847) reported algal growth colouring Antarctic icebergs, pack and fast ice. Over 50 species, mainly neritic diatoms with some chrysophytes and dinoflagellates, are known to colonize this uniquely polar habitat. The communities occur in three major zones within the ice sheet: the surface infiltration zone, the main ice zone and the brash or platelet ice zone. On icebergs they occupy ice shelves and other surfaces within the euphotic zone.

The infiltration zone develops when the weight of snow cover forces the surface of free-floating pack ice below sea level, or when ice floes or fast ice jam below high tide level along a coast. Sea water rises through pores and cracks and part freezes to form an ice–water matrix. Considerable algal growths have been observed in this zone. Whitaker (1977a) found almost pure colonies of *Navicula glaciei* Van Heurck developing in a coastal tide crack infiltration zone at Signy Island (60°43'S, 45°36'W), South Orkney Islands.

Algae have been observed at various levels in the main ice zone. Hoshiai (1972) found two distinct bands formed of different species in the sea ice near Syowa Station (69°00'S, 39°35'E). An upper band, 35 cm thick and dominated by *Fragilariopsis* and *Nitzschia* spp. formed in autumn below 30 cm of ice, and a lower 7 cm band of *Amphiprora*, *Nitzschia* and *Stephanopyxis* spp. developed under 1.1 m of ice in spring. In McMurdo

TABLE I

Important phytoplankton species in the Antarctic marine flora

			Sub-Antarctic zone	Antarctic zone	
				Low latitude	High latitude
BACILLARIOPHYCEAE					
Centrales					
Asteromphalus hookeri Ehr.	endemic	oceanic	.	+	+
Asteromphalus hyalinus Karsten	cosmopolitan	neritic/oceanic	.	+	+
Biddulphia weissflogii Janisch in Grunow		neritic	.	Sp-eSu	e-mSu
Chaetoceros atlanticum Cleve	cosmopolitan	oceanic	Su	Au	Au
Chaetoceros bulbosum (Ehr.) Heiden	endemic	neritic	Su	lSu	Au
Chaetoceros criophilum Castr.	bipolar	oceanic	Au	Au	lSu
Chaetoceros dichaeta Ehr.	cosmopolitan	oceanic	Su	Su	Au
Chaetoceros flexuosum Mangin	endemic	neritic	.	.	e-mSu
Chaetoceros neglectum Karsten	endemic	neritic	Su	lSu	Au
Chaetoceros schimperianum Karsten	endemic	neritic/oceanic	+	+	.
Chartcotia actinochilus (Ehr.) Hust.	endemic	neritic	.	.	.
Corethron criophilum Castr.	cosmopolitan	neritic/oceanic	Au	Au	lSu
Corethron criophilum f. inerme (Karsten) Castr.	endemic	neritic/oceanic	eSu	Su	.
Coscinodiscus bouvet Karsten	endemic	neritic	+	+	.
Coscinodiscus centralis Ehr.	cosmopolitan	oceanic	.	.	.
Coscinodiscus furcatus Karsten	endemic	oceanic	.	.	.
Coscinodiscus marginatus Ehr.		oceanic	.	.	.
Coscinodiscus oculoides Karsten	endemic?	neritic	eSu	.	.
Coscinodiscus oculusiridis Ehr.	endemic	neritic/oceanic	.	Su	.
Coscinodiscus oppositus Karsten	endemic	oceanic	.	.	+
Coscinodiscus tabularis Grun.	endemic	oceanic	.	.	.
Dactyliosolen antarcticus Castr.	cosmopolitan	oceanic	Au	Au	lSu
Eucampia balaustium Castr.	endemic	oceanic	Su	Su	Au
Leptocylindrus mediterraneus (H.Per.) Hasle	cosmopolitan	neritic	.	.	.
Porosira glacialis (Grun.) Cleve	bipolar	neritic	.	.	.
Porosira pseudodenticulata (Hust.) Zhuse	endemic	oceanic	.	.	.
Rhizosolenia alata Brightw.	cosmopolitan	oceanic	.	.	.
Rhizosolenia chunii Karsten	endemic	oceanic	Su	Au	Au

Taxon	Distribution	Habitat				
Rhizosolenia curvata Zacharias	endemic	oceanic	Su	·	·	Au
Rhizosolenia cylindrus Cleve	cosmopolitan	oceanic	Su	·	Au	Au
Rhizosolenia hebetata Bailey var subacuta Grun. f. semispina (Hensen) Gran	cosmopolitan	oceanic	ˡSu	·	Au	Au
Rhizosolenia imbricata var shrubsolei (Cleve) Van Heurck	cosmopolitan	oceanic	eSu	Su	Su	ˡSu
Rhizosolenia simplex Karsten	endemic	oceanic	·	·	·	·
Rhizosolenia styliformis Brightw. var. polydactyla (Castr.) Peragallo	cosmopolitan	neritic	·	·	·	·
Thalassiosira antarctica Comber	endemic	neritic/oceanic	eSu	e-mSu	·	+
Thalassiosira gracilis (Karsten) Hust.	endemic	neritic/oceanic	·	·	·	·
Thalassiosira gracilis (Karsten) Hust. Var. expecta Fryxell & Hasle	endemic	neritic/oceanic	·	·	·	·
Thalassiosira gravida Cleve	cosmopolitan (cold waters)		·	·	·	·
Thalassiosira lentiginosa (Janisch) G. Fryxell	endemic	oceanic				
Thalassiosira perpusilla Kozlova,	endemic	oceanic				
Thalassiosira ritscheri (Hustedt) Hasle	endemic					
Thalassiosira tumida (Janisch) Hasle,	endemic	neritic/oceanic	·	·	·	·
Pennales						
Nitzschia barbieri M.Per.	endemic	neritic	·	·	+	+
Nitzschia curta (Van Heurck) Hasle	endemic	neritic	+	+	+	+
Nitzschia cylindrus (Grun.) Hasle	bipolar	neritic	·	+	+	+
Nitzschia kerguelensis (O'meara) Hasle	endemic	neritic/oceanic	Sp–Su	Sp–Su	+	+
Nitzschia lineata Hasle	endemic	neritic	·	·	+	+
Nitzschia obliquecostata (Van Heurck) Hasle	endemic	neritic	+	+	+	+
Nitzschia ritscheri (Hust.) Hasle	endemic	oceanic	+	+	+	+
Nitzschia sublineata Hasle	endemic	neritic	+	+	+	+
Nitzschia closterium (Ehr.) W.Sm	cosmopolitan	neritic	eSu	Su	Su	ˡSu
Nitzschia decipiens Hust.	endemic	neritic	·	·	+	+
Nitzschia lecointei Van Heurck	endemic	neritic	·	·	·	·
Nitzschia subcurvata Hasle	endemic	neritic	+	+	+	+
Nitzschia fraudulenta Cl.	cosmopolitan	neritic/oceanic	·	Sp–Su	Sp–Su	·
Nitzschia prolongatoides Hasle	endemic	oceanic	+	Su	Su	Su
Nitzschia turgiduloides Hasle	endemic	neritic/oceanic	Su	·	Su	Su
Nitzschia tugidula Hust.	cosmopolitan	oceanic	+	·	·	·
Nitzschia bicapitata Cl.	cosmopolitan	oceanic	Su	·	·	·

TABLE I (contd)

			Sub-Antarctic zone	Antarctic zone	
				Low latitude	High latitude
Synedra reinboldii Van Heurck	endemic	neritic/oceanic	.	Au	lSu
Thalassionema nitzschioides (Grun.) Hust.	cosmopolitan	oceanic	.	.	.
Thalassiothrix antarctica Schimper ex Karsten	endemic	oceanic	Au	Au	lSu
Thallassiothrix longissima Cleve & Grun.			.	.	.
DINOPHYCEAE					
Ceratium lineatum (Ehr.) Cleve	cosmopolitan	oceanic	+	+	+
Ceratium pentagonum Gourret f. *grandis* Margin	cosmopolitan	oceanic	+	+	.
Dinophysis antarcticum Balech	endemic		.	+	+
Dinophysis tuberculata Mangin	endemic		.	+	+
Protoperidinium antarcticum (Schimper) Balech	endemic		.	+	+
Protoperidinium applanatum (Mangin) Balech	endemic	oceanic	Su	lSu	lSu
Protoperidinium affine (Balech) Balech	endemic		.	+	+
SILICOFLAGELLATAE					
Dictyocha speculum Lemm.	cosmopolitan	oceanic	eSu	Su	lSu
COCCOLITHOPHORIDAE					
Gephyrocapsa huxleyi (Lohm.) Reinhardt	cosmopolitan	oceanic	+	.	.
Haptophyta					
Phaeocystis antarctica Karsten	cosmopolitan		.	+	Su

Period of main standing crop: Sp, spring; Su, summer; Au, autumn; e, early; m, mid; l, late.

Sound (77°30'S, 165°00'E), *Nitzschia, Amphiprora* and *Coscinodiscus* spp. dominated a community forming a 20 cm thick layer at the bottom of ice 2.4 m thick (Hoshiai, 1972). Ackley *et al.* (1978) found significant levels of chlorophyll *a* throughout the whole depth of ice in the Weddell Sea with *Nitzschia cylindrus* (Grun) Hasle and *Nitzschia curta* (Van Heurck) Hasle dominating the 18 species of algae detected.

The brash or platelet ice zone consists of a layer of ice crystals not yet consolidated into the main mass of the ice sheet. It forms a matrix of small pockets of water, continuous with the brine held in the intercrystal lattice of the main ice and with the general water column. The layer may be 1–2 m thick in McMurdo Sound. Bunt and Wood (1963) identified *Pleurosigma, Nitzschia, Amphiprora, Biddulphia, Coscinodiscus* and *Asteromphalus* as the main genera in the McMurdo Sound community.

The coastal ice foot and the underside of inshore fast ice can support rich microalgal growth. At Signy Island *Navicula glaciei, Nitzschia sublineata* Hasle and *Nitzschia curta* dominated a community of eight diatoms and a dinoflagellate on the undersurface of 140 cm thick fast ice (Whitaker, 1977a,b). Forty-five species were found in an ice foot community which was dominated by *Navicula glaciei* and *Nitzschia curta* (Richardson and Whitaker, 1979). The Gauss Expedition (1901–1903) collected almost pure colonies of a *Schizonema* sp. and a *Colletonema* sp. from icebergs (Vanhöffen, 1902). Whitaker (1977a) observed an extraordinarily dense growth of diatoms whilst diving around a grounded berg in Borge Bay, Signy Island. About 50 species formed dense 5 cm thick layers, dominated by *Biddulphia punctata* Greville at depths of up to 17 m. Growth was particularly luxuriant on a platform 5–8 m below the water surface.

The source of the algae would appear to be the sea water which forms the ice or floods the surface (Meguro, 1962). Algal cells may be caught up by ice crystals when they form on the sea bed or during the time they are passing up through the water column (Bunt, 1968). The ice certainly forms a favourable substrate for neritic forms, extending their range into oceanic areas (p. 375). On release through melting of the ice the plants presumably survive in the plankton, but they do not appear to make a significant contribution to it during the period of maximum plankton production.

2.3 The benthic flora

About 700 species of benthic macroalgae belonging to 300 genera are recorded for the Southern Ocean (Delépine, 1966; Neushul, 1968; Zaneveld, 1968). More than 30 genera and 250 species are founded on Southern Ocean material and of these approximately half the genera are monotypic and apparently endemic (Table II). Unfortunately the taxonomy is unreli-

TABLE II

Number of species of benthic macroalgae by taxonomic group and region

	Species total	Percent	Sub-Antarctic			Low Antarctic			High Antarctic		
			Total	Total endemic	Percent endemic	Total	Total endemic	Percent endemic	Total	Total endemic	Percent endemic
Chlorophyta	20	19.4	19	3	15.8	9	3	33.3	3	2	66.7
Phaeophyta	28	27.2	22	9	40.9	15	11	73.3	6	5	83.3
Rhodophyta	55	53.4	40	33	70.0	36	33	91.7	10	10	100
Total	103	100	81			61			19		
Percentage of total	100		78.6			59.2			18.5		

able because many descriptions have been based on poor material and inadequate field notes. Papenfuss (1962) has pointed out that a detailed structural study of new and type material and a reappraisal of all published work is essential. A significant start has been made by Papenfuss (1964) and Lamb and Zimmerman (1977), but only a few genera have been covered so far. Furthermore many areas within the sub-Antarctic and Antarctic zones have not been studied and consequently the geographic distribution of most benthic algal species is sparsely documented. Neushul (1968) has presented a tentative distribution scheme but already new records have invalidated many details. It is difficult to draw many conclusions other than that most species appear to have a circumpolar distribution and that the warmer waters of the sub-Antarctic zone contain the most species (Tables II and III). Skottsberg (1962) distinguishes a sub-Antarctic flora using the 0°C surface water isotherm as a rough guide. Many genera of the sub-Antarctic zone are not found in the Antarctic zones and vice vera. South Georgia appears to be situated on the boundary having representatives from all three zones (Skottsberg, 1962; Neushul, 1968).

There is a vertical succession of plant species on most Antarctic shores, but few general conclusions on zonation can be drawn because of the limited number of detailed surveys. The vertical range of a species may vary considerably according to the substrate, wave exposure and the intensity of ice scour (Table IV). The filamentous green algae *Urospora penicilliformis* (Roth.) Areschoug and *Ulothrix australis* Gain commonly form a conspicuous green band on rocks around high tide level (approximately 2 m above mean low water) on sub-Antarctic and Antarctic islands and on the Antarctic Peninsula. *Porphyra endiviifolium* (A. and E. S. Gepp) Chamberlain, a rather curious green Rhodophycophyte, occurs in rock crevices at this level. *Monostroma* sp. and *Chaetomorpha* sp. have been reported at 1.5 m above mean low water at Palmer Station, Anvers Island (64°46′S, 64°03′E) (Stockton, 1973). Macroalgae are sparse in very shallow water (0–5 m below mean low water) because of the abrasive action of sea ice. The only species on exposed rock are the encrusting calcareous red algae *Lithophyllum aequabile* (Foslie) Foslie and *Lithothamnium granuliferum* Foslie, which also occur in rock pools. The only obligate submerged marine lichen *Verrucaria serpuloides* Lamb grows in this region and down to 9 m below mean low water. Several other lichen species occur in the splash zone. Foliose algae can only survive in cracks and crevices unless they have a short annual life cycle, for example *Adenocystis utricularis* (Bory) Skottsberg (Richardson, 1980). *Porphyra* spp., *Iridaea obovata* Kutz., *Leptosomia simplex* (A. and E. S. Gepp) Kyelin, *Phaeurus antarcticus* Skottsberg, *Curdiea racovitzae* Hariot, *Monostroma hariotii* Gain and *Phyllophora antarctica* A. and E. S. Gepp have been recorded; and most of

TABLE III

Some important Antarctic benthic algae (after Papenfuss, 1964)

	Status	Sub-Antarctic zone	Antarctic zone	
			Low latitude	High latitude
CYANOPHYTA				
Calothrix crustacea Born. & Flak.	cosmopolitan	+	·	·
Entophysalis conferta (Kütz.) Drouet & Daily	cosmopolitan	+	·	·
Entophysalis deusta (Menegh.) Drouet & Daily	cosmopolitan	+	·	·
Lyngbya confervoides Gom.	cosmopolitan	+	·	·
Oscillatoria nigroviridis Gom.	cosmopolitan	+	·	·
Phormidium submenbranaceum Gom.	cosmopolitan	+	·	·
Plectonema calothrichoides Gom.	cosmopolitan	+	·	·
Chlorophyta				
Blidingia minima (Nägeli ex Kütz.) Kylin	cosmopolitan	+	·	·
Cladophora incompta J. D. Hooker & Harvey	endemic	+	·	·
Cladophora radiosa (Suhr.) De Toni	cosmopolitan?	+	·	·
Cladophora rupestris (L.) Kütz	cosmopolitan	+	·	·
Codium fragile (Suringar) Hariot	cosmopolitan	+	·	·
Codium tomentosum Stackhouse	cosmopolitan	+	+	·
Enteromorpha bulbosa (Suhr.) Montagne	cosmopolitan	+	+	·
Enteromorpha intestinalis (L.) Greville	cosmopolitan	+	·	·
Entocladia viridis Reinke	cosmopolitan	+	+	·
Lambia antarctica (Skottsb.) Délepine	endemic	·	+	·
Monostroma applanatum Gain	endemic	+	+	·
Monostroma hariotii Gain	cosmopolitan	+	+	+
Prasiola crispa (Lightfoot) Menegh.	cosmopolitan	+	·	+
Rhizoclonium ambiguum (J. D. Hooker & Harvey) Kützing	?	+	·	·
Rhizoclonium riparum (Roth.) Harv.	endemic	+	·	·
Spongomorpha pacifica (Montagne) Kütz	endemic	+	+	+
Ulothrix australis Gain	cosmopolitan	+	+	·
Ulothrix flacca (Dillwyn) Thuret	cosmopolitan	+	·	·
Ulva lactua L.	cosmopolitan	+	·	·
Ulva lactua Auct. (Non L.)	cosmopolitan	+	·	·
Ulva rigida (C. Agardh.) Thuret	cosmopolitan	+	·	·

CHRYSOPHYTA

Species	Distribution				
Antarctosaccion applanatum (Gain) Délepine	endemic		+			.

PHAEOPHYTA

Species	Distribution				
Adenocystis utricularis (Bory) Skottsb.	endemic	+	+	+	
Alethocladus corymbosus (Dickie) Sauvageau	endemic	+	.	+	
Acoseira mirabilis Skottsb.	endemic	+	+	.	
Caepidium antarcticum Agardh.	endemic	+	+	+	
Colpomenia sinuosa (Roth.) Derb. & Solier	cosmopolitan?	+	.	.	
Cystophaera jacquinotii (Montagne) Skottsberg	endemic	.	+	.	
Desmarestia anceps Montagne	endemic	+	+	.	
Desmarestia ligulata (Lightfoot) Lamouroux	cosmopolitan	+	+	+	+
Desmarestia menziesii J. Agardh	cosmopolitan	+	+	+	+
Desmarstia rossii J. D. Hooker & Harvey	endemic	+	+	+	+
Desmarestia willii Reinsch	endemic	+	+	+	+
Durvillea antarctica (Chamisso) Hariot		+	.		
Durvillea caepaestipes (Montagne) Chapman & Diken	endemic	+	.	.	
Ectocarpus constanciae Hariot	endemic	+	.	+	
Ectocarpus exiguus Skottsberg	endemic	+	.	+	
Feldmannia globifera (Kütz) Hamel	cosmopolitan	+	.	+	
Giffordia granulosa (Smith) Hamel	cosmopolitan	+	.	+	
Giffordia mitchelliae (Harv.) Hamel	cosmopolitan	+	.	+	
Geminocarpus geminatus (J. D. Hooker & Harvey) Skottsb.	endemic	+	+	.	+
Lessonia fuscescens Bory	cosmopolitan	+	+	.	+
Lithoderma antarcticum Skottsb.	endemic	+	.	.	
Macrocystis pyrifera (L.) c. Agardh.	cosmopolitan	.	+[a]	+	+[a]
Pylaiella littoralis (L.) Kjellman	cosmopolitan	+	.	+	
Petalonia fuscia (Müller) Kuntze	cosmopolitan	+	.	+	
Phaeoglossum monacanthum Skottsb.	endemic	.	+	.	+
Phaeurus antarcticus Skottsb.	endemic	.	+	.	+
Phillogigas grandifolius (Gepp) Skottsb.	endemic	+	+	.	+
Scytosiphon lomentaria (Lyngb.) Endlicher	cosmopolitan	+	+[a]	.	+[a]
Scytothamnus fasciculatus (J. D. Hooker & Harvey) Cotton	endemic	+	+	+	+

TABLE III contd

	Status	Sub-Antarctic zone	Antarctic zone	
			Low latitude	High latitude
Sphacelaria furcigera Kütz	cosmopolitan	+	·	·
Stereocladon rugulosus (Bory) Hariot	endemic	+	+	+
RHODOPHYTA				
Antarctocolax lambii Skottsb.	endemic	·	+	·
Antithamnion antarcticum Kylin	endemic	·	+	·
Bangia fuscopurpurea (Dillw.) Lyngb.	cosmopolitan	+	·	·
***Ballia callitricha* (Agardh) Kütz.**	endemic	+	+	+
Bostrychia mixta J. D. Hooker & Harvey	S. circumpolar	+	·	·
Bostrychia vaga J. D. Hooker & Harvey	endemic	+	·	·
Callophyllis tenera J. Agardh	endemic	+	+	·
Callophyllis variegata (Bory) Kützing	cosmopolitan	+	+	·
Centroceras clavulatum (Agardh) Montagne	cosmopolitan	+	·	·
Ceramium rubrum (Hudson) C. Agardh	cosmopolitan	+	·	·
Chaetangium fastigiatum (Bory) J. Agardh	endemic	+	·	·
Corallina goughensis Chamberlain	endemic	+	·	·
Corallina officinalis L.	cosmopolitan	+	+	·
***Curdiea racovitzae* Hariot**	endemic	·	+	·
Delesseria epiglossum J. Agardh	endemic	+	·	·
Delesseria lancifolia (J. D. Hooker) J. Agardh	endemic	+	+	·
Delesseria staphanocarpa (A. & E. S. Gepp) Skottsberg	endemic	·	+	·
Delisea pulchra (Greville) Montagne	endemic	+	·	·
Dermatolithon nodulosum Chamberlain	endemic	+	·	·
Gelidium regulare Baards.	endemic?	+	·	·
Georgiella confluens (Reinsch) Kylin	endemic	·	+	·
***Gigartina papillosa* (Bory) Setchell & Gardner**	endemic	+	+	·
Gymnogongrus antarcticus Skottsb.	endemic	·	+	·
Herposiphonia paniculata Baards.	endemic	+	·	·
***Hildenbrandia lecannellieri* Hariot**	endemic	+	?	·
***Iridaea obovata* Kutz.**	endemic	+	+	+
***Iridaea laminarioides* Bory**	cosmopolitan	+	·	+
Iridaea undulosa Bory	S. hemisphere	+	·	·

	1	2	3	Distribution
Kallymenia antarctica Hariot	+	+	+	endemic
Leptosomia simplex (A. & E. S. Gepp) Kylin	+	·	·	endemic
Lythophyllum aequabile (Foslie) Foslie	·	+	+	endemic
Lithophyllum subantarcticum (Foslie) Foslie	·	+	+	endemic
Lithothamnion antarcticum (J. D. Hooker & Harvey) Foslie	·	+	+	endemic
Lithothamnion granuliferum Foslie	·	+	+	endemic
Lithothamnion neglectum (Foslie) Foslie	·	+	+	endemic
Lithothamnion schmitzii (Hariot) Heydrich	·	+	+	endemic
Lophurella hookeriana (J. Agardh) Falkenb.	·	·	+	endemic
Lophurella patula (J. D. Hooker & Harvey) De Toni	·	·	+	endemic?
Lophosiphonia scopulorum (Harv.) Womersley	·	+	+	S. hemisphere
Myriogramme mangini (Gain) Skottsberg	·	+	+	endemic
Myriogramme smithii (J. D. Hooker & Harvey) Kylin	+	+	+	endemic
Pantoneura plocamioides Kylin	·	+	·	endemic
Phycodrys antarctica	·	·	·	
Phycodrys quercifolia (Bory) Skottsberg	+	+	+	endemic
Phyllophora antarctica A. & E. S. Gepp	+	·	·	endemic
Phyllophora appendiculata Skottsberg	·	+	+	endemic
Picconiella plumosa (Kylin) De Toni	·	+	+	endemic
Plocamium coccineum (Hudson) Lyngbye	+	+	+	bipolar
Plocamium hookeri Harvey	·	+	+	endemic
Plocamium secundatum (Kützing) Kützing	·	+	+	endemic
Plumariopsis eatoni (Dickie) De Toni	·	+	+	endemic
Polysiphonia abscissa J. D. Hooker & Harvey	+	+	+	endemic
Polysiphonia boergesenni Baards.	·	+	+	endemic?
Polysiphonia howei Hollenb. apud W. R. Taylor	·	+	+	cosmopolitan
Porphyra endiviifolium (A. & E. S. Gepp) Chamberlain	·	·	·	endemic
Porphyra tristanensis Baards.	·	+	+	endemic
Porphyra umbilicalis (L.) Kütz.	+	·	+	cosmopolitan
Rhodoglossum revolutum Baards.	·	+	+	endemic
Rhodomenia palmatiformis Skottsb.	·	·	+	endemic
Schizoseris laciniata (Kütz.)	+	+	+	endemic

[a] Indicates presence at South Georgia only; ?, status uncertain.

these species have also been found in rock pools where they are similarly protected from ice action. However, the bottom of many pools is covered entirely with a thick diatom felt (e.g. *Melosira sphaerica* Karsten at Signy Island (T.M.W.)). The nitrogenophil *Enteromorpha bulbosa* (Suhr) Montagne occurs in pools and on rocks receiving excrement from bird colonies (Lamb and Zimmerman, 1977; Hastings, 1977).

The vegetation becomes richer with depth. The shallow water species *Curdiea*, *Leptosomia*, *Iridaea*, *Ascoseira mirabilis* Skottsberg and *Gigartina papillosa* (Bory) Setchell and Gardner appear in increasingly more exposed positions. *Desmarestia ligulata* (Lightfoot) Lamouroux, *D. anceps* Montagne and *D. menziesii* J. Agardh often dominate the flora down to 10 m below mean low water and extend down to 25 m. Below this the largest Antarctic brown alga, *Phyllogigas grandifolius* (A. and E. S. Gepp) Skottsberg tends to be dominant and has been reported well below 50 m (Zaneveld, 1966a; Hastings, 1977; Lamb and Zimmerman, 1977). Below 40 m the communities gradually become sparse again. However, several species have been recorded from depths in excess of 100 m, e.g. *Phycodrys antarctica*, *Leptosomia simplex*, *Plocamium coccineum* (Hudson) Lyngbye, *Desmarestia menziesii*, *Monostroma hariotii*, *Phaeoglossom monacanthum* Skottsberg and *Phyllogigas grandifolius*. *Ballia callitricha* (Agardh) Kützing has a reported upper limit of 37 m (Zaneveld, 1966a, 1968; Skottsberg, 1962). The many records of apparently macroalgal material from great depths, often in excess of 300 m, present an interesting problem for phycologists (p. 398). Some records can be discounted as being the product of recorded depth errors or uprooted plants recently transported by currents or ice (Skottsberg and Neushul, 1960; Skottsberg, 1962; · Neushul, 1965; Zaneveld, 1968), but enough apparently reliable records remain to establish the occurrence of plants living at these depths (Lund, 1959; Wilce, 1967; Zaneveld, 1968).

Several small macroalgae have been reported as epiphytes, e.g. *Plocamium coccineum*, *Myriogramme smithii* (Hooker and Harvey) Kylin and *M. mangini* (Gain) Skottsberg, the latter being itself a common host for *Georgiella confluens* (Rausch) Kylin. *Antarctocolax lambii* Skottsberg is a tiny parasite on the deep water red alga *Picconiella plumosa* (Kylin) G. de Toni (Lamb and Zimmerman, 1977).

Macroalgae in general have a wide variety of growth strategies and life cycles and Antarctic species are no exception. *Adenocystis utricularis* (Bory) Skottsberg and *Monostroma hariotii* Gain are annuals appearing suddenly on bare rock or on encrusting red algae in early summer. Growth is rapid and maturation is attained in 6–8 weeks after which the plants disintegrate leaving microspores to survive the winter.

Leptosomia simplex, which sprouts anew from a permanent holdfast

TABLE IV

Vertical zonation on Antarctic and sub-Antarctic shores

Depth	Sub-Antarctic (After Chamberlain, 1965; Knox, 1960)	Northern (After Stockton, 1973; Neushul, 1968)	Southern (After Zaneveld, 1965)
EHWS	Lichens Blue-green algae Verucaria sp. Porphyria tristanensis Hildenbrandia Blidingia minima	Lichens	**Ulothris australis** **Prasiola crispa**
MLLW	**Iridaea laminarioides** **Rhodoglossum revolutum** Durvillaea antarctica	Monostroma, Ulothrix/ **Chaetomorpha**, Urospora **Curdiea racovitzae** Adenocystis utricularis	"BARREN ZONE" (Diatoms in summer)
ELWS	**Dermatolithum, Lithophyllum** Lithothamnium	**Lithophyllum** **Lithothamnion** Leptosomia simplex Adenocystis utricularis	**Monostroma hariotii** **Hildenbrandia lecanellieri** **Phyllophora antarctica** **Iridaea obovata**
−10 m			Plocamium coccineum
−20 m	**Macrocystis pyrifera**	**Gigartina papillosa** **Plocamium coccineum** **Desmarestia anceps** **Desmarestia menziesii** **Desmarstia ligulata**	Leptosomia simplex
−30 m		**Phyllogigas grandifolium**	**Phyllogigas grandifolium**
−40 m		Piconiella plumosa Delisea pulchra Lambia antarctica	
−50 m			
−60 m			Ballia calitricha

each season, is described as pseudoperennial. At Petermann Island (65°10'S, 64°10'W) new growth appears in early October and reaches maturity in December, when numerous tetraspores are borne on lateral shoots. The tetraspores germinate the following October and produce a short sterile shoot in the first summer season. Development is completed the following summer. Few adult plants escape destruction by ice scour and so the life cycle may be also considered biennial (Gain, 1912). Another pseudoperennial is *Myriogramme manginii* whose tough, brown, irregularly-branched stipes persist throughout the winter and produce foliose fronds in January or later (Lamb and Zimmerman, 1977).

The majority of the macroalgae are true perennials, but little is known about their growth. Hastings (1977), in the most complete study to date of an Antarctic perennial, demonstrated a markedly seasonal pattern of growth in the endemic *Phyllogigas grandifolius*. Photosynthate accumulation started in September at Signy Island and growth followed a sigmoid curve. Elongation of the lamina was slow in September and October and ash weight per unit area decreased. There was then a phase of rapid elongation and increasing photosynthesis and carbon accumulation rates which reached a maximum in early December. Although surface light flux was at a maximum in late December, light penetration was reduced at this time by phytoplankton and later by suspended sediment. Growth rate decreased until May, after which no growth was recorded. An increasing ash content indicated utilization of stored carbon for maintenance and possibly the formation of reproductive structures. Mannitol (storage carbon) minimum and ash weight maximum occurred in late winter (August).

There is no record of any study on the microphytobenthos which includes a great variety of epipelic, epilithic and epiphytic microalgae, primarily diatoms. Fragmentary evidence suggests that in general benthic diatoms in shallow water proliferate in early summer before any significant phytoplankton growth occurs. However Lamb and Zimmerman (1977) observed massive epiphytic diatom growths around the Melchior Islands (64°19'S, 62°57'W) during the midsummer period. When one of us (T.M.W.) observed a similar phenomenon in Borge Bay, Signy Island—webs of *Biddulphia punctata* and *Nitzschia sublineata* covering *Desmarestia* at 8 m depth—the growth occurred during a temporary reduction in phytoplankton density. The microphytobenthos persists at least until the end of March around Anvers Island (Krebbs, 1973) and even as far south as Rothera Point, Adelaide Island (67°34'S, 68°08'W), where a diatom film covered otherwise bare rocks down to approximately 5 m (T.M.W.).

3. Factors Influencing Physiology

Forty-five years ago Hart (1934) reviewed the possible factors limiting the activities of the phytoplankton in the Antarctic zones. He concluded that of the major nutrients only silicate was likely to be limiting and then only in certain areas. He made passing reference to the effect of "minute traces of iron and of soil washings" but at that time plant physiologists were only just becoming aware of the effects of trace elements. Hart thought that it was the physical features of the environment (light intensity and duration, ice, surface water stability and currents) that exerted the "strongest influence upon phytoplankton production in the far south". Since Hart's conclusions were published there has been a considerable increase in knowledge of plant physiology and ecology in general, but little direct knowledge gained with respect to Antarctic species. To the factors selected by Hart as important have been added biological factors such as grazing and settling rates, but there has been no further evaluation, as will be discussed.

3.1 Macronutrients

The *Discovery* Investigations showed that concentrations of nitrate, phosphate and silicate were rather high in the surface waters of all Southern Ocean zones, and remained so throughout the year, in contrast to temperate and tropical seas other than their upwelling regions (Deacon, 1937a; Clowes, 1938). The silicate content could fall below detectable levels in certain northern areas of the Southern Ocean, presumably during periods of maximum diatom production. Upwelling of the Warm Deep Water at a divergence in the region between westerly and easterly winds (Chapter 6) is generally thought to provide a rich supply of macronutrients to the surface waters of the southern Antarctic zone. The concentrations gradually decrease as the surface waters move away from the continent. Additional nutrients may be supplied from the Weddell Drift Divergence (60°00′–62°30′S, 35°00′W–30°00′E), the Scotia Sea Divergence (61°00′–58°00′S, 42°00′W–63°00′W), Koopman's Bouvet Divergence (57°00′S, 61°00′W) (Mackintosh, 1972) and an upwelling area near 58°00′S, 48°00′W (Movchan, 1975). There may be another area of upwelling in the sub-Antarctic zone near the Antarctic Convergence (Movchan, 1975). Recorded values for the macronutrients range from 0.18 to 30.0 μg-at l^{-1} NO_3-N, 0.01 to 2.2 μg-at l^{-1} PO_4-P and 0.18 to 90.0 μg-at l^{-1} SiO_3-Si. Summer minimum values often exceed the winter maximum values recorded in lower latitudes. Mean values are often given, but they are of little value because they are only the means of recorded values and are unlikely to reflect either the areal, seasonal or annual situation.

Nutrient availability can affect plants in two main ways. It can be yield limiting, in which case the maximum amount of biomass attained is determined by the least available nutrient; or it can be rate limiting, in which case plants are only able to take up the nutrients at reduced rates and growth rate becomes sub-optimal. High nutrient concentrations remain after the period of maximum production in most areas of the Southern Ocean. El-Sayed (1971b) measured concentrations of 2.49 μg-at l^{-1} NO_3-N, 2.02 μg-at l^{-1} PO_4-P and 68.00 μg-at l^{-1} SiO_3-Si during a bloom of phytoplankton which covered more than 15,500 km² of the southern Weddell Sea off the Filchner Ice Shelf. Chlorophyll a values as high as 123 μg l^{-1} were recorded. Therefore yield limitation through macronutrient levels would appear unlikely in the Southern Ocean in general. It may occur however in sheltered inshore areas (Mandelli and Burkholder, 1966; Bienati *et al.*, 1977).

Under rate limiting conditions nutrient utilization, photosynthetic effciency and cell composition may vary considerably (Droop, 1973). Uptake of salts by phytoplankton cells is an energy-dependent process following the laws of enzymatic uptake kinetics, although there is no firm evidence that the uptake is in fact enzyme mediated. Rate limitation is usually expressed in terms of the concentration of a nutrient at which the uptake rate by a species is half the maximum rate, and it is termed the k constant. The concentration at which uptake becomes limited is determined by many factors, of which temperature is one (Thomas and Dodson, 1974), and varies from species to species (Chu, 1943). It is unfortunate therefore that most experimental determinations of k have been made over the temperature range of 8–25°C and that there are no data on Antarctic species.

Thomas (1970) showed rate limitation in a natural mixed population of diatoms and dinoflagellates when NO_3-N fell below 3 μg-at l^{-1}. Uptake k constants were 0.75 μg-at l^{-1} and 1.5 μg-at l^{-1} for NO_3-N and NH_4-N respectively. In *Skeletonema costatum* (Grev.) Cleve the NO_3-N constant is less than 0.22 μg-at l^{-1} (Falkowski and Stone, 1975) and in *Ditylum brightwellii* (West) Grunow it is 0.4 μg-at l^{-1} (Eppley and Coatsworth, 1968). Nitrate is probably rate limiting below 1.5 μg-at l^{-1} for many marine microalgae (Goering, 1971) with k constants ranging from 0.1 μg-at l^{-1} to 6.5 μg-at l^{-1} (Thomas and Dodson, 1974; Eppley *et al.*, 1969; Eppley and Thomas, 1969).

Fewer data are available on phosphate-uptake rate limitation in marine plants, but it has been known for many years that *Nitzschia closterium* (Ehrenberg) W. Smith divides more slowly when PO_4-P concentrations fall below 0.53 μg-at l^{-1} (Ketchum, 1939). Known k constants for marine algae fall between 0.12 μg-at l^{-1} and 0.60 μg-at l^{-1} PO_4-P (Thomas and

Dodson, 1968; Yull Rhee, 1973). Paasche (1973) obtained SiO_3–Si uptake k constants between 0.80μg-at l^{-1} and 3.37μg-at l^{-1} for *Skeletonema costatum*, *Thalassiosira decipiens* (Grunow) Jørgensen, *Thalassiosira pseudonana*, *Ditylum brightwellii* and a *Licmorphora* sp. The uptake kinetics only conformed to the Michaelis-Menton pattern if account was taken of a residual 0.5–1.5μg-at l^{-1} of unavailable bound SiO_3–Si.

Extrapolation of the data for application in the Southern Ocean must be done with extreme caution because little is known about low temperature uptake kinetics. Macronutrients are unlikely to be rate limiting in most surface waters, but just south of the Antarctic Convergence silicate could be in short supply, promoting the post-maximal summer diatom decrease (Hart, 1942; Holm-Hansen *et al.*, 1977). Phosphate and nitrate can become limiting in enclosed inshore waters. In Borge Bay, Signy Island, summer minima in 1973–1974 were 0.34μg-at l^{-1} PO_4–P and 1.16μg-at l^{-1} NO_3–N. Additions of phosphates and nitrates, separately and in combination, indicated that PO_4–P was rate limiting below 0.59μg-at l^{-1} for a natural mixed phytoplankton population dominated by *Thalassiosira antarctica* Comber (Whitaker, 1977b).

Few data are available on the nutrient environment of the ice associated diatoms. Bunt and Lee (1970) found that at the peak of the growing season in McMurdo Sound the concentration of NO_3–N in ice, interstitial water and water 5 m below the ice was 4.35, 7.07 and 7.70μg-at l^{-1} respectively. The corresponding PO_4–P values were 0.75, 2.16 and 2.16μg-at l^{-1}. Presumably the nutrients are concentrated with other salts when water molecules are extracted from the sea water in the formation of ice (Chapter 6). They remain in the interstitial brine until utilized by the plants. They can be replenished by the draining down of brine from higher levels, when increasing ice thickness raises the ice sheet further out of the water, and by washing down of ions through the ice during surface melt in summer (Ackley *et al.*, 1978; Oradovskii, 1974). These elements do not appear to be the dominant factors limiting yield or productivity of ice-associated algae. However these algae are often associated with zones of high pH, probably caused by removal of carbon dioxide during photosynthesis. Extreme values of pH 9.20 and 9.61 have been reported (Hoshiai, 1972; Oradovskii, 1974). As pH rises there is a shift away from free carbon dioxide towards a predominance of bicarbonate and then carbonate ions. Some algae are able to use bicarbonate ions directly, but it is possible that this increase in pH could limit the productivity of any obligate-free carbon dioxide user. Carbon limitation is most unusual in marine environments and does not appear to be a factor in Antarctica.

No data are available for benthic algae but it would seem unlikely that macronutrient limitation is ever a dominant factor controlling growth. The plants are adnate on rocks or other plants and washed by constantly changing water moved by currents and tidal action. The macroalgae also have much greater storage capability than phytoplankton.

3.2 Micronutrients

There is very little information on the concentration of micronutrients in the Southern Ocean and their effect on the plant populations. Carlucci and Cuhel (1977) after studying the distribution and significance of vitamins B_{12}, thiamine and biotin in the Indian Ocean sector concluded that most of the phytoplankton do not require vitamins. Vitamins are produced by bacteria and phytoplankton, and are utilized by vitamin-requiring organisms at rates approaching the rates at which they are produced. The vitamin-requiring phytoplankton also utilize vitamins produced in highly productive areas which have been transported to other locations by the movements of water masses. The results of this investigation also suggested that naturally occurring vitamin B_{12} concentrations could limit growth of vitamin-requiring diatoms. However, it seems unlikely that the limitation could be of great ecological importance. Trace metals may be important in limiting plant growth. Volkovinskii (1966) found a positive correlation between phytoplankton production and levels of manganese and molybdenum in the Weddell Sea. Cobalt, zinc, copper and vanadium may be important (El-Sayed, 1968), as may iron (Fogg, 1977). Chelating agents should also be considered, for it is now known that by binding ions they may make them more readily available for plant uptake (Barber and Ryther, 1969), or reduce any phytotoxic effects (Davey et al., 1973). This field seems a profitable one for future research. The areas of highest productivity in the Southern Ocean are known to be in shallow water (shelf frontal zones are normally areas of upwelling and mixing (Bowman and Esaias, 1978) and even the proximity of the bottom can induce local upwelling) and in deep water near divergence zones and where different water masses mix (all areas where trace elements may be supplied).

3.3 Temperature

Gran (1932) and Hart (1934) thought that Antarctic marine plants were fully adapted to low temperatures. However, recent experimental evidence indicates that although many plants are obligate psychrophiles showing a sharp metabolic drop-off above 10°C, their various metabolic rates are sub-optimal over the range of temperatures naturally occurring in the Southern Ocean. Eppley (1972) related specific growth, μ (the ratio of increase in cell substance per unit of cell substance as a function of time), to temperature ($t°C$) by the equation

$$\log_{10}\mu = 0.0275t - 0.07$$

This predicts a μ value of 0.76 at $-1.8°C$, but Antarctic plants studied so far show much lower values. *Nitzschia sublineata*, a prominent member of the sea ice flora, was found to have a μ value of 0.34 doublings day^{-1} *in situ* at $-1.5°C$ in McMurdo Sound when the population was in the logarithmic growth phase (Bunt, 1968). Optimum temperature for growth was 5–7°C; at higher temperatures the growth rate fell and temperatures in excess of 10°C were generally lethal. Thirteen other diatoms and a dinoflagellate, also prominent members of the McMurdo Sound ice community, showed similar behaviour.

Growth-rate data from the *Eltanin* cruises provide a peak μ value of 0.33 doublings day^{-1} for phytoplankton populations and in many cases maximal rates were close to 0.1 doublings day^{-1}. Whitaker (1977b) obtained a mean value of 0.18 doublings day^{-1} for *Thalassiosira antarctica* Comber at temperatures of -0.4 to $-0.5°C$ during the primary spring increase in Borge Bay, Signy Island. Drew (1977) found that rates of photosynthesis considerably greater than those occurring at *in situ* temperatures (0.0–1.0°C) could be obtained at temperatures up to 15°C when studying 13 benthic macroalgae from Borge Bay, Signy Island. *Phyllogigas grandifolius*, *Desmarestia anceps* and a *Leptosomia* sp. more than doubled their gross photosynthesis rates, but *Ascoseira mirabilis* Skottsberg merely increased its rate by about 15%—some indication of adaptation. However, the overall effect of low temperature appears to be beneficial to Antarctic plants, as will be seen in the next section.

3.4 Light

Limitation of available light intensity, duration and spectra is a particularly important factor in the biology of Antarctic marine plants. First, the southern Antarctic zone beyond 66°S latitude is subject to polar night, the duration of which increases with latitude (60 days at 70°S, 100 days at 75°S). Secondly, the height of the sun above the horizon is relatively lower for a greater part of the year than in temperate and tropical latitudes. The low angle of incidence of the sun's rays increases the reflection from the sea surface. The reduced submarine light has a longer path through the water, which affects the spectral composition of light in each metre stratum through increased absorption of long and short wave-lengths. The period of effective submarine light per day is also reduced. Thirdly, the Southern Ocean is particularly stormy. Although disturbance of the surface may have relatively little effect on the total radiation entering the water (Ångstrom, 1925), air bubbles probably reduce transmission through the surface waters considerably (Powell and Clarke, 1936). Fourthly, 56% of the Southern Ocean (20.0×10^6 km²) is covered with ice during the winter. Most of this breaks up, floats north and melts during the summer, but approximately 3.5×10^6 km² remains as fast and pack ice, mainly in the Weddell and Ross Seas (Chapter 6, Fig. 4). The ice and especially the associated snow cover reduce the amount of submarine illumination considerably and change its spectral composition. Finally, decreasing light intensities with depth are an even greater problem for benthic algae in regions where the abrasive action of icebergs, pack and fast ice severely restricts the area of shallow water suitable for colonization. Some Antarctic marine plants appear to be adapted to low light levels, but current information suggests that the adaptation does not involve changing the enzymatic content of the cell as described by Jørgensen (1964, 1969) for some diatoms, or the pigment content as in *Chlorella* (Steemann-Nielsen and Jørgensen, 1968).

The relationship between available light intensity and photosynthetic rate can be described by a rectangular hyperbolic function (Soeder and Stengal, 1974). The equation of the curve is affected to a considerable extent by temperature (Fig. 2) and the effects of light intensity and temperature on photosynthetic rate must be considered together.

The effect of temperature on the compensation point light intensity is of particular importance. The compensation point light intensity is that at which the production of carbon by photosynthesis exactly balances carbon loss through other metabolic processes (as indicated by respiration). Growth occurs when light levels are above the compensation point light intensity. Photosynthesis is affected less by change in temperature than the other metabolic processes. This is largely because the initial stage of photosynthesis is a photochemical dissociation of water; the subsequent processing is by chemical reactions and consequently temperature dependent. Therefore at sub-optimal light levels, light controls photosynthetic rate. Consequently, in the cold waters of the Southern Ocean the rate of respiration (or carbon loss) is suppressed more than the photosynthetic rate (or carbon gain). The result is a proportionate increase in net production for a given light intensity and the compensation point light intensity is correspondingly lowered. This is a valuable adjustment for all Antarctic plants—marine, freshwater and terrestrial (Kanwisher, 1966; Collins, 1977; Fogg, 1977; Priddle, 1980a,b). It is not an adaptation in the strict sense but a direct response to temperature which is beneficial. However, gross fixation is very small.

Extremely low compensation point light intensities have been reported for some Antarctic marine plants. Bunt (1964a,b) found that the compensation point light intensity for a mixed population of sea ice algae was between

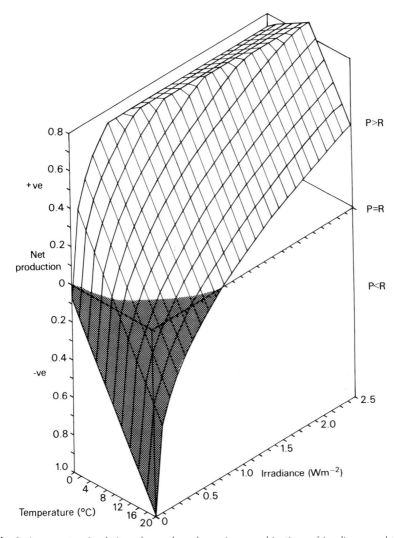

Fig. 2. A computer simulation of growth under various combinations of irradiance and temperature. (Kindly provided by Dr J. Priddle and based on *Drepanocladus* data published in Priddle, 1980b.) P, photosynthesis; R, respiration.

0.433 W m^{-2} and 0.865 W m^{-2} (2.5–5.0 ft candles) and for phytoplankton 10–15 m below the ice 0.865 W m^{-2} (5.0 ft candles). In later work on the diatom *Nitzschia sublineata* colonizing the brash ice layer in McMurdo Sound, Bunt (1968) found a compensation intensity of 0.349 W m^{-2} (0.0005 langley min^{-1}). In contrast Drew (1977) found relatively high compensation point values of 2–26 W m^{-2} for 13 species of macroalgae in Borge

Bay, Signy Island. The algae included the endemic species *Ascoseira mirabilis* and *Phyllogigas grandifolius*. Drew compared his results with data obtained for similar species from temperate regions and concluded that the Antarctic species he had studied showed no obvious adaptation to the extreme conditions of their enviroment. They had chlorophyll contents very similar to their temperate counterparts and photosynthesis and re-spiration rates also very similar to temperate species in winter. He sug-gested that the similarity of the respiration rates was to be expected since even temperate algae have low Q_{10} values for respiration in the 0–10°C range during the winter in Britain.

The depth at which the light intensity is equal to the compensation intensity is called the compensation depth, and the zone above this depth is called the euphotic zone. This naturally varies from species to species but for convenience it has generally been considered to lie above the depth at which the light intensity is 1% of incident radiation at noon. This may have no application to Antarctic plants, because Burkholder and Mandelli (1965) found more than one-half of the phytoplankton chlorophyll *a* below the 1% euphotic zone in inshore and offshore areas of the Bellingshausen Sea. In the absence of specific compensation point intensity measurements it is probably better to consider the euphotic zone as extending to at least the depth where the light intensity is reduced to 0.25 W m^{-2} (approximately 0.1% of incident illumination) (El-Sayed and Turner, 1977; Holm-Hansen *et al.*, 1977; El-Sayed, 1978). This depth may vary between 40 and 200 m. Holm-Hansen (1974) has suggested that "photobiology" studies should extend to at least 500 m in all latitudes. Drew (1977) discounts Zaneveld's (1968) suggestion of active growth of benthic algae by phototrophic means at depths as great as 600 m in the Southern Ocean. He pointed out that Jerlov and Koczy (1951) found $1 \times 10^{-7}\%$ of surface irradiance at 600 m which could only represent 0.0004 W m^{-2} on the sunniest day possible. Facultative heterotrophy has often been postulated for both phytoplankton and phytobenthos. Available evidence suggests that few algae have this ability and no species is likely to compete successfully with bacteria for the low amounts of dissolved organic nutrients available in natural waters. Another hypothesis is that plants may be capable of the phototrophic assimilation of dissolved organic substances under very low light condi-tions. The process may give higher yields of growth per unit of light energy than normal photosynthesis (Fogg and Horne, 1970). Low compensation points could make such abilities unnecessary for most, if not all, Antarctic plants. Fogg (1977) thought that growth as a result of normal photosyn-thetic assimilation of carbon dioxide exceeding respiration, even at very low light intensities at near zero temperatures, could account for the observed biomasses. Drew (1977) concluded that it did not seem necessary to consider heterotrophy to account for the growth of most of the phyto-benthos at Signy Island, despite the relatively high compensation points recorded and the low light intensities prevailing even in the summer.

Although beneficial during the greater part of the year, adaptation to low light intensities can be disadvantageous at times during the summer when high light intensities may inhibit phytoplankton growth. This is a normal effect under conditions where photochemical energy fixation exceeds the carbon assimilation capacity of the cell (Ryther, 1956). Holm-Hansen (1974), however, pointed out that photoinhibition is not necessarily a simple relationship, but depends on the immediate history of the cells, nutrient concentrations and temperature as well as light intensity. Assimilation numbers commonly do not indicate photoinhibition, and he suggested that some profiles which have been interpreted as showing surface inhibition could indicate instead that there is greater grazing pressure in surface levels. Workers on U.S.S. *Eltanin* have observed photoinhibition in surface phytoplankton when mean light intensities exceeded about $1.7 \, \text{W m}^{-2}$ throughout 8 h (70 g cal cm^{-2} half light day^{-1}). No photoinhibition was observed on cloudy days when mean light intensities were in the range 0.49–$0.73 \, \text{W m}^{-2}$ throughout 8 h (20–30 g cal cm^{-2} half light day^{-1}) (Holm-Hansen *et al.*, 1977). Burkholder and Mandelli (1965) recorded saturation light intensities of 2.69–$7.27 \, \text{W m}^{-2}$ for mixed populations of phytoplankton from inshore and offshore areas of the Bellingshausen Sea. Inhibition of the surface phytoplankton was observed at intensities ranging from 7.27–$8.10 \, \text{W m}^{-2}$. Cold water phytoplankton and perhaps the phyto-benthos appear to have a metabolic preadaptation which increases survival chances during the long dark winter. This prevents maximal productivity during the brief summer, but a higher metabolic rate, with associated higher respiration rate and compensation light intensity point, would only serve to extend the "winter" period. However, more experimental work is urgently needed in this field (see Jones, 1978).

The spectral composition of submarine light is important because each type of plant photosynthetic pigment absorbs the various wavelengths to a different degree, and the pigment composition varies between major plant groups (Baatz, 1941; Harder and Bedeke, 1957; Strickland, 1965). Chromatic adaptation has been reported (Stanbury, 1931; Brody and Emerson, 1959), but no information is available on the spectral needs of Antarctic plants.

If a plant is to achieve a net gain of carbon (growth) within a certain time, the period when it receives light of above compensation intensity must be greater than the period when it receives light of less intensity. Growth may therefore be curtailed by daylength and by vertical movement within the water column. Hastings (1977) showed that daylength was as important as light intensity in promoting growth in *Phyllogigas grandifolius*, an endemic benthic macroalga of circumpolar distribution. Reduction of the period an individual phytoplankton cell stays within the euphotic zone has been put forward as the main (Gran, 1932; Hasle, 1956), or as a major (Saijo and Kawashima, 1964; El-Sayed *et al.*, 1964) limitation of primary production within the Southern Ocean. Phytoplankton are carried out of the euphotic zone by water movement in areas of downwelling (convergence zones) and primary production in these areas of the Southern Ocean appears to be exceptionally low. Over the greater area of the world ocean, however, phytoplankton movement is brought about by wind-generated turbulence, the effective depth of which is largely controlled by the stability of the water column.

3.5 Stability of the water column

The depth of the Antarctic Surface Water increases with decreasing latitude as the newly formed water mixes with the Warm Deep Water (Chapter 6). The boundary layer has been recorded at 100–150 m in 67°S latitude and 150–200 m in 64°S latitude (Deacon, 1933, 1937a). Stability in the Antarctic Surface Water is slight during winter because of the very small differences in temperature and salinity with depth. The water is homogeneous to at least 100 m. Hydrological conditions change in spring, as sea and land ice melt and dilute the surface layers with fresh water. The temperature of the less saline water is raised 1–2°C by solar radiation which increases the stability of the surface layers. On calm sunny days near the ice edge and inshore, the discontinuity layer may lie within 5–10 m of the surface and the temperature difference may be 3°C. This layer is quickly dispersed by wind action and ordinarily near the ice the discontinuity layer is at 20–30 m. The presence of loose pack ice aids stability by physically damping down wave action. Some of the immediate increase in phytoplankton biomass recorded following the break-up of ice is no doubt due to the release of ice-associated diatoms (Hart, 1934; Walsh, 1969). A period of maximum production often follows, but this is by different species and the increased productivity must be due to the imposed stability. El-Sayed (1978) has suggested that the high primary production (up to $1.56 \, \text{g C m}^{-2} \text{day}^{-1}$) recorded in 1968 over more than 15,500 km^2 of the southern Weddell Sea may have been due to a strong pycnocline (plane of separation between two layers of water of different density) produced by the melting of ice at the edge of the Filchner Ice Shelf. The sharpness of the discontinuity layer decreases and its depth increases with distance from the ice edge, and as the season advances, because of mixing by wind action. This could explain in part the time difference in onset of the period of maximum production in the various regions (see pp. 375–377); the ice melt and surface water warming, and therefore most stable surface water, moves southward as summer progresses. It could also explain in part the greater productivity recorded in neritic areas which receive run-off from land throughout the summer, and especially in sheltered areas such as the Gerlache Strait (64°30′S, 62°20′W) (Burkholder and Sieburth, 1961; Burkholder and Mandelli, 1965; El-Sayed, 1968). The *Discovery* Investigations found that the depth to which wind action was generally effective in overturning the water column in the open ocean (the depth of frictional resistance (Ekman, 1928)) ranged from 60 to 80 m and the water was fairly uniform to a depth of 80 m, especially after storms (Deacon, 1933). On a recent (1979) R.R.S. *Discovery* cruise in sector 20°E to 30°E longitude one of us (R.B.H.) observed the discontinuity layer at 112 m after a two-day storm in latitude 56°S.

The depth of the Sub-Antarctic Surface Water also varies with latitude, having been recorded as 1100 m deep at 45°S latitude and 1450 m deep at 40°30′S latitude (Deacon, 1937a). It consists of a surface water mass originating in more temperature zones and, underneath, the Antarctic Surface Water moving north from the Antarctic Convergence (Chapter 6). The two water masses are well mixed together at their common boundary and it is difficult to distinguish them from temperature and salinity profiles. Strong westerly winds are prevalent throughout the sub-Antarctic zone. Vertical mixing of the surface layers is particularly vigorous over an area extending 160–240 km north of the Antarctic Convergence. Temperature and salinities are uniform to depths of 150 m. Salinity was uniform to 300–400 m at 80°W longitude (Deacon, 1937a). In the northern part of the zone the surface water remains homogeneous to 60–80 m (Deacon, 1937a).

The depth to which the surface waters can be mixed without stopping plant growth is called the critical depth (Sverdrup, 1953). It is usually less than five times the compensation depth. In view of the revised definition for the euphotic zone for Antarctic phytoplankton given above it would seem unlikely that the mixed layer is ever as great as the euphotic zone in any part of the stormy Southern Ocean. However, a deep mixed layer throughout most of the growing season could keep primary production well below its potential maximum.

3.6 Other factors

Although other factors have been put forward as of probable importance in controlling primary production or plant biomass, such as the settling out of the phytoplankton from the euphotic zone and grazing down by zooplankton, no studies have been directed to assess their importance in the Southern Ocean as far as we know. During periods of maximum production phytoplankton cells may become buoyant, presumably because of lipids stored in the cytoplasm (Smayda and Boleyn, 1965). At other times some turbulence is necessary to stop plant cells sinking out of the euphotic zone, even though most algae have morphological adaptations to increase the surface area to volume ratio, or otherwise reduce the sinking rate, and flagellates are capable of some weak movement. However, during ice-free periods in the Southern Ocean excessive turbulence is more likely to be the dominant factor. Plant loss through settling out is not of ecological importance at these times. Sometimes an inverse relationship between zooplankton and plant biomass has been recorded (Hart, 1942; Volkovinskii, 1969), but there do not appear to be the productivity data to confirm that the relationship is a result of grazing although clearly this is the most likely cause.

A summary of all the known variables affecting plant biomass and productivity is given in Fig. 3.

4. Primary Production

4.1 The phytoplankton

As is common in other world oceans, neritic areas and areas of the Southern Ocean where there is upwelling appear to be considerably more productive than deep or open ocean areas. The levels of productivity recorded are comparable with those from similar areas of high productivity in other latitudes. Values in excess of $10\,mg\,m^{-3}$ and $2\,g\,m^{-2}\,day^{-1}$ have frequently been measured for chlorophyll a and carbon fixation respectively (Burkholder and Sieburth, 1961; Burkholder and Mandelli, 1965; Mandelli and Burkholder, 1966; El-Sayed, 1966, 1968, 1971a; Horne et al., 1969; Bienati et al., 1977; Bonner et al., 1978; and others). In contrast, chlorophyll a values for the open ocean are rarely reported as high as $1.0\,mg\,m^{-3}$ and are usually half that value. Daily production in excess of $1.0\,g\,C\,m^{-2}\,day^{-1}$ has been recorded, but more commonly values are close to $0.2\,g\,C\,m^{-2}\,day^{-1}$ (El Sayed et al., 1964; Mandelli and Burkholder, 1966; El-Sayed, 1966, 1970a; and others). Again these values are comparable with those recorded for open ocean areas in lower latitudes. The open ocean area of the Southern Ocean is 12 times larger than the combined neritic and upwelling areas. Consequently it must supply the bulk of the primary production, though at a low rate of productivity.

Considerable caution must be exercised in any attempt to extrapolate annual production from these figures. Relatively few observations have yet been made in this vast ocean, and the methods and techniques currently used have many limitations (El-Sayed, 1966; Holm-Hansen, 1974). Obser-

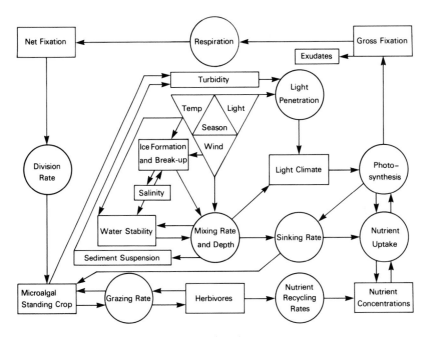

Fig. 3. The variables affecting plant biomass and productivity.

vations of standing crop and production rates have been made in isolation, both in time and space, as dictated by logistics and the overall scientific workload of research vessels, and not by the biology of the plants. No research worker appears to have been able to take into account the apparent seasonal progression of maximum production with latitude demonstrated by Hart (1934, 1942), either during the planning or execution stage. No account appears to have been taken of the phenomenon during the analysis stage either. Hart's description is most likely a simplistic one. What probably happens is that productivity increases during one or more calm periods occurring within the time framework constructed by Hart. A ship may pass through all these "seasonal" zones within a few hours or days. The chances of being present at the right time and place for the plants to be in the necessary physiological state to give maximum productivity during the observations and experiments are low. The plants may have recently undergone a period of considerable productivity and the products could have been either consumed by zooplankton or dispersed by storms. At the time of observation, productivity could be limited by some environmental factor or the physiological state of the cells. If the former is identified, the probable conclusion would be that the conditions were normal and prevalent for the area and therefore that the productivity measured was typical.

Seasonal progression of maximum productivity with latitude, modified by sea state and wind force, could explain the wide variation in productivity between areas within the same regions of the Southern Ocean recorded by most workers. In certain cases however, closer examination of the geographic position of the more productive open ocean areas suggests that they may relate to submerged banks and ridges where upwelling could occur. The productive Station 12 of *Eltanin* Cruise 46 reported by El-Sayed and Jitts (1973) appear to lie in the vicinity of the Banzare Bank (58°50'S, 77°44'E).

Opportunity is often taken to measure continuously the standing crop of the surface layer while research vessels are underway. Large variations in apparent standing crop have been observed and again this could reflect the biological and topographical phenomena mentioned. The method also give rise to further sources of error. Summer surface light conditions are rarely optimal for photosynthesis and the main plant concentrations are frequently at lower depths, where light levels correspond to 12–25% of incident light intensity (El-Sayed and Jitts, 1973; El-Sayed, 1978). These light levels have been recorded at various depths between 10 and 120 m. The relative value of surface measurements only, as compared with integrated measurements for the euphotic zone, is well illustrated by El-Sayed (1970a). Surface measurements gave mean recorded chlorophyll *a* values of 1.40 and 0.36 mg m^{-3} respectively for the Atlantic and Pacific regions of the Southern Ocean, but over the same time period the integrated values for the euphotic zone (1% incident light level) were 14.92 and 11.55 mg m^{-2} respectively. The corresponding radiocarbon uptake values were 4.87 and 1.22 mg C m^{-3} h^{-1}, 42.82 and 32.01 mg C m^{-2} h^{-1}. If the euphotic zone had been defined by the 0.1% or the 0.01% level, the integrated values for the two regions would probably have been the same. Lorenzen (1970) has frequently been quoted as having demonstrated a reasonably good agreement between surface chlorophyll *a* values and integrated productivity values for the entire euphotic zone. The concept has led to the development of remote sensing devices such as the coastal zone colour scanner on the satellite Nimbus 7, which analyses the spectral pattern of upwelling irradiance from the upper layers of the sea. However, Lorenzen actually said that

> on the basis of this exercise (statistical comparison of surface to euphotic zone chlorophyll *a* and surface chlorophyll *a* to euphotic zone primary production) one must conclude that surface chlorophyll *a* measurements are worthwhile taking if one is limited in a sampling programme. On the other hand if precise information on depth, chlorophyll content or primary productivity of the euphotic zone is desired, it would be advisable to measure those parameters. Statistical procedures operate on the average, and one must realise that unusual events are easily missed when using statistical averages.

The data presented by El-Sayed (1970a) would suggest that the latter comment could be an understatement. To be of any value horizontal profiling must be calibrated frequently against vertical profiles. Remote sensing will only be of value as a long-term monitoring device and only after considerably more field work has produced accurate figures for Southern Ocean production and a greater understanding of the factors controlling it.

Closing water bottles at discrete depths has been the most frequently used method of obtaining data for integrated estimations of plant biomass within the euphotic zone, determining the distribution of plants within the water column and obtaining samples for use in productivity experiments. Regardless of the criteria on which the sampling depths have been chosen (light levels, position of the thermocline, standard depths, etc.) the chances of actually sampling the depth of maximum biomass and/or productivity are low. Strickland (1968) has suggested that the estimated concentrations at a given depth could be wrong by a factor of two or more and estimates of biomass beneath a unit area could be in error by as much as 25%. Furthermore, the lowest sample has often been from a depth where the light level corresponds to the 1% incident light level. Net photosynthesis frequently occurs below this, and there are records of more than half the biomass occurring at greater depths (Burkholder and Mandelli, 1965; Horne *et al.*, 1969).

Estimates of plant standing crop are usually made from chlorophyll *a* values. Measurement of chlorophyll *a*, either photometrically or fluorometrically, involves relatively simple techniques readily adapted to shipboard operations. Unfortunately, few users of these methods in the Southern Ocean have attempted to distinguish between living chlorophyll *a* and breakdown pigments contained by, or released from, dead and dying cells. *In vivo* fluorometric techniques permit continuous profiling and provide real-time data. Errors arise because *in vivo* chlorophyll *a* molecules can only be excited and made to fluoresce if they are not actually engaged in photosynthesis. The process is therefore dependent on light intensity and nutrients status, etc., and constantly varying (Kiefer, 1973; Loftus and Seliger, 1975; Harris, 1978). Herbicides have been used to inhibit photosynthesis and maximize the quantum fluoresence yield. DCMU (3-(3,4 dichlorophenyl)-1,1 dimethylurea) has been used in both laboratory and field experiments (Loftus and Seliger, 1975; Samuelsson and Öquist, 1977; Slovacek and Hannan, 1977), and Tranter *et al.* (1979) have recently used DCMU in continuous-flow, surface fluorescence profiling studies. This technique may be an important advance which will come into common usage. However, Harris (1980) has recently questioned the effectiveness of the technique with the type of fluorometers normally employed in the field. Clearly more evaluation studies are required. There will still be the need to measure frequently the proportion of broken-down pigment molecules which also fluoresce. However, the main problem in estimating phytoplankton biomass from chlorophyll *a* measurements lies in the fact that the chlorophyll *a* to carbon ratio varies by an order of magnitude between different physiological states of the same cell and between species (Banse, 1977).

Measurement of plant biomass is of limited value unless accompanied by measurement of concurrent zooplankton grazing rates and loss of plant cells through senescence and death, or some variables indicative of these phenomena. An area of low plant biomass could be highly productive and support a large zooplankton population. Radiocarbon uptake measurements are assumed to give a more direct indication of the actual productivity of the plant population during the period of experimentation. However, there is always some question as to what is actually being measured (Dring and Jewson, 1979). Currently it is the only technique sensitive enough to measure the low rates of productivity frequently encountered. It is in the application of the technique that most errors arise (Holm-Hansen, 1974; Fogg, 1977). First, the photosynthetic behaviour of plants confined to small bottles differs considerably in both laboratory and *in situ* experiments from those in highly turbulent water, which are subjected to changing light intensity and wavelength stress as they move up and down the water column (Gieskes *et al.*, 1979). Secondly, in laboratory experiments samples from different depths have been subjected to standard light and temperature regimes with the same interval for adaptation. Both temperature and light conditions may not be optimum for some of the species present. Again, the experimental conditions do not relate to natural conditions.

The sources of error described are not unique to investigations of Southern Ocean planktonic primary production. They are common to all aquatic plant biomass and primary productivity studies and reflect the present state of the science. Given enough data, it is relatively straightforward to calculate the production of a single station, but even this has rarely been done in the Antarctic. However, it is much more diffcult to calculate the regional production of the Southern Ocean because the basic data are so fragmentary. The several estimates of phytoplankton annual production made over the last 15 years have ranged in precision from intuitive guesswork to complicated calculations based on many assumptions (Table V). The more recent values have suffcient grounding in fact to permit one to conclude that the phytoplankton of the Southern Ocean does not appear to be any more productive per unit area than that of any other ocean except the Arctic Ocean. This is in complete contrast to earlier ideas on its productivity.

TABLE V

Estimates of phytoplankton annual production

Author	Area of ocean (10⁶ km²)	Area of ocean Comments	Productivity	Productivity Comments	Production (10⁹ tonnes year⁻¹)	General comments
Anderson and Banse, 1961	Not stated		$0.2–0.5$ g Cm⁻² day⁻¹	Production can be calculated[c]	$0.26–0.64$	The first estimate?
Ryther (in Hill), 1963	Not stated		"of the order of 100 g Cm⁻² year⁻¹"	Production can be calculated[c]	0.35	Uses Hart's *Discovery* data
Currie, 1964	Not stated		43 g Cm⁻² year⁻¹		1	Specifically does not consider neritic areas
El-Sayed, 1967	23.8 (March) 11.8 (Sept)	Uses Mackintosh and Brown (1956) estimate of open-water (4.5 and 9 × 10⁶ mile²)	21.24 × 10⁶ tonnes C day⁻¹ / 10.5 × 10⁶ tonnes C day⁻¹	Multiplies average photosynthetic rates (mg Cm⁻² h⁻¹) by the number of sunshine per year	3.3^a limits $4.5–2.2$	El-Sayed (1978) comments "based on more productive areas"
Ryther, 1969	Not stated	?(23.0 × 10⁶ km²) Uses means of Mackintosh and Brown (1956)	100 g Cm⁻² year⁻¹ Pacific mean	Multiplies average photosynthetic rates of each of 153 stations mg Cm⁻² h⁻¹ by the number of hours sunshine predicted	2.3^a	
El-Sayed, 1971	17.8		42.82 mg Cm⁻² h⁻¹ Atlantic mean / 32.01 mg Cm⁻² h⁻¹		3.03^a	
Holm Hansen et al., 1977	32.0		134 mg Cm⁻² day⁻¹	Calculations not stated by authors	0.65^b	
El-Sayed, 1978	38.1	Shelf area 2.1 Open ocean 36.0	134 mg Cm⁻² day⁻¹ gives 16 g Cm⁻² year⁻¹	Calculations not stated by author	0.61^b	See above (El-Sayed, 1967)

[a]Antarctic production only; [b]Antarctic and sub-Antarctic production; [c]production calculated using an area of 35 × 10⁶ km².

4.2 Ice-associated (sympagic) algae

Chlorophyll *a* values of 407.22 and 304.98 mg m^{-3} and carbon fixation rates of 1080.0 and 797.4 mg m^{-3} h^{-1} have been recorded for ice-associated algae in Martha Strait (66°35'S, 67°00'W) and Marguerite Bay (68°30'S, 68°30'W) respectively (Burkholder and Mandelli, 1965). The methods used for studying ice-associated primary production are the same as those used for phytoplankton and the same limitations apply. The most serious source of error in estimates of annual production stems from the inaccessibility of the majority of the algae to the research worker. One can only guess as to the extent, productivity and importance of this food source. Burkholder and Mandelli (1965) diluted the slush containing the ice communities with sea water at about the same temperature before carrying out the radiocarbon fixation experiments. They concluded that, if ice algae *in situ* have a similar activity and if all the sea ice remaining in summer contained a biomass of similar magnitude, then the productivity of the algae would be 4.94 × 10^5 tonnes C day^{-1}. This would give an annual production of approximately 5 × 10^7 tonnes C year^{-1} assuming a growing season of about 100 days, a valuable contribution equivalent to 12% of the annual phytoplankton production estimated by El-Sayed (1978). However, Bunt (1968) gave a much lower estimate of 3 × 10^4 tonnes C year^{-1}, only equivalent to 0.005% of the annual phytoplankton production figure.

4.3 The benthic flora

In the sub-Antarctic waters around Îles Kerguelen (49°30'S, 69°30'E), 3.4–22.5 kg m^{-2} fresh weights have been recorded for *Macrocytis* and *Durvillea* (Delépine, 1976). However, the standing crops are lower in the colder Antarctic waters where the giant kelps do not occur. A maximum fresh weight of 3.7 kg m^{-2} (0.82 kg dry weight (d.w.)) was reported for a dense patch of *Phyllogigas grandifolius* at Signy Island (Hastings, 1977). White and Robins (1972) found a mean fresh weight of 1.37 kg m^{-2} on four horizontal sites and Richardson (1980) a mean fresh weight of 980 g m^{-2} (260 g d.w.) at 30 hard substrate sites at the same location. It is possible that biomass estimates from higher latitudes will show even lower values for standing crop.

No production data are available for sub-Antarctic benthic algae. *Phyllogigas grandifolius* was found to have a mean annual productivity of 1.53 kg m^{-2} for a mean standing crop of 813 g m^{-2} at Signy Island (Hastings, 1977). Drew (1977) showed that five macroalgae from the same location were capable of fixing 0.42–4.8 mg C g^{-1} h^{-1}. All these values compare favourably with data for seaweeds in warmer waters (Westlake, 1963; Jupp and Drew, 1974).

Accurate measurements of the annual production of specific plant communities can be made, because the same community can be identified throughout the year and studied using physical techniques for measuring growth increments, as well as radiocarbon techniques. It is not as easy to distinguish between macroalgal and epiphytic microalgal productivity, but it is not important to do so in this context. Attempts to estimate meaningful values for benthic annual production fail because the amount of data is so small, substrates are known to be very diverse but have not been quantified, and vast areas of the Antarctic coastal zone are inaccessible to research workers.

4.4 Total annual primary production

An accurate assessment of annual primary production will be a vital component of any mathematical model built to study the effectiveness of management plans for the sensible commercial exploitation of the living resources of the Southern Ocean. Clearly no reliable value is yet available. Estimates of the biomass and production of organisms at higher trophic levels are even more speculative. There is a danger that commercial pressures will result in these speculative data being used for estimating the potential annual yield of krill, fish, squid, etc., from the Southern Ocean. El-Sayed (1978) has shown the limitation inherent in using present estimates of primary production and limited knowledge of trophic efficiencies and pathways to estimate the overall biological productivity (Table VI). Although man is increasing his utilization of benthic macroalgae, the predominant interest in harvesting krill, fish, seals and whales demands that accurate estimates of the biomass and annual production of phytoplankton and ice-associated algae be given priority by the marine botanist. The contribution of ice-associated algae may be vital at certain times of the year to zooplankton, but available evidence suggests that their overall contribution as a food source is small compared to the phytoplankton. Extensive investigation of ice-associated algae would involve considerable logistical resources. Therefore it is recommended that current effort be concentrated on the phytoplankton.

Continuing to monitor the phytoplankton of the Southern Ocean using conventional techniques would probably supply sufficient information to reduce the errors outlined and permit an accurate estimate of the primary production. However, the time required would be unacceptable if a mathematical model is to be ready to guide the utilization of living resources. Multi-ship international investigations, co-ordinated through BIOMASS,

TABLE VI

Estimates of potential yield (in metric tonnes ($\times 10^9$) per year) at various trophic levels using three estimates of primary production in the Southern Ocean

Annual primary production $(g\,Cm^{-2})$	Trophic level	Ecological efficiency factor					
		10%		15%		20%	
		Carbon	Wet Wt.	Carbon	Wet Wt.	Carbon	Wet Wt.
100[a]	Phytoplankton	3.80	38.0	3.80	38.0	3.80	38.0
	Herbivores	0.38	3.8	0.57	5.7	0.76	7.6
	Primary carnivores	0.038	0.38	0.09	0.9	0.15	1.5
43[b]	Phytoplankton	1.63	16.3	1.63	16.3	1.63	16.3
	Herbivores	0.163	1.63	0.24	2.4	0.33	3.3
	Primary carnivores	0.016	0.16	0.04	0.4	0.07	0.7
16[c]	Phytoplankton	0.61	6.1	0.61	6.1	0.61	6.1
	Herbivores	0.061	0.61	0.09	0.9	0.12	1.2
	Primary carnivores	0.006	0.06	0.01	0.1	0.02	0.2

[a](Ryther, 1963); [b](Currie, 1964); [c](Holm-Hansen *et al.*, 1977).

are an attempt to increase the rate of data acquisition and should permit synoptic observational and experimental work which should answer some of the criticism of current work (El-Sayed, 1966). These investigations mark the movement of Southern Ocean biology away from a survey to an experimental approach.

The modern approach to Southern Ocean biology does mean that only restricted areas can be investigated, but more extensive horizontal profiling and remote sensing can be used to extrapolate the annual production of much larger regions, guided by detailed biological and environmental observations.

5. Conclusion

Available evidence indicates that the primary production is no greater than that of any other world ocean except the Arctic Ocean. This conclusion questions currrent ideas on secondary production. Is the secondary production of the Southern Ocean really outstanding—or is the amount of production more apparent than elsewhere because it is concentrated to a large extent into relatively few, relatively large, commercially valuable animals such as krill, fish, squid, birds, seals and whales? If secondary production is outstanding, is it because the zooplankton are able to use the products of primary production more efficiently—perhaps because the plants live longer in the cold waters? This would mean the animals had more living, and therefore, more nutritive matter to eat than detritus, even at great depths. Alternatively, the detritus may have more nutritional value than similar material at lower latitudes because bacterial action seems to be reduced in Antarctic waters (Wiebe and Hendricks, 1974; Morita et al., 1977). Nemoto (1966) investigated chlorophyll pigments in the stomachs of several euphausids. Near-surface feeders such as *E. similis* G. O. Sars had the highest percentages of undegraded chlorophyll pigments present and produced abundant faecal pellets. In contrast, deeper-living species had degraded chlorophyll pigments present and were presumed to be feeding on the rain of faecal pellets. Perhaps the faecal pellets of adult *E. superba* Dana form food for the deeper living larval stages, and the faecal pellets provide a more nutritious diet than would be possible at lower latitudes, because of the colder surface waters and the limited bacterial activity. Secondary production could also be outstanding because the reduced number of trophic layers in the food web means that less energy is lost from the ecosystem.

Antarctic marine botanical research should concentrate on the phytoplankton of the open ocean, and especially on those taxonomic, physiological and ecological problems which will lead directly to a better understanding of the factors controlling productivity and to a more accurate estimate of annual production. These are identified as changes in species composition related to time and environmental variation, estimates of productivity throughout the water column to depths determined by the chlorophyll *a* profiles, and the effect on productivity of trace elements (including chelating agents), stability of the water column, grazing and natural mortality. Research on benthic algae should continue at the present level and serendipitous research should take place on ice-associated algae. However, commercial pressures and economy of time, scientists, ships and other materials demand that the major effort be concentrated on phytoplankton.

6. References

Ackley, S. F., Taguchi, S. and Buck, K. R. (1978). Primary production in sea ice of the Weddell region. *Army Cold Regions Research and Engineering Laboratory Reports* **78–19**, 21 pp.

Ångstrom, A. (1925). On the albedo of various surfaces of ground. *Geographical Annals* **7**, 323–342.

Baatz, I. (1941). Die Bedeutung der Lichtqualität für Wachstum und Stoffproduktion Planktontischer Meeresdiatomeen. *Planta* **31**, 726–766.

Baker, A. de C. (1954). The circumpolar continuity of Antarctic plankton species. "*Discovery*" *Reports* **27**, 201–218.

Balech, E., El-Sayed, S. Z., Hasle, G., Neushul, M. and Zaneveld, J. S. (1968).

Primary productivity and benthic marine algae of the Antarctic and sub-Antarctic. *Antarctic Map Folio Series* **10**, 12 pp.

Banse, K. (1977). Determining the carbon to chlorophyll ratios of natural phytoplankton. *Marine Biology* **41**, 199–212.

Barber, R. T. and Ryther, J. H. (1969). Organic chelators: factors affecting primary production in the Cromwell Current upwelling. *Journal of Experimental Marine Biology and Ecology* **3**, 191–199.

Beklemischev, K. V. (1958). O shirotnoi zonal 'nostï v raspredelenii Antarkticheskogo fitoplanktona (Latitudinal zoning of Antarctic phytoplankton). *Informatsionnyy Byulleten' Sovetskoy Antarkticheskoy Ekspeditsii* **3**, 35–56. [English translation (1964) **1**, 113–114.]

Beklemishev, K. V. (1960). O printsipkh fitogeograficheskogo razdeleniia antarkicheskoï pelagicheskoï oblasti. (Concerning the phytogeographic division of the Antarctic pelagic region). *Informatsionnyy Byulleten' Sovetskoy Antarkticheskoy Ekspeditsii* **19**, 43–46. [English translation (1964) **2**, 272–276.]

Bienati, N. L., Comes, R. A. and Spiedo, H. (1977). Primary production in Antarctic waters: seasonal variation and production in fertilized samples during the summer cycle. *In* "Polar Oceans" (M. J. Dunbar, ed.), pp. 377–389. Arctic Institute of North America.

Bonner, W. N., Clarke, A., Everson, I., Heywood, R. B., Whitaker, T. M. and White, M. G. (1978). Research on krill in relation to the Southern Ocean ecosystem by the British Antarctic Survey. *International Council for the Exploration of the Sea. C.M. 1978/L* **23**, 6 pp.

Bowman, M. J. and Esaias, W. E. (eds) (1978). "Oceanic Fronts in Coastal Processes". Springer-Verlag, Berlin.

Brody, M. and Emerson, R. (1959). The effect of wavelengths and intensity of light on the proportion of pigments in *Porphyridium cruentum*. *American Journal of Botany* **46**, 433–440.

Bunt, J. S. (1964a). Primary productivity under sea ice in Antarctic waters. I. Concentrations and photosynthetic activities of microalgae in the waters of McMurdo Sound, Antarctica. *Antarctic Research Series* **1**, 13–26.

Bunt, J. S. (1964b). Primary productivity under sea ice in Antarctic waters. II. Influence of light and other factors on the photosynthetic activities of Antarctic marine microalgae. *Antarctic Research Series* **1**, 27–31.

Bunt, J. S. (1968). Some characteristics of microalgae isolated from Antarctic sea ice. *Antarctic Research Series* **11**, 1–14.

Bunt, J. S. and Lee, C. C. (1970). Seasonal primary production in Antarctic sea ice at McMurdo Sound, 1967. *Journal of Marine Research* **28**, 304–320.

Bunt, J. S. and Wood, E. J. F. (1963). Microbiology of Antarctic sea-ice. *Nature* (*Lond.*) **199**, 1254–1258.

Burkholder, P. R. and Mandelli, E. F. (1965). Carbon assimilation of marine phytoplankton in Antarctica. *Proceedings of the National Academy of Science of the United States of America* **54**, 437–444.

Burkholder, P. R. and Sieburth, J. M. (1961). Phytoplankton and chlorophyll in the Gerlache and Bransfield Straits of Antarctica. *Limnology and Oceanography* **6**, 45–52.

Carlucci, A. F. and Cuhel, R. L. (1977). Vitamins in the South Polar Seas: distribution and significance of dissolved and particulate vitamin B_{12}, thiamine and biotin in the Southern Ocean. *In* "Adaptations within Antarctic Ecosystems" (G. A. Llano, ed.), pp. 115–128. Smithsonian Institution, Washington, D.C.

Cassie, V. (1963). Distribution of surface phytoplankton between New Zealand and Antarctica, December 1957. *Scientific Reports, Transantarctic Expedition 1955-1958* **7**, 11 pp.

Chamberlain, Y. M. (1965). Marine algae of Gough Island. *Bulletin of the British Museum (Natural History) Lond. E. Botany* **3**, 175–232.

Chu, S. P. (1943). The influence of the mineral composition of the medium on the growth of planktonic algae. Part 2: the influence of the concentration of inorganic nitrogen and phosphate phosphorus. *Journal of Ecology* **31**, 109–148.

Clowes, A. J. (1934). Hydrology of the Bransfield Strait. *"Discovery" Reports* **9**, 1–64.

Clowes, A. J. (1938). Phosphate and silicate in the Southern Ocean. *"Discovery" Reports* **19**, 1–120.

Collins, N. J. (1977). The growth of mosses in two contrasting communities in the maritime Antarctic: measurement and prediction of annual production. *In* "Adaptations within Antarctic Ecosystems" (G. A. Llano, ed.), pp. 921–933. Smithsonian Institution, Washington, D.C.

Currie, R. I. (1964). Environmental features in the ecology of Antarctic seas. *In* "Biologie Antarctique" (R. Carrick, M. W. Holdgate and J. Prevost, eds), pp. 87–94. Hermann, Paris.

Davey, E. W., Morgan, M. J. and Erickson, S. J. (1973). A biological measurement of the copper complexation capacity of seawater. *Limnology and Oceanography* **18**, 993–997.

Deacon, G. E. R. (1933). A general account of the hydrology of the South Atlantic Ocean. *"Discovery" Reports* **7**, 171–238.

Deacon, G. E. R. (1937a). The hydrology of the Southern Ocean. *"Discovery" Reports* **15**, 1–124.

Deacon, G. E. R. (1937b). Notes on the dynamics of the Southern Ocean. *"Discovery" Reports* **15**, 125–152.

Delépine, R. (1966). La végétation marine dans l'Antarctique de l'Quest comparée à celle des Îles Australes Françaises. Conséquences biogéographiques. *Compte rendu de la Société de biogéographie* **374**, 52–68.

Delépine, E. (1976). Note préliminaire sur la répartition des algues marine aux Îles Kerguelen. *Comité National Français des Recherches Antarctiques* **39**, 153–159.

Drew, E. A. (1977). The physiology of photosynthesis and respiration in some Antarctic marine algae. *British Antarctic Survey Bulletin* No. 46, 59–76.

Dring, M. J. and Jewson, D. H. (1979). What does ^{14}C-uptake by phytoplankton really measure? A fresh approach using a theoretical model. *British Phycological Journal* **14**, 122–123.

Droop, M. R. (1973). Some thoughts on nutrient limitation in algae. *Journal of Phycology* **9**, 264–272.

Ehrenberg, C. G. (1844). Einige vorlaufige resultate der Untersuchungen der von der Sudpolreise des Capitain Ross, so wie von der Herren Schayer und Darwin. Zugkommenen Materialen. *Monatsbericht der Preuss Akademie des Wissenschaften* 1844, 182–207.

Ekman, V. W. (1928). A survey of some theoretical investigations in ocean currents. *Journal du Conseil, Conseil permanent international pour l'exploration de la mer* **3**, 295–397.

El-Sayed, S. Z. (1966). Prospects of primary productivity studies in Antarctic waters. *In* "Symposium on Antarctic Oceanography" (R. I. Currie, ed.), pp. 227–239. Scott Polar Research Institute, Cambridge.

El-Sayed, S. Z. (1968). Primary productivity. *Antarctic Map Folio Series* **10**, 1–3.

El-Sayed, S. Z. (1970a). On the productivity of the Southern Ocean (Atlantic and Pacific Sectors). *In* "Antarctic Ecology" (M. W. Holdgate, ed.), pp. 119–135. Academic Press, London and New York.

El-Sayed, S. Z. (1970b). Phytoplankton production of the South Pacific and the Pacific Sector of the Antarctic. *In* "Scientific Exploration of the South Pacific" (W. S. Wooster, ed.), pp. 194–210. National Academy of Sciences, Washington, D.C.

El-Sayed, S. Z. (1971a). Dynamics of trophic relations in the Southern Ocean. *In* "Research in Antarctica" (L. O. Quam, ed.), pp. 73–91. American Association for the Advancement of Science, Washington, D.C.

El-Sayed, S. Z. (1971b). Observations on a phytoplankton bloom in the Weddell Sea. *Antarctic Research Series* **17**, 301–312.

El-Sayed, S. Z. (1973a). Biological oceanography. *Antarctic Journal of the United States* **8**, 93–100.

El-Sayed, S. Z. (1973b). Biological oceanographic investigations during the Marion–Dufresne Cruise 8. *Antarctic Journal of the United States* **11**, 184–186.

El-Sayed, S. Z. (Convenor) (1977). "Biological Investigations of Marine Antarctic Systems and Stocks (BIOMASS) 1. Research Proposals", 79 pp. Scott Polar Research Institute (SCAR), Cambridge.

El-Sayed, S. Z. (1978). Primary productivity and estimates of potential yields in the Southern Ocean. *In* "Polar Research to the Present and Future" (M. A. McWhinnie, ed.), pp. 141–160. West View Press, Colorado.

El-Sayed, S. Z. and Jitts, H. R. (1973). Phytoplankton production in the southeastern Indian Ocean. *In* "The Biology of the Indian Ocean" (B. Zeitzschel, ed.), pp. 131–142. Springer-Verlag, Berlin.

El-Sayed, S. Z. and Turner, J. T. (1977). Productivity of the Antarctic and tropical/sub-tropical regions: a comparative study. *In* "Polar Oceans" (M. J. Dunbar, ed.), pp. 463–501. Calgary Arctic Institute of North America, Calgary.

El-Sayed, S. Z., Mandelli, E. F. and Sugimura, Y. (1964). Primary organic production in the Drake Passage and Bransfield Strait. *Antarctic Research Series* **1**, 1–11.

Eppley, R. W. (1972). Temperature and phytoplankton growth in the sea. *Fishery Bulletin, Fish and Wildlife Service, United States Department of Interior* **70**, 1063–1085.

Eppley, R. W. and Coatsworth, J. L. (1968). Uptake of nitrate and nitrite by *Ditylum brightwellii*—kinetics and mechanisms. *Journal of Phycology* **4**, 151–156.

Eppley, R. W. and Thomas, W. H. (1969). Comparison of half-saturation constants for growth and nitrate uptake of marine phytoplankton. *Journal of Phycology* **5**, 375–379.

Eppley, R. W., Rogers, J. N. and McCarthy, J. J. (1969). Half-saturation constants for uptake of nitrate and ammonium by marine phytoplankton. *Limnology and Oceanography* **14**, 912–920.

Falkowski, P. G. and Stone, D. P. (1975). Nitrate uptake in marine phytoplankton: energy sources and the interaction with carbon fixation. *Marine Biology* **32**, 77–84.

Fogg, G. E. (1977). Aquatic primary production in the Antarctic. *Philosophical Transactions of The Royal Society* **B279**, 27–38.

Fogg, G. E. and Horne, A. J. (1970). The physiology of Antarctic freshwater algae.

In "Antarctic Ecology" (M. W. Holdgate, ed.), Vol. 2, pp. 632–638. Academic Press, London and New York.

Fryxell, G. A. and Hasle, G. R. (1979). The genus *Thalassiosira*: species with internal extensions of the strutted processes. *Phycologia* **18**, 379–394.

Fukase, S. (1962). Oceanographic condition of surface water between the south end of Africa and Antarctica. *Antarctic Record* **15**, 53–110.

Gain, L. (1912). La flora Algologique des régions Antarctiques et Subantarctiques. *Documents Scientifique Deuxième Expedition Antarctique Française. Botanique* 218 pp.

Gaudichaud, C. (1826). Botanique. *In* "Voyage autour du monde sur l'Uranie et la Physicienne, pendant 1817–1820" (L. Freycinet, ed.), 512 pp. Paris.

Gieskes, W. W. C., Kraay, G. W. and Baars, M. A. (1979). Current ¹⁴C methods for measuring primary production: gross underestimates in oceanic waters. *Netherlands Journal of Sea Research* **13**, 58–78.

Goering, J. J. (1971). The role of nitrogen in eutrophic processes. *In* "Microbial Aspects of Pollution" (G. A. Sykes and F. A. Skinner, eds), pp. 43–68. Academic Press, London and New York.

Gran, H. H. (1932). Phytoplankton: methods and problems. *Journal du Conseil. Conseil permanent international pour l'exploration de la mer* **8**, 343–358.

Harder, R. and Bederke, B. (1957). Ueber Wachstumversuche mit Rot und Gruenalgen (*Porphyridium cruentum, Trailliella intricata, Chlorella pyrenoidosa*) in verschiedenfarbigem, energiegleichen Licht. *Archiv für Mikrobiologie* **28**, 153–172.

Hardy, A. C. and Gunther, E. R. (1935). The plankton of the South Georgia whaling grounds and adjacent waters 1926–1927. *"Discovery" Reports* **11**, 1–456.

Harris, G. P. (1978). Photosynthesis, productivity and growth: the physiological ecology of phytoplankton. *Archiv für Hydrobiologie: Beihefte: Ergebnisse der Limnologie* **10**, 1–171.

Harris, G. P. (1980). The relationship between chlorophyll *a* fluorescence, diffuse attenuation changes and photosynthesis in natural phytoplankton populations. *Journal of Plankton Research* **2**, 109–127.

Hart, T. J. (1934). On the phytoplankton of the south-west Atlantic and the Bellingshausen Sea. *"Discovery" Reports* **8**, 1–208.

Hart, T. J. (1937). *Rhizosolenia curvata* Zacharias, an indicator species in the Southern Ocean. *"Discovery" Reports* **16**, 413–446.

Hart, T. J. (1942). Phytoplankton periodicity in Antarctic surface waters. *"Discovery" Reports* **21**, 261–356.

Hasle, G. R. (1956). Phytoplankton and hydrography of the Pacific part of the Antarctic Ocean. *Nature (Lond.)* **177**, 616–617.

Hasle, G. R. (1968). Marine diatoms. *Antarctic Map Folio Series* **10**, 6–8.

Hasle, G. R. (1969). An analysis of the phytoplankton of the Pacific Southern Ocean: abundance, composition and distribution during the Brategg Expedition, 1947–48. *Hvalrådets skrifter* **52**, 1–168.

Hastings, R. M. (1977). An investigation into the primary productivity of the Antarctic macro-alga *Phyllogigas grandifolius* (A. and E. S. Gepp) Skottsb. Unpublished thesis, University of St. Andrews.

Hendey, N. I. (1937). The plankton diatoms of the Southern Seas. *"Discovery" Reports* **16**, 151–364.

Holm-Hansen, O. (1974). Review and critique of primary productivity measurements. *Report, California Co-operative Oceanic Fisheries Investigations* **17**, 53–56.

Holm-Hansen, O., El-Sayed, S. Z., Franceschini, G. A. and Cuhel, R. L. (1977).

Primary production and the factors controlling phytoplankton growth in the Southern Ocean. *In* "Adaptations within Antarctic Ecosystems" (G. A. Llano, ed.), pp. 11–50. Smithsonian Institution, Washington, D.C.

Hooker, J. D. (1847). Flora Antarctica. Pt. 55. Algae. *In* "The Botany of the Antarctic Voyage", Vol. II, pp. 454–519. Reeve Brothers, London.

Horne, A. J., Fogg, G. E. and Eagle, D. J. (1969). Studies *in situ* of the primary production of an area of inshore Antarctic sea. *Journal of the Marine Biological Association of the United Kingdom* **49**, 393–405.

Hoshiai, T. (1972). Diatom distribution in sea ice near McMurdo and Syowa stations (1972). *Antarctic Journal of the United States* **7**, 84–85.

Hustedt, F. (1958). Diatomeen aus der Antarktis und dem Südatlantik. *Wissenschaftliche Ergebnisse der Deutschen Antarktischen Expedition, 1938–39* **2**, 103–191.

Jerlov, N. G. and Koczy, F. (1951). Photographic measurements of daylight in deep water. *Report. Swedish Deep Sea Expedition. Physics and Chemistry* **3**, 62–69.

Jones, R. I. (1978). Adaptation to fluctuating irradiance by natural phytoplankton communities. *Limnology and Oceanography* **23**, 920–926.

Jørgensen, E. G. (1964). Adaptation to different light intensities in the diatom *Cyclotella meneghiniana* Kütz. *Physiologia plantarum* **17**, 136–145.

Jørgensen, E. G. (1969). The adaptation of plankton algae. IV. Light adaptation in different algal species. *Physiologia plantarum* **22**, 1307–1315.

Jupp, B. P. and Drew, E. A. (1974). Studies on the growth of *Laminaria hyperborea* (Gunn.) Fosl. I. Biomass and productivity. *Journal of Experimental Marine Biology and Ecology* **15**, 185–196.

Kanwisher, J. W. (1966). Photosynthesis and respiration in some seaweeds. *In* "Some Contemporary Studies in Marine Science" (H. Barnes, ed.), pp. 407–420. Allen and Unwin, London.

Ketchum, B. H. (1939). The absorption of phosphate and nitrate by illuminated cultures of *Nitzschia closterium. American Journal of Botany* **26**, 399–407.

Kiefer, D. A. (1973). Fluorescence properties of natural phytoplankton populations. *Marine Biology* **22**, 263–269.

Knox, G. A. (1960). Littoral ecology and biogeography of the Southern Oceans. *Proceedings of the Royal Society* **B152**, 577–624.

Koslova, O. G. (1962). Vidouoi sostav diatomougkh vodoroslei v vodakh Indiiskogo sektoia Antarktiki (Species composition of diatoms from the waters of the Indian Ocean sector of the Antarctic). *Trudy Instituta okeanologii Akademiya nauk SSSR Moskva* **61**, 1–18.

Koslova, O. G. (1964). Diatomovye vodorosli Indiïskogo i Tikhookeanskogo sektorov Antarktiki. (Diatoms in the Indian and Pacific sectors of the Antarctic). Moscow, Nauka. 168 pp. [English Translation (1966). Jerusalem. Israel Programme for Scientific Translation. 191 pp.]

Krebs, W. N. (1973). Ecology of Antarctic marine diatoms. *Antarctic Journal of the United States* **8**, 307–309.

Lamb, I. M. and Zimmerman, M. H. (1977). Benthic marine algae of the Antarctic Peninsula. *Antarctic Research Series* **23**, 130–229.

Loftus, M. E. and Seliger, H. H. (1975). Some limitations of the *in vivo* fluorescence technique. *Chesapeake Science* **16**, 79–92.

Lorenzen, C. J. (1970). Surface chlorophyll as an index of the depth, chlorophyll content and primary productivity of the euphotic layer. *Limnology and Oceanography* **15**, 479–480.

Lund, S. (1959). The marine algae of East Greenland. II. Geographic distribution. *Meddelelser om Grønland* **156**, 1–72.

Mackintosh, N. A. (1972). Life cycle of Antarctic krill in relation to ice and water conditions. *"Discovery" Reports* **36**, 1–94.

Mandelli, E. F. and Burkholder, P. (1966). Primary production in the Gerlache and Bransfield Straits of Antarctica. *Journal of Marine Research* **24**, 15–27.

Meguro, H. (1962). Plankton ice in the Antarctic Ocean. *Antarctic Record* **14**, 72–79.

Montagne, J. F. C. (1845). "Plantes Cellulaires. Voyage au Pole Sud sur l'Astrolabe et la Lélée sous Dumont d'Urville pendant 1837–40. Botanique", Vol. 1. Paris.

Montagne, J. F. C. (1846). Cryptogames cellulaires. Algues, Lichens, Hépatiques et Mousses. *In* "Voyage autour du monde exécuté pendant les années 1836 et 1837, sur la corvette La Bonité commandée par A. N. Vaillant. Botanique", Vol. 1, pp. 1–163. Paris.

Morita, R. Y., Griffiths, R. P. and Hayasaka, S. S. (1977). Heterotrophic activity of microorganisms in Antarctic waters. *In* "Adaptations within Antarctic Ecosystems" (G. A. Llano, ed.), pp. 99–113. Smithsonian Institution, Washington, D.C.

Movchan, O. A. (1975). (Distribution of phytoplankton in the Scotia Sea in relation to the vertical circulation of the water). *Okeanologiia* **15**, 485–487. [English Translation (1976). *Oceanologyy* **15**.]

Nemoto, T. (1966). Feeding of baleen whales and krill, and the value of krill as a marine resource in the Antarctic. *In* "Symposium on Antarctic Oceanography" (R. I. Currie, ed.), pp. 240–253. Scott Polar Research Institute (SCAR), Cambridge.

Neushul, M. (1965). Diving observations of sub-tidal Antarctic marine vegetation. *Botanica marina* **8**, 234–243.

Neushul, M. (1968). Benthic marine algae. *Antarctic Map Folio Series* **10**, 9–10.

Oradovskii, S. G. (1974). (Marine chemistry. Investigation of the chemical composition of Antarctic sea ice). *Okeanologia* **14**, 64–70. [English Translation (1974). *Oceanology* **14**.]

Paasche, E. (1973). Silicon and the ecology of marine plankton diatoms. II. Silicon uptake kinetics in five diatom species. *Marine Biology* **19**, 262–269.

Papenfuss, G. F. (1962). Problems in the taxonomy and geographical distribution of Antarctic marine algae. *In* "Biologie Antarctique" (R. Carrick, M. Holdgate and J. Prevost, eds), pp. 155–160. Hermann, Paris.

Papenfuss, G. F. (1964). Catalogue and bibliography of Antarctic and sub-Antarctic benthic marine algae. *Antarctic Research Series* **1** (Suppl.), 76 pp.

Powell, W. M. and Clarke, G. L. (1936). The reflection and absorption of daylight at the surface of the ocean. *Journal of the Optical Society of America* **26**, 111-120.

Priddle, J. (1980a). The production ecology of benthic plants in some Antarctic lakes. I. *In situ* production studies. *Journal of Ecology* **68**, 141–153.

Priddle, J. (1980b). The production ecology of benthic plants in some Antarctic lakes. II. Laboratory physiology studies. *Journal of Ecology* **68**, 155–166.

Richardson, M. G. (1980). The distribution of Antarctic marine macroalgae related to depth and substrate. *British Antarctic Survey Bulletin* No. 49, 1–13.

Richardson, M. G. and Whitaker, T. M. (1979). An Antarctic fast-ice food-chain: observations on the interaction of the amphipod *Pontageneia antarctica* Chevreux with ice-associated microalgae. *British Antarctic Survey Bulletin* No. 47, 107–115.

Ryther, J. H. (1956). Photosynthesis in the ocean as a function of light intensity. *Limnology and Oceanography* **1**, 61–70.

Ryther, J. H. (1963). Geographic variations in productivity *In* "The Sea" (M. N. Hill, ed.), Vol. 2, pp. 347–380. Wiley, London.

Ryther, J. H. (1969). Photosynthesis and fish production in the sea. *Science* **166**, 72–76.

Saijo, Y. and Kawashima, T. (1964). Primary production in the Antarctic Ocean. *Journal of the Oceanographical Society of Japan* **19**, 190–196.

Samuelsson, G. and Öquist, G. (1977). A method for studying photosynthetic capacities of unicellular algae based on *in vivo* chlorophyll fluorescence. *Physiologia plantarum* **40**, 315–319.

Skottsberg, C. J. F. (1962). Antarctic phycology. *In* "Biologie Antarctique" (R. Carrick, M. Holdgate and J. Prevost, eds), pp. 147–154. Hermann, Paris.

Skottsberg, C. J. F. and Neushul, M. (1960). *Phyllogigas* and *Himantothallus*, Antarctic Phaeophyceae. *Botanica marina* **2**, 164–173.

Slovacek, R. E. and Hannan, P. J. (1977). *In vivo* fluorescence determinations of phytoplankton chlorophyll *a*. *Limnology and Oceanography* **22**. 919–925.

Smayda, T. J. and Boleyn, B. J. (1965). Experimental observations on the floatation of marine diatoms. I. *Thalassiosira* c.f. *nana*, *Thalassiosira rotula* and *Nitzschia seriata*. *Limnology and Oceanography* **10**, 499–509.

Soeder, C. and Stengel, E. (1974). Physico-chemical factors affecting metabolism and growth rate. *In* "Algal Physiology and Biochemistry" (W. D. P. Stewart. ed.), pp. 714–740. Blackwell, Oxford.

Stanbury, F. A. (1931). The effect of light of different intensities, reduced selectively and non-selectively, upon the rate of growth of *Nitzschia closterium*. *Journal of the Marine Biological Association of the United Kingdom* **17**, 633–653.

Steemann-Nielsen, E. (1952). The use of radioactive carbon (^{14}C) for measuring organic production in the sea. *Journal du Conseil. Conseil permanent international pour l'exploration de la mer* **18**, 177-140.

Steemann-Nielsen, E. and Jørgensen, E. G. (1968). The adaptation of plankton algae, I, general part. *Physiologia Plantarum* **21**, 401–413.

Stockton, W. L. (1973). An intertidal assemblage at Palmer Station. *Antarctic Journal of the United States* **8**, 305–307.

Strickland, J. D. H. (1965). Phytoplankton and marine primary production. *Annual Review of Microbiology* **19**, 127–162.

Strickland, J. D. H. (1968). A comparison of profiles of nutrient and chlorophyll concentrations taken from discrete depths and by continuous recording. *Limnology and Oceanography* **13**, 388–391.

Sverdrup, H. V. (1953). On conditions for the vernal blooming of phytoplankton. *Journal du Conseil, Conseil Permanent international pour l'exploration de la mer* **18**, 287–295.

Thomas, W. H. (1970). Effect of ammonium and nitrate concentration on chlorophyll increases in natural tropical Pacific phytoplankton populations. *Limnology and Oceanography* **15**, 386–394.

Thomas, W. H. and Dodson, A. N. (1968). Effects of phosphate concentration on cell division rates and yield of a tropical oceanic diatom. *Biological Bulletin, Marine Biological Laboratory, Woods Hole, Mass.* **134**, 199–208.

Thomas, W. H. and Dodson, A. N. (1974). Effect of interactions between temperature and nitrate supply on the cell division rates of two marine phytoflagellates. *Marine biology* **24**, 213–217.

Tranter, D. J., Parker, R. R. and Vaudrey, D. J. (1979). *In vivo* chlorophyll *a* fluorescence in the vicinity of warm core eddies off the coast of New South Wales. 1 September 1978. *C.S.I.R.O. Division of Fisheries and Oceanography Reports* **105**, 28 pp.

Vanhöffen, E. (1902). Biologische Beobachtungen. *Deutsche Sudpolar-Expedition* **2**, 39–45.

Vladimirskaya, E. V., Makarov, R. R., Maslennikov, V. V. and Movchan, O. A. (1976). (Some traits of phytoplankton distribution in the southern part of the Scotia Sea in spring). *Okeanologiia* **16**, 1069–1074. [English translation (1976). *Oceanology* **16**.]

Volkovinskii, V. V. (1966). Studies of primary production in the waters of the South Atlantic Ocean. *Abstracts of papers presented at the Second International Oceanography Congress* (Moscow) 1966, 386–387.

Volkovinskii, V. V. (1969). Izmereniya pervichnoi produktsii v More Skotiya. (Measurements of plankton production in the Scotia Sea). *Trudy Vsesoyuznyĭ nauchnoissledovatel'skiĭ institut morskogo rybnogo khozyaĭstva i oceanografii Moskva* **66**, 160–167. [National Lending Library (UK) Translation 5922.]

Walsh, J. J. (1969). Vertical distribution of Antarctic phytoplankton, II. Comparison of phytoplankton standing crops in the Southern Ocean with that of the Florida Strait. *Limnology and Oceanography* **14**, 86–94.

Westlake, D. F. (1963). Comparison of plant productivity. *Biological Reviews* **38**, 385–425.

Whitaker, T. M. (1977a). Sea-ice habitats of Signy Island (South Orkneys) and their primary productivity. *In* "Adaptations within Antarctic Ecosystems" (G. A. Llano, ed.), pp. 75–82. Smithsonian Institution, Washington, D.C.

Whitaker, T. M. (1977b). "Plant production in inshore waters of Signy Island, Antarctica". Unpublished thesis, London University.

White, M. G. and Robins, M. W. (1972). Biomass estimates from Borge Bay, Signy Island, South Orkney Islands. *British Antarctic Survey Bulletin* No. 31, 45–50.

Wiebe, W. J. and Hendricks, C. W. (1974). Distribution of heterotrophic bacteria in a transect of the Antarctic Ocean. *In* "Effect of Ocean Environment on Microbial Activities" (R. R. Colwell and R. Y. Morita, eds), pp. 524–535, Baltimore University Park Press, Baltimore.

Wilce, R. T. (1967). Heterotrophy in arctic sublittoral seaweeds: an hypothesis. *Botanic marina* **10**, 185–197.

Wimpenny, R. S. (1966). "The Plankton of the Sea". Faber, London.

Yull Rhee, G. (1973). A continuous culture study of phosphate uptake, growth rate and polyphosphate in *Scenedesmus* sp. *Journal of Phycology* **9**, 495–506.

Zaneveld, J. S. (1966a). Vertical zonation of Antarctic and sub-Antarctic benthic marine algae. *Antarctic Journal of the United States* **1**, 211–213.

Zaneveld, J. S. (1968). Benthic marine algae, Ross Island to Balleny Islands. *Antarctic Map Folio Series* **10**, 10–12.

8

Marine benthos

M. G. White

1. Introduction

There is now a considerable literature about the Antarctic marine benthic
ecosystem and a comprehensive account would demand the dedication of a
complete volume. The reviews by Hedgpeth (1969, 1970, 1971), Dell (1972)
and Arnaud (1974) are most useful sources of descriptions of the principal
characteristics of the benthos. This account offers a view concentrating on
recent developments. The benthic marine flora and demersal fish are considered in Chapters 7 and 10.

Scientific observations of the marine benthic environment began with the
early expeditions to the region which were principally concerned with geographical exploration. Inevitably, the majority of the research was carried
out on collections made from ocean-going vessels and the results of these
observations can be found in the scientific reports and narratives of the
various national expeditions (Dell, 1972). The Belgian Antarctic Expedition (1897–1899) to the South Shetland Islands and the Antarctic Peninsula
in the *Belgica* was the first expedition to the region to make systematic
collections of benthic material. Notable marine collections from the
Southern Ocean were made during the voyages of HMS *Challenger*
(1872–1876) and by the *Discovery* Investigations (1925–1937) and the
Soviet Antarctic Expedition (1955–1958). The results of research by the
Discovery Investigations were published in the "*Discovery*" *Reports* which
remain standard reference works.

Until 15 years ago the majority of benthic collections were obtained from
large vessels at offshore sites by the use of remote sampling methods.
Samples from the sea-floor were often taken incidentally during a programme to investigate the flora and fauna of the water column. The research was mainly descriptive and was often carried out by specialists

ANTARCTIC ECOLOGY VOL. 2
ISBN 0 12–439502–3

unfamiliar with the field conditions, who worked without much contact with others investigating polar material. Consequently modern taxonomists and ecologists find that much of their effort is devoted to unravelling the tangles of the past. The early taxonomic literature on Antarctic benthos shows abundant cases of aberrations due to sexually dimorphic or polymorphic species being described as separate species; arthropod species being recorded as blind because the preservative in which they were stored had leached the pigment from their eyes; and the same species being described independently on several occasions—all of which led to extensive synonymies for most taxa.

The advent of permanently-occupied research stations in the Antarctic, during and following the International Geophysical Year (1957), and the co-operative attitudes resulting from the Antarctic Treaty, have led to significant advances in our understanding of the marine benthos. The qualitative collections made from large research vessels in deep water have been complemented by year-round ecological and physiological investigations of the nearshore benthic communities. The use of self-contained diving techniques during the past 15 years has greatly assisted these studies, because it has enabled marine biologists to make *in situ* observations and use reliable quantitative sampling procedures. Quantitative and experimental research has been concentrated near to the stations of each participating nation. For example, that of the U.S.A. is centred on McMurdo Sound and the west coast of the Antarctic Peninsula; that of the U.S.S.R. is centred at Haswell Islands; of Britain, at the South Orkney Islands and South Georgia; that of Argentina is carried out on the west coast of the Antarctic Peninsula. Numerous sites around the Antarctic Continent and at most of the Antarctic island groups are involved. Research stations are well distributed throughout the region but the distance between them is considerable, and so comparative studies should be considered with caution. Dell (1972) points out that, although the centres of activity are dispersed, the environmental conditions are remarkably similar at given latitudes. This suggests that any differences observed tend to be due to phenomena such as the degree of isolation, the routes of dispersal and the rates of colonization rather than direct effects of the physical environment. Thus, attempts to compare benthic community assemblages at different geographical locations are probably unjustified.

Appreciation of the more obvious characteristics of the Antarctic benthic communities (including high biomass; gigantism; high levels of endemism; an incomplete range of invertebrate groups, e.g. few cirripedes or decapods; the relative absence of pelagic larval stages as agents of dispersal and colonization) was based on few observations. However, recent quantitative investigations have confirmed the widespread occurrence of these characteristics and the causative factors. Additional features such as high species diversity, high abundance, prolonged longevity, slow growth rates, and delayed maturation, have been shown to be typical. Detailed laboratory investigations have led to a systematic analysis of physiological adaptations and in particular a critical appraisal of metabolic compensation to a cold, highly seasonal environment. Communities from unusual environments such as those under permanent ice-shelves have been described for the first time and analysis of coastal benthos has provided evidence for the presence of both local and global pollutants.

2. Abundance and Diversity

2.1 Biomass

Marine biologists who have investigated the Antarctic benthos have been impressed by the startling contrast between the obvious impoverishment of the terrestrial ecosystem and the richness of the nearshore benthic communities. The high biomass of the marine fauna was mistakenly interpreted as being indicative of a very high annual primary production and high secondary production. Neritic primary production was shown to be moderately high (86–289 g C m^{-2} year^{-1}, Horne et al., 1969; Whitaker, 1982) but the high benthic biomass was found to be the result of slow growth, delayed maturation and longevity.

Benthic communities in shallow water are subject to the disruptive effects of abrasion by ice and plucking by anchor-ice (White, 1973; Dayton et al., 1974), and so the sessile epibenthos is restricted to deciduous groups or sheltered habitats like rocky crevices and overhangs. Errant groups, such as the gastropod molluscs, pycnogonids, echinoderms, fish and crustaceans are widely distributed. Soft bottom sediments support rich infaunal communities dominated by lamellibranch molluscs, polychaetes and amphipod crustaceans.

The dominant groups below the level of persistent ice-scour by sea ice are sessile, particle-feeding organisms. Large areas of the sea bed are covered by hexactinellid sponges, desmosponges, hydroids, tunicates, polyzoans, sedentary polychaetes, lamellibranch molluscs, actinarians, scleractinian corals and holothurians (Fig. 1).

The general observation that high biomasses are found on shelf areas in the Antarctic is supported by few quantitative data. Ushakov (1964), using grab sampling techniques, found biomass levels of about 1.3 kg m^{-2} on the Antarctic continental shelf in the Indian Ocean Sector. More recent observations by Propp (1970), White and Robins (1972), Hardy (1972) and Platt

Fig. 1. Sessile invertebrate groups from benthos at South Orkney Islands.

TABLE I

Biomass of nearshore benthos at three Antarctic localities (from Propp, 1970; White and Robins, 1972; Hardy, 1972; Platt, 1980)

Depth range (m)	Flora (g m^{-2})			Fauna (g m^{-2})			
	Haswell Islands	Signy Island	South Georgia	Haswell Islands	Signy Island Infauna	Signy Island Epifauna	South Georgia
2–10	a	1040 1230 1723	2000–15,000	20–257	1500	137–200	99–279
10–25	a	—	2000–15,000	550	2600	—	34–229
25–30	0	218 1487	1000	1000	—	53–1347	—
30	0	0	—	3000	—	200	—

a Macro-algae present in small quantities.

(1980), have shown that the elevated biomass on the outer shelf continues into nearshore locations, as sessile filter-feeding organisms on hard substrates and infaunal assemblages dominated by lamellibranchs, polychaetes and amphipods (Table I). Sessile invertebrates may be replaced in rocky areas in shallow water by macroalgae with a similar or higher biomass than the faunal standing crop. This is particularly so where the giant kelp, *Macrocystis pyrifera*, occurs at the northern islands such as South Georgia.

2.2 Density

Few data are as yet available to demonstrate the ranges of densities of individual benthic organisms in the Antarctic. The high densities noted by casual observers, reinforced by associated taxonomic difficulties, have served to deter further investigation.

Comparisons between communities are complicated by the use of different sampling and extraction techniques, familiar problems to benthic ecologists since Ryther (1963) demonstrated the relationship between biomass, abundance and species diversity when estimated by different extraction procedures.

Table II illustrates density values from three widely separated sites in the Southern Ocean compared with selected information from other seas. The observations by Richardson and Hedgpeth (1977) demonstrate high densities at the shallower sampling sites and reduction of about one order of magnitude at those sites below 300 m. They also illustrate differences in apparent abundance caused by screens of different aperture. At shallow sites the use of a 0.5 mm screen rather than a 1.0 mm mesh size nearly trebled the range of density values and doubled the average densities from 18,412 to 39,965 individuals m^{-2}. Observations by Lowry (1975) at two different sites in Arthur Harbour, sampled at regular intervals over an annual cycle, produced rather lower average densities although the range of densities was of the same order.

Oceanographic observations in McMurdo Sound by Littlepage and Pearse (1962) and Littlepage (1965) showed low levels of oxygen concentration in areas where currents brought water from under the Ross Ice Shelf. Dayton and Oliver (1977) showed a most interesting contrast between sites around McMurdo Sound that were influenced by water flowing out from under the Ross Ice Shelf (west), and sites open to circulation from the open sea (east). Presumably a water body that has traversed the sea bed under the ice-shelf has less potential to support production by the uncovered shallow water benthic communities because it will have been depleted of nutrients by biological activity under the shelf. Thus, the McMurdo Sound (west) benthic communities were found to be about one order of magnitude less

TABLE II
Comparison of benthic faunal abundance at Antarctic, Arctic, Temperate and Sub-tropical locations

Location	Depth (m)	Screen aperture	Abundance (individuals m^{-2})		Source
			Range	Average	
McMudro Sound, East	20	0.5		118,712	Dayton and Oliver (1977)
	20	0.5		155,573	
	30	0.5		145,781	
McMurdo Sound, West	30	0.5		2184	
	30	0.5		45,294	
	40	0.5		10,036	
Ross Sea	500	0.5		1960	
Arthur Harbour, Anvers Island and Bismarck Strait	5–75	1.0	3954–34,251	18,412	Richardson and Hedgpeth (1977)
	5–75	0.5	9440–86,514		
	300–700	1.0		1530	
	300–700	1.0		2891	
	300–700	0.5		1876	
	300–700	0.5		4362	
Arthur Harbour, Anvers Island	30	1.0	3264–14,756	7629	Lowry (1975)
		1.0	2244–11,747	6285	
King Edward Cove, South Georgia	5	1.0		31,150	Platt (1980)
	6	1.0		2490	
	11	1.0	390–3260	1618	
Gay Head–Bermuda	487	0.5		8653	Dayton and Oliver (1977)
	2086	0.5		2154	
California Massachusetts	4	0.5		84,709	Haven (1967)
	Intertidal	0.5		80,450	
Massachusetts Buzzard Bay		0.2		9985	Sanders (1960)
Massachusetts Bermuda	Outer Shelf	0.2	6000–13,000		Sanders (1968)
	slope	0.2	6000–23,000		
	Abyssal rise	0.2	1500–3000		
Gulf Stream Sargasso Sea	Abyss	0.2	150–270		Sanders (1968)
	Abyss	0.2	30–150		
Virginia: York River	1–3	0.25		44,204	Haven (1967)
	1–3	1.0		5448	
	6–12	0.25		4904	
	6–12	1.0		928	
Arctic: Frustration Bay Baffin Island Disk Bugt Disk Bugt		2.0		243	Ellis (1960)
		1.5		1295	
	Shallow	1.0		1299	
	Deep	1.0		1134	

abundant than those in the east. The most striking feature of Dayton and Oliver's observations in McMurdo Sound was the extremely high densities (among the highest recorded anywhere—up to 155,000 individuals m^{-2}) on the sponge spicule sediments, compared with observations from other regions (Table II).

The values reported by Platt (1980) for the South Georgia benthos show high levels of abundance at the shallowest sites with a rapidly diminished density at sites deeper than 6 m. This was probably due to limitation by the substrates. King Edward Cove is a partially enclosed flooded glacial basin in which very fine soft sediments predominate at depth and limit colonization by macrobenthic invertebrates.

Richardson and Hedgpeth (1977) suggested that the high densities at Arthur Harbour may be a result of high primary production in shallow water. They noted dense growths of attached macroalgae which, they believe, provides an abundant food source for the macrobenthos. It has been observed elsewhere (Whitaker, 1977) that much of the annual primary production in neritic waters in the Antarctic will be transmitted by sedimentation directly to the benthic communities.

The stability of the physical environment coupled with a slow growth rates will tend to lead to the evolution of efficient, stable community structures with low annual turnover rates. This type of community will support a higher biomass, or alternatively higher number of individuals per unit of organic matter than the less stable, less efficient assemblages characteristic of physically fluctuating environments.

In all oceans the benthos of the inner continental shelf is generally considered to be richer in species and numbers than in deeper water. Wigley and McIntyre (1964) attributed this phenomenon to the abundant zooplankton in the overlying water. The relationship between neritic production and density of animals is supported by the results of Dayton and Oliver (1977) from McMurdo Sound. The highest densities occurred in the sponge mats of eastern McMurdo Sound. Sponge mats offer a wide range of microhabitats that enhance both density and diversity to levels beyond that which a normally graded marine sediment is capable of supporting.

Antarctic macrobenthic communities exhibit high abundance largely owing to the high (but seasonal) primary production and the diverse substrate characteristics.

2.3 Diversity

The Antarctic benthic communities are grossly under-sampled and analysis of new collections from poorly-investigated geographical locations or unusual habitats invariably produces a surprisingly large number of species new to the region. Most Antarctic research organizations have a substantial back-log of undescribed collections and few of them have been sufficiently well analysed to provide quantitative estimates of faunal diversity. Comparisons are often difficult because of non-standard procedures. However, despite the incompleteness and unevenness of sampling, crude assessments of the diversity of the macrobenthos suggest that these communities have a relatively high species richness.

Table III compares selected groups of invertebrates from the Antarctic and Arctic and indicates that the Antarctic fauna is some 50–100% richer in numbers of species represented in each of these groups.

TABLE III

Comparison of the number of species recorded from certain groups of the Antarctic and Arctic macrobenthos

Group	Antarctic	Arctic	Source
Molluscs	875	224	Powell (1965)
Polychaetes	650	300	Zenkevitch (1963) Ushakov (1955)
Amphipods	470	262	Hartman (1967) Knox and Lowry (1977)
Bryzoans	310	200	Zenkevitch (1963) Bullivant (1969)
Sponges	300	200	Zenkevitch (1963) Koltun (1969)
Isopods	299	49	Kussakin (1967)
Ascidians	129	47	Zenkevitch (1963) Kott (1969a,b, 1971)
Pycnogonids	100	29	Fry (1964) Zenkevitch (1963)

Lowry (1975) examined the macrobenthic faunal characteristics of a pair of stations sampled throughout the annual cycle at Arthur Harbour, Antarctic Peninsula. Analysis of the samples demonstrated that no single species dominated the communities. By using the indices H, the annual mean diversity index and R, a measure of the degree of potential diversity, Patten (1962) was able to show that the yearly mean diversity was 3.9866 bits individual^{-1} ($R = 0.1947$) at station I and 3.7500 bits individual^{-1} ($R = 0.2370$) at station II. These are high species diversity values close to the theoretical maximum.

An independent investigation by Richardson and Hedgpeth (1977) studied a series of similar collections from Arthur Harbour from a wide range of habitats (Table IV). They used a slightly different diversity index, H' (Pielon, 1966) and also examined species richness SR (Margalef, 1958), evenness J' (ratio of observed diversity to maximum theoretically possible,

Pielon, 1966) and equitability E (ratio of observed species to theoretical maximum number adjusted for individual abundance within each species, Lloyd and Ghelardi, 1964). The values derived for the Arthur Harbour macrobenthos were compared with similar observations by Boesch (1972) for the North Carolina shelf. The diversity values (H') were shown to be similar in both localities but the species richness (SR) was much higher and the equitability values (E) were much lower at Arthur Harbour. The Antarctic collections were obtained during the austral summer and so the increase in abundance of some species, owing to seasonal recruitment, was thought to be responsible for the low equitability values.

TABLE IV

Station, depth, number of species (S), number of individuals $(N) > 1.0$ mm, > 0.5 m, species diversity (H'), evenness (J'), equitability (E), and species richness (SR) at each station. Vicinity of Arthur Harbour, Antarctic Peninsula (after Richardson and Hedgpeth, 1977)

Station	Depth (m)	S	$N > 1.0$ mm	$N > 0.5$ mm	H'	J'	E'	SR
3	300–700	81	1317	2891	4.92	0.78	0.56	13.04
4	300–700	67	1876	4362	4.85	0.80	0.64	11.04
2	75	117	13,751	28,369	4.43	0.64	0.27	13.68
1	65	71	11,717	26,780	3.66	0.60	0.25	8.40
5	50	64	7200	19,460	3.39	0.57	0.23	8.04
11	43	79	13,231	22,700	3.74	0.59	0.25	9.24
12	18	95	26,469	55,049	4.06	0.62	0.26	10.29
13	23	105	20,486	55,718	3.98	0.59	0.22	12.02
14	30	92	29,180	86,514	3.66	0.56	0.21	10.00
9	30	84	20,549	47,623	3.76	0.59	0.24	9.35
10	15	77	34,251	69,363	3.16	0.50	0.17	8.09
6	18	56	12,061	19,836	3.30	0.57	0.25	6.77
7	5–7	60	16,583	32,077	3.74	0.64	0.33	6.81
8	50	43	3954	9440	2.05	0.38	0.12	5.81

The observation of high species diversity and species richness in the stable, low temperature environment of Arthur Harbour supports the conclusion of Sanders (1968), that species diversity is enhanced in physically stable environments.

Lowry (1975) came to a similar conclusion. He noted that the mean diversity value at Arthur Harbour Stations I (3.9866) and II (3.7500) were comparable to results from York River, Massachusetts (3.3096–3.7604) given by Haven (1967). They were very much higher than the values derived by Grassle (1967) for sites in Buzzards Bay, Massachusetts (1.5575–3.4658), where the annual primary production rates are similar to those for Arthur Harbour, but the physical conditions are much more variable. Grassle (1967) found high average diversity values (4.770–4.780) for communities off the North Carolina coast, but there the faunal density is about three times lower than at Arthur Harbour.

High population density lowers the theoretical maximum diversity, but R values for Arthur Harbour communities indicate that they are near to their theoretical maximum diversity. Lowry (1975) concluded that there appeared to be two conflicting factors influencing the structure of communities: a passive force in the form of a stable environment that allowed high diversity, complexity and community stability, and an active force in the form of a rich food supply that tended to increase density and thereby reduce diversity.

Whatever the controlling factors, it has become evident that Antarctic benthic communities are not only characterized by high biomass and abundance but also an unexpected species richness, promoted for the most part by environmental stability and enhanced niche availability.

One curious feature of the evolutionary trends within the benthic invertebrate groups is that, although species diversity is high, it is often only so because of speciation within a few families of an order. One might expect recent colonizers of the Southern Ocean to show low levels of speciation and the more ancient autochthenous groups to exhibit radiation. Yet in the Antarctic, the autochthenous groups often demonstrate both evolutionary conservatism and extensive speciation. Most phyla exhibit this feature and it is well illustrated, for example, by the Malacostraca among the isopods. The majority of the more ancient families are represented by few genera which are often monospecific, but three families, Antarcturidae, Serolidae and the Munnidae, account for at least one-half of the Antarctic species. The geographical distribution of these species seems to correspond to former Gondwanian association. For example, of the 55 species of *Antarcturus*, 25 are found north of the Antarctic Convergence. Twelve of these are found in South and Central America, seven in Australia/New Zealand, two in South Africa, one each in East Indies, Galapagos, Fiji and one from the Pacific deep sea. *Serolis* species exhibit a similar distribution whereas members of the Munnidae are also distributed in the northern hemisphere.

Similar types of distribution and species diversity occur in the other invertebrate phyla and the skewed diversity levels within groups with similar evolutionary history must to some extent reflect evolutionary "success".

3. Affinities

Several authors have discussed the biogeographical relationships of the marine faunas of the southern hemisphere. Some have considered the distribution of many different phyla in their analysis (Ekman, 1953; Hedgpeth,

1969, 1970; Dell, 1972). Others have presented accounts based on the distribution and affinities of a particular group; for example, fish (Andriashev, 1965); polychaetes and amphipods (Knox and Lowry, 1977); isopods (Kussakin, 1967); molluscs (Powell, 1965); echinoderms (Fell *et al.*, 1969); ascidians (Kott, 1969a); sponges (Koltun, 1969); amphipods (Thurston, 1972); macroalgae (Knox, 1960).

The regional divisions proposed by these authors are very similar although differences in nomenclature and geography are apparent. The scheme proposed by Knox (1960) is most divergent from the others, largely because it is mainly based on macroalgae distribution and is therefore confined to a description of shallow-water biotas.

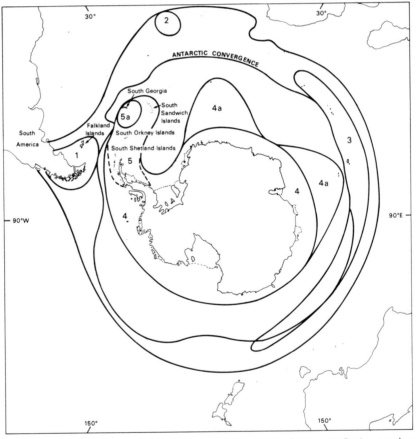

Fig. 2. Biogeographical Zones (after Hedgpeth, 1969): (1–3) Sub-Antarctic Region (southern limit—the Antarctic Convergence)—(1) Magellanic sub-region. (4–5) Antarctic Region (northern limit—the Antarctic Convergence)—(4) Continental sub-region; (4a) extensions of Continental sub-region; (5) Scotia sub-region; (5a) South Georgia District.

The biogeographical regions described by Hedgpath (1969, 1970) are based on 12 phyla from numerous habitats (Fig. 2). Here, the Antarctic Region, covering the whole of the area to the south of the Antarctic Convergence, is divided into two sub-regions, the Western Antarctic (composed of the Antarctic Peninsula and the Scotia arc) and the Continental Antarctic. The Sub-Antarctic Region includes the area between the Antarctic Convergence and the Sub-tropical Convergence. New Zealand is not included in the Sub-Antarctic Region but southern South America is included. Magellanic and Kerguelen sub-regions are recognized within the Sub-Antarctic Region. The majority of other biogeographers have followed this system giving greater or lesser emphasis to lower biogeographic units.

Hedgpeth, drawing on the records of Dell (1972) and Powell (1965), recognized four principal benthic faunal components for Antarctic molluscs.

(1) Circumcontinental species.
(2) Species confined to the Weddell Sea, Antarctic Peninsula and Bellinghausen Sea.
(3) Species restricted to the Scotia Ridge.
(4) Species characteristic of the sub-Antarctic islands.

The affinities of these faunal components suggest that they originated from:

(1) A relic autochthenous fauna.
(2) A fauna derived from adjacent deep-water basins.
(3) A fauna dispersing from South America via the Scotia arc.
(4) A fauna which has spread in the opposite direction from the Antarctic northwards along the Scotia arc.

This results in a largely circumpolar fauna with some regionalization resulting from recent migration via shallow water routes (Fig. 3). The other benthic phyla were found to have very similar distribution patterns but showed differences in the proportions of the component elements.

Kussakin (1967) suggested that the isopods are a most suitable group for biogeographical investigations because they are largely benthic and non-migratory. They are richly represented in the Southern Ocean in varied habitats and physical conditions and do not have pelagic larval stages to aid dispersal. Preston's Coefficient of faunal diversity (z) (Preston, 1962a,b) is essentially the number of species common to both areas in each of two geographical areas. By the use of this coefficient Kussakin (1967) divided the Antarctic and sub-Antarctic into 12 geographical zones and analysed the affinities of the littoral, sub-littoral, pseudo-abyssal and bathyl faunas. The value $z = 0.27$ is considered to be a critical level; below it the areas

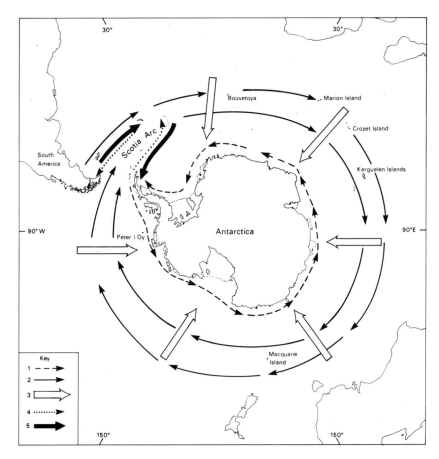

Fig. 3. Origins and dispersal of the Antarctic marine fauna (after Knox and Lowry, 1977). (1) Dispersal by East Wind Drift; (2) dispersal by West Wind Drift; (3) migration of deepwater groups; (4) northward migration on Scotia arc; (5) southward migration on Scotia arc.

compared are samples of some larger unit while higher values of z indicate that the faunas of these areas show some degree of isolation.

Up to now the lack of data from the South Orkney Islands has prevented proper analysis of the biogeography of the Scotia arc, but recent additional observations from this island group have enabled reappraisal of the affinities of the isopod fauna at the species and generic levels (Tables V, VI), and have demonstrated the robustness of Hedgpeth's biogeographical conclusions.

TABLE V
Preston Coefficients of dissimilarity for isopod genera of faunal components at different
Antarctic localities

Locality	Number of Genera	Locality	Number of Genera	Genera in Common	(%)	Preston Coefficients z_1	z_2
S. Orkney Is.	27	S. Shetland Is.	17	14	82	0.390	0.377
S. Orkney Is.	27	South Georgia	25	21	84	0.229	0.254
S. Orkney Is.	27	Antarctic Peninsula	23	20	87	0.247	0.254
S. Orkney Is.	27	Continental Antarctic	43	24	56	0.326	0.323
S. Shetland Is.	17	South Georgia	25	14	56	0.374	0.366
S. Shetland Is.	17	Antarctic Peninsula	23	15	65	0.374	0.292
S. Shetland Is.	17	Continental Antarctic	43	15	35	0.414	0.344
South Georgia	25	Antarctic Peninsula	23	21	91	0.160	0.170
South Georgia	25	Continental Antarctic	43	20	47	0.430	0.401
Antarctic Peninsula	23	Continental Antarctic	43	20	47	0.390	0.353

z_1, Preston Coefficient calculated from known distributions. z_2, Preston Coefficient calculated from data smoothed for discontinuous distributions.

The values of the more realistic coefficient, z_2 at the generic level were found to be about 0.27 or below, indicating that much of the isopod fauna at the localities examined in the Western Antarctic should be considered to be part of a larger biogeographical unit at the generic level. The faunas of the Antarctic Peninsula, South Georgia and the South Orkney Islands all showed sufficient affinity for these localities to be components of a discrete region, the Western Antarctic Region. The fauna from the South Shetland Islands exhibited unexpected isolation which is likely to be due to under-sampling rather than real insularity.

Relatively low levels of affinity were observed between the isopod fauna of the Antarctic Peninsula and the Continental Antarctic. This can be interpreted as due to the very high level of endemism which occurs among the Continental Antarctic fauna. Most isopod species that occur along the Antarctic Peninsula also occur in the Continental Antarctic Region whereas many species found around the Antarctic Continent do not occur as members of the Antarctic Peninsula fauna (Table V).

The values of z_1 and z_2 at the species level were all considerably above $z = 0.27$ indicating some form of faunal isolation of the areas examined. The closest faunal links appeared to be between the fauna of the Continental Antarctic and the Antarctic Peninsula and the Antarctic Peninsula and the South Shetland Islands. This is quite different to the calculated affinities at the generic level, but is very much as expected because of the close geological and geographical associations between these areas (Table VI).

TABLE VI

Preston coefficients of dissimilarity for isopod species occurring at different Antarctic localities

Locality	Number of species	Locality	Number of species	Species in Common	(%)	Preston Coefficients z_1	z_2
S. Orkney Is.	65	S. Shetland Is.	24	14	58	0.677	0.476
S. Orkney Is.	65	South Georgia	47	23	49	0.657	0.632
S. Orkney Is.	65	Antarctic Peninsula	46	25	54	0.621	0.598
S. Orkney Is.	65	Continential Antarctic	99	29	29	0.713	0.660
S. Shetland Is.	24	South Georgia	47	12	26	0.707	0.590
S. Shetland Is.	24	Antarctic Peninsula	46	14	30	0.613	0.539
S. Shetland Is.	24	Continental Antarctic	99	12	12	0.747	0.537
South Georgia	47	Antarctic Peninsula	46	18	39	0.689	0.689
South Georgia	47	Continental Antarctic	99	16	16	0.774	0.658
Antarctic Peninsula	46	Continental Antarctic	99	30	30	0.606	0.487

z_1, Preston Coefficient calculated from known distributions. z_2, Preston Coefficient calculated from data smoothed for discontinuous distributions.

The index calculated for species affinities from known distribution data (z_1) produces a result similar to that given by the observations made by Thurston (1972), which indicated that the closest associations were to be found between the fauna of the South Shetland Islands and the Antarctic Peninsula, the fauna of the South Orkney Islands and the Antarctic Peninsula, and the fauna of the Antarctic Peninsula and the Continental Antarctic.

The Preston Coefficients calculated from smoothed (and therefore more reliable) data (z_2) indicated that the stronger associations were between the South Shetland Islands, the Antarctic Peninsula and the South Orkney Islands, and the Antarctic Peninsula and the Continental Antarctic. The isopod fauna of South Georgia was demonstrated to be rather isolated from the rest of the western Antarctic fauna at the species level. Conversely the link between the eastern and western Antarctic isopod fauna at the species level was confirmed. The isopod fauna of the South Orkney Islands showed closest affinity with the fauna of the South Shetland Islands and the Antarctic Peninsula; this is compatible with recent descriptions of the geological relationships of the western Antarctic (Dalziel and Elliott, 1971).

Most polar biologists have been impressed by the distinctiveness of the Antarctic fauna, particularly the high level of endemism at the species level. Species endemism typically ranges between 57 and 95% whereas generic endemism is always much lower (Table VII). High levels of endemism result from speciation during long periods of isolation. Factors such as significant hydrological barriers, the lack of shallow water bridges and wide geographical separation, are accentuated in the Antarctic fauna because the dominant invertebrate components reproduce without pelagic larval stages thereby reducing dispersal and enhancing isolation (White, 1977; Picken, 1980). It is, therefore, no surprise to find that not only the Antarctic fauna but also each island group tend to have a high proportion of endemic species (Table VIII).

TABLE VII

Comparison of endemism in selected benthic groups

Group	Genera (%)	Species (%)	Source
Fish	70	95	Andriashev (1965)
Amphipoda	39	90	Knox and Lowry (1977)
Echinodermata	27	73	Ekman (1953)
Echinoidea	25	77	Pawson (1969b)
Pycnogonida	14	90	Fry (1964)
Isopoda and Tanaidacea	10	66	Kussakin (1967)
Holothuroidea	5	58	Pawson (1969a)
Polychaeta	5	57	Knox and Lowry (1977)

The affinities indicated by the benthic fauna at the generic and species level, as illustrated by a typical group such as the isopoda, are consistent with the hypothesis of Fry (1964) that the high level of endemism was indicative of a long period of isolation and an independent evolution of the Antarctic fauna.

TABLE VIII

Comparison of total number of species and genera of isopods at different Antarctic localities and the level of endemism

Locality	Total species	Endemic	(%)	Total genera	Endemic	(%)
S. Orkney Islands	67	19	28.4	27	0	0
S. Shetland Islands	24	4	16.7	17	0	0
Antarctic Peninsula	47	5	10.6	23	0	0
South Georgia	46	12	26.1	25	0	0
Western Antarctic	106	40	37.7	38	0	0
Continental Antarctic	99	45	45.5	43	8	19
Antarctic Region	180	130	72.2	52	15	29

Analysis of the biogeographical affinities of the isopod fauna of the Antarctic and sub-Antarctic confirm the patterns observed for other benthic phyla and support the conclusions on the sub-division of this region of the southern hemisphere which were proposed by Hedgpeth (1969; 1970).

These results also support the division of the Antarctic into Eastern and Western Regions, and the lack of strong links between faunas to the north and south of the Antarctic Convergence. Thus, the Antarctic Convergence is a real oceanographic barrier for the benthic fauna as well as for the more directly affected planktonic communities.

4. Life Beneath Ice-shelves

It has long been suspected that organisms live under the extensive ice-shelves around the Antarctic Continent. Fish, echinoderms and other benthic organisms have been found on the surface of the Ross Ice Shelf (Debenham, 1959), well away from the ice-front, in areas of net ice abla-tion. Benthic organisms have been caught through natural fractures in the ice-shelf (Littlepage and Pearse, 1962); fish have been caught under the ice-shelf in George VI Sound (Heywood and Light, 1975), at a considerable distance from the open sea. Organisms collected in these situations were largely errant species which could have strayed under the ice-shelves and were therefore not necessarily part of a resident sub-shelf community. However, the quality of water flowing out from under the Ross Ice Shelf suggested depletion by biological communities under the shelf (Littlepage and Pearse, 1962; Littlepage, 1965).

A systematic study of the sub-shelf communities has been undertaken by United States biologists in collaboration with those of a number of other nations, by drilling through the Ross Ice Shelf, more than 400 km from the open sea. Preliminary observations confirmed the existence of organisms beneath the ice-shelf (Lipps et al., 1977; Azam et al., 1978) and suggested that basic metabolic processes tended to be slow; dissolved organic mater-ial turnover was estimated to be 1–10 years (Holm-Hansen et al., 1978).

It was expected that the Ross Ice Shelf either concealed a typical Antarctic fauna or a sparse but still diverse fauna, yet subsequent observa-tions revealed neither. Lipps et al. (1978, 1979), using a variety of tech-niques, demonstrated the dominant components to be a sparse errant crustacean fauna of copepods, mysids, euphausiids, amphipods and isopods. The sediments were virtually devoid of infauna or sessile epifauna. Under-water television similarly pictured sediments showing no evidence of bio-logical activity or epifaunal organisms (Ronan et al., 1978). Microbial biomass, as evidenced by ATP concentration, was measured in the water column and sediments and found to be highest at the sea-floor. However, the concentrations were only equivalent to 1 mg bacterial $C\,m^{-2}$ (Holm-Hansen et al., 1979) which is much lower than normally found in continental shelf sediments and similar to that expected in abyssal conditions where nutrient levels are impoverished.

It remains to be seen whether these observations from one site are typical of conditions under the Ross Ice Shelf as a whole or of other shelves around the Antarctic, but such observations should provide interesting indications of the structure and energetics of ecosystems remote from direct primary production, and the adaptations of organisms found in them.

5. Ecological Strategies

Antarctic poikilotherms exhibit a number of features such as slow and seasonal growth, delayed maturation, longevity, large size, low fecundity, large egg size, non-pelagic larval development, seasonal reproduction and low metabolic rate, that appear to be an associated suite of mechanisms by which the organisms respond to cold, highly seasonal environments where primary production is confined to a brief period during the summer.

5.1 Development

In the oceans overall the abundance of pelagic larval stages from benthic invertebrates is typical of the neritic zooplankton community. About 70% of all benthic species reproduce by pelagic development yet at high latitudes very few benthic species appear to produce pelagic larvae (Thorson, 1950), although the detailed reproductive pattern of only a small proportion is known. Where it has been described the majority of species reproduce by non-pelagic modes of development, which usually involve some form of brood protection. In addition, extensive plankton sampling in the Southern Ocean has yet to produce more than isolated collections of larval stages from benthic invertebrates.

Invertebrate groups that normally reproduce by brooding, such as the Amphipoda and Isopoda, are well represented in the Antarctic marine fauna, whereas the benthic crustacean groups that are dominant components elsewhere, such as Decapoda and Cirripedia, are poorly represented. In this example, the amphipods and isopods can be considered to be pre-adapted and therefore readily able to colonize high latitude habitats. This does not explain why the higher orders of the Malacostraca, which also brood and might therefore be considered to be pre-adapted, seem to be excluded from faunas at high latitudes. In other phyla, such as the Porifera, Mollusca, Annelida and Echinodermata, the marine orders are more evenly represented but a much larger proportion of the species undergoes non-pelagic development than of those found in lower latitudes. For example, 80% of Antarctic sponges are either viviparous or exhibit brood protection, whereas only about 55% of those in the Tropical or Temperate environments reproduce in this manner (Arnaud, 1974). Brooding and the production of large yolky eggs deposited in egg capsules is common in Arctic molluscs (Thorson, 1950; Ockelmann, 1958, 1965) and this trend also occurs in Antarctic molluscs (Dell, 1972; Picken, 1979).

The widespread avoidance of the planktotrophic route of development, so typical of benthic invertebrates elsewhere, must be an indication of the unsuitable conditions in the upper water column for larval development. Even the early larval development of major components of the zoo-plankton, such as *Euphausia superba*, takes place at depth rather than in the euphotic zone (Mackintosh, 1972; Marr, 1962).

A number of explanations have been proposed for this. It avoids the hazards of the upper water column, where marked changes in salinity can occur during the summer due to sea ice melting and freshwater run-off from the land; also juveniles hatch in suitable habitats for colonization rather than being swept off in ocean currents (Ostergreen, 1912).

The overall seasonal periodicity of the production cycle is very predic-table (Arnaud, 1977) but perturbations by ice make local production highly variable (White, 1977). Thorson (1950) suggested that in polar environ-ments the cold combined with the characteristic short period of primary production inhibit the completion of pelagic development of larvae before food becomes scarce. Non-pelagic development, involving adaptations such as large yolky eggs, brood protection or viviparity, ensures successful development of the larvae, despite the unfavourable environment. This general conclusion is supported by recent field observations on a range of benthic invertebrates (Arnaud, 1974, 1977) and gastropod molluscs (Simpson, 1977; Picken, 1979, 1980). Large eggs will result in large robust juveniles (Amio, 1963) which should have a better chance of survival than smaller juveniles (Smith and Fretwell, 1974; Spight, 1976). Consideration of the total energy requirements of reproduction in different environments suggests that lecithotrophic larvae will be favoured in conditions of poor food supply and low water temperature (Chia, 1970; Vance, 1972).

The absence of pelagic larvae is a serious handicap to dispersal and colonization, and the high levels of species endemism among the majority of Antarctic benthic animals testify to its effect. The selective pressures on these species to adopt a non-pelagic development in high latitude environ-ments must be very powerful because those species which do reproduce pelagically, such as the Antarctic limpet *Nacella concinna*, and the echino-derms *Odontaster validus* and *Sterechinus neumayeri*, are widely distri-buted and form a dominant component of the shallow water benthos in terms of occurrence and biomass.

5.2 Growth

It is generally accepted that polar marine invertebrates grow slowly (Kinne, 1970), and there is a considerable body of literature which demonstrates that lowered temperature reduces growth (De March, 1978). However, reduced growth in organisms experimentally acclimated to lowered environmental temperatures does not explain slow growth rates in groups normally inhabiting cold-water environments. Indeed, there are reports of polar species that appear to grow rapidly. For example, it has been established that sponges of the genus *Mycale* grow rapidly in comparison with others in the same habitat in McMurdo Sound (Dayton *et al.*, 1974), and the Antarctic mollusc *Adamussium colbecki* grows at similar rates and to a similar size as temperate-water pectens (White, 1975).

White suggested that relict species may be better adapted and therefore grow more quickly than more recent colonizers of the polar environments, but this now seems to be a rather simplistic approach. Clarke (1980) posed the question: do polar marine invertebrates really grow slowly? Everson (1977) noted that Antarctic poikilotherms show a wide range of absolute growth rates (Fig. 4). When he compared the growth of six species of

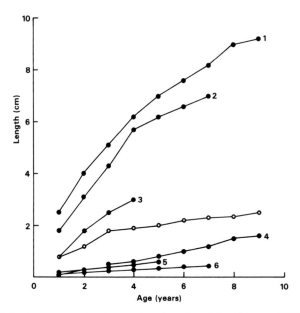

Fig. 4. Growth in temperate and polar species of mollusc (after Everson, 1977). ○, *Venus striatula* at Millport, U.K.; ●, polar species: (1) *Laternula elliptica*; (2) *Adamussium colbecki*; (3) *Gaimardia trapesina*; (4) *Yoldia eightsi*; (5) *Kidderia bicolor*; (6) *Lissarca miliaris*.

Antarctic molluscs with that of the temperate species *Venus striatula*, three species were found to grow faster and the others more slowly than the example from lower latitudes. These species came from a wide range of ecological niches, and a more valid comparison can be made by investigating the relative rates for species with similar maximum size and ecology. Ralph and Maxwell (1977a,b,c) found, when such a comparison was made, that polar species grow more slowly than their temperate-water counterparts. Similar results have been demonstrated for fish (Everson, 1977; Arnaud, 1977) and echinoderms (Pearse, 1965), and Luxmoore (1982) demonstrated a clear relationship between latitude and relative rate of increase in size after hatching in the Crustacea (Fig. 5).

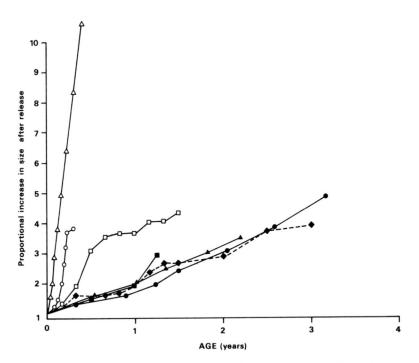

Fig. 5. Growth of temperate and Antarctic Crustacea (after Luxmoore, 1981). ●, *Serols cornuta*; ▲, *Serolis polita*; ■, *Chorismus antarcticus* (Clarke and Lakhani, 1979); ◆, *Hippomedon femoratus* (Bregazzi, 1972); △, *Idotea baltica* (Strong and Daborn, 1979); ○, *Dynamene bidentata* (Holdich, 1968); □, *Cirolana imposita* (Shafir and Field, 1980). Solid symbols, Antarctic species.

Clarke (1980) concluded that low environmental temperature was no bar to fast absolute growth rate, but even so (wherever it was possible to make valid comparisons) polar species grew more slowly than related species of similar ecology and potential maximum size from warmer water. In common with others, he noted that growth was often markedly seasonal and, since temperatures fluctuate very little at high latitudes, concluded that food was a major regulating factor.

Slow growth at later stages in the life-history of polar invertebrates is anticipated in the very earliest stages; embryonic development in many groups is very slow. Wear (1974) demonstrated the direct relationship between temperature and embryonic development in caridean Crustacea. Bregazzi (1972), by comparing the brooding interval of amphipod Crustacea from different geographical locations, demonstrated the considerably increased length of the period between release of the eggs into the marsupium and the release of the juveniles in polar species, as well as a much longer period of development from hatching to maturity (Table IX). The Antarctic benthos is dominated by invertebrate groups that adopt some form of direct development or brood protection and all those species studied so far show a similar trend towards protracted embryonic development (Picken, 1980). This effect is the result of two factors operating together: large egg-size, which slows development independent of temperature, and low temperature (A. Clarke, personal communication).

In many groups, slow growth is coupled with delayed maturation and prolonged gametogenesis. This is best known in the Antarctic echinoderms and fish but is also indicated in other phyla. It was initially demonstrated that batches of eggs due to be spawned in up to three successive seasons were to be found in the female gonads of *Notothenia neglecta* (Everson, 1970) and *Odontaster validus* (Pearse, 1965), and subsequent observations have shown that in Antarctic poikilotherms as a whole gametogenesis extending over more than one season is a common phenomenon (White, 1977).

5.3 Large size

Slow growth, delayed maturation, prolonged gametogenesis and embryonic development, result in enhanced longevity and large size in Antarctic invertebrates. This combination of factors which delay maturation and extend the period until first breeding will usually enhance longevity in comparison with species that rapidly complete their reproductive cycle; however, the reason why invertebrates should exhibit large overall size, rather than deferred maturation with the same range of size as in lower latitude species, is not at all obvious. Descriptions of giant members of the Antarctic benthos are common; pycnogonids, isopods, sponges, amphipods and free-living nematodes are usually given as examples. The phenomenon of "gigantism" is real, rather than perceived, because of inadequate sampling; it has been tested for the range of invertebrate groups (Arnaud, 1974) and amphipod Crustacea in particular (De Broyer, 1977), and it was clearly demonstrated that species of larger than average size are represented more often than usual in the Antarctic benthic communities. Within the Antarctic region the trend is progressive, and Luxmoore (1982) has shown that the ubiquitous serolid Isopoda demonstrated a clear trend towards increase in the size at maturity in species with a more southerly distribution.

TABLE IX

Duration of brood incubation in polar and temperate Amphipoda

Region/species	Incubation duration	Ambient temperature (°C)	Authority
Antarctic			
Orchomene plebs	5 months		Pearse (1963)
Bovallia gigantea	7 months		Thurston (1970)
	6–8 months	−2 to 1	Bone (1972)
Hippomedon femoratus	6 months	−2 to 1	Bregazzi (1972)[a]
Tryphosella kergueleni	6 months	−2 to 1	Bregazzi (1972)
Arctic or boreal			
Parathemisto lilbellula	several months		Dunbar (1957)
Gammarus wilkitzkii	5–6 months		Barnard (1959)
Pontoporeia affinis	3–4 months	3–4	Mathisen (1953)
Pallasea quadrispinosa	2–2½ months		Mathisen (1953)
Temperate			
Gammarus pulex	3 months (winter)		Hynes (1955)
	16–17 days (summer)		Sexton (1924)
Gammarus duebeni	19–20 days	20	Forsman (1951)
	47–49 days	4–6	
	12½ days	20	Kinne (1953)
	19 days	14	
	14 days	18	Hynes (1954)
	54–59 days	4.7	
Gammarus locusta	9–10 days (summer)		Sexton (1924)
Gammarus zaddachi	10 days	20	Kinne (1960)
	15 days	14	Kinne (1961)
Marinogammarus obtusatus	13 days	6–9	Sheader and Chia (1970)
Crangonyx pseudogracilis	48 days	3.5	Hynes (1955)
	14–17 days	15	
	8 days	23	Embody (1912)
Corophium volutator	about 17 days		Watkin (1941)

[a] As Cheirimidon femoratus.

There is a subtle evolutionary interplay between, on the one hand, large size, which reduces potential predation and increases individual fecundity, thereby enhancing population recruitment, balanced, on the other hand, by slow development and delayed maturation that together increase the period of exposure to individual mortality. McLaren (1966) demonstrated the potential selective advantage to the pelagic chaetognath *Sagitta elegans* of attaining large size and thereby producing more offspring, even though this required another year's growth. Similar evolutionary trends must be operating in the Antarctic benthic invertebrates where female size is critical, because large lecithotrophic eggs, brooding and non-pelagic larval development is widespread (Picken, 1980) (Fig. 6). Investigation of the energetics of various reproductive strategies by Chia (1970) have demonstrated that it is less energetically expensive to produce few yolky eggs than numerous non-yolky eggs.

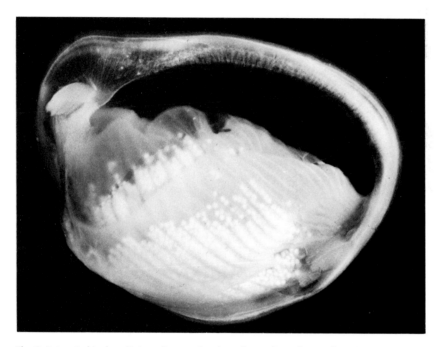

Fig. 6. Antarctic bivalve, *Gaimardia trapesina*, brooding embryos in mantle cavity.

A development of this theme with Antarctic species (as direct attempt to measure the different energy expenditure of planktotrophic and lecithotrophic reproduction in caridean Crustacea from different environments (Clarke, 1979)), demonstrates that the mean individual annual reproductive effort of the polar species was significantly less than that of temperate species (Table X). Clarke (1980) also points out that there are equally strong indications of a reduced reproductive effort in the polar opisthobranch *Philine gibba* (Seager, 1979) and the brooding bivalve *Lissarca miliaris* (Richardson, 1980).

TABLE X

Annual individual female reproductive effort in two temperate and two Antarctic caridean crustaceans (after Clarke, 1979)

Species	x̄ ± SE	Regression of egg fresh weight (mg) on female fresh weight (g)				
		b	SE	Intercept	r²	F	n
Freshweight eggs/ fresh weight female (g/g)							
Chorismus antarcticus	0.171 ± 0.003	170.67	10.97	−0.70	0.90	241.3	28
Pandalus montagui	0.243 ± 0.006	222.02	21.76	37.37	0.74	104.1	39
Notocrangon antarcticus	0.119 ± 0.003	153.91	5.04	−91.45	0.98	934.4	23
Crangon crangon	0.165 ± 0.004	151.08	10.96	22.61	0.74	190.1	68

5.4 Metabolism

The concept of cold-adapted metabolism is firmly established in the literature (Dunbar, 1968), the energetics of polar poikilotherms described as being characterized by an elevated metabolic rate when compared to the metabolic rates of ectotherms from warmer environments. The foundation for this relationship stems from observations by Krogh (1914, 1916) on oxygen consumption by fish over a wide range of temperatures. The results of experiments on fish by Wohlschlag (1960, 1964) and Scholander *et al.* (1953); on amphipods by Armitage (1962), Rakusa-Suszczewski and Klekowski (1973); on euphausiids by McWhinnie (1964); and on isopods by George (1977), seem to support the generality of the phenomenon. Cold-adapted metabolism also gained considerable acceptance because it conveniently explained the widely recognized observation that polar poikilotherms exhibit slow growth rates, delayed maturation and prolonged gametogenesis. It was logical to argue that if activity levels and feeding rates were broadly similar among poikilotherms from polar and warmer marine environments then an elevated rate of metabolism must result in reduced potential for growth and reproduction.

This assertion has now been challenged (see below) and there is a growing body of biochemical and physiological data which refutes the concept of cold-adapted metabolism.

Basal metabolism, usually estimated by oxygen consumption, is a difficult parameter to measure because other activities such as digestion, feeding, movement, gametogenesis and growth also require oxygen and so must also be measured or eliminated. Differences between systematic groups occur in the proportion of each element of an energy budget, and so valid comparisons may be inhibited. A reasonable approximation can be made by measuring the routine oxygen consumption of an acclimatized quiescent organism where extra activities are controlled. By the use of carefully controlled experimental technique and experimentally robust organisms, useful comparative estimates of basal metabolism can be achieved.

Holeton (1973, 1974) demonstrated that polar fish are very sensitive to physiological stress resulting from experimental procedures, and showed that when reliable techniques were used a wide range of species had low routine oxygen consumption rates. Well-controlled experiments with polar benthic invertebrates (White, 1975; Maxwell, 1977; Ralph and Maxwell, 1977b,c) demonstrated that they also had low metabolic rates during experiments conducted at ambient temperatures (Figs 7, 8).

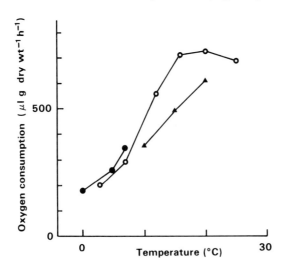

Fig. 7. Oxygen consumption of bivalve molluscs. ●, *Gaimardia trapesina* (polar); ○, *Mytilus edulis* (temperate); ▲, *Donax vittatus* (temperate) (after Maxwell, 1977).

The failure to demonstrate elevated metabolic rates, "cold-adapted" in the sense of Dunbar (1968), under controlled experimental conditions has largely led to this empirical concept being abandoned. Everson (1977) concluded that in Antarctic marine invertebrates, there is no detectable elevation of routine metabolism, and by inference basal metabolic rate, of the magnitude originally suggested by Scholander *et al.* (1953) or Wohlschlag (1960, 1964). White (1975) argued that it was ecologically "illogical" for natural selection to act on polar poikilotherms in a way that resulted in an energetically "wasteful" process, and that evolutionary processes

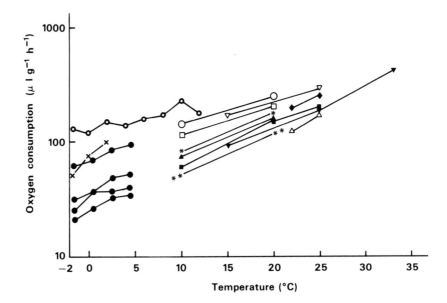

Fig. 8. Comparisons of oxygen consumption of Crustacea from a range of environments (after White, 1975). ×, *Paramoera walkeri* (Klekowski et al., 1973); ○, *Orchomene chilensis* (Armitage, 1962); ■, *Idotea baltica* (Khmelela, 1973); ▲, *Idotea ochotensis* (Khmelela, 1973); △ *Limnoria* sp. (Eltringham, 1965); ◆, *Ligia oceanica* (Ellenby, 1951); □, *Asellus aquaticus* (Fox and Simmons, 1933); ○, *Asellus intermedius* (Edwards, 1960); ▼, *Ligia beaudiana* (Wieser, 1972); ★★, *Armadillidium vulgare* (Saito, 1969); ★, *Armadillidium vulgare* (Saito, 1969); ▽, *Ligidium japonicum* (Saito, 1969); ●, *Glyptonotus antarcticus* (White, 1975).

demonstrably lead to selection for the conservation of energy rather than its expenditure; none the less, he was unable to show why slow growth was normal.

However, having set aside the phenomenon of "cold-adapted metabolism" (in the sense of Dunbar, 1968) another paradox was revealed. If inhabiting low temperature environments does not appear to impose a consequential metabolic burden, why then are the growth and development processes of polar poikilotherms still generally slow? Clarke (1980) has reviewed the data available and suggests that basal enzyme processes or protein metabolism possibly account for the apparent inconsistency.

Hochachka and Somero (1973) and Hazel and Prosser (1974) have suggested that if metabolism is to proceed at comparable rates in poikilo-therms from different environmental temperatures then some form of cel-lular and molecular compensation must evolve. Lowering the energy threshold of an enzyme reaction is one way to compensate for decreased ambient temperature. No observations are available for invertebrate poikilotherms, but a detailed study of the characteristics of selected

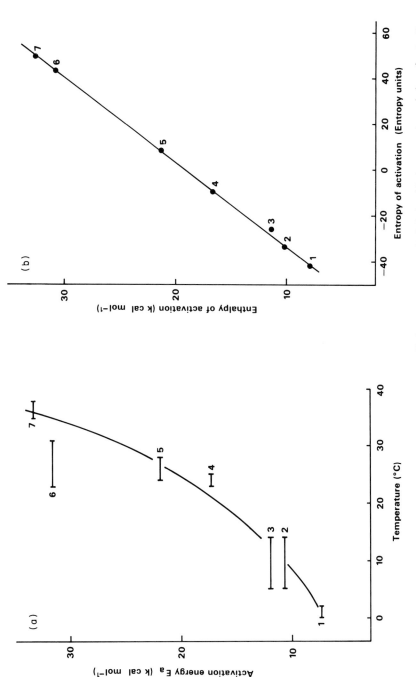

Fig. 9. (a) Arrhenius activation energies of ATP-ase in fish from a range of habitat temperatures. (b) Relationship between the enthalpy of activation and entropy of activation for ATP-ase in fish from a range of habitat temperatures. (1) *Notothenia rossii*; (2) *Gadus virens*; (3) *Gadus morhua*; (4) *Amphiprion sebea*; (5) *Carassius auratus*; (6) *Tilapia nigra*; (7) *Tilapia grahami* (after Johnstone and Goldspink, 1975).

enzymes in fish adapted to a wide range of environmental temperatures shows that the Arrhenius activation energy is positively correlated with habitat temperature (Johnstone et al., 1979) (Fig. 9). However, it appears common for adaptation to low temperature to be accompanied by a reduction in the thermal stability of the molecule, and Johnstone and Goldspink (1975) have investigated the adaptation of myofibrillar ATPase and suggest that this is possible because the molecule has a more open structure. Such an open structure would mean that a cold-water enzyme variant would degrade more quickly than a warm-water variant and, although this may not occur at the temperatures to which the enzymes are adapted, it may well explain why stenothermy is so frequently observed in cold-water poikilotherms (DeVries, 1977).

The turnover of protein in polar poikilotherms will be the resultant of lower degradation rates (owing to lower environmental temperature) and the elevated degradation rates of protein adapted to function at low temperatures. The data available suggest that protein synthesis is not fully temperature compensated (Matthews and Haschemeyer, 1978), although it is not obvious why protein synthesis should be unique in being strictly temperature dependent. Comparison of protein synthesis in fish generally (Matthews and Haschemeyer, 1978) and Antarctic species (Smith and Haschemeyer, 1980), shows that fish from a wide range of ambient temperatures exhibit a decrease in protein sythesis rate with temperature represented by an approximate Q_{10} of about 2.4. A departure from this relationship was noted in polar species from McMurdo Sound, where the rate of liver protein synthesis was elevated by about two-fold above expected levels. This elevation above expected levels implies that adaptation to temperatures below 5°C carries an increased burden of protein degradation, even though this will still be below rates in temperate fish. This also implies the possibility of slightly elevated rates of basal oxygen consumption, not to the extent necessary to support the levels implied in "cold-adapted metabolism" but, interestingly, of the same order as the "residual" elevation found by Holeton (1973). Until the natural range of variation of basal metabolism is fully understood it will not be possible to decide whether increased protein synthesis at low temperatures will be reflected in elevated metabolic rate (Clarke, 1980).

5.5 Conclusions

Seasonal response of growth rates, development and reproductive cycles to the seasonal environment is widely reported among benthic invertebrates from the polar regions and because of the very small variations in temperature these seasonal variations are usually attributed to the marked differences in food availability. Herbivores are the most directly affected, but it is now clear that predators also exhibit seasonal growth and development (Luxmoore, 1982). White (1977) proposed that the majority of components of the reproductive strategy of polar invertebrates are responses to the seasonal availability of food and the manner in which it is partitioned throughout the life-history of the organism (Fig. 10). A number of different strategies are equally well adapted to the polar environment, but most involved protracted development and a conservative utilization of resources.

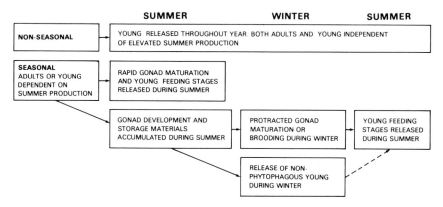

Fig. 10. The reproductive strategies of Antarctic marine poikilotherms (after White, 1977).

It can reasonably be concluded from the earlier discussion of the concept of cold-adapted metabolism (according to which excessively elevated basal metabolic rate in cold-water environments conveniently diminishes energy available for growth and reproduction), that it is no longer tenable. Yet reduced growth is still the most obvious feature of organisms from low temperature environments, and increased protein synthesis only partially explains this phenomenon.

Clarke (1980) draws these observations together and suggests that reduced basal metabolism, reduced growth, reduced reproductive effort and the assumption that energy expenditures due to feeding, movement and other activities are comparable between different environments, indicate that polar adaptations tend toward an overall reduction in energy utilization (Fig. 11). He illustrates this from his own observations on Crustacea, where a comparison between species living at temperate (10°C) and polar (0°C) environmental temperatures would result in basal metabolism being reduced by 55%, growth by 40% and reproductive effort by 30%.

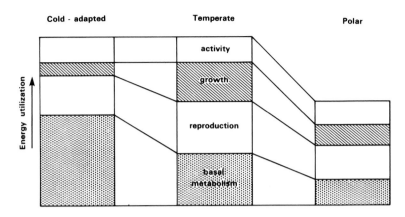

Fig. 11. Representation of effects of "cold-adapted metabolism" and polar-adapted metabolism in relation to the total annual energy intake of a temperate water benthic marine invertebrate (after Clarke, 1980).

Southwood (1977) proposes that K-strategies would be expected in environments where the conditions are highly stable, such as the deep sea, or else where environmental variations are highly predictable. The Antarctic marine environment is thermally stable and the marked variations in food availability are for the most part predictable (Arnaud, 1977; Clarke, 1979). It must be remembered, however, that whereas general seasonal primary production is highly predictable, actual local food availability is less predictable, and that this has led to the extensive use of non-pelagic reproductive processes among the sessile invertebrate groups even though this imposes severe limits on dispersal (White, 1977).

Nevertheless, it is overwhelmingly apparent that Antarctic poikilotherms have adopted a whole range of K-adapted qualities—slow growth, protracted development, reduced effort, low basal metabolic rate, large yolky eggs, advanced newly-hatched juvenile stages, seasonal breeding, deferred maturity, increased longevity, and large size—which act together so as to adapt organisms to cold and long periods with little or no primary production, the major features of the Antarctic marine environment. Organisms which have been selected for reduced annual individual energy uptake will be most successful in colonizing the Antarctic environment. Seemingly incongruous features such as slow growth and low metabolic rate, where rapid development and growth would appear possible, should be genetically determined and part of the overall strategy for successful survival in a highly seasonal Antarctic marine ecosystem.

6. Future Research

The Southern Ocean is large by any standards, and the components of the Antarctic marine benthic ecosystem have been found to be as diverse and complex as those from any other ocean. Some research on the benthos was carried out during the early twentieth century, but it is only since the establishment of permanent shore stations during the past 25 years that year-round or quantitative sampling has been carried out, or detailed laboratory investigations have been possible. The fauna and flora, particularly from the shallow shelf areas, is greatly undersampled, a considerable back-log of collections to be analysed exists, and relatively few good autecological investigations have been completed. It cannot be over-emphasized that there remains an important requirement for basic (but now unfashionable) descriptive systematic and ecological studies to be carried out, so that hypotheses about how the benthic communities are organized and the manner in which the ecosystem interacts with the environment can be tested with reliable quantitative data.

Primary production studies have been in progress for some time and data even exist for establishing the whole annual cycle at a number of sites. Yet the decomposition cycle, by which nutrients are recycled to the flora, has attracted very little attention. It is important that research into decomposition is carred out in parallel with production estimates, because these results would determine the constraint within which the whole ecosystem has to partition its component energy transfer pathways and rates. It is likely that such observations would have considerable bearing on our understanding of the principal adaptations of the Antarctic benthos.

The Antarctic is remote from major primary sources of pollution and so the region is ideal for base-line investigations of global pollutants. Some areas have been locally affected by the building of research stations and logistic facilities or by past whaling activities. These provide suitable opportunities to study the disruption of more or less pristine ecosystems or their recovery after the initial disruption. The marine benthos, being composed of potentially long-lived species and acting as a zone of accumulation, is well suited for such investigations; the preliminary studies made so far (e.g. Platt, 1979; Clarke and Law, 1981) show considerable promise.

Because the Antarctic marine environment is characterized by marked seasonal variations, it is important in ecological or physiological research that whenever possible year-round observations are made; otherwise there is a significant likelihood of misinterpreting the biology of polar organisms. Significant advances in understanding the manner in which they are adapted to low temperature environments have been made, but even so quite basic questions are as yet unresolved, such as: why do organisms in cold water grow slowly? Why are there so few pelagic larval stages of benthic invertebrates occurring in the water column? How do those few species that have pelagic larvae differ from the majority of other species? Why are species in the Antarctic so strongly K-adapted? Is low temperature an important factor in the marine environment, or are seasonal fluctuations or the disruptive intervention of ice more critical? Are adaptations exhibited by terrestrial polar invertebrates paralleled by or different to those of aquatic poikilotherms at high latitudes?

All are problems under active investigation but none is satisfactorily resolved. Obviously, considerable scope for research into the Antarctic marine benthic ecosystem exists in almost all biological disciplines. Its unexpected species diversity means that, as a system, it is rather less readily amenable to investigation than the terrestial or freshwater ecosystems, but, none the less, the accessible nearshore benthos and the large robust species found there, will prove to be a fertile area for research into the underlying mechanisms of polar adaptation.

7. References

Amio, M. (1963). A comparative embryology of marine gastropods, with ecological emphasis. *Journal of the Simnoseki College of Fisheries* **12**, 229–358.

Andriashev, A. P. (1965). A general review of the Antarctic fish fauna. *In* "Biogeography and Ecology in Antarctica" (J. Van Mieghem and P. Van Oye, eds), pp. 491–550. Junk, The Hague.

Armitage, K. B. (1962). Temperature and oxygen consumption of *Orchomonella chilensis* (Heller) (Amphipoda: Gammeroidea). *Biological Bulletin, Marine Biological Laboratory, Woods Hole, Mass.* **123**, 225–232.

Arnaud, P. M. (1974). Contribution à la bionomie marine benthique des régions antarctiques et subantarctiques. *Téthys* **6**, 465–656.

Arnaud, P. M. (1977). Adaptations within the Antarctic marine benthic ecosystem. *In* "Adaptions within Antarctic Ecosystems" (G. A. Llano, ed.), pp. 135–137. Gulf Publishing Co., Houston.

Azam, F. D., Holm-Hansen, O., Campbell, L., Carlucci, A. and Williams, P. (1978). Occurrence and metabolic activity of living organisms under the Ross Ice Shelf. *Transactions of the American Geophysical Union* **59**, No. 4, 308.

Barnard, J. L. (1959). Epipelagic and under-ice Amphipoda of the central Arctic Basin. *In* "Scientific Studies at Fletcher's Ice Island, T-3, 1952–1955" (V. C. Bushnell, ed.), pp. 115–152, Geophysical Research Centre, Bedford, Mass.

Boesch, D. F. (1972). Classification and community structure of macrobenthos in the Hampton Roads area, Virginia. *Marine Biology* **21**, 226–244.

Bone, D. G. (1972). Aspects of the biology of the Antarctic amphipod *Bovallia gigantea* Pfeffer at Signy Island, South Orkney Islands. *British Antarctic Survey Bulletin* No. 27, 105–22.

Bregazzi, P. K. (1972). Life cycles and seasonal movements of *Cheirimedon femoratus* (Pfeffer) and *Tryphosella kergueleni* (Miers) (Crustacea: Amphiphoda). *British Antarctic Survey Bulletin* No. 30, 1–34.

Bullivant, J. S. (1969). Bryozoa. *Antarctic Map Folio Series*, (American Geographical Society) **11**, 22–23.

Chia, F. S. (1970). Reproduction of Arctic marine invertebrates. *Marine Pollution Bulletin* **1**, No. 5, 78–79.

Clarke, A. (1979). On living in cold water: K-strategies in Antarctic benthos. *Marine Biology* **55**, No. 2, 111–119.

Clarke, A. (1980). A reappraisal of the concept of metabolic cold adaptation in polar marine invertebrates. *Biological Journal of the Linnean Society* **14**, No. 1, 77–92.

Clarke, A. and Lakhani, K. H. (1979). Measures of biomass, moulting behaviour and the pattern of early growth in *Chorismus antarcticus* (Pfeffer). *British Antarctic Survey Bulletin* No. 48, 61–88.

Clarke, A. and Law, R. (1981). Aliphatic and aromatic hydrocarbons in benthic invertebrates from two sites in Antarctica. *Marine Pollution Bulletin* **12**, No. 1, 10–14.

Dalziel, I. W. D. and Elliot, D. H. (1971). Evolution of the Scotia arc. *Nature* **233**, 246–252.

Dayton, P. K. and Oliver, J. S. (1977). Antarctic soft-bottom benthos in oligotrophic and eutrophic environments. *Science* **197**, 55–58.

Dayton, P. K., Robilliard, R. T., Paine, R. T. and Dayton, L. B. (1974). Biological accommodation in the benthic community at McMurdo Sound, Antarctic. *Ecological Monographs* **44**, 105–128.

Debenham, F. (1959). "Antarctica: the Story of a Continent". Jenkins, London.

De Broyer, C. (1977). Analysis of the gigantism and dwarfness of Antarctic and Sub-Antarctic Gammaridean Amphipoda. *In* "Adaptations within Antarctic Ecosystems" (G. A. Llano, ed.), pp. 327–334. Gulf Publishing Co., Houston.

Dell, R. K. (1972). Antarctic benthos. *Advances in Marine Biology* **10**, 1–216.

De March, B. G. E. (1978). The effects of constant and variable temperature on the size, growth and reproduction of the freshwater amphipod *Hyalella azteca* (Sanssure). *Canadian Journal of Zoology* **56**, 1801–1806.

De Vries, A. L. (1977). The physiology of cold adaptation in polar marine poikilotherms. *In* "Polar Oceans" (M. J. Dunbar, ed.), pp. 409–420. Arctic Institute of North America, Calgary.

Dunbar, M. J. (1957). The determinants of production in northern seas: a study of the biology of *Themisto libellula* Mandt. *Canadian Journal of Zoology* **35**, No. 5–6, 797–819.

Dunbar, M. J. (1968). "Ecological Development in Polar Regions". Prentice-Hall, Englewood Cliffs, N. J.

Edwards, R. W. and Learner, M. A. (1960). Some factors affecting the oxygen consumption of *Asellus*. *Journal of Experimental Biology* **37**, 706–718.

Ekman, S. (1953). "Zoogeography of the Sea". Sidgwick and Jackson, London.

Ellenby, C. (1951). Body size in relation to oxygen consumption and pleopod beat in *Ligia oceanica* (L). *Journal of Experimental Biology* **28**, 492–507.

Ellis, D. V. (1960). Marine infaunal benthos in Arctic North America. *Technical papers of the Arctic Institute of North America* **5**, 1–53.

Eltringham, S. K. (1965). The respiration of *Limnoria* (Isopoda) in relation to salinity. *Journal of the Marine Biological Association of the United Kingdom* **45**, 145–152.

Embody, G. C. (1912). A preliminary study of the distribution, food and reproductive capacity of some freshwater amphipods. *Internationale Revue de gesamten Hydrobiologie und Hydrographie* Ser. 2 **3**, No. 4, 1–33.

Everson, I. (1970). Reproduction in *Notothenia neglecta* Nybelin. *British Antarctic Survey Bulletin* No. 23, 81–92.

Everson, I. (1977). Antarctic marine secondary production and the phenomenon of cold adaptation. *Philosophical Transactions of the Royal Society* **B279**, 55–66.

Fell, H. B., Holzinger, T. and Sherraden, M. (1969). Ophiuroidea. *Antarctic Map Folio Series*, (American Geographical Society) **11**, 42–43.

Forsmann, B. (1951). Studies in *Gammarus duebeni* Lillj., with notes on rock pool organisms in Sweden. *Zoologiska bidrag från Uppsala* **29**, 215–237.

Fox, H. M. and Simmons, B. G. (1933). Metabolic rates of aquatic arthropods from different habitats. *Journal of Experimental Biology* **10**, 67–74.

Fry, W. G. (1964). The pycnogonid fauna of the Antarctic continental shelf. *In* "Biologie Antarctique" (R. Carrick, M. W. Holdgate and J. Prévost, eds), pp. 263–270. Hermann, Paris.

George, R. Y. (1977). Dissimilar and similar trends in Antarctic and Arctic marine benthos. In "Polar Oceans" (M. J. Dunbar, ed.), pp. 392–407. Arctic Insitute of North America, Calgary.

Grassle, J. F. (1967). "Influence of environmental variations on species diversity in benthic communities of the continental shelf and slope". Ph.D.Thesis. Duke University, Durham, North Carolina.

Hardy, P. (1972). Biomass estimates for some shallow-water infaunal communities at Signy Island, South Orkney Islands. *British Antarctic Survey Bulletin* No. 31, 93–106.

Hartmann, O. (1967). Polychetous annelids collected by the USNS *Eltanin* and *Staten Island* cruises, chiefly from Antarctic seas. *Allan Hancock Monographs in Marine Biology* **2**, 1–387.

Haven, D. S. (1967). An animal–sediment study in the lower York River, Virginia. Concentration of suspended radioactive wastes into bottom desposits. Final report to United States Atomic Energy Commission, Washington, D.C.

Hazel, J. R. and Prosser, C. L. (1974). Molecular mechanisms of temperature compensation in poikilotherms. *Physiological Reviews* **54**, 620–670.

Hedgpeth, J. W. (1969). Introduction to Antarctic zoogeography. *Antarctic Map Folio Series* (American Geographical Society) **11**, 1–9.

Hedgpeth, J. W. (1970). Marine biogeography of the Antarctic regions. *In* "Antarctic Ecology" (M. W. Holdagate, ed.), Vol. I, pp. 97–104. Academic Press, London and New York.

Hedgpeth, J. W. (1971). Perspectives of benthic ecology in Antarctica. *In* "Research in the Antarctic" (L. O. Quam, ed.), pp. 93–136. American Association for Advancement of Science, Washington.

Heywood, R. B. and Light, J. J. (1975). First direct evidence of life under Antarctic shelf ice. *Nature* **254**, No. 5501, 591–592.

Hochachka, P. W. and Somero, G. N. (1973). "Strategies of Biochemical Adaptation". Saunders, Philadelphia.

Holdich, D. M. (1968). Reproduction, growth and bionomics of *Dynamene bidentata* (Crustacea: Isopoda). *Journal of Zoology* **156**, 137–153.

Holeton, G. F. (1973). Respiration of arctic char (*Salvelinus aplinus*) from a high arctic lake. *Journal of the Fisheries Research Board of Canada* **30**, 717–723.

Holeton, G. F. (1974). Metabolic cold adaptation of polar fish: fact or artefact? *Physiological Zoology* **47**, 137–152.

Horne, A. J., Fogg, G. E. and Eagle, D. J. (1969). Studies *In situ* of the primary production of an area of inshore Antarctic Sea. *Journal of the Marine Biological Association of the United Kingdom* **49**, 393–405.

Holm-Hansen, O., Azam, F., Campbell, L., Carlucci, A. F. and Karl, D. M. (1978). Microbial life beneath the Ross Ice Shelf. *Antarctic Journal of the United States* **13**, No. 4, 129–130.

Holm-Hansen, O., Carlucci, A. F. and Azam, F. (1979). Biological studies of the water column and sediments under the Ross Ice Shelf. *Antarctic Journal of the United States* **14**, No. 5, 160–161.

Hynes, H. B. N. (1954). Ecology of *Gammarus duebeni* Lilljeborg and its occurrence in fresh water in western Britain. *Journal of Animal Ecology* **23**, No. 1, 38–84.

Hynes, H. B. N. (1955). The reproductive cycle of some British freshwater Gammaridae. *Journal of Animal Ecology* **24**, No. 2, 352–387.

Johnstone, I. A. and Goldspink, G. (1975). Thermodynamic activation parameters of fish myofibrillar ATPase enzyme and evolutionary adaptations to temperature. *Nature* **257**, 620–622.

Johnstone, I. A., Walesby, N. J., Davidson, W. and Goldspink, G. (1979). Further studies on the adaptation of fish myofibrillar ATPases to different cell temperatures. *Pflügers Archiv fur die gesamte Physiologie des Menschen und der Tiere* **371**, 257–262.

Khmelela, N. N. (1973). "Biology and Energy Budget in Marine Pillbugs (*Idotea baltica basteri*)". Naukovo Dumka, Kiev.

Kinne, O. (1953). Zur Biologie and Physiologie von *Gammarus dueveni* Lillj. *Zeitschrift fur wissenschaftliche Zoologie* **157**, No. 4, 427–491.

Kinne, O. (1960). *Gammarus salinus* einige Daten über den Umwelteinfluss auf Wachstum, Häntungsfolge, Hertzfrequenz und Eientwicklungsdaner. *Crustaceana* **I**, No. 3, 208–217.

Kinne, O. (1961). Growth, moulting frequency, heart beat, number of eggs and incubation time in *Gammarus zadlachi* exposed to different environments. *Crustaceana* **II**, No. 1, 26–36.

Kinne, O. (ed.) (1970). Temperature: Invertebrates. *In* "Marine Ecology", pp. 407–514. Wiley Interscience, London.

Klekowski, R. Z., Opalinski, K. W. and Rakusa-Suszczewski, S. (1973). Respiration of antarctic Amphipoda *Paramoera walkeri* Stebbwig during the winter season. *Polskie Archiwum hydrobiologii* **20**, 301–308.

Knox, G. A. (1960). Littoral ecology and biogeography of the southern oceans. *In* "A Discussion on the Biology of the Southern Cold Temperate Zone" (C. F. A. Pantin, ed.). *Proceedings of the Royal Society* **B152**, 577–627.

Knox, G. A. and Lowry, J. K. (1977). A comparison between the benthos of the Southern Ocean and the North Polar Ocean with special reference to the Amphipods and the Polychaeta. *In* "Polar Oceans" (M. J. Dunbar, ed.), pp. 423–462. Arctic Institute of North America, Calgary.

Koltun, V. M. (1969). Porifera. *Antarctic Map Folio Series* (American Geographical Society) **11**, 13–14.

Kott, P. (1969a). Antarctic Ascidiacea. *Antarctic Research Series* **13**, 1–239.

Kott, P. (1969b). Ascidiacea. *Antarctic Map Folio Series* (American Geographical Society) **11**, 43–44.

Kott, P. (1971). Antarctica Ascidiacea II. *Antarctic Research Series* **17**, 11–82.

Krogh, A. (1914). The quantitative relations between temperature and standard metabolism in animals. *Internationale Zeitschrift für physikalisch-chemische Biologie* **1**, 491–508.

Krogh, A. (1916). "The Respiratory Exchange of Animals and Man". Longmans, London.

Kussakin, O. G. (1967). Fauna of Isopoda and Tanaidacea in the coastal zones of the Antarctic and Subantarctic waters. Biological zones of the Antarctic and Subantarctic waters. *Biological Reports of the Soviet Antarctic Expeditions* (1955–1958). *Akidemiya nauk SSSR Zoologischeskii Institut, Issledovaniya a Fauny morei* , 220–389.

Lipps, J. H., Krebs, W. N. and Temnikow, N. K. (1977). Microbiota under Antarctic ice Shelves. *Nature* **265**, No. 5591, 232–233.

Lipps, J. H., Delaca, T. E., Farmer, J., Showers, W., Ronan, T. E., Clough, J., Raymond, J. and Bedford, J. (1978). Benthic marine biology, Ross Ice Shelf Project. *Antarctic Journal of the United States* **13**, No. 4, 139–141.

Lipps, J. H., Ronan, T. E., and Delaca, T. E. (1979). Life below the Ross Ice Shelf, Antarctica. *Science* **203**, 447–449.

Littlepage, J. L. (1965). Oceanographic investigations in McMurdo Sound, Antarctica. *In* "Biology of the Antarctic Seas II" (G. A. Llano, ed.). *Antarctic Research Series* **5**, 1–37.

Littlepage, J. L. and Pearse, J. S. (1962). Biological and oceanographic observations under an Antarctic Ice Shelf. *Science* **137**, No. 3531, 679–681.

Lloyd, M. and Ghelardi, R. J. (1964). A table for calculating the "equitability" component of species diversity. *Journal of Animal Ecology* **33**, 217–225.

Lowry, J. K. (1975). Soft bottom macrobenthic community of Arthur Harbour, Antarctica. *Antarctic Research Series* **23**, 1–19.

Luxmoore, R. A. (1982). Moulting and growth in serolid isopods. *Journal of Experimental Marine Biology and Ecology* **56**, 63–85.

McLaren, I. A. (1966). Adaptive significance of large body size and slow growth of the chaetograth *Sagitta elegans* in the Arctic. *Ecology* **47**, No. 5, 852–855.

McWhinnie, M. A. (1964). Temperature responses and tissue respiration in Antarctic crustaceans with particular reference to the krill *Euphausia superba*. *Antarctic Research Series* (American Geophysical Union) **1**, 63–72.

Mackintosh, N. A. (1972). Life cycle of Antarctic krill in relation to ice and water conditions. *Discovery Reports* **36**, 1–94.

Margalef, R. (1958). Information theory in ecology. *General Systems* **3**, 36–71.

Marr, J. (1962). The natural history and geography of the Antarctic krill (*Euphausia superba* Dana). *"Discovery" Reports* **32**, 38–464.

Mathisen, O. A. (1953). Some investigations on the relict crustaceans in Norway with special reference to *Pontoporeia affinis* Lindström and *Pallasea quadrispinosa* G. O. Sars. *Nytt magasin for zoologi* **I**, No. 1, 49–86.

Matthews, R. W. and Haschemeyer, A. E. V. (1978). Temperature dependency of protein synthesis in toadfish liver *in vivo*. *Comparative Biochemistry and Physiology* **61B**, 479–484.

Maxwell, J. G. H. (1977). "Aspects of the biology and ecology of selected Antarctic invertebrates". Ph.D. thesis, University of Aberdeen.

Ockelmann, W. K. (1958). Marine Lamellibranchiata. The zoology of East Greenland. *Meddelelser om Grønland* **122**, No. 4, 1–256.

Ockelmann, W. K. (1965). Development types in marine bivalves and distribution along the Atlantic coast of Europe. *In* "Proceedings of the First European Malacological Congress, 1962" (L. R. Peake and J. F. Cox, eds), pp. 25–35. Conchology Society of Great Britain and the Malacology Society, London.

Ostergreen, H. (1912). Über die Brutpflege der Echinodermen in den sudpolaren Kustengebeiten. *Zeitschreiffe wissenschaftliche Zoologische* **101**, 325–341.

Patten, B. C. (1962). Species diversity in net phytoplankton of Raritan Bay. *Journal of Marine Research* **20**, 57–75.

Pawson, D. L. (1969a). Holothuroidea. *Antarctic Map Folio Series* (American Geographical Society) **II**, 36–38.

Pawson, D. L. (1969b). Echninoidea. *Antarctic Map Folio Series* (American Geographical Society) **II**, 38–41.

Pearse, J. S. (1963). Marine reproductive periodicity in polar seas: a study of two invertebrates at McMurdo Station, Antarctica. *Ecological Society of America, Bulletin* **44**, No. 2, 43.

Pearse, J. S. (1965). Reproductive periodicities in several contrasting populations of *Odontaster validis* Koehler, a common Antarctic asteroid. *Antarctic Research Series* (American Geophysical Union) **5**, 39–85.

Picken, G. B. (1979). Non-pelagic reproduction of some Antarctic prosobranch gastropods from Signy Island, South Orkney Islands. *Malacologia* **19**, No. 1, 109–28.

Picken, G. B. (1980). Reproductive adaptations of Antarctic benthic invertebrates. *Biological Journal of the Linnean Society* **14**, No. 1, 67–75.

Pielon, E. C. (1966). The measurement of diversity in different types of biological collections. *Journal of Theoretical Biology* **13**, 131–144.

Platt, H. M. (1979). Exploitation and pollution in Antarctica: a case history. *Progress in Underwater Science* **5**, 188–200.

Platt, H. M. (1980). Ecology of King Edward Cove, South Georgia: Macro-benthos and the benthic environment. *British Antarctic Survey Bulletin* No. 49, 231–238.

Powell, A. W. B. (1965). Mollusca of Antarctic and Subantarctic seas. *In* "Biogeography and Ecology in Antarctica" (J. Van Mieghem and P. Van Oye, eds), pp. 333–380. Junk, The Hague.

Preston, F. W. (1962a). The cannonical distribution of commonness and rarity, Part 1. *Ecology* **43**, 185–215.

Preston, F. W. (1962b). The cannonical distribution of commonness and rarity, Part 2. *Ecology* **43**, 410–432.

Propp, M. V. (1970). The study of the bottom fauna at Haswell Islands by scuba diving. *In* "Antarctic Ecology" (M. W. Holdgate, ed.), Vol. I, pp. 239–241. Academic Press, London and New York.

Rakusa-Suszczewski, S. and Klekowski, R. Z. (1973). Biology and respiration of the Antarctic amphipod (*Paramoera walkeri* Stebbing) in the summer. *Polski archiwum hydrobiologii* **20**, 475–488.

Ralph, R. and Maxwell, J. G. H. (1977a). Growth of two Antarctic lammelibranchs: *Adamussium colbecki* and *Laternula elliptica*. *Marine Biology* **42**, 171–175.

Ralph, R. and Maxwell, J. G. H. (1977b). The oxygen consumption of the Antarctic limpet *Nacella* (*Patinigera*) *concinna*. *British Antarctic Survey Bulletin* No. 45, 19–23.

Ralph, R. and Maxwell, J. G. H. (1977c). The oxygen consumption of the Antarctic lamellibranch *Gaimardia trapesina trapesina* in relation to cold adaptation in polar invertebrates. *British Antarctic Survey Bulletin* No. 45, 41–46.

Richardson, M. D. and Hedgpeth, J. W. (1977). Antarctic soft-bottom, macroben-thic community adaptations to a cold, stable, highly productive, glacially affected environment. *In* "Adaptations within Antarctic Ecosystems" (G. A. Llano, ed.), pp. 181–196. Gulf Publishing Co., Houston.

Richardson, M. G. (1980). The ecology and reproduction of the brooding Antarctic bivalve, *Lissarca miliaris*. *British Antarctic Survey Bulletin* No. 49, 91–155.

Ronan, T. E., Lipps, J. H and Delaca, T. E. (1978). Sediments and life beneath beneath the Ross Ice Shelf (J-9), Antarctica. *Antarctic Journal of the United States* 13, No. 4, 141–142.

Ryther, J. M. (1963). Geographical variations in productivity. *In* "The Sea" (M. N. Hill, ed.), Vol. 2, pp. 347–380. Wiley, New York.

Saito, S. (1969). Energetics of isopod populations in the forest of central Japan. *Researches in Population Ecology, Kyoto University* II, 229–258.

Sanders, H. L. (1960). Benthic studies in Buzzards Bay III. The structure of the soft bottom community. *Limnology and Oceanography* 5, 138–153.

Sanders, H. L. (1968). Marine benthic diversity; a comparative study. *American Naturalist* 102, 243–282.

Scholander, P. F., Flagg, W., Waters, V. and Irving, L. (1953). Climatic adaptation in arctic and tropical poikilotherms. *Physiological Zoölogy* 26, 67–92.

Seager, J. R. (1979). Reproductive biology of the Antarctic opisthobranch *Philine gibba* Strebel. *Journal of Experimental Marine Biology and Ecology* 41, 51–74.

Sexton, E. W. (1924). The moulting and growth-stages of *Gammarus*, with descrip-tions of the normals and intersexes of *Gammarus chevreuxi*. *Journal of the Marine Biological Association of the United Kingdom* 13, No. 2, 340–401.

Shafir, A. and Field, J. G. (1980). Population dynamics of the isopod *Cirolana imposita* Barnard in a kelp-bed. *Crustaceana* 39, No. 2, 185–195.

Sheader, M. and Chia, F. S. (1970). Development, fecundity and brooding behaviour of the amphipod *Marinogammarus obtusatus*. *Journal of the Marine Biological Association of the United Kingdom* 50, No. 4, 1979–1999.

Simpson, R. D. (1977). The reproduction of some littoral molluscs from Macquarie Island (Sub-Antarctic). *Marine Biology* 44, 125–142.

Smith, C. C. and Fretwell, S. D. (1974). The optimal balance between size and number of offspring. *American Naturalist* 108, 499–506.

Smith, M. A. K. and Haschemeyer, A. E. V. (1980). Protein metabolism and cold adaptation in Antarctic fishes. *Physiological Zoölogy* 54, 373–382.

Southwood, T. R. E. (1977). Habitat, the templet for ecological strategies? *Journal of Animal Ecology* 46, 337–365.

Spight, T. M. (1976). Ecology of hatching size for marine snails. *Oecologia* 24, 283–294.

Strong, K. W. and Daborn, G. R. (1979). Growth and energy utilisation of inter-tidal isopod *Idotea baltica* (Pallan) (Crustacea: Isopoda). *Journal of Experimen-tal Marine Biology and Ecology* 41, 101–123.

Thorson, G. (1950). Reproduction and larval ecology of marine bottom inverte-brates. *Biological Reviews* 25, 1–45.

Thurston, M. H. (1970). Growth in *Bovallia gigantea* Pfeffer (Crustacea: Amphipoda). *In* "Antarctic Ecology" (M. W. Holdgate, ed.), pp. 269–278. Academic Press, London and New York.

Thurston, M. H. (1972). The Crustacea Amphipoda of Signy Island, South Orkney Islands. *British Antarctic Survey Scientific Report* No. 71, 127 pp.

Uschakov, P. V. (1955). Polychaetes from the seas in the Far East. *Opredelitch po Faune USSR* **56**, 1–445.

Uschakov, P. V. (1964). Some characteristics of the distribution of bottom fauna off the coast of East Antarctica. *Informatsionnyi byulleten Sovetskoi antarkticheskoi ekspeditsii* **40**, 287–292.

Vance, R. R. (1972). On reproductive strategies in marine benthic invertebrates. *American Naturalist* **107**, 339–352.

Watkin, E. E. (1941). The yearly life-cycle of the amphipod *Corophium volutator*. *Journal of Animal Ecology* **10**, No. 1, 77–93.

Wear, R. G. (1974). Incubation in British decapod crustacea and the effects of temperature on the rate and success of embryonic development. *Journal of the Marine Biological Association of the United Kingdom* **54**, 745–762.

Whitaker, T. M. (1977). Sea ice habitats of Signy Island (South Orkneys) and their primary productivity. *In* "Adaptations within Antarctic Ecosystems" (G. A. Llano, ed.), pp. 75–82. Gulf Publishing Co., Houston.

Whitaker, T. M. (1982). Primary production of phytoplankton off Signy Island, South Orkney Islands, the Antarctic. *Proceedings of the Royal Society of London* **B214**, 169–189.

White, M. G. (1973). Aspects of the biological significance of ice in the marine environment. *Proceedings of the Challenger Society* **4**, No. 3, 145–146.

White, M. G. (1975). Oxygen consumption and nitrogen excretion by the giant Antarctic isopod *Glyptonotus antarcticus* Eights in relation to cold-adapted metabolism in marine polar poikilotherms. *Proceedings of the 9th European Marine Biological Symposium* 707–724.

White, M. G. (1977). Ecological adaptations by Antarctic poikilotherms to the polar marine environment. *In* "Adaptations within Antarctic Ecosystem" (G. A. Llano, ed.), pp. 197–208. Gulf Publishing Co., Houston.

White, M. G. and Robins, M. W. (1972). Biomass estimates from Borge Bay, Signy Island, South Orkney Islands. *British Antarctic Survey Bulletin* No. 31, 45–50.

Wieser, W. (1972). Oxygen consumption and ammonia excretion in *Ligia beaudiana* (M-E). *Comparative Biochemistry and Physiology* **43**, 869–876.

Wigley, R. L. and McIntyre, A. D. (1964). Some quantitative comparisons of offshore meiobenthos and macrobenthos south of Martha's Vineyard. *Limnology and Oceanography* **9**, 485–493.

Wohlschlag, D. E. (1960). Metabolism of an Antarctic fish and the phenomenon of cold adaptation. *Ecology* **41**, 287–292.

Wohlschlag, D. E. (1964). Respiratory metabolism and ecological characteristics of some fishes in McMurdo Sound, Antarctica. *Antarctic Research Series* (American Geophysical Union) **1**, 33–62.

Zenkevitch, L. A. (1963). "Biology of the Seas of the USSR". Allen and Unwin, London.

9

Zooplankton

I. Everson

1. Introduction

In Chapter 7 it is estimated that the annual primary production south of the Antarctic Convergence is around 610 million tonnes. This large amount of phytoplankton in turn serves to maintain the large and diverse zooplankton communities. The literature on Southern Ocean zooplankton is dominated by studies on a single species, *Euphausia superba*, the Antarctic krill, which as well as being of enormous interest ecologically is also a resource of considerable commercial potential. In spite of this there is some evidence to suggest that other species or groups, such as the copepods, are as significant in the ecosystem in terms of biomass and production although, because of their supposed lesser importance to higher predators and their lack of commercial potential, they have received less attention.

2. Species Composition

Although the Antarctic Convergence is generally accepted as being the northern limit of the Antarctic zone the fact that it is a surface-water phenomenon and subject to some variation means that it does not represent a major barrier to many zooplankters. As a result the Southern Ocean planktonic fauna does include some species that are frequently found as far north as the Sub-tropical Convergence. Mackintosh (1934), from an analysis of a large number of plankton samples, was able to identify the following groups based on the temperature of the water in which they were caught.

Warm-water species

(a) Practically confined to water above 3°C: *Euphausia vallentini*.
(b) Typical warm-water species: *Eucalanus* sp., *Candacia* sp., *Hetero-*

ANTARCTIC ECOLOGY VOL. 2
ISBN 0 12–439502–3

rhabdus sp., *Euphausia triacantha*, *Calanus simillimus*, *Pleuro-mamma robusta*.

(c) Warm-water species found in colder regions: *Limacina balea*, *Pareu-chaeta* sp., *Parathemisto gaudichaudii*, *Euphausia frigida*.

Widespread species

(d) Species found on all isotherms but with a slight preference for warmer water: *Primno macropa*, *Spongiobranchia australis*, *Thysannoessa* sp., *Rhincalanus gigas*.

(e) Neutral species: *Haloptilus* sp., *Euchirella* sp., *Solmundella* sp., *Cyllopus* spp.

(f) Species found on all isotherms but with a slight preference for colder water: *Calanus acutus*, *Vibilia antarctica*, *Calanus propinquus*.

Cold-water species

(g) Cold-water species which occur in large numbers anywhere south of the 3°C isotherm: *Euphausia superba*, *Cleodora sulcata*, *Salpa fusiformis*, *Tomopteris* sp. *Metridia gerlachei*, *Clione antarctica*, *Limacina helcina*, *Pyrostephos vanhoffeni*.

(h) Species typical of the coldest regions, which rarely or never approach the convergence: *Sibogita borchgrevinki*, *Mimophys arctica*, *Vanadis antarctica*, *Diphyes antarctica*, *Eusirus antarcticus*, *Haloptilus ocellatus*.

Neritic species

(i) *Antarctomysis maxima*, *Euphausia crystallorophias*.

An indication of the geographical range of these groups can be gauged from an examination of the temperature charts in Chapter 6 in relation to the categories listed above and it is clear from this that there is no clear demarcation between the species composition of the Southern Ocean and the major ocean basins to the north. Rather there is a gradual transition from north to south. The fact that many species occur within quite clearly marked temperature bands and that these same thermal zones are more or less circumpolar indicates that many species may have a circumpolar distribution.

3. Distribution

3.1 Geographical distribution

From an analysis of a large number of plankton samples Baker (1954) concluded that the more important zooplankters had a circumpolar distribution. This result does not, however, necessarily indicate that there is a single population of each species, a fact that is of limited consequence for most species but is of extreme importance for krill due to its commercial potential.

On a presence or absence basis several species do appear to be present literally everywhere in the Southern Ocean. The chaetognaths *Sagitta gazellae* and *Eukrohnia hamata* were found in almost all the samples examined by David (1958) and the same was true of the copepods *Calanoides acutus*, *Calanus propinquus* and *Rhincalanus gigas* (Baker, 1959) and the euphausiid *Thysannoessa*. There are however some interesting exceptions, particularly in species that are known to occur over the whole latitudinal range of the Southern Ocean. Two such examples are *Salpa* sp. and *Euphausia superba*. It is possible that this patchy distribution is a result of vertical migration (either diurnal or seasonal) beyond the range of the sampling nets, but from Baker's analysis this seems unlikely. There does, however, seem to be some correlation between the tendency to produce swarms and the tendency to be absent from net hauls made in localities within the species' known distributional range.

Zooplankton swarms in the Southern Ocean are formed either by rapid multiplication, as is the case with *Salpa thompsoni*, or else by large numbers of individuals of the same species congregating. Observations suggest that the salps are for the most part widely distributed, and for most of the time present in low densities, but under favourable conditions they reproduce rapidly and thus produce swarms. Such a pattern is therefore very likely to result in an extremely discontinuous distribution. These features are not present in some of the other swarming species such as *E. superba* and *Parathemisto gaudichaudii*, both of which have a life span of at least one year and are thus unable to take advantage of locally favourable conditions by reproducing rapidly. All the same their biomass must be fairly high throughout the year. Swarming in these species is also certainly related to food availability and is therefore discussed more fully in the section on feeding. It is important to remember that the swarms mentioned above do represent very high concentrations of individuals—far higher than is normal for zooplankton. However, the normal processes contributing to the discontinuous distribution of zooplankton discussed by Henry *et al.* (1978) almost certainly apply in the Southern Ocean in the same way that they do elsewhere.

3.2 Vertical migration

The phenomenon of vertical migration may be considered under two broad headings depending on the time scale: seasonal migrations in which much of the summer is spent in the surface water, and a diurnal pattern in which the hours of darkness are spent near to the surface. Both types of migration pattern are exhibited by some Southern Ocean zooplankters.

Examples of species which spend the summer months in the surface layers and descend into the Warm Deep Water in winter are:

Rhincalanus gigas Ommaney (1936)
Calanoides acutus Andrews (1966)
Calanus propinquus Voronina (1972)
Eukrohnia hamata David (1958, 1965)
Sagitta gazellae David (1955)
Parathemisto gaudichaudii Kane (1966)

In discussing this migration pattern Mackintosh (1937) showed that the extent of the migration would mean that for the most part the zooplankters would spend about half the year in the Warm Deep Water with its southerly movement and about half the year in the surface water with its northerly movement. Although these water movements are not diametrically opposite (see Chapter 6 for fuller details) they are a mechanism by which the creatures involved can be maintained within latitudinial bands in the Southern Ocean. Several species have an extensive diurnal migration pattern and some examples are set out in Table I. The two species *E. frigida* and *E. triacantha* do have a clearly discernible migration pattern which would take them from the Warm Deep Water in daytime to the surface water at night. The situation with *E. superba* is much less clear, because it is established that this species does migrate vertically, but only on rare occasions has a recognizable pattern been discernible (see Marr, 1962; Mohr, 1976; and Fischer and Mohr, 1978).

TABLE I

Vertical migration of some Southern Ocean euphausiids (Mauchline and Fisher, 1969)

Species	Average day depth (m)	Average night depth (m)	Total vertical range (m)
Euphausia superba	100–10	70–0	900–0
E. frigida	500–250	100–50	750–0
E. triacantha	500–250	250–0	750–0

My own results from the Scotia Sea and around South Georgia (Fig. 1) in March 1980 indicate that in the open ocean there is a clearly-defined diurnal migration pattern, the krill being close to or at the surface at night but at about 100 m during daylight. The situation is quite different in the seas around South Georgia where no clearly defined migration was recognizable although there was a cycle of daytime swarming and night-time dispersion. The reasons for this are probably the local high concentration of krill in conjunction with the local water circulation.

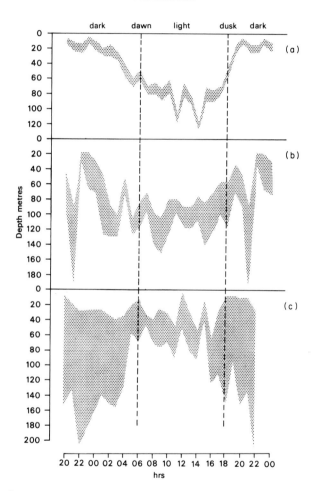

Fig. 1. Diurnal variation in the average depth distribution of krill. (a) Open ocean, Scotia Sea; (b) average distribution around South Georgia; (c) a krill patch north of South Georgia in April 1980.

Euphausia superba is for the most part herbivorous and, for a zoo-plankter, is long-lived. This means that the main body of krill food will occur in the surface water and that there is likely to be a great seasonal variation in its availability. Also, because the life span of krill is several years, the size frequency distribution of krill present at a given locality at a particular time is likely to be quite broad. In an extensive review of migration patterns, Baker (1978) describes an ideal pattern of daily variation in vertical distribution for zooplankton of large body size that feed on "non-migratory food" (Fig. 2). In general, the distribution patterns follow the normally expected cycle but there are "tails of distribution", upwards in daylight and downwards at night. Baker explains that

> The tail upward to the surface during the middle of the day results from selection favouring individuals with poor food collection success the previous night performing an upward migration to the feeding zone some time during the day. Optimum stay-time in the feeding zone is shorter during the day than during the night. The "tail" downward after dusk results partly from individuals that fed during the day initiating upward migration later than those that did not and partly from individuals which achieved rapid feeding success initiating downward migration. As more and more individuals initiate downward migration the vertical distribution becomes more even. Optimum stay-time at lower levels is less at night than during the day. As more individuals migrate upwards for a second or third feeding bout, a second concentration in surface waters occurs, followed by initiation of downward migration at dawn.

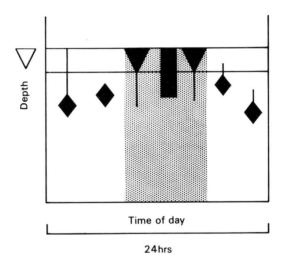

Fig. 2. Ideal pattern of daily variation in vertical distribution of zooplankters of large body size such as krill (Reproduced with permission from Baker, R. R. "The Evolutionary Ecology of Animal Migration" Hodder and Stoughton).

How then does this relate to krill? If it is considered in relation to swarming behaviour (discussed in detail later) there is quite good agreement between theory and fact. Pavlov (1969) has suggested that krill swarm as part of a feeding cycle; the animals are dispersed whilst feeding; when they are replete they swarm and sink; they remain in swarms until they require more food at which time they return to the surface to feed. To a very great extent this cycle is dependent on food availability and the time required for the animals to pass food through their gut. The time it takes for an individual to feed to repletion will depend on its size (larger krill taking longer than smaller ones) and how much food is available. The time taken in digesting the food will also be size dependent (longer for larger krill). A possible relationship is shown in Fig. 3.

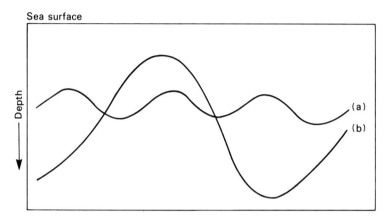

Fig. 3. Suggested range and periodicity of vertical migration in (a) small and (b) large krill, *Euphausia superba.*

On the assumption that swarms are formed when krill are replete, some patterns of swarming (and thus vertical migration) can be postulated. We can see that the periodicity of the feeding pattern will depend on the available food and on the size of the krill, with the result that the cycle will have little correlation with the diet cycle (except that the light regime must have a major influence during the day), and that the vertical extent of the movement will depend on size (digestion time).

The observed diurnal vertical distribution of krill is quite complicated (Fig. 1) although the main features can be explained reasonably well; they are summarized below.

Observation	Suggested explanation
Krill occur at surface at night	Normal diurnal pattern (Baker 1978).
Krill occur at surface in daylight	"Requirement for food" stimulus overrides "light stimulus" (Baker 1978).

Krill of different size groups   Different amplitude or migration for
occur in separate layers at   different-sized krill (Everson and
certain times   Ward, 1980).

These explanations are related to food availability and do not necessarily apply for very high or very low phytoplankton concentrations. Such conditions may be encountered frequently in selected areas during the summer (see Chapter 7) and low phytoplankton concentrations will be encountered everywhere in winter. Clearly this is a topic worthy of a great deal more study.

3.3 Swarming

It has been well known for a long time that zooplankton is not evenly distributed, even in areas of essentially uniform physical and chemical characteristics. The Southern Ocean is no exception to this as, probably without exception, all species vary in abundance quite markedly even within limited areas. There are in addition several examples of extreme patchiness. Mention has already been made of examples from three groups: the euphausiid *E. superba*, the salp *Salpa thompsoni* and the amphipod *Parathemisto gaudichaudii*.

Krill swarms have been described by several workers (e.g. Marr, 1962; Nemoto *et al.*, 1981; Shevtsov and Makarov, 1969) and all agree they are of an amorphous, continually changing shape. Their size varies from only a metre or so to several kilometres in extent (Cram, 1978) and although they are sometimes visible at the surface they are more frequently "seen" on echo-sounders. The density of krill within swarms is thought to be quite high. Based on visual observations of swarms Marr (1962) estimated that there was one krill per eight cubic metres of water in a swarm or about $6\,kg\,m^{-3}$. Other estimates, based on echo-sounder indications in conjunction with net hauls, indicate a density of from 1.5 to $33\,kg\,m^{-3}$ with most swarms falling at the lower end of the range and generally below $6\,kg\,m^{-3}$ (Moiseev, 1970; Makarov *et al.*, 1970; Nemoto and Nasu, 1975; Nemoto *et al.*, 1981). The mechanisms causing krill swarm formation are by no means fully understood, although as described earlier there does seem to be a close link with a feeding cycle and, from my own observations, with ambient light level. Observations on a large patch of krill just north of South Georgia in April 1980 indicated that during the day the krill were aggregated into dense swarms but at night they were dispersed throughout the top 200 m, their density at this time being about $10\,m^{-3}$ (Everson, 1982). It is clear that krill swarms do arise as a result of many individuals congregating; this is in contrast to salp swarms where for the most part the swarms arise as a result of rapid budding.

The ability of salps to reproduce rapidly when feeding conditions are favourable means that the incidence of swarms will be highest during the summer when primary production is greatest (Foxton, 1966). On the assumption that one of the factors causing krill to swarm is food availability it is to be expected that swarming will be greatest during the summer months. Although Marr (1962) found no evidence to support this hypothesis the results of Mackintosh (1973) lend support to the theory. He estimated densities of krill (weight per standard net haul) by applying correction factors to net haul catches for time of day, size of net and size of krill. His results are summarized in Table II.

TABLE II

Corrected mean catch of krill and mode of catch frequency distribution for different periods of the year (from Mackintosh, 1973)

Period	Mean catch (g)	Mode of catch frequency distribution (g)	Number of hauls
Oct–Dec	54	10·00–17·78, 1·00–1·78	142
Jan–Mar	518	3·60–5·62	243
April	42	3·16–5·62	25
Oct–April	325	3·16–5·62	410

The modal frequencies for three of the periods under consideration are the same, whilst the fourth period has two modes, one on each side of the mode of the other periods. This relative evenness indicates that a similar situation, in terms of average overall biomass, is being sampled throughout the period. By contrast there is a very great difference between the arithmetic means for the spring and autumn in comparison to that for the summer. The approximately ten-fold increase in the summer is almost certainly due to the presence of swarms—a few very large samples producing a very large effect on the mean (the difference is almost certainly not due to production as Mackintosh surmised, because growth over the period is nowhere near fast enough). Although there are no results for the middle of winter the indications are that swarming is likely to be much less than during the summer.

4. Ecology

4.1 Growth

There is in the literature very little information on growth in Antarctic zooplankton. Furthermore, although the species for which information is available are sometimes described as being the most important members of the zooplankton, this may not necessarily be so, and their characteristics may not be typical of zooplankton as a whole. The best information available is for the herbivores *Euphausia superba*, *Calanoides acutus*, the omnivore *E. triacantha*, and for the carnivores *Parathemisto gaudichaudii* and *Sagitta gazellae*.

Let us consider first of all the herbivores. There is disagreement over the life span of *E. superba*, although it is agreed that peaks of growth occur during the primary production season (Ruud, 1932; Marr, 1962; Mackintosh, 1972). In the season during which they spawn for the first time growth is much less, presumably because a large proportion of the available assimilated energy is diverted to gamete production. Between the summer peaks are the unproductive winter months when growth is virtually nil. *Calanoides acutus* likewise has a period of minimum growth during the winter and maximum

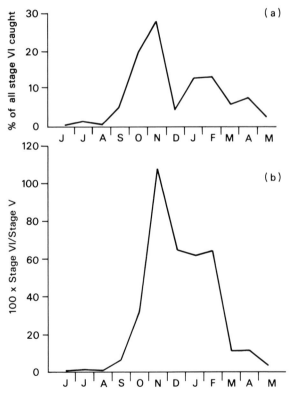

Fig. 4. *Calanoides acutus*: seasonal frequency of occurrence of copepodites in net hauls. (a) Stage VI and (b) percentage of stage VI in combined catches of stages V and VI (data from Andrews, 1966).

growth during the months of November–March. Andrews (1966) has assumed that the summer growth period leads to the production solely of overwintering stage IV and V copepodites. However, the presence of two peaks of abundance of stage VI copepodites during the summer (Fig. 4a) suggests that those spawned early in October and November may be maturing and spawning in the following February. A similar situation may also occur in *Rhincalanus gigas* Ommaney (1936) although this has been challenged by Voronina (1968) (see section 4.2).

In *Euphausia triacantha*, Baker (1959) has derived an unambiguous growth curve (Fig. 5), based on analysis of size frequency distribution from net hauls throughout the year. Baker notes that, during the first summer, growth is about 2.5 mm per month, but slows to about 1.0 mm per month from May to August. The rate increases again during the second summer to about 1.7 mm per month, but after March little or no further growth takes place. It is interesting that in this species some growth occurs during the winter months and this probably reflects the omnivorous nature of its diet, as detritus and zooplankton would be available at this time.

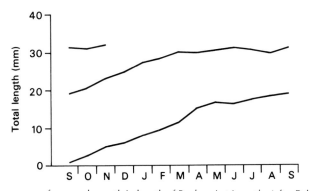

Fig. 5. Average curve of seasonal growth in length of *Euphausia triacantha* (after Baker, 1959).

Although, as described above, the growth season for *E. superba* is known, it is not clear at what rate growth occurs. Marr (1962), from a very large number of samples, thought the krill took about two years to reach 5 cm in length. Both he and Mackintosh (1972), however, had noted a few individuals of an intermediate size (around 3 cm) during the summer months, but this intermediate size group made up a very small proportion of the total population. Recent expeditions have found large numbers of these intermediate-sized krill, and these have been so abundant on occasions as to indicate that they may constitute an additional year class (Ivanov, 1970).

There can be no doubt that this intermediate size group is frequently present and is not a sampling artefact—how then can it be explained? There are three possible explanations for it. It is:

(a) an extra year class;
(b) the result of mixing of krill from different regions and, by implication, with differing growth rates;
(c) the result of spawning at different times of the year.

Let us consider each of these in turn. If it were an additional year class, the intermediate size group would be present all the year round and be at least as abundant as the year class composed of the largest individuals. Apart from *Discovery* Investigations, there appears to be virtually no year round sampling of krill and, since *Discovery* found very few intermediate-sized krill, there is only negative information for the period when growth would be at a minimum and a year class most easily recognized. Furthermore, the intermediate size class is neither consistently present nor is it very often as abundant as the other size classes.

The intermediate size group has been recognized in samples of krill from all areas (Mackintosh, 1973) including some from the East Wind Drift, the area where krill grow slowest, and there is no locality having slower growth with which these could mix. Thus although mixing is a convenient explanation for the intermediate size group it is almost certainly not valid.

It has been known for a long time that spawning in *E. superba* takes place during at least the months from November to April, with a peak during February and March. Spawning during the early summer months, typical of high latitude euphausiids, is restricted to the larger krill which are thought to be spawning for a second time; it is possible that the larvae resulting from this spawning do form that intermediate size group. There is no information on growth rates of early larvae during the early summer months so it is impossible to predict exactly the growth pattern of these early larvae. However, some idea of the pattern may be indicated by comparison with *E. triacantha*, a species which spawns during the spring and whose early life history stages are spent growing during the productive summer season. Applying the growth rate of *E. triacantha* during its first summer to a larva of approximately 4.5 mm length (a reasonable starting point for *E. superba*), if the growth is followed through to the following season these individuals would be the same size as the intermediate size group. Such a hypothetical approach cannot answer the question, but it does suggest a possible explanation and thus indicates lines for further study.

At this stage mention must also be made of other information concerning growth in *E. superba*. Laboratory experiments on growth in krill have failed to provide results which are in any way compatible with the creatures growing to 50 mm in two years. This is almost certainly because in no case has it been possible to provide a reasonable simulation of natural conditions for the experiments (see Mackintosh, 1967; Clarke, 1976; McWhinnie *et al.*, 1976). Another point is that growth rate of *E. superba* in terms of weight increment per day would need to be much faster than for any other euphausiid (Mauchline and Fisher, 1969), although it can be argued that this is because they spend a far greater proportion of the time growing during the productive season rather than preparing to spawn (see Everson, 1977).

The controversy over growth in *E. superba* is largely confined to the first two years of its life span; does it in effect grow to 30 mm or 50 mm in length during this period? It seems clear that it is normal for a significant proportion of the krill to live for one or two years after they have reached 5 cm in length. As the maximum size to which krill grow is rarely more than 6 cm, it is not possible to detect these older year classes from size frequency distributions. By following the development stages in the gonads it has, however, been possible to show that krill spawn for a second or even a third time (Makarov, 1975) and that these subsequent spawnings will clearly depend on the abundance of the larger individuals, which in turn depends on predation rate and time. The level of predation by the initial whale stocks may have been such as to virtually eliminate the repeat spawning and thus, if this is the cause of the intermediate size group, that group also. Certainly, the intermediate size group seems to be more frequently encountered nowadays when the predation pressure from whales is much less.

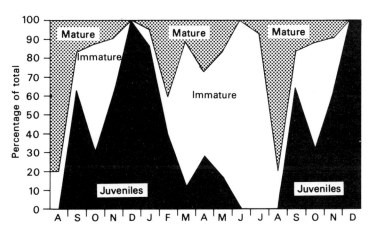

Fig. 6. *Parathemisto gaudichaudii*: percentage frequency of juvenile, immature and mature specimens in net hauls (data from Kane, 1966).

Contrasting growth patterns are shown by the two carnivorous zoo-plankters. The amphipod *Parathemisto gaudichaudii* has a peak of growth during the summer period (Kane, 1966), but during the winter there is virtually no growth at all. This pattern is superficially very similar to that of *Calanoides acutus* and *Euphausia triacantha*, except that it is clear that physiological changes are taking place in the amphipod leading to matur-ation in the early spring (Fig. 6). This species is thus able to release a large number of juveniles early in the spring, which can feed on the early life history stages of the herbivores when they appear at the start of the primary production season. Kane (1966) considered that generally the *Parathemisto* have a life span of one year, but that a very small number of individuals survive to breed again in a second year.

From the information available, the chaetognath *Sagitta gazellae* appears to be capable of breeding in most months of the year (David, 1955). The result of this is that, except at certain times when vertical migration separates the different age classes, it is difficult to interpret size frequency distribu-tions. David was able to follow growth by one age group through the winter and spring months. He showed that growth was more or less steady at about 5 mm per month from about May until November (Fig. 7). Since *S. gazellae* spawn when 75–80 mm long and growth during the summer is more rapid it is inferred that they reach sexual maturity in about a year.

Winter growth has also been noted in some other species; for example the tunicate *Salpa thompsoni* is thought to grow at a rate of about 6–8 mm a month during this period (Foxton, 1966). Bearing in mind that this species is a filter feeder and that food is therefore likely to be limited during this period, its growth rate is quite exceptional. It is unfortunate that the con-fused nature of summer size frequency distributions makes estimation of growth at that time impossible.

4.2 Life histories

The marked seasonality of the primary production (see Chapter 7) imposes a similar seasonality on the reproductive cycles of many zooplankters. For example, the herbivores need to take in sufficient food to enable them to produce their reproductive products in time for the resulting larvae to get an adequate start prior to the winter.

The life history of one of the dominant copepods, *Calanoides acutus*, has been described by Andrews (1966). During the winter months the population is composed almost entirely of stage IV and stage V copepodites (Fig. 8). In the spring they migrate to the surface water and become sexually mature (stage VI). Egg laying begins in November and reaches a peak during December and January, with the result that soon afterwards the stage I and II

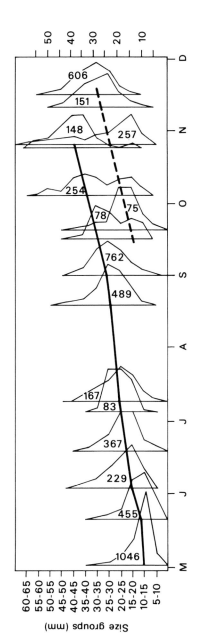

Fig. 7. The growth of *Sagitta gazellae*, based upon counts and measurements of specimens taken in shallow oblique 1 m nets. The number of individuals in each haul or set of hauls are added. A probable mean average growth curve has been added (Reproduced with permission from David, 1955).

copepodites appear and grow rapidly to stage III. Prior to winter most of these have grown to stage IV or V and these in turn form the spawning population in the following spring. Andrews' results also indicate the presence of two maxima of stage VI abundance during the summer (Fig. 4a), a phenomenon also noted in *Rhincalanus gigas*. In an extensive investigation Ommaney (1936) came to the conclusion that *Rhincalanus gigas* had two spawning seasons during the year. He considered that spawning occurred first of all during the spring at about the same time as in *Calanoides acutus*, but that the copepodites from this spawning reached maturity during the summer and spawned in the later summer or early autumn. The copepodites arising from this spawning would then grow during the winter to stage III or IV and spawn during the spring. Voronina (1968) has challenged this conclusion and considers that only one spawning occurs during the year.

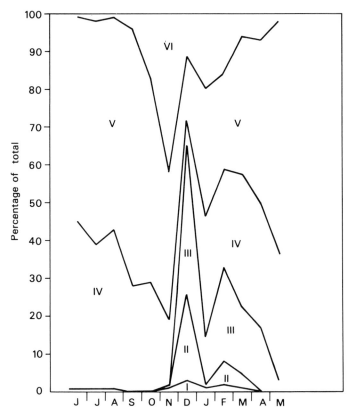

Fig. 8. Seasonal copepodite composition of *Calanoides acutus* in the top 100 m of the water column (data from Andrews, 1966).

Although it has been confirmed that *R. gigas* does spawn in the autumn at the southern end of its range, Voronina considers that this is a result of latitudinal shift in the breeding season and that, bearing in mind the temperature change over the distributional range, it is to be expected that spawning will be later further south. The release of eggs during the autumn at the southern end of the range will mean that the early copepodites will not be able to grow very much at this time, because primary production is nearing its winter minimum. This situation may also be characteristic of *Calanoides acutus* if the spawning season is determined by the monthly ratio of Vs and VIs (Fig. 4b). This tends to indicate more or less continuous spawning from October to March that could be correlated with latitude. The results from all these studies are based on large numbers of samples and these in turn are likely to have an averaging effect, leading to indications of a prolonged spawning season rather than two peaks. Thus on balance it seems that both species could complete a generation during the summer, but there must also be some latitudinal shift in spawning time.

Calanoides acutus and *Rhincalanus gigas* as well as being significant components of the zooplankton are also, for copepods, quite large when fully mature (6 mm). There are in addition many other species that are significantly smaller and these could conceivably go through more than one generation during the course of a summer and still overwinter as stage IV or stage V copepodites.

The euphausiid *Euphausia triacantha* takes two years to reach maturity and spawn (Baker, 1959). Since spawning occurs in the spring the larvae have a full primary production season in which to grow, prior to the onset of winter. By contrast *E. superba* has been known to spawn during most of the summer months. The peak of spawning activity occurs well into the summer, with the result that during the winter, first year *E. superba* are much smaller than first year *E. triacantha*. It is not at all clear how long it takes *E. superba* to grow to sexual maturity, although it is evident that it must take at least two years (see section 4.1). The prolonged spawning season may be in part due to the extended latitudinal range of the species. Mackintosh (1972) suggests that spawning occurs earlier in warmer areas and, from examination of the results from many net hauls, has suggested mean spawning dates for the main areas of krill abundance. It is also known that in some years a significant proportion of the mature krill live through the winter and spawn again in the following spring (Makarov, 1975). Larvae resulting from this spring spawning may well grow as fast as, or even faster than, those of *E. triacantha*—the size they reach will depend on their size when they start feeding (earliest *E. superba* larvae hatching prior to *E. triacantha*) and the time at which they start breeding. In any case their size at age distribution is likely to be significantly different to that of larvae resulting from the normal summer spawning.

The early life history of *E. superba* has been described by Marr (1962) and the morphological structure of the larvae by Fraser (1936). Descriptions of the larval stages of other Southern Ocean euphausiids are given by John (1937). Marr deduced that the eggs were released at the surface and then sank to a depth of around 2000 m during which they went through the initial cleavage stage. On hatching, the nauplii migrate upwards, going through a metanaupliar stage to arrive at the surface as first calyptopes (Fig. 9). The duration of this developmental ascent is thought to be about 2–4 weeks. It has recently been shown that this developmental ascent is a characteristic of Southern Ocean euphausiids, as it has been recognized in *E. triacantha*, *E. frigida* and *Thysannoessa* (Makarov, 1978).

The carnivorous amphipod *Parathemisto gaudichaudii* has a very similar annual cycle to *Calanoides acutus*. Based on the frequency of occurrence of three developmental stages, Kane (1966) demonstrated that, for the most part, the life cycle was completed in one year, although a few individuals did not die after spawning, but lived on to spawn again and possibly even for a further year. Typically, ovarian maturation occurs during the late winter and early spring, with the result that small individuals are released from the brood pouch from August onwards. By the end of the summer most of the population is at the juvenile stage and by July mature specimens are starting to appear. This species therefore has a fairly restricted breeding season which produces large numbers of young stages during the spring. In contrast to this the chaetognath *Sagitta gazellae* has been found in reproductive condition in most months of the year and, although maturation and spawning almost certainly occur in deep water (David, 1955), little definite is known about this, due to difficulties in sampling the mature stages in quantity at great depths. Despite the deep spawning habit of the species the earliest larvae have been found at the surface, where they remain for several months, and in the northern part of their range (north of the Antarctic Convergence) grow at about 5 mm per month. South of the Antarctic Convergence they reach sexual maturity when about 75 mm long and then migrate to the deep water to spawn.

The life history of *Salpa thompsoni* is much more complicated than for any of the other species considered so far. This is because it is capable of reproducing both sexually and asexually and as a result is present in two morphologically distinct types—the solitary and aggregate forms. The important features of this complicated life history have been described by Foxton (1966). The solitary form develops from embryos released in March and April and these form the nucleus of the overwintering population. In the spring these individuals release chains of buds (the

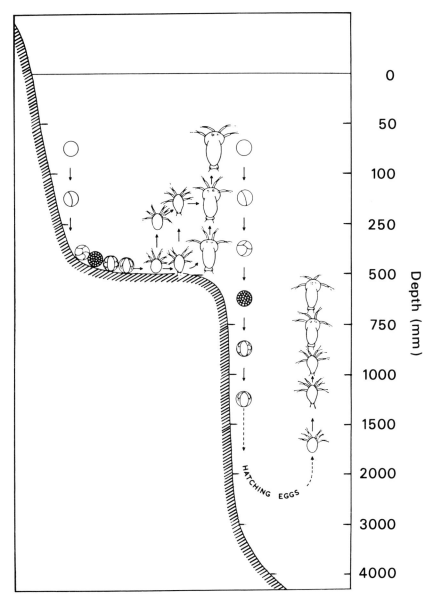

Depth (mm)

0

50

100

250

500

750

1000

1500

2000

3000

4000

HATCHING EGGS

Fig. 9. Development of sinking eggs of *Euphausia superba* in shelf and oceanic water, showing how hatching in the shallower conditions gives rise to occurrences of nauplii and metanauplii unusually close to the surface (Reproduced with permission from Marr, 1962).

aggregate form) which lead to a massive increase in numbers during the summer season. During the summer both aggregate and solitary forms are present in the plankton.

Each aggregate bears a single ovum which, after fertilization, develops within the "parent" supported and nurtured by a "placenta". When 4–5 mm in length the embryo is released and the embryonic organs gradually regress as the solitary assumes its free-living existence. The aggregate form is produced by budding from the stolon, and Foxton estimates that each solitary could produce as many as 800 buds. There is thus an alternation of generations which, because aggregates are at their most abundant during the summer, probably requires one year to complete.

4.3 Feeding, chemical composition and annual cycles

The food of zooplankton may be roughly divided into three broad categories: diatoms, dinoflagellates, etc., filtered from the water; other zooplankton; detritus.

The first category, since it is composed almost entirely of plant material, is abundant during the summer and almost totally absent during the winter. By contrast zooplankton are present to a significant extent in all months of the year so that the second category, and as a result the third category, will be present throughout the year.

Some examples of species that filter phytoplankton from the water have already been mentioned and from these certain seasonal patterns can be seen among them. With the exception of *Salpa thompsoni*, growth is limited to the summer months. Similarly, the final maturation of the gonads in most herbivores occurs at this time. Both of these activities require input of energy over and above that for maintenance, and it is only to be expected that there will be a close synchrony between them and the primary production season. What is equally important is the mechanism by which the animals survive the winter. Probably without exception this is achieved by the establishment of depot lipid during the summer and the metabolism of this store during the winter. This is demonstrated for the copepod *Calanoides acutus* and euphausiid *Euphausia crystallorophias* in Figs 10 and 11. In *Calanoides acutus* the lipid store is present as oil globules contained within the oil sac of stage IV, V and VI copepodites (Andrews, 1966). The overwintering stages IV and V do, however, show interesting differences. Relatively few IVs achieve a full oil sac before the onset of winter. This may be because they continue to divert energy to growth rather than establishing maximal food reserves. The relatively high oil content remaining in spring is probably an aid to the production of eggs coincident with the phytoplankton bloom. The lipid store in both these species is predominantly wax. The establishment of lipid stores during the summer months has also been demonstrated for the copepods *Rhincalanus gigas* and *Pareuchaeta antarctica* and the euphausiid *E. triacantha*. As *Pareuchaeta antarctica* is carnivorous it is capable of obtaining food all year-round and thus shows little fluctuation in seasonal lipid content (Fig. 10). This difference between carnivorous and herbivorous zooplankton is also related to the type of lipid used as an energy store. Species capable of feeding year-round (such as *Pareuchaeta*) tend to store triglycerides whereas those which fast overwinter (such as *Calanoides acutus*) tend to store less readily mobilized lipid such as wax esters (see Sargent, 1976). Interestingly enough, *E. superba* has generally been found to contain very little if any wax and this may indicate that krill can feed year-round (implying a strong reliance on food other than phytoplankton during the winter—it is recorded as occasionally feeding on detritus and other zooplankton (Pavlov, 1969)), or else reflect the fact that the results are from specimens that have just completed reproduction and are just beginning to lay down their winter lipid store.

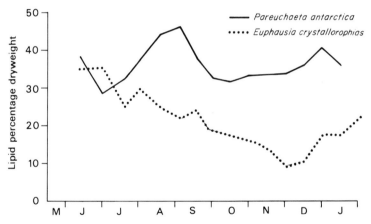

Fig. 10. Seasonal change in lipid content of two Antarctic crustaceans, *Pareuchaeta antarctica* and *Euphausia crystallorophias* (data from Littlepage, 1964).

The carnivorous zooplankters, with the exception of *Pareuchaeta* (a copepod) and *Parathemisto*, do not tend to lay down depot lipids and, because the biomass of smaller zooplankton in the top 1000 m is more or less constant throughout the year (Foxton, 1956), thus maintaining a continuous food supply, they do not have to live through periods of food shortage. The continuous feeding activity throughout the winter almost certainly releases a great deal of detritus which will provide an alternative food source for some species.

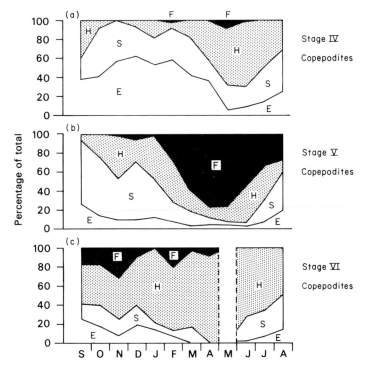

Fig. 11. *Calanoides acutus:* monthly variation in oil contained within the oil sac by four subjective categories E, empty; S, very little; H, half full; F, full (data from Andrews, 1966).

TABLE III

Comparative synopsis of main seasonal cycles in Southern Ocean zooplankton

Cycle	Carnivorous	Herbivorous	Krill
Growth	Year-round. Except *Parathemisto* which has strong peak in summer	Summer only. Except salp which also grow in winter	Summer
Reproduction	± independent of season. Except *Parathemisto* which closely linked to season	Short period in summer	Two spawnings in summer
Feeding	Year-round	Summer only	Assumed summer only but possibly feeds year-round
Biochemical	No depot lipid. Except *Pareuchaeta* which has large wax store and *Parathemisto* which has "moderate" store	Establish wax rich depot lipids in summer	Effectively no depot lipid

A comparative synopsis is given in Table III of some of the main annual cycles present in herbivorous and carnivorous zooplankton which confirms their expected close correlation with the availability of food. However, what is particularly interesting is the degree to which *E. superba* deviates from the normal herbivore standard and yet is the most significant component of the zooplankton.

5. Biomass and Production

The enormous difference in physical size, activity and absolute density of the vast range of species making up the zooplankton has presented enormous problems in making realistic estimates of standing stock. For the most part the estimates that have been made exclude the physically large creatures, such as medusae and salps, mainly because of their low frequency of occurrence in plankton hauls, which gives them an unrealistic weighting in statistical analyses. In addition species known to be quite active, such as krill, are certainly able to avoid plankton nets with efficiencies varying with the conditions under which the samples have been taken. For these reasons krill are often excluded from any analyses. Unfortunately there is little information to indicate what reliance can be placed on the various "quantitative" estimates that have been made.

Most of the estimates that have been made generally consider copepods as the dominant group in the zooplankton. Foxton (1956) showed that, although there was a clearly marked seasonal cycle with a peak during the summer for zooplankton in the top 50 m, the biomass over the top 1000 m was more or less constant throughout the year. This is because many species undergo a marked seasonal vertical migration and also have a life span of about a year.

A list of standing crop estimates has been given by Everson (1977) which range from about 10 to 100 mg m^{-3} over the top 1000 m. Taking a median value of about 50 mg m^{-3} and multiplying this up for the total area of the Southern Ocean of 36 million km^2, gives a total standing crop of around 180 million tons. This figure should be treated with a great deal of reserve, because it is derived from sampling data that may not be totally representative of zooplankton as a whole and it does not include krill. Some consider krill represents only a minor component (Voronina, 1966) but it may constitute as much as 50% of the herbivorous zooplankton.

I have not found reliable figures for total zooplankton production, although indirect estimates of krill production based on consumption by the dominant predators have been made. Naturally the accuracy of these figures depends on a good knowledge of the ecological energetics of the predators. For some, such as the whales and seals, these figures are probably fairly reliable, although for some such as squid there is only the knowledge that krill form a significant part of their diet and that squid are a significant component of the ecosystem. The estimated consumption rates for krill by the key predators are listed below:

	Estimated consumption per annum (Million tons)	Reference
Present whale stocks	43	Laws, 1977
Seals (1972, 1982)	64, 128	Chapter 12
Birds	33	Chapter 11
Squid	(100?)	Everson, 1977
Fish	?	

These estimates and the respective interactions are discussed in more detail in Chapter 14.

6. Exploitation

The Antarctic krill, because of its high annual production and its habit of congregating into dense swarms, has attracted considerable interest from some of the major fishing nations of the world. In the early 1960s the U.S.S.R. began exploratory fishing for krill using midwater trawls and also a specially-developed side trawl. Catch rates during this exploratory period were rather poor and rarely more than one ton per hour fishing. More recently other nations (Japan, West Germany, East Germany, Poland, Chile and Taiwan) have sent expeditions to the Southern Ocean with the specific purpose of evaluating the commercial potential of krill. The most successful fishing methods have used specially-developed midwater trawls. These have a fine mesh in the cod end and a small mouth opening, as it has been found that krill are not "herded" by the coarse meshes in the wings of pelagic trawls in the same way as pelagic fish are (for a fuller description of fishing methods see Eddie, 1977; Everson, 1978).

Although krill swarms have been seen at the surface they are most easily detected by echo-sounders. Because of their small size and lack of any structure that would make them good acoustic reflectors they can only be readily detected by high frequency echo-sounders and then only at close range, because of the high attenuation. This is no great disadvantage since krill are generally most abundant in the top 100 m of the water column. The very high densities often encountered in krill swarms mean that swarms are also frequently seen on lower frequency fishfinders.

Examples of catch rates by a commercial vessel carrying out exploratory fishing as part of a resource evaluation programme are set out in Table IV.

TABLE IV

Catch rates of Antarctic krill by F. M. S. Weser during the 1975–1976 season (Kock and Neudecker, 1977)

Locality	Catch rate (ton h^{-1} fishing)
North-east of South Georgia	24·1
East of South Georgia	15·6
Between South Orkneys and South Georgia	28·8

With catch rates of this order it is clear that a trawler, if allowed to operate on a purely commercial basis would be capable of catching around 100 tons a day. Such a catch rate is at present beyond the processing capability of fishing vessels and it is clear that developments will need to be made in processing krill on a large scale before any large scale expansion of the fishery is likely to occur.

The high unit cost of krill and krill products caused by the remoteness of the resource from recognized markets and the limited throughput currently possible has probably been one of the key factors in keeping the total krill catch to a relatively low level. The development of the fishery is catalogued in Table V. Although the total catch is currently of the order of 600,000 tons this is neither large in fishery terms nor in relation to the estimated total

TABLE V

Estimated total annual catch of krill (data from Everson, 1978; F. A. O., 1981)

Season	Catch (tons)	Main fishing nations
1961/1962	4	U.S.S.R.
1963/1964	70	U.S.S.R.
1964/1965	306	U.S.S.R.
1966/1967	?	U.S.S.R.
1967/1968	140	U.S.S.R.
1969/1970	100	U.S.S.R.
1970/1971	1300	U.S.S.R.
1971/1972	2100	U.S.S.R.
1972/1973	7459	U.S.S.R., Japan
1973/1974	22,543	U.S.S.R., Japan
1974/1975	39,981	U.S.S.R., Japan, Chile
1975/1976	2787	U.S.S.R., Japan, Chile, West Germany, Poland
1976/1977	122,532	U.S.S.R., Japan, Poland, Taiwan
1977/1978	142,803	U.S.S.R., Japan, Poland
1978/1979	386,882	U.S.S.R., Japan
1979/1980	424,660	U.S.S.R., Japan, Poland

annual production of the resource. However, it should be remembered that krill is the dominant component in the diet of a wide variety of species in the Southern Ocean and therefore the size to which the fishery is permitted to expand should be decided in relation to the other consumer stocks. At the moment there is no international agreement which includes conservation of krill although such an agreement, The Convention for the Conservation of Antarctic Marine Living Resources, has recently been signed. It is to be hoped that this agreement, whilst allowing for expansion in the krill fishery, will also maintain the resource and its consumers at an optimal level in the long term (see also Chapter 15).

7. References

Andrews, K. J. H. (1966). The distribution and life-history of *Calanoides acutus* (Giesbrecht). *"Discovery" Reports* **34**, 117–162.

Baker, A. de C. (1954). The circumpolar continuity of Antarctic plankton species. *"Discovery" Reports* **27**, 201–218.

Baker, A. de C. (1959). The distribution of *Euphausia triacantha* Holt and Tattersall. *"Discovery" Reprots* **29**, 309–339.

Baker, R. R. (1978). "The Evolutionary Ecology of Animal Migration". Hodder and Stoughton, London.

Clarke, A. (1976). Some observations on krill (*Euphausia superba* Dana) maintained alive in the laboratory. *British Antarctic Survey Bulletin* No. 43, 111–118.

Cram, D. L. (1978). "Preliminary results of the 1978 krill acoustics and remote sensing study and their relevance to FIBEX". Draft paper submitted to the SCAR/SCOR Group of Specialists on Living Resources of the Southern Ocean.

David, P. M. (1955). The distribution of *Sagitta gazellae* Ritter-Zahoney. *"Discovery" Reports* **27**, 235–278.

David, P. M. (1958). The distribution of the chaetognatha of the Southern Ocean. *"Discovery" Reports* **29**, 199–228.

David, P. M. (1965). The chaetognatha of the Southern Ocean. *In* "Biogeography and Ecology in Antarctica" (J. Van Mieghem and P. Van Oye, eds), pp. 296–323. Junk, The Hague.

Eddie, G. C. (1977). "The Harvesting of Krill". Southern Ocean Fisheries Survey Programme GLO/SO/77/2. F.A.O., Rome.

Everson, I. (1977). "The Living Resources of the Southern Ocean". Southern Ocean Fisheries Survey Programme GLO/SO/77/1. F.A.O., Rome.

Everson, I. (1978). Antarctic fisheries. *Polar Record* **19**, 233–251.

Everson, I. (1982). Diurnal variations in mean volume backscattering strength of an Antarctic krill (*Euphausia superba*) patch. *Journal of Plankton Research* **4**, 155–162.

Everson, I. and Ward, P. (1980). Aspects of Scotia Sea zooplankton. *Biological Journal of the Linnean Society* **14**, 93–101.

F.A.O. (1981). "Yearbook of Fishery Statistics, Vol. 50. Catches and Landings 1980". F.A.O., Rome.

Fischer, W. and Mohr, H. (1978). Verhaltensbeobachtungen an Krill (*Euphausia superba* Dana). *Archiv für Fischereiwissenschaft* **29**, 71–79.

Foxton, P. (1956). The distribution of the standing crop of zooplankton in the Southern Ocean. "*Discovery*" *Reports* **28**, 191–236.

Foxton, P. (1966). The distribution and life-history of *Salpa thompsoni* Foxton with observations on a related species *Salpa gerlachei* Foxton. "*Discovery*" *Reports* **34**, 1–116.

Fraser, F. C. (1936). On the development and distribution of the young stages of krill (*Euphausia superba*). "*Discovery*" *Reports* **14**, 1–192.

Henry, L. R., McGowan, J. A. and Wiebe, P. H. (1978). Patterns and processes in the time-space scales of plankton distributions. *In* "Spatial Pattern in Plankton Communities" (J. H. Steele, ed.), pp. 277–327. Plenum Press, New York.

Ivanov, B. E. (1970). On the biology of the Antarctic krill (*Euphausia superba* Dana). *Marine Biology* **7**, 340–351.

John, D. D. (1937). The southern species of the genus *Euphausia*. "*Discovery*" *Reports* **14**, 195–324.

Kane, J. E. (1966). The distribution of *Parathemisto gaudichaudii* (Guér.) with observations on its life-history in the 0° to 20°E sector of the Southern Ocean. "*Discovery*" *Reports* **34**, 163–198.

Kock, K.-H. and Neudecker, A. (1977). Krillfange im atlantischen Sektor der Antarktis. *Informationen für die Fischwirtschaft* **24**, 8–12.

Laws, R. M. (1977). Seals and whales of the Southern Ocean. *Philosophical Transactions of the Royal Society* **B279**, 81–96.

McWhinnie, M. A., Denys, C. and Schenborn, D. (1976). Biology of krill (*Euphausia superba*) and other antarctic invertebrates. *Antarctic Journal of the United States* **11**, 55–58.

Mackintosh, N. A. (1934). Distribution of the macroplankton in the Atlantic sector of the Antarctic. "*Discovery*" *Reports* **9**, 65–160.

Mackintosh, N. A. (1937). The seasonal circulation of the Antarctic macroplankton. "*Discovery*" *Reports* **16**, 365–412.

Mackintosh, N. A. (1967). Maintenance of living *Euphausia superba* and frequency of moults. *Norsk Hvalfangst-Tidende* **56**, 97–102.

Mackintosh, N. A. (1972). Life cycle of Antarctic krill in relation to ice and water conditions. "*Discovery*" *Reports* **36**, 1–94.

Mackintosh, N. A. (1973). Distribution of post larval krill in the Antarctic. "*Discovery*" *Reports* **36**, 95–156.

Makarov, R. R. (1975). A study of the second maturation of Euphausiid (Eucarida, Euphausiacea) females. *Zoologicheskii Zhurnal* **54**, 670–681.

Makarov, R. R. (1978). Vertical distribution of Euphausiid eggs and larvae off the northeastern coast of South Georgia Island. *Oceanology* **15**, 708–711.

Makarov, R. R., Naumov, A. G. and Shevtsov, V. V. (1970). The biology and the distribution of the Antarctic krill. *In* "Antarctic Ecology" (M. W. Holdgate, ed.), Vol. I, pp. 173–176. Academic Press, London and New York.

Marr, J. W. S. (1962). The natural history and geography of the Antarctic krill (*Euphausia superba* Dana). "*Discovery*" *Reports* **32**, 33–464.

Mauchline, J. and Fisher, L. R. (1969). "The Biology of Euphausiids". Advances in Marine Biology, Vol. 7. Academic Press, London and New York.

Mohr, H. (1976). Tagesezeitlich bedingte Rhythmik im Verhalten von halbwüchsigem Krill (*Euphausia superba*). *Informationen für die Fischwirtschaft* **23**, 132–134.

Moiseev, P. A. (1970). Some aspects of the commercial use of the krill resources of the Antarctic seas. *In* "Antarctic Ecology" (M. W. Holdgate, ed.), Vol. I, pp. 213–216. Academic Press, London and New York.

Nemoto, T. and Nasu, K. (1975). Present status of exploitation and biology of krill in the Antarctic. *In* "Oceanology International 1975. Conference Papers", pp. 353–360. BPS Exhibitions Ltd, Brighton and London.

Nemoto, T., Doi, T. and Nasu, K. (1981). Biological characteristics of krill caught in the Southern Ocean. *In* "Biological Investigations of Marine Antarctic Systems and Stocks (BIOMASS)" (S. Z. El-Sayed, ed.), Vol. II, pp. 47–63. Scientific Committee on Antarctic Research, Cambridge.

Ommaney, F. D. (1936). *Rhincalanus gigas* (Brady), a copepod of the southern macroplankton. *"Discovery" Reports* **13**, 277–384.

Pavlov, V. Ya. (1969). The feeding of krill and some features of its behaviour. Trudy VNIRO **66**, 207–222. [M.A.F.F. Translation NS No. 94.]

Ruud, J. T. (1932). On the biology of southern Euphausiidae. *Hvalradets Skrifter* **2**, 1–105.

Sargent, J. R. (1976). The structure, metabolism and function of lipids in marine organisms. *In* "Biochemical and Biophysical Perspectives in Marine Biology" (D. C. Malins and J. R. Sargent, eds), Vol. 3, pp. 149–212. Academic Press, London and new York.

Shevtsov, V. V. and Makarov, R. R. (1969). On the biology of Antarctic krill. *Trudy VNIRO* **66**, 177–206. [M.A.F.F. Translation NS No. 91.]

Voronina, N. M. (1966). the zooplankton of the Southern Ocean: some study results. *Oceanology* **6**, 557–563.

Voronina, N. M. (1968). The distribution of zooplankton in the Southern Ocean and its dependence on the circulation of water. *Sarsia* **34**, 277–284.

Voronina, N. M. (1972). Vertical structure of a pelagic community in the Antarctic. *Oceanology* **12**, 415–420.

10

Fish biology

I. Everson

1. Species Composition and Distribution

The very remoteness of the Southern Ocean and, until recently, its freedom from human habitation has meant that detailed knowledge of its ichthyofauna has only been available this century. Of the 20,000 or so modern fish species only 120 are found south of the Antarctic Convergence and most of these are found exclusively in that area.

The majority of species are restricted to the continental shelf or the shelf area surrounding the island groups. In general, the depth of water over Antarctic continental shelf habitats is much greater than in other oceans (Adie, 1964) and in no sea is there a continuous shallow-water "bridge" between Antarctica and the continents to the north. A direct consequence of this is a high degree of endemism amongst Antarctic species. The same is not true of the deep-water fauna where only about half the species are restricted to the Antarctic zone (Table I). This fact is not surprising because differences between deep-water habitats in different oceans are much less extreme.

In contrast to the other oceans of the world the Southern Ocean does not appear to contain any densely-schooling obligate pelagic species. This is particularly surprising, bearing in mind the availability of large amounts of krill over much of the region. Those species present, the most common being the myctophids *Electrona antarctica*, *Gymnoscopelus braueri*, *Bathylagus antarcticus*, *Notolepis coatsi* and *Cyclothone microdon* and the nototheniid *Pleuragramma antarcticum*, do however, feed largely on krill (DeWitt and Hopkins, 1977; Andriashev, 1965).

The dominant group of Antarctic fish is the Notothenoidei whose four families Nototheniidae, Harpagiferidae, Bathydraconidae and Channichthyidae include about 75% of all species. The Nototheniidae is the

TABLE I
The number of genera and species in each family found in the Antarctic, showing the number restricted to the Antarctic and the number also found farther north

Family	Antarctic only		Antarctic and farther north		Totals	
	Genera	Species	Genera	Species	Genera	Species
Geotriidae	0	0	1	1	1	1
Myxinidae	0	0	1	1	1	1
Rajidae	0	3	2	1	2	4
Synaphobranchidae [a]	0	0	1	1	1	1
Halosauridae [a]	0	0	1	1	1	1
Muraenolepidae	0	2	1	1	1	3
Moridae	0	0	2	2	2	2
Gadidae	0	0	1	1	1	1
Macrouridae [a]	0	4	5	3	5	7
Brotulidae [a]	0	1	1	0	1	1
Zoarcidae	3	8	3	3	6	11
Nototheniidae	4	31	2	3	6	34
Harpagiferidae	4	14	1	1	5	15
Bathydraconidae	8	15	0	0	8	15
Channichthyidae	9	15	1	0	10	15
Congiopodidae	1	1	0	0	1	1
Liparidae	0	5	3	0	3	5
Bothidae	0	1	1	1	1	2
TOTALS						
All families	29	100	27	20	56	120
All but abyssal families	29	95	19	15	48	110

[a]Denotes a bathyal or abyssal family (DeWitt, 1971).

largest of the families; most are sedentary demersal species although some have become adapted to living closely associated with the undersurface of sea ice (DeVries, 1978). The group also includes *Pleuragramma*, a totally pelagic species. The genera *Notothenia* and *Trematomus* have recently been examined in detail by Anderson and Hureau (1979) who have reclassified them into three genera, *Patagonotothen* (species found typically in the Patagonian region), *Pagothenia* (described originally by Nichols and Lamonte (1936) but recently absorbed within the genus *Trematomus*) and *Notothenia* (the type genus described by Richardson (1844) but now including the subgenera *Paranotothenia*, *Gobionotothen*, *Lindbergia* and *Lepidonotothen* erected by Balushkin (1976) and *Trematomus* described by Boulenger (1902)). The species present in the Antarctic zone now included in each genus are listed below:

Patagonotothen (*Notothenia*) *larseni*
Pagothenia (*Trematomus*) *brachysoma*

P. (Trematomus) borchgrevinki
Notothenia (Notothenia) coriiceps neglecta
N. (Notothenia) coriiceps coriiceps
N. (Notothenia) rossii rossii
N. (Notothenia) rossii marmorata
N. (Notothenia) microlepidota
N. (Paranotothenia) magellanica
N. (Gobionotothen) gibberifrons
N. (Gobionotothen) acuta
N. (Gobionotothen) angustifrons
N. (Gobionotothen) marionensis
N. (Gobionotothen) cyanobrancha
N. (Lindbergia) mizops
N. (Lindbergia) nudifrons
N. (Lepidonotothen) kempi
N. (Trematomus) newnesi
N. (Trematomus) nicolai
N. (Trematomus) bernacchii
N. (Trematomus) vicarius
N. (Trematomus) centronotus
N. (Trematomus) pennelli
N. (Trematomus) eulepidotus
N. (Trematomus) lepidorhinus
N. (Trematomus) scotti
N. (Trematomus) hansoni
N. (Trematomus) lonnbergii

2. Ecology

2.1 Size and growth

The Antarctic ichthyofauna is dominated by small species, fewer than half the species grow to 25 cm in length and only about 12 grow to more than 50 cm (Andriashev, 1965). Based on an index "the mean species length" (the sum of the total lengths of the largest individuals of each species in a family divided by the number of species), Andriashev has shown that the Channichthyidae, the group which lack a respiratory pigment, are in fact the largest. Andriashev's calculated values are:

Mean species length (cm)

Harpagiferidae	15
Bathydraconidae	26
Nototheniidae	36
Channichthyidae	43

The relationship between length and weight has been studied in a number of species. In general the relationship can be adequately described by a simple cubic of the form:

$$\text{weight} = \text{constant} \times (\text{length})^3$$

In some cases, and particularly for larger sizes, the cubic relation provides a poor fit and in those circumstances a more accurate exponent has been determined. This is generally slightly less than 3. Information on length/weight relationships for some species is summarized in Table II.

TABLE II

Length/weight relationships for some species of Antarctic fish

Species	Relationship	Locality	Reference
Raja georgianus	$W = (0.21\ L)^3$	South Georgia	Calculated from results of Permitin, 1969
Micromesistius australis	$W = (0.21\ L - 1.3)^3$	Scotia Sea	Estimated from Shubnikov *et al.*, 1969
Notothenia neglecta	$W = 0.029\ (SL)^3$ $W = 0.028\ (SL)^3$ $\log W = 2.92 \log SL - 4.45$	Signy I. Terre Adélie	Everson, 1970[a] Hureau, 1970
N. rossii rossii	$\log W = 2.76 \log SL - 4.06$	Kerguelen	Hureau, 1970
N. rossii marmorata	$W = 0.029\ L^{2.85}$	South Georgia	Crisp and Carrick, 1975
N. magellanica	$\log W = 2.87 \log SL - 4.2$	Kerguelen	Hureau, 1970
Pseudochaenichthys georgianus	$W = (0.213\ L)^3$	Scotia Sea	Dubrovskaya and Makarov, 1969
Chaenocephalus aceratus	$W = (0.189\ L)^3$	Scotia Sea	Dubrovskaya and Makarov, 1969
Channichthys rhinoceratus	$W = 47.8 \times 10^{-6} L^{2.75}$	Kerguelen	Hureau, 1966

W, weight; L, length; SL, standard length.

Several workers have found recognizable annual growth structures in otoliths, scales and bones of some species and have used these to provide age/length and age/weight keys. The Channichthyidae are a consistently difficult group as far as age determination is concerned; they do not possess scales and their otoliths frequently have patterns of marks which are open to more than one interpretation. The methodology has recently been reviewed by Everson (1981).

Length (cm) at Age (years) for Antarctic fish

Species	Locality	Sex	Length	I	II	III	IV	V	VI	VII	VIII	IX	X	XI	XII	XIII	XIV	XV	XVI	XVII	Reference
Micromesistius australis	South Orkney	♂	TL				45	47	48	50	50	51	53								Shubiknov et al., 1969
		♀	TL			46	48	49	49	50	52	53	65								
	Patagonia	♂	TL			44	45	46	47	49	50	—	55								
	Patagonia	♀	TL			44	46	47	48	49	51	52	58								
Notothenia neglecta	Signy	♀	SL					22	24	26	27.5	29	30.5	31.8	33.0	34.1	35.0	35.8			Everson, 1970a
	Terre Adélie	♀	SL						18.2	21.4	24.6	27.8	31.0	34.2	37.4	40.6					Hureau, 1970
	Signy	♂	SL					22.5	24.6	26.4	28.0	29.4	30.4	31.6	32.5	33.4	34.1	34.7			Everson, 1970
	Terre Adélie	♂	SL					16.5	18.5	20.4	22.3	24.2	26.2	28.1	30.0	31.9					Hureau, 1970
Notothenia rossii	South Georgia		TL	7	—	22	28	32	44	51♀/50♂	59/57	61/59	64/62	67/64	70/65	72/68	72/69				Olsen, 1954
	South Georgia		TL		19.2	26.9	33.4	42.8	45.8	51.3	54.7	59.6	64.3	—	67.0	—		79.0			Freytag, 1980
	S. Shetlands		TL					40.1	43.8	46.9	51.8	55.3	58.1	61.1	64.5	67.7					
	Kerguelen		SL	11.2	17.1	23.5	32.1	39.3	50/48	55♀/53♂	60/—	—/61									Hureau, 1970
Notothenia magellanica	Kerguelen		SL	12.1	18.0	23.4	26.6	30.3	33.1	36.5											Hureau, 1970
Notothenia cyanobrancha	Kerguelen	♀	SL	4.8	7.2	10.4	15.0	18.9	21.0	22.8	24.2										Hureau, 1970
	Kerguelen	♂	SL	4.8	7.7	9.9	14.2	18.4	20.7	22.5	24.2										
Notothenia macrocephala	Kerguelen		SL	12.1	18.0	23.4	26.6	30.0	33.1	36.5											Hureau, 1970
Notothenia bernacchii	Terre Adélie	♀	SL	4.5	7.0	10.2	14.4	17.0	18.5	19.8	21.3	22.8	24.4								Hureau, 1970
	Terre Adélie	♂	SL	4.5	7.0	10.2	13.6	15.1	16.7	18.5											
Notothenia hansoni		♀	SL				17.6	19.0	21.6	24.1	25.7	—	29.5								Hureau, 1970
		♂	SL			15.8	16.7	18.0	19.5	20.5	21.9										
Champsocephalus gunnari	South Georgia	♀	TL			26.6	32.1	34.2	36.5	37.6	39.5	40.5	40	41							Olsen, 1955
		♂	TL			26.8	32.5	34.9	36.3	36.7	38.2	41	—	41	42						
Channichthys rhinoceratus	Kerguelen		SL		14.8	22.3	26.0	34.0	37.0	39.7	41.0	42.5	—	—	47.5						Hureau, 1966

TL = total length, SL = standard length.

Information available on size at age is given in Table III. In general growth tends to be slow with the result that for older fish, there is quite a large variation about the size for each age in comparison to the annual growth increment. This has meant that for many species there have been problems in fitting growth curves to size at age data. A summary of the constants for the Bertalanffy equation fitted to results for several species of Antarctic fish is given in Table IV.

TABLE IV

Bertalanffy growth constants for some species of Antarctic fish

Species		K	L_∞ (cm)	W_∞ (g)	t_0 (years)	Reference
(1) *Notothenia neglecta*	♀	0.091	45.5	2744	−1.7	Everson, 1970a
(2) *Notothenia neglecta*	♂	0.129	39.5	1728	−0.8	Everson, 1970a
(3) *N. rossii rossii*	♀	0.13	90		−0.62	Hureau, 1970
(4) *N. rossii rossii*	♂	0.13	80		−1.69	Hureau, 1970
(5) *N. rossii marmorata*	I–V[1]	0.15	75		0.1	Everson, 1970a (data from Olsen, 1954)
(6) *N. rossii marmorata*	V–XIV[1]	0.29	75		3	Everson, 1970a (data from Olsen, 1954)
(7) *N. magellanica*		0.26	40		0.4	Hureau, 1970
(8) *N. cyanobrancha*		0.186	33.5		0.5	Hureau, 1970
(9) *N. macrocephala*		0.26	40		−0.4	Hureau, 1970
(10) *N. bernacchii*	♀	0.127	35		0.05	Hureau, 1970
(11) *N. bernacchii*	♂	0.178	27.5		0.5	Hureau, 1970
(12) *N. hansoni*	♀	0.093	45		−1.2	Hureau, 1970
(13) *N. hansoni*	♂	0.111	30.5		−3.1	Hureau, 1970

The constant L_∞ of the Bertalanffy equation represents the maximum size to which the animal can grow and the constant K is a measure of the rate at which it will approach this upper asymptote. The value of K will itself be dependent on physiological rates within the animal as well as on density dependent factors within the population. The constant t_0 is the origin of the curve and is dependent to a great extent on larval development rate and physiological changes in early life. The values of L_∞ and K have been plotted (Fig. 1) and it can be seen that there are several distinct groups.

The species *Notothenia neglecta*, *N. hansoni* and female *N. bernacchii* all have slow growth rates and grow to a maximum size of 30–45 cm. These results are from Pointe Géologie and Signy Island where the seasonal temperature regimes are similar although the former is colder for slightly longer (Hureau, 1970; Everson, 1970a). All these species feed predominantly on benthic invertebrates.

It is interesting that male *N. bernacchii* have similar growth characteristics to *N. cyanobrancha* from Îles Kerguelen. This may reflect a more effi-

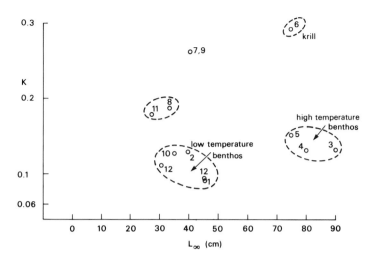

Fig. 1. Plot of Bertalanffy coefficient K, against asymptotic length L_∞ for Antarctic fish species referred to in Table IV. Key: (1) *Notothenia neglecta* ♀; (2) *N. neglecta* ♂; (3) *N. r. rossii* ♀; (4) *N. r. rossii* ♂; (5) *N. r. marmorata*, age I–V; (6) *N. r. marmorata*, age V–XIV; (7) *N. magellanica*; (8) *N. cyanobrancha*; (9) *N. macrocephala*; (10) *N. bernacchii* ♀; (11) *N. bernacchii* ♂; (12) *N. hansoni* ♀; (13) *N. hansoni* ♂.

cient utilization of food or alternatively that the males have to divert less energy to production of gametes. At Kerguelen, where the summer sea temperature reaches +7°C and in winter goes down to +2°C, most species grow relatively rapidly to a moderate size. The exception is *Notothenia rossii* which grows slowly but to a greater ultimate size. During the latter part of its life *N. rossii* at South Georgia has a much faster growth rate which is probably related to its change of diet from benthic invertebrates to krill.

Bearing in mind that the value of K is partially density dependent, it will be very interesting to see to what extent this has changed as a result of recent commercial fishing at Kerguelen and South Georgia.

It is clear from the results reported so far that Antarctic fish in general have a long life span and yet only grow to a moderate size. How then does this relate to growth by fish from other regions? In an analysis of a variety of marine organisms Everson (1977a) used the factor:

$$\text{size ratio} = \log_e \frac{\text{length at time } (t+1)}{\text{length at time } (t)}$$

to provide general comparisons. Plotting the size ratio against the size at the start of the year, it was shown that Antarctic fish tended to have a slower growth rate than other cold-water species (e.g. Yellow-tailed flounder from

Canada) although similar to the Arctic char. The only species that grew as fast as the Arctic cod (*Gadus morhua*) was *Notothenia rossii* when feeding on krill. Thus, although the amount of data available is very strictly limited, it does confirm that Antarctic fish grow more slowly than temperate-water species and at about the same rate as those from other cold regions.

TABLE V

Age and size at sexual maturity for Antarctic fish

Species	Sex	Sexual maturity			Locality	Reference
		Age	Length (cm)	Weight (g)		
Raja georgianus	♀		60		South Georgia	Permitin, 1969
Micromesistius australis	♂	(4)[a]	45.3		Scotia Sea	Shubnikov *et al.*, 1969
M. australis	♀	(3)[a]	46.4		Scotia Sea	Shubnikov *et al.*, 1969
Notothenia gibberifrons	♀		35[b]	400	South Georgia	Permitin and Sil'yanova, 1971
Notothenia neglecta	♂	8	30		Signy Island	Everson, 1970a,b
N. neglecta	♀	7	29		Signy Island	Everson, 1970a,b
N. neglecta	♂	7	18	190	Terre Adélie	Hureau, 1970
N. neglecta	♀	8	22.5	300	Terre Adélie	Hureau, 1970
N. rossii	♂	7	48	1700	Îles Kerguelen	Hureau, 1970
N. rossii	♀	8	55	2700	Îles Kerguelen	Hureau, 1970
N. rossii marmorata	♂	5 (min)	40 (min)		South Georgia	Olsen, 1954
N. rossii marmorata	♀	6 (min)	45 (min)		South Georgia	Olsen, 1954
N. magellanica	♂+♀	(6–7)	25	500	Îles Kerguelen	Hureau, 1970
Champsocephalus sp.		4			South Georgia	Olsen, 1955
Champsocephalus sp.	♂	4	21–26		South Georgia	Permitin, 1973
Champsocephalus sp.	♀	4	21–25		South Georgia	Permitin, 1973
Chaenocephalus sp.		(9)[c]			South Georgia	Olsen, 1955
Channichthys rhinoceratus		5	34	435	Îles Kerguelen	Hureau, 1966
Pseudochaenichthys sp.	♂	4–6	40–48		South Georgia	Permitin, 1973
Pseudochaenichthys sp.	♀	4–6	44–50		South Georgia	Permitin, 1973
Chionodraco sp.	♂		31–36		?	Permitin, 1973
Chionodraco sp.	♀		33–37		?	Permitin, 1973

[a]This is inferred since the authors state that only sexually mature fish were caught.
[b]In this paper mention is made only of mature fish; the size quoted is of the smallest specimen. By comparison with my own unpublished observations at Signy Island this would approximate to the size at sexual maturity.
[c]All the fish were sexually mature and aged nine or more.

2.2 Reproduction

A direct consequence of the slow growth rate and long life span of most Antarctic fish is the fact that many do not reach sexual maturity until they are more than five years old, although they probably breed annually thereafter. Published information on age and size at sexual maturity is summarized in Table V.

Gonad development and maturation progress synchronously in individuals of the same species with the result that the spawning season is generally of limited duration. In the species studied so far, spawning typically takes place in summer or early winter, at which time large yolky eggs are laid on the sea bed. It is, however, very interesting that the earliest breeding season occurs in species that are commonly found close to the Antarctic Continent, although the majority of studies have been carried out in more northerly waters. The results tend to indicate that there is probably a relationship between annual temperature regime (more or less equivalent to latitude) and the spawning season (Fig. 2). Most of the values included in Fig. 2 are estimates based on gonad development stages observed during a brief period in summer and inevitably these will be valid only to perhaps the nearest two months. Bearing this in mind, and the lack of information from "intermediate" areas, the relationship between latitude and spawning season seems quite reasonable. There are two possible explanations for this: either the spawning season is controlled by the rate of gonad production and the season during which it can take place, or else it is controlled by the hatching of the larvae and their dependence on the plankton. Both of these points are discussed more fully later.

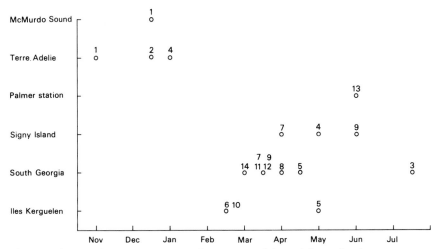

Fig. 2. Midpoints of spawning seasons for Antarctic fish at different localities. Key: (1) *Trematomus bernacchii*; (2) *T. hansoni*; (3) *Notothenia gibberifrons*; (4) *N. neglecta*; (5) *N. rossii*; (6) *N. magellanica*; (7) *Notothenia nudifrons*; (8) *Champsocephalus*; (9) *Chaenocephalus*; (10) *Channichthys*; (11) *Pseudochaenichthys*; (12) *Chionodraco*; (13) *Harpagifer bispinis*; (14) *Parachaenichthys georgicus*.

Descriptions of the development and final maturation of the gonads have been given for several species by Dearborn (1965), Everson (1970b) and Hureau (1970), and subjective maturation stages were described by Everson (1977b). In *Notothenia neglecta* the ovary starts to increase in size during November after being more or less constant at about 3% of the total body weight for the preceding six months (Fig. 3). The increase is gradual until March when there is a rapid increase, so that the gonad is nearly twice its March size when spawning occurs in May. The reduction in gonad size at spawning does not leave the ovary totally devoid of ova because many small ova, which will form the next year's spawn, have already been formed in it. The final maturation of the testis begins during December when there is a steady increase in size until spawning in May. There is then a steady reduction in size due to release and resorption of sperm. A generalized pattern is indicated in Fig. 4, which, if due allowance is made for differences in timing, is applicable to most Nototheniiformes.

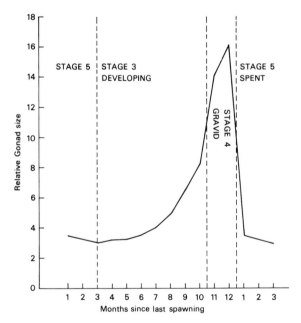

Fig. 3. Probable seasonal pattern of relative female gonad size (gonad weight/total weight) × 100. Morphological characteristics of stages: (1) Immature—ovary small, firm; no ova visible to naked eye. (2) Maturing virgin—ovary ¼ length body cavity, firm, full of eggs. (3) Developing—ovary large, contains eggs of two sizes. (4) Gravid—ovary large; when opened large ova spill out. (5) Spent—ovary flaccid, contains few large and many small ova.

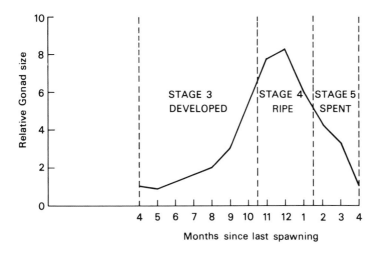

Fig. 4. Probable seasonal pattern of relative male gonad size. Morphological characteristics of stages: (1) Immature—testis small, translucent. (2) Developing—testis small, white, convoluted. (3) Developed—testis large, white, convoluted; no milt produced when cut. (4) Ripe—testis large, opalescent white; milt produced when cut. (5) Spent—testis smaller, dirty white in colour.

Although the final maturation processes in each species do appear to be more or less in synchrony, there is a slight variation in timing which can be related to size. The most striking example is that of *Notothenia cyano-brancha* from Îles Kerguelen, where fish which are spawning for the first time do so at the end of January although the peak of spawning by the remainder of the population occurs at the end of April (Hureau, 1970). A similar situation occurs in *Notothenia neglecta* at Signy Island where, based on the gonad index, final maturation and spawning by female fish of the smallest mature size group occurs about a month before the remainder of the population (Fig. 5). The analogous situation does not appear to occur in male fish, although mature sperm are present in testes in April (Everson, 1970b), and as can be seen from Fig. 5, spawning is probably completed earlier in smaller than larger fish. The opposite situation may be the case for the channichthyid, *Champsocephalus gunnari* where, in pre-spawning condition, the average egg dry weight is greatest in larger fish, indicating either that final maturation occurs earlier in older fish, or else that larger fish tend to produce larger eggs (Kock, 1979).

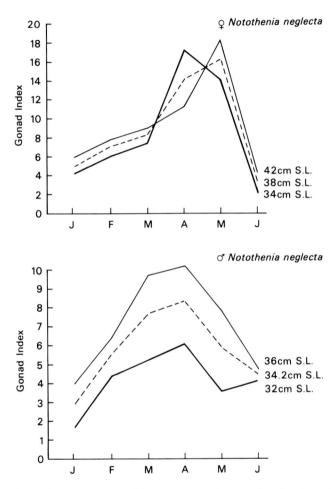

Fig. 5. Gonad Index for first six months of the year for *Notothenia neglecta* female (top) and male (bottom) at Signy Island (Everson, unpublished data). Points derived from regression lines for each month of general form: Gonad index = A + B (standard length—mean standard length for month).

The large size of the ova has meant that the process of yolk deposition takes more than one year. In *Notothenia neglecta*, in the years before the females become fully mature, the ovary slowly develops to about one-quarter the length of the body cavity. The ova at this stage are about 0.5 mm in diameter. When the fish becomes mature for the first time these ova enlarge and take up a great deal more yolk; at the same time yolk deposition begins in a new generation of ova. There are thus two distinct size groups of yolky oocytes present in the mature ovary. Yolk deposition probably continues throughout most of the year in both types of yolky oocyte, although the greatest increase occurs in the largest ova in the months immediately prior to spawning (Fig. 6). Because there are yolky eggs present in the ovary throughout the year, the ovary in post-spawning condition still contains many clearly recognizable eggs and these are the main reason for the ovary constituting about 3% of the body weight at this time (Fig. 3). It is not clear what the adaptative advantage to the fish is in taking two years to lay down yolk in the oocytes. The physiological processes within the fish, controlling the rate of yolk deposition, may mean that for some reason it is less efficient for the process to take one year. There may also be a link with the short production season which may permit the rapid deposition prior to spawning. However, this does imply that food is more readily available or contains some essential component at this time—such major changes have not been identified in benthic invertebrates, the major food component.

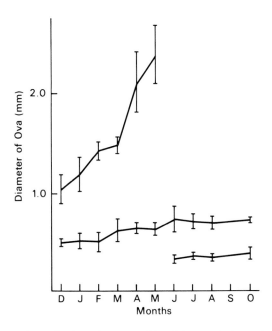

Fig. 6. The diameter of *Notothenia neglecta* ova with yolk by months (mean ± 1 s.d.).

The production of large yolky eggs has, as a consequence, meant that the fecundity must generally be quite low (Table VI). The relative fecundity

TABLE VI
Egg size, fecundity and spawning period for Antarctic fish

Species	Egg diameter (mm)	Fecundity × 10⁻³	Spawning period	References
Micromesistius australis			Spring	Hart, 1946; Weiss, 1974
Merluccius hubbsii	0.8–0.9(P)		December	Ciechomski and Weiss, 1974
Muraenolepis microps (South Georgia)	(0.7)	86–428 330–529 g⁻¹ t.w.	(Winter?)	Permitin, 1973
Notothenia gibberifrons		50–100	Jul–Aug	Permitin and Sil'yanova, 1971
N. neglecta (South Orkneys)	3.0(D)	10–30 (12 g⁻¹ t.w.)	May	Everson, 1970b
	3	10.1–14.7 (8–16 g⁻¹ t.w.)		Permitin and Sil'yanova, 1971
(Terre Adélie)	1.2	20–30 (13–20 g⁻¹ t.w.)	January	Hureau, 1970
N. rossii rossii	3.0(D)	46–53 (15–17 g⁻¹ t.w.)	May	Hureau, 1970
N. rossii marmorata	4.8(D)	20–120	Apr–May	Permitin and Sil'yanova, 1971
N. magellanica	1.2(P)	60–70 (50–58 g⁻¹ t.w.)	Feb–Mar	Hureau, 1970
N. rossii rossii	3.0(D)	46–53 (15–17 g⁻¹t.w.)	May	Hureau, 1970
N. rossii marmorata	4.8(D)	20–120	Apr–May	Permitin and Sil'yanova, 1971
N. magellanica	1.2(P)	60–70 (50–58 g⁻¹ t.w.)	Feb–Mar	Hureau, 1970
N. cyanobrancha (Kerguelen)	1.6	(300 g⁻¹ t.w.)	Jan/Feb[a] Apr/May	Hureau, 1970
N. kempi (South Orkneys)	1.3	100–170 g⁻¹ t.w.		Permitin and Sil'yanova, 1971
N. larseni (South Orkneys)	2.0	64–104 g⁻¹ t.w.		Permitin and Sil'yanova, 1971
(South Georgia)	(2.0)	140–195 g⁻¹ t.w.		Permitin and Sil'yanova, 1971
N. nudifrons	1.9	104–122 g⁻¹ t.w.		Permitin and Sil'yanova, 1971
(South Shetlands)	2.3	35–51 g⁻¹ t.w.		Permitin and Sil'yanova, 1971
N. angustifrons (South Sandwich)	1	202–352		Permitin and Sil'yanova, 1971
N. hansoni (Terre Adélie)	3–3.5	7–12 17.5–16.7 g⁻¹ t.w.	Jan/Feb	Hureau, 1970
N. bernacchii	3.5–4(D)	1.5–2.5	Oct	Hureau, 1970
Parachaenichthys georgianus	3.4(D)	14.1 (10.7 g⁻¹ t.w.)		
Psilodraco breviceps		1.34 74	(Autumn)	Permitin, 1973
Chaenocephalus aceratus	4.7		(June)	Everson, 1968
(South Orkneys)	3.9	(9.3–9.4) 5–6 g⁻¹ t.w.		Permitin, 1973
(South Georgia)		7.4–22.6 9–5 g⁻¹ t.w. 5.9–18.0 5.1–8.1 g⁻¹ gutfree weight		Permitin, 1973 Kock, 1979

Species	Egg diameter (mm)	Fecundity × 10⁻³	Spawning period	References
Pagothenia borchgrevinki	3.6	1.5–3.0 (mean 2.12)	June	Andriashev, et al., 1979
Dissostichus mawsoni	4–4.3(D)		(Nov/Dec)[b]	Yukhov, 1971
Champsocephalus sp. (South Georgia)	1.9–2.2		April	Olsen, 1955
Champsocephalus sp.	3.4–4		May	Lönnberg, 1905
Champsocephalus sp. (South Georgia)	2.6	4–23 15–16 g⁻¹ t.w.		Permitin, 1973
(South Orkneys)		8.4 14 g⁻¹ t.w.		Permitin, 1973
Channichthys rhinoceratus	4.5	6–14	Feb/Mar	Hureau, 1966
Pseudochaenichthys georgianus	4	5.8–10.9	Mar/Apr	Permitin, 1973
Chionodraco sp.	3.7–5.0	2.5–4 5 g⁻¹ t.w.	Mar/Apr	Permitin, 1973

[a]Spawning on first occasion.
[b]Comparison of the process of final ovarian maturation in this species with N. neglecta from Signy Island suggests that spawning may occur in the middle of winter and not Nov/Dec.
P = pelagic eggs, D = demersal eggs, t. w. = total weight.

(number of eggs constituting one season's spawn divided by the total weight of the fish) does vary greatly between species and within the same species from different localities. Because the relative fecundity is a function of the volume of the ovary it is to be expected that there will be an exponential relationship between this factor and the egg diameter (Fig. 7). The species which have been found to produce the largest eggs are the channichthyids, the more southern *Notothenia* spp. (previously included in the genus *Trematomus*) and the largest of the *Notothenia* spp. The smaller *Notothenia* spp., which are found at the northern end of the Antarctic zone, tend to produce the smallest eggs. Where several species have been studied at one locality the results tend to indicate that there is a negative exponential relationship between the relative fecundity and size. Because there is an inverse correlation between egg size and the relative fecundity, it is probably true to say that for fish of the same size the egg size will be larger in higher latitudes. This conclusion has been suggested by several workers although there is very little published information with which to make valid comparisons. Permitin and Sil'yanova (1971) have published some results, summarized in Table VII, which support this view.

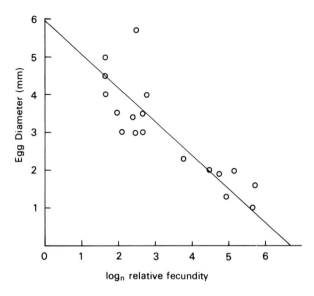

Fig. 7. Relationship between egg diameter and relative fecundity for Antarctic Nototheniiformes (calculated from data in Hureau, 1970; Everson, 1970b; Permitin, 1971; Permitin and Sil'yanova, 1973).

TABLE VII
Fecundity and egg size in Antarctic fish

Species	Locality	Length (cm)	Relative fecundity	Egg size (mm)
Notothenia	S. Georgia	17–18	166	1.3–2.0
larseni	S. Orkneys and S. Shetlands	17–18	79	1.6–2.0
N. nudifrons	S. Georgia	14–15	122	1.2–1.9
	S. Orkneys and S. Shetlands	14–15	46	1.5–2.3
	S. Georgia	17–18	104	1.2–1.9
	S. Orkneys and S. Shetlands	17–18	47	1.5–2.3

The same paper includes some interesting results for *Notothenia gibberifrons*. In this species at South Georgia and the South Orkneys there appear to be two types designated by their relative fecundity. One group has a relative fecundity of around 55 whilst the other is around 110. From an analysis of the results of White and North (1979), who give measurements of 49 *N. gibberifrons* from South Georgia caught in February 1978, it can be shown, using probability paper, that the gonad index (gonad weight/total weight × 100) frequency distribution is bimodal with mean values at 2.75 and 0.95 (Fig. 8). As this species probably spawns in August it is very likely that the final rapid maturation process had only just commenced at the time these fish were caught. The ovaries of mature fish would therefore contain the ova for two spawning periods, whereas ovaries of fish preparing to spawn for the first time in the following year would contain yolky eggs for only one spawning. The same is probably true of the fish that Permitin examined. In ovaries where maturing ova are quite small it is very difficult to distinguish microscopically between those eggs which will form the current year's spawn and those which will mature the following year. It therefore seems very likely that the high values of relative fecundity were caused by inadvertently counting the eggs responsible for two years' spawn. The relative fecundity for *N. gibberifrons* is probably therefore about 55.

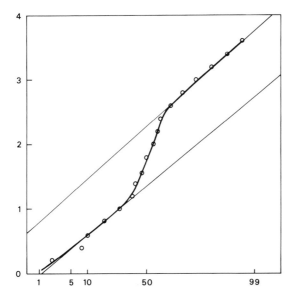

Fig. 8. Cumulative frequency distribution of gonad index of female *Notothenia gibberifrons*, arithmetic probability paper plot (*n* = 49; data from White and North, 1979).

Marshall (1953) noted that Antarctic fish characteristically produce large yolky eggs and suggested that this conferred several advantages on the developing larvae. These were that relative to larvae from small eggs the larvae would hatch at a more advanced stage, have a smaller food requirement per unit weight and, being larger, would be capable of swimming more actively in search of food. Even though relatively large, the early post larva will only be large enough to feed extensively on the smallest components of the zooplankton. These food items, principally larval copepods, will be most abundant during the period immediately following the commencement of the summer phytoplankton bloom. Theoretically, therefore, the larval development needs to be synchronized in such a way that the larvae have utilized all their yolk reserves at about the same time as the copepod larvae are at their peak of abundance. Although the complete story has not been followed through in any one species, there is sufficient information to indicate that it is substantially correct.

Spawning dates are fairly well known for a reasonable number of species (Table VIII) although development rates have only been studied in a few. Information on the time from spawning to hatching is summarized in Table IX.

TABLE VIII
Egg size and spawning time for Antarctic fish

Spawning period	Egg size (mm)	Species
Spring (Nov–Dec)	2.5–3.5	*Trematomus bernacchii, T. hansoni*
Summer (Jan–Feb)	1	*Notothenia neglecta* (Terre Adélie) *N. magellanica*
Autumn (Mar–June)	2–4	*Notothenia nudifrons* (*N. augustifrons*) *N. neglecta* (Scotia arc) *N. rossii* *N. kempi* *N. gibberifrons* *N. larseni* (*Dissostichus mawsoni*) *Champsocephalus gunnari* *Chaenocephalus aceratus* *Pseudochaenichthys georgianus* *Chionodraco* sp. *Channichthys rhinoceratus*

From Hureau, 1966, 1970; Everson, 1970b; Permitin, 1973; Keysner *et al.*, 1974; Permitin and Sil'yanova, 1971.

Based on the known spawning dates it is possible to determine a calendar of events (Fig. 9) in the early life history for two species, *Harpagifer bispinis* and *Notothenia neglecta*, which fits well with the cycles of primary production and thus the production of copepod larvae as food (Daniels, 1979; North and Burchett, personal communication). These two examples probably indicate the norm as far as the majority of Nototheniiformes is concerned. This in turn indicates that the spawning dates are geared to producing larvae in time for the primary production bloom, rather than being dependent on the time of the year that is most favourable for adult fish to complete the final maturation of their gonads.

TABLE IX
Time from spawning to hatching for Antarctic fish

Species	Locality	Time of spawning–hatching (days)	Reference
Harpagifer bispinis	Arthur Harbour	56–126	Daniels, 1979
Notothenia neglecta	Signy Island	175	Twelves, 1972
N. neglecta	Signy Island	130	Jones, 1978

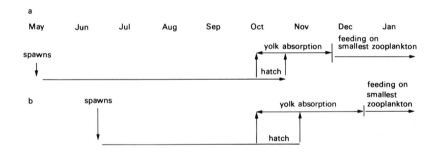

Fig. 9. Schematic representation of egg and larval development in two Antarctic fish: (a) *Notothenia neglecta* and (b) *Harpagifer bispinis*.

2.3 Food

The diet of most of the nototheniids that have been studied can best be described as catholic. Amphipoda, one of the dominant invertebrate groups, are abundant in the nearshore benthos throughout the year and naturally these figure largely in the diet of many species. In an analysis of the stomach contents of four species of fish at Signy Island, Richardson (1975) identified 26 species of amphipod, which probably include most of the species commonly present in the area in which he was working. Few studies have been as exhaustive as Richardson's in identifying prey species, but my own observations tend to indicate that predation on other suitable groups is no less comprehensive.

A complete list of species would be inappropriate in this chapter due to

TABLE X
Diet of Antarctic fish

	Authority	Locality	Fish	Salps	Mysidacea	Euphausia	Parathemisto	Cnidaria/Ctenophora	Other benthos	Echinodermata	Other Crustacea	Decapoda	Isopoda	Amphipoda	Cephalopoda	Bivalvia	Gastropoda	Polychaeta	Algae
Raja georgianus	(1)	SG	16		24	10		1		1	1	18	3	6	2			10	
Notothenia gibberifrons	(1)	SG	1.5	x	5	11	1.5	8	1	6		3	9	10	2	3		29	x
N. rossii marmorata	(3)	SG	3		1	4	1.5	82											
N. rossii marmorata	(3)	SG	3	1	8	80	3	3											
juvenile	(4)	SG	/	/	/	//					/								
adult	(4)	SG		/			/	/		/	/	/	/	/					
N. rossii rossii	(5)	K		/	/	/	/	/		/	/	/	/						
juvenile	(6)	K	38			6						6	51	10		x	1	6	18
N. magellanica	(6)	K	16								4	24	40	19		19	8	3	34
N. magellanica	(7)	O				//													
Dissostichus mawsoni	(8)	O	/												//				
Dissostichus eleginoides	(1)	SG	84		7	1						7			/				
Champsocephalus sp.	(1)	SG	3		30	38	24			1							x		
Champsocephalus sp.	(4)	SG				//	xx	x						x					
Pseudochaenichthys sp.	(1)	SG	40		2	48				x		10							
Chaenocephalus sp.	(1)	SG	15		48	11													
Chaenocephalus sp.	(9)	SG	//											/					
Pleuragramma sp.	(10)	O				//								/					
Micromesistius sp.		SO				//													

	Authority	Locality	Fish	Salps	Mysidacea	Euphausia	Parathemisto	Cnidaria/Ctenophora	Other benthos	Echinodermata	Other Crustacea	Decapoda	Isopoda	Amphipoda	Cephalopoda	Bivalvia	Gastropoda	Polychaeta	Algae
Muraenolepis microps	(1)	SG	8		12	4	1			3		1	27	14	13				7
Notothenia kempi	(1)	SG	4	4	4	17	6	8		3	2	2	3	11	16		1	13	
Notothenia larseni	(1)	SG	1		5	31	31			<1			1	11			1		
Notothenia nudifrons	(1)	SG	1	1	1	24				2			3	11	31			27	27
Notothenia gibberifrons 0–50 m	(12)	P							8					36	76	23	9	46	
N. gibberifrons 51–100 m	(12)	P				3			6					32	61	24	13	59	
N. gibberifrons 100–150 m	(12)	P				4			33					4	48	23	8	56	
N. gibberifrons 150–200 m	(12)	P							32						9	57			42
Notothenia bernacchii	(6)	TA				5			4					19	27		28	15	2
Trematomus hansoni	(6)	TA				45			12					7	14		5	17	1
Notothenia cyanobrancha	(6)	K	2						1			9		54	29		7	7	7
Notothenia macrocephala	(6)	K										3		30	18		1	43	2
Trematomus newnesi <8 cm	(13)	SO						80							70	1	3	1	1
T. newnesi >8 cm	(13)	SO						25							90			3	5
Harpagifer bispinis	(13)	SO						7						7	90			7	
Notothenia neglecta	(6)	TA	7						1					17	56		11	3	5
N. neglecta summer	(2)	SO	8			2								73	100	36	31	25	67
N. neglecta winter	(2)	SO	17	2	3	18								46	88	22	11	15	13

Figures indicate the percentage frequency occurrence of a particular item.
/ = present, // = dominant item, x = present but unquantifiable.
Localities: SG, South Georgia; SO, South Orkney Islands; K, Îles Kerguelen; O, Oceanic; P, Antarctic Peninsula; TA, Terre Adélie.
Authorities: (1) Permitin and Tarverdiyeva, 1972; (2) Everson, unpublished results; (3) Tarverdiyeva, 1972; (4) Olsen, 1954; (5) Keysner *et al.*, 1974; (6) Hureau, 1970; (7) DeWitt, 1971; (8) Yukhov, 1971; (9) Olsen, 1955; (10) DeWitt and Hopkins, 1977; (11) Permitin, 1969; (12) Moreno and Osorio, 1977; (13) Richardson, 1975.

the differing emphasis placed on the identification within the groups, but the following major groups figure prominently in the diet of many species: Algae, Bivalvia, Gastropoda, Amphipoda, Isopoda, Mysidacea, Euphausiacea, Polychaeta, Pisces. A résumé of dietary data is set out in Table X.

Algae form an unusually large component in the diet of several species, e.g. in *Notothenia neglecta* at both Terre Adélie and Signy Island (Arnaud and Hureau, 1966; Everson, 1977a) and indicates a feeding strategy that includes several seaweeds.

The molluscs form a significant component in the diet in most of the areas studied although it is interesting that bivalves are taken hardly at all in the Terre Adélie region. This probably reflects the major species composition in the benthos of the higher latitudes, because where bivalves are abundant (e.g. *Yoldia*, *Laternula* at Signy and *Gaimardia* at Kerguelen) they are frequently eaten (Permitin and Tarverdiyeva, 1972; Richardson, 1975; Hureau, 1970; Everson, 1977a). The wholly demersal species, such as *Notothenia gibberifrons*, as well as feeding on molluscs and crustacea, also eat large numbers of polychaetes such as *Neanthes*, *Aglaophamus* and *Scoloplos*.

Although most species are demersal in habit they do feed opportunistically on pelagic prey and this probably accounts for the occasionally high incidence of mysids and euphausiids in the samples. Permitin and Tarverdiyeva (1972) derived an "index of food similarity" for some of the dominant species near to South Georgia and from their analysis and the results they give in support several feeding groups are recognizable. These are:

(a) Fish and krill feeders. Examples are *Dissostichus eleginoides* and *Pseudochaenichthys georgianus*.

(b) Mainly plankton feeders. The dominant prey species for this group are *Euphausia superba*, *Parathemisto* and Mysidacae. Examples are *Notothenia larseni*, adult *N. rossii* and *Champsocephalus gunnari*.

(c) Nectobenthos. The dominant prey for this group are benthic crustacea although fish, krill and mysids are taken opportunistically. Examples are *Raja georgianus*, *Chaenocephalus aceratus* and juvenile *N. rossii*.

(d) Benthos. The dominant prey for this group are Polychaetes, Amphipoda, Isopoda and Mollusca. Examples are *N. gibberifrons*, *N. kempi* and *N. nudifrons*.

Most of the fish that Permitin and Tarverdiyeva studied are more or less restricted to the shelf area and it is an interesting point that large concentrations of feeding fish are rarely, if at all, found in the open ocean. The Antarctic silverfish, *Pleuragramma antarcticum*, although commonly present in high latitudes, never seems to be as abundant as its main food type, krill (DeWitt and Hopkins, 1977), suggests it could be. The same is true of the myctophids which although widespread are rarely caught in great numbers. This may be an indication of the lack of diversification by the fish of the region. If true, it would be surprising in view of the fact that many species feed on krill extensively in the shelf area. Alternatively, it could be an indication that krill are found most abundantly in the shelf areas of the continent and its surrounding islands.

2.4 Annual cycles

Mention has already been made of the annual cycle in the gonads of certain species of Antarctic fish, but there are several additional cycles which are equally recognizable and which warrant consideration.

Earlier in this chapter we saw how an approximately cubic relationship existed between the weight and the length of individual fish and this feature is often used by fish population analysts to derive a condition factor. For Antarctic fish a convenient general formula is:

$$\text{condition factor } C = 100 \times \text{weight}/(\text{length})^3$$

because this generally gives values of 1–5. Hureau (1970) determined this factor for six species of Antarctic fish and although he found that generally C decreased with increasing age (the exceptions were *Notothenia hansoni* and male *N. bernacchii*), there was no recognizable seasonal cycle in addition to that imposed by the gonad cycle. For *Notothenia neglecta* at Signy Island, however, there does appear to be a marked seasonal cycle (Fig. 10) which, although obviously affected by the gonad cycle, does have some interesting characteristics of its own.

During the months prior to spawning C reaches a peak which then declines to a post-spawning low level. In females the peak is interrupted by a decline in April (equally marked in each year of the study) that is probably related to the final maturation of the ovaries. There is a slight increase during the middle of winter, which would indicate that the fish are feeding, although in the spring there is a further decline before the increase in the summer prior to spawning.

There are two further factors that might also bear some relationship to the condition factor. These are the feeding cycle and those cycles associated with energy stores. Furthermore, if a feeding cycle is implicated as having some correlation with the condition factor, then this in turn might have some correlation with seasonal cycles of activity.

Hureau (1970) noted the strong correlation between the gonad cycle and the liver index cycle (liver index = 100 × liver weight/total weight) in all of

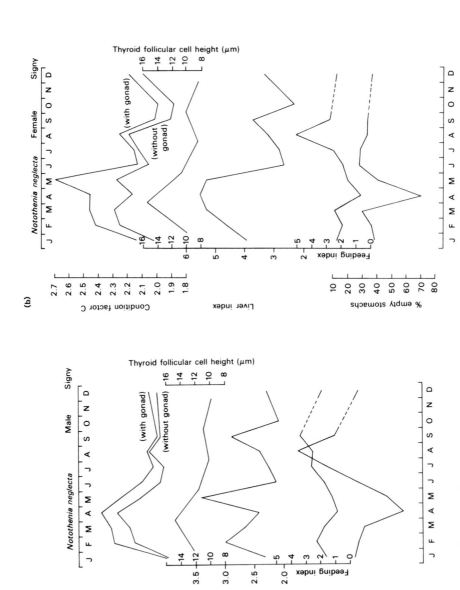

Fig. 10. Some seasonal cycles in *Notothenia neglecta*. (a) male and (b) female. Liver index = 100 × liver weight/(total weight−gonad); Feeding index = 100 × food weight/total weight.

the six species that he studied. Interestingly, *Notothenia neglecta* at Terre Adélie has a peak in the liver index one month prior to spawning in female fish and during the month of spawning for males. The same pattern is present for this species at Signy Island although the cycle immediately prior to the peak is quite different for the two sexes. During the months leading up to spawning there is a progressive decline in the male liver index which is linked to a progressive decline in feeding activity (as measured by the proportion of fish stomachs examined that contained food) (Fig. 10). In female fish there is a progressive increase in liver index to a peak one month prior to spawning. Neither sex feeds very much prior to spawning and this, with the probable translocation of energy stores from the liver to the ovary in the females, is responsible for the post-spawning minimum. During the winter months there is an increase in feeding activity which is marked by an increase in the liver index until October, at which time there is another minimum. This spring minimum is almost certainly associated with feeding activity in some way, although the proportion of stomachs containing food is quite high. A change in feeding activity at this time has been suggested by Everson (1970) based on the average size (which reached a minimum in the same month at all sampling stations) and the proportion of mature fish in the catch. This minimum was thought to be associated with the return to the inshore waters of Weddell and elephant seals, both of which eat large fish.

Although it is not possible to rigorously compare the situation in *N. neglecta* with the species that Hureau studied, his conclusions and the results he presents indicate an essentially similar pattern in the months leading up to spawning. The spring minimum in *N. neglecta* may well have its analogue in other species, but the timing and extent of this will depend very much on the predators involved, their presence and cycles of activity.

A further annual cycle has been detected by Twelves *et al.* (1975), who studied the thyroid gland of *Notothenia neglecta*. They found that the maximum thyroid activity occurred during the summer (sea temperature greater than $-0.4°C$) and that this was significantly higher than during the winter (sea temperature less than $-1.5°C$). They found that although the cycle of thyroid activity followed that of gonad size fairly closely, there was no significant correlation between the mean follicular cell height and the relative gonad size of individual fish, which suggests that the two are independent. Various authors have detected correlations between thyroid activity and growth as well as temperature and metabolism (see reviews by Love, 1970; Simpson, 1978; Donaldson *et al.*, 1979). Twelves *et al.* (1975) detected significant seasonal differences in the follicular cell height of *Notothenia neglecta* thyroids which they related to temperature. Furthermore, their data follow reasonably closely those for condition factor presented here (Table XI).

TABLE XI

Condition factor and thyroid activity in sexually mature *Notothenia neglecta* at Signy Island

Month	Male		Female	
	Condition factor	Follicular cell height (μm)	Condition factor	Follicular cell height (μm)
Sept.–Oct.	2.06	9.85	1.90	10.2
Nov.–Dec.	2.06	8.92	2.09	8.48
Jan.–Feb.	2.12	—	2.16	10.00
Mar.–April	2.27	13.95	2.27	15.40
May–June	2.10	10.73	2.16	10.67
July–August	2·05	9·24	2·15	8·63

The correlation is very much closer for male than female fish. However, if the data for September/October are excluded from the calculation then the value of r for females is vastly improved (Table XII). The fact that the correlation coefficient for females can be improved if the spring data are excluded is of interest, particularly as we have already seen that at this time of year there is some interruption in the feeding and liver index rhythms. If the liver index is compared with the follicular cell height then the situation is quite different, because the significant correlation here is only with the female fish and although we can improve the male correlation coefficient by excluding data from March/April it is still not significant even at the 10% level.

TABLE XII

Correlation coefficients (r) for the relationships between follicular cell height and condition factor and FCH and liver index in *Notothenia neglecta* at Signy Island

Follicular cell height	Condition factor	Liver index
Male	0·982 ($N = 5$)	0·142 ($N = 5$) (0·742)[b] ($N = 4$)
Female	0·509 ($N = 6$) (0·948)[a] ($N = 5$)	0·855 ($N = 6$)

[a]Excludes September–October values; [b]excludes March–April values.

These results tend to indicate that although there are, as one would expect, great similarities between these annual cycles in the two sexes there are major differences associated with the reproductive cycle. A tentative explanation follows. During the summer months final maturation of the gonads occurs; this requires greater mobilization of food reserves for females than males and hence at this time the liver would be most active. The level of activity would be influenced to a large extent by thyroid hormone. During the spring the maturation of ova has already begun and this would be via the liver supplying energy. Male fish have no such constraints on their metabolic activity so that one could assume that energy may be stored in the musculature rather than in the liver.

Clearly these conclusions are very speculative, but they do indicate a possible series of interactions. However, they relate only to one species, *Notothenia neglecta* at Signy Island and there is obviously much scope for further studies of the rates and mechanisms of energy transfer in other species.

3. Adaptations

Two important characteristics of the Antarctic marine environment are a narrow seasonal range of variation in temperature and a temperature itself near to or at the freezing point of sea-water. In one respect the relative stability of the thermal environment has permitted the Antarctic fish to evolve in such a way that their whole metabolism is most efficient at low temperature but they have had to compensate by evolving systems to prevent freezing. Various workers have considered the effects and adaptations resulting from this, such as stenothermy, freezing resistance, metabolic adaptation and white bloodedness in Channichthyids and these are described here.

3.1 Stenothermy

A direct result of the continuously low environmental temperature to which Antarctic fish are exposed has been the development of extreme stenothermy. Examples of incipient lethal temperatures are given in Table XIII and these indicate a high degree of cold stenothermy. Furthermore, even after prolonged periods of acclimation the upper and lower lethal temperatures are not altered (DeVries, 1978).

3.2 Freezing avoidance

Sea-water has a freezing point of about $-1.8°C$, the precise freezing point depending almost entirely on the salinity—the higher the salinity, the lower the freezing point. Most marine invertebrates have body fluids which contain as much as, if not more, dissolved salts than the surrounding medium; thus, under normal circumstances, freezing will present no problem to them. Fish on the other hand have much more dilute body fluids and their salt concentra-

TABLE XIII

Seasonal thermal tolerances of two Antarctic fish

Species	Water temperature and/or thermal history (°C)	Incipient lethal temperature (°C)	
		lower	upper
Rhigophila dearborni	−1·5 acclimated to +4	−1·9 −1·4	+7 +8
Pagothenia borchgrevinki	−1·9 acclimated to +4	−2·0 −1·9	+7 +8

tion can only be responsible for depressing the freezing point to about −0.7°C. Since temperatures lower than this occur in most seasons over much of the Southern Ocean, the fish must clearly have some additional adaptation to avoid freezing. There are two possibilities: either they can maintain their body temperature at about that of the environment by minimizing metabolic heat loss or they can develop an "antifreeze". The body temperature of Antarctic fish follows fairly closely that of the environment (Smith, 1972), indicating that control of metabolic heat loss is not the main method used.

In spite of the fact that Antarctic fish have only slightly more sodium and chloride ions in their blood than temperate fish, their blood freezing point is still higher than the freezing point of sea-water, the difference being far more than can be explained solely by the differences in salt concentrations. During the past decade a series of macromolecules have been identified which possess unique antifreeze properties. These antifreezes act in non-colligative manner by lowering the freezing point without affecting the melting point. Their structure is relatively simple, being composed of repeating groups involving the amino acids Alanine and Threonine and the sugars Galactose and *N*-acetyl galactosamine (DeVries, 1978).

It is not precisely clear how these antifreezes function but it is speculated that by binding to the ice surface they restrict further ice formation to regions of high curvature (Lin *et al.*, 1976; Raymond and DeVries, 1976), which in turn can only occur at lower temperatures (DeVries, 1978), thus depressing the freezing point.

3.3 Metabolic adaptation

The consistently low environmental temperatures present in the Southern Ocean mean that rates of biochemical reactions will be much lower than they would be in temperate regions. In spite of this Antarctic fish are still sufficiently active to live, grow and reproduce, totally within the Antarctic zone.

Adaptation at the tissue level has been found for several species (Lin *et al.*, 1974; Somero *et al.*, 1968) and also in terms of direct enzyme activity (Somero, 1969; Johnston and Walesby, 1977). These results show that at low environmental temperatures enzymes from Antarctic fish are more efficient catalysts than those from temperate waters.

At the whole-animal level elevated oxygen uptake rates have been thought of as being indicative of cold adaptation (Wohlschlag, 1964), although Holeton (1974) considers these rates are probably an artefact of the experimental technique (fish from low temperature environments take longer to achieve a steady resting level than warm-water fish). Bearing in mind that any evolutionary change of this type is unlikely to occur solely in those enzyme systems associated with activity and not those affecting other ecological aspects, Everson (1977a) looked at growth-rate in relation to warm-water fish. In general, growth rates are slow (see section 2.1), indicating little by way of adaptation, at least in comparison with the elevated respiratory levels reported by Wohlschlag.

The fact that adaptation at the enzyme level has been clearly demonstrated indicates that some tangible form of adaptation should be manifested at the whole animal level. However, a time comparison can only be made by examining both growth and metabolism under controlled conditions. Under such conditions it is not unreasonable to expect that growth and metabolism of Antarctic fish, when measured at low temperatures, will be higher than those of ecologically similar temperate-water fish. Since growth rates in Antarctic fish are by and large slow, any difference should only be very slight and thus not at all easy to demonstrate convincingly.

3.4 White bloodedness

There has been a great deal of interest in the respiratory physiology of Antarctic fish ever since it was firmly established by Matthews (1931) and Ruud (1954, 1965) that the Channichthyidae have no haemoglobin or any respiratory pigment in their blood. Several workers have examined the blood of other Antarctic fish and they have drawn attention to the lower concentrations of haemoglobin and the reduced numbers of erythrocytes present compared with fish from tropical and temperate waters. In general, haemoglobin concentrations for Antarctic fish fall within the range 4–6 g 100 ml^{-1} blood as compared to 7–12 g 100 ml^{-1} for normal teleosts. Similarly, erythrocyte counts generally fall within the range 0.5–1.0×10^6 mm^{-3} blood as compared to 1–2×10^6 mm^{-3} for most other teleosts (Tyler, 1960; Kooyman, 1963; Hureau, 1966; Everson and Ralph, 1968). A notable exception, for which unfortunately there is very little information, is *Parachaenichthys georgianus*, which Everson and Ralph (1968) found to have very low haemoglobin concentration and erythrocyte counts, although more recent results from a sample of five fish showed erythrocyte counts to be 501 ± 45, haemoglobin concentration 1.93 ± 0.66 and packed cell volume $33\% \pm 11$ (Everson, unpublished results).

Against this background of information, several physiologists have studied the Channichthyidae in order to determine how they extract sufficient oxygen from the water and transport it around their bodies. The problems may be considered under the following main headings:

(a) How does the overall oxygen uptake rate compare with other Antarctic fish?
(b) How is the oxygen extracted from the water?
(c) How is it transported around the body?
(d) What, if any, restrictions are forced on the Channichthyidae by their unique oxygen uptake system?

Estimates of oxygen uptake rate with respect to weight have been made by several workers. Bearing in mind the difficulties in comparing oxygen uptake rates between species (see Section 3) the general conclusion is that the oxygen uptake rate for Channichthyids is about the same as or only slightly lower than that for red-blooded fish (Scholander *et al.*, 1953; Wohlschlag, 1960, 1962, 1964; Ralph and Everson, 1968; Hemmingsen *et al.*, 1969; Holeton, 1970; Hemmingsen and Douglas, 1970, 1977). To explain this it is necessary to invoke some major modifications to the normal red-blooded fish's oxygen system.

The major site for gaseous exchange in fish is typically the gills but since Channichthyids do not possess scales it has been suggested that cutaneous respiration may be a significant process. Hemmingsen and Douglas (1970) did obtain some estimates for oxygen uptake rate through the skin over the main part of the body. They estimated that the skin was responsible for 2.8–3% of the total oxygen uptake. Holeton (1975) has pointed out that if Channichthyids maintained isometric proportioning as they grew then an exponent b of 0.67 in the relationship:

$$\text{surface area} = a \times \text{weight}^b$$

would be expected. In terms of skin surface area this exponent is 0.58 whereas for gill surface area it is 1.06. He therefore concludes that the effect of cutaneous respiration declines with increasing size, and since Channichthyids are some of the largest fish in the Antarctic this pathway cannot be the dominant one. Holeton describes seven other features which support this conclusion. These are:

(1) The gills receive 100% of the cardiac output whereas the skin receives only a fraction.

(2) The gills receive venous blood of low PO_2, ensuring a high diffusion gradient between water and blood whereas the skin receives well-oxygenated arterial blood.

(3) The gills are highly organized structures with an efficient counter-current flow arrangement between blood and water.

(4) The gills are associated with a branchial pump which ensures convection of water over them.

(5) The blood-to-water distance is shorter in the gills than it is in the skin by at least an order of magnitude (Walvig, 1960; Steen and Berg, 1966) in the case of *Chaenocephalus aceratus*.

(6) Water passes on both sides of the secondary lamellae of the gills while it passes only one side of most of the skin capillaries.

(7) When the fish are hypoxic, they increase water convection over their gills (Hemmingsen *et al.*, 1969; Hemmingsen and Douglas, 1970; Holeton, 1970).

It is quite clear therefore that cutaneous respiration can only be of secondary importance to the Channichthyidae.

Having concluded that the gills are the major site for gaseous interchange, we must now look for adaptations there. Estimates of the absorptive area of the gills have been made, which indicate that the absorptive area per unit body weight is not significantly different in Channichthyids as compared with red-blooded Antarctic fish, or the Arctic char (*Salvelinus alpinus*) (Hughes, 1966; Steen and Berg, 1966; Holeton, 1975; Jakubowski and Byczkowska-Smyk, 1970). Although the absorptive surface is no greater in Channichthyids, the bore of the blood vessels in the gills has been found to be significantly greater in all species examined with the exception of *Champsocephalus esox* (Steen and Berg, 1966; Jakubowski and Byczkowska-Smyk, 1970). This increase in size almost certainly reduces the vascular resistance to blood flow (Holeton, 1970).

It is known that generally at low temperature haemoglobin typically becomes less efficient, although there is a significant level of low temperature adaptation in Antarctic fish haemoglobin (Grigg, 1967). The result of this is that the oxygen-carrying capacity of the blood of red-blooded Antarctic fish is about nine times that of Channichthyids (Holeton, 1970). Clearly, since Channichthyids and red-blooded fish extract oxygen from the water at roughly similar rates, the former will need to pump blood at a very much faster rate. Knowing the oxygen uptake rate, the oxygen tension in afferent and efferent blood and the oxygen-carrying capacity of the blood, the gill blood flow (cardiac output) may be calculated from the Fick principle. Everson and Ralph (1970) estimated cardiac output for *Chaenocephalus aceratus* to be about ten times that of an equivalent-sized cod, whilst Holeton (1970) found a several-fold difference between this species and red-blooded fish from the same locality.

Pumping blood at a faster rate can be achieved by increasing the heart rate (beats min^{-1}) or the stroke volume or both. Holeton (1970) has demonstrated that the resting heart rate is essentially the same for *C. aceratus*, *Notothenia gibberifrons*, *N. neglecta* and *Parachaenichthys charcoti*, indicating that the compensation must be by increasing the stroke volume and therefore the size of the heart. Assuming that ventricle weight is a reasonable index of heart size, the Channichthyids have been shown to have hearts approximately three times the size of those in comparably-sized red-blooded fish (Everson and Ralph, 1970; Twelves, 1972; Holeton, 1975). Using the product of ventricle weight and resting heart rate to give a measure of resting cardiac output Holeton (1970) estimated that *Chaenocephalus aceratus* pumps three to four times as much blood as red-blooded Antarctic fish. However, since the blood oxygen capacity is only about one-tenth that in red-blooded fish, the actual amount of oxygen transported is much less in the Channichthyidae. Based on his observation that *C. aceratus* utilizes 63% of the oxygen-carrying capacity of its blood when at rest, Holeton (1970) calculated that *Notothenia gibberifrons* would use only 25%, *N. neglecta* 21% and *Parachaenichthys charcoti* 33% under similar conditions. Such a difference, Holeton points out, may facilitate diffusion by ensuring a high blood-to-tissue PO_2 gradient; this is less important for red-blooded fish because of the Bohr and Root effects of haemoglobin.

An increased heart size in Channichthyidae necessarily requires a larger blood volume in order to maintain a sufficient reservoir for the heart to pump. This suggestion has been confirmed by Hemmingsen and Douglas (1970) and Twelves (1972) who estimated the blood volume to be 7.6–9.2% of the body size, significantly more than that of typical teleosts. The figure may, however, be somewhat inflated because, as Holeton (1975) points out, the body musculature is less than in most teleosts, thus giving a lower weight per unit length.

Although from the point of view of oxygen transport the lack of haemoglobin can be considered disadvantageous, the greatly reduced number of formed elements in the blood does mean that the viscosity is reduced. Although it is not easy to estimate the viscosity (more practically the resistance to flow in capillaries) of blood because of the presence of the formed elements and the flexibility of the vessels, experiments do suggest an approximately two-fold difference in favour of Channichthyids (Hemmingsen and Douglas, 1970; Twelves, 1972).

Resistance to flow is a function of capillary diameter as well as viscosity. The Poiseuille equation states that resistance to laminar flow in tubes varies as the fourth power of their radius. The average capillary diameter of

Channichthys rugosus is 17 μm while for other red-blooded fish the diameter is 10 μm; this would provide an approximately eight-fold difference. Thus the energy costs per unit volume of blood pumped must be much lower for the Channichthyid; however, due to its lower oxygen capacity, it must pump a larger volume of blood.

The Channichthyid circulatory system can therefore be described as one of large volume operating at low pressure and, because of the physical constraints of solubility of gases in liquids, the blood-to-tissue PO_2 gradient must be much higher than for red-blooded fish. The pumping system presumably has some significant advantages for Channichthyids over red-blooded fish, particularly in terms of energy. However, the low oxygen capacity of the blood does mean that the fish are intolerant of low ambient oxygen tensions. Cold waters, such as are characteristic of the Southern Ocean, can hold quite large amounts of oxygen and furthermore the percentage saturation is generally quite high. Under normal conditions therefore the low resistance to hypoxia of Channichthyids (Holeton, 1970) is probably no great physiological disadvantage. It does, however, suggest why the group is virtually restricted to the Southern Ocean.

4. Biomass and Production

Ecological research on Antarctic fish has been concentrated on a few selected species in limited areas and the result of this is that there is very little generalized information available. At Signy Island, Everson (1970a) estimated the biomass of *Notothenia neglecta*, the dominant species in shallow water, to be 194 kg ha^{-1} and the annual production to be about 0.34 g g^{-1}. In that study no account was taken of the other species present although some, such as *N. rossii* in shallow water and *N. gibberifrons* in deeper water, probably formed a significant component of the total fish biomass. These results therefore will only give an indication of the fish biomass and production in the nearshore environment. Wider-ranging surveys have certainly been carried out using commercial nets although little information has so far been published. Hureau (1980) estimated the standing stock of fish on the shelf area around Îles Kerguelen to be about 120,000 tonnes or about 24 kg ha^{-1}. This survey was undertaken using a small beam trawl which would almost certainly have missed most of the large fish (the exceptions being the rays which were sampled in some quantity), which would make the greatest contribution to the total biomass. It is also possible that the results are low as a result of the commercial fishing carried out in the area in the years prior to the survey.

Estimates of fish production have also been made by summing the estimated total food consumption of the major predators. The most recent results are summarized below:

Estimated consumption of fish in the Antarctic
(see Chapters 11, 12 and Laws, 1977)
(tonnes $\times 10^3$)

Whales	1129
Seals (1972, 1982)	6244, 8261
Birds	6750
	————
Total	15,554

No detailed specific breakdown is available for these consumption figures and it is impossible to subdivide the figures even into major habitat groups. Although pelagic fish do occur in the Southern Ocean and are frequently eaten by birds (the remains of myctophids have been found in shag colonies (Everson, unpublished)), they are probably unlikely to form a major part of the total. It is more likely that the total figure comprises mainly the dermersal species which are dominated by the nototheniiformes.

The demersal fish are, for the most part, restricted to the continental and island shelf areas which together cover an area of approximately 2.2 million km² (excluding ice shelves) (Everson, 1977b). The total consumption of fish if averaged over the whole shelf area is therefore about 7.1 tonnes km⁻². This approximate figure for production of fish is quite close to that derived for *N. neglecta* at Signy Island.

A further indication of fish production may be gained from an analysis of reported catches. Recently, FAO (1978) has produced a species breakdown of the major fish catches in the Southern Ocean taken in recent years and these are summarized in Tables XIV and XV. In an analysis of these catches Everson (1977b) considered that the greater part (and perhaps all) of the reported catch from area 48 was taken from the South Georgia area and similarly that the catch from area 58 was largely from Îles Kerguelen. Unfortunately, no information is available on fishing effort during this period and it is therefore impossible to estimate the biomass and production by anything but the simplest rule of thumb methods. From the observed fishing strategy around South Georgia it is likely that the very high fishing effort resulting from the activities of a large fleet of vessels from the U.S.S.R. removed the greater part of the standing stock. It is not unreasonable, therefore, to assume that the standing stock around South Georgia prior to that season was around 500,000 tonnes. Applying this value to the generalized equation proposed by Gulland (1970)

$$\text{yield} = 0.5 \times M \times \text{initial biomass}$$

where M is the natural mortality coefficient. Using a value of M of 0.36 based on the results of Everson (1970a) for *Notothenia neglecta* gives a yield estimate of 90,000 tonnes. This generalized equation assumes that fishing is for the most part aimed at mature fish.

TABLE XIV

The reported catches of fish (tonnes) in the Atlantic sector of the Southern Ocean (FAO Statistical Area 48). Data from FAO (1978, 1979)

Species	1970/ 1971	1971/ 1972	1972/ 1973	1973/ 1974	1974/ 1975	1975/ 1976	1976/ 1977	1977/ 1978
Notothenia rossii	403,100	11,800	—	—	—	11,400	8320	5143
N. gibberifrons	—	—	—	—	—	5100	3070	15,997
N. squamifrons	—	400	400	1600	300	500	5100	468
Dissostichus eleginoides	—	—	—	—	—	—	1656	922
Other Nototheniidae	—	—	—	—	—	—	4751	3004
Chaenocephalus aceratus	—	—	—	—	—	—	293	2277
Champsocephalus gunnari	5800	5200	2100	1000	—	22,400	109,603	154,312
Pseudochaenichthys georgianus	—	—	—	—	—	—	1608	13,674
Total	408,900	17,400	2500	2600	300	39,400	134,401	195,797

TABLE XV

The reported catches of fish (tonnes) in the Indian Ocean sector of the Southern Ocean (FAO Statistical Area 48). Data from FAO (1978, 1979)

Species	1970/ 1971	1971/ 1972	1972/ 1973	1973/ 1974	1974/ 1975	1975/ 1976	1976/ 1977	1977/ 1978
Notothenia rossii	149,700	37,400	2500	24,100	7800	4300	35,255	10,997
N. squamifrons	26,500	51,000	3100	29,400	6900	5300	20,600	12,796
Pleuragramma antarcticum	—	—	—	—	—	—	—	234
Champsocephalus gunnari	49,900	15,700	7200	46,100	9900	7400	54,708	29,135
Channichthys rhinoceratus	—	—	—	—	—	—	—	82
Dissostichus eleginoides	—	—	—	—	—	—	—	201
Total	226,100	104,100	12,800	99,600	24,600	17,000	110,563	53,445

Everson (1970a) calculated that approximately one-third of the total production was attributable to sexually mature fish and if this factor is applied to the estimate of production based on consumption by predators the production by mature fish is 2.1 tonnes km^{-2} or 85,000 tonnes and this can be considered equivalent to the yield figure calculated above. These results are summarized in Table XVI.

TABLE XVI

Biomass and production estimates (tonnes) for the South Georgia fish stocks (Everson, 1977b)

Estimate	Estimate based on		
	Reported catch	*Notothenia neglecta*	Predator consumption
Standing stock	500,000	680,000	—
Total production	—	230,000	254,684
Production by mature fish	90,000	77,000	85,000

The closeness of these estimated values is no real indicator of precision since each has some quite large error factors which could make a large difference to the final figures. They are, however, a good indication of the situation at South Georgia and in the absence of more precise information do serve to give some indication of the potential size of the fishery.

5. Exploitation

In recent years there has been a steady increase in the total world fish catch to such an extent that many traditional fisheries are now at their maximum level. This has caused many nations with a deepwater fishing capability to look to new areas such as the Southern Ocean. Attention has focussed on the Southern Ocean initially because of krill, a potentially large resource, but because krill processing technology is still developing, the major effort has been aimed at fish. Thus, although finfish were probably not the most important long-term target for most fishing fleets, they have been very heavily fished.

A major problem in determining the magnitude of the Southern Ocean fish catch has been the fact that until recently fish caught in the Southern Ocean were included as "Unspecified Demersal Percomorphs" and referred to fishing areas to the north such as S. W. Atlantic Ocean (Everson, 1977b). When this situation was recognized, FAO redefined the boundaries of its reporting areas and requested a breakdown of catches by key species. As a result of this, information is now available for most areas for the past few years and these largely confirm the provisional estimates made by Everson (1977b). The catch figures by species are set out in Tables XIV and XV.

The greater part of the fishing effort has been concentrated in two regions, the Kerguelen area and the South Georgia area. The first area to be extensively fished was South Georgia when Soviet trawlers began operating there in the late 1960s. The catches have varied considerably from year to year with a very large peak during the 1970–1971 season. Two species have dominated the catches, *Notothenia rossii* and *Champsocephalus gunnari*, although their proportions in the total catches have changed with time such that early on *N. rossii* predominated whilst more recently *Champsocephalus* is the dominant species. This change is probably due to very heavy aimed fishing for *N. rossii* in the early years reducing the standing stock, thus causing the effort to be transferred to the other species. The difference may also have been due to the differing marketability of the respective species, although this seems very unlikely since the 403,100 tons of *N. rossii* taken in 1970–1971 must have represented a very high proportion of the initial standing stock.

The peak of fishing activity around Kerguelen occurred a year after that at South Georgia and although the initial catches contained a large proportion of *N. rossii* this declined to 20–30% from the 1972–1973 season onwards. The proportion of other species in the catches has also remained more or less stable from then onwards. This tends to mitigate against the suggestion of a change in consumer preference away from *N. rossii* mentioned above.

In addition to the Nototheniids and Channichthyids listed in Tables XIV and XV, small catches of southern blue whiting (*Micromesistius australis*) and Patagonian hake (*Merluccius hubbsii*) have been made in the Atlantic sector of the Southern Ocean. The fact that the reported catches are quite small indicates that any southward migration of these species from Patagonia is not very extensive since both would be as sought after as those forming the major components in the catch.

Hard data are not currently available to make firm predictions of what effect these levels of exploitation will have on the stocks. Some rough estimates were made by Everson (1977b) who considered that the MSY for South Georgia was probably about 50,000 tonnes year^{-1} and for Kerguelen something less than 80,000 tonnes year^{-1}. A further estimate for Kerguelen has been made by Hureau (1980) of 20,000 tonnes year^{-1}, although this is based on a survey using beam trawls, a biassed form of sampling gear. Considering these figures in relation to the reported catches clearly indicates that the catches are much larger than can be sustained. This in turn clearly indicates the need for more adequate control and better data on which to base management strategies (see also Chapter 15).

6. References

Adie, R. J. (1964). Geological history. In "Antarctic Research. A Review of British Scientific Achievement in Antarctica." (Sir Raymond Priestley, R. J. Adie and G. de Q. Robin, eds), pp. 118–162. Butterworths, London.

Anderson, N. C. and Hureau, J. C. (1979). Proposition pour une nouvelle classification des Nototheniidae (Pisces, Perciformes, Nototheniidae). Cybium 3e série, 6, 47–53.

Andriashev, A. P. (1965). A general review of the Antarctic fish fauna. In "Biogeography and Ecology in Antarctica" (J. van Mieghem and P. van Oye, eds), pp. 343–402. Junk, The Hague.

Andriashev, A. P., Butskaya, N. A. and Faleeva, T. I. (1979). Polovye tsikly antarkticheskikh ryb Trematomus bernacchii i Pagothenia borchgrevinki (Nototheniidae) v sviazi s adaptatsiei k usloviiam obitaniia. Doklady Akademii Nauk SSSR 248, No. 2, 499–502.

Arnaud, P. and Hureau, J.-C. (1966). Régime alimentaire de trois Téléostéens Nototheniidae antarctiques (Terre Adélie). Bulletin de l'Institut océanographique 66, 1–24.

Balushkin, A. V. (1976). A brief review of Nototheniidae (Notothenia and related genera). In "Zoogeografiya i Sistematika Ryb", pp. 118–134. Nauka, Leningrad.

Boulenger, G. A. (1902). Pisces. Report of the Collections of Natural History, Southern Cross Expedition, 174–189.

Ciechomski, J. D. de and Weiss, G. (1974). Distribution de huevos y larvas de merluzza, Merluccius merluccius hubbsi, en las aguas de la plateforma de la Argentina y Uruguay en relacion con la anchoita, Engraulis anchoita, y las condiciones ambientales. Physis 33A, 185–198.

Crisp, D. T. and Carrick, S. M. (1975). Some observations on the growth and length:weight relationship of the South Georgia cod Notothenia rossii marmorata Fischer during the first four years of life. Journal of Fish Biology 7, 407–409.

Daniels, R. A. (1979). Nest guard replacement in the Antarctic fish Harpagifer bispinis: possible altruistic behavior. Science 205, 831–833.

Dearborn, J. H. (1965). Reproduction in the Nototheniid fish Trematomus bernacchi Boulenger at McMurdo Sound, Antarctica. Copeia No. 3, 302–308.

DeVries, A. L. (1978). The physiology and biochemistry of low temperature adaptations in polar marine ectotherms. In "Polar Research. To the Present, and the Future" (M. A. McWhinnie, ed.), pp. 175–202. AAAS Selected Symposium No. 7. Westview Press, Boulder.

DeWitt, H. H. (1971). Coastal and deep-water benthic fishes of the Antarctic. Antarctic Map Folio Series (American Geographical Society) Folio 15, 10 pp.

DeWitt, H. H. and Hopkins, T. L. (1977). Aspects of the diet of the Antarctic silverfish, Pleuragramma antarcticum. In "Adaptations within Antarctic Ecosystems" (G. A. Llano, ed.), pp. 557–567. Smithsonian Institution, Washington, D.C.

Donaldson, E. M., Fagerlund, U. H. M., Higgs, D. A. and McBride, J. R. (1979). Hormonal enhancement of growth. In "Fish Physiology" (W. S. Hoar, D. J. Randall and J. R. Brett, eds), Vol. VIII, pp. 455–597. Academic Press, New York and London.

Dubrovskaya, T. A. and Makarov, O. E. (1969). Technochemical characteristics of fish from the Scotia Sea and their use of food. Trudy VNIRO 66, 311–317. National Lending Library Translation No. RTS 5597.

Everson, I. (1968). Larval stages of certain Antarctic fishes. *British Antarctic Survey Bulletin* No. 16, 65–70.

Everson, I. (1970a). The population dynamics and energy budget of *Notothenia neglecta* Nybelin at Signy Island, South Orkney Islands. *British Antarctic Survey Bulletin* No. 23, 25–50.

Everson, I. (1970b). Reproduction in *Notothenia neglecta* Nybelin. *British Antarctic Survey Bulletin* No. 23, 81–92.

Everson, I. (1977a). Antarctic marine secondary production and the phenomenon of cold adaptation. *Philosophical Transactions of the Royal Society* **B297**, 55–66.

Everson, I. (1977b). "The Living Resources of the Southern Ocean." Southern Ocean Fisheries Survey Programme GLO/SO/77/1. FAO, Rome.

Everson, I. (ed.) (1981). "Antarctic Fish Age Determination Methods", BIOMASS Handbook No. 8. Scientific Committee on Antarctic Research, Cambridge.

Everson, I. and Ralph, R. (1968). Blood analyses of some Antarctic fish. *British Antarctic Survey Bulletin* No. 15, 59–62.

Everson, I. and Ralph, R. (1970). Respiratory metabolism of *Chaenocephalus aceratus*. *In* "Antarctic Ecology" (M. W. Holdgate, ed.), Vol. I, pp. 315–319. Academic Press, London and New York.

FAO (1978). "Southern Ocean (Major Fishing Areas 48, 58, 88). Nominal Catches by Countries and Species, 1971–77", FAO Fisheries Circular no. 648, FIDI/C648. FAO, Rome.

FAO (1979). "Yearbook of Fishery Statistics, Vol. 46. Catches and Landings, 1978." FAO, Rome.

Freytag, G. (1980). Length, age and growth of *Notothenia rossii marmorata* Fischer 1885 in the west Antarctic waters. *Archiv fur Fischereiwissenschaft* **29**, 71–79.

Grigg, G. C. (1967). Some respiratory properties of the blood of four species of Antarctic fishes. *Comparative Biochemistry and Physiology* **23**, 139–148.

Gulland, J. A. (1970). Food chain studies and some problems in world fisheries. *In* "Marine Food Chains" (J. H. Steele, ed.), pp. 296–315.

Hart, T. J. (1946). Report on trawling surveys on the Patagonian continental shelf. *"Discovery" Reports* **23**, 226–408.

Hemmingsen, E. A. and Douglas, E. L. (1970). Respiratory characteristics of the hemoglobin-free fish *Chaenocephalus aceratus*. *Comparative Biochemistry and Physiology* **33**, 733–744.

Hemmingsen, E. A. and Douglas, E. L. (1977). Respiratory and circulatory adaptations to the absence of hemoglobin in chaenichthyid fishes. *In* "Adaptations within Antarctic Ecosystems" (G. A. Llano, ed.), pp. 479–487. Smithsonian Institution, Washington, D.C.

Hemmingsen, E. A., Douglas, E. L. and Grigg, G. C. (1969). Oxygen consumption in an Antarctic hemoglobin-free fish, *Pagetopsis macropterus*, and in three species of *Notothenia*. *Comparative Biochemistry and Physiology* **29**, 467–470.

Holeton, G. F. (1970). Oxygen uptake and circulation by a hemoglobinless antarctic fish (*Chaenocephalus aceratus* Lonnberg) compared with three red-blooded antarctic fish. *Comparative Biochemistry and Physiology* **34**, 457–471.

Holeton, G. F. (1974). Metabolic cold adaptation of polar fish: fact or artefact? *Physiological Zoology* **47**, 137–152.

Holeton, G. F. (1975). Respiration and morphometrics of hemoglobinless Antarctic icefish. *In* "Respiration of Marine Organisms" (J. J. Cech, D. W.

Bridges and D. B. Horton, eds), pp. 198–211. The Research Institute of the Gulf of Maine, South Portland.

Hughes, G. M. (1966). The dimensions of fish gills in relation to their function. *Journal of Experimental Biology* **45**, 177–195.

Hureau, J.-C. (1966). Biologie de *Chaenichthys rhinoceratus* Richardson, et problème du sang incolore des Chaenichthyidae, poissons des mers australes. *Bulletin de la Société zoologique de France* **91**, 735–751.

Hureau, J.-C. (1970). Biologie comparée de quelques poissons antarctiques (Nototheniidae). *Bulletin de l'Institut océanographique* **68**, 1–244.

Hureau, J.-C. (1980). La faune ichthyologique du secteur indien de l'océan antarctique et estimation du stock de poissons autour des îles Kerguelen. *Mémoires du Muséum national d'histoire naturelle* **43**, 235–247.

Jakubowski, M. and Byczkowska-Smyk, W. (1970). Respiratory surfaces of white-blooded fish *Chaenichthys rugosus* Regan (Perciformes). *Polskie Archiwum Hydrobiologii* **17**, 273–281.

Johnston, I. A. and Walesby, N. J. (1977). Molecular mechanisms of temperature adaptation in fish myofibrillar adenosine triphosphate. *Journal of Comparative Physiology* **119**, 195–206.

Jones, S. (1978). "Marine Assistant's Report. Fish Investigations." British Antarctic Survey unpublished report.

Keysner, E. E., Tot, V. S. and Shilov, V. N. (1974). Characteristics of the behaviour and biological cycles of the marbled Notothenia (*Notothenia rossii*) in relation to bottom topography, bottom materials and currents. *Journal of Ichthyology* **14**, 610–613.

Kock, K. H. (1979). On the fecundity of *Champsocephalus gunnari* Lonnberg 1905 and *Chaenocephalus aceratus* Lonnberg 1906 (Pisces, Channichthyidae) off South Georgia Island. *Meeresforschung* **27**, 177–185.

Kooyman, G. L. (1963). Erythrocytes analysis of some antarctic fishes. *Copeia* No. 2, 457–458.

Laws, R. M. (1977). Seals and whales of the Southern Ocean. *Philosophical Transactions of the Royal Society* **B279**, 81–96.

Lin, Y., Dobbs, G. H. and DeVries, A. L. (1974). Oxygen consumption and lipid content in red and white muscles of antarctic fish. *Journal of Experimental Zoology* **189**, 379–385.

Lin, Y., Raymond, J. A. and DeVries, A. L. (1976). Compartmentalization of NaCl in frozen solutions of antifreeze glycoproteins. *Cryobiology* **13**, 334–340.

Lonnberg, E. (1905). The fishes of the Swedish South Polar Expedition. *Wissenschaftliche Ergebnisse der Schwedischen Sudpolarexpedition, 1901–1903* (5 Zoology) **1**, 1–69.

Love, R. M. (1970). "The Chemical Biology of Fishes". Academic Press, London and New York.

Marshall, N. B. (1953). Egg size in arctic, antarctic and deep-sea fishes. *Evolution* **7**, 328–341.

Matthews, L. H. (1931). "South Georgia. The British Empire's Subantarctic Outpost", p. 36. Simpkin Marshall, London.

Moreno, C. A. and Osorio, H. H. (1977). Bathymetric food habits in the Antarctic fish, *Notothenia gibberifrons* Lonnberg (Pisces: Nototheniidae). *Hydrobiologia* **55**, 139–144.

Nichols, J. T. and Lamonte, F. R. (1936). *Pagothenia*, a new Antarctic genus. *American Museum Novitates* No. 839, 1–4.

Olsen, S. (1954). South Georgian cod (*Notothenia rossii marmorata* Fischer). *Norsk Hvalfangsttidende* **43**, 373–382.

Olsen, S. (1955). A contribution to the systematics and biology of Chaenichthyid fishes from South Georgia. *Nytt Magasin for Zoologi* **3**, 79–93.

Permitin, Yu. E. (1969). New data on the species composition and distribution of fishes in the Scotia Sea. *Journal of Ichthyology* **9**, 167–181.

Permitin, Yu. E. (1973). Fecundity and reproductive biology of icefish (Channichthyidae), fish of the family Muraenolepidae and dragonfish (Bathydraconidae) of the Scotia Sea (Antarctica). *Journal of Ichthyology* **13**, 204–215.

Permitin, Yu. E. and Sil'yanova, Z. S. (1971). New data on the reproductive biology and fecundity of fishes of the genus *Notothenia* (Richardson) in the Scotia Sea (Antarctica). *Journal of Ichthyology* **11**, 693–705.

Permitin, Yu. E. and Tarverdiyeva, M. I. (1972). Feeding of some species of Antarctic fishes in the South Georgia Island area. *Journal of Ichthyology* **12**, 104–114.

Ralph, R. and Everson, I. (1968). The respiratory metabolism of some antarctic fish. *Comparative Biochemistry and Physiology* **27**, 299–307.

Raymond, J. A. and DeVries, A. L. (1976). Bioluminescence in McMurdo Sound, Antarctica. *Limnology and Oceanography* **21**, 599–602.

Richardson, J. (1844). Description of a new genus of Gobioid fish. *Annual Magazine of Natural History* **13**, 461–462.

Richardson, M. G. (1975). The dietary composition of some antarctic fish. *British Antarctic Survey Bulletin* Nos 41/42, 113–120.

Ruud, J. T. (1954). Vertebrates without erythrocytes and blood pigment. *Nature* **173**, 848–850.

Ruud, J. T. (1965). The ice fish. *Scientific American* **213**, 108–114.

Scholander, P. F., Flagg, W., Walters, V. and Irving, L. (1953). Climatic adaptation in arctic and tropical poikilotherms. *Physiological Zoology* **26**, 67–92.

Shubnikov, D. A., Permitin, Yu. E. and Voznyak, S. P. (1969). Some data on the biology of poutassou *Micromesistius australis* Norman. *Trudy VNIRO* **66**, 299–306. [National Lending Library Translation RTS 5595.]

Simpson, T. H. (1978). An interpretation of some endocrine rhythms in fish. *In* "Rhythmic Activity of Fishes" (J. E. Thorpe, ed.), pp. 55–68. Academic Press, London and New York.

Smith, R. N. (1972). The freezing resistance of Antarctic fish: I. Serum composition and its relation to freezing resistance. *British Antarctic Survey Bulletin* No. 28, 1–10.

Somero, G. N. (1969). Enzyme mechanisms of temperature compensation: immediate and evolutionary effects of temperature on enzymes of aquatic poikilotherms. *American Naturalist* **103**, 517–530.

Somero, G. N., Giese, A. C. and Wohlschlag, D. E. (1968). Cold adaptation in the Antarctic fish *Trematomus bernacchii*. *Comparative Biochemistry and Physiology* **26**, 223–233.

Steen, J. B. and Berg, T. (1966). The gills of two species of haemoglobin-free fishes compared to those of other teleosts—with a note on severe anaemia in an eel. *Comparative Biochemistry and Physiology* **18**, 517–526.

Tarverdiyeva, M. I. (1972). Daily food consumption and feeding patterns of the South Georgia cod (*Notothenia rossii marmorata*) and the Patagonian toothfish (*Dissostichus eleginoides* Smitt) (fam. Nototheniidae) in the South Georgia area. *Journal of Ichthyology* **12**, 684–692.

Twelves, E. L. (1972). Blood volume of two Antarctic fishes. *British Antarctic Survey Bulletin* No. 31, 85–92.

Twelves, E. L., Everson, I. and Leith, I. (1975). Thyroid structure and function in two Antarctic fishes. *British Antarctic Survey Bulletin* No. 40, 7–14.

Tyler, J. C. (1960). Erythrocite counts and hemoglobin determinations for two antarctic Nototheniid fishes. *Stanford Ichthyological Bulletin* **7**, 199–201.

Walvig, F. (1960). The integument of the icefish *Chaenocephalus aceratus* (Loennberg). *Nytt Magasin for Zoologi* **6**, 111–120.

Weiss, G. (1974). Hallazgo y descripcion de larvas de la polaca *Micromesistius australis* en aguas del sector Patagonico Argentino (Pisces Gadidae). *Physis* **33A**, 537–542.

White, M. G. and North, A. W. (1979). Offshore Biological Programme: ichthyological data. *British Antarctic Survey Data* No. 2, 25 pp.

Wohlschlag, D. E. (1960). Metabolism of an antarctic fish and the phenomenon of cold adaptation. *Ecology* **41**, 287–291.

Wohlschlag, D. E. (1962). Antarctic fish growth and metabolic differences related to sex. *Ecology* **43**, 589–597.

Wohlschlag, D. E. (1964). Respiratory metabolism and ecological characteristics of some fishes in McMurdo Sound, Antarctica. *In* "Biology of the Antarctic Seas" (M. O. Lee, ed.). *Antarctic Research Series* **1**, pp. 33–62. American Geophysical Union, Washington, D.C.

Yukhov, V. L. (1971). The range of *Dissostichus mawsoni* Norman and some features of its biology. *Journal of Ichthyology* **11**, 8–18.

11

Seabirds

J. P. Croxall

1. Introduction

With the vast extent of ocean and small area of ice- and snow-free land in Antarctic and sub-Antarctic regions it is hardly surprising that nearly all the birds of these areas should be seabirds. Furthermore they chiefly belong to the two most marine-adapted of all groups, the procellariforms (albatrosses, petrels etc.) and penguins.

On a world basis for both groups the greatest diversity of species is to be found in the New Zealand area but many species and by far the greatest numerical concentrations occur in sub-Antarctic and Antarctic regions. The few other seabirds in these areas—shags *Phalacrocorax*, skuas *Catharacta*, terns *Sterna* and a gull *Larus*—are at most essentially inshore feeders and as, except for skuas, they have been rather little studied, only limited reference will be made to them in this account. Sheathbills *Chionis* spp. are excluded from consideration as even the inter-tidal element in their foraging does not really qualify them as seabirds. For recent research on *C. minor* and a review of work on *C. alba* see Burger (1979, 1980).

There have been several previous reviews of Antarctic seabirds which have emphasized particular groups or standpoints, e.g. taxonomy (Murphy, 1964; Voous, 1965), distribution (Watson *et al.*, 1971), role of climate (Stonehouse, 1964), petrels (Mougin, 1975), penguins (Stonehouse, 1967, 1975), comprehensive field guides (Prévost and Mougin, 1970; Watson, 1975) but perhaps the most useful ecologically were those of Carrick and Ingham (1967, 1970) where much general information is tabulated, and the principal studies that had taken place since Murphy's (1936) classic work noted. A recent review of taxonomic interrelationships within the Procellariiformes (Harper, 1978) contains much of relevance to Antarctic seabirds.

ANTARCTIC ECOLOGY VOL. 2
ISBN 0 12-439502-3

Even concentrating on ecological aspects and thus neglecting many behavioural and physiological studies, the literature is now so extensive that selective treatment is still essential. I shall therefore try to cover areas hitherto not extensively reviewed, with particular attention to research on trophic relations and population structure and dynamics. Nevertheless such work needs, and can only be fully appreciated on the basis of, a sound knowledge of species' breeding biology. Thus, after reviewing the species involved and their distribution patterns, I shall summarize briefly the main features of penguin and petrel breeding cycles with special reference, wherever possible, to work concluded since 1970. In general and for selected species these can then be evaluated with reference to food and feeding ecology and population structure and dynamics. Finally, energetic requirements and the possible level of impact of seabird populations on Antarctic marine living resources will be discussed.

With these selective aims, directed particularly to topics of considerable current interest, on many of which research has only recently been initiated, I am inevitably drawing extensively on the work that I know best, which is principally that in progress by British workers. There are, however, several other active seabird research programmes with similar aims, particularly involving South Africa at Marion Island (e.g. van Zinderen Bakker, 1971a; Williams *et al.*, 1975, 1979; Siegfried, 1978); France at Terre Adélie (recently mainly physiology and behaviour, e.g. Jouventin, 1971; Le Maho *et al.*, 1976; Guillotin and Jouventin, 1979) and at Îles Crozet (e.g. Despin *et al.*, 1972; Barrat *et al.*, 1976); Australia at Macquarie Island, U.S.A. and New Zealand in the Ross Sea (e.g. Ainley and DeMaster, 1980; Ainley *et al.*, 1983; Spurr, 1975, 1977; Young, 1981) and the U.S.A. in the Antarctic Peninsula area (e.g. Parmelee *et al.*, 1977; Trivelpiece and Volkman, 1979; Volkman *et al.*, 1981).

2. Zoogeography

2.1 Boundaries and species

Important sources of distributional data that have appeared since the tabulation by Carrick and Ingham (1970) are Watson *et al.* (1971), Prévost and Mougin (1970), Segonzac (1972), Despin *et al.* (1972), Barrat and Mougin (1974), Derenne *et al.* (1974, 1976b), Fevolden and Sømme (1978), Prince and Payne (1979), Warham and Bell (1979), Jones (1980) and Berruti *et al.* (1981).

The breeding seabirds of most islands and island groups relevant to this account are shown in Table I (most Latin names are in Appendix I). It is, however, difficult to define rigorously the species, and limits of the area, under consideration. In these latitudes it is usual to distinguish circumpolar life zones, principally based on climatological and oceanographical phenomena. These zones tend to be less well defined for seabirds which are frequently constrained, by the shortage of available breeding areas, to breed where they can, but are able to compensate by being often wide-ranging at sea. Two well defined zonal boundaries are the Antarctic Convergence (separating Antarctic and sub-Antarctic zones) and the northern limit of permanent pack ice, defining the limit of the cold Antarctic sub-zone. As a breeding bird only one species (Antarctic petrel) is entirely restricted to the latter sub-zone but a number of others (e.g. emperor penguin, Antarctic skua, Adélie penguin, snow petrel) have their greatest concentrations here, although also occurring on the Antarctic Peninsula. The latter, with its associated island groups, comprises the maritime Antarctic sub-zone and provides a bridge facilitating the intermingling along an essentially north–south axis, of Antarctic species and those more typical of the sub-Antarctic islands.

Local conditions, climatological, oceanographic and topographical, all influence the composition of the avifauna of the islands lying near the Antarctic Convergence. South Georgia and Heard Island (and Bouvetøya) are the only islands lying well south of this convergence but South Georgia being larger, with more varied topography and closer to a continental land mass, has several additional species more typical of islands at or north of the convergence such as Macquarie and Kerguelen. Both these islands and especially Kerguelen may have acquired species (notably *Pterodroma* spp.) from islands to their north but in spite of this Macquarie has a rather reduced species diversity although this may be the result of the elimination of some smaller seabirds by introduced mammalian predators.

The seabirds at the Prince Edward and Crozet Islands, which lie just to the north of the Convergence and close enough for the cold Antarctic sub-surface water to upwell against them, are essentially similar to those at Kerguelen. Other islands further north of the Antarctic Convergence are the Auckland and Campbell Islands and the Falkland Islands. These have some species whose presence reflects the islands' proximity to New Zealand and South America respectively but in general they lack some colder water species and also some of the warmer water species widespread in the Indian Ocean. The seabird situation in the New Zealand area is particularly complex but the avifauna of the Antipodes (and Bounty) Islands appears to resemble that of the Auckland and Campbell Islands rather than that of the Snares and Stewart Islands. These latter have closer links with the mainland and with the Chatham Islands, which lie very close to the Sub-tropical Convergence.

TABLE I

Breeding distribution of Antarctic and sub-Antarctic seabirds

	Antarctic Continent	Bouvet I.	Antarctic Peninsula	South Sandwich I.	South Orkney I.	South Shetland I.	Falkland I.	Campbell I.	Auckland I.	Antipodes I.	South Georgia	Heard I.	Macquarie I.	Kerguelen I.	Crozet I.	Prince Edward I.	Marion I.	Gough I.	Tristan da Cunha	St. Paul I.	Amsterdam I.
SPHENISCIFORMES																					
Aptenodytes forsteri*	+		+																		
Aptenodytes patagonicus*		+					+				+	+	+	+	+	+	+	+	+		
Pygoscelis adeliae*	+		+	+	+	+															
Pygoscelis papua*			+			+	+		+		+	+	+	+	+	+	+				
Pygoscelis antarctica*	+	+	+	+	+	+					+										
Eudyptes chrysocome*					(+)		+	+		+		+	+	+	+	+	+	+[a]	+	+[a]	+[a]
Eudyptes chrysolophus[b]*		+	(+)		+						+	+	+	+	+	+	+		+		
Eudyptes sclateri								+	+	+											
Megadyptes antipodes								+	+												
Spheniscus magellanicus							+														
PROCELLARIIFORMES																					
Diomedea exulans*									+	+	+		+	+	+	+	+				+[c]
Diomedea epomophora								+	+												
Diomedea melanophrys*							+	+	+	+	+	+	+	+	+	+	+				
Diomedea chrysostoma*								+		+	+		+	+	+	+	+				
Diomedea chlororhynchos*														+	+	+	+	+	+		+
Diomedea cauta									+												
Phoebetria fusca*														+	+	+	+	+	+		+
Phoebetria palpebrata*								+	+	+	+	+	+	+	+	+	+				
Macronectes giganteus*	+	+	+			+	+				+	+	+	+	+	+	+				
Macronectes halli*								+	+	+	+		+	+	+	+	+				
Thalassoica antarctica*	+		+																		
Daption capense*	+	+	+			+		+	+	+	+	+	+	+	+						
Fulmarus glacialoides*	+	+	+			+															
Pagodroma nivea*	+	+	+			+															
Pachyptila belcheri*							+							+	+						
Pachyptila desolata*				+					+	+	+	+	+	+	+	+	+				
Pachyptila vittata																		+	+		
Pachyptila salvini*															+	+	+				
Pachyptila crassirostris*									+			+									
Pachyptila turtur*							+	+	+				+	+	+	+	+	+	+		
Halobaena caerulea*											+		+	+	+	+	+				
Pterodroma macroptera*	(+)													+	+	+	+	+	+		(+)
Pterodroma lessoni*									+	+			+	+	+		+				

	Amsterdam I. / St. Paul I.	Gough I. / Tristan da Cunha	Marion I. / Prince Edward I.	Crozet I.	Kerguelen I.	Macquarie I.	Heard I.	South Georgia	Antipodes I.	Auckland I.	Campbell I.	Falkland I.	South Shetland I. / South Orkney I. / South Sandwich I.	Antarctic Peninsula	Bouvet I.	Antarctic Continent
Pterodroma brevirostris*	(+)	+ +	+ +	+ +	+ ~											
Pterodroma mollis*	(+)	+ +	+ +	+ +	+ +											
Pterodroma incerta		+ +														
Procellaria aequinoctialis*	(+)	+ +	+ +	+ +	+ +	(+)			+ + +	+ + + +	(+)	+				
Procellaria cinerea*	(+)	+ +	+ +	+ +	+ +	+			+ + +		(+)	+				
Puffinus griseus	+															
Puffinus carneipes	+															
Puffinus gravis		+ +										+				
Puffinus assimilis	+ ~	+ +														
Oceanites oceanicus*		+ +	+	+ +	+ +	+	+	+ +	+	+ +	+	+	+ +	+	+ +	+
Fregetta tropica*	+	+ +		+	+		+	+ +				+		+		
Fregetta grallaria	+	+ +	+	+		~						+				
Garrodia nereis*	(+)	+ +	+	+	+	~	+ +	+	+	+	(+)	+				
Pelagodroma marina		+ +	+	+	+	+				+						
Pelecanoides georgicus*	(+)	+ +	+ +	+	+ +		+ +	+ +	+	+ + +	+ +	+				
Pelecanoides urinatrix*	(+)	+	+ +	+ +	+ +	+	+	+	+	+	+	+				
PELECANIFORMES																
Phalacrocorax albiventer[d]*						+	+	+				+	+	+		
Phalacrocorax atriceps*							+			+		+	+	+		
Phalacrocorax magellanicus												+				
Phalacrocorax campbelli									+ +	+	+ +					
Phalacrocorax melanoleucos										+						
CHARADRIIFORMES																
Catharacta maccormicki*	+												+ +	+ +	+ +	+
Catharacta lonnbergi*		+	+ +	+ +	+ +	+ +	+ +	+ +	+ +	+ +	+ +	+ + +	+ + +	+ + +	+ ~	
Larus dominicanus*	+											+ +	+	+		
Larus maculipennis												+				
Larus novae-hollandiae										+	+					
Larus scoresbii												+				
Sterna fuscata	+															
Sterna vittata*	+	+	+	+ +	+ +	+	+	+	+	+	+	+	+	+	+	+
Sterna virgata*	+				+ +					+						
Sterna hirundinacea												+				
Anous stolidus		+														
Total	11	21	26	34	30	21	17	26	20	24	18	22	16	14	11	10

[a] Sometimes separated as E. moseleyi, [b] Includes E. schlegeli, [c] Described as D. amsterdamensis (Roux et al., 1983), [d] includes P. verrucosus, (+) probable or former breeding species, * species of chief interest (see p. 538).

St Paul and Amsterdam Islands in the Indian Ocean and Tristan da Cunha and Gough Island in the South Atlantic Ocean belong to the temperate sub-Antarctic zone, lie near the Sub-tropical Convergence and have some species with distinctly sub-tropical affinities.

In this chapter most attention will be given to species breeding in the Antarctic zone and at the islands near the Antarctic Convergence, (i.e. the seven penguins, six albatrosses, 18 petrels, three storm petrels, two diving petrels, the two shags and five Charadriiformes marked* in Table I). Data on species at the more northerly islands will chiefly be used for comparative purposes, especially where they assist interpretation of the adaptations shown by the more southerly distributed species.

Information on the breeding distribution of these seabirds has been used to derive indices of faunal similarity between the various island groups and on the basis of this a system of faunal provinces, super-provinces and sub-regions was developed (Barrat and Mougin, 1974). Such an approach is probably over-elaborate for an area where much of the breeding distribution reflects the sparsity of suitable locations, but the analysis does emphasize the quite marked differences between three basic groupings:

(a) the temperate sub-Antarctic islands (Tristan/Gough and Amsterdam/St Paul)
(b) Greater Antarctica and the Antarctic Peninsula
(c) the rest

Remaining relationships chiefly reflect geographical proximity but recent discoveries at South Georgia (Prince and Payne, 1979; Prince and Croxall, 1983) will have emphasized its affinities to the Indian Ocean sub-Antarctic islands and reduced its overall similarity to Heard Island.

2.2 Taxonomy and speciation

The philopatry of juvenile birds and the fidelity of seabirds to the same breeding site in successive seasons greatly reduces the amount of interchange between island populations of seabirds. This must have the effect of accentuating any differences that develop within populations. These are fairly well marked in prions (see later) but much less so in other seabirds, although there is a general lack of measurements from adequate samples of birds of similar status. Nevertheless, much greater geographical differentiation is recognizable on the basis of circum-Antarctic zones.

Zonal or latitudinal speciation has occurred in several genera resulting in distinct species or subspecies inhabiting different life zones. This is particularly marked in the temperate sub-Antarctic sub-zone which has distinct races of rockhopper penguin, wandering albatross, cape pigeon, white-chinned petrel and black-bellied storm petrel (Murphy, 1936; Watson, 1975). In more southerly-distributed species there are also well-marked (but probably fundamentally clinal) disjunctions in gentoo penguin (Stonehouse, 1970a) and Wilson's storm petrel (Roberts, 1940; Beck and Brown, 1972).

At the species level zonal differences have become somewhat obscured by both members of a species pair (each presumably evolved within a single zone) co-occurring at certain sub-Antarctic islands. The sooty albatrosses (Fig. 1) show a situation with only limited contact. In giant petrels (Fig. 2) this contact is more extensive (and further complicated by the uncertain status of populations at Gough Island and the Falkland Islands (Bourne and Warham, 1966; Johnstone et al., 1976; Devillers and Terschuren, 1980;

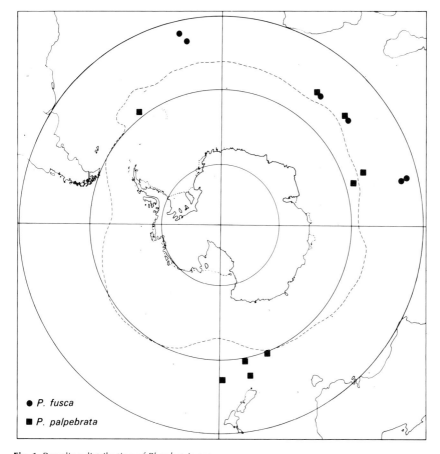

Fig. 1. Breeding distribution of *Phoebetria* spp.

Voisin and Bester, 1983) which may be worthy of taxonomic recognition at some level). The *Eudyptes* penguins (Fig. 3) and small *Diomedea* albatrosses (mollymauks) (Fig. 4) each show considerable local speciation in the New Zealand area and have a more northerly-distributed species (rockhopper penguin and yellow-nosed albatross) that has made some incursions further south. As Carrick and Ingham (1967) noted, the rarity of rockhopper penguin at South Georgia is surprising (as it and macaroni penguin co-occur abundantly elsewhere) and the reasons for the exact distribution pattern of the three widespread mollymauks are also unclear. The distinction between macaroni penguin and royal penguin (whether at species or subspecies level) is one of the few fairly clear-cut examples of geographically replacing taxa within a zone.

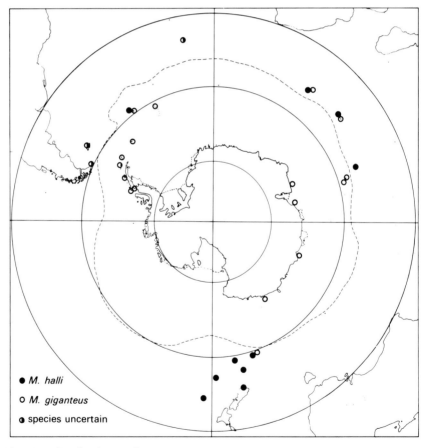

Fig. 2. Breeding distribution of *Macronectes* spp.

As Bourne (1968) first demonstrated, the diving petrels (Fig. 5) show an interesting combination of zonal differentiation at both species and subspecies level with the two widespread sub-Antarctic species being derived from different source populations which are zonally differentiated at the species level in the South America area but apparently only at the subspecies level in the New Zealand area.

Some groups, however, have more complex patterns of distribution and variation and have suffered a variety of taxonomic treatments. Recently Devillers (1977, 1978) has reviewed the southern skuas, reaffirming the essential distinctiveness of the Antarctic skua *Catharacta maccormicki* (although its most northerly populations hybridize with the brown skua *C. (s) lonnbergi* at various localities on the Antarctic Peninsula) from the

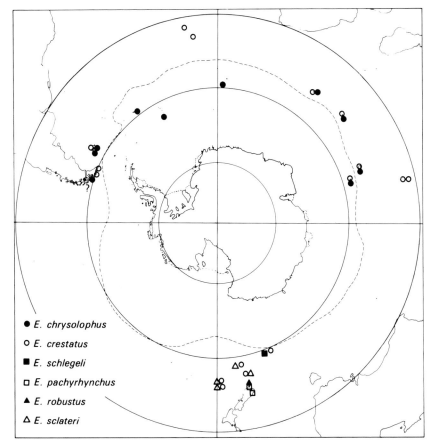

● *E. chrysolophus*

○ *E. crestatus*

■ *E. schlegeli*

□ *E. pachyrhynchus*

▲ *E. robustus*

△ *E. sclateri*

Fig. 3. Breeding distribution of *Eudyptes* spp.

more northerly taxa and suggesting that *C. (s) chilensis* is also worthy of specific rank. This leaves *C. (s) antarctica* of the Falkland Islands and south-east Argentina and *C. (s) lonnbergi* as subspecies of the northern hemisphere *C. skua*. Further study is needed, particularly of the *C. lonnbergi* assemblage, which is polymorphic and unlikely to be closely related to *C. skua*.

With the shags of the subgenus *Leucocarbo*, Devillers and Terschuren (1978) have suggested that *P. atriceps* blue-eyed shag should be united with *P. albiventer* king shag, but this does not tackle the central problem of the status of the several largely allopatric island populations of the two "species" especially in the Indian Ocean (see Voisin, 1970; Derenne *et al.*, 1974).

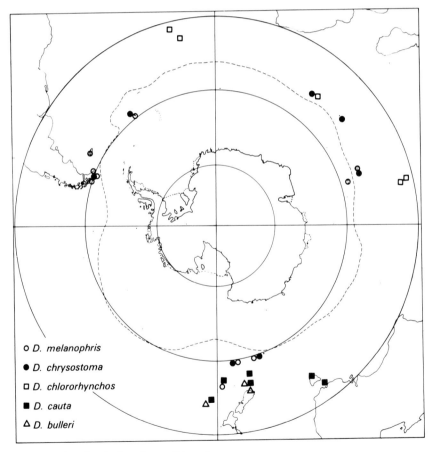

○ *D. melanophris*

● *D. chrysostoma*

□ *D. chlororhynchos*

■ *D. cauta*

△ *D. bulleri*

Fig. 4. Breeding distribution of some *Diomedea* spp.

The prions (Fig. 6) are a particularly complex group and a varying number of species (compare Cox, 1979; Harper, 1980) have been recognized. Not only have zonal and latitudinal diversification taken place, but nearly every island has morphometrically distinguishable populations, often belonging to at least two distinct lineages (often separated as the subgenera *Pseudoprion* and *Pachyptila*). It would seem that *P. vittata* and *P. salvini* are northerly and southerly vicariates of a basically north of the Antarctic Convergence taxon. *P. desolata* almost exclusively occurs south of the convergence with *P. belcheri* its northern replacement. Distinctions

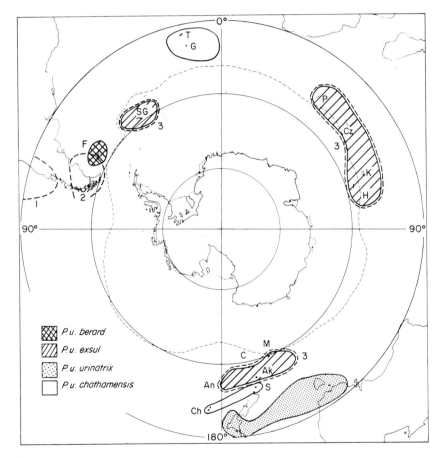

Fig. 5. Breeding distribution of *Pelecanoides* spp. (after Payne and Prince, 1979). Distribution of *P. urinatrix* taxa enclosed by solid lines. *P. garnoti:* ——1——, *P. magellani:* ——2——, *P. georgicus:* ——3——. Key: Ak, Auckland Islands; An, Antipodes; Ch, Chatham; Cz, Crozet; F, Falklands; G, Gough; H, Heard; K, Kerguelen; M, Macquarie; P, Prince Edward; S, Stewart; SG, South Georgia; T, Tristan da Cunha.

between *P. crassirostris* and *P. turtur* are still uncertain. There are already
indications of dietary (Harper, 1972; Imber, 1981), habitat and breeding
season differences between some taxa and ecological work, especially
where several taxa coexist, should greatly assist the resolution of taxonomic
problems.

Finally, the status of the two, morphometrically distinguishable, populations of snow petrel (Prévost, 1969) remains enigmatic.

Although it is reasonable to interpret some seabird distribution patterns
in terms of their evolution in (and presumably therefore adaptation to)
certain oceanic zones this does not help to understand the interactions that
occur when two related species from contiguous zones seek to breed at the
same site. Nor does it make clear, for these and other species, what factors

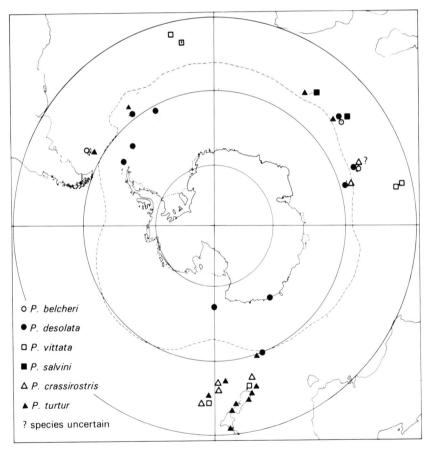

Fig. 6. Breeding distribution of *Pachyptila* spp.

influence the northern and southern limits of their breeding distribution. To understand more of this we must turn to details of species' breeding biology and feeding ecology.

3. Breeding Dispersion and Habitat

The nature of available substrate and its topography are obviously important influences on colony size and breeding density and there are significant variations between sites. Nevertheless, the reviews of breeding dispersion, colony size and preferred habitat by Carrick and Ingham (1967) for Antarctic seabirds generally and by Croxall and Prince (1980a) for South Georgia do suggest the existence of some species-characteristic patterns.

In general, of course, seabirds are colonial and the only consistent exceptions in the Antarctic, apart perhaps from the often solitary cliff-nesting light-mantled sooty albatross, are the charadriiform species (skuas, terns, gull). These defend isolated nest territories and, in the case of some skuas, feeding territories based on portions of penguin colonies (Müller-Schwarze and Müller-Schwarze, 1977; Trillmich, 1978; Trivelpiece et al., 1980). Sheathbills, which also scavenge in penguin colonies, are similar in this latter respect (Burger, 1979), and nest solitarily in crevices.

The burrow-dwelling habit, confined to the smaller and medium sized petrels (up to white-chinned petrel size), is best developed at the sub-Antarctic (and further north) islands where large areas of peaty grassland are found. Rather little is known about colony size and breeding density and much may depend on the precise configuration of the terrain and on the nature of microhabitat preferences, some of the more obvious of which have been portrayed by Richdale (1965), Woods (1970) and Derenne and Mougin (1976). At Bird Island, South Georgia, the densities of occupied burrows per $100 \, m^2$ for white-chinned petrel, blue petrel and dove prion can reach 14, 72 and 103 respectively (I. Hunter, unpublished data). Most species seem to prefer tussock slopes but steep tussock cliffs are certainly preferred by common diving petrels, while dove prion, grey-faced petrel and some other species breed successfully in completely flat areas.

There are frequently differences between species in depth, length and conformation of tunnels and in particularly suitable sites a number of species may breed in the same area. There are often substantial differences in abundance of the various burrowing species at a single site or island and it is not at all clear to what extent these may relate to availability or nature of substrate or topography. Other habitats suitable for burrow excavation include screes, moraine debris and moss banks and these are used principally by storm petrels (moss banks) and South Georgia diving petrels (fine compacted scree and moraine debris). The two species of diving petrels thus represent an extreme case of preference for quite different breeding habitats.

Storm petrels commonly breed in crevices, especially in coarse scree and cliffs; other crevice nesters include snow petrel and the prions *P. turtur* and *P. crassirostris*, these three requiring much larger interstices than the storm petrels. Prions also enlarge existing cavities in cliffs and the dove prion is one of the few true tussock burrowing species which also utilizes rock crevice sites much further south.

The surface nesting habit is virtually restricted to the larger seabirds and although bulkier birds possess relatively greater insulation they usually select sheltered sites and particularly so towards the south of their ranges. Apparently, however, the very small grey-backed storm petrel usually enlarges cavities at the base of big tussock stools (Carrick and Ingham, 1967; Woods, 1975). Cape pigeon, Antarctic fulmar and Antarctic petrel, with their preference for sheltered ledges, provide a link between the crevice-nesting snow petrel and the sheltered open sites used by giant petrels.

The remaining surface nesters are albatrosses and penguins. Most albatrosses tend to nest in compact colonies on tussock slopes but the sooty albatrosses breed in very small groups, even singly, often on tussock cliffs and the wandering albatross usually in dispersed groups on flatter areas. Like giant petrels, the use of level sites may relate to its general clumsiness on land and difficulties in becoming airborne. With the albatrosses the different nest situations also correlate with marked differences in courtship behaviour. Thus the wandering albatross uses the large spaces around its nest for its complex and vigorous display, culminating in the well known "dancing" sequences; black-browed and grey-headed albatrosses have shorter bouts of more static displays; an important element of the cliff nesting light-mantled sooty albatross courtship is the highly co-ordinated simultaneous flight display by both members of the pair. It would be interesting to know what behavioural adaptations are shown by yellow-nosed albatross on Gough Island where the colonies are under a canopy of tall *Phylica* scrub and the individuals more spaced out than other mollymauks.

Most penguins breed on flat sites and some, like the emperor penguin (sea ice) and king penguin (beaches or adjacent areas, often near glaciers, presumably because the outflow keeps the topography suitably obstacle-free) are essentially confined to these. At the Indian Ocean islands some macaroni penguin colonies are on flat beaches, but at South Georgia it is confined to steep slopes by the sea. Distinct habitat preferences are often attributed to the pygoscelid penguins (e.g. White and Conroy, 1975) but these are by no means consistent between sites (Volkman and Trivelpiece,

1982) and it is likely that Adélie and chinstrap have broadly overlapping requirements. The gentoo penguin, while preferring flat sites, has catholic tastes, being found on beaches, tussock and even in boulder areas. The principal penguin breeding on boulder beaches is the rockhopper and the shelter given by such habitat to this, the smallest penguin in the area, is the nearest that any Antarctic penguin comes to being a burrowing species, like the essentially sub-tropical *Spheniscus* and *Eudyptula* species.

Given even the very imprecise habitat preferences indicated, the availability of suitable breeding terrain clearly has the potential to influence the number and distribution of breeding seabirds. It is unlikely that its role in limiting breeding numbers is of overriding importance as, for most species in most parts of the Antarctic, adequate breeding sites would seem superabundant. In some cases this impression may, however, be misleading. For instance, not all grass-covered land, or even all tussock areas, are suitable for every burrowing species. Also, at South Georgia, the cliffs and particularly those on the more sheltered north side of the island, do not seem to provide the abundance of crevices and rock ledges of the type used by snow petrels and cape pigeons farther south. This may even be implicated in the rarity of both species as breeding birds at South Georgia, the snow petrel being restricted to rock crevices above the tussock line and the cape pigeon, which is abundant in the surrounding waters, only breeding on a few cliffs (Prince and Payne, 1979).

On a broader basis the nature of available habitat clearly affects the general distribution of species. Foremost perhaps is the restriction of terrain suitable for burrowing activities to the sub-Antarctic islands. This places an enforced southern limit on the breeding range of species which cannot adapt to or do not already utilize ledge and crevice habitats. This applies to all petrels of the genera *Pterodroma*, *Procellaria* and *Halobaena* and apparently to some prions *Pachyptila*, although not *P. desolata*.

Grassland is also important in other ways. Thus, in contrast to giant petrels, albatrosses appear to depend on the presence of adequate vegetation for construction of their massive nests, and their southern limit of breeding may coincide with the distribution of suitable plant material.

The procellariforms that are able to breed successfully in high latitudes (e.g. south of 60°S) comprise three crevice-nesting species: Wilson's storm petrel (which is so small that it effectively still lives underground), snow petrel and dove prion (both of which would probably be vulnerable to skua predation in more open sites), three ledge-inhabiting species (cape pigeon, Antarctic petrel, Antarctic fulmar) and one species of more open sites (southern giant petrel). These species choose progressively more sheltered sites the further south they breed and other problems, such as drifts of snow and debris (e.g. Roberts, 1940; Brown, 1966), probably intensify the problem of nest site selection and make it difficult to assess the amount of fully suitable habitat available. Dove prion, except for one, probably no longer extant colony on the Antarctic continent (Watson, 1975), does not appear to extend farther south than the islands off the Antarctic Peninsula. In the far south small petrels (unless small enough to escape normal ambient conditions by entering the substrate, like Wilson's storm petrel) may have difficulty finding enough sufficiently sheltered sites to minimize the relatively greater heat loss from a small body. The remaining species are considerably larger and this correlates to some extent with their ability to occupy sites of increasing exposure (Mougin, 1968). With increased size, however, goes delay in acquisition of homeothermy by the chick, and longer brooding (and overall fledging) periods, all placing greater demands on the adults—in addition to any difficulties in finding large enough sheltered sites to minimize heat loss. Thus a medium-sized species may present the best compromise and this may in turn have influenced their wide distribution and great abundance in high latitudes. The fact that all these species, except the storm petrel, belong to the group of fulmarine petrels, suggests that there may have been other features in the biology of this group which pre-adapted them for life in these areas. Some evidence for this will appear later (p. 573).

Although there are many parts of the Antarctic (and especially the coasts of the continent itself) totally unsuitable for breeding seabirds, it is particularly difficult to see direct habitat restrictions on distribution of penguins. It has been noted, however, that both *Aptenodytes* species require flat breeding sites (so they can move with an egg balanced on their feet) and nearly all emperor penguin colonies are in particularly sheltered sites on sea ice (Budd, 1961)—yet breeding space is superabundant at all these.

Thus, in some very broad ways and perhaps also in a few specific ones, substrate and climate exert some fundamental influences on the general breeding distribution of Antarctic seabirds. They are chiefly linked to the absence of suitable breeding substrates or to climatic (and ecological) rigours proving more suitable for species that evolved under a particular combination of constraints, rather than for species from other zones. Indirectly, through its influence on the nature and seasonality of the marine environment, the climate has determined the basic background against which the ecological adaptations of the species concerned must be viewed and it is appropriate now to consider these.

4. Timing of Breeding Season

The duration of the breeding season, from egg laying to chick fledging, for species for which adequate data are available, is shown in Fig. 7. It is the

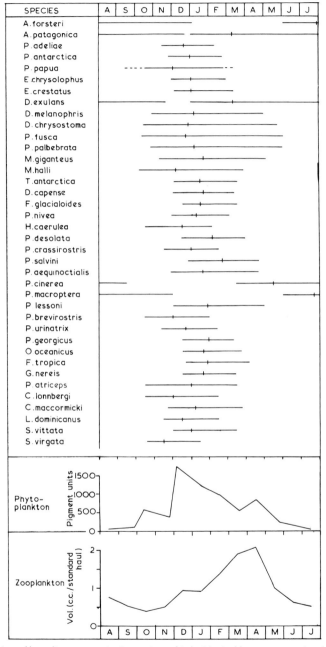

Fig. 7. Timing of breeding seasons in Antarctic seabirds. Vertical bars represent hatching dates. Phytoplankton and zooplankton data from Hart (1942) and Foxton (1956) respectively.

overall pattern which is of principal interest, as the actual durations shown can only be approximations, for various reasons.

First, there are differences in the time of the onset of breeding at various sites. Characteristically the more northerly populations of most species breed 2–3 weeks earlier than the more southerly ones. This is in line with the earlier onset of milder conditions further north and for some species (e.g. rockhopper penguin) there is even a correlation between mean annual sea temperature and laying date (Warham, 1972). Other relevant climate data are summarized by Stonehouse (1964, 1967, 1970b). This distinction is better marked between sub-Antarctic islands and the Antarctic Continent and Peninsula than between the islands near the Sub-tropical Convergence and the sub-Antarctic islands. For some species in particularly critical environments, the difference can be seen within a zone, e.g. emperor penguins at Pointe Géologie (66°S) breed three weeks earlier than those at Cape Crozier (78°S) (Prevost, 1961). In Wilson's storm petrel, however, the reverse is true and the populations at Kerguelen (Paulian, 1953) and Signy Island (Beck and Brown, 1972) breed three weeks later than those at Terre Adélie (Lacan, 1971). Why nest sites become habitable slightly earlier at Terre Adélie than at Signy Island, and what other factors may operate, is not clear.

In some species there are differences in timing between sites at similar latitudes. In general these differences seem least in procellariforms, although the data are not extensive, and are smaller than those related to longitude. This is not so for royal penguin, however, which breeds 2–3 weeks earlier at Macquarie than at Heard (Carrick and Ingham, 1967); South Georgia dates agree with the latter. Gentoo penguin shows perhaps the greatest variation in timing and although some differences probably relate to latitude it is difficult to believe that this is the only factor operating. Thus birds lay in June at Marion (van Zinderen Bakker, 1971), July–August at Crozet (Despin, 1972), August at Kerguelen (Paulian, 1953), September–October at Macquarie (Carrick and Ingham, 1967), mid-October at Heard (Downes et al., 1959), usually late October at South Georgia (personal observation) and Signy Island and in mid-November near the species' southern limit at Petermann Island (Gain, 1914).

Secondly, even in a single general area, a few species show poor synchrony of breeding, eggs being laid over two or more months. Many, perhaps most, Antarctic seabirds are relatively highly synchronized (eggs laid during less than three weeks), this being attributable to the short period of favourable conditions and to their predominantly colonial habit, with social behaviour and any anti-predator adaptations tending to promote synchrony of early season events. The exceptions can be grouped as follows:

(i) medium-sized petrels of lower latitudes, e.g. *Procellaria aequinoctialis* (Mougin, 1975 and unpublished data from South Georgia), *P. cinerea* (Barrat, 1974), *Pterodroma macroptera* (Mougin, 1975), which are rather dispersed breeders, with very long chick fledging periods and, as two of them breed in winter, seasonal environmental factors may be generally less of a constraint.

(ii) storm petrels *O. oceanicus* and *F. tropica* at some sites (e.g. Signy Island, Beck, 1970; Beck and Brown, 1971, 1972) but not at others (e.g. Terre Adélie, Lacan, 1971). The asynchrony at Signy Island was attributed to climatic effects causing unpredictable timing of mortality which would favour early breeders in one season and late breeders in another, thus maintaining a broad spread of laying dates (Beck and Brown, 1972); it is not clear why this does not apply equally at other sites. The dove prion, another crevice nester, also shows poorer synchrony at Signy than elsewhere (Tickell, 1962).

(iii) the brown skua, southern black-backed gull, *Larus dominicanus* and Antarctic tern *Sterna vittata*, which are essentially solitary species in Antarctic regions and, for the first two, where the availability of scavengeable food from different sources (e.g. seal beaches, penguin colonies, petrel areas) for different groups of birds may play a part. It is interesting that the giant petrels, also important scavengers, are well synchronized, but this may be because at the northern sites both species occur and there is a selection pressure to maintain reproductive isolation whereas at southern sites (with only the southern giant petrel) the season is too short to permit significant asynchrony. Similarly the Antarctic skua is, as expected, a highly synchronized breeder, even though many birds are purely scavengers.

(iv) king and gentoo penguins. The former has an unusual breeding cycle, involving maintaining chicks in winter and late breeding by parents that have successfully fledged a chick in spring (see p. 554). Failed breeders may start again at almost any time in the summer. Reasons for the well attested lack of synchrony in gentoo penguins are less clear but it has been suggested (Croxall and Prince, 1980a) that as an inshore feeding species with a relatively small foraging range, this may be an adaptation to reduce intraspecific competition especially during the chick rearing and adult premoult fattening periods. Interestingly the Antarctic tern and the Antarctic shags are also inshore feeding species that often appear very poorly synchronized and there are suggestions that the same may be true for diving petrels (Carrick and Ingham, 1967; Payne and Prince, 1979) and possible that this might apply, in part, to other inshore feeding species like prions and storm petrels.

Thirdly, there are season to season variations in laying dates at a single site or colony. These are often caused by climatic factors (e.g. late breakout of sea ice, snow and ice blocking nest burrows etc.) and are often reflected in breeding success (see p. 585). Even so the variation is seldom more than a week or so and for some species, colony or population mean laying dates are consistent to within a week over many years. The gentoo penguin is again anomalous (Despin, 1972; Croxall and Prince, 1979) with a five week difference in two successive seasons at South Georgia; it has been suggested that differences in food availability may account for this.

Notwithstanding these complications, the basic pattern of timing of seabird breeding seasons inevitably reflects the pronounced seasonality of the environment and in particular the timing of the increase in marine primary and secondary production. This is portrayed in Fig. 7 using data on phytoplankton production from Hart (1942) and zooplankton (excluding krill) biomass in the upper 50 m from Foxton (1956).

Most seabirds commence breeding early in the season (and for most large species and those in the far south probably as early as practicable) so that the principal demand for food (during rapid chick growth and once the chick has fledged) can coincide with the period of high resource availability. Even larger species, like albatrosses, which must lay earlier to fledge a chick by May and must therefore form an egg and undergo lengthy incubation fasts when zooplankton levels are still relatively low, seem to be able to maintain body weight during incubation (Prince et al., 1981; Croxall and Ricketts, 1983). Smaller species can be flexible in the timing of breeding and this is shown by the fact that several small petrels lay midway through the season (and still fledge chicks in April). Some small petrels do breed early but in several there is evidence that they may do this to reduce direct competition, particularly during the chick-rearing phase, with closely related and/or ecologically similar species.

Thus the blue petrel and the fulmar prion P. crassirostris (which do not themselves coexist) breed earlier than all other prions with which they thus have essentially mutually exclusive chick-rearing periods. The two diving petrels, the two Procellaria petrels, the three Pterodroma petrels and Antarctic and Kerguelen terns are similarly distinct and although the six week laying difference between the giant petrels (consistent for all sites where both occur) may be mainly related to maintaining reproductive isolation, this too creates some differences in prey exploited, at least at South Georgia (Hunter, 1983).

Although the general pattern of breeding during the period of main zooplankton abundance is clear cut there are five species with a significant proportion of their breeding activity in winter. The most celebrated of these is the emperor penguin and it is appropriate briefly to digress and review the adaptations which permit it to breed under the most extreme environmental conditions of any bird. Its basic breeding strategy is not difficult to appreciate, as were emperor penguins to lay in spring, their chicks would, even assuming a somewhat improved growth rate, be quite unable to fledge before the winter. Consequently laying takes place in late summer with adults in peak condition for the long fasts and extreme conditions ahead and the chick is reared throughout the winter. It fledges in midsummer at only about 60% of adult body weight (Prévost, 1961), the lowest proportion for any penguin, presumably because this offers the best compromise between chick survival and the provision of sufficient time for adults to moult and return to breeding condition by the end of the summer.

To cope with the problems of incubation and brooding fasts in which adults lose up to 40% of their body mass (Prévost, 1961) in temperatures which may drop to $-48°C$, the emperor penguin shows a number of adaptations. Its lower ambient critical temperature (below which metabolic rate must be increased to maintain body temperature at a constant level) is $-10°C$ (Le Maho et al., 1976) ($-5°C$ in king penguins; Le Maho, 1977). Its thermal conductance (Pinshow et al., 1976; Le Maho et al., 1976) is similar to that for other penguins and thus the low critical temperature is not simply due to excellent insulation. Not only is the emperor penguin a very large bird (twice as heavy as the king penguin) but its appendages (flipper, bill) are about 25% smaller in proportion than other penguins (Stonehouse, 1967). Furthermore, its flippers and feet have vascular countercurrent heat exchangers (for reducing heat expenditure in cold air) that proliferate twice as much as king and three times as much as Adélie penguins (Trawa, 1960). Heat loss is also minimized in the nasal passages (where Adélie and gentoo penguins recover 83% of the respiratory heat added to cold inhaled air (Murrish, 1973)). The subcutaneous fat is only 2.3 cm thick and plays a minor role in thermal insulation compared to the very long double-layered and high density feathers.

All these adaptations combined, however, still only contribute to the lower critical temperature of $-10°C$ and additional behavioural adaptations are needed to combat the effects of long fasts at consistently low temperatures. This is achieved principally by huddling, which may involve up to 5000 birds at ten per m² (Prévost, 1961). The huddle as a whole moves very slowly with the wind and windward birds move along the flanks and then into the centre until they are once again exposed at the rear, so that no birds are continually exposed on the periphery of the group. It has been calculated that huddling reduces the theoretical daily loss of body weight by 25–50% (Prévost, 1961). Huddling is not seen in adult king penguins, which breed with constant interindividual distances, presumably because air temperatures rarely exceed its lower critical temperature. Chicks in winter, however, frequently huddle in groups.

Successful emperor penguin adults can apparently breed in successive seasons. The king penguin has a more complex breeding system. At South Georgia laying occurs in early December, chicks are raised to 90% of adult weight by June and then fed only sporadically (fasts of up to three months) until the following spring when they are fed regularly again and fledge in November–December. The parents, however, cannot return to breeding condition until about March and a much smaller chick then over-winters (though high mortality occurs), which does not fledge until well into the next summer so that the parents cannot breed again that year (Stonehouse, 1960). At Îles Crozet it appears that adults, when success-ful, breed in alternate seasons (Barrat, 1976). It seems paradoxical that in the milder sub-Antarctic climate king penguins should be unable to breed annually either by raising a chick through the winter like the emperor penguin or by laying two months earlier and fledging a chick at 80% adult weight in April. It has been suggested (Croxall and Prince, 1980a) that late laying may be a result of competition for squid food with the large population of elephant seals which have a breeding distribution coextens-ive with king penguins and pup during September. Also South Georgia and Macquarie, both with relatively small king penguin populations, have vast elephant seal herds (Chapter 12).

It is not clear why small chicks cannot be raised slowly during the winter. Breeding biennially at a climatically clement time of the year might place less strain on adults than breeding annually in severe condi-tions. However, emperor and king penguins start breeding at much the same ages and emperor penguin has a mean annual survival that is very high for any penguin (Table VII). Alternatively, annual breeding might be associated with greater loss of fledglings. Only 18.9% of emperor pen-guin chicks (fledging at 60% adult weight) survive their first year (Mougin and van Beveren, 1979) in marked contrast to the mean annual survival of immature king penguins (which fledge at about adult weight) of 93% (Jouventin and Mougin, 1981).

Winter breeding in the remaining species (wandering albatross, grey petrel and great-winged petrel) can probably be interpreted as taking advantage of the reduced competition for resources in winter where climatic conditions are suitable, although the time needed to raise as large a fledgling as the wandering albatross may be an important constraint. In these latitudes such a strategy seems possible only for species well adapted to catching squid (and possibly fish too) because crustaceans are certainly unavailable in sufficient quantities in winter. Furthermore, for energetic reasons, it is probably a strategy mainly available to burrowing species (like the petrels) at climatically fairly mild islands. The size of the wandering albatross chick and its acquisition of homeothermy well before the onset of winter are probably important factors in its ability to survive over winter.

5. Breeding Biology

5.1 General patterns

The basic pattern of events during the breeding season is very similar for most procellariforms and penguins and, in the former case, is little different from that recorded in studies of northern hemisphere species. Thus potential breeding birds arrive at the colony some weeks before egglaying (males often before females) and a period of courtship behaviour, pair bond formation (or re-establishment) and burrow prospecting or nest building (or modification of burrow/nest of previous season) ensues, the exact details depending on the past reproductive history of the birds involved. The duration of this period is usually about 25–30% that of the time from egglaying to chick fledging and a more detailed discussion can be found in Mougin (1975). After copulation the female generally departs to sea for a period often lasting 2–3 weeks and returns immediately before egglaying. This is usually regarded (e.g. Warham, 1964; Lack, 1968) as enabling her to find additional food to aid in egg-formation. In petrels the males are often (usually?) absent from the colony during the day but frequently (normally?) return at night; in albatrosses males spend more time at the nest. Egglaying follows quickly on the female's return and she departs after a usually very short incubation shift. Incubation duties are then alternated by the parents until the chick hatches. It is then brooded for a while in alternating shifts by one parent while the other feeds it; subsequently both parents feed the chick, which gains weight rapidly, accumulating substantial fat reserves, to a peak weight normally substantially in excess of adult-weight. Thereafter it continues to be fed, often with gradually decreasing frequency while body tissue, muscles, feathers, etc. grow, but weight decreases until fledging, as the fat reserves are utilized, in most Antarctic species; in the more temperate shearwaters *P. tenuirostris, P. griseus* and *P. gravis*, however, the chicks are rarely fed in the last fortnight before departure.

In penguins the males usually arrive to take up nest territories in advance of the females and there is no real pre-laying exodus of either sex (although in several species both birds of the pair are not always present at the nest). After laying, alternating incubation and brooding shifts are taken by each parent. In eudyptid penguins these shifts are much longer than in pygoscelid species. In most penguins, chicks fledge at a weight below that of adults and there is usually little decline from a peak weight prior to fledging. Chicks do not fledge until body moult is completed and eudyptid penguin adults normally cease feeding at this stage whereas in some species (e.g. gentoo) parental attention may continue for some time afterwards.

Most penguins (except *Aptenodytes* spp.) lay at least two eggs and (except *Eudyptes* spp.) can often rear more than one chick. Unlike procellariforms, limited re-laying is usually possible (not *Eudyptes*) and incubation commences with the first egg (not *Eudyptes*; see Burger and Williams, 1979), this being characteristic also of the Antarctic shags, skuas, gulls and terns. Chicks thus hatch asynchronously and often only the older one(s) survive(s). Penguin chicks often leave the actual nest site at the end of brooding and in several species (particularly *Aptenodytes* spp., Adélie and gentoo) large "crêches" develop. The offspring of skuas, gulls and terns are nidifugous and usually seek cover near the nest when their parents are absent.

These patterns and relationships will be familiar to all ornithologists and fairly recent information on the breeding biology of shags (Derenne *et al.*, 1976a; Williams and Burger, 1979), skuas (Le Morvan *et al.*, 1967; Burton, 1968; Spellerberg, 1969, 1970, 1971; Wood, 1971, 1972; Müller-Schwarze and Müller-Schwarze, 1973; Johnston, 1973; Barré, 1976; Jones and Skira, 1979; Jouventin and Guillotin, 1979; Moors, 1980; Williams, 1980a,b,e; Trivelpiece and Volkman, 1982; Young, 1978), southern black-backed gulls (Kinsky, 1963; Fordham, 1964) and Antarctic and Kerguelen terns (Parmelee and Maxson, 1975; Parmelee, 1977; Stahl and Weimerskirch, 1982) can be found in the literature. These species will not be discussed further here.

For the most significant groups, procellariforms and penguins, however, it is possible to make a comparative synopsis of the principal features of breeding season events rather than to discuss the species individually in detail.

The basic data for these comparisons are given in Appendix 1. It should be stressed that these are mean values taken from the literature. In many cases data are sparse and some anomalous values may simply reflect inadequate observations. Information on adult weight is particularly difficult to find for birds of equivalent status and by no means all figures are for breeding birds at the laying stage. A concerted international effort is now being made to collate weight data for Antarctic seabirds so that reliable values for these and other computations may be provided.

Egg weights are also unlikely to be standardized because not all measurements were made at laying and bird eggs, on average, lose 16% of their weight during incubation due to water loss. The best relationship presently available (Drent, 1975) gives a relationship between water loss (mg day^{-1})

and fresh egg weight (W in g) of $15.2\,W^{0.74}$, but, at least for some Procellariiformes, this gives results nearly double true weight loss (unpublished data).

A number of additional species have been incorporated for comparative purposes, either so that a whole genus (albatrosses) is represented, or to include just extralimital species or, in one or two cases, so that the position of well known north temperate species may be ascertained.

Only the most general (and anomalous) features of the various groups will be mentioned here; when the many gaps in information are filled, a more comprehensive and sophisticated analysis should be possible and such an undertaking has been foreshadowed independently in the work of Warham (1975). In particular the trends of each component group within the procellariforms should be examined more closely as it is likely that we are dealing with a set of curves and relationships rather than a single basic relationship for the order as a whole.

5.2 Eggs and incubation

Larger birds lay heavier eggs and this is as true for Procellariiformes (Fig. 8) and Sphenisciformes (Fig. 9) as for other groups of birds. However, the eggs of smaller birds are proportionately larger (i.e. in relation to their own body weight; see Figs 10, 11). In the procellariforms it seems likely that the precise nature of the relationship differs for several of the distinct taxonomic groups (e.g. storm petrels, albatrosses). For their size, diving petrels and penguins (relative to procellariforms) appear to lay rather small eggs. Most penguins, however, lay more than one egg. The eudyptid penguins are unusual in that they lay eggs of unequal size, the first (20–60% smaller than the second) usually only hatching in rockhopper, fiordland and Snares crested penguins and, even there, the chick only being raised if the second egg fails to hatch. In the most extreme case, macaroni penguin, most first eggs are lost (during territorial fighting etc.) in the 3–4 days before the second is laid. Warham (1975) proposed that the dissimilar eggs exist to deal with the high degree of egg loss resulting from selection favouring aggressive males, like Lack (1968) assuming that enough first eggs replaced lost second ones, for the former to act as a kind of reserve into which, however, it is not worth placing a full complement of resources. Williams (1980c), however, showed that macaroni penguins at Marion Island hatched no first eggs and suggested (Williams, unpublished) that the egg-size dimorphism functions to ensure rapid and predetermined brood reduction in a species apparently unable to lay a large "functional" egg first.

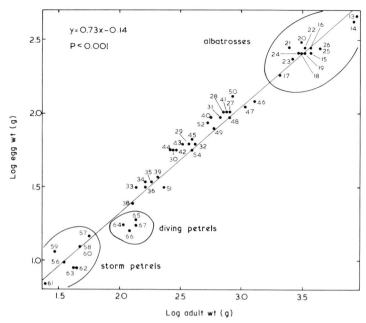

Fig. 8. Relationship between egg weight and adult weight in Antarctic Procellariiformes. Numbers refer to Appendix I.

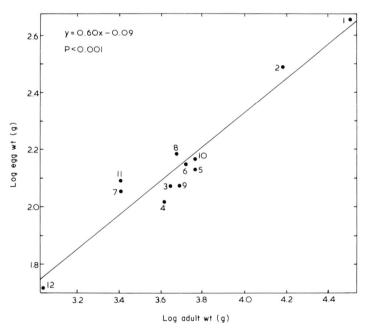

Fig. 9. Relationship between egg weight and adult weight in Antarctic Sphenisciformes. Numbers refer to Appendix I.

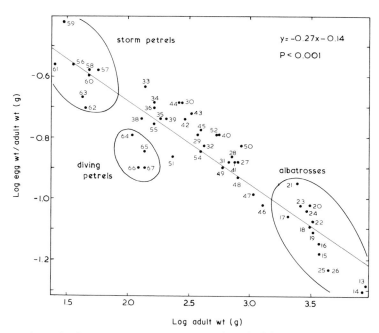

Fig. 10. Relationship between proportionate egg weight and adult weight in Antarctic Procellariiformes. Numbers refer to Appendix I.

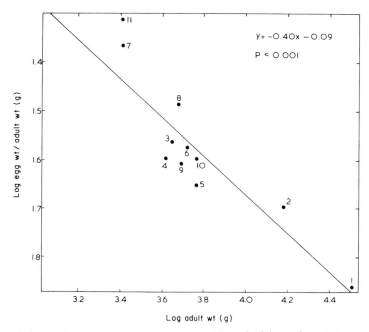

Fig. 11. Relationship between proportionate egg weight and adult weight in Antarctic Sphenisciformes. Numbers refer to Appendix I.

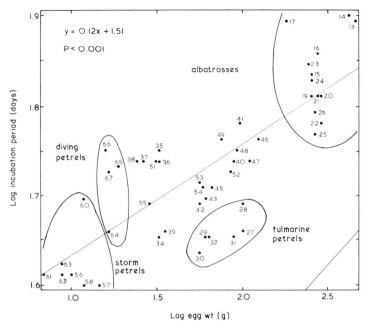

Fig. 12. Relationship between incubation period and egg weight in Antarctic Procellariiformes. Numbers refer to Appendix I. Lower regression line is that of Rahn and Ar (1974) for all birds.

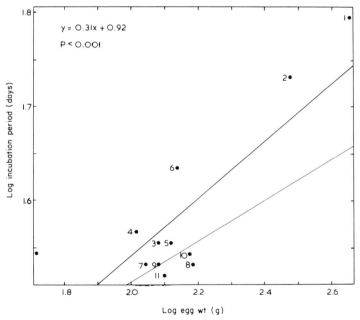

Fig. 13. Relationship between incubation period and egg weight in Antarctic Sphenisciformes. Lower regression line is that of Rahn and Ar (1974) for all birds. Numbers refer to Appendix I.

It is also well established that egg weight and incubation period are positively correlated (Heinroth, 1922). The relationship for 475 species of birds (Rahn and Ar, 1974) is plotted in Figs 12 and 13 and it is clear that procellariforms (but penguins to a much lesser extent) lie significantly above this line; that is they have unusually long incubation periods. Warham (1971) suggested that this pertains to their low incubation temperature but this is not supported by presently available data (Drent, 1975; Ricklefs and Rahn, 1979). In Lack's (1968) view, long incubation periods are, with long fledging periods, a reflection of depressed overall growth rates which evolved where resource availability was low in relation to foraging ability of parents. Petrels in general do have long breeding periods, considering they have only a single chick to raise, but not every species shows a good correlation between length of incubation and fledging periods (see Fig. 15). Within the group several points are apparent, apart from the general one that considerably greater variation (compare Figs 8 and 12) has been introduced, presumably reflecting the greater scope for operation of environmental variables. The smaller fulmarine petrels have exceedingly short incubation periods (as have giant petrels compared with most albatrosses), while relatively long periods are shown by several albatrosses, all prions except dove prion and all diving petrels except *P. georgicus*.

The incubation period is divided into a number of separate shifts, of fairly equal length but with a tendency for the shift or shifts prior to hatching to be shorter, ensuring that on hatching the chick receives a meal quickly. This tendency is most marked in large birds with long incubation shifts (e.g. albatrosses) where shift length decreases from about the midpoint of incubation. In smaller petrels it is often only the penultimate shift that is noticeably shorter. For the wandering albatross (Tickell, 1968; Croxall and Ricketts, 1983), cape pigeon (Pinder, 1966; Mougin, 1968; Isenmann, 1970a), and snow petrel (Brown, 1966; Isenmann, 1970b) it is well established that, excluding the short first and last shifts, females take slightly shorter shifts than males with a mean difference of about 0.5–1.0 days per shift. While it is probable that a similar pattern may apply to other species (see Mougin, 1975), although not to grey-faced petrel (Imber, 1976) nor soft-plumaged petrel (Mougin, 1975) whose males have shorter shifts than females, any advantage to the female is largely offset by the fact that she invariably takes the first incubation shift and usually the last one also so that total time spent incubating by both sexes is often very similar. Interspecific variation in mean shift length (sexes combined) is substantial (see Table II). Larger birds, with longer incubation periods, tend to take longer shifts. However, some fulmarine petrels appear to have very short shifts and *Pterodroma* petrels very long shifts (greater than the albatrosses). Surprisingly, wandering and royal albatrosses may often have shorter shifts than mollymauks.

TABLE II
Number and duration of incubation shifts (excluding first and last) in
Antarctic Procellariiformes

Species	Mean no. shifts	Mean length (days)	Reference
Wandering albatross	10	8.1	Tickell, 1968
	8	10.3	Barrat, 1976
	6	12.1	Croxall, unpublished
Royal albatross	10	7.2	Richdale, 1952
Black-browed albatross	6	11.1	Tickell and Pinder, 1975
Grey-headed albatross	6	11.5	Tickell and Pinder, 1975
Light-mantled sooty albatross	5	15	Thomas, et al., 1983
	5	14	Mougin, 1970
Sooty albatross	7	9.5	Berruti, 1979
Northern giant petrel	8	8	Mougin, 1975
Southern giant petrel	9	6.5	Conroy, 1972
	11	5.3	Hunter, in press
Cape pigeon	15	3.6	Mougin, 1968
	12	3.7	Pinder, 1966
Antarctic fulmar	11	4	Mougin, 1975
Snow petrel	13	3.8	Mougin, 1968
	5	8.4	Brown, 1966
	8	5.7	Isenmann, 1970b
Dove prion	15	3	Tickell, 1962
Fairy prion	c. 10	5.6	Richdale, 1965b
	c. 20	2.4	Harper, 1976
Grey-faced petrel	3	15.6	Imber, 1976b
Kerguelen petrel	3	13	Mougin, 1975
Mottled petrel	3	13.1	Warham et al., 1977
Blue petrel	c. 9	c. 5	Prince, unpublished
White-chinned petrel	5	9.6	Mougin, 1975
Sooty shearwater	c. 10	5	Richdale, 1963
Short-tailed shearwater	4	c. 12.5	Marshall and Serventy, 1956b
Wilson's storm petrel	c. 16	2.5	Beck and Brown, 1972
	c. 33	1.2	Lacan, 1971
Black-bellied storm petrel	c. 13	3	Beck and Brown, 1971
White-faced storm petrel	c. 10	4.5	Richdale, 1965a
Common diving petrel	c. 55	1	Richdale, 1965a

It was believed by Lack (1968) that these inter- and intra-specific differences should relate to foraging range and ease of food finding. Circumstantial evidence that could be interpreted as supporting this comes from chick growth rates (see p. 571). These are particularly rapid in fulmarine petrels (suggesting abundant resources), very slow in gadfly petrels (suggesting very dispersed resources) and correlate with different shift lengths in Wilson's storm petrel at Signy Island and Terre Adélie. Nevertheless, it is not clear why species with good levels of available food should waste feeding time by undertaking frequent changeovers at the nest and the relationship between body size, type of nest site and weight loss in incubating birds needs investigating to see to what extent rate of weight loss may influence shift duration. With wandering, grey-headed and black-browed albatrosses most birds have little difficulty maintaining weight throughout incubation (Prince *et al.*, 1981; Croxall and Ricketts, 1983) although the poor performance of some individuals may ultimately pre-judice their chick-rearing ability (Croxall and Ricketts, 1983).

In penguins the pattern of incubation shifts is extremely variable, ranging from the usually daily changeovers in gentoo penguin to stints of over a month in eudyptid species. Figure 14 gives a simplified diagrammatic version of the duration of periods ashore and at sea for breeding penguins of both sexes throughout the whole breeding season. Of the pygoscelid penguins the gentoo is not shown, as once incubation commences, it has a pattern of usually daily changeovers (at South Georgia and Marion Island;

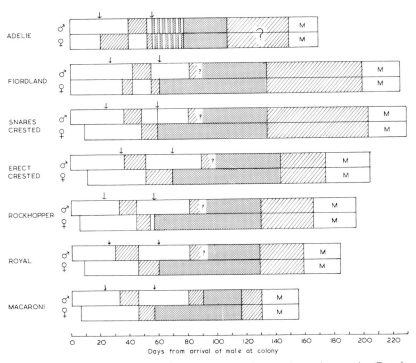

Fig. 14. Duration and timing of breeding season events in some Antarctic penguins (Data from, in turn: Taylor, 1962 and Spurr, 1975; Warham, 1974a; Warham, 1974b; Warham, 1972b; Warham, 1963; Warham, 1971b; Croxall, unpublished). First arrow; mean laying date second egg; second arrow; mean hatching date; cross-hatched; at sea; strippled; feeding chicks; blank; in colony; M; moult. Periods of unknown duration indicated by ?

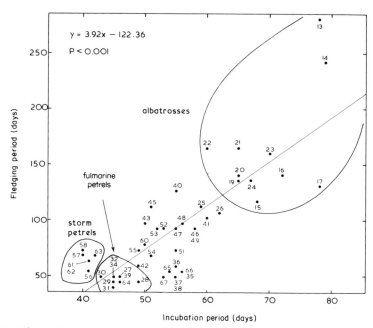

Fig. 15. Relationship between duration of fledging and incubation period in Antarctic Procellariiformes. Numbers refer to Appendix I.

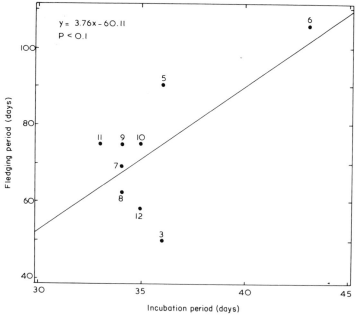

Fig. 16. Relationship between duration of fledging and incubation period in Antarctic Sphenisciformes. Numbers refer to Appendix I.

at Îles Crozet, Despin (1972) recording mean shifts of 2.8 days for females and 3.3 days for males) and this is essentially maintained throughout the chick rearing period. There are inadequate published data to construct a diagram for chinstrap penguin, although it is suggested (Conroy *et al.*, 1975) that its incubation shifts are shorter (mean 2–8 days), and visits to feed chicks more frequent, than in the Adélie penguin. In the Adélie the female sometimes takes the first shift which is then short (six days) but followed by a normal length (15 days) male shift (Spurr, 1975).

With the eudyptid penguins the basic pattern is fairly consistent, only the Fiordland penguin, where the male takes the first incubation shift and the female has two (not one) periods at sea before the chick hatches, deviating. The overall duration of the cycle is roughly in relation to breeding latitude (see Fig. 3) but it is noteworthy that the much smaller rockhopper penguin takes longer than the other two sub-Antarctic species or subspecies. These are of similar size but the macaroni penguin at South Georgia has a shorter season than the royal penguin at Macquarie. This is because it has a reduced chick rearing period and spends less time at sea, particularly before moult. Indeed the duration of the premoult fattening period is the single event most responsible for the differences in overall length of eudyptid penguin breeding seasons.

While one might interpret the long shifts in the Adélie penguin as an adaptation necessary when a considerable extent of fast ice may need to be crossed to reach feeding areas early in the season, it is not clear why the eudyptid penguins have such very long shifts, unless early in the season they need to travel very much further than when feeding chicks to find suitable feeding grounds.

A general correlation between length of incubation and fledging periods has long been recognized and this is confirmed for procellariforms (Fig. 15) but not significantly so for penguins (Fig. 16). Imbalance between the duration of the two periods is shown for wandering (13) and royal albatross (14) and two tropical albatrosses (21 and 22), also gadfly petrels (except Kerguelen petrel (42)) and storm petrels (except *Pelagodroma* (37)) which have longer fledging periods, and prions (except *P. desolata* (54)) and diving petrels (except *P. georgicus* (41)) which have shorter fledging periods. These latter two groups (except for the two anomalous species), however, show very long incubation periods compared with egg size and thus their fledging periods are essentially redressing the previous imbalance.

With such data it is inappropriate to make more detailed interspecific comparisons but it should be noted that some differences probably relate partly to different relationships between chick and egg weights, and between chick hatching and fledging weights and to differences in environ-

TABLE III

Chick growth data for Antarctic penguins and procellariiforms

Species	Asymptote (g)	Growth constant[b]	$t_{10}-t_{90}$ (days)	Mean daily weight gain[b] (g)	(as % asymptote)	Reference
Emperor penguin	13,000	0.046	89	113	0.87	Stonehouse, 1953
King penguin	12,000	0.10	74	130	1.08	Stonehouse, 1960
Adélie penguin	4200	0.168	29	116	2.76	Taylor and Roberts, 1962
	2310	0.174	28	70	3.03	Sapin–Jaloustre & Bourlière, 1951
	4200	0.12	37	91	2.16	Sladen, 1958
	3940	0.146	30			Volkman and Trivelpiece, 1980
Chinstrap penguin	3650	0.156	34	86	2.35	Despin, 1977
	4025	0.127	35			Volkman and Trivelpiece, 1980
Gentoo penguin	5100	0.116	45	87	1.69	Despin, 1977
	6230	0.074	c.50	c.75	1.19	Despin, 1972
	5300	0.12	46	85	1.66	Croxall, unpublished
Macaroni penguin	3200	0.128	37	69	2.16	Croxall, unpublished
Rockhopper penguin	2750	0.132	45	49	1.78	Warham, 1963
Fiordland crested penguin	3000	0.092	46	52	1.74	Warham, 1974
Yellow-eyed penguin	6000	0.08	72	67	1.11	Richdale, 1957
Jackass penguin	1750	0.09	52	27	1.54	Cooper, 1977
Little blue penguin	1100		38	23	2.07	Kinsky, 1960
Wandering albatross	11,500	0.026	164	56	0.49	Tickell, 1968

Royal albatross	10,900		105	83	0.76	Richdale, 1952
Black-browed albatross	5000	0.048	57	70	1.40	Ricketts and Prince, 1981
Grey-headed albatross	4700	0.042	60	63	1.33	Ricketts and Prince, 1981
Light-mantled sooty albatross	3450	0.043	62	45	1.30	Thomas, et al., 1983
Northern giant petrel	5850	0.047	70	66	1.13	Hunter, in press
Southern giant petrel	6000	0.040	59	79	1.31	Hunter, in press
Antarctic fulmar	1200	0.121[a]	30	32	2.7	Mougin, 1967
Cape pigeon	680		27	20	3.0	Mougin, 1968
	480		25	16	3.2	Pinder, 1966
Snow petrel	500	0.194[a]	23	17	3.5	Isenmann, 1970b
Dove prion	215	0.183[a]	25	6.9	3.2	Prince, unpublished
	220	0.160[a]	28	6.6	2.86	Tickell, 1962
Salvin's prion	c.190	0.151[a]	31	5.9	3.01	Derenne and Mougin, 1976
Fairy prion	c.150	0.145[a]	26	4.6	3.33	Harper, 1976
Narrow-billed prion	235	0.107	29	6.5	2.76	Strange, 1980
Blue petrel	290	0.136[a]	33	7.2	2.61	Prince, unpublished
White-headed petrel	c.900		55	13	1.45	Barré, 1976
White-chinned petrel	1850	0.043	62	24	1.29	Prince, unpublished
Grey petrel	1220		c.55	18	1.45	Barrat, 1974
Sooty shearwater	c.750		36	17	2.22	Richdale, 1945
Wilson's storm petrel	62	0.041	45	1.1	1.8	Beck and Brown, 1972
	68	0.077	19	2.8	4.2	Lacan, 1971
White-faced storm petrel	c.65	0.120	c.25	2.08	3.1	Richdale, 1965a
Common diving petrel	c.160	0.129[a]	30	4.27	2.7	Payne and Prince, 1979
South Georgia diving petrel	145	0.165[a]	24	4.8	3.3	Payne and Prince, 1979

K_L for all penguins; K_G for all Procellariiformes, except ^{a}, which K_L.
^{b} Over period $t_{10}-t_{90}$.

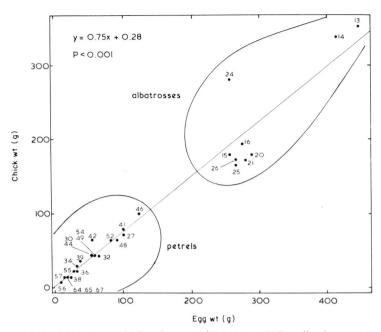

Fig. 17. Relationship between chick and egg weights in Antarctic Procellariiformes. Numbers refer to Appendix I.

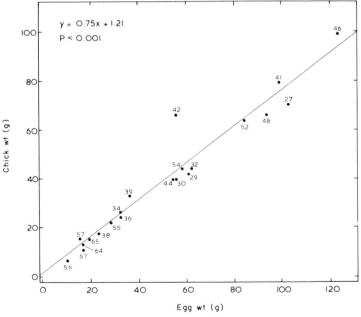

Fig. 18. Relationship between chick and egg weights in smaller Antarctic Procellariiformes. Numbers refer to Appendix I.

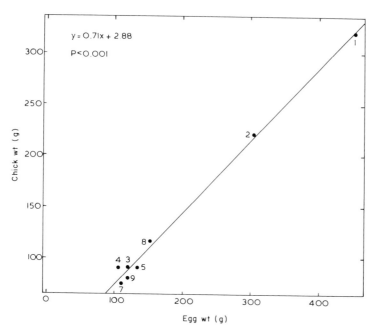

Fig. 19. Relationship between chick and egg weights in Antarctic Spheniciformes. Numbers refer to Appendix I.

ment. One might suggest, for instance, that the longer fledging period of wandering albatross, when compared with royal albatross, might be partly explained in these ways, but also seems to involve different growth rates (Table III).

The eudyptid penguins form a group with no obvious trends but the Adélie penguin has a proportionately very short fledging period whereas that of the gentoo penguin is proportionately long (although it is difficult to determine the true fledging period in this species because there is some parental care of chicks ashore for some time after one might judge them independent—and certainly when they are obtaining some food for themselves).

5.3 Chicks, fledging period and growth

The weight of chicks at hatching is, for most species, closely correlated with egg weight (Figs 17–19). As with eggs, larger birds have larger chicks but the reverse is true if they are considered in proportion to adult body weight (Figs 20, 21). The absence of reliable hatching weights reduces the number

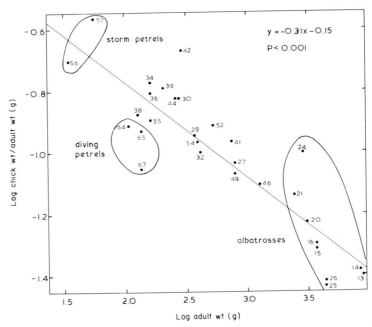

Fig. 20. Relationship between proportionate chick weight and adult weight in Antarctic Procellariiformes. Numbers refer to Appendix I.

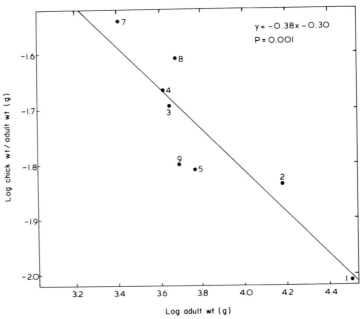

Fig. 21. Relationship between proportionate chick weight and adult weight in Antarctic Sphenisciformes. Numbers refer to Appendix I.

of points on this graph and the scatter suggests that there may exist within the Procellariiformes family-specific trends that are not parallel to the overall one for the order.

For their size giant petrels and the nominate race of common diving petrel and especially narrow-billed prions (Strange, 1980) have particularly small hatchlings, whereas Kerguelen petrel and light-mantled sooty albatross apparently have relatively large ones, but the data for these last two species need verifying.

After hatching, chicks are brooded by their parents until they can cope alone with the rigours of their immediate environment. In burrow-dwelling species the parents leave the chick alone, at least during the day, after only 2–3 days and before it has acquired homeothermy, the ambient temperature of the burrow being high enough for this not to be a problem. For surface nesting species, however, brooding persists through the stages of the chick being covered by the brood patch, then by the underparts of the adult and finally being merely sheltered by the adult. Even in the smaller petrels (e.g. Antarctic fulmar) this takes nearly three weeks (Mougin, 1975). This progressive acquisition of homeothermy has been described for several Antarctic seabirds (e.g. Voisin, 1968, 1969; Mougin, 1968, 1970) and the topic reviewed in some detail for petrels by Mougin (1975); it is not proposed to deal further with it here. The energy costs and other adaptations associated with growth and development of homeothermy have been assessed for king penguin (Barré, 1978; Barré and Rouanet, 1982) and Leach's storm petrel (Ricklefs et al., 1980a).

The fledging periods of procellariforms and penguins are given in Appendix 1. Inevitably the length of this period is correlated with the disparity between hatchling and adult size (i.e. the amount of growth that has to be undertaken) but in Fig. 22 there is a substantial scatter of points (so much so for penguins that the relationship is barely significant and is not plotted) and more species seem to fledge chicks faster or slower than conform to the average relationship. Noteworthy, however, are the fast fledging giant petrels (25, 26) and other fulmarine petrels (27, 29, 32) and the slow fledging warmer water *Puffinus* (52, 55) and *Pterodroma* (41, 42) petrels, a tropical albatross (21) and light-mantled sooty albatross (24).

It is preferable, however, for those species where such data exist, to examine the actual rates of chick growth. Ricklefs (1967, 1968, 1973) has shown that chick growth in birds can be compared by using the best fitting of the three standard growth equations (Gompertz, logistic, von Bertalanffy) to the weight data. Originally (Ricklefs, 1968) the Gompertz equation was applied to penguin data and it has been used again recently (Despin, 1977) but all penguin data are undoubtedly best fitted by the logistic equation and this conclusion is substantiated by Volkman and Trivelpiece (1980)

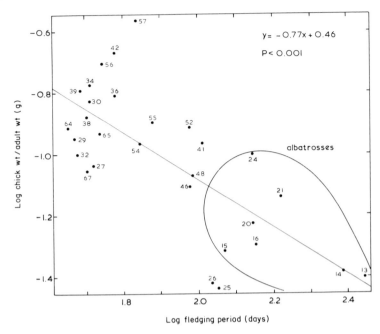

Fig. 22. Relationship between proportionate chick weight and fledging period in Antarctic Procellariiformes. Numbers refer to Appendix I.

who independently analysed penguin growth data. Nevertheless, the basic form of the appropriate curve does not give particularly good fits with growth data from seabirds and although comparisons can be made by using only the "linear" portion of the curve (usually approximated by computing growth over the time taken to grow from 10 to 90% of asymptote weight (t_{10}–t_{90}; see Ricklefs (1973)), this latter statistic and the growth curves themselves are very sensitive to the asymptote value selected. Thus it is often difficult to calculate growth constants from age–weight graphs in the literature.

Nevertheless, until further developments in growth simulation take place, it is feasible to compare seabird growth using the growth constant K for curves fitted by the Gompertz and logistic equations and also to calculate the rate of growth over the t_{10}–t_{90} period. Both these are inversely related to adult body weight. In Table III approximate values of K, t_{10}–t_{90} and the mean increment (g day^{-1}) during the latter, also expressed as a proportion of the asymptote (to correct partially for body weight scaling effects) are presented. All computations are made on the data presented in the source reference, except that the values calculated by Volkman and Trivelpiece (1980) have been used direct. Not all studies provided data adequate to calculate K but estimates of mean daily increment for $t_{10}-t_{90}$ could usually be made.

It is, in any case, the comparative aspects that are of interest here. Thus the emperor and king penguin might appear similar overall but early growth (in winter in the emperor penguin, in summer in the king penguin) is much slower in the former which takes nearly four times as long to achieve a tenfold weight increase (Stonehouse, 1970b). Emperor penguin chicks fledge at only 60% of adult weight whereas king penguin chicks reach 90% of adult weight before virtually fasting throughout the winter and finally increasing again to fledging weight the following spring. Of the pygoscelid penguins the Adélie has the fastest growth rate, followed by chinstrap and then gentoo. This corresponds roughly with the trend to more northerly breeding distributions and suggests that in the species of higher latitudes a shorter fledging period is achieved by faster growth rate, providing the level of food resources can sustain this. Data from Terre Adélie (Sapin-Jaloustre and Bourlière, 1951) give very rapid growth rates, but, as Volkman and Trivelpiece (1980) noted, very low asymptote weights and poor survival up to crèche stage which may have reflected lack of food. Sladen's (1950) data are also anomalous, giving very slow growth rates (and he recorded incubation shifts twice as long as any other workers) and it may have been an unusual season locally. Of the crested penguins, macaroni and rockhopper have the highest growth constants, but, by proportionate weight, the former achieves the larger weight increases.

In procellariform growth to peak weight, within the normal trend for larger birds to have slower growth, there are several anomalies. Thus the small fulmarine petrels have exceptionally fast growth for their weight; in contrast *Procellaria* and *Pterodroma* petrels have very slow growth rates approximating to those of the much larger albatrosses. It is clearly no coincidence that the former group should be widely and abundantly distributed in high latitudes and the latter confined, in the Antarctic, to low latitudes, the two groups virtually replacing each other. Only those medium-sized species with short breeding seasons would have been able to take full advantage of the rich food available in the immediate vicinity of the Antarctic continent. Whether the fulmarine petrels already possessed short incubation and fledging periods or whether they were developed as the niche became available is uncertain, but they are shared by *Fulmarus glacialis*, their sole northern hemisphere representative. Although most members of the group have been studied to some extent (Mougin, 1967, 1968; Maher, 1962; Pinder, 1966; Brown 1966; Beck, 1969) and their apparent suitability from the viewpoint of environmental considerations was noted earlier (p. 548), it is not clear what facets of their biology and ecology enabled fulmarine petrels, rather than other groups, to take advantage of the opportunity and which are the key adaptations that maintain the situation today.

The lengthy breeding season of the *Pterodroma* and *Procellaria* petrels, and the disproportionate length of the fledging period, seem (see later) to be related to the long intervals at which chicks are fed, which is presumably a reflection of where they feed and the nature and dispersion of their prey.

Wilson's storm petrels at Signy grow much slower than those at Terre Adélie, taking nearly twice as long to reach peak values. Although this would fit with breeding latitude, the discrepancy is a very large one and judging from data for other storm petrels (e.g. Harris, 1969; Richdale, 1965a), the Signy value is rather extreme for the family.

The South Georgia diving petrel grows significantly faster than any race of the common diving petrel and, as Payne and Prince (1979) emphasized, it has shortened both incubation and fledging periods in comparison with its coexisting congener. This may be attributable to its breeding later, when food resources are more abundant.

It should be emphasized that most data in Table III derive from a single study in one season using rather few individuals and thus detailed comparison of species patterns is inadvisable. Nevertheless, with black-browed and grey-headed albatrosses where large samples were used, their quite small differences in growth rate do appear to represent species-characteristic differences and are of real significance in influencing the duration of the breeding season (Ricketts and Prince, 1981).

There has been considerable recent discussion concerning growth strategies (e.g. O'Connor, 1977; Ricklefs, 1979) and while this has mainly involved questions of whether resources are allocated to growth of components with currently highest functional priority (but with regard for future needs) and whether there exist physiological bottlenecks limiting growth rates, much information of relevance to seabird growth has emerged. In particular Ricklefs (1979) showed that for many precocial birds (in their growth patterns he regards procellariforms as semi-precocial rather than semi-altricial), the development period may be determined by the slowest growing tissue, which tends to be the skeletal muscle of the legs, and in late growth the pectoral muscles (Ricklefs *et al.*, 1980b). He further suggested that the large fat stores of procellariform chicks may also function as an energy sink, increasing the nestling's capacity to accumulate calories, and thereby additional protein and other nutrients, which may be more limiting. The slow growth of many tropical seabirds (mainly gulls, terns and Pelecaniformes; there is suggestive evidence here of similar phenomena in tropical petrels and albatrosses) is thought to be related to energy or particular nutrient constraints. Although procellariforms as a group grow slowly there is apparently such a variation in growth rates, even between related species, in the Antarctic that the interrelationship between growth rate, diet, meal size and feeding frequency should be a particularly fruitful field for further study.

6. Food and Feeding Ecology

6.1 Food

Carrick and Ingham (1967) reviewed the nature of the prey of Antarctic seabirds, but like a recent summary for Procellariidae (Mougin, 1975), this was chiefly based on observed stomach contents analysed on the basis of frequency of occurrence of main prey types. As Ashmole and Ashmole (1967) noted, such information is unsatisfactory and can be misleading as it emphasizes the presence of indigestible remains (and especially squid beaks). For thorough interpretation it is necessary to have information on numbers of individuals and total weight of each prey class with the latter the most important single measure, particularly if calculations of population consumption, etc. are desired.

The main results of the very few fully quantitative studies involving Antarctic seabirds are presented in Table IV. All except some samples from grey-faced petrels (Imber, 1973) were obtained from adults (usually about to feed their chicks), thus avoiding the problems of food accumulation that arise when samples are taken from chicks. Since Carrick and Ingham's (1967) review, a number of useful qualitative analyses or quantitative analyses of certain components of the diet (e.g. squid beaks) have been published. These have involved sooty and light-mantled sooty albatrosses (based on squid beaks in regurgitated pellets: Berruti, 1979; Berruti and Harcus, 1978), wandering albatrosses (squid from chicks or pellets: Imber and Russ, 1975; Clarke et al., 1981), northern and southern giant petrels (pellets and chick regurgitations: Conroy, 1972; Johnstone, 1977), white-chinned petrels (squid beaks from chicks: Imber, 1976a), cape pigeons (chick regurgitations: Beck, 1969), various prions (regurgitations and stomach samples: Imber, 1981), and blue-eyed shags (squid beaks and fish remains from pellets: Schlatter and Moreno, 1976); some mention of diet can be found in most of the main papers on general biology and some additional unpublished data are given in Croxall and Prince (1980a) and Prince (1982).

Before we consider some of the results of the more detailed studies, on the basis of all available information (and interpreting the qualitative studies on the basis of the qualitative and quantitative comparisons in the detailed studies—especially Imber (1973, 1981), Prince (1980a,b)—the following greatly simplified breakdown of species' principal natural dietary preferences can be suggested.

TABLE IV

Percentage composition by weight of diet of various Antarctic seabirds

Species	Main prey classes					Crustacean prey				Locality	Reference
	Squid	Fish	Lamprey	Crustacea	Carrion	Euphausiids	Decapods	Amphipods	Copepods		
Adélie penguin	+	39		61		98[a]		2	+	Cape Crozier	Emison, 1968
Adélie penguin		+		100		100		+		S. Shetland I.	Volkman et al., 1981
Chinstrap penguin		4		96		100		+		S. Shetland I.	Croxall and Furse, 1980
Chinstrap penguin		+		100		100		+		S. Shetland I.	Volkman et al., 1981
Gentoo penguin		15		85		100		+		S. Shetland I.	Volkman et al., 1981
Gentoo penguin		32		68		100		+		South Georgia	Croxall and Prince, 1980a
Macaroni penguin		2		98		100		+		South Georgia	Croxall and Prince, 1980a
Macaroni penguin		25		75		75[b]		+		S. Shetland I.	Croxall and Furse, 1980
Black-browed albatross	21	38		40	+	95	2.5	2.5		South Georgia	Prince, 1980b
Grey-headed albatross	49	24		16		96	2	2		South Georgia	Prince, 1980b
Light-mantled sooty albatross	47	11		41	+	89	10	1		South Georgia	Thomas, 1982
Northern giant petrel	2	3		22	73	100				South Georgia	Hunter, 1983
Southern giant petrel	1	1		21	77	100				South Georgia	Hunter, 1983
Dove prion	1	2		97		60		8	32	South Georgia	Prince, 1980a
Broad-billed prion		2		97		6[c]	+	20	72	Chatham I.	Imber, 1981
Blue petrel	1	8		91		90	1	5	4	South Georgia	Prince, 1980a
White-chinned petrel	47	24		29		96	2	2		South Georgia	Prince, unpublished
Grey-faced petrel	58	28		12		17[e]	54	+		New Zealand	Imber, 1973
South Georgia diving petrel				100		76		4	20	South Georgia	Payne and Prince, 1979
Common diving petrel		30		100		15		17	68	South Georgia	Payne and Prince, 1979
White-faced storm petrel				70		67[d]		14	+	Chatham I.	Imber, 1981
Grey-backed storm petrel	+			100[f]		7[c]		7		Chatham I.	Imber, 1981

Euphausiids were all *E. superba* except: [a]99% *E. crystallorophias*, [b]50% *Thysanoessa macrura*, [c]*Nyctiphanes australis*, [d]mainly *N. australis* and *Nematoscelis megalops*; remaining crustaceans (19%) were brachyurans, stomatopods and mysids.
[e]Remaining crustaceans (28%) were mysids.
[f]85% were larvae/juveniles of *Lepas australis* (Cirripedia).
+ Present in small quantities.

Crustacea: *Eudyptes* spp., *Pygoscelis* spp., *D. melanophris, Phoebetria* spp., *Daption, Pagodroma, Thalassoica, Fulmarus, Halobaena, Pachyptila* spp., *Pelecanoides* spp., storm petrels.

Squid: *Aptenodytes* spp., *Diomedea* spp., (except *D. melanophris*) *Phoebetria* spp., *Macronectes* spp. (at some localities), *Fulmarus, Procellaria* spp., *Pterodroma* spp., *Puffinus* spp.

Fish: *Aptenodytes forsteri, Pygoscelis papua, P. adeliae* (continent), some *Diomedea* spp., *Halobaena, Phalacrocorax* spp. (some squid), *Sterna vittata* (and crustacea?).

Other: *Macronectes* spp. (carrion), *Catharacta* spp. (eggs, chicks, small petrels, also fish and crustacea in *C. maccormicki*), *Larus* (beach invertebrates), *Sterna virgata* (insects etc.).

Further breakdown on the basis of diet type within these categories is impossible for fish (usually highly digested; various Nototheniidae, Chaenichthyidae, Myctophidae and *Pleurogramma* are frequently recorded in the Antarctic). With increasing ability to identify squid on the basis of beaks alone (see Clarke, 1962, 1980 for methods) more detailed analysis of this dietary component is now possible and some significant differences in the size and species of squid taken by different seabirds are emerging, e.g. for the four albatrosses breeding at South Georgia (Croxall and Prince, 1980a; Clarke *et al.*, 1981; Clarke and Prince, 1981). In other cases similar species appear to take much more similar squid (e.g. Berruti (1979) on the two *Phoebetria* albatrosses at Marion Island).

In studies so far most crustaceans consumed are krill *Euphausia superba* except near the Antarctic continent where this is replaced by *E. crystallorophias* and in the New Zealand area where other euphausiids such as *Thysanoessa macrura* and *Nyctiphanes australis* may also be locally important. Small differences in the size of euphausiids taken by species, populations or sexes have been found during various studies (e.g. Emison, 1968; Ainley and Emison, 1972; White and Conroy, 1975; Croxall and Furse, 1980; Croxall and Prince, 1980b; Volkman *et al.*, 1981) but because euphausiid populations themselves apparently show considerable local variation it is not clear to what extent these are the result of differential selection or feeding in different areas. Other groups of crustacea may be important, e.g. copepods in the diet of broad-billed and dove prion (and probably *P. salvini* also), diving petrels and possibly storm petrels. Amphipods and particularly *Parathemisto gaudichaudii* may be important to *Pachyptila belcheri* (Harper, 1972; Strange, 1980) and there were significant differences in the proportions taken by blue petrel and dove prion of amphipod species common to the diet of both (Prince, 1980a).

In more northerly petrels euphausiids may play a less significant role, and other groups (decapods, mysids, barnacle larvae) may predominate, as Imber (1973, 1981) found for grey-faced petrels and grey-backed storm petrels, although these studies were conducted at or north of the Subtropical Convergence. The presence of large numbers of lampreys in the diet of the grey-headed albatrosses at South Georgia is intriguing and perhaps only intelligible if they become free-living prior to returning to their natal South American streams (Potter *et al.*, 1979).

There are a number of other interesting features in the dietary information. Firstly, there are some important differences in the food of closely related (or otherwise rather similar) species, e.g. diving petrels, black-browed and grey-headed albatrosses, dove prion and blue petrel and the significance of this in terms of minimizing direct competition has been discussed in the papers concerned and reviewed by Croxall and Prince (1980a). With further detailed studies doubtless other examples will be recognized.

Secondly, certain diets can be tentatively correlated with other aspects of species' biology. Thus it will be difficult for most seabirds to find crustaceans in the Antarctic in winter as most remaining stocks will be at some depth. Therefore such seabirds must either move north out of the Antarctic regions (as do the black-browed albatross, Wilson's storm petrel and macaroni penguin—and probably some other species) or turn to catching squid and fish.

We have very little information on the winter diets of summer breeding species, except for sooty and great shearwaters off Newfoundland (Brown *et al.*, 1981), but doubtless those that already take squid and fish prey in summer continue to do so in winter. It is not surprising that gentoo penguin (which alone of the small penguins takes much fish) is essentially a resident species at the sub-Antarctic islands. The very early breeding of at least some of the population at most localities may also be assisted by having a prey resource available before the crustacean stocks become abundant.

All *Pterodroma* and *Procellaria* petrels probably take mainly squid. These seabirds were identified as having particularly long fledging periods and evidence is accumulating that squid tend to be a fairly well dispersed resource (most known squid predators feed their chicks rather infrequently) and that at least some species are of poor nutritive quality (Croxall and Prince, 1982a). The two smaller albatrosses that feed largely on squid have significantly longer chick fledging periods than the black-browed albatross, which feeds extensively on krill, and this has also been attributed to the influence of a squid diet (Prince, 1980b; Prince & Ricketts, 1981). Furthermore, the long fledging period in *D. chrysostoma* and *Phoebetria* spp. is important in influencing their frequencies of breeding as these are species that, if successful, do not breed the following season. This is true too for the wandering albatross which also predominantly feeds on squid but this, being much larger, has a very much longer chick fledging period anyway. Nevertheless, the relationships between diet, chick growth rate, length of fledging period and breeding periodicity in albatrosses deserve much further study.

This brief review of diets has only dealt with the solid portion of meals fed to chicks. Procellariforms (but not penguins) also feed their chicks a substantial quantity of liquid (50% in small albatrosses (Prince, 1980b); 40% in blue petrel, 20% in dove prion (Prince, 1980a) but apparently none in diving petrels (Warham, 1977a)), which is now confirmed to be dietary in origin (Clarke and Prince, 1976; Warham *et al.*, 1976). It has usually been assumed that food digestion is accompanied by water elimination and that the lipid-rich oil is an important adaptation ensuring that birds feeding far from the breeding colony give their chick a highly-concentrated meal. There is now evidence, however, that, at least with mollymauks, different prey types are associated with liquids of different lipid content, only krill meals having substantial quantities of associated lipid—and then only 27% of liquid by weight (Clarke and Prince, 1980). Thus there may well be no real concentration of lipid by the parent and it is possible that the water transferred is itself important to the water balance of the chick (cf. Warham, 1977a).

6.2 Feeding ecology

Complementary to an accurate knowledge of what seabirds eat is information on how they catch their prey and where they find it. This subject has recently been reviewed by Croxall and Prince (1980a) for seabirds at South Georgia (where most of the detailed studies of diet have been carried out).

6.2.1 Feeding methods

There are two fundamental marine feeding techniques shown by Antarctic seabirds, pursuit diving and surface feeding. The former is particularly characteristic of penguins and the large *Aptenodytes* spp. (feeding on squid and fish) reach 235–265 m (Kooyman *et al.*, 1971, 1982) whereas the krill-eating chinstrap penguin did not exceed 70 m, and 40% of dives were shallower than 10 m (Lishman and Croxall, 1983). Other diving species are the shags which are characteristically inshore species, often associated with kelp beds where younger stages of many Antarctic fish mature, and diving petrels, which probably feed only in the upper few metres of the water column. Diving petrels and penguins in particular show clear morphological and anatomical adaptations for diving (Kuroda, 1967; Kooyman, 1975); these are less obvious in shags.

A greater degree of subdivision of the essentially surface-feeding habit is possible. Using the terminology of Ashmole (1971) probably nearly all the remaining seabirds "surface seize" to catch prey, although not all will rely on this technique to the same extent. "Dipping" is probably characteristic of the storm petrels, which patter near the surface and the gadfly petrels (*Pterodroma* spp.) and blue petrel which swoop down from a height. Plunging is typical of the terns and has been recorded occasionally for storm petrels and some albatrosses. Surface diving is perhaps most prevalent amongst petrels, particularly *Puffinus* and *Procellaria* species, but it is also used by albatrosses and diving petrels. In some ways the most specialized technique is that of certain prions (*P. desolata*, *P. salvini* and *P. vittata*) that have broad deep bills and a comb-like lamella fringing the inside of the upper mandible through which they expel water to filter out small prey organisms.

Most seabirds are opportunistic scavengers but some obtain most of their food in this way, whether from the sea or on land. Pre-eminent are giant petrels and Johnstone (1977, 1979) has detailed the various types of carrion that they acquire and some of the interactions that occur between the two species. Skuas, particularly brown skua (and southern black-backed gull) also scavenge and detailed studies of their effect on, and rôle in, penguin colonies have been made by Young (1963a), Müller-Schwarze and Müller-Schwarze (1975), Trivelpiece *et al.* (1980) and Trivelpiece and Volkman (1982). Young (1963a) showed that some Antarctic skuas, particularly those which do not have territories including portions of penguin colonies, are capable of subsisting by catching fish and even crustaceans at sea. Such habits are rarely, if at all, shown by the brown skua and it is significant that the more marine of these two skuas has longer wings more adapted for foraging at sea (and also for more extensive migratory journeys).

Feeding methods are obviously related to the morphology of the species concerned and Warham (1977b) has reviewed wing shapes and wing loadings of a number of species, while Ainley (1977) related feeding techniques to buoyancy indices; in both cases any correlations are of the most general kind as we lack precise data on flight capabilities and understanding of the adaptive significance of small scale differences in wing shape and area. There are also general relationships between prey type and bill shape and structure. Thus the "filter feeding" dove prion feeds principally on copepods, whereas blue petrel, often recognizing prey from a distance, catches consistently larger organisms (Prince, 1980a). The narrow but powerful hook-tipped bills of gadfly petrels presumably aid in immobilizing the squid they swoop down on or, in the case of *Procellaria* petrels, seize at the sea surface. Albatross bills are razor sharp at the edges and hook tipped and they appear to be well equipped to handle quite large fish and especially squid (Clarke *et al.*, 1981).

6.2.2 Foraging range

Until the movements of known breeding birds can be directly monitored we rely on indirect evidence for the distance seabirds travel to find food and the areas which they visit.

For breeding birds the length of incubation shifts and particularly the time between successive visits to feed a chick can give an indication of potential foraging range. Chick feeding frequency is often determined from daily chick weighings but this method becomes increasingly inaccurate with smaller birds and may lead to underestimates of as much as 55% (Harper, 1976). Using information from a variety of sources, Croxall and Prince (1980a,b) provided estimates of the time between successive feeds by the same parent for South Georgia penguins and petrels that varied between at least twice daily (giant petrel) and every 5–6 days (wandering albatross). Using other information available in the literature, including a parental absence period of eight days in grey-faced petrels (Imber, 1976b), and assuming that related species show similar patterns, this approach can be extended to the other Antarctic seabirds. In Table V these are classified as inshore (at least one feed by each parent per day), offshore (each parent visits at about two-day intervals) and pelagic (interval at least three days). A few species are placed in intermediate categories. Penguins and petrels cannot be compared directly as, taking reasonable swimming and flight speeds (see Croxall and Prince, 1980a for details), gentoo, macaroni and king penguins might have theoretical feeding radii of *c.* 30 km, *c.* 115 km and *c.* 500 km respectively whereas albatrosses and petrels in each of the three main categories might have radii of 300 km, 900 km and 1200–2000+ km. These distances assume direct flight without stopping and so are maxima, but provide a basis for comparison.

The differing ability of species to feed at different distances from a breeding colony can be important in reducing direct competition (Croxall and Prince, 1980a), particularly for species whose diets are broadly similar, e.g. gentoo and macaroni penguins at South Georgia, both of which extensively take mature krill (Croxall and Prince, 1980b).

The existence of different feeding areas for species of similar potential foraging ranges has also been suggested (on the basis of at-sea observations) for the two *Phoebetria* albatrosses at Marion Island (Berruti, 1979)—*P. fusca* foraging north and *P. palpebrata* south of the Antarctic

TABLE V

Feeding zones of Antarctic seabirds

	Inshore	Intermediate	Offshore	Intermediate	Pelagic
Diving	Gentoo penguin Shags Diving petrels	Chinstrap penguin	Macaroni penguin Adelie penguin	King penguin	
Surface feeding	Storm petrels Diving petrels Giant petrels Antarctic skua Antarctic tern	Prions	Black-browed albatross Grey-headed albatross Snow petrel Antarctic fulmar Cape pigeon	Blue petrel Antarctic petrel	Wandering albatross Sooty albatrosses White-chinned petrel Grey-faced petrel Grey petrel Kerguelen petrel White-headed petrel

Convergence—and for *P. palpebrata* and *D. melanophris* at South Georgia (Thomas, 1982). Other cases might be recognized with more observations at critical times of year.

If any group of seabirds co-occurring at a single breeding station is studied closely it seems likely that even the most similar species will show significant differences in diet, feeding methods or foraging range and that, overall, they will show a considerable range of different combinations of adaptations. As Croxall and Prince (1980a) emphasize for South Georgia, these, together with differences in timing of the breeding season, may well provide adequate ecological isolating mechanisms to ensure that in normal circumstances direct competition for food is avoided, at least in summer.

Abnormal conditions, however, such as the absence of krill swarms from the vicinity of South Georgia in 1977–1978 and the subsequent breeding failure of some krill-eating species (Croxall and Prince, 1979), provide evidence that direct competition may not be negligible in these circumstances and may thus have been important in shaping the adaptations that have been described.

There are two final points worth mentioning here. First, the time of feeding may differ between species. Surface-feeding species may only be able to obtain prey regularly at night when krill (and fish and squid predators) rise to the surface. The subject of nocturnal feeding has been extensively discussed by Imber (1973) but we still lack any direct observations. Diving species suffer from no such feeding time restrictions and at least some penguins probably do part of their feeding during the day—and often spend the night at the breeding colony.

Secondly, there will be many local differences in the availability of food in the vicinity of breeding colonies. On a larger scale there is some evidence for this when comparisons are made between South Georgia and other sub-Antarctic islands. Thus the macaroni penguin at South Georgia has chicks that grow faster, and adults that have a much shorter premoult fattening period than any other eudyptid and particularly shorter than the same species at Marion Island (Williams *et al.*, 1977) and the royal penguin at Macquarie Island (Warham, 1971b, and see Fig. 17). This is the best evidence but data in Berruti (1979) suggest that at Marion Island the light-mantled sooty albatross brings fewer feeds to its chick which has a longer fledging period there, perhaps as a result of both this and of an apparently greater dependence on squid, than at South Georgia. In normal seasons the gentoo penguin seems to enjoy better breeding success at South Georgia than elsewhere (cf. Croxall and Prince, 1979; Despin, 1972; van Zinderen Bakker, 1971b; Williams, 1980d).

South Georgia, with its extensive continental shelf and proximity to the Antarctic Convergence while being surrounded by nutrient-rich cold waters, may thus have a particularly favourable marine environment and one that has been very successfully exploited by its vast macaroni penguin population. Further south, seabirds are by no means evenly distributed and their breeding and feeding concentrations may equally reflect differences in the productivity of the adjacent marine environment. The differences in species' breeding ecology consequent on this may be small but yet highly significant if the marine environment changes, e.g. through krill and fish harvesting.

7. Breeding Success

The proportion of eggs hatched and chicks fledged is recorded in many papers on breeding biology. Such information (for some summarized data see Mougin, 1975; Berruti, 1979; Croxall and Prince, 1979) suggests it is rare for chicks to fledge from more than half the eggs laid and indicates that albatrosses and giant petrels may normally have greater (and more consistent) breeding success than penguins, and especially than the smaller burrowing petrels. However, samples are usually small, and differences between seasons, sites and colonies large, whilst the studies themselves probably cause some disturbance, especially to small petrels. Direct natural predation is rare, skuas being usually (giant petrels, sheathbills and gulls occasionally) responsible, and normally involves abandoned eggs or chicks, although in sub-Antarctic regions skuas excavate healthy chicks from their burrows. Introduced predators (rats and particularly cats), however, take a heavy toll of eggs and chicks of burrowing petrels. Breeding success, especially in relation to environmental conditions and age and experience of parents, has been best studied with penguins. Jouventin (1975) and Yeates (1968, 1975) showed direct relationships between the severity of environmental conditions and egg and chick losses in emperor penguin and Adélie penguin respectively. With the latter species Stonehouse (1963) and Ainley and Le Resche (1973) also demonstrated the importance of the timing of ice break-out in spring (influencing the distance birds have to travel to find food); early break-out was correlated with good breeding success at Cape Crozier (Ainley and Le Resche, 1973) and Cape Royds (Yeates, 1968).

Although fledging success is very variable between seasons and despite different environmental circumstances at various breeding colonies the mean number of eggs laid by Adélie penguin has only varied between 1.81 and 1.86 per pair over numerous extensive studies (Sladen, 1958; Taylor, 1962; Reid, 1964; Yeates, 1968; Ainley and Schlatter, 1971; Spurr, 1975; Trivelpiece and Volkman, 1982), except for a value of 1.61 at Cape Bird in

1968–1969 attributed to reduction of clutch size by many birds in poor condition due to unusual ice conditions (Spurr, 1975).

Pack-ice conditions, ice-blocked burrows or snow-covered nest sites may delay onset of breeding in species generally (many references in the literature) and may even result in adults feeding and chicks fledging at less than optimum times. Mild winter weather has also been noted to coincide with high wandering albatross breeding success (Croxall and Prince, 1979; Croxall, 1979). The relationship between breeding success and colony size (better in larger colonies; Oelke, 1975) and nest position (better in central than peripheral birds; Tenaza, 1971; Spurr, 1975) have been investigated in the Adélie penguin. The latter result probably reflects the tendency for younger birds (which lay fewer (Tenaza, 1971), smaller (Yeates, 1968) eggs) to breed at the periphery of colonies (cf. Coulson, 1968). The influence of age on breeding success has been extensively studied in Adélie penguin (Sladen *et al.*, 1968; Ainley and Schlatter, 1972; Ainley *et al.*, 1983). Age affected laying date, clutch size, incubation routine (but not incubation period), egg fertility and hatching and fledging success. Experience, even of only one previous breeding season, improved hatching and fledging success, although no effect on the other factors could be detected. In royal penguin Carrick (1972) showed that the incidence of breeding and breeding success increased with age. In the Adélie penguin chick weights at fledging also increased with the age of the parents and similar differences in peak weight have been found when comparing the progeny of mature (>25 years old) and young (10–15 years old) grey-headed albatrosses (Prince, unpublished). The quality of feeding territories has also been shown to influence breeding success in Antarctic and brown skuas (Young, 1963b; Trillmich, 1978; Trivelpiece *et al.*, 1980) but it is likely that it is increased feeding ability with greater age and experience that is relevant to penguins and other pelagic seabirds.

Despite all the variables (i.e. environment, colony size, nest position, age) that may influence growth rate and breeding success there has been increasing recognition that long-term studies of such topics, with appropriate methodology, may be particularly valuable for monitoring the response of Antarctic seabirds to changes in marine living resources, and especially those that may follow the advent of large-scale commercial exploitation of krill and fish. Proposals have been made to monitor selected species at geographically widespread sites (SCAR, 1979, 1980). A review of general concepts and certain active investigations (Croxall and Prince, 1979) stressed the importance of, where possible, simultaneously monitoring several species at a single site. This paper and Croxall and Kirkwood (1979) also presented further evidence for increases in breeding numbers and range of Antarctic seabirds, especially penguins. These have been long interpreted as due to improved breeding and fledging success and survival consequent on enhanced availability of krill following the reduction in numbers of Antarctic baleen whales. However, winter food resources must also be adequate to sustain these increased bird populations and enhanced opportunities for scavenging at fishing boats may be important in this.

8. Non-breeding Season Events

8.1 Moult

Information is sparse on the timing and duration of moult in Antarctic seabirds and only for the southern black-backed gull is a reasonably comprehensive picture available (Kinsky, 1963). The only clear patterns seem to be that in petrels body moult usually commences during the incubation period (Marshall and Serventy, 1956a; Warham, 1962, 1967; Beck, 1969; Conroy, 1972; Berruti, 1979) but that primary feather moult takes place at sea after chicks have fledged. In the cape pigeon (Beck, 1969) and probably the snow petrel (Maher, 1962), however, primary moult commences shortly before chicks fledge, and, as it lasts about 85 days in the cape pigeon (Beck, 1969), is completed by May before the start of winter conditions. An early start to primary moult was also noted for the southern giant petrel (Warham, 1962; Conroy, 1972) and has now been shown to be characteristic of breeding birds of both giant petrel species (although on average slightly later in *M. halli*) and in male *M. giganteus* it commences at egg-laying and is suspended during chick growth (Hunter, 1984). This early onset of wing moult may prove to be typical of the larger petrels that breed in high latitudes, permitting them to undertake a process requiring major energy expenditure while food levels are still high. The smaller crevice-nesting petrels, at least at Signy, showed no signs of primary moult while breeding (Beck, 1970).

Tickell and Pinder (1975) noted that, unlike other albatrosses (Harris, 1973), *D. melanophris* does undergo some body moult while breeding. This is doubtless a concomitant of an annual breeding strategy with the shorter time available for moult between successive breeding attempts. The pattern of primary moult in these albatrosses is a complex one with several moult "centres" in the wing and complete renewal of plumage certainly takes more than one year in *D. melanophris* and more than two years in *D. chrysostoma* (Prince, unpublished).

In failed breeders primary moult may begin within a week of egg or chick loss. Non-breeding birds also moult during the breeding season and

Warham (1967) suggested, on the basis of data from the white-headed petrel, that as birds get older they may begin moult progressively later.

Penguins come ashore for a complete moult during a comparatively brief and well-defined period (see Fig. 14) in anticipation of which they accumulate considerable fat reserves which are lost during the moult fast. Pre-breeding birds come ashore to moult progressively later in succeeding years as shown by data for the royal penguin (Carrick, 1972) and in gentoo but not macaroni penguin failed breeders normally commence moult earlier than successful birds (Croxall, unpublished). There is clearly substantial scope for more intensive studies of moult, particularly in the large petrels and albatrosses.

8.2 Migrations and movements

A review of this topic is outside the scope of this chapter and only brief comments on some salient features will be made. Pelagic distributions have been the subject of numerous papers recording bird sightings. There were reviewed briefly by Voous (1965), general distributions summarized by Watson (1975) and there are relevant recent papers by van Zinderen Bakker (1971c), Tickell and Woods (1972), Johnstone (1974), Johnstone and Kerry (1976), Kock and Reinsch (1978), Linkowski and Rembizewski (1978), Naito *et al.* (1979), Ainley and Jacobs (1981), Thurston (1982) and Jouventin *et al.* (1982). Wilson's storm petrels (Roberts, 1940) and at least some Antarctic skuas (records from Japan (Voous, 1965) and as far north as Greenland (Parmelee, 1976)) are transequatorial migrants, as are several temperate sub-Antarctic species, e.g. sooty shearwater (Richdale, 1963), great shearwater, mottled petrel and Tasmanian short-tailed shearwater (Serventy, 1957). Inevitably most other Antarctic seabirds also tend to move northwards in winter but rarely past the sub-tropical zone. Those that breed at high latitudes are (except the emperor penguin) virtually compelled to move at least to the pack-ice edge.

Related species seem often to show different degrees of winter movement. Thus snow and Antarctic petrels maintain a high Antarctic distribution but the other fulmarine petrels range much further north even into the Humboldt and Benguela cold surface-water currents off South America and South Africa, respectively. Black-browed albatross populations move well north in winter whereas grey-headed albatrosses remain in the high latitudes (Tickell, 1967; Prince, 1980b) and different black-browed albatross populations may even have different wintering areas. Those from the Falkland Islands and South Georgia frequent South America and South Africa respectively (Tickell, 1967). That the gentoo penguin is more sedentary than the other penguin species has already been noted.

The only regular migrant from the northern hemisphere is the Arctic tern *Sterna paradisaea*, which occurs in Antarctic and sub-Antarctic waters from September to April and completes wing and tail moult before returning north (principally to North Atlantic ocean areas) to breed.

Probably all Antarctic species have a wide dispersal of juvenile birds shortly after fledging, although this has only been well documented, on the basis of recoveries from ringed chicks, for the southern giant petrel (Tickell and Scotland, 1961; Conroy, 1972), and the wandering albatross (Tickell and Gibson, 1968).

9. Population Structure and Dynamics

Seabirds are well known to be long-lived (i.e. having low annual mortality, especially as adults) and to delay breeding until they are several years old. Despite also being easy to capture, mark and recapture, there have been few detailed long-term population studies carried out on Antarctic seabirds except for two major studies involving penguins (Carrick, 1972; Ainley and DeMaster, 1980). Large numbers of birds have been ringed, however, and this does provide some information on the earliest age at which species breed, average age at first breeding and an indication of mean annual mortality of breeding adults (Table VI), topics reviewed in greater detail by Croxall (1982b).

In four penguins and one albatross, one shearwater and one skua, females start breeding before males; only in the southern giant petrel does the reverse appear to happen. The age of onset of breeding is variable, from two years in the common diving petrel to ten years in the sooty albatross, with a suggestion of substantial differences between sites in wandering and black-browed albatrosses. For most species it takes several years from the time when breeding is first recorded for half that year-group to be breeding.

Data on annual survival are derived from recapture data in a variety of ways and it is probably only safe to say that for most species (particularly large albatrosses and fulmarine petrels) it may reach 95% per annum. Diving petrels seem to be a notable exception and all penguins, except the emperor penguin, have an adult survival of only 82–87%.

As adults, few species have any important natural predators. Skuas take numerous storm petrels, diving petrels and prions (and blue petrels and probably *Pterodroma* species of similar size) at night when these arrive to feed their chicks (and this may have been important in the evolution of burrow-dwelling habits); some leopard and fur seals patrol offshore from penguin colonies and take incoming and outgoing birds and also occasional shags; giant petrels take recently-fledged penguins and the occasional small petrel. Feral cats, however, take large numbers of adult burrowing petrels, up to the size of (and possibly including) white-chinned petrels, and are directly responsible for substantial reductions in the numbers of such petrels at some sub-Antarctic islands (Warham, 1967; Mougin, 1969, 1970c; Despin *et al.*, 1972; Jones, 1977, 1980). At Marion Island it is estimated that cats consume about 455,000 petrels of seven species (chiefly dove prions (60%) and the *Pterodroma* spp.) each year (van Aarde, 1980). At Kerguelen the total annual consumption is assessed as 1.2 million birds, probably mainly prions (Pascal, 1980).

In terms of mean life expectancy the smaller petrels may reach 10–15 years of age and the albatrosses and giant petrels at least 25. Some individuals will, of course, live much longer than this and there are field records of 16-year-old Adélie penguins (Ainley and DeMaster, 1980) and 19-year-old yellow-eyed penguins (Richdale, 1957). Wandering albatrosses and snow petrels over 35 years old are still breeding at South Georgia and Signy Island.

Estimation of survival in pre-breeding years is particularly difficult as some young birds may not return to their natal area for several years after fledging and "new" birds may continue to appear even after the majority of that cohort is already breeding. Unlike procellariforms, all pre-breeding penguins come ashore to moult and there is an increasing tendency to do this at their natal colony as they get older. Even in the wandering albatross, with long-deferred maturity, 1% of birds return to their natal area at age two and large numbers (over 25% of a fledged cohort) have appeared by age four, some three seasons before breeding is first observed. This general pattern (though for most species with a more rapid transition to breeding status) is probably typical of most seabirds. Knowing egg, chick and breeding adult mean mortality, estimates of the level of juvenile mortality necessary to keep the population stable can be made (see e.g. Tickell, 1968; Mougin, 1975; Barrat *et al.*, 1976). Assuming, probably reasonably, that the bulk of this mortality is sustained in the first year after fledging, it can be estimated that perhaps only one-third of birds fledged will survive this period, although in the very long-lived species with long-deferred maturity (e.g. wandering albatross) over one-half the birds fledged may survive.

There is increasing evidence that after losses in the first year of life pre-breeding birds may survive well until they commence breeding attempts, when mortality is then high until the survivors become established breeders. Preliminary data of this kind for wandering albatrosses were presented by Croxall (1982) and similar data are accumulating for grey-headed and black-browed albatrosses (Prince *et al.*, in preparation). In these two species, for several hundred birds currently aged 12–17, mean

TABLE VI

Age of first breeding and mean annual adult survival in Antarctic and sub-Antarctic seabirds

Species	Age of first breeding		Mean annual survival[a]	Locality	Reference
	Minimum	Average			
Emperor penguin	3♀ 4♂	5.2 (5♀ 5.8♂)	0.95[b]	Terre Adélie	Mougin and Van Beveren, 1979; Guillotin and Jouventin, 1979
King penguin	4		0.82	Crozet	Barrat, 1976; Jouventin and Mougin, 1981
Adélie penguin	3♀ 4♂	4.7♀ 6.8♂	0.61–0.70	Cape Crozier	Ainley and DeMaster, 1980[c]
Chinstrap penguin	3			Signy	B.A.S. data
Gentoo penguin	2			South Georgia	Croxall, unpublished
Royal penguin	5	7♀ 8♂	0.86	Macquarie	Carrick, 1972
Yellow-eyed penguin	2	2.1♀ 3.2♂	0.87	New Zealand	Richdale, 1957
Little penguin	2	3–4	0.86	Australia	Reilly and Cullen, 1979, 1981
Royal albatross	8		0.97	New Zealand	Richdale, 1952
Wandering albatross	7♀ 9♂	10.6♀ 11.0♂	0.96	South Georgia	Tickell, 1968; Croxall, 1982
Black-browed albatross	4		0.96	Crozet	Barrat et al., 1976
	8	11	0.92	South Georgia	Prince et al., unpublished
	4			Kerguelen	Pascal, 1979
Grey-headed albatross	9	13	0.95	South Georgia	Prince et al., unpublished
Buller's albatross			0.89	New Zealand	Richdale and Warham, 1973
Sooty albatross	10		0.95	Crozet	Weimerskirch, 1982

Species				Adult survival[a]	Locality	References
Light-mantled sooty albatross						
Southern giant petrel	4♂ 7♀	7	c.10	0.96	Macquarie	Kerry and Colback, 1972
					Signy	B.A.S. data; Conroy, 1972
Northern giant petrel	6			c.0.90	Terre Adélie	Mougin, 1975
Antarctic fulmar				0.90–0.95	South Georgia	Hunter, in press
					Terre Adélie	Mougin, 1975; Guillotin and Jouventin, 1980
Cape pigeon	3	6		0.93–0.96	Signy	Beck, 1969; Hudson, 1966
Snow petrel	4	6		0.93–0.96	Signy	B.A.S. data; Hudson, 1966
					Terre Adélie	Guillotin and Jouventin, 1980
Antarctic prion	5	6–7		0.93(0.94–0.95)	Signy	B.A.S. data
Fairy prion	3	5–6		>0.84	New Zealand	Richdale, 1965b
Sooty shearwater	?6	4–5		c.0.94	New Zealand	Richdale, 1963
Short-tailed shearwater	5	6.2 (5.8♀ 6.6♂)		0.93–0.94	Australia	Serventy, 1967
Wilson's storm petrel	3	?4		0.91	Signy	Beck and Brown, 1972
Common diving petrel	2	2		0.75	New Zealand	Richdale, 1965a
Antarctic skua	3	5.5 (5.2♀ 6.2♂) 6♀ 6.5♂			Terre Adélie	Jouventin and Guillotin, 1979
Sub-Antarctic skua	4			0.94	Cape Crozier	Wood, 1971, 1972
					Crozet	Barré, 1976
Blue-eyed shag	3	4–5		0.91	Signy	Burton, 1968
					Signy	B.A.S. data

[a]Of established breeding birds, [b]of birds >1 year old, [c]Survival estimates new revised upwards (to c. 0.80) (Ainley et al., 1983).

annual survival from fledging in 93.5 and 90.5% respectively. By these ages black-browed albatrosses are completely recruited into the breeding population. However, some grey-headed albatrosses are still in the throes of their first few breeding attempts and might be expected to sustain greater losses then but whenever a grey-headed albatross breeds successfully it has a year as a non-breeder and this may reduce any cumulative effect of breeding stress. The interplay of age, experience, breeding status and breeding periodicity is ideally studied with known-age cohorts of long-lived birds and should therefore be an important area of Antarctic bird research.

The most detailed work to date on these lines comes from a ten-year study of Adélie penguins at Cape Crozier (Ainley and DeMaster, 1980; Ainley et al., 1983) and additional important comparative insights are provided by the work of Carrick (1972) on the sub-Antarctic royal penguin at Macquarie Island and Richdale (1957) on the cold temperate yellow-eyed penguin in southern New Zealand. Survivorship curves for these species are shown in Fig. 23 where it is clear that Adélie penguins show the poorest survival both as juveniles and adults and the latter is confirmed from Table VII where the mean annual survival of breeding adults is, at 70%, about 15% lower than the other two. Ainley and DeMaster (1980) show that age, sex and breeding status significantly affect mortality and in particular that mortality is very high for young breeders, but decreases markedly with age especially in females (Fig. 24). With non-breeders mortality is very low but increases slightly with age. This has some important effects on population age structure, notably that with high early mortality in females older birds are chiefly males which started breeding late, often failed to breed and were relatively unsuccessful when they did (Ainley, 1978; Ainley and DeMaster, 1980).

Carrick (1972) showed that in royal penguins weight on first arrival at the colony was an excellent index of whether a bird would breed or not. Early season reserves, with a five week incubation fast ahead, are likely to be particularly critical for eudyptid penguins. A more detailed analysis of the royal penguin data might help to explain some of the differences in population structure between the three penguins. Thus yellow-eyed penguins breed when young and survive well in a mild climate (but their total population is low); royal penguins breed when relatively old and survive well in a moderate climate (and are very abundant); Adélie penguins breed at an intermediate age and survive poorly in a harsh climate (but are extremely abundant). It is probable that the intensity of competition for food around the breeding places, availability of winter food, climate and perhaps predator activity all influence the population demography but the relative importance of these is unknown at present.

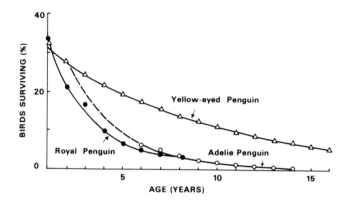

Fig. 23. Survivorship curves for Adélie, royal and yellow-eyed penguins (data respectively from Ainley and DeMaster, 1980; Carrick, 1972; Richdale, 1957). Copyright © 1980, The Ecological Society of America.

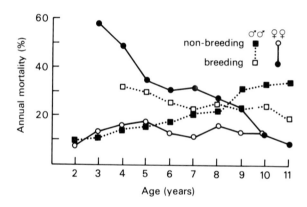

Fig. 24. Mean annual mortality of Adélie penguins with respect to age (from Ainley and DeMaster, 1980). Copyright © 1980, The Ecological Society of America.

Emperor penguins have particularly unusual population structure and dynamics. The very high survival rate of adults (95% per annum) is balanced by a very low (19%) rate of recruitment into the breeding population (Mougin and van Beveren, 1979). This is not due to low fledging success but probably relates directly to chicks fledging at only 60% of adult weight. King penguin chicks, in contrast, fledge at adult weight, survive well as immatures (93% per annum) but have lower (82%) annual survival as adults (Jouventin and Mougin, 1981).

10. Energetics

10.1 Species requirements

Knowledge of energy requirements is of considerable importance in understanding ecological adaptations, whether pertaining to chicks, breeding or non-breeding adults. Much reliance has been placed on the use of equations, relating body weight to energy consumption, derived from relatively few studies of energy requirements that have been made (reviewed by Kendeigh *et al.* 1977). Such equations, however, only permit estimation of basal (BMR) or existence (EMR) metabolic rate and the relationship between these and resting and active metabolic rates is very imperfectly understood. Baudinette and Schmidt-Nielsen (1974) suggested that resting metabolic rate might be about 1.7 times basal and the demands of swimming (Prange and Schmidt-Nielsen, 1974), flapping flight (Bernstein *et al.*, 1973) and gliding flight (Baudinette and Schmidt-Nielsen, 1974) have been roughly assessed as four, six and two times resting metabolic rate. Kooyman *et al.*, (1976) showed that for Adélie penguins immersed (but not swimming) in water at 5°C, metabolic rate was 3.6 times that resting in air and response to cold ambient temperatures may be an additional energy cost imposed on Antarctic birds. As most of these figures are highly generalized there is a real need for fresh studies, particularly in the field.

For seabirds, studies of chick budgets should be comparatively straightforward once meal sizes, the composition of the diet by weight and the energy values of the main prey items are known, and provided that the quantity and composition of excreted material can be assessed. Despite chick demands changing rapidly with growth it should be possible to determine approximately the amount of food required for successful fledging as has been done for the jackass penguin (Cooper, 1977).

The budgets of active adults are particularly difficult to assess, as even if labelled isotopes (e.g. Utter and Le Febvre, 1970; Hails and Bryant, 1979) are used to estimate total energy costs over a known period, it will usually be difficult to obtain a breakdown of activity (e.g. time spent flapping, gliding, resting, feeding, etc.) over this time. Nevertheless, an indication of the cost of a typical foraging trip would be a great improvement on present knowledge. Preliminary information for king, macaroni and gentoo penguins suggests that the daily cost of foraging during chick rearing is about 2.5–3.5 times BMR (Kooyman *et al.*, 1982; Davis *et al.*, 1983).

During the breeding season most seabirds spend long periods ashore, especially during incubation and chick brooding and, in the case of penguins, also during moult. A graph of the typical pattern of weight change during a breeding season for macaroni penguin is shown in Fig. 25. The

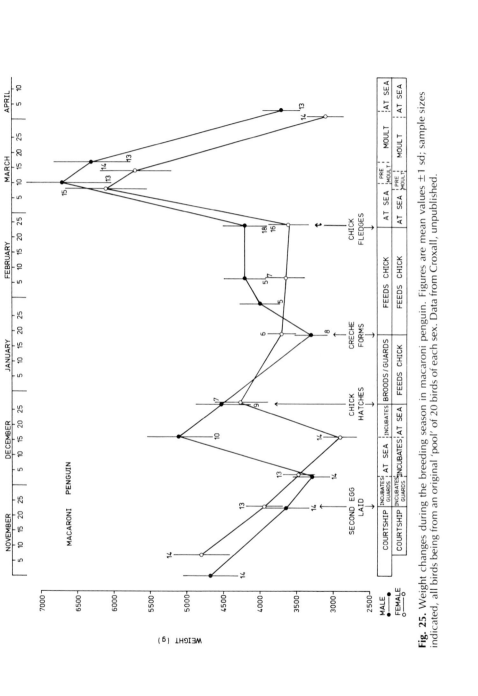

Fig. 25. Weight changes during the breeding season in macaroni penguin. Figures are mean values ±1 sd; sample sizes indicated, all birds being from an original 'pool' of 20 birds of each sex. Data from Croxall, unpublished.

periods when the birds are fasting and inactive offer an excellent opportunity for measuring weight loss and calculating mean daily energy expenditure. To do this requires knowledge of the composition of the material
lost and only recently have data on this appeared. Earlier workers had
assumed that *c.* 95% of the loss comprised fat, but Groscolas and Clement
(1976), for fasting emperor penguins and Williams *et al.* (1977), for moulting, fasting rockhopper and macaroni penguins, obtained respectively
values of 55.5% fat, 9.2% protein and 38% fat, 12% protein (of which half
was due to loss of old feathers and new sheaths), the residue being water.
Using these values Croxall (1982) reviewed available data on fasting weight
loss in petrels and penguins and compared the calculated energy costs with
those of predicted BMR and with oxygen consumption data for penguins.
All data, and especially the last, indicate that fat is unlikely to comprise
much more than 50% of the fast weight loss. Overall results are summarized in Fig. 26. Although data are available for only 13 petrels, these
include three sub-Antarctic albatrosses (wandering, grey-headed, black-
browed) and two storm (black-bellied, Wilson's) and two cool-temperate
petrels (grey-faced, mottled). Data are available for only seven penguin
species during incubation fasts, but 13 of 17 species have been weighed
during moult fasts. Proportionate weight loss is not independent of body
weight and scales to the −0.33 for petrels and to the −0.32 and −0.24 for
incubating and moulting penguins, respectively. Average daily costs of

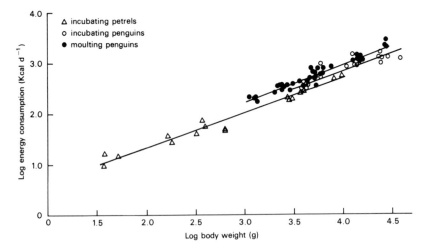

Fig. 26. Log-log relationships between energy consumption and body weight in incubating
petrels and incubating and moulting penguins. The least-squares regression line for each data set
is shown; the equations and full data are in Croxall (1982).

incubation in petrels were assessed as 1.3 times BMR (range 0.8–2.0), of incubation in penguins as 1.4 times BMR (range 1.0–1.6) and of moulting in penguins as 2.0 times BMR (range 1.6–2.4).

10.2 Population requirements

Information on activity costs and energy budgets leads naturally to a consideration of overall food consumption of seabird populations and their role in marine ecosystem, a topic of considerable relevance to the Southern Ocean system.

Several general studies of energy flow in northern hemisphere seabird communities have been made (e.g. Belopolskii, 1961; Sanger, 1972; Wiens and Scott, 1975; Furness, 1978) but even though reliable data are available on many aspects, all involve substantial assumptions. Furness (1978) analysed the sensitivity to error of the parameters he used and concluded that, although these varied between species, population size and structure, the multiplicand and exponent of the Kendeigh equation and the relationship of standard to active metabolic rate were of particular importance generally.

These constraints are equally relevant to Antarctic systems where they are exacerbated by particularly poor knowledge of the costs of swimming in the vitally important penguins and by the lack of reliable information on seabird numbers. This is attested by comparing estimates presented by Mougin and Prévost (1980) and Williams et al. (1979) for the relatively easily estimated surface breeding species, where discrepancies of several hundred per cent are not infrequent; the latter seems the more realistic, except for its very low value for macaroni penguin.

With present knowledge it is probably premature to attempt to assess the role of birds in Southern Ocean systems but simplified attempts have been made e.g. Croxall and Prince (in Everson, 1977), Mougin and Prévost (1980). The latter represents a detailed evaluation but although it acknowledges the inadequacy of much of the available data there are still drawbacks to the estimates made and the methodology used, which preclude uncritical acceptance. Thus the breeding numbers of eudyptid penguins are excessively high (cf. Williams et al., 1979; Croxall and Prince, 1979) and those of the smaller petrels extremely low. The non-breeding portion of penguin populations is assessed as over twice the breeding stock, which is greatly at variance with information on penguin demography (see p. 590). The division of penguins into Antarctic and sub-Antarctic categories is misleading, as all the macaroni/royal penguin populations are apparently included in the former. Thus bird numbers and biomass generally, and particularly the proportion of these found in the Antarctic, will be over-estimated. In contrast, the assumption that active metabolic costs will only be 40% greater than existence metabolism is unconventional (see p. 594), and will result in an underestimate of energy costs and food consumption.

It is not possible to present a detailed re-evaluation here but modifying Mougin and Prévost (1980) on the basis of data in Croxall and Kirkwood (1979), Croxall and Prince (1979, 1980a), the references cited by Williams et al. (1979) and unpublished information, some very approximate figures for Southern Ocean bird biomass and energy requirements can be derived (Table VII). These are based simply on estimated total population size and use of standard equations for existence metabolism.

They emphasize the pre-eminent role of penguins (which would remain even if some very substantial increases to procellariform populations were made). Thus, in terms of biomass and consumption, all birds in the Antarctic are effectively penguins and two-thirds of these are Adélie penguins; in sub-Antarctic regions 80% of birds are penguins and 50% macaroni penguins.

From the quantitative studies of diet (and assuming unstudied species are similar to their studied relatives) consumption of krill probably accounts for about 78% of the total (B.A.S. unpublished data), the remainder being about equally fish and squid. These themselves eat krill and if standard relationships between primary and secondary consumers (Humphreys, 1979) are used then the sum of direct and indirect consumption by seabirds is raised to c. 115 million tonnes, which is slightly larger than whale, and two-thirds seal consumption calculated by similar methods (Grenfell and Lawton, 1979).

Furthermore, the original computation of bird energy consumption was made on the basis of existence metabolic rates and we have seen earlier that active values are at least twice, and perhaps even four times greater, which would make the total direct plus indirect consumption in excess of that of seals. Such figures should be treated with extreme caution and simply emphasize the importance of seabirds in the Southern Ocean system and also our need of better data to evaluate that role more accurately.

More realistic estimates of seabird consumption can be made for better-known areas and Croxall and Prince (1982b) made a preliminary attempt to do this for seabirds at South Georgia, using extensive empirical data from studies there. They concluded that breeding seabirds in their breeding seasons consume about 1.7 m tons of food, about 88% of which is krill, and 80% of which is taken by macaroni penguins and 17% by dove prions. If immature penguins and failed breeders are included, a further 0.8 m tons are consumed, and the total annual consumption must be in the region of 3 m tons.

TABLE VII

Biomass and energy consumption of Antarctic seabirds

	Sub-Antarctic		Antarctic		Total	
	Biomass (tonnes × 10^6)	Energy consumption (kcal × 10^{12} y^{-1})	Biomass (tonnes × 10^6)	Energy consumption (kcal × 10^{12} y^{-1})	Biomass (tonnes × 10^6)	Energy consumption (kcal × 10^{12} y^{-1})
Penguins	410	22.3	198	14.1	608	36.4
Other species	53	5.1	3	0.5	56	5.6
Total	463	27.4	201	14.6	664	42.0

While the role of seabirds as predators on marine resources is of great importance, they also play a significant (perhaps pre-eminent) role in providing nutrients for terrestrial ecosystems and this has been extensively studied recently at Marion Island (Burger *et al.*, 1978; Siegfried *et al.*, 1978; Williams and Berruti, 1978; Williams *et al.*, 1978).

11. Conclusions

In this chapter I have tried to outline the principal areas of current research and topics of particular interest against the background of a general review of Antarctic seabird ecology.

There is increasing interest in species interactions in the Southern Ocean ecosystem, particularly from the point of view of harvesting and management (May *et al.*, 1979) and the role of seabirds is one of the least understood. It is natural, therefore, that attention should be turned to population energy requirements and consumption but this should not obscure the considerable variety of important ecological work that can be carried out with Antarctic seabirds.

Of particular interest is the relationship between breeding strategy (timing and duration of breeding season, breeding periodicity and age of first breeding, annual mortality, etc.) and physiological and dietary adaptations and limitations. Important studies have been carried out on one or the other of these main areas but rather few have sought to use a full range of techniques to study the whole problem simultaneously. The work on penguins (particularly emperor, Adélie and royal) and grey-headed and black-browed albatrosses referred to earlier gave indications of the complex nature of the interrelationships between age, experience, behaviour, physiology and diet. They have all demonstrated the importance of working with known age individuals and, given the longevity and delayed sexual maturity of Antarctic seabirds, this demands foresight and long term studies. Nevertheless, the ease with which these birds can be handled and manipulated in the Antarctic is such that the rewards of fully integrated studies can be very considerable and one would expect many of the more significant future developments in the understanding of seabird ecology to come from the work currently in progress in the Antarctic.

12. References

Ainley, D. G. (1977). Feeding methods in seabirds: a comparison of polar and tropical nesting communities in the eastern Pacific Ocean. In "Adaptations within Antarctic Ecosystems" (G. A. Llano, ed.), pp. 669–685. Smithsonian Institution, Washington, D.C.

Ainley, D. G. (1978). Activity patterns and social behaviour of non-breeding Adélie penguins. Condor 80, 138–146.

Ainley, D. G. and DeMaster, D. P. (1980). Survival and mortality in a population of penguins. Ecology 61, 522–530.

Ainley, D. G. and Emison, W. B. (1972). Sexual size dimorphism in Adélie penguins. Ibis 114, 267–271.

Ainley, D. G. and Jacobs, S. S. (1981). Seabird affinities for ocean and ice boundaries in the Antarctic. Deep Sea Research 28A, 1173–1185.

Ainley, D. G. and Le Resche, R. E. (1973). The effects of weather and ice conditions on breeding in Adélie penguins. Condor 75, 235–239.

Ainley, D. G. and Schlatter, R. P. (1972). Chick raising ability in Adélie penguins. Auk 89, 559–566.

Ainley, D. G., Le Resche, R. E. and Sladen, W. J. L. (1983). "Breeding Biology of the Adélie Penguin". University of California Press, Berkeley.

Ashmole, N. P. (1971). Sea bird ecology and the marine environment. In "Avian Biology" (D. S. Farner and J. R. King, eds), Vol. 1, pp. 112–286. Academic Press, London and New York.

Ashmole, N. P. and Ashmole, M. J. (1967). Comparative feeding ecology of sea birds of a tropical oceanic island. Bulletin of the Peabody Museum of Natural History 24, 1–131.

*Barrat, A. (1974). Note sur le pétrel gris Procellaria cinerea. Comité National Français des Recherches Antarctiques 33, 19–24.

*Barrat, A. (1976). Quelques aspects de la biologie et de l'écologie du manchot royal (Aptenodytes patagonica) des îles Crozet. Comité National Français des Recherches Antarctiques 40, 9–52.

Barrat, A. and Mougin, J. L. (1974). Données numériques sur la zoogéographie de l'avifaune antarctique et subantarctique. Comité National Français des Recherches Antarctiques 33, 1–18.

Barrat, A., Barré, H. and Mougin, J. L. (1976a). Données écologiques sur les grands albatros Diomedea exulans de l'île de la Possession (archipel Crozet). Oiseau 46, 143–155.

Barrat, A. et al. (1976b). Recherches écologiques sur les oiseaux de l'archipel Crozet. Comité National Français des Recherches Antarctiques 40, 1–220.

Barré, H. (1976a). Le skua subantarctique Stercorarius skua lonnbergi (Mathews) à l'île de la Possession (îles Crozet). Comité National Français des Recherches Antarctiques 40, 77–105.

Barré, H. (1976b). Pterodroma lessonii (Garnot) à l'île de la Possession (îles Crozet). Comité National Français des Recherches Antarctiques 40, 61–76.

Barré, H. (1978). Dépense énergétique du poussin de manchot royal Aptenodytes patagonicus (J. F. Miller) au cours de la croissance. Journal of Physiology (Paris) 74, 555–561.

---

*Principal references for data in Appendix I.

Barré, H. and Rouanet, J.-L. (1982). Metabolisme énergétique du poussin de manchot royal au cours de la croissance: problème de l'emancipation thermique. *Comité National Français des Recherches Antarctiques* **51**, 357–362.

Baudinette, R. V. and Schmidt-Nielsen, K. (1974). Energy cost of gliding in herring gulls. *Nature* (Lond.) **248**, 83–84.

Beck, J. R. (1969). Food, moult and age of first breeding in the cape pigeon *Daption capensis* Linnaeus. *British Antarctic Survey Bulletin* No. 21, 33–44.

Beck, J. R. (1970). Breeding seasons and moult in some smaller Antarctic petrels. *In* "Antarctic Ecology" (M. W. Holdgate, ed.) Vol. 1, pp. 542–550. Academic Press, New York and London.

Beck, J. R. and Brown, D. W. (1971). The breeding biology of the black-bellied storm petrel *Fregetta tropica*. *Ibis* **113**, 73–90.

Beck, J. R. and Brown, D. W. (1972). The biology of Wilson's storm petrel, *Oceanites oceanicus* (Kuhl), at Signy Island, South Orkney Islands. *British Antarctic Survey Scientific Reports* **69**, 1–54.

Belopol'skii, L. O. (1961). "Ecology of Sea Colony Birds of the Barents Sea". [Israel Program of Scientific Translations.]

Bernstein, M. H., Thomas, S. P. and Schmidt-Nielsen, K. (1973). Power input during flight of fish crow *Corvus ossifragus*. *Journal of Experimental Biology* **58**, 401–410.

Berruti, A. (1979). The breeding biologies of the sooty albatrosses *Phoebetria fusca* and *P. palpebrata*. *Emu* **79**, 161–175.

Berruti, A. and Harcus, T. (1978). The cephalopod prey of the sooty albatrosses *Phoebetria fusca* and *P. palpebrata* at Marion Island. *South African Journal of Antarctic Research* **8**, 99–108.

Berruti, A., Griffiths, A. M., Imber, M. J., Schramm, M. and Sinclair, J. C. (1981). The status of seabirds at Prince Edward Island. *South African Journal of Antarctic Research* **10/11**, 31–32.

Bourne, W. R. P. (1968). Notes on the diving petrels. *Bulletin of the British Ornithologist's Club* **88**, 77–85.

Bourne, W. R. P. and Warham, J. (1966). Geographical variation in giant petrels of the genus *Macronectes*. *Ardea* **54**, 45–67.

Brown, D. A. (1966). Breeding biology of the snow petrel *Pagodroma nivea* (Forster). *Australian National Antarctic Research Expedition Reports*, Ser. B **89**, 1–63.

Brown, R. G. B., Barker, S. P., Gaskin, D. E. and Sandeman, M. R. (1981). The foods of great and sooty shearwaters *Puffinus gravis* and *P. griseus* in eastern Canadian waters. *Ibis* **123**, 19–30.

Budd, G. M. (1961). The biotopes of emperor penguin rookeries. *Emu* **61**, 171–189.

Burger, A. E. (1979). Breeding biology, moult and survival of lesser sheathbills *Chionis minor* at Marion Island. *Ardea* **67**, 1–14.

Burger, A. E. (1980). "Behavioural ecology of lesser sheathbills *Chionis minor* at Marion Island". Ph.D. thesis, University of Cape Town.

Burger, A. E. and Williams, A. J. (1979). Egg temperature of the rockhopper penguin and some other penguins. *Auk* **96**, 100–105.

Burger, A. E., Lindeboom, M. and Williams, A. J. (1978). Mineral energy contributions of guano of selected species of birds to the Marion Island terrestrial ecosystem. *South African Journal of Antarctic Research* **8**, 59–70.

Burton, R. W. (1968). Breeding biology of the brown skua, *Catharacta skua lonnbergi* (Mathews) at Signy Island, South Orkney Islands. *British Antarctic Survey Bulletin* No. 15, 9–28.

Carrick, R. (1972). Population ecology of the Australian black-backed magpie, royal penguin and silver gull. In "Population ecology of migratory birds: a symposium". United States Department of the Interior Wildlife Research Report No. 2, 41–99.

Carrick, R. and Ingham, S. E. (1967). Antarctic sea birds as subjects for ecological research. In "Proceedings of the Symposium on Pacific Antarctic Sciences, Tokyo, 1966". JARE Scientific Reports Special Issue No. 1, 151–184.

Carrick, R. and Ingham, S. E. (1970). Ecology and population dynamics of Antarctic seabirds. In "Antarctic Ecology" (M. W. Holdgate, ed.) Vol. 1, pp. 505–525. Academic Press, New York and London.

Clarke, A. and Prince, P. A. (1976). The origin of stomach oil in marine birds: analyses of the stomach oil from six species of subantarctic procellariiform birds. Journal of Experimental Marine Biology and Ecology 23, 15–30.

Clarke, A. and Prince, P. A. (1980). Chemical composition and calorific value of food fed to mollymauk chicks at Bird Island, South Georgia. Ibis 122, 488–494.

Clarke, M. R. (1980). Cephalopoda in the diet of sperm whales of the Southern Hemisphere and their bearing on sperm whale biology. "Discovery" Reports 37, 1–324.

Clarke, M. R. and Prince, P. A. (1981). Cephalopod remains in regurgitations of black-browed albatross, Diomedea melanophris, and grey-headed albatross D. chrysostoma at South Georgia. British Antarctic Survey Bulletin No. 54, 1–7.

Clarke, M. R., Croxall, J. P. and Prince, P. A. (1981). Cephalopod remains in regurgitations of the wandering albatross at South Georgia. British Antarctic Survey Bulletin No. 54, 9–21.

*Conroy, J. W. H. (1972). Ecological aspects of the biology of the giant petrel, Macronectes giganteus (Gmelin) in the maritime Antarctic. British Antarctic Survey Scientific Reports 75, 1–74.

Conroy, J. W. H., Darling, O. W. H. and Smith, H. G. (1975). The annual cycle of the chinstrap penguin (Pygoscelis antarctica) on Signy Island, South Orkney Islands. In "The Biology of Penguins" (B. Stonehouse, ed.) pp. 353–362. Macmillan, London.

Cooper, J. (1977). Energetic requirements for growth of the jackass penguin. Zoologica Africana 12, 201–213.

Coulson, J. C. (1968). Differences in the quality of birds nesting in the centre and on the edges of a colony. Nature (Lond.) 217, 478–479.

Cox, J. B. (1979). Some remarks on the breeding distribution and taxonomy of the prions (Procellariidae: Pachyptila). Records of the South Australian Museum 18, 91–121.

*Cramp, S. and Simmons, K. E. L. (eds) (1977). "The Birds of the Western Palearctic", Vol. 1. Oxford University Press, Oxford.

Croxall, J. P. (1979). Distribution and population changes in the wandering albatross Diomedea exulans L. at South Georgia. Ardea 67, 15–21.

Croxall, J. P. (1982a). Energy costs of incubation and moult in petrels and penguins. Journal of Animal Ecology 51, 177–194.

Croxall, J. P. (1982b). Aspects of the population demography of Antarctic and sub-Antarctic seabirds. Comité National Français des Recherches Antarctiques 51, 479–488.

Croxall, J. P. and Furse, J. R. (1980). Food of chinstrap penguins Pygoscelis antarctica and macaroni penguins Eudyptes chrysolophus at Elephant Island group, South Shetland Islands. Ibis 122, 237–245.

Croxall, J. P. and Kirkwood, E. D. (1979). "The Breeding Distribution of Penguins on the Antarctic Peninsula and Islands of the Scotia Sea". British Antarctic Survey, Cambridge.

Croxall, J. P. and Prince, P. A. (1979). Antarctic seabird and seal monitoring studies. *Polar Record* **19**, 573–595.

*Croxall, J. P. and Prince, P. A. (1980a). Food, feeding ecology and ecological segregation of seabirds at South Georgia. *Biological Journal of the Linnean Society* **14**, 103–131.

Croxall, J. P. and Prince, P. A. (1980b). The food of gentoo penguins *Pygoscelis papua* and macaroni penguins *Eudyptes chrysolophus* at South Georgia. *Ibis* **122**, 245–253.

Croxall, J. P. and Prince, P. A. (1982a). Calorific content of squid (Mollusca: Cephalopoda). *British Antarctic Survey Bulletin* No. 55, 27–31.

Croxall, J. P. and Prince, P. A. (1982b). A preliminary assessment of the impact of seabirds on marine resources at South Georgia. *Comité National Français des Recherches Antarctiques* **51**, 501–509.

Croxall, J. P. and Ricketts, C. (1983). Energy costs of incubation in the wandering albatross *Diomedea exulans*. *Ibis* **125**, 33–39.

Davis, R. W., Kooyman, G. L. and Croxall, J. P. (1983). Water flux and estimated metabolism of free-ranging gentoo and macaroni penguins at South Georgia. *Polar Biology* **2**, 41–46.

*Derenne, P. and Mougin, J.-L. (1976). Les Procellariiformes à nidification hypogée de l'île aux Cochons (archipel Crozet). *Comité National Français des Recherches Antarctiques* **40**, 149–176.

*Derenne, P., Lufbery, J. X. and Tollu, B. (1974). L'avifaune de l'archipel Kerguelen. *Comité National Français des Recherches Antarctiques* **33**, 57–87.

*Derenne, P., Mary, G. and Mougin, J.-L. (1976a). Le cormoran à ventre blanc, *Phalacrocorax albiventer melanogenis* (Blyth) de l'archipel Crozet. *Comité National Français des Recherches Antarctiques* **33**, 57–87.

*Derenne, P., Mougin, J.-L., Steinberg, C. and Voisin, J.-F. (1976b). Les oiseaux de l'île aux Cochons, archipel Crozet. *Comité National Français des Recherches Antarctiques* **40**, 107–148.

*Despin, B. (1972). Note préliminaire sur le manchot papou *Pygoscelis papua* de l'île de la Possession (archipel Crozet). *Oiseau* **42**, no. spéc., 69–83.

Despin, B. (1977a). Croissances comparées des poussins chez les manchots du genre *Pygoscelis*. *Comptes Rendus, Academie des Sciences* (Paris) Ser. D **285**, 1135–1136.

*Despin, B. (1977b). Biologie du damier du cap, *Daption capense* à l'île de la Possession (archipel Crozet). *Oiseau* **47**, 149–157.

*Despin, B., Mougin, J.-L. and Segonzac, M. (1972). Oiseaux et mammifères de l'île de l'Est, archipel Crozet. *Comité National Français des Recherches Antarctiques* **31**, 1–106.

Devillers, P. (1977). The skuas of the North American Pacific coast. *Auk* **94**, 417–429.

Devillers, P. (1978). Distribution and relationships of the South American skuas. *Gerfaut* **68**, 374–417.

Devillers, P. and Terschuren, J. A. (1978). Relationships between the blue-eyed shags of South America. *Gerfaut* **68**, 53–86.

Devillers, P. and Terschuren, J. A. (1980). Les petrels géants (*Macronectes*) des îles Falklands et du sud de l'Amerique du Sud. *Gerfaut* **70**, 447–454.

Downes, M. C., Ealey, E. H. M., Gwynn, A. M. and Young, P. S. (1959). The birds of Heard Island. *Australian National Antarctic Research Expedition Reports*, Ser. B **1**, 1–135.

Drent, R. H. (1975). Incubation. *In* "Avian Biology" (D. S. Farner and J. R. King, eds), Vol. V, pp. 333–420. Academic Press, London and New York.

Duroselle, T. and Tollu, B. (1977). The rockhopper penguin (*Eudyptes chrysocome moseleyi*) of Saint Paul and Amsterdam Islands. *In* "Adaptations within Antarctic Ecosystems" (G. A. Llano, ed.) pp. 579–604. Smithsonian Institution, Washington, D.C.

Emison, W. B. (1968). Feeding preferences of the Adélie penguin at Cape Crozier, Ross Island. *In* "Antarctic Bird Studies", Antarctic Research Series Vol. 12 (O. L. Austin Jr, ed.), pp. 191–212. American Geophysical Union, Washington, D.C.

Everson, I. (1977). "The Living Resources of the Southern Ocean". Food and Agriculture Organisation of the United Nations, United Nations Development Programme. (Southern Ocean Fisheries Survey Programme GLO/SO/77/1.)

Fevolden, S. E. and Sømme, L. (1977). Observations on birds and seals at Bouvetøya. *Norsk Polarinstitut Arbok* 1976, 367–371.

Fordham, R. A. (1964). Breeding biology of the southern black-backed gull. *Notornis* **11**, 3–34, 110–126.

Foxton, P. (1956). The distribution of the standing crop of zooplankton in the Southern Ocean. *"Discovery" Reports* **28**, 191–236.

Furness, R. W. (1978). Energy requirements of seabird communities: a bioenergetics model. *Journal of Animal Ecology* **47**, 39–53.

Gain, L. (1914). Oiseaux antarctiques. *Deuxième Expedition Antarctique Français 1908–1910* **2**, 1–200.

Grenfell, B. T. and Lawton, J. H. (1979). Estimates of the krill consumed by whales and other groups in the Southern Ocean: 1900 and the present (unpublished manuscript).

Groscolas, R. and Clément, C. (1976). Utilisation des réserves énergétiques au cours du jeûne de le reproduction chez le manchot empereur *Aptenodytes forsteri*. *Comptes Rendus, Academie des Sciences* (Paris) Ser. D **282**, 297–300.

Guillotin, M. and Jouventin, P. (1979). La parade nuptiale du manchot empereur et sa signification biologique. *Biology of Behaviour* **4**, 249–267.

Guillotin, M. and Jouventin, P. (1980). Le petrel des neiges à Pointe Geologie. *Gerfaut* **70**, 51–72.

Gwynn, A. M. (1953). The egg-laying and incubation periods of rockhopper, macaroni, and gentoo penguins. *Australian National Antarctic Research Expedition Reports*, Ser. B **1**, 1–29.

Hails, C. J. and Bryant, D. M. (1979). Reproductive energetics of a free-living bird. *Journal of Animal Ecology* **48**, 471–482.

Harper, P. C. (1972). The field identification and distribution of the thin-billed prion (*Pachyptila belcheri*) and the Antarctic prion (*Pachyptila desolata*). *Notornis* **19**, 140–175.

*Harper, P. C. (1976). Breeding biology of the fairy prion (*Pachyptila turtur*) at the Poor Knights Islands, New Zealand. *New Zealand Journal of Zoology* **3**, 351–371.

Harper, P. C. (1978). The plasma proteins of some albatrosses and petrels as an index of relationship in the Procellariiformes. *New Zealand Journal of Zoology* **5**, 509–548.

Harper, P. C. (1980). The field identification and distribution of the prions (genus

Pachyptila) with particular reference to the identification of storm-cast material. *Notornis* **27**, 235–286.

*Harris, M. P. (1969). The biology of storm petrels in the Galapagos Islands. *Proceedings of the California Academy of Sciences* **37**, 95–165.

*Harris, M. P. (1970). The biology of an endangered species, the dark-rumped petrel (*Pterodroma phaeopygia*), in the Galapagos Islands. *Condor* **72**, 76–84.

*Harris, M. P. (1973). The biology of the waved albatross of Hood I. Galapagos. *Ibis* **115**, 213–236.

Hart, T. J. (1942). Phytoplankton periodicity in Antarctic surface waters. *"Discovery" Reports* **21**, 261–356.

Heinroth, O. (1922). Die Beziehungen zwischen Vogelgewicht, Eigewicht, Gelegegewicht und Brutdauer. *Journal of Ornithology* **70**, 172–285.

Hudson, R. (1966). Adult survival estimates for two Antarctic petrels. *British Antarctic Survey Bulletin* No. 8, 63–73.

Humphreys, W. F. (1979). Production and respiration in animal populations. *Journal of Animal Ecology* **48**, 427–454.

Hunter, S. (1983). The food and feeding ecology of the giant petrels *Macronectes halli* and *M. giganteus* at South Georgia. *Journal of Zoology* (Lond.) **200**, 521–538.

Hunter, S. (1984). Moult in the giant petrels *Macronectes halli* and *M. giganteus* at South Georgia. *Ibis* **126**.

Hunter, S. (in press). Breeding biology and population dynamics of giant petrels *Macronectes* spp. at South Georgia. *Journal of Zoology* (Lond.).

Imber, M. J. (1973). The food of grey-faced petrels (*Pterodroma macroptera gouldi* (Hutton)), with special reference to diurnal vertical migration of their prey. *Journal of Animal Ecology* **42**, 645–662.

Imber, M. J. (1976a). Comparison of the prey of the black *Procellaria* petrels of New Zealand. *New Zealand Journal of Marine & Freshwater Research* **10**, 119–130.

*Imber, M. J. (1976b). Breeding biology of the grey-faced petrel *Pterodroma macroptera gouldi*. *Ibis* **118**, 51–64.

Imber, M. J. (1981). Diets of storm petrels *Pelagodroma* and *Garrodia* and of prions *Pachyptila* (Procellariiformes). *In* "Proceedings of the Symposium on Birds of the Sea and Shore, 1979" (J. Cooper, ed.), pp. 63–88. African Seabird Group, Cape Town.

Imber, M. J. and Russ, R. (1975). Some foods of the wandering albatross (*Diomedea exulans*). *Notornis* **22**, 27–36.

*Isenmann, P. (1970a). Note sur la biologie de reproduction comparée de damiers du cap *Daption capensis* aux Orcades du Sud et en Terre Adélie. *Oiseau* **40**, no. spéc., 135–141.

*Isenmann, P. (1970b). Contribution à la biologie de reproduction du pétrel des neiges (*Pagodroma nivea* Forster); le problème de la petite et de la grande forme. *Oiseau* **40**, 99–134.

Johnston, G. C. (1973). Predation by southern skuas on rabbits on Macquarie Island. *Emu* **73**, 25–26.

Johnstone, G. W. (1974). Field characters and behaviour at sea of giant petrels in relation to their oceanic distribution. *Emu* **74**, 209–218.

Johnstone, G. W. (1977). Comparative feeding ecology of the giant petrels *Macronectes giganteus* (Gmelin) and *M. halli* (Mathews). *In* "Adaptations within Antarctic Ecosystems" (G. A. Llano, ed.), pp. 647–668. Smithsonian Institution, Washington, D.C.

Johnstone, G. W. (1979). Agonistic behaviour of the giant petrels *Macronectes giganteus* and *M. halli* feeding at seal carcasses. *Emu* **79**, 129–132.

Johnstone, G. W. and Kerry, K. R. (1976). Ornithological observations in the Australian sector of the Southern Ocean. *Proceedings of the 16th International Ornithological Congress*, 725–738.

Johnstone, G. W., Shaughnessy, P. D. and Conroy, J. W. H. (1976). Giant petrels in the South Atlantic: new data from Gough Island. *South African Journal of Antarctic Research* **6**, 19–22.

Jones, E. (1977). Ecology of the feral cat *Felis catus* (L.) (Carnivora: Felidae) on Macquarie Island. *Australian Wildlife Research* **4**, 249–262.

Jones, E. (1980). A survey of burrow-nesting petrels at Macquarie Island based upon remains left by predators. *Notornis* **27**, 11–20.

Jones, E. and Skira, I. J. (1979). Breeding distribution of the great skua at Macquarie Island in relation to numbers of rabbits. *Emu* **79**, 19–23.

Jouventin, P. (1971). Comportement et structure sociale chez le manchot empereur. *Terre et la Vie, Revue d'Écologie* **25**, 510–586.

Jouventin, P. (1975). Mortality parameters in emperor penguins *Aptenodytes forsteri*. *In* "The Biology of Penguins" (B. Stonehouse, ed.) pp. 435–446. Macmillan, London.

Jouventin, P. and Guillotin, M. (1979). Socio-ecologie du skua antarctique à Pointe Géologie. *Terre et la Vie, Revue d'Écologie* **33**, 109–127.

Jouventin, P. and Mougin, J.-L. (1981). Les strategies adaptatives des oiseaux de mer. *Terre et la Vie, Revue d'Écologie* **35**, 217–272.

Jouventin, P., Mougin, J.-L., Stahl, J.-C., Bartle, J. A. and Weimerskirch, H. (1982). Données préliminaires sur la distribution pélagique des oiseaux des terres australes et antarctiques Françaises. *Comité National Français des Recherches Antarctiques* **51**, 427–436.

Kendeigh, S. C., Dol'nik, V. R. and Gavrilov, V. M. (1977). Avian energetics. *In* "Granivorous Birds in Ecosystems" (J. Pinowski and S. C. Kendeigh, eds), pp. 127–204. Cambridge University Press, Cambridge.

Kerry, K. R. and Colback, G. C. (1972). Follow the band! Light-mantled sooty albatross on Macquarie Island. *Australian Bird Bander* **10**, 61–62.

Kinsky, F. C. (1963). The southern black-backed gull (*Larus dominicanus* Lichtenstein); measurements, plumage colour, and moult cycle. *Record of the Dominion Museum* **4**, 149–219.

Kock, K-H. and Reinsch, H. H. (1978). Ornithological observations during the German Antarctic Expedition 1975/1976. *Beiträge zur Vogelkunde Leipzig* **24**, 305–328.

Kooyman, G. L. (1975). The physiology of diving in penguins. In "The Biology of Penguins" (B. Stonehouse, ed.), pp. 115–137. Macmillan, London.

Kooyman, G. L., Drabek, C. M., Elsner, R. and Campbell, W. B. (1971). Diving behavior in the emperor penguin *Aptenodytes forsteri*. *Auk* **88**, 775–795.

Kooyman G. L., Gentry, R. L., Bergman, W. P. and Hammel, H. T. (1976). Heat loss in penguins during immersion and compression. *Comparative Biochemistry and Physiology* **54A**, 75–80.

Kooyman, G. L., Davis, R. W., Croxall, J. P. and Costa, D. P. (1982). Diving depths and energy requirements of king penguins. *Science* **217**, 726–727.

Kuroda, N. H. (1967). Morpho-anatomical analysis of parallel evolution between diving petrel and ancient auk, with comparative osteological data of other species. *Miscellaneous Reports of the Yamashina Institute for Ornithology and Zoology* **5**, 2 (28), 111–137.

*Lacan, F. (1971). Observations écologiques sur le pétrel de Wilson (*Oceanites oceanicus*) en Terre Adélie. *Oiseau* **41**, no. spéc., 65–89.

Lack, D. (1968). "Ecological Adaptations for Breeding in Birds". Methuen, London.

Le Maho, Y. (1977). The emperor penguin: a strategy to live and breed in the cold. *American Scientist* **65**, 680–693.

Le Maho, Y., Delclitte, P. and Chatonnet, J. (1976). Thermoregulation in fasting emperor penguins under natural conditions. *American Journal of Physiology* **231**, 913–922.

Le Morvan, P., Mougin, J.-L. and Prévost, J. (1967). Écologie du skua antarctique (*Stercorarius skua maccormicki*) dans l'Archipel de Pointe Géologie (Terre Adélie). *Oiseau* **37**, 193–220.

Linkowski, T. B. and Rembiszewski, J. M. (1978). Distribution of seabirds of Argentina coast and the feeding habits of the bird fauna in the Drake Passage and Scotia Sea. *Polish Archives of Hydrobiology* **25**, 717–727.

Lishman, G. S. and Croxall, J. P. (1983). Diving depths of the chinstrap penguin *Pygoscelis antarctica*. *British Antarctic Survey Bulletin* No. 61, 21–26.

Maher, W. J. (1962). Breeding biology of the snow petrel near Cape Hallett, Antarctica. *Condor* **64**, 488–499.

Marshall, A. J. and Serventy, D. L. (1956a). Moult adaptations in relation to long distance migration in petrels. *Nature* (Lond.) **177**, 943.

Marshall, A. J. and Serventy, D. L. (1956b). The breeding cycle of the short-tailed shearwater *Puffinus tenuirostris* (Temminck) in relation to transequatorial migration and its environment. *Proceedings of the Zoological Society of London* **127**, 489–510.

May, R. M., Beddington, J. R., Clark, C. W. and Laws, R. M. (1979). Management of multi-species fisheries. *Science* **205**, 267–277.

Moors, P. J. (1980). Southern great skuas on Antipodes Island, New Zealand: observations on foods, breeding and growth of chicks. *Notornis* **27**, 133–146.

*Mougin, J.-L. (1967). Étude écologique des deux espèces de fulmars: le fulmar atlantique (*Fulmarus glacialis*) et le fulmar antarctique (*Fulmarus glacialoides*). *Oiseau* **37**, 57–103.

*Mougin, J.-L. (1968). Étude écologique de quatre espèces de pétrels antarctiques. *Oiseau* **38**, no. spéc., 2–52.

*Mougin, J.-L. (1969). Notes écologiques sur le pétrel de Kerguelen *Pterodroma brevirostris* de l'île de la Possession (archipel Crozet). *Oiseau* **39**, no. spéc., 58–81.

Mougin, J.-L. (1970a). Observations écologiques sur les grands albatros (*Diomedea exulans*) de l'île de la Possession (archipel Crozet) en 1968. *Oiseau* **40**, no. spéc., 16–36.

Mougin, J.-L. (1970b). Les albatros fuligineux *Phoebetria palpebrata* et *P. fusca* de l'île de la Possession (archipel Crozet). *Oiseau* **40**, no. spéc., 37–61.

Mougin, J.-L. (1970c). Le pétrel à menton blanc *Procellaria aecquinoctialis* de l'île de la Possession (archipel Crozet). *Oiseau* **40**, no. spéc., 62–96.

Mougin, J.-L. (1975). Écologie comparée des Procellariidae Antarctiques et Sub-antarctiques. *Comité National Français des Recherches Antarctiques* **36**, 1–195.

Mougin, J.-L. and Prévost, J. (1980). Évolution annuelle des effectifs et des biomasses des oiseaux Antarctiques. *Terre et la Vie, Revue d'Écologie* **34**, 101–133.

Mougin, J.-L. and van Beveren, M. (1979). Structure et dynamique de la population de manchots empereur *Aptenodytes forsteri* de la colonie de l'archipel de Pointe Geologie, Terre Adélie. *Comptes Rendus, Academie des Sciences* (Paris) Ser. D **289**, 157–160.

Müller-Schwarze, D. and Müller-Schwarze, C. (1973). Differential predation by south polar skuas in an Adélie penguin colony. *Condor* **75**, 127–131.

Müller-Schwarze, D. and Müller-Schwarze, C. (1977). Interactions between south polar skuas and Adélie penguins. *In* "Adaptations within Antarctic Ecosystems" (G. A. Llano, ed.) pp. 619–646. Smithsonian Institution, Washington, D.C.

Murphy, R. C. (1936). "Oceanic Birds of South America", Vols 1 and 2. American Museum of Natural History, New York.

Murphy, R. C. (1964). Systematics and distribution of Antarctic petrels. *In* "Biologie Antarctique" (R. Carrick, M. W. Holdgate and J. Prévost, eds), pp. 349–358. Hermann, Paris.

Murrish, D. E. (1973). Respiratory heat and water exchange in penguins. *Respiratory Physiology* **19**, 262–270.

Naito, Y., Nasu, K. and Suzuki, H. (1979). Distribution of Antarctic seabirds in the outer margin of the summer pack ice area. *Antarctic Record* **66**, 50–63.

O'Connor, R. J. (1977). Differential growth and body composition in altricial passerines. *Ibis* **119**, 147–166.

Oelke, H. (1975). Breeding behaviour and success in a colony of Adélie penguins, *Pygoscelis adeliae*, at Cape Crozier, Antarctica. *In* "The Biology of Penguins (B. Stonehouse, ed.), pp. 363–395. Macmillan, London.

Orton, M. N. (1968). Notes on Antarctic petrels, *Thalassoica antarctica*. *Emu* **67**, 225–229.

Parmelee, D. F. (1976). Banded south polar skua found in Greenland. *Antarctic Journal of the United States* **11**, 111.

*Parmelee, D. F. (1977). Adaptations of Arctic terns and Antarctic terns within Antarctic ecosystems. *In* "Adaptations within Antarctic Ecosystems" (G. A. Llano, ed.), pp. 687–702. Smithsonian Institution, Washington, D.C.

Parmelee, D. F. and Maxson, S. J. (1975). The Antarctic terns of Anvers Island. *Living Bird* **13**, 233–250.

Parmelee, D. F., Fraser, W. R. and Neilson, D. R. (1977). Birds of the Palmer Station area. *Antarctic Journal of the United States* **12**, 15–21.

Pascal, M. (1979). Données écologiques sur l'albatros à sourcils noir *Diomedea melanophris* (Temminck) dans l'archipel des îles Kerguelen. *Alauda* **47**, 165–172.

Pascal, M. (1980). Structure et dynamique de la population de chats harets de l'archipel des Kerguelen. *Mammalia* **44**, 161–182.

Paulian, P. (1953). Pinnipèdes, cétacés, oiseaux des îles Kerguelen et Amsterdam. *Mémoires de l'Institut Scientifique de Madagascar, Série A* **8**, 111–234.

Payne, M. R. and Prince, P. A. (1979). Identification and breeding biology of the diving petrels *Pelecanoides georgicus* and *P. urinatrix exsul* at South Georgia. *New Zealand Journal of Zoology* **6**, 299–318.

Pinder, R. (1966). The cape pigeon *Daption capensis* Linnaeus at Signy Island, South Orkney Islands. *British Antarctic Survey Bulletin* No. 8, 19–47.

Pinshow, B., Fedak, M. A., Battles, D. R. and Schmidt-Nielsen, K. (1976). Energy expenditure for thermoregulation and locomotion in Emperor Penguins. *American Journal of Physiology* **231**, 903–912.

Potter, I. C., Prince, P. A. and Croxall, J. P. (1979). Data on the adult marine and migratory phases in the life cycle of the Southern Hemisphere lamprey, *Geotria australis* Gray. *Environmental Biology of Fishes* **4**, 65–69.

Prange, H. D. and Schmidt-Nielsen, K. (1970). The metabolic cost of swimming in ducks. *Journal of Experimental Biology* **53**, 763–777.

Prévost, J. (1961). "Écologie du Manchot Empereur". Hermann, Paris.

Prévost, J. (1969). A propos des pétrels des neiges de la Terre Adélie. *Oiseau* **39**, no. spéc., 33–49.

Prévost, J. and Mougin, J.-L. (1970). "Guide des Oiseaux et Mammifères des Terres Australes et Antarctiques Françaises". Delachaux et Niestlé, Neuchâtel.

Prince, P. A. (1980a). The food and feeding ecology of blue petrel (*Halobaena caerulea*) and dove prion (*Pachyptila desolata*). *Journal of Zoology* (Lond.) **190**, 59–76.

Prince, P. A. (1980b). The food and feeding ecology of grey-headed albatross *Diomedea chrysostoma* and black-browed albatross *D. melanophris*. *Ibis* **122**, 476–488.

Prince, P. A. (1982). The black-browed albatross *Diomedea melanophris* population on Beauchêne Island, Falkland Islands. *Comité National Français des Recherches Antarctiques* **51**, 111–117.

Prince, P. A. and Payne, M. R. (1979). Current status of birds at South Georgia. *British Antarctic Survey Bulletin* No. 48, 103–118.

Prince, P. A. and Ricketts, C. (1981). Relationships between food supply and growth in albatrosses: an interspecies fostering experiment. *Ornis Scandinavica* **12**, 207–210.

Prince, P. A., Ricketts, C. and Thomas, G. (1981). Weight loss in incubating albatrosses and its implication for their energy and food requirements. *Condor* **83**, 238–242.

Rahn, H. and Ar, A. (1974). The avian egg: incubation time and water loss. *Condor* **76**, 147–152.

Reid, B. E. (1964). The Cape Hallett Adélie penguin rookery, its size, composition and structure. *Record of the Dominion Museum* **5**, 11–37.

Reilly, P. N. and Balmford, P. (1975). A breeding study of the little penguin *Eudyptula minor* in Australia. *In* "The Biology of Penguins" (B. Stonehouse, ed.), pp. 161–187. Macmillan, London.

Reilly, P. N. and Cullen, J. M. (1979). The little penguin *Eudyptula minor* in Victoria, I: mortality of adults. *Emu* **79**, 97–102.

Reilly, P. N. and Cullen, J. M. (1981). The little penguin *Eudyptula minor* in Victoria, II: breeding. *Emu* **81**, 1–19.

Richdale, L. E. (1945). The nestling of the sooty shearwater. *Condor* **47**, 45–62.

Richdale, L. E. (1952). Post-egg period in albatrosses. *Biological Monographs* **4**, 1–66.

Richdale, L. E. (1957). "A Population Study of Penguins". Oxford University Press, Oxford.

Richdale, L. E. (1963). Biology of the sooty shearwater *Puffinus griseus*. *Proceedings of the Zoological Society of London* **141**, 1–117.

Richdale, L. E. (1965a). Biology of the birds of Whero Island, New Zealand with special reference to the diving petrel and the white-faced storm petrel. *Transactions of the Zoological Society of London* **31**, 1–86.

Richdale, L. E. (1965b). Breeding behaviour of the narrow-billed prion and the broad-billed prion on Whero Island, New Zealand. *Transactions of the Zoological Society of London* **31**, 87–155.

Richdale, L. E. and Warham, J. (1973). Survival, pair bond retention and nest site tenacity in Buller's mollymauk. *Ibis* **115**, 257–263.

Ricketts, C. and Prince, P. A. (1981). Comparison of growth of albatrosses. *Ornis Scandinavica* **12**, 120–124.

Ricklefs, R. E. (1967). A graphical method of fitting equations to growth curves. *Ecology* **48**, 978–983.

Ricklefs, R. E. (1968a). Patterns of growth in birds. *Ibis* **110**, 419–451.

Ricklefs, R. E. (1968b). On the limitations of brood size in passerine birds by the ability of adults to nourish their young. *Proceedings of the National Academy of Sciences of the United States of America* **61**, 847–851.

Ricklefs, R. E. (1973). Patterns of growth in birds II. Growth rate and mode of development. *Ibis* **115**, 177–201.

Ricklefs, R. E. (1979). Adaptation, constraint and compromise in avian postnatal development. *Biological Reviews* **54**, 269–290.

Ricklefs, R. E. and Rahn, H. (1979). The incubation temperature of Leach's storm petrel. *Auk* **96**, 625–627.

Ricklefs, R. E., White, S. C. and Cullen, J. (1980a). Energetics of postnatal growth in Leach's storm petrel. *Auk* **97**, 566–575.

Ricklefs, R. E., White, S. C. and Cullen, J. (1980b). Postnatal development of Leach's storm petrel. *Auk* **97**, 768–781.

Roberts, B. B. (1940). The life cycle of Wilson's petrel *Oceanites oceanicus* (Kuhl). *British Graham Land Expedition 1934–37 Scientific Reports* **1**, 141–194.

Roux, J.-P., Jouventin, P., Mougin, J.-L. and Weimerskirch, H. (1983). Un nouvel albatros (*Diomedea amsterdamensis* nova species) découvert sur l'île Amsterdam (37°50′S, 77°35′E). *Oiseau* **53**,1–11.

*Rowan, M. K. (1951). The yellow-nosed albatross, *Diomedea chlororhynchos* at its breeding grounds in the Tristan da Cunha group. *Ostrich* **22**, 139–155.

*Sagar, P. M. (1979). Breeding of the cape pigeon (*Daption capense*) at the Snares Islands. *Notornis* **26**, 23–36.

Saint-Romas, G. and Le Maho, Y. (1976). Décroissance pondérale au cours des premiers jours de jeûne chez le manchot empereur (*Aptenodytes forsteri*). *Comptes Rendus, Academie des Sciences* (Paris) Sér. D **283**, 1097–1099.

Sanger, G. A. (1972). Preliminary standing stock and biomass estimates of seabirds in subarctic Pacific region. *In* "Biological Oceanography of the Northern Pacific Ocean" (A. Y. Takenouti, ed.), pp. 589–611. Idemitsu Shoten, Tokyo.

Sapin-Jaloustre, J. and Bourlière, F. (1951). Incubation et developpement chez le manchot Adélie *Pygoscelis adeliae*. *Alauda* **19**, 65–83.

Schlatter, R. P. and Moreno, C. A. (1976). Habitos alimentarios del cormoran antartico, *Phalacrocorax atriceps bransfieldensis* (Murphy) en Isla Green, Antartica. *Serie Cientifica, Instituto Antartico Chileno* **4**, 69–88.

Scientific Committee on Antarctic Research (1979). Fifteenth Meeting of SCAR, Chamonix 16–26 May 1978. Appendix A. Working Group on Biology. *Polar Record* **19**, 304–312.

Scientific Committee on Antarctic Research (1980). "Antarctic bird Biology". *BIOMASS Report Series* No. 8.

Segonzac, M. (1970). La nidification du puffin à pieds pales (*Puffinus carneipes*) a l'île Saint-Paul. *Oiseau* **40**, 131–135.

Segonzac, M. (1972) Données récentes sur la faune des îles Saint-Paul et Nouvelle Amsterdam. *Oiseau* **42**, no. spéc., 3–68.

Serventy, D. L. (1957). The banding of *Puffinus tenuirostris* (Temminck). *CSIRO Wildlife Research* **2**, 51–59.

Serventy, D. L. (1967). Aspects of the population ecology of short-tailed shearwater *Puffinus tenuirostris*. *Proceedings of the 14th International Ornithological Congress*, 165–190.

Serventy, D. L., Serventy, V. and Warham, J. (1971). "The Handbook of Australian Sea-birds". A. H. and A. W. Reed, Wellington.

Siegfried, W. R. (1978). Ornithological research at the Prince Edward Islands: a review of progress. *South African Journal of Antarctic Research* **8**, 30–34.

Siegfried, W. R., Williams, A. J., Burger, A. E. and Berruti, A. (1978). Mineral and energy contributions of eggs of selected species of seabirds to the Marion Island terrestrial ecosystem. *South African Journal of Antarctic Research* **8**, 75–87.

Sladen, W. J. L. (1958). The pygoscelid penguins. 1, Methods of study. 2, The Adélie penguin *Pygoscelis adeliae* (Hombron and Jacquinot). *Falkland Islands Dependencies Survey Scientific Reports* **17**, 1–97.

Sladen, W. J. L., Wood, R. C. and Monaghan, E. P. (1968). Antarctic avian population studies 1967–68. *Antarctic Journal of the United States* **3**, 247–249.

Sorensen, J. H. (1950). The light-mantled sooty albatross at Campbell Island. *Cape Expedition Series Bulletin* **8**, 1–30.

Spellerburg, I. F. (1969). Incubation temperatures and thermoregulation in the McCormick skua. *Condor* **71**, 59–67.

Spellerburg, I. F. (1970). Body measurements and colour phases of the McCormick skua *Catharacta maccormicki*. *Notornis* **17**, 280–285.

Spellerburg, I. F. (1971). Aspects of McCormick skua breeding biology. *Ibis* **113**, 357–363.

Spurr, E. B. (1975). The breeding of the Adélie penguin *Pygoscelis adeliae* at Cape Bird. *Ibis* **117**, 324–338.

Spurr, E. B. (1977). Adaptive significance of the reoccupation period of the Adélie penguin. *In* "Adaptations within Antarctic Ecosystems" (G. A. Llano, ed.), pp. 605–618. Smithsonian Institution, Washington, D.C.

Stahl, J.-C. and Weimerskirch, H. (1982). La segregation écologique entre les deux espèces de sternes des îles Crozet. *Comité National Français des Recherches Antarctiques* **51**, 449–456.

Stonehouse, B. (1953). The emperor penguin *Aptenodytes forsteri* Gray. 1. Breeding behaviour and development. *Falkland Islands Dependencies Survey Scientific Reports* **6**, 1–33.

Stonehouse, B. (1960). The king penguin *Aptenodytes patagonica* of South Georgia. 1, Breeding behaviour and development. *Falkland Islands Dependencies Survey Scientific Reports* **23**, 1–81.

Stonehouse, B. (1963). Observations on Adélie penguins (*Pygoscelis adeliae*) at Cape Royds, Antarctica. *Proceedings of the 13th International Ornithological Congress*, 766–769.

Stonehouse, B. (1964). Bird Life. *In* "Antarctic Research" (R. Priestley, R. J. Adie and G. de Q. Robin, eds), pp. 219–239. Butterworth, London.

Stonehouse, B. (1967). The general biology and thermal balances of penguins. *In* "Advances in Ecological Research" (J. B. Cragg, ed.), Vol. 4, pp. 131–196. Academic Press, New York and London.

Stonehouse, B. (1970a). Geographic variation in gentoo penguins, *Pygoscelis papua*. *Ibis* **112**, 52–57.

Stonehouse, B. (1970b). Adaptation in polar and subpolar penguins (Spheniscidae). *In* "Antarctic Ecology" (M. W. Holdgate, ed.), Vol. 1, pp. 526–541. Academic Press, New York and London.

Stonehouse, B. (ed.) (1975). "The Biology of Penguins". Macmillan, London.

*Strange, I. J. (1980). The thin-billed prion, *Pachyptila belcheri*, at New Island, Falkland Islands. *Gerfaut* **70**, 411–445.

*Swales, M. K. (1965). The sea-birds of Gough Island. *Ibis* **107**, 17–42, 215–229.

Taylor, R. H. (1962). The Adélie penguin *Pygoscelis adeliae* at Cape Royds. *Ibis* **104**, 176–204.

Taylor, R. H. and Roberts, H. S. (1962). Growth of Adélie penguin (*Pygoscelis adeliae* Hombron and Jacquinot) chicks. *New Zealand Journal of Science* **5**, 191–197.

Tenaza, R. (1971). Behavior and nesting success relative to nest location in Adélie penguin (*Pygoscelis adeliae*). *Condor* **73**, 81–92.

Thomas, G. (1982). The food and feeding ecology of the light-mantled sooty albatross at South Georgia. *Emu* **82**, 92–100.

Thomas, G., Croxall, J. P. and Prince, P. A. (1983). Breeding biology of the light-mantled sooty albatross at South Georgia. *Journal of Zoology,* (Lond.). **199**, 123–135.

Thurston, M. H. (1982). Ornithological observations in the South Atlantic Ocean and Weddell Sea, 1959–1964. *British Antarctic Survey Bulletin* No. 55, 77–104.

Tickell, W. L. N. (1962). The dove prion *Pachyptila desolata* Gmelin. *Falkland Islands Dependencies Survey Scientific Reports* **33**, 1–55.

Tickell, W. L. N. (1967). Movements of black-browed and grey-headed albatrosses in the South Atlantic. *Emu* **66**, 357–367.

Tickell, W. L. N. (1968). The biology of the great albatrosses, *Diomedea exulans* and *Diomedea epomophora*. *In* "Antarctic Bird Studies", Antarctic Research Series, Vol. 12 (O. L. Austin, Jr, ed.), pp. 1–55. American Geophysical Union, Washington, D.C.

Tickell, W. L. N. and Gibson, J. D. (1968). Movements of wandering albatrosses *Diomedea exulans*. *Emu* **68**, 7–20.

*Tickell, W. L. N. and Pinder, R. (1975). Breeding biology of the black-browed albatross *Diomedea melanophris* and grey-headed albatross *D. chrysostoma* at Bird Island, South Georgia. *Ibis* **117**, 433–451.

Tickell, W. L. N. and Scotland, C. D. (1961). Recoveries of ringed giant petrels *Macronectes giganteus*. *Ibis* **103a**, 260–266.

Tickell, W. L. N. and Woods, R. W. (1972). Ornithological observations at sea in the South Atlantic Ocean, 1954–1964. *British Antarctic Survey Bulletin* No. 31, 63–84.

Trawa, G. (1970). Note préliminaire sur la vascularisation des membres des sphéniscidés de Terre Adélie. *Oiseau* **40**, no. spéc., 142–156.

Trillmich, F. (1978). Feeding territories and breeding success of south polar skuas. *Auk* **95**, 23–33.

Trivelpiece, W. and Volkman, N. J. (1979). Nest site competition between Adélie and chinstrap penguins: an ecological interpretation. *Auk* **96**, 675–681.

Trivelpiece, W. and Volkman, N. J. (1982). Feeding strategies of sympatric south polar (*Catharacta maccormicki*) and brown skuas (*C. lonnbergi*). *Ibis* **124**, 50–54.

Trivelpiece, W., Butler, R. G. and Volkman, N. J. (1980). Feeding territories of brown skuas (*Catharacta lonnbergi*). *Auk* **97**, 669–676.

Utter, J. M. and Le Febvre, E. A. (1970). Energy expenditure for free flight by the purple martin (*Progne subis*). *Comparative Biochemistry and Physiology* **35**, 713–719.

van Aarde, R. J. (1980). The diet and feeding behaviour of feral cats, *Felis catus*, at Marion Island. *South African Journal of Wildlife Research* **10**, 123–128.

van Zinderen Bakker, E. M. Jr (1971a). Comparative avian ecology. *In* "Marion and Prince Edward Islands. Report on the South African Biological and Geological Expedition 1965–1966" (E. M. van Zinderen Bakker Sr, J. M. Winterbottom and R. A. Dyer, eds), pp. 161–172. A. A. Balkema, Cape Town.

van Zinderen Bakker, E. M. Jr (1971b). A behaviour analysis of the gentoo penguin. *In* "Marion and Prince Edward Islands. Report on the South African Biological and Geological Expedition 1965–1966" (E. M. van Zinderen Bakker, Sr, J. M. Winterbottom and R. A. Dyer, eds), pp. 257–272. A. A. Balkema, Cape Town.

van Zinderen Bakker, E. M. Jr (1971c). Birds observed at sea. *In* "Marion and Prince Edward Islands. Report on the South African Biological and Geological Expedition 1965–1966" (E. M. van Zinderen Bakker Sr, J. M. Winterbottom and R. A. Dyer, eds), pp. 249–250. A. A. Balkema, Cape Town.

*Voisin, J.-F. (1968). Les pétrels géants (*Macrconectes halli* et *Macronectes giganteus*) de l'île de la Possession. *Oiseau* **38**, no. spéc., 95–122.

*Voisin, J.-F. (1969). L'albatros hurleur *Diomedea exulans* à l'île de la Possession. *Oiseau* **39**, no. spéc., 82–106.

*Voisin, J.-F. (1970). On the specific status of the Kerguelen shag and its affinities. *Notornis* **17**, 286–290.

Voisin, J.-F. and Bester, M. N. (1981). The specific status of giant petrels *Macronectes* at Gough Island. *In* "Proceedings of the Symposium on Birds of the Sea and Shore, 1979" (J. Cooper, ed.), pp. 215–222. African Seabird Group, Cape Town.

Volkman, N. J. and Trivelpiece, W. (1980). Growth in pygoscelid penguin chicks. *Journal of Zoology* (Lond.) **191**, 521–530.

Volkman, N. J. and Trivelpiece, W. (1981). Nest-site selection among Adélie, chinstrap and gentoo penguins in mixed species rookeries. *Wilson Bulletin* **93**, 243–248.

Volkman, N. J., Presler, P. and Trivelpiece, W. (1981). Diets of pygoscelid penguins at King George Island, Antarctic. *Condor* **82**, 373–378.

Voous, K. H. (1965). Antarctic birds. *In* "Biogeography and Ecology in Antarctica" (J. van Mieghem and P. van Oye, eds) *Monographiae Biologicae* Vol. 15, pp. 649–689. Junk, The Hague.

Warham, J. (1956). The breeding of the great-winged petrel *Pterodroma macroptera*. *Ibis* **98**, 171–185.

Warham, J. (1958). The nesting of the shearwater *Puffinus carneipes*. *Auk* **75**, 1–14.

Warham, J. (1962). The biology of the giant petrel *Macronectes giganteus*. *Auk* **79**, 139–160.

Warham, J. (1963). The rockhopper penguin, *Eudyptes chrysocome*, at Macquarie Island. *Auk* **80**, 229–256.

Warham, J. (1964). Breeding behaviour in Procellariiformes. *In* "Biologie Antarctique" (R. Carrick, M. W. Holdgate and J. Prévost, eds), pp. 389–391. Hermann, Paris.

Warham, J. (1967). The white-headed petrel *Pterodroma lessoni* at Macquarie Island. *Emu* **67**, 1–22.

Warham, J. (1971a). Body temperatures of petrels. *Condor* **73**, 214–219.

*Warham, J. (1971b). Aspects of breeding behaviour in the royal penguin (*Eudyptes chrysolophus schlegeli*). *Notornis* **18**, 91–115.

*Warham, J. (1972a). Breeding seasons and sexual dimorphism in rockhopper penguins. Auk **89**, 86–105.

*Warham, J. (1972b). Aspects of the breeding biology of the erect-crested penguin Eudyptes sclateri. Ardea **60**, 145–184.

*Warham, J. (1974a). The Fiordland crested penguin Eudyptes robustus. Ibis **116**, 1–27.

*Warham, J. (1974b). The breeding biology and behaviour of the Snares crested penguin. Journal of the Royal Society of New Zealand **4**, 63–108.

Warham, J. (1975). Relations of body size among Procellariiformes. Emu **74** (suppl.), 323–324.

Warham, J. (1977a). The incidence, functions and ecological significance of petrel stomach oils. Proceedings of the New Zealand Ecological Society **24**, 84–93.

Warham, J. (1977b). Wing-loading, wing shapes and flight capabilities of Procellariiformes. New Zealand Journal of Zoology **4**, 73–83.

Warham, J. and Bell, B. D. (1979). The birds of the Antipodes Islands, New Zealand. Notornis **26**, 121–169.

Warham, J., Watts, R. and Dainty, R. J. (1976). The composition, energy content and function of the stomach oils of petrels (Order Procellariiformes). Journal of Experimental Marine Biology and Ecology **23**, 1–13.

Warham, J., Keeley, B. R. and Wilson, G. J. (1977). Breeding of the mottled petrel. Auk **94**, 1–17.

Watson, G. E. (1975). "Birds of the Antarctic and Subantarctic". American Geophysical Union, Washington, D.C.

Watson, G. E. et al. (1971). Birds of the Antarctic and Subantarctic. Antarctic Map Folio Series **14**, 1–18.

Weimerskirch, H. (1982). La stratégie de reproduction de l'albatros fuligineux à dos sombre. Comité National Français des Recherches Antarctiques **51**, 437–447.

White, M. G. and Conroy, J. W. H. (1975). Aspects of competition between pygoscelid penguins at Signy Island, South Orkney Islands. Ibis **117**, 371–373.

Wiens, J. A. and Scott, J. M. (1975). Model estimation of energy flow in Oregon coastal seabird populations. Condor **77**, 439–452.

Williams, A. J. (1978). Mineral and energy contributions of petrels (Procellariiformes) killed by cats, to the Marion Island terrestrial ecosystem. South African Journal of Antarctic Research **8**, 49–53.

Williams, A. J. (1980a). The effect of attendance by three adults upon nest contents and chick growth in the southern great skua. Notornis **27**, 79–85.

Williams, A. J. (1980b). Aspects of the breeding biology of the subantarctic skua at Marion Island. Ostrich **51**, 160–167.

Williams, A. J. (1980c). Offspring reduction in macaroni and rockhopper penguins. Auk **97**, 754–759.

Williams, A. J. (1980d). Aspects of the breeding biology of the gentoo penguin, Pygoscelis papua. Gerfaut **70**, 283–295.

Williams, A. J. (1980e). Variation in the weight of eggs and its effect on the breeding biology of the great skua. Emu **80**, 198–202.

Williams, A. J. and Berruti, A. (1978). Mineral and energy contributions of feathers moulted by penguins, gulls and cormorants to the Marion Island terrestrial ecosystem. South African Journal of Antarctic Research **8**, 71–74.

Williams, A. J. and Burger, A. E. (1979). Aspects of the breeding biology of the imperial cormorant, *Phalacrocorax atriceps*, at Marion Island. *Gerfaut* **69**, 407–423.

Williams, A. J., Burger, A. E., Berruti, A. and Siegfried, W. R. (1975). Ornithological research on Marion Island. *South African Journal of Antarctic Research* **5**, 48–50.

Williams, A. J., Siegfried, W. R., Burger, A. E. and Berruti, A. (1977). Body composition and energy metabolism of moulting eudyptid penguins. *Comparative Biochemistry and Physiology* **56A**, 27–30.

Williams, A. J., Burger, A. E. and Berruti, A. (1978). Mineral and energy contributions of carcasses of selected species of seabirds to the Marion Island terrestrial ecosystem. *South African Journal of Antarctic Research* **8**, 53–59.

Williams, A. J., Siegfried, W. R., Burger, A. E. and Berruti, A. (1979). The Prince Edward Islands: a sanctuary for seabirds in the Southern Ocean. *Biological Conservation* **15**, 59–71.

Wood, R. C. (1971). Population dynamics of breeding skuas of unknown age. *Auk* **88**, 805–814.

Wood, R. C. (1972). Population study of south polar skuas (*Catharacta maccormicki*) age one to eight years. *Proceedings of the 15th International Ornithological Congress*, 705–706.

Woods, R. W. (1970). The avian ecology of a tussock island in the Falkland Islands. *Ibis* **112**, 15–24.

Woods, R. W. (1975). "The Birds of the Falkland Islands". Anthony Nelson, Oswestry.

Yeates, G. W. (1968). Studies on the Adélie penguin at Cape Royds 1964–65 and 1965–66. *New Zealand Journal of Marine and Freshwater Research* **2**, 472–496.

Yeates, G. W. (1975). Microclimate, climate and breeding success in Antarctic penguins. *In* "The Biology of Penguins" (B. Stonehouse, ed.), pp. 397–409. Macmillan, London.

Young, E. C. (1963a). Feeding habits of the south polar skua *Catharacta maccormicki*. *Ibis* **105**, 301–318.

Young, E. C. (1963b). The breeding behaviour of the south polar skua *Catharacta maccormicki*. *Ibis* **105**, 203–233.

Young, E. C. (1978). Behavioural ecology of *lonnbergi* skuas in relation to environment in the Chatham Islands, New Zealand. *New Zealand Journal of Zoology* **5**, 401–416.

Young, E. C. (1981). The ornithology of the Ross Sea. *Journal of the Royal Society of New Zealand* **11**, 287–315.

Appendix I. Some penguin and petrel weights[a] and duration of incubation and fledging periods

No.[b]	Species		Adult weight (g)	Egg weight (g)	Chick weight[c] (g)	Incubation period (days)	Fledging period (days)	Total (days)
1	Emperor penguin	Aptenodytes forsteri	32,550	450	320	62	170	232
2	King penguin	A. patagonicus	15,150	302	220	54	350	404
3	Adélie penguin	Pygoscelis adeliae	4400	120	90	36	50	86
4	Chinstrap penguin	P. antarctica	4150	104	90	37	54	91
5	Gentoo penguin	P. papua	5890	133	92	36	70–90	106–126
6	Yellow-eyed penguin	Megadyptes antipodes	5200	138		43	106	149
7	Rockhopper penguin	Eudyptes chrysocome	2600	111	75	34[d]	70	104
8	Macaroni penguin	E. chrysolophus	4700	154	116	34	62	96
9	Fiordland penguin	E. pachyrhynchus	4880	120	78	34	75	109
10	Erect-crested penguin	E. sclateri	5900	149		35	75	110
11	Snares crested penguin	E. robustus	2560	125		33	75	108
12	Little blue penguin	Eudyptula minor	1100	52		35	58	93
13	Wandering albatross	Diomedea exulans	8730	448	352	78	278	356
14	Royal albatross	D. epomophora	8290	416	340	79	240	319
15	Black-browed albatross	D. melanophrys	3790	257	181	68	116	184
16	Grey-headed albatross	D. chrysostoma	3790	276	195	72	141	213
17	Yellow-nosed albatross	D. chlororhynchos	2060	180		78	130	208
18	Buller's albatross	D. bulleri	3100	257				200
19	Shy albatross	D. cauta	3290	259		65	135	200
20	Black-footed albatross	D. nigripes	3090	291	180	65	140	205
21	Laysan albatross	D. immutabilis	2450	279	175	65	165	230
22	Waved albatross	D. irrorata	3290	284		60	167	227
23	Sooty albatross	Phoebetria fusca	2510	243		70	160	230
24	Light-mantled sooty albatross	P. palpebrata	2840	258	280	69	140	209
25	Southern giant petrel	Macronectes giganteus	4500[e]	268	167	59	112	171
26	Northern giant petrel	M. halli	4500	268	174	62	108	170
27	Antarctic fulmar	Fulmarus glacialoides	775	103	71	46	52	98
28	Northern fulmar	F. glacialis	720	101	68	49	46	95
29	Snow petrel	Pagodroma nivea major	373	56	40	45	47	92
30	Snow petrel	P. nivea nivea	270	56		43	51	94
31	Antarctic petrel	Thalassoica antarctica	680	90		45	42	87
32	Cape pigeon	Daption capense	425	63	43	45	48	93
33	Narrow-billed prion	Pachyptila belcheri	132	31	13	47	49	96
34		P. desolata	162	33	27	45	51	96

No.	Common name	Species						
35	Broad-billed prion	*P. vittata*						
36	Salvin's prion	*P. salvini*	180	33	25	56	53	109
37	Fulmar prion	*P. crassirostris*	162	32		55	60	115
38	Fairy prion	*P. turtur*	130	26		55	50	105
39	Blue petrel	*Halobaena caerulea*	200	24	33	55	50	105
40	Grey-faced petrel	*Pterodroma macroptera*	560	36		46	49	95
41	White-headed petrel	*P. lessonii*	750	90	80	55	125	180
42	Kerguelen petrel	*P. brevirostris*	300	99	65	60	102	162
43	Mottled petrel	*P. inexpectata*	323	56		49	60	109
44	Soft-plumaged petrel	*P. mollis*	265	61	40	50	97	147
45	Dark-rumped petrel	*P. phaeopygia*	385	54		50	91	141
46	White-chinned petrel	*Procellaria aequinoctialis*	1270	66	100	51	110	161
47	Grey petrel	*P. cinerea*	1040	124		58	94	152
48	Sooty shearwater	*Puffinus griseus*	787	110	66	55	93	148
49	Flesh-footed shearwater	*P. carneipes*	600	93		56	97	153
50	Great shearwater	*P. gravis*	834	77		58	92	150
51	Little shearwater	*P. assimilis*	225	125		55	72	127
52	Short-tailed shearwater	*P. tenuirostris*	530	31	64	53	94	147
53	Wedge-tailed shearwater	*P. pacificus*	500	85		52	93	145
54	Manx shearwater	*P. puffinus*	400	56	44	51	70	121
55	Audubon's shearwater	*P. lherminieri*	165	58	21	49	75	124
56	Wilson's storm petrel	*Oceanites oceanicus*	36	29	7	41	55	96
57	Black-bellied storm petrel	*Fregetta tropica*	56	10	15	40	68	108
58	White-bellied storm petrel	*F. grallaria*	46	15		40	75	115
59	Grey-backed storm petrel	*Garrodia nereis*	29	12				
60	White-faced storm petrel	*Pelagodroma marina*	47	11		50	80	130
61	British storm petrel	*Hydrobates pelagicus*	25	12		41	66	107
62	Leach's storm petrel	*Oceanodroma leucorhoa*	45	7		41	66	107
63	Madeiran storm petrel	*O. castro*	42	9		42	69	111
64	South Georgia diving petrel	*Pelecanoides georgicus*	106	17	13	46	45	91
65	Common diving petrel	*P. urinatrix exsul*	134	19	16	54	54	108
66	Common diving petrel	*P. u. chathamensis*	124	16		56	54	110
67	Common diving petrel	*P. u. urinatrix*	136	17	12	53	50	103

Data from references cited in Lack (1968), superseded or modified by those marked* in reference list.

[a] Sexes combined.

[b] For reference to Figs 8–13, 15–22.

[c] Weight at hatching.

[d] For *E. c. moseleyi* at Amsterdam I. recorded as 29 days (Duroselle and Tollu, 1977).

[e] Recent data show *M. halli* to be slightly heavier than *M. giganteus* at South Georgia (Hunter, in press).

12

Seals

R. M. Laws

1. Introduction

The Southern Ocean is wide and deep, with a narrow and deep continental shelf, much of it covered by floating ice shelves. The sea south of
the Antarctic Convergence comprises 35 million km^2 and is cold but rich in
food (Chapter 6). The circumpolar zone of fast ice and pack ice is a barrier
to some seal species, although all six Antarctic seals have been recorded in
it, but it also provides a platform on which they haul out.

It was not until the turn of this century that accurate information on the
animal life of the region began to accumulate, although Gray (1844) had
described the seals. Being more conspicuous than most other Antarctic
animals, they attracted particular attention and a number of early accounts
described their taxonomy, appearance and behaviour (Allen, 1880; Barrett-
Hamilton, 1902; Brown, 1913; Bruce, 1913a,b; Trouessart, 1906; Wilson,
1907). Expeditions in the 1930s greatly extended our knowledge of the two
most abundant species (Bertram, 1940; Lindsey, 1937, 1938; Perkins,
1945). The biology of Antarctic seals has previously been reviewed by a
number of authors (Bonner and Laws, 1964; Erickson and Hofman, 1974;
King, 1964; Laws, 1964; Øritsland, 1970a; Ray, 1970; Scheffer, 1958;
Turbott, 1952).

Although few in number of species (six out of 36 pinniped species), each
species represents a separate genus (six out of 19 world wide) and several
are very abundant. One, the crabeater seal, *Lobodon carcinophagus*,
comprises at least half the total world stocks of pinnipeds. As a group it has
been estimated that they amount to about 56% of the world stocks and,
because individuals tend to be larger than other seals, about 79% of the
total biomass of pinnipeds (Laws, 1977a). However, population increases
in the last decade suggest that they may account for considerably more than

ANTARCTIC ECOLOGY VOL. 2
ISBN 0 12-439502-3

these proportions (this chapter). Their importance cannot be denied, both on account of their basic scientific interest, as a basis for former industries and as a potential future resource (Chapter 15). Finally, a number of the more significant developments in marine mammal and more general mammalian studies owe much to the results of research on Antarctic seals, for example in age determination, reproduction, population dynamics, behaviour and diving physiology.

2. Zoogeography and Distribution

2.1 General

Six species are discussed: the Antarctic (Kerguelen) fur seal, *Arctocephalus gazella*; the southern elephant seal, *Mirounga leonina*; the crabeater seal, *Lobodon carcinophagus*; the Ross seal, *Ommatophoca rossii*; the leopard seal, *Hydrurga leptonyx*; and the Weddell seal, *Leptonychotes weddellii*. Their characteristics are summarized by Ray (1970). The seals are intermediate between the birds (restricted to land except for the emperor penguin) and the whales (completely aquatic) in their requirements for breeding sites (land or sea ice).

Like many other Antarctic animals, the seals are essentially distributed in circumpolar latitudinal zones except where the Antarctic Peninsula and Scotia arc intervene, extending the breeding distribution of some high latitude species northwards (e.g. Weddell and leopard seals) and of some lower latitude species southwards (e.g. elephant seal and fur seal) (Fig. 1). The influence on pinniped distribution of a continuous coastline and pack ice zone in the south, and very discontinuous coastlines to the north (the surrounding Antarctic and sub-Antarctic islands and the other southern continents), is clearly apparent. Further north in the Southern Hemisphere, speciation has led to a proliferation of seven fur seal and three sea lion species associated with island groups or temperate continental shores. This contrasts with the Northern Hemisphere where there are only two fur seals and two sea lions (confined to the North Pacific), but 16 true seals. An obvious influence on speciation is that physiographically, the Arctic region is the reverse of the Antarctic. A deep ocean centred on the North Pole and at sub-Arctic and temperate latitudes large land masses—containing inland seas and broken by three oceans—contrast with a high continent centred on the pole, surrounded in lower latitudes by a continuous circumpolar ocean with islands or relatively short coastlines at sub-Antarctic and southern temperate latitudes.

Climate and substrate are the main factors limiting breeding distributions. The distributions of food organisms may also be important; for example the crabeater seal is an obligate krill feeder. Important physical boundaries affecting overall distributions are the Antarctic Convergence and the Sub-tropical Convergence (Chapter 6). Most of the continental coast is fringed by shelf ice cliffs or ice foots, which prevent breeding on land. The southern limit for successful breeding colonies of elephant and fur seals is governed by air temperatures and the presence of sea ice in spring.

The greatest numbers of seals are found in the pack ice zone, but there are stragglers even of the pack ice seals to temperate waters. They fall into two groups, essentially land breeding (fur and elephant seals) and ice breeding (Weddell, crabeater, Ross and leopard seals). This has consequences for their distribution and breeding behaviour, although the division is not absolute. The breeding distribution of three species is strictly limited to south of the Antarctic Convergence (crabeater, Ross and Weddell seals). Of those breeding on sea ice, pupping is restricted to fast ice in the Weddell seal (and elephant seal when it occurs). In their social organization and breeding behaviour the six species range from solitary to gregarious, and from largely monogamous to highly polygnous. The Weddell, fur and elephant seals exhibit varying degrees of territoriality and polygyny, almost certainly because they have a firm unmoving substrate for pupping and lactation (section 4).

2.2 Breeding distribution

The distribution of breeding sites is shown in Fig. 1. With the exception of a small colony on Marion Island, the breeding range of the Antarctic fur seal is limited to islands south of the Antarctic Convergence and north of about 65°S (Bonner, 1981). The main breeding stock is on Bird Island, Willis Islands, and the neighbouring coast of South Georgia. Smaller colonies are present at the South Orkney Islands, South Shetland Islands, Elephant and Clarence Islands, South Sandwich Islands, Bouvetøya, Heard and Mac-Donald Islands and Îles Kerguelen. Individuals tagged on Bird Island have later been observed breeding on South Georgia and as summer visitors to the South Orkney Islands, Elephant Island and Tierra del Fuego (Payne, 1979a; Hunt, 1973).

The situation at Marion Island is unique, because the most southerly large breeding population of *Arctocephalus tropicalis* and the most northerly breeding population of *A. gazella* are found there, respectively 7000 and 300, and appear to hybridize (Condy, 1978).

The main elephant seal population centres are South Georgia, Kerguelen and Heard Islands and Macquarie Island (Laws, 1960; Fig. 1). The group of

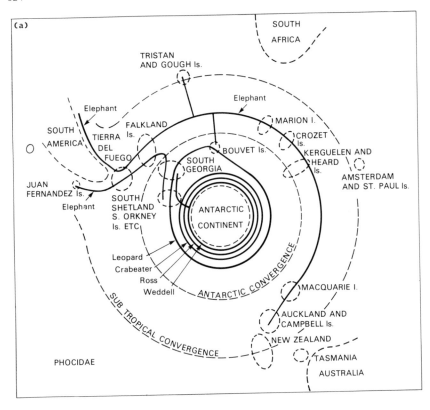

Fig. 1. Diagram of the geographical distribution of southern seals. The thick lines are drawn to join breeding localities of (a) Phocidae, (b) Otariidae.

breeding colonies centred on South Georgia probably includes South American coasts, Falkland Islands, South Orkney Islands, South Shetland Islands and possibly South Sandwich Islands and Bouvetøya. The Kerguelen group includes Heard Island, Marion and Prince Edward Islands, Crozet Island, Amsterdam and St. Paul Islands; and the Macquarie Island group includes Campbell Island, Auckland Island and Antipodes Islands (Laws, 1960).

Although branding and tagging experiments have demonstrated movements within the geographical areas covered by these three main groups, no interchange between them has yet been observed. Dickinson (1967) reported tag returns that showed movements from South Georgia to the South Orkney Islands, southern Argentina, and Tierra del Fuego, but not outside this region. Scolaro (1976) has reported movements from Peninsula Valdes, Argentina, to the Falkland Islands. Hunt (1973) observed on

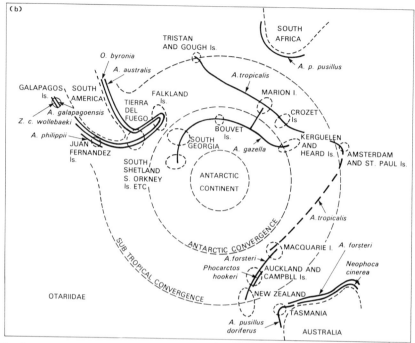

Fig. 1b

Elephant Island eight elephant seals tagged as pups at South Georgia or the South Orkney Islands. Ingham (1967) reported movements of seals branded at Macquarie Island that were later seen at Campbell Island, Chatham Islands, New Zealand and Tasmania; branded seals from Heard Island have been seen at Îles Kerguelen, Marion Island and the Antarctic continent. Although 374 of over 10,000 elephant seals marked at Îles Kerguelen had been registered up to 1977, none had been seen on other breeding islands (Van Aarde and Pascal, 1980). Six subadults marked on the Antarctic continent were later observed at Kerguelen.

No evidence for transferrin polymorphism was found in 18 samples of serum from *M. leonina* examined by Seal *et al.* (1971b), and so cannot be used to typify genetic stocks.

Births have also been reported from South Africa, Tasmania, Antarctic Peninsula, as far south as Avian Island (67°46′S) (Laws, 1960; Müller Schwarze *et al.*, 1978; British Antarctic Survey, unpublished records) and from Greater Antarctica, where several births have been recorded since 1973 at Peterson Island (66°27′S, 11°30′E) near Casey Station (Murray, 1981). Numbers hauling out there to moult are increasing; near Davis Station (68°38′S, 77°58′E) several hundred elephant seals haul out to moult, but there has been no breeding. A major difference between Casey and Davis is that at Casey there is nearby open water during much of the year.

Weddell seal breeding colonies have been recorded from fast ice areas adjacent to the Antarctic continent and off-lying islands in every region which man has visited at the appropriate time of year. The island groups include South Sandwich Islands, South Orkney Islands, Bouvetøya, Balleny Islands. At South Georgia a very small breeding population has been known for many years at Larsen Harbour, which produced annually less than 30 pups (Bonner, 1958).

The long term tagging programmes at McMurdo Sound and Signy Island have shown fidelity to the general area of the colony of birth with no evidence for long range movements. The same applies to tagging carried out in the Vestfold Hills area. Blood samples collected from four widely separated areas around the Antarctic Continent (at longitudes 62°52′E, 77°58′E, 110°32′E and 166°45′E) showed protein polymorphisms and indicated significant differences in three transferrin types, which is not unexpected if there is some measure of birth site fidelity (Shaughnessy, 1969). Seal et al. (1971a,b) reached similar conclusions, an additional region sampled, the Weddell Sea, suggesting isolation of that population compared with the Ross Sea. These results support the conclusion that there are genetically separate breeding populations of Weddell seals, but further studies are needed.

The other three species appear to have a circumpolar breeding distribution in the pack ice (inferred from distributions in the summer, non-breeding, season). For logistical reasons direct observations in the pack ice at the time of the breeding season are difficult to make and so are very few and confined to the Antarctic Peninsula (Siniff et al., 1979; Bengtson and Siniff, 1981), and the vicinity of the South Orkney Islands (Øritsland, 1970b). The crabeater seal breeds in spring in the pack ice wherever there is access for haul out, which, in practice restricts it to a zone near the periphery of the pack ice. Studies of protein and enzyme polymorphisms have given no indication of genetically separate sub-populations and so homogeneity is inferred (Seal et al., 1971a,b). Two adult male crabeater seals were recovered two years later in the same area where they were tagged (Siniff et al., 1980).

The breeding distribution of the leopard seal is probably very similar to that of the crabeater seal in consolidated pack ice, and in the non-breeding season a consistent crabeater seal — leopard seal association has been demonstrated by Gilbert and Erickson (1977). Breeding has also been reported from Îles Kerguelen (Scheffer, 1958). There is no evidence of protein polymorphism in the species (Seal et al., 1971a,b) and it is assumed, as for the crabeater seal, that it is genetically homogeneous.

Eight suckling Ross seals with pups were recorded by Tikhomirov (1975) south of the Scott Islands (67°24′S, 179°55′W); one was recorded by Solyanik (1964) near the South Sandwich Islands (56°00′S, 26°30′W); and one has been recorded by Thomas *et al.* (1980) near the west coast of the Antarctic Peninsula (64°21′S, 62°47′W). Valette (1906) observed a pup at the South Orkney Islands and Øritsland (1970b) collected seven foetuses near the group (60°35′S, 45°30′W) in September and October. This supports the view that the Ross seal breeding distribution is, like the non-breeding distribution, circumpolar, but there may be greater numbers between 6°E and 6°W than elsewhere in the Antarctic (Condy, 1976). No evidence of transferrin polymorphism was found in Ross seals, but the sample size was too small for the results to be significant (Seal *et al.*, 1971a,b).

2.3 Non-breeding distribution

The non-breeding distribution is less well-known for fur, elephant and Weddell seals but better understood for the pack ice breeding species.

Almost nothing is known about the pelagic distribution of the fur seal, adults of which are absent from the breeding islands between May and October. It is not known whether there is a directional migration, or a widespread dispersal northwards or westwards from South Georgia. The bones of a seal tagged as a pup at Bird Island in January 1973 were recovered nine months later 2000 km to the west in Tierra del Fuego, Chile (Payne, 1979a) and juveniles have been seen at South Georgia with tightly-fitting neck collars of rope and other materials. Payne (1979a) and Bonner and McCann (1982) described these. The former suggested that they most likely had been attached by fishermen in South American waters, but it now seems probable that they had become attached accidentally as the seals were swimming. Payne believed that this and other evidence suggested that there may be a directed migration similar to that of the northern fur seal, *Callorhinus ursinus*, in the North Pacific. If there is a similar migration in *A. gazella* it could well have gone undetected at the low population levels of the last 150 years and with the difficulty of separating *A. gazella* in the field from the southern fur seal *A. australis*.

In the case of the elephant seal the marking returns show that the species is very widely distributed at sea when not ashore for breeding or moulting—up to 1500 miles from their breeding grounds (Ingham, 1967; Dickinson, 1967; Hunt, 1973; Laws, 1960; van Aarde and Pascal, 1980; Murray, 1981; Scolaro, 1976). It has, unusually, been recorded in pack ice (Laws, unpublished observations) and as far south as the Antarctic Continent (see above); also from South Africa (Best, 1971; Kettlewell and

Rand, 1955), Tasmania (Davies, 1961), New Zealand (Daniel, 1971), Mauritius and Rodriguez Islands (Stoddart, 1972).

3. Abundance and Habitat Preferences

3.1 Total numbers and overall densities

A recent summary of methods of counting Antarctic seals and relevant literature was given by Laws (1980). For colonial breeders (fur, Weddell and elephant seals) counts of pups are raised by a factor related to the age structure to give estimates of total population size. For pack ice species estimates are derived from stratified random strip counts.

The Antarctic fur seal has undergone one of the most rapid population increases recorded for any marine mammal (Payne, 1977; Laws, 1979) following its near extinction in the nineteenth century, the cessation of commercial sealing in the early years of this century, and the subsequent implementation of rational conservation measures (Chapter 15). The most recent account, based mainly upon Payne's (1977, 1978) studies, is by Bonner (1981). After the early exploitation it was thought to be extinct until small numbers were seen at Bird Island, South Georgia, in the 1930s, probably representing a relict population of no more than a hundred or so. It was not until 1957 that serious studies were initiated and counts made between 1957 and 1963, and 1972–1975, when the size of the colonies made counting difficult. Between 1958 and 1972 the annual rate of increase was shown to be 16.8% and from 1972 to 1975, 14.5%. The annual pup production in 1975 was carefully assessed by Payne (1977, 1978) at about 90,000. Further studies by the British Antarctic Survey indicate that the rate of increase at Bird Island has decreased but daughter colonies on the mainland of South Georgia continue to increase very rapidly. Bonner (1981) estimated that the annual pup production in 1978 was 135,000 corresponding to a total population of about 554,000, and by 1982 it was estimated that there were probably over 900,000 (Fig. 2, Table II).

Laws (1973, 1981) gave the results of counts at the South Orkney Islands where other daughter colonies produced about 69 pups in 1974, representing only a 2% annual increase during the previous three years; however, pup production in the largest colony increased from 28 in 1965 to 47 in 1974, an annual rate of 6%, though still far below the South Georgia rate. In the other southern colonies similarly small rates of increase have been reported (Bonner, 1981). In recent years there has been an increase in the number of breeding sites to include Signy Island (British Antarctic

Survey, unpublished reports), but the current status of the other colonies in the group is not known.

Laws (1960), on the basis of information then available, concluded that the total mid-year population of southern elephant seals was 600,000 ± 100,000. This has been updated by McCann (in press) to *c*. 750,000, the South Georgia stock comprising 350,000, Macquarie Island 136,000, Îles Kerguelen 157,000 and Heard Island 80,000. At Marion Island Condy (1977a) showed that since 1951 there had been an average annual decline of 5% to an estimated population of 4500 in 1978 (see section 9.3).

The crabeater seal is "perhaps the most abundant large mammal in the world" (Kooyman, 1981a). Censuses in the shifting pack ice zone have produced estimates ranging from 2 to 5 million (Scheffer, 1958) up to 75 million (Erickson *et al.*, 1971). The true population size lies somewhere in between and Kooyman (1981a) has emphasized the difficulties of counting a species which occupies a vast range and is under the surface and invisible for most of the time.

The most carefully planned and executed population estimates of the four Antarctic pack ice seals are those described by Erickson *et al.* (1971), Siniff *et al.* (1970) and by Gilbert and Erickson (1977), based on investigations made from icebreakers, in 1968, 1969, 1972 and 1973. These authors also summarize earlier attempts. Owing to the very high logistic costs of operating in pack ice and the vast area to be covered, these operations may not be repeated and other methods of assessing population status need to be developed (sections 7.6 and 9.1).

Reliable estimates of population size required, first, counts of seals hauled out on the pack ice in relation to ice type and cover, in sample areas, preferably randomly located strips, in order to calculate densities (Laws, 1980). These counts were made from surveys conducted by helicopters, ice breakers and low-level aerial photography. Secondly, an estimate was made of the total area of pack ice and its stratification by types of floe and their packing; this is available from satellite imagery (Chapter 6). Seal densities have been shown to be inversely related to the area of pack ice available for haul out (Eklund and Atwood, 1962; Erickson *et al.*, 1971). Thirdly, an appropriate estimation procedure must be applied to the data collected. Adjustments are necessary to allow for fluctuations during the day of numbers hauled out and the densities obtained are likely to be conservative, because even when peak numbers are on the ice there is likely to be an unknown but substantial proportion of the population in the water, which may be as high as 50% (Smith, 1973; see also section 5.4).

Gilbert and Erickson (1977) concluded that there were six residual pack ice regions (Fig. 2) which were consistent in their pattern from year to year in summer and, taking into account the results presented by Siniff *et al.*

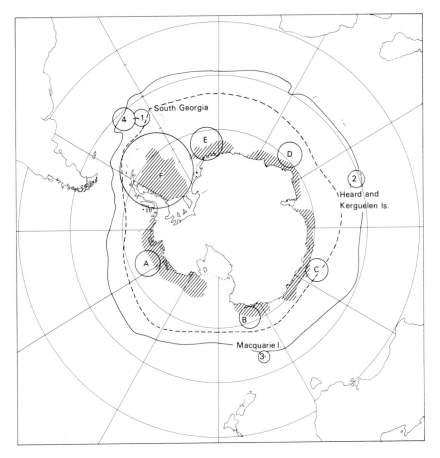

Fig. 2. The Southern Ocean, showing the Antarctic Convergence (continuous line); pack ice extent in October (broken line); Gilbert and Erickson's (1977) ice-breeding seal populations associated with residual pack ice regions (A-F); elephant seal breeding stocks (1–3); Antarctic fur seal (4). Areas of circles are proportional to estimated population sizes.

(1970), estimated their overall seal densities in February to March, within the range 1.86 to 6.56 km^{-2}, to reach a total conservative population estimate of 14,858,000 crabeater seals. Using their *summary* data (p. 375) and following their method of calculation, I reached a somewhat different result, summarized in Table 1 and Fig. 2. However, as they point out, the juvenile segment of the population is probably under-represented and the recorded densities are likely to be low. A total of 15 million may well be conservative and a current population of 30–40 million or more is not unlikely, as the species appears to have been increasing (section 9.5).

TABLE I

Crabeater seal population estimates for six residual pack ice regions, 1968–1973

Region	Pack ice area (km²)	Seal density (km⁻²)	Population
Amundsen-Bellingshausen Sea	359,000	3.32	1,193,000
Oates Coast	254,000	1.86	472,000
Wilkes Land	415,000	1.86	772,000
Queen Maude Land	429,000	1.86	798,000
Halley Bay region	257,000	6.56	1,686,000
		(7.50)	(1,927,000)
Weddell Sea	1,257,000	6.56	8,247,000
		(7.50)	(9,422,000)
Total (average)	2,971,000	4.43	13,174,000
		(4.83)	(14,349,000)

Figures in parentheses based on mean of 1968 and 1969 censuses.

It could be objected (Kooyman, 1981a) that extrapolation from the numbers in the relatively small areas surveyed (totalling some $10,500 \text{ km}^2$) to some 3 million km^2 of pack ice is unjustified, but it was carried out using acceptable procedures and the extrapolation is conservative and gives the best estimates of numbers yet available. (Gilbert and Erickson give some indication of the differing variances of the estimates for different species, presumably influenced by their differing abundances, behaviour patterns and types of distributions). Also, the fact that the 1968 and 1969 censuses in the Weddell Sea gave very different seal densities which then had to be extrapolated to widely different total pack ice areas, but nevertheless produced not too dissimilar results, promotes confidence. In 1968, during the surveys in January, February and March, there were $2,758,000 \text{ km}^2$ of loose pack in the Weddell Sea and during the surveys in 1969, $1,648,500 \text{ km}^2$. This is reflected in inversely proportional crabeater seal densities during the surveys and yet the population estimates were 8,246,800 and 10,597,500 respectively. The mean of these estimates is 9,422,150 and the variation of the 1968 and 1969 totals is $\pm 12\%$ of this mean. It appears to indicate a remarkable consistency for the crabeater seal population estimates. Figure 2 shows the estimated population sizes associated with six residual pack ice regions. In percentage terms these represent 92.36% crabeater, 1.35% leopard, 1.35% Ross and 4·93% Weddell seal. Erickson *et al.* (1971) concluded that the species composition of seals in the pack ice remains remarkably consistent, but in inshore areas these proportions change. For example, Ray (1970) found 43% Weddell seals in counts at the western side of the Ross Sea. Estimates of the total populations of all six species are given in Table II and amounted to some 18 million in the early 1970s, possibly rising to some 33 million in 1982 (section 9).

TABLE II
Estimated total abundances of the Antarctic seal populations

Species	Population size 1982 (thousands)	Status
Fur seal	930	Increasing
Elephant seal	750	Stable, some decreasing
Crabeater seal	15,000–30,000	Increasing
Leopard seal	220–440	Increasing
Ross seal	220	Not known
Weddell seal	800	Stable, some colonies decreasing
Total	17,920–33,140	Increasing

3.2 Habitat preferences

On land in the breeding season the Antarctic fur seal shows a preference for rocky shores and small beaches in sheltered coves (Bonner, 1968) and at other times of the year it is found both in these situations, in more open bays and, at South Georgia, in tussock grass areas behind the beaches. The elephant seal tends to occupy larger, more open beaches in the breeding season and is found on these and in muddy wallows in low-lying tussock grass at South Georgia. At more southerly colonies breeding occurs on inshore fast ice or on land and the moulting pods occupy wallows in summer (Laws, 1956a).

The pack ice seals show preferences for particular ice types (Fig. 3). In spring the Weddell seal forms pupping colonies on the fast ice, along shore lines, associated with broken ice, tide cracks and hummocking, which facilitates the maintenance of holes for hauling out (Stirling, 1971a; Siniff *et al.*, 1977; Kooyman, 1981c). Kooyman has described the awesome conditions that the most southerly colony at White Island has to cope with in order to feed under the 100 m thick shelf ice. After the breeding season there is a movement into the pack ice away from the coast. In the pack they are nearly always single and are found throughout the pack ice, although densities are probably higher closer to land or fast ice. Their peak haul out time during the day varies seasonally but is at about 14 h in summer (Gilbert and Erickson, 1977, and Fig. 8). A proportion of the population winters under the fast ice, keeping open breathing holes with their teeth (Kooyman, 1981c).

In contrast, the crabeater seal is usually found near the outer edge of the pack ice region, the highest densities having been recorded in summer within 120 km of the ice edge. The densities are most closely correlated with dominant floe size, not ice cover, and in summer they are most abundant in cake and brash ice of about 7–8 oktas cover; densities are lowest in areas with larger floes (Gilbert and Erickson, 1977). These authors suggest that this is related to food availability and that krill is most abundant near the ice edge, associated with the sympagic diatoms (Chapter 7) on which it feeds. However, they were not able to confirm, in the Amundsen and Bellingshausen Seas, the correlation between crabeater density and chlorophyll *a* content reported by Siniff *et al.* (1970) in the Weddell Sea.

Peak haul out periods for crabeaters are around midday, with some regional and year to year variability (Condy, 1977b and Fig. 9). According to Erickson *et al.* (1971) and Hofman (cited by Gilbert and Erickson, 1977), body length frequency analyses of samples from pack ice and nearshore locations "indicated that most of the juvenile segment of the population was absent from the pack ice when the censuses were conducted".

Their winter distribution is not known, but it is likely to be in the peripheral pack ice zone, because in some years large numbers of crabeater seals have been recorded at Signy Island, South Orkney Islands, which is near the pack ice edge (Mansfield, personal communication; British Antarctic Survey, unpublished report). Racovitza (1900), during the drift of the *Belgica*, observed southerly movement of crabeaters as leads opened up in the spring, and a northward movement in autumn was recorded during the drift of the *Endurance* in the Weddell Sea (Bertram, 1940).

In spring their family groups (section 4.1) are associated with larger hummocked floes, and the immatures can be found in large concentrations of several thousands, associated with the fast ice remaining in bays (Bengtson and Siniff, 1981).

Leopard seals are observed in summer as solitary animals and show higher densities near the pack ice edge, like the crabeater. Even in summer relatively few are seen in inshore waters, where their predatory activities in the vicinity of penguin colonies have attracted much attention (Laws, 1981). They are correlated with similar ice types and show similar daytime haul out patterns to crabeater seals. Little is known of their winter behaviour, but there is a seasonal cycle in their occurrence at Macquarie Island which is probably related to the nearness of the pack ice edge (Rounsevell and Eberhard, 1980).

Ross seals are usually observed as solitary individuals and their higher

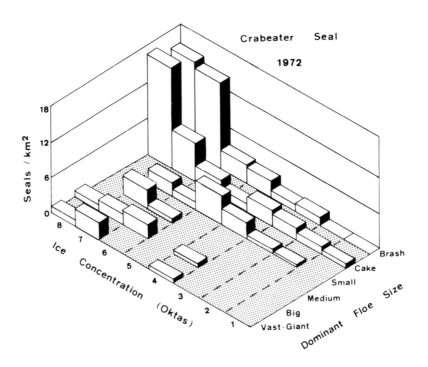

Crabeater Seal

1972

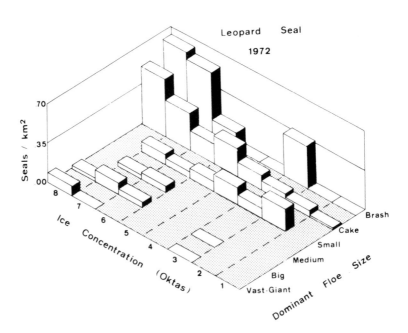

Leopard Seal

1972

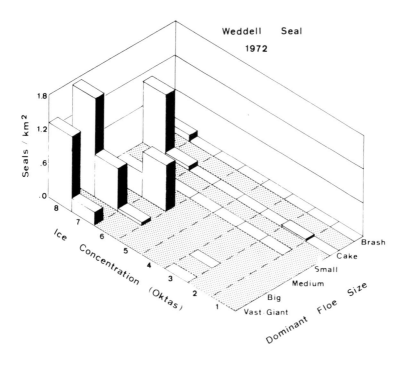

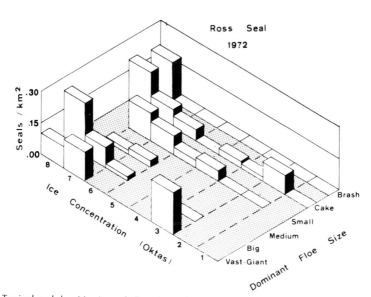

Fig. 3. Typical seal densities in each floe size and ice concentration class, for the four pack ice species (Gilbert and Erickson, 1977). By permission of the Smithsonian Institution Press from *Adaptations within Antarctic Ecosystems: Proceedings of the Third SCAR Symposium on Antarctic Biology*, G. A. Llano, ed., Smithsonian Institution, Washington, D.C.

densities are associated with larger floes than is the case with other species, typically where ice cover is about 6–8 oktas (Gilbert and Erickson, 1977). The peak haul out is around 1430–1530 h, which may reflect a diurnal vertical movement of the fish and squid on which they feed.

4. Social Organization

4.1 Ice breeding species

None of the ice breeding seals form concentrations as dense as those of the land breeding species, even in the breeding season. Probably the most solitary is the Ross seal. We know virtually nothing of their social organization, and they remain almost unstudied during the breeding season. During the summer in the regions surveyed by Gilbert and Erickson (1977) their closest observed spacing was 1 km and the average overall density was about $0.09\,\mathrm{km^{-2}}$ in summer and probably about $0.02\,\mathrm{km^{-2}}$ in spring. The estimated densitites change by season and from year to year according to the amount of pack ice available as a platform for hauling out, which varies from 3 to 19 million $\mathrm{km^2}$ in an average year (Chapter 6), but regionally may show much greater fluctuations. Not surprisingly, Ross seals are almost invariably solitary, although groups of up to 13 have been recorded (Laws, 1964).

Leopard seal densities in summer were similar ($0.14\,\mathrm{km^{-2}}$) and again we know little of their social organization; densities during the pupping season were probably about $0.02\,\mathrm{km^{-2}}$.

Conversely crabeater seals are sometimes found in summer in local aggregations of up to 600 within a radius of 5 km (Gilbert and Erickson, 1977) and in larger numbers on fast ice (Siniff et al., 1979). However, the overall mean density was about $4.83\,\mathrm{km^{-2}}$ in summer (Table 1) and probably about $0.5\,\mathrm{km^{-2}}$ in winter and spring. In summer most are single animals, but the mean group sizes recorded ranged from 1.29 to 2.22 in summer, varying in different areas and years. Statistical analysis of the group size frequency distributions indicated that there is some degree of sociability in summer (Gilbert and Erickson, 1977).

The crabeater pupping season is from late September until early November, with a peak in early to mid-October (Siniff et al., 1979), but owing to their inaccessibility in the pack ice at this time, virtually nothing was known of their breeding behaviour until a few years ago; our knowledge is still sparse compared with other seal species. Valette (1906) reported many young of 1–3 months in December at the South Orkneys, indicating births in September–November. King (1957) described a pup collected near Port

Lockroy, and summarized previous records. Øritsland (1970b) observed males paired with non-pregnant adult females and also several family groups containing an adult female, her pup and a mature male. Corner (1972) gave a detailed account of the behaviour of such a family group over a 12-day period.

Since 1975 several expeditions to the general area of the Bransfield Strait in October–November have been devoted to such investigations (Siniff and Bengtson, 1977; Siniff et al., 1979; Bengtson and Siniff, 1981). This work indicated that crabeater seal densities (0.7–$0.8 \, \mathrm{km}^{-2}$) are much lower than in summer, but there is some evidence of clumping; on one day for example six family groups were found within 2 km of each other.

It seems that family groups form when a pregnant female hauls out to give birth on a suitable floe and is joined by a male, before or after parturition; only twice was a female-pup pair seen without a male in attendance. Fig. 4 shows the probable timing of events. The family group appears to remain within a small area, usually on one floe, until the pup is weaned. Such groups were seen along the Antarctic Peninsula between 7 October and 4 November. They usually occupied hummocked floes and the male often occupied the elevated parts of the floe, showing a characteristically alert posture and behaviour. The pup was almost invariably alongside and touching its mother. The male makes periodic advances towards the female, presumably testing her sexual receptivity. He positions himself as close as possible to her but if he comes too close she chases him away; older males are typically very scarred about the head and neck from females' bites.

The duration of the suckling period is not reliably known, but is probably no more than about four weeks (section 8.2.2). Weaning appears to be initiated when the male becomes dominant and drives the female from the pup; this is presumably associated with the weakening of the female who has lost about 50% of her initial weight by the time of weaning.

The male defends the family group against other adult males, leopard seals and humans, protecting his right to mate when the female comes into oestrus. Intraspecific competition is not infrequent despite the wide spacing, and changes in male occur, although usually the resident male successfully maintains his position, defending an area of about 50 m radius around the female.

As the pup grows the distance between the male and female decreases, and when it is weaned they become a male-female pair, maintaining close contact; the male prevents the female from leaving the floe, often biting her on the upper back and neck, so that characteristically she becomes covered in blood. This is probably precopulationary behaviour and the female returns the male aggression. Attempted mounting has been observed, but

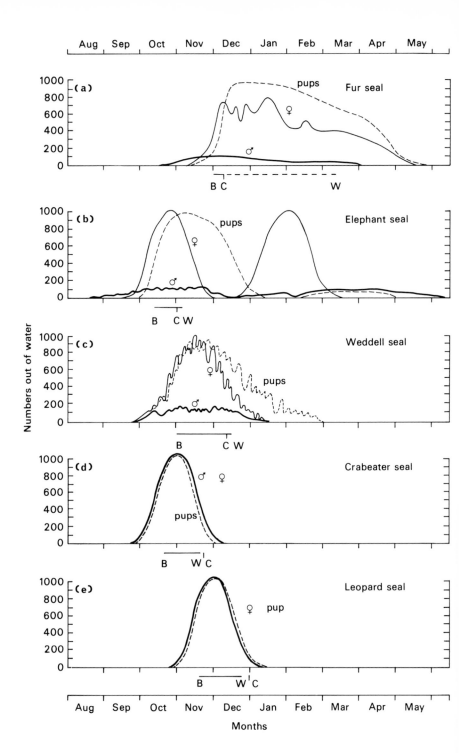

not a successful one. Most ice breeding seals mate in the water (Stirling, 1975) but the effort expended by the male crabeater in remaining close to the female strongly suggests that mating of the parous females, at least, occurs on the ice. From post mortem examination it was found that almost all females in family groups had not yet ovulated; of those in mated pairs 60% had not ovulated, but the majority of lone females had already ovulated and a corpus luteum was forming (Bengtson and Siniff, 1981), suggesting that ovulation occurs shortly after weaning of the pup, not before as in most other pinnipeds studied. The occurrence of these solitary females suggests that the male–female bond is a temporary one as would be expected. Mating of newly mature females may typically occur in the water and they appear to ovulate later in the season than older females (Bengtson and Siniff, 1981).

It seems likely that, after copulating with one female, the male will actively search in the pack ice for another by smell and, when near, by sight, but the number of impregnations a male achieves must be small compared with the Weddell, elephant and fur seals (see below).

In spring also, large close concentrations are found in some fast ice areas; they consist of animals that are mainly younger than those involved in the breeding groups. Almost no aggressive behaviour is seen in these aggregations and they may form because the pack ice and the water beneath it is dominated by aggressive males at this time, or they may have an anti-predator function. Groups of up to 50 of these younger animals are also seen in the vicinity of the fast ice aggregations swimming together along the edge of the fast ice in unison.

The mating strategies of the leopard and Ross seals are even less well understood than in the crabeater seal. This is because they are much less abundant species—with estimated total populations less than 2% of that of the crabeater—and in the case of the Ross seal probably frequenting denser and more remote pack ice regions. The opportunities for study are therefore even more limited.

From the few observations made, it appears that the leopard seal gives

---

Fig. 4. Diagrammatical representation of breeding season activities of Antarctic seals. (a) Fur seal, Bird Island, haul out of mature males and females for parturition, lactation and mating. Average dates of birth (B), conception (C) and weaning (W) are indicated. Note suckling period is broken by feeding trips to sea. Data to early March from Bonner (1968), extrapolated to May from other reports. (b) Elephant seal, South Georgia, as above. Adult haul out for moult in January–May is also shown (Data from Laws (1956a) and McCann (1980a)). (c) Weddell seal, McMurdo Sound, haul out of mature males, females and pups on fast ice for breeding; fluctuating curves reflect aquatic activity (data from Kauffman et al. (1975)). (d) Crabeater seal, Antarctic Peninsula, family groups and mated pairs in pack ice. Hypothetical curve represents current ideas (see text). (e) Leopard seal, Antarctic Peninsula, female and pup pairs on ice. Hypothetical curve inferred from very limited observations.

birth in November and December in the Antarctic Peninsula region, perhaps a month later than the crabeater (Fig. 4); groups in the pupping season consist exclusively of female and pup pairs on the ice floes. At this time males are seen cruising in the water, looking for crabeater seal pups (see section 5.2.2) and no interactions between them and female and pup leopard seals have been seen (DeMaster *et al.*, 1980; Siniff, 1982; Tikhomirov, 1975; Laws, personal observation). Mating was thought to occur well after weaning, probably in January–March (Harrison, 1969; Harrison *et al.*, 1952; Sinha and Erickson, 1972; Siniff *et al.*, 1980), and is probably aquatic. Wild (1923) described a "fight" on 9 February when one seal leaped repeatedly to 6 feet out of the water, thought to have been "courtship behaviour" by Hamilton (1939). However, recent work by Siniff and Stone (in press) indicates that mating occurs around the end of December.

Very few Ross seal females with pups have ever been recorded. The only records appear to be: one at the South Orkney Islands (Valette, 1906); one at the South Sandwich Islands (Solyanik, 1964); one off the Antarctic Peninsula (Thomas *et al.*, 1980); and eight near the Balleny Islands (Tikhomirov, 1975). In addition, Øritsland (1970b) reported foetuses in seven Ross seals collected near the South Orkney Islands between 23 September and 29 October. The Balleny Islands pups were estimated to have been born between 3 and 18 November, and the Antarctic Peninsula pup seen on 14 November was thought to be new born. Again the indication is of later pupping than in the crabeater and the Ross seal breeding pattern is probably similar to the leopard seal (Fig. 4).

The Weddell seal is quite different in its social organization from the other ice breeding species. Several key papers review earlier work and are the source of much of the following information (Stirling, 1969a, 1971a; Kaufman *et al.*, 1975; Siniff *et al.*, 1977).

In summer, outside the breeding season, Weddell seals probably move to the outer limits of the fast ice and the inner zones of the pack ice. Dispersal may be very limited in this species; one would expect it to involve mainly younger animals, but no great numbers of subadults have been reported from the outer pack ice and Weddell seal densities in the pack tend to be no higher than Ross and leopard seal densities, although its population abundance is several times larger (section 3.1).

They are nearly always single in the pack ice in summer; the largest group found was four (Gilbert and Erickson, 1977), although larger aggregations are found hauled out on land; Laws (1981) recorded a close-packed group of 61 on Laurie Island, South Orkney Islands. The mean density in the pack ice in summer was $0.14 \, \text{km}^{-2}$; in winter it may be about $0.02 \, \text{km}^{-2}$, assuming an even spacing as the pack ice expands. Most Antarctic research stations are near the shore, but although the Weddell seal's preferred habitat is inshore fast ice there are few sightings in winter. Possible explanations of this are that they spend the winter under the ice and rarely haul out; that they make local movements, perhaps to nearby polynyas (areas of open water in the sea ice); or that most of the population migrates north, leaving small numbers of adults to winter. In fast ice the species must keep breathing holes open, which they do by using their procumbent incisor and canine teeth (Fig. 5).

In spring the pupping colonies form on the near shore sea ice. Their location is determined by physical factors governing access to the sea—such as ice movement caused by icebergs, glaciers, tide cracks—and not by exposure or snow drifting. The first available breathing holes in spring become the loci of the discrete pupping colonies and these holes are enlarged to permit haul out. The colonies therefore tend to be located in areas of perennial cracks.

Even during the breeding season several females share a single breathing hole, giving birth to the pup on the sea ice surrounding it. The females show a clear fidelity to a colony for pupping in successive years; this is possible owing to the predictability and stability of the fast ice, in contrast to the shifting pack ice on which the other ice breeding seals pup, but similar to fur seals and elephant seals which have even more stable pupping areas.

During the winter and spring there is intraspecific competition for space, and non-breeding seals and subadults are excluded from the preferred breeding areas. They are permitted to enter during the summer and autumn after the breeding organization has broken down, but the proportion of subadults decreases as one enters more stable fast ice areas. The pupping season is September–November, depending on latitude, being later in more southerly colonies (section 8.1). Where the sea ice breaks up early in lower latitudes, they may pup on land, and the small relict colony at South Georgia is on land. In McMurdo Sound, Ross Sea, where the most thorough investigations have been carried out, the mean pupping date is late October, the pregnant females haul out a few days before parturition and nearly all pups have been born by mid-November (Fig. 4).

The mature female ovulates just before the pup is weaned in late November–December and underwater mating occurs then; it has been observed, but only once (Kaufman *et al.*, 1975). There is a diurnal pattern of haul out activity, mainly around midday. The bond between mother and pup is strong and interspecific aggression on the surface at this time means that females are more widely spaced from other seals (about 6.5 m) than later in the season (about 3 m) (Stirling, 1969a). During the first half of the suckling period the female leaves the pup very infrequently. The pups first enter the water at 2–3 weeks old and underwater play between mother and pup was observed; suckling was attempted underwater but was not seen to be successful.

In the pupping colonies there are more females than males on the surface of the fast ice and the dominant adult males are beneath it, defending aquatic territories. They exclude other males from the use of their breathing holes, but not the females. Although the female body size is slightly greater than the male (section 7.5), polygyny is indicated by the holding of these territories, but because the male must periodically return to his breathing hole, defence of the territory is interrupted. Nevertheless, it seems clear that dominant males can restrict access to the females by competitors. This conclusion is also supported by the fact that the adult sex ratio is disproportionately in favour of the female, and especially so in the vicinity of the pupping colonies.

Underwater behaviour has been studied by television camera (Kaufman et al., 1975) and acoustic tagging of males (Siniff et al., 1977), and social interactions have been observed. Males join the colony at about the time the first females haul out. Three classes of males have been described in association with the pupping colonies: transient males remained for a few days and then moved on; basking males spent most of their time on the surface—some were wounded and recovering from underwater battles; territorial males spent most of their time underwater.

The underwater territories are orientated along the tide crack in the pupping colony. Circumstantial evidence indicated that the three-dimensional territories were vigorously defended in fights with other males. The basking males appeared more often from the end of November and it was assumed that they had been displaced from their territories. A typical underwater territory declined from 6.5 m^2 on 19 November, to 4.5 m^2 on 30 November and to 3 m^2 on 6 December. This decrease may be due to more territorial males acquiring territories along the tide crack, but this is unconfirmed. It would be analogous to the change in size of the land territories of fur seals (McCann, 1980b) and elephant seals (Laws, 1956a; McCann, 1980a, 1981a,b), described below.

4.2 Land breeding species

The two land breeding species, the fur seal and elephant seal, are highly polygynous and gregarious in their breeding behaviour, and also form large aggregations at other times.

The preferred breeding beaches of the Antarctic fur seal are of rock or shingle, with easy access to the sea, but above the reach of storms. At Bird Island, South Georgia, the males, which have been at sea during the winter, come ashore and establish territories averaging 60 m^2 in late October, 2–3 weeks before the cows haul out to pup (Fig. 4). The territory size declines during the season as other bulls arrive from the sea. Pupping occurs about two days after haul out and harems averaging ten cows form. Pupping is very synchronized, 50% of the pups being born by 4 December and 80% within a 17 day period (Payne, 1978). Mating occurs about eight days post-partum and at the peak period the male territories average about 22 m² in area. Territories are held from late October to late December for an average period of 34 days (1–53 days), during which the bulls do not feed (McCann, 1980b).

After the mating season the males abandon their territories but the cows continue to suckle the pups for 110–115 days. Unlike the bulls, which return to sea until they haul out later in the summer to moult, the cows make the first feeding trip to sea immediately after mating, and this and subsequent ones last 3–6 days, interspersed with 2–5 day periods of suckling the pups on land (Bonner, 1968; Doidge and Croxall, 1983). This pattern is reflected in the microstructure of the dentine layers in the teeth of the pups (Payne, 1978). As a result, the cow is with the pup only for 44% of the time to weaning, or about 48–51 days (Bonner, 1968).

From early September to late May there are always some elephant seals ashore. In September the bulls arrive from the pelagic feeding grounds and shortly afterwards the cows haul out to give birth (Fig. 4). They are gre-garious and form groups, not strictly speaking harems, which quickly at-tract the larger bulls to take up station among them. When they give birth to the pups eight days after hauling out they are tied to land, in contrast to the fur seal, until the pup is weaned. Both cows and bulls go without food on the breeding beaches, the female for over three weeks and some males for up to three months. The cow groups enlarge as they attract other arrivals and the larger groups may have several bulls among them. One of these is clearly dominant except in the very large groups, and on the periphery are subordinate bulls lower in the dominance hierarchy. Usually a vocal threat is sufficient to maintain dominance; if this is not a deterrent the beachmaster will rear up, indicating his size; and if this is still inadequate fights ensue, but are usually of short duration and rarely result in serious injuries (Laws, 1956a, 1960).

The cow comes into oestrus at 19 days post-partum (Laws, 1956b, 1960), is receptive for about four days (McCann, 1980a) and is usually mated several times by dominant bulls, although as she departs from the beach a subor-dinate male may mate with her. On a typical beach at South Georgia the great majority of matings were achieved by a small minority of the bulls, the two top ranking bulls achieving 57% of observed copulations (McCann, 1981a). These intense activities mean that the beachmasters probably have only two or three seasons of such dominance (Le Boeuf, 1974) and then die at sea—because very few dead ones are seen ashore.

While ashore, both sexes live on their reserves of blubber and lose weight rapidly, the bulls owing to the energy used in maintaining their position and repeated matings, the cows by transferring it to the pups as milk (section 5.6).

4.3 Comparison of mating systems

4.3.1 Terrestrial breeding and the evolution of polygyny

Bartholomew (1970) pointed out that polygyny appeared early in pinniped history and was closely associated with the evolution of amphibious habits. He presented a schematic model linking key attributes and functions with positive feedback loops, illustrating his thesis that, given marine feeding and terrestrial parturition, the normal physiological and behavioural characters of eutherian mammals are apt to lead to the establishment of polygyny—that is organized polygamy. The pinnipeds are unique in combining two key attributes: they are adapted, anatomically and physiologically, to exploit marine food resources and yet they give birth on land or sea ice; feeding behaviour and breeding behaviour occur in completely different habitats.

The aquatic adaptations of seals include large size and also make them less mobile on land than other mammals. Their gregariousness makes it possible for them to become concentrated into the limited breeding areas, in some cases forming extremely close-packed breeding colonies. One male can fertilize many females and in polygynous pinnipeds the males have evolved to be much larger than the females (section 7·5), because only those males vigorous and aggressive enough to maintain position among the females can participate in the breeding process.

Male aggressiveness and sex drive are high in the breeding season, controlled in part by testosterone, but most males are effectively excluded from the breeding population by their failure to establish themselves among the breeding females. Males holding territories for the longest period have opportunities to fertilize more females than other males; a successful male might produce 80 male offspring in his lifetime, an unsuccessful one which never held a territory might produce none. The selective force is very obvious.

Fat stored in the blubber serves as an energy source during fasting and large animals can go for longer without food than smaller ones, because of the more favourable ratio of surface area to metabolic rate. Territory maintenance depends on this. The females are less intolerant of each other and reach high densities on the beach, but the aggressive behaviour of the males leads, through threats and fights, to a relatively stable spaced-out population of males among the females, which results in local female: male sex ratios as high as 100:1. The territories of the males are quite small and this is probably determined by the poor terrestrial locomotion which makes defence of larger territories physically impossible. Even if a male could defend a larger territory, there is a limit to the number of females he could serve. In short, it is clear that, linked by multiple feedback loops with other attributes, there must be extremely strong selection for male aggressiveness, large size, vigour, large canines, protective shields of skin or fur, structures used in visual and vocal threats, and the capacity for prolonged fasting—all of which contribute to territory maintenance. As a result pinnipeds, and especially the southern elephant seal, show the most extreme development of sexual dimorphism that occurs in mammals (section 7.5.2).

Complementary to these male attributes, Bartholomew listed female qualities favouring a brief, synchronous annual breeding period, namely: a short post-partum oestrus, high sexual receptivity during oestrus, and delayed implantation of the blastocyst. The advantages of the first two are obvious and delayed implantation (which is almost universal among pinnipeds) may also help to synchronize the pupping season and so the next oestrus (section 8.2.3).

Also, the pups are advanced at birth and require minimal parental attention—being partially deserted from 4–5 days in the Antarctic fur seal and completely independent from 23 days in the southern elephant seal.

Bartholomew pointed out that the development of polygyny in the elephant seal is so extreme as to be near the limit; male activity reduces pup survival and their terrestrial mobility is so limited that if much larger, they could not defend a territory. He also suggested that female gregariousness is carried to seemingly non-functional extremes. While it is necessary if polygyny is to occur in seals, a less dense spacing should be advantageous, by decreasing pup mortality, preventing the accumulation of numbers within a territory in excess of male capacity, and decreasing the incidence of infection and disease. But gregariousness in females should be reinforced by positive selection and in balance with the territorial behaviour, which results in the exclusion of some males from breeding, so as to maintain the reproductive performance at some optimum level.

Writing before the demonstration that male Weddell seals have aquatic territories (Kaufman *et al.*, 1975), Bartholomew considered that the extreme mobility of pinnipeds in the water, combined with the difficulty of maintaining a three-dimensional territory in a medium without boundaries, precluded the establishment of stable aquatic territories in which females can aggregate. He believed that the polygynous system would break down if copulations occurred in the water, because non-territorial males could then participate. The sea lion *Zalophus californianus* provides an example in which aquatic copulation is frequent and polygyny less extreme than in species in which aquatic copulations are less frequent. The Weddell seal may represent a further development of this tendency to reduced polygyny, even though aquatic territories are held.

4.3.2   Factors in the evolution of ice breeding systems

The reversed sexual size dimorphism of the Antarctic ice breeding seals is interesting, particularly in the polygynous territorially-breeding Weddell seal. We know that the extremely dimorphic and polygynous elephant seal can successfully maintain harems and breed on sea ice (Laws, 1956a); the limiting factor seems to be pup survival in an unpredictable environment, when the fast ice breaks up. Large fluctuations in crabeater seal recruitment from year to year may partly reflect year to year variations in pack ice stability at the breeding season (see section 9.4). Further south where the fast ice is more persistent, other limiting factors, such as food availability, climate and the establishment and maintenance of breathing and exit holes through the fast ice may come into play. But why does the Weddell seal not show more highly polygynous behaviour and direct sex dimorphism? In principle the male should be able to hold harems on the surface, like the elephant seal, and surface mating could evolve as it appears to have done in the crabeater seal. The answer may be along the following lines.

The other ice breeding seals occupy the pack ice zone, with apparently unlimited space for breeding. It has been suggested that this would lead to a breakdown of polygyny (Stirling, 1975) or prevent its development. However, the environment is not uniform but patchy and its units, the floes which define the area to be defended, are not usually large enough in the outer pack ice, to hold more than one family group (Siniff, 1982). The spacing of female crabeaters appears to be strongly influenced by the distances between floes and by floe size. The females defend their pups, as other species do, and the males defend the females. Some Arctic pack ice seals aggregate in pupping colonies. Siniff (1982) suggests that predators may have played an important role in the evolution of crabeater behaviour (see section 5.2), resulting in mating on the ice (although copulation has never actually been observed); precopulatory behaviour in the water would probably attract large predators and lead to increased vulnerability. The leopard seal, which appears to copulate under water and is not gregarious, is possibly able to cope with the only other large predator, the killer whale, *Orcinus orca*; the Ross seal, unlike the crabeater seal, is found in regions of heavier ice and does not overlap in its distribution with the leopard, to the extent that the crabeater does; it is also much less abundant. It is therefore less likely to be the prey of leopard seals, and at the same time, is less vulnerable to killer whales in the denser pack ice, like the Weddell seal in fast ice regions.

Where mating is mainly underwater, as in the Weddell (and as appears to be the case in the leopard and Ross seals), the advantage may be thought to lie, not in male size, but in agility underwater where smaller size may be an advantage. In the Weddell seal it is significant that most intraspecific male wounds are around the genital region and the rear of the body; in marked contrast, the highly polygynous and dimorphic elephant and fur seal male and the male crabeater, have wounds around the head and neck. Also, because of the opportunities to feed when they are in the water, there is presumably less of a selective advantage in the ability to fast and lay down large food reserves in the form of blubber. In the baleen whales, as opposed to the toothed whales (especially the sperm whale *Physeter catodon*), there is a reversed size dimorphism and Whitehead (1981) has also speculated that agility may be more advantageous to the male humpback whale (*Megaptera novaeangliae*) than mere body size.

Why then, as mating of the crabeater occurs on the floes, has the male remained smaller than the female? There would seem to be some advantage accruing to larger males, even in a "monogamous" system, and this must be outweighed by disadvantages (or additional advantages in smaller size). One obvious consideration is that, given the present system, adapted to the presence of aquatic predators in the outer pack ice region, a male which was larger than the female might force early weaning, with consequently reduced reproductive success because of lowered pup survival. Added to this is a possible advantage in greater agility if the mating of newly mature females is aquatic and males compete at this time. Defending a single female produces fewer rewards than defending a group for mating rights (but in this species group defence is not advantageous, because of the increased vulnerability of larger groups to predators, as compared with many widely dispersed small groups).

Among ice breeding seals, the direction of sexual dimorphism is not obviously related to variations in mating strategy. It may be significant that in the eight species comprising the related grouping of the Antarctic phocids, Lobodontinae, monk seal, *Monachus* and bearded seal, *Erignathus*, the female tends to be larger than the male, whereas the reverse occurs in all the other phocids, suggestive of a long established ancestral condition.

A survey of the Arctic ice-breeding seals also suggests that it may be a trait that is independent of breeding strategy. Thus, the closest parallel with the crabeater appears to be the larga seal, *Phoca largha*, in which pairs form ten days before pupping and territory is defended around the natal floe; groups are separated by about 0·25 km. The adults are found near the edge of the pack ice and immatures deeper in the pack (Bigg, 1981). The grey seal, *Halichoerus grypus*, where it breeds on drift ice, appears to behave similarly (Hook and Johnels, 1972). Species that appear to show parallels with the leopard and Ross seals are the ribbon seal, *Phoca fasciata*, and bearded seal, *Erignathus barbatus*, in which the female is solitary and males are absent until she approaches oestrus (Burns, 1981a,b). The harp seal, *Phoca groenlandica*, probably mates on the surface of large floes 2–3 weeks post-partrum, when weaning is completed, but forms large spaced aggregations (Ronald and Healey, 1981). The ringed seal, *Phoca hispida*, may be territorial like the Weddell seal, but is not thought to be polygynous and is not very gregarious (Frost and Lowry, 1981). The hooded seal, *Cystophora cristata*, shows strong sexual dimorphism in favour of the male and yet only female-pup pairs are found, although they are accompanied by 1–7 males, which often remain in the water (Reeves and Ling, 1981), presumably constituting a competitive hierarchy with the dominant male maintaining his mating rights to the female.

This indicates that even among the Arctic ice-breeding phocids (in which the male is larger than the female—and in *Cystophora* markedly so), there are selective pressures against the formation of female—pup aggregations on the ice defended by a dominant male. The factors operating may be related to the difficulties of defending a group of females in the unstable environment, to aquatic mating, and/or the presence of dangerous large predators, the polar bear and man, on the ice.

Why then has the Weddell seal not adopted above-ice mating and the opportunity this would seem to afford to father more pups? First, there are no significant aquatic predators in the fast ice region and so no apparent disadvantage from this cause in aquatic mating concentrations. Secondly, there are predictable annual tide cracks along which the pupping colonies form and which can therefore be considered as a resource required by females for reproduction. Siniff (1982) suggested that, "Rather than defending the female directly, it is advantageous [for individual males] to defend sections of the tide crack, since their mating success is thus increased." Thirdly, even if the mating success is not increased relative to harem-breeding organization, but merely potentially equal, there may be advantages to the male in remaining in the water where energy expenditure may be less than on the surface and opportunities for feeding may occur; on the surface defending females he would have to fast, like the elephant, fur and crabeater seals.

5. Food Consumption and Feeding Behaviour

There are great difficulties in establishing the quantitative and qualitative aspects of feeding in Antarctic seals. The vast area they occupy, the inaccessibility of the pack ice and fast ice regions, and our inability to observe feeding directly except on rare occasions, all contribute to make this a poorly known aspect of their ecology. The widely scattered observations that have been made indicate that there is regional variability in the food taken, and that there may be seasonal variation and changes with age; in the present state of knowledge only tentative quantitative conclusions are possible. However, some generalizations can be made, mainly on the basis of records of stomach contents of collected animals. The food preferences of the Antarctic seals may be summarized as follows: fur seals take almost exclusively krill in the breeding season; elephant seals consume squid and fish; Weddell seals take mainly fish and cephalopods; Ross seals take mainly cephalopods and fish; crabeater seals eat krill almost exclusively; leopard seals take krill, penguin, other seals, fish and cephalopods (Laws, 1977b).

5.1 Stomach analyses

The most recent review, restricted to the pack ice seals, is by Øritsland (1977) who included literature up to the early 1970's, the best documented investigations being by Dearborn (1965) on the Weddell seal. He considered earlier records together with data from an exploratory sealing expedition to the Scotia Sea area in 1964 (Øritsland, 1970b); a total of over 300 stomachs has been examined, relating to the pack ice zone. Øritsland (1977) lists the frequencies of food items in the stomachs of 48 Weddell seals, 254 crabeater seals, 159 leopard seals (including 35 faecal samples); 29 Ross seals, four elephant and one fur seal. Each food item was scored according to whether it occurred alone (100), with one other item (50), with two others (33) and so on. The relative frequency was then given as a percentage of the sum of all scores, by species and observer, in the categories krill, other crustaceans, cephalopods, lamellibranchs, ascidians, holothurians, fish, penguins, other birds, seal, carrion, algae, gravel, miscellaneous.

None of the Weddell seal stomachs was empty (presumably because empty stomachs were not reported); of the other species, 70% of crabeater stomachs were empty, 55% of leopard seals, 53% of Ross seals, 75% of elephant seals and the single fur seal stomach was empty. Of the combined sample of stomachs containing food items there were 48 Weddell seals, 100 crabeater seals, 159 leopard seals, 21 Ross seals and one elephant seal. His analysis indicated that Weddell seals on average take 53% fish, 11% cephalopods, only 1% krill and 35% of other invertebrates; crabeater seals take 94% krill, 3% fish and 2% squid; leopard seals take 37% krill, 26% birds, mainly penguins, 13% other seals, 13% fish, 8% cephalopods and 3%

TABLE III

Food items recorded from the stomachs of Antarctic seals

	Weddell	Crabeater	Leopard	Ross	Elephant	Fur
Crustacea	*Euphausia superba* (*E. crystallorophias*) *Antarctomysis ohlini* (*A. maxima*) *Cirolana* sp. *Epimeria* sp. *Eusirus microps* *Chorismus antarcticus* *Crangon antarcticus* Isopods[4] Amphipods[4]	*E. superba* (*E. crystallorophias*)	*E. superba* (*E. crystallorophias*)	Amphipods[1] *E. superba*	Amphipods *Nectocarcinus antarcticus*[3]	*E. superba*[2] (*E. crystallorophias*)
Cephalopoda	*Psychroteuthis glacialis* *Pareledone charcoti* *Moroteuthis knipovitchi*[4] *Kondakovia longimanna*[4] ?*Crystalloteuthis* sp.[4] *Brachioteuthis picta*[4] *Gonatus antarcticus*[4] Octopod sp.	"Octopus" *Gonatus antarcticus*	"Octopus" "Squid"	"Octopus" "Cuttlefish" *Moroteuthis* sp.[1] Onychoteuthid sp.[1] Oegopsid spp.[1]	Cephalopods[5,6,7,8] Architeuthidae[9] Onychoteuthidae *Gonatus antarcticus*[10] *Moroteuthis knipovitchi*[10] *Kondakovia longimanna*[10] ?*Psychroteuthis* sp.[10] ?*Crystalloteuthis* sp.[10] Octopodidae[10]	Ommastrephidae[2] (probably *Stenoteuthis* or *Dosidicus*) Onychoteuthidae (probably *Onychoteuthis banksi*)[2] Enoploteuthidae[2]
Other invertebrates	Lamellibranch Holothurian Ribbon worms?		Lamellibranch Ascidian		Small sea creatures[6] Lamellibranchs[8] Brachiopods	
Pisces	*Notothenia coriiceps* *Pleurogramma antarcticum* *Dissostichus mawsoni*	"Small fish" Paralepididae *Chaenichthys* sp.	*Paralepis atlantica*	Myctophidae Bathydraconidae	*Notothenia* spp.[5] Flounders[11] Fish[6,7] *Notothenia*	Nototheniidae[2] *Notothenia rossii*[2]

Cryodraco antarcticus
Pagetopsis macropterus
Gymnodraco acuticeps
Trematomus sp.[12]
Chaenocephalus
  aceratus
Elasmobranchs

coriiceps[8]

Pygoscelis papua
Eudyptes chrysolophus[13]

Aves

Aptenodytes forsteri
A. patagonica
Pygoscelis adeliae
P. antarctica
P. papua
Eudyptes robustus[14]
Spheniscus
  magellanicus[15]
Macronectes sp.
Pelecanoides sp.
Halobaena coerulea
Pachyptila sp.
Pelecanoides urinatrix
Phalacrocorax atriceps[16]
Daption capensis[17]
Larus dominicanus[17]
Tern spp.[18]

Monotremata

Ornithorynchus
  anatinus[16]

Mammalia   Blubber[4]

Lobodon carcinophagus
Leptonychotes weddelli
Mirounga leonina
Arctocephalus gazella[16]
Otaria flavescens[19]

Notes: Except where otherwise stated the references are given in Oritsland's (1977) review; parentheses, probable occurrence.
1, King (1969); 2, Bonner (1968); 3, Yaldwyn (1958); 4, Clarke and Macleod (1982b); 5, Ling and Bryden (1981); 6, Csordas (1965); 7, Murphy (1914);
8, Laws (1956a); 9, Matthews (1929); 10, Clarke and Macleod (1982a); 11, Sorensen (1950); 12, Kooyman (1981d); 13, Bonner and Hunter (1982);
14, Horning and Fenwick (1978); 15, Markham (1971); 16, Kooyman (1981b); 17, Ealey (1954); 18, Roberts (1951); 19, Hamilton (1934).

other invertebrates; Ross seals take 64% cephalopods, 22% fish, 9% krill, and 5% other invertebrates. Table III summarizes the food items recorded by Øritsland (1977) and other investigators.

A recent study by Clarke ·and Macleod (1982b) analysed the stomach contents of eight Weddell seals taken at Deception Island, South Shetland Islands; seven of the stomachs contained fish remains and six of these had "much" fish, five of them teleosts and one elasmobranchs. Five stomachs contained crustacea and of these, five had *Euphausia superba*, one had isopods and two each contained an amphipod. All contained stones. From 336 lower beaks of cephalopods found in the stomachs, they were able to estimate the frequency of eight species, 6 squid and 2 octopuses. The maximum number of lower beaks in one stomach was 180 and the maximum number of species seven. Despite the small number of stomachs sampled, there was an indication of a seasonal shift in food; in March the beaks consisted almost entirely of squid; in April squids and octopods were represented and by July the contents were almost entirely octopods. They were able to estimate from the beaks, the size of the fresh cephalopods, the numerical composition by species and the percentage distribution by weight of cephalopod flesh represented. An octopod ?*Pareledone* sp. was most abundant numerically (33.6%) followed by *Moroteuthis knipovitchi* (31.0%), and ?*Psychroteuthis glacialis* (28.7%). By weight of flesh *M. knipovitchi* was again predominant (48.5%), followed by ?*P. glacialis* (23.3%) and ?*Pareledone* sp. (21.9%). This supports the suggestion that whereas fish are the main food at McMurdo Sound, occurring in 97% of stomachs with food, Weddell seals in the Antarctic Peninsula area may tend to feed more frequently on cephalopods (Kooyman, 1981c). Kooyman refers also to the seasonal variations in food available, especially the occurrence of *Dissostichus mawsoni* at McMurdo Sound, which is limited to October–December. There are also age-related variations, and a transitional period after weaning when mainly crustaceans are taken (Lindsey, 1937; Bertram, 1940).

Laws (1956a) noted that young elephant seals also take amphipods in shallow water and algal fragments are found in stomachs. He observed an elephant seal eating a large *Notothenia* at the surface. Of the 139 stomachs examined, only six contained any fresh items and none were full; 23 contained cephalopod remains, six had fish, and three had both fish remains and cephalopod beaks; in the 35 stomachs containing food items, cephalopods and fish were found in respectively 83% and 26% of stomachs. Of the fresh remains one stomach contained cephalopod flesh and five had fish. Matthews (1929) found cephalopod beaks in 35% of the stomachs he examined and no trace of other foods. Murphy (1914) found as many as 100 beaks in a single stomach and in one cow killed just after it came ashore he found fifteen fish 25 cm long. On the basis of this evidence Laws (1956a) concluded that elephant seals probably feed mainly on fish in inshore waters and on cephalopods elsewhere; there is no cause to reject this conclusion and it is assumed that the elephant seals' year round diet probably includes about 75% cephalopods and 25% fish (Laws, 1977b; McCann, in press). In Chapter 10 it was shown that there are changes in feeding activity of inshore fish, and the proportion of mature fish is at a minimum in October; it was suggested that this was related to the return of Weddell and elephant seals to inshore waters.

Clarke and Macleod (1982a) have analysed the feeding pattern represented by the stomach contents of 11 elephant seals taken at Signy Island between November and May. The only recognizable food items were cephalopod beaks. Eight species of cephalopods from 5–6 families were identified from the lower beaks. In terms of estimated fresh weight an octopod of average weight over 5 kg, probably ?*Pareledone*, accounted for 60% of the intake, but was represented by only five lower beaks, all from one seal. Next in importance was a Gonatid, *G. antarcticus*, representing 15% by estimated weight of flesh, accounting for 42% of the beaks. An Onychoteuthid, *Moroteuthis knipovitchi*, comprised 9.6% by estimated fresh weight and 14% of lower beaks. Another, *Kondakovia longimanna*, represented 6.6% of the fresh weight and 4% of the lower beaks. A Psychroteuthid comprised 6% of the beaks and 4.8% of the fresh weight. The other two identified species, both Cranchiids, comprised only 4% of the beaks and 0.2% of the estimated fresh weight. An unidentified teuthoid was found in 56% of stomachs containing lower beaks.

Clarke and Macleod commented that four species, *G. antarcticus*, *M. knipovitchi*, *P. glacialis* and *Crystalloteuthis* sp., are represented by animals in the size range eaten by sperm whales, *Physeter catodon* and one, *K. longimanna*, is at the lower end of this size range. Referring to their earlier analysis of Weddell seal stomachs, they concluded that there is a "real difference between the teuthoids sampled by the Weddell and elephant seals", indicating a "real preference by the seal species" despite the different geographical locations, because the two most abundant cephalopods are present in the sea at both island groups.

Of the cephalopods represented in Ross seal stomachs, 92% were "small", and the fish recorded were equally divided between "large" and "small" (Øritsland, 1977). In contrast, Barrett-Hamilton (1902) said that "it feeds exclusively on large cephalopods" and King (1969) observed that they feed on larger squid (up to 7 kg with a mantle length of 70 cm) than other seals. Pierard and Bisaillon (1979) believed that they show anatomical adaptations for swallowing large prey. However, their teeth are small, the incisors and canines sharp and recurved, either for holding cephalopods or tearing them (Fig. 5).

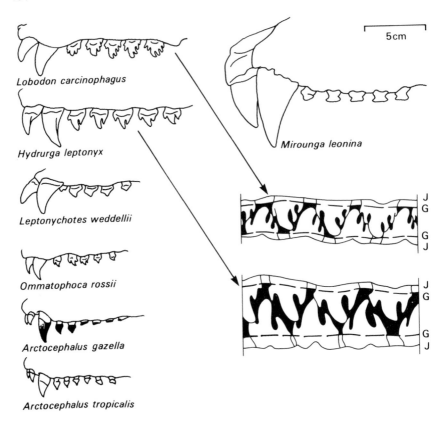

5cm

Lobodon carcinophagus

Hydrurga leptonyx

Mirounga leonina

Leptonychotes weddellii

J
G

G
J

Ommatophoca rossii

Arctocephalus gazella

J
G

G
J

Arctocephalus tropicalis

Fig. 5. Maxillary dentitions of six Antarctic seals and one sub-Antarctic species. Inset, enlarged diagram of opposed jaws to show sieve (J, jaw; G, gumline).

The crabeater and leopard seals appear to take more krill than other species and their cheek teeth are rather similar (Fig. 5), suggesting similar feeding habits. Those of the crabeater show multiple cusps, perhaps the most complex of any carnivore, and the leopard seal's are only slightly less complicated. In both species the teeth occlude to leave a very small gap and presumably act as a sieve. King (1961) described the straining mechanism of the crabeater, including a bony projection on the mandible which closes the gap behind the last, upper cheek tooth, and the scoop-like lower jaw. Racovitza (1900) described its feeding as swimming, mouth open, in the krill swarms, like baleen whales (see Chapter 13) and King considered it uneconomic for the species to catch one krill at a time. However, the only detailed reports of feeding behaviour describe it as catching invertebrates one by one (Wilson, in Kooyman, 1981a) by a sucking action of the lips (Tomo, personal communication).

Øritsland (1977) concluded that overall the leopard seal takes 37% krill in its diet, but Hofman *et al.* (1977) found a higher proportion (87%). They suggested that there was an age-related transition, with younger animals taking krill more frequently than older, more experienced animals whose larger size enables them to take other seals and penguins. More recently Stone and Siniff (1983) have broadly confirmed Øritsland's conclusions on the overall proportional frequency of occurrence of prey. From 52 stomach samples and 16 faecal samples examined during November–March, along the west coast of the Antarctic Peninsula, they found 54% krill; 27% penguin, mainly Adélie; 25% seal, mostly crabeater; 8% fish and 6% squid, "with little difference due to age, sex or season". Øritsland's (1977) 38 samples from the pack ice comprised 58% krill, 16% penguin, 12% fish, 9% cephalopods, and 3% seal. These percentages are not directly comparable but other evidence (section 5.2.2.) indicates that seal are under-represented in the latter sample. Re-analysing the combined samples suggests that the relative proportions are: 50% krill; 20% penguins; 14% seal; 9% fish and 6% cephalopods.

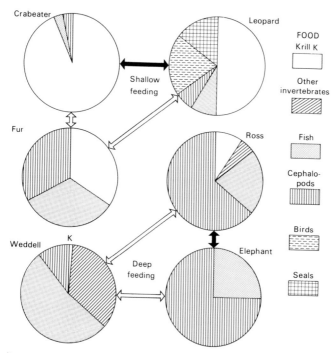

Fig. 6. Pie diagrams to show percentage composition of stomach samples of Antarctic seals. Black arrows, major similarities in diet; white arrows, minor similarities in diet.

The fur seal is also predominantly a krill feeder at South Georgia and Bonner (1968) noted two types of faeces: bright pinkish-red associated with crustaceans; and less commonly greyish with fish bones and scales. He suggested that *A. gazella* has perhaps specialized for a diet of krill "which may account for the unusual reduction of the post canine teeth". They have the smallest post-canine teeth of any Arctocephaline (Repenning *et al.*, 1971). However, the similarity with the squid-feeding elephant seal is perhaps more striking and the reduction of the cheek teeth is in marked contrast to other crustacean feeders—crabeater, leopard and ringed seals (*Phoca hispida*) for example—and in the toothed whales, species that feed on squid usually have fewer and smaller teeth than those feeding on fish (Chapter 13). The discoloration of the post-canine teeth characteristic of *A. gazella* may be due to squid ink. Also, *A. gazella* is unique in the very conspicuous abrasion on the medial surfaces of the cheek teeth—which seems at variance with a near exclusive diet of krill, although Bonner suggested it was due to abrasion by the krill exoskeletons. Squid beaks, fish and penguins are also found in *A. gazella* stomachs (Bonner, 1981) and further north *A. tropicalis*, formerly thought to be conspecific with *A. gazella*, takes squid and penguins at Île Amsterdam and fish, squid and euphausids at Marion Island. It is concluded that the diet of *A. gazella* is approximately 34% krill, 33% cephalopods and 33% fish (Laws, 1977b).

The overall conclusions about seal diets are shown diagrammatically in Fig. 6.

5.2 Leopard seal predation on penguins and seals

5.2.1 Penguins

Traditionally the leopard seal is well known as a predator of penguins, especially Adélie penguins, *Pygoscelis adeliae* (Barrett-Hamilton 1901; Wilson, 1907; Hamilton, 1939; Scheffer, 1958), but this is probably because most early observations were by shore-based observers in the vicinity of penguin rookeries where leopard seals are seen to chase and eat penguins. This behaviour was described by Müller-Schwarze and Müller-Schwarze (1975), Penney and Lowry (1967) and Hunt (1973). Early in the season at Cape Crozier leopard seals penetrate the thin fast ice from beneath to take penguins walking on top. Later they intercept adult penguins inshore, on feeding trips to and from the ocean, and the chicks during their short annual exodus from the colony. They catch and kill the penguins in the water and dismember them by powerful jerks of the head. This is a temporary seasonal resource when the birds are concentrated for breeding and they disperse in winter to the pack ice fringes. Also there are probably only a few pioneering males at the rookeries (Penney and Lowry, 1967). In the study by Müller-Schwarze and Müller-Schwarze (1975), all seals observed catching penguins at high latitudes along continental shores and at the Antarctic Peninsula, where the sex could be identified, were males. Kooyman (1981b) points out that in lower latitudes such as the Antarctic Peninsula coasts there are many leopard seals, but sightings of them catching penguins are unusual. Müller-Schwarze and Müller-Schwarze (1975) suggest that penguin colonies below about 10,000 pairs are not exploited by leopard seals, but at South Georgia they are regularly sighted at king penguin colonies smaller than this.

5.2.2 Other seals

Five other pinnipeds are listed in Table III as prey of leopard seals. Of these the crabeater seal is undoubtedly the most important food. Scars typically borne by crabeater seals were long thought to be due to killer whales, but evidence has recently accumulated implicating leopard seals (Siniff and Bengtson, 1977; Siniff *et al.*, 1979; Stone and Siniff, 1983; Siniff, 1982; Laws, unpublished). Fresh killer whale slash marks are closer spaced and different from fresh leopard seal cuts. Crabeater seals older than a year are seldom attacked and fresh wounds on adults are rare. Laws (1977a) reported that in samples taken in the summer, 83% of fresh wounds were on animals less than 18 months old. Most animals with fresh wounds are aged about ½–1 year old, and are about 175–210 cm long, mean 192.7 cm (Siniff and Bengtson, 1977) (Fig. 7). According to Stone and Siniff (1983) weaned pups do not begin to show fresh wounds until late February. Presumably younger pups do not survive an encounter with a leopard seal, because of their inexperience, but the chance of escaping improves with time and so the frequency of survivors "increases in the population through late summer to a level that approaches the proportion of adults bearing scars inflicted by leopard seals." By one year of age the probability of being eaten if a leopard seal is encountered approaches zero and in November the leopard seals switch to the new pup crop. Thus, whereas Øritsland (1977) recorded only 3% of stomachs collected in September–October with seal, Stone and Siniff (1983) in November–March recorded 25% with seal remains.

Laws (unpublished) measured the spacing of 94 pairs of scars which had a mean separation of 6.79 ± 1.46 (S.D.) cm; the killer whale tooth spacing is only 3.57 ± 0.46 cm and for leopard seals 5.74 ± 0.81; the ratio between tooth spacing and scar separation was 1 : 1.183. The mean standard length of 1125 crabeater seals more than a year old was 228.4 cm, and assuming that the spacing of the scars had increased since they were inflicted, in proportion to the growth in length of the seals, application of the ratio above

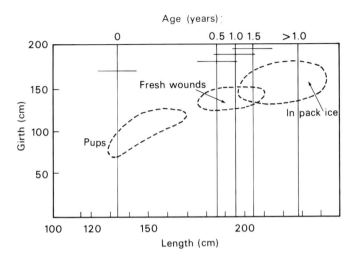

Fig. 7. Ellipses of plots of length against girth for crabeater seals. Mean lengths s.d. ±1 are shown for age groups 0, 0.5, 1.0, 1.5 years and all seals >1.0 year old (after Siniff and Bengtson, 1977).

predicted a length of 193 cm for the mean body length at origin, remarkably close to the observed 192.7 cm of Siniff and Bengtson (1977). This is equivalent to an age of about 4–5 months (Fig. 12), or February–March, which is in close agreement with Stone and Siniff (1983).

It seems therefore that most scars are inflicted in the middle of the first year, as the probability of escaping increases. Siniff and Bengtson (1977) recorded 78% of crabeater seals in the pack ice with leopard seal scars, and according to Siniff (1982), 83% of crabeaters examined were scarred and had escaped leopard seals. Condy (1976) reported 62.5%, 63% and 25.2% scarred in three cruises near the Weddell Sea, but a mere 3.0 and 3.2% of Ross seals showed such scars.

5.3 Fasting

The two land breeding species undergo quite lengthy fasts in the breeding season and the elephant seal also during the moult. The other species may fast to a greater or lesser degree during the breeding season. Laws (1956a) reported that 90% of the elephant seals he examined had empty stomachs.

In the elephant seal there is a more complete separation of the aquatic and terrestrial phases of its life than for any other pinniped (Carrick *et al.*, 1962b). From regular counts made at the South Orkney Islands, Laws (1956a) concluded that adult males were ashore for more than eight weeks in the breeding season (say 60 days) and for slightly less (say 50 days) during the summer while they undergo a "catastrophic moult", when epidermis as well as hair is shed in patches. The adult females were ashore for 28–30 days in the breeding season and about 32 days for the moult (Fig. 4). Younger animals of both sexes spent slightly shorter periods ashore than the adult females. Carrick *et al.* (1962a) stated that at Macquarie Island the actual moult period was 18–19 days, but there was a pre-moult haul out of up to 13 days and a post-moult period of up to 11–28 days, increasing with age. They summarized the mean duration of the total moult haul out as: immature cows, 24 days (range 18–34 days); mature cows, 28.5 days (22–39); immature males, 26.5 days (18–39); younger sub-adult bulls 28.0 days (17–43); older sub-adult bulls 33.0 days (25–42 days). There is also a winter haul out of individuals of most ages at Macquarie Island, but not at Heard Island, South Georgia, or Signy Island, which have more rigorous climates.

Laws (1960) showed that the average oil yield of the catch of bulls at South Georgia declined by about 11% a month from September to November, though this may partly reflect a change in the age of the catch. Laws (1956a) found that the males occasionally broke their fast during the moult but not the females, who formed aggregations further from the sea. Of the stomachs he examined 84% contained sand and small stones, which some were observed to ingest on land and regurgitate before departure. There were fewer such stomachs in spring and autumn.

Fur seal bulls hold territories for an average of 34 days, during which time they do not feed (section 4.2). Although the cows suckle the pups for 110–115 days they make frequent feeding trips to sea. The moulting of adult females begins about 5 February, and of males about 11 February, so that moult is in full swing by the end of that month. It probably lasts about five months according to Bonner (1968) and, unlike the elephant seal, cows in full moult continue to suckle their young and return to sea to feed (Fig. 4).

There is less information about the other species, but breeding and moulting appear to have less effect on their feeding rates. However, 53–75% of all specimens examined had empty stomachs (section 5.1). Bertram (1940) noted that in the Weddell seal the intensity of feeding decreases during the moult but doesn't stop. Wilson (1907) reported that crabeaters were "replete with food" although moulting; he thought Ross seals starved "for a week or two during moult". Gwynn (1953) concluded that the moult "doesn't seem to interfere with normal activities" in leopard seals. In contrast, Ashwell-Erickson *et al.* (1983) concluded that two Northern Hemisphere species fed infrequently during the moult period, and their basic metabolic rate fell by 10%.

In the breeding season, territory-holding male Weddell seals remain in the water and are thought to feed; according to Kaufman *et al.* (1975) and Tedman and Bryden (1979), females probably lose about 40% of their body weight during a lactation period of 45–50 days (Lindsey, 1937; Siniff, 1982). Siniff *et al.* (1971) suspected that the cow fasted for the first 14 days, but later made longer dives representing feeding or territorial activity. Siniff *et al.* (1977) in their experiments found a significantly greater weight loss in animals in a colony as compared with experimental animals held five miles out from shore and consider that when food resources are available nursing Weddell seals will utilize them.

From observations on the behaviour of crabeater seals it seems clear that neither male nor female feeds during the suckling period (section 4.1) and Øritsland (1977) reported a significant increase in the relative frequency of empty stomachs in September and October. From 27 August to 10 September, 75% were empty and from 11 to 31 October 84% were empty. He found no similar pattern in the other species taken. The average sternal blubber thickness of female crabeaters decreased during the breeding season from 67 mm during 1–8 October to 53 mm during 19–31 October. In February/March, Laws and Baird (in prep.) found that it averaged only 34–43 mm but was increasing.

To summarize, for the purpose of estimating annual food consumption, the crabeater fasting period is about 30 days in aggregate; but it may be shorter in the Weddell and its duration is unknown in the Ross and leopard seals. The male fur seal undergoes a breeding fast of about 34 days on average; the female in aggregate fasts for about 50 days, while nursing (section 4.2). Neither sex appears to fast significantly while moulting. The adult male elephant seal fasts on average for about 110 days in aggregate, the adult female for about 60 days and younger animals for, say, 50 days.

5.4 Feeding and diving behaviour

Virtually nothing is known about the aquatic behaviour of the elephant seal. Except when in inshore waters, it probably feeds at depth because, first, the very similar northern elephant seal, *M. angustirostris*, takes prey species usually found between 100–300 m (Huey, 1930); secondly, they take similar prey to the deep-diving sperm whale (see section 5.1; chapter 13); and thirdly, their eyes have a visual pigment—a "deep sea rhodopsin"—resembling that of deep water fishes and Lythgoe and Dartnall (1970) speculate that it is an adaptation for detecting the bioluminescence of deep-water squids. The Ross seal is believed to feed at depth, from the evidence of its stomach contents and its enormous eyeballs.

Kooyman (1981c,d) obtained exciting results by using time depth recorders (TDR's) attached to free-diving Weddell seals. Experiments are possible because the seals are indifferent to Man and use breathing and haul-out holes in thick stable ice. As a result, in this species diving ability is

better known than for any other marine mammal. Dives to 200–400 m
(approximately the depths at which the Antarctic cod is caught) were
common and the deepest measured, to 600 m, was essentially to the sea
floor, so deeper dives may be undertaken. The usual duration of such
feeding dives is 15 min or less. A typical pattern based on one individual's
diving behaviour, over four days in September, is presented diagrammatically in Fig. 8. At McMurdo Sound where these studies were made, fish
were found in 97% of stomachs that contained any food (Dearborn, 1965),
and Dartnall and Lythgoe (1970) concluded from the nature of its visual
pigment that the species feeds on fishes that are not luminescent.

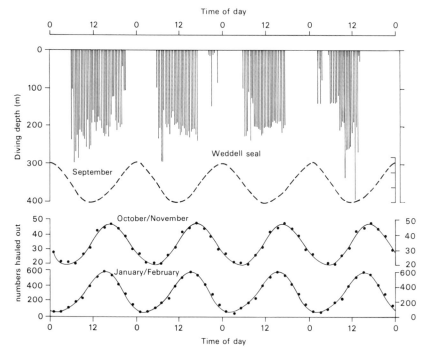

Fig. 8. Above, diagrammatical representation of typical Weddell seal time/depth diving pattern
over 4 days in September (after Kooyman, 1981d), and the described haul out pattern for
September. Below, actual haul out cycle for McMurdo Sound Weddell seals during October/
November and January/February, repeated over four days for comparison with the diving
pattern of the experimental animal (data from Kaufman et al., 1975; Stirling, 1969c).

Kooyman (1981d) investigated these seals during September, a month at
the equinox during which day length increases from 6½ to 16½ hours. Fewer
animals were at the surface during the day as they preferred to dive then
(Fig. 8).

He identified two types of dive; deep dives and exploratory dives. The daytime dives were also more rigorous—to depths averaging about 120 m and up to 600 m compared with an average to 40 m and a maximum of 270 m at night—and there were more exploratory dives during the day. Night exploratory dives, when they occurred, were shallow, and Kooyman concluded that vision is important for orientation. He summarized the difference between the two types of dives as follows:

DEEP DIVES	EXPLORATORY DIVES
Short duration (5–25 min)	Long duration (20–73 min)
Short distance from hole (<1 km)	Long distance (to >12 km)
Below familiar ice topography	Often below unfamiliar ice
Working depth (? 200–400 m) in low ambient light levels	Depth: always in visual contact with surface
One component of point of origin (surface) is constant	Point of origin held on constant heading by seal

Kooyman (1968, 1981d) described his other experiments on the physiology of diving and the adaptations which have made it possible for a mammal to adopt this extraordinary way of life.

The spring diurnal pattern of night activity changes during the summer so that in October/November, the breeding season, the haul out pattern shows a peak on the ice at about 16.00–18.00 h (Kaufman et al., 1975). Siniff et al. (1970) also described the 24-hour activity pattern in November/December as actively aquatic from about midnight to 09.00–10.00 and least active from noon to about 19.00 h. In January/February the peak haul out is at 13.00–14.00 h (Stirling, 1969a). (Erickson et al. (1971) and Gilbert and Erickson (1977) reported a similar haul out pattern of Weddell seals in pack ice.) In Fig. 8, these results are shown diagrammatically. It is predicted that the March (equinoctial) haul out pattern should be the same as for September.

Possibly the presumed deep-feeding elephant and Ross seals have a similar diurnal cycle. Gilbert and Erickson (1977) observed most Ross seals between 14.00–15.00 h in January/February. Condy (1977b) reported peak numbers hauled out between 10.00–12.00 h in January; he reviewed the observations of other workers.

Recently Kooyman and Davis (1980) have deployed TDRs attached to fur seals at Bird Island, South Georgia, with similarly exciting results. In Fig. 9 a typical diving pattern of a female fur seal, feeding on krill offshore during four days in the summer, is shown. Like the Weddell seal, there is a diurnal pattern, but with most diving activity at night. The dive depths are not so great in the fur seal, never to more than 100 m, and mostly to about 20–50 m; the dives are to shallower depths at night (the broken line suggests

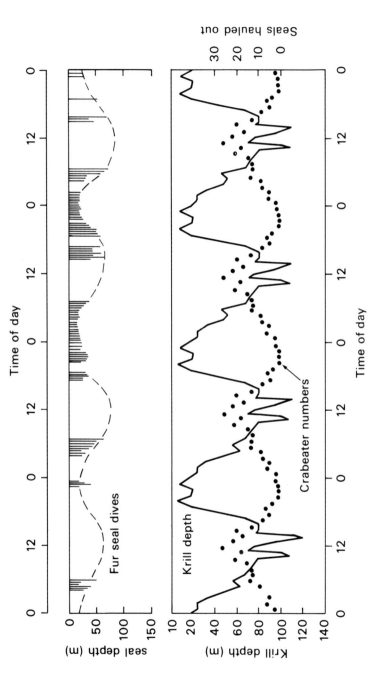

Fig. 9. Diagrammatic representation of typical fur seal diving patterns over four days in January (data kindly provided by Kooyman); compared with a diurnal variation in mean depth of krill in Scotia Sea in summer (from Chapter 9, Fig. 1), and diurnal variation in crabeater seal numbers hauled out in pack ice on 21, 23 and 25 January at about 69°S 4°E (data from Condy, 1977b). (Lower plots are repeated over four days for comparison with diving pattern.)

the possible form of the depth fluctuations). For comparison, the diurnal variation in the mean depth of krill in the Scotia Sea in summer is shown (Chapter 9, Fig. 1). This is shallower at night and deeper during the day and is clearly correlated with the diving pattern of fur seals. Croxall (personal communication), in a more intensive analysis of a larger sample, has compared the number of dives made against krill availability above 75 m for different times of day and finds that there is a close correlation indicating peak feeding between 21.00 and 07.00 h.

Limited evidence suggests that the crabeater seal has a similar feeding strategy, for maximum numbers are in the water when krill are expected to be near the surface (Fig. 9) (Erickson et al., 1971; Condy, 1977b; Gilbert and Erickson, 1977). It is therefore probable that the crabeater, like the fur seal, feeds at relatively shallow depths. Nocturnal feeding has the advantage of exposure to what solar radiation there is during the day.

From its diet and dive durations the leopard seal would also be expected to be a predominantly shallow diver, and to follow the crabeater pattern when feeding on krill. Erickson et al. (1971), obtained limited data suggesting peak haul out in the pack ice during the nine hours from 09.00 to 18.00 (73% of leopard seals observed). Gilbert and Erickson (1977) reported that leopard seals paralleled crabeater seals in their haul out pattern, and both species showed peak haul out about midday and "were most active in the water, presumably feeding, at night" (Hofman et al., 1977). Diving behaviour was described; when feeding on krill, leopard seal dives averaged 2.64 min and crabeaters' 3.82 min, suggesting (on the basis of Weddell seal descent rates of 35 m min^{-1} and ascent rates of 50 m min^{-1} (Kooyman, 1968)) average depths of about 56 m and 81 m respectively, that is similar to the fur seal. Only two penguin kills were observed in more than 1200 h of observation, although there was a penguin colony in the vicinity, because the leopard seals at Palmer Station "had a nocturnal activity period that was out of phase with the diurnal activity of adelie penguins."

To summarize diving behaviour, then: the elephant, Ross and Weddell seals appear to dive regularly to depths of several hundred metres at least (the former two species perhaps to greater depths than the Weddell) and with diurnal patterns that may vary seasonally. The fur, crabeater and leopard seals are probably shallow divers, usually to about 60–80 m in summer at least, mainly feeding at night and hauled out on land or ice or swimming at the surface during the day (Fig. 9).

5.5 Amounts of food eaten

It was concluded in section 5.3 that elephant seals feed for some 255–315 days annually according to age and sex; fur seals for 315–331 days; and pack ice seals for about 335 days. The incidence of recent feeding as indicated by the proportion of empty stomachs was $c.$ 25–47% (section 5.3) for the pack ice seals.

The quantities of food consumed are difficult to estimate. According to Øritsland (1977) the average meal sizes were: Weddell seal, 23 kg; leopard seal, 16 kg; crabeater seal, 8 kg; Ross seal 6 kg. The maximum Weddell seal stomach contents weighed 68 kg (Calhaem and Christoffel, 1969) and Murphy (1948) recorded a leopard seal with 64 kg of king penguins. These probably did not represent daily consumption because seals may either take several meals a day or have prolonged feeding periods (Figs. 8 and 9); leopard seals may feed less intensively for several days after a substantial meal, like other large carnivores. Captive seals give some idea of daily feeding rates: 6–10% of body weight, less for elephant seals (Keyes, 1968); 4–7% (Geraci, 1975); adults 6%, young 10% (Ray, in Sergeant, 1973); 5% (Samuelsen, in Øritsland, 1977); 7.6% (Sergeant, 1973); 5% (Blix et al., 1973). These estimates of 4–10% are for captive animals, relatively inactive and at higher and more constant temperatures than wild Antarctic seals.

Laws (1977b) accepted Øritsland's (1977) tentative estimate of average daily food intake as 7% of body weight for the pack ice seals, and a similar rate for fur seals, but 6% for elephant seals when not fasting. (These compare with 3–4% body weight for large whales, about 4% for killer whales and about 4–11% for dolphins (Chapter 13).) Applying the percentages for seals to the feeding periods given above suggests a daily intake, averaged over the year, of 55 g food kg^{-1} for the elephant seal, 62 g kg^{-1} for the fur seal and 64 g kg^{-1} for the pack ice seals. The average annual food consumption is about 20 times mean body weight for elephant seals; 23 times for fur seals; and about the same for pack ice seals.

The energetic value of the different foods varies: for krill it is about 4.2–4.5 kJ g^{-1} wet weight (Clarke and Prince, 1980); for lipid-rich myctophid fish 5.6–8.0 kJ g^{-1}; and for Notothenia about 4.1 kJ g^{-1}; compared with 3.5 kJ g^{-1} (range 2.9–4.5) for squid (Croxall and Prince, 1982). Thus the ratio of energy content of krill:fish:squid eaten by seals is probably about 1.00:0.94:0.80. For seal prey it is about 20.5 kJ g^{-1}, that is 4–5 times the energy content of krill. For penguins it is probably rather similar.

5.6 Energy requirements

Numbers tend to under-emphasize and biomass to over-emphasize the importance of large mammals in the ecosystem and energy gives a more realistic assessment. Unfortunately, it is difficult to measure in large free-living marine mammals, but can be estimated (see Chapter 13). This provides another way to estimate seals' food intake, which is to calculate their energy expenditure and hence requirements, but there have been very few studies of seal bioenergetics. Lavigne *et al.* (1982) reviewed the literature up to 1976. Other recent studies were by Stewart and Lavigne (1980), Naumov and Chekunova (1980) and Fedak and Anderson (1982).

Naumov and Chekunova (1980), using the crabeater as an example, calculated energy expenditure and needs from generally accepted equations for mammal energy balances. They estimated that a 190 kg female crabeater seal (the calculated population mean weight is 193 kg, see section 9) expends about 6445 kCal day^{-1} (27,004 kJ day^{-1}) on resting metabolism (this compares with 4800 kCal day^{-1} (20,112 kJ day^{-1}) for a 160 kg grey seal, *Halichoerus grypus* (Fedak and Anderson, 1982) and seems to be about right); heat transferred was 7200 kCal day^{-1} (30,168 kJ day^{-1}), and 3222 kCal day^{-1} (13,500 kJ day^{-1}) in swimming; making a total metabolic energy expenditure of 16,867 kCal day^{-1} (70,672 kJ day^{-1}). Growth energy requirements were calculated as 782 kCal day^{-1} (3277 kJ day^{-1}).

The special energy demands of reproduction for the female were calculated as: 190 kg female body equivalent to 929,100 kCal (3893 × 10^3 kJ); neonate weight 97,800 kCal (409,782 kJ) receiving 378,400 (1585 × 10^3 kJ) in milk during 4–5 week suckling period, or 40.7% of the total energy of the maternal body. This calculation excluded uterine enlargement, placenta and foetal membranes, although this is small, and so the female spends over 51% of its energy resource on reproductive metabolism.

Fedak and Anderson (1982) obtained information from serial weighings of free-living grey seals and their pups and calculated the efficiency of lactation. This species has an average lactation period of only 18 days. The average female weight loss was 3.60 kg day^{-1} and the pup weight gain was 1.64 kg day^{-1}. Females used over 30,000 kCal day^{-1} (125,580 kJ day^{-1}) for maintenance and milk production. Pups consumed 17,000 kCal day^{-1} (71,162 kJ day^{-1}) in milk and can convert 14,000 kCal day^{-1} (58,600 kJ day^{-1}) into growth and stored fat. Over 80% of the females' energy resources were used to feed their pups and the gross efficiency of the transfer was about 57%. Female grey seals increased their daily energy expenditure by a factor of six during lactation, and in energetic terms lactation is the most critical period of the annual reproductive cycle.

Naumov and Chekunova (1980) calculated that their 190 kg crabeater seal must consume 10.4% of its body weight (20 kg) daily to satisfy energy requirements of 22,062 kCal day^{-1} (92,440 kJ day^{-1}), but considered that it feeds intensively for only 120 days a year, and for 200 days eats enough (15 kg) to maintain its resting metabolism. Averaged over the year, this represents 14.8 kg day^{-1} or 7.8% of body weight, which is fairly close to the figure of 7% assumed in section 5.5.

6. Ecological Separation

The preceding sections give some idea of the degree of ecological separation of the six seal species. The mechanisms responsible include geographical distribution, habitat preferences, food preferences, feeding behaviour, diving adaptations and breeding behaviour. The main factors thought to be involved are summarized by species in Table IV.

Geographical distributions have been discussed in section 2, breeding and non-breeding distributions often being different within a species and between species. Within the range of a species, conspicuous habitat preferences have been identified in terms of substrate when out of the water (land, fast ice or pack ice types) (section 3.2) and in terms of diving depths—the fur seal, crabeater and leopard probably being generally shallow divers and elephant, Ross and Weddell seals generally deep divers (section 5, Figs. 6, 8 and 9). These horizontal and vertical distributions are related to food preferences which may also vary seasonally (e.g. Weddell, fur seal, section 5.1). Shallow divers tend to be essentially krill-based feeders (crabeater, leopard and fur seals) although the fur seal may dive deeper after squid and fish. The deep-diving species (elephant, Ross and Weddell seals) tend to pursue squid and fish, but species show preferences within these groups (e.g. elephant and Weddell seals, section 5.1) even though the latitudinal geographical separation would minimize potential competition. Additional evidence of feeding separation is provided by the adaptive radiation of jaws and teeth (section 5.1, Fig. 5). Finally, this three-dimensional separation is maintained by clear differences in social and breeding behaviour (section 4), and reproductive physiology (section 8), which would limit opportunities for interbreeding.

These ecological differences all tend to reduce competition within the group although there is substantial overlap, especially between crabeater and leopard seals. Other vertebrate and invertebrate groups are potentially in competition with the seals. The squid, fish, bird and baleen whale populations feed on krill and their distributions overlap those of the krill-eating seals. With the exception of the fur seal, however, the krill-eating seals are associated with the pack ice whereas the birds and whales—and probably fish and squid—are more northerly in distribution, or tend to feed outside the pack ice, or at different depths. Flying birds are limited to near-surface feeding, but penguins may be in substantial competition, some species covering depths down to 265 m (Kooyman *et al.*, 1982).

The squid and fish eating groups, the petrels and albatrosses, penguins and toothed whales, are less likely to compete with the pack ice seals than with elephant and fur seals. King penguins and sperm whales may well compete with elephant and fur seals and some food species are common to

TABLE IV

Ecological separation of Antarctic seals, promoted by geographical distribution, habitat preferences and food habits

| SPECIES | DISTRIBUTION | | | FEEDING | | |
| | Breeding | Non-breeding | | Teeth | Food | Depth |
		Summer	Winter			
Fur seal	Land; colonial; sub-Antarctic islands; maritime Antarctic, South Shetlands. Rocky coasts. Beaches— boulders or large pebbles	Dispersal north (to South America?) and south to pack ice edge	Northward dispersal at sea	Canines large; post-canines reduced	Krill, fish and cephalopods	To 70 m for krill; probably deeper for cepha- lopods and fish
Elephant seal	Land; colonial; South America, Falkland Islands, sub-Antarctic Islands; maritime Antarctic.	Dispersal north to South America and south to pack ice edge	Northward pelagic dispersal	Canines large; post-canines reduced	Cephalopods and fish	To 300 m or more; possibly unlimited.

Leopard seal	Beaches—sand or small pebbles. Sub-Antarctic; Falkland Islands; South American coasts. Pack ice medium-sized hummocked floes. Female and pup	Pack ice periphery; sub-Antarctic and Cold Temperate islands and coasts. Southward shift	Pack ice periphery, and sub-Antarctic and Cold Temperate islands and coasts. Northward shift	Canines large; post-canines large; multi-cusped	Krill, fish, cephalopods, penguins and seals	Mainly shallow, ? to c. 70 m for krill; ? deeper for fish and cephalopods
Crabeater seal	Pack ice periphery—medium-sized hummocked floes. Triads, mated pairs. Immatures often on fast ice	Pack ice—cake and brash ice	Pack ice periphery	Canines small; post-canines large; multi-cusped	Krill	Shallow; ? to c. 70 m
Ross seal	Pack ice—probably as leopard seal	Dense pack ice—large floes	Pack ice	Canines very small, sharp; post-canines very small	Cephalopods	Deep
Weddell seal	Fast ice or land; colonial	Dispersal to pack ice near coasts or on fast ice	Fast ice, and pack ice nearby	Canines large; incisors procumbent; postcanines reduced	Fish, cephalopods, benthos	To 600 m or more; possibly unlimited

the diets of both groups. Emperor penguins and bottle-nosed whales may compete with Ross and Weddell seals. However, until we know more about the feeding of these groups it is not possible to be more specific.

7. Growth and Development

7.1 Introduction

In this section ecological aspects of growth in Antarctic seals are discussed. Bryden (1972) reviewed growth of marine mammals, including gross aspects, the development of tissues and the development of organs, but he had limited data on the Antarctic seals; the earlier studies were presented and growth shown to be determinate. More general aspects of linear dimensions and body weight are considered here, including foetal and neonatal growth, and results from additional studies are now available. Methods of individual age determination make possible the construction of growth curves from birth onwards. In addition the seasonal synchrony of birth dates (Fig. 4 and section 8) facilitates the study of foetal growth, and some workers have studied growth to weaning and later by means of known-age (marked) animals.

7.2 Foetal growth

The annual reproductive cycle is discussed in section 8 where it is shown that delayed implantation is a feature in most if not all species; the period between conception and implantation varies, according to species, from about a week to about four months. Gestation periods are usually just under a year (Figs. 4 and 17, Table V). Thus, the period of active foetal growth varies from 7.5 months in the elephant seal to 9.0 months in the Weddell and 9.5 months in the leopard seal. Huggett and Widdas (1951) showed that plots of foetal growth in length and $W^{\frac{1}{3}}$ are more or less linear. The growth in foetal length for five species is shown in Fig. 17. The length at birth varies widely, from 64 cm in the fur seal to 125 cm in the elephant seal—a doubling—and the birth weight from 5.65 kg to 47 kg—an over eight-fold difference. Larger birth weights are in general achieved by an acceleration in the rate of foetal growth. Thus the mean daily increment in length ranges between 2.8 mm in the fur seal to 5.5 mm in the elephant seal. The average post-implantation daily increment in weight ranges from $c.25$ g in the fur seal to $c.170$–210 g, in the elephant seal, roughly a seven- to eight-fold difference.

The range given for the elephant seal reflects the population differences in neonatal weight. Thus at Marion Island it was 37.8 ± 1.7 kg, at Kerguelen 38.9 ± 4.3 kg, Macquarie Island 37.4 kg, South Georgia 45.2 ± 5.7 kg, and Signy Island 47.4 ± 4.5 kg (Condy, 1980; McCann, 1981b). Almost certainly there are similar population differences in other species.

Laws (1959) showed birth size is roughly proportional to maternal size but there are variations. The birth weight as a percentage of adult weight is about 8.3% in the Weddell seal, 10% in the elephant seal, 13.5% in the crabeater seal and 14.9% in the fur seal (from data above and in section 7.5.2). Because a single pup is born, with rare exceptions, the individual new-born is relatively larger than in other carnivores and is weaned within 23 days in the very large elephant seal, in 45–50 days in the smaller Weddell seal and 110–115 days in the much smaller fur seal.

7.3 Postnatal growth to weaning

Several studies of immediate postnatal weight gain have been carried out. Where the records extend beyond weaning there is, as expected, an initial decline after weaning.

The fur seal shows the slowest rate of growth, from 5.65 kg at birth to 15.25 kg at weaning (110 days) (means of sexes combined), a mean daily rate of 8.7 g (Payne, 1979b). At the other extreme is the elephant seal at Signy Island which grew from 47 kg at birth to 205 kg at weaning (23 days), a mean daily rate of 6.9 kg! (Laws, 1953b, 1960). Pups increased their weight by 50% in the first week, doubled it in 11 days, trebled it in 17–18 and had more than quadrupled it at weaning (Laws, 1953b). Some individual pups showed a mean daily growth rate of 12.0 kg day^{-1}. Growth curves to weaning for three other elephant seal populations have been compared by Condy (1980); the lowest rate was shown by the Macquarie Island pups, the mean being 5.5 kg day^{-1} (Carrick et al., 1962a).

The Weddell seal grows from 24–29 kg at birth to about 110–140 kg at weaning about 45–50 days post-partum (Tedman and Bryden, 1979; Kooyman, 1981c; Stirling, 1969a). The crabeater seal birth weight is similar and it grows to about 110 kg at weaning (the largest pup weighed was 113 kg, Bengtson and Siniff, 1981).

7.4 Age determination

Methods of age determination for seals were reviewed by Laws (1962). Two methods are in use for Antarctic seals, apart from tagging and recapture. The first and most useful is based on seasonal growth layers that can be counted in thin sections or cross-sectional surfaces in the dentine and

Fig. 10. (a) Transverse section viewed with transmitted light of a canine tooth from a 14-year-old female elephant seal. Black circles indicate pupping lines from age four years. (b) Longitudinal section viewed with transmitted light of third post-canine tooth from a 33-year-old female crabeater seal, to show cementum layers. Black circles indicate annual increments. Sexual maturity at five years.

cementum of the teeth (Laws, 1952, 1953a; McCann, 1981b; Payne, 1978) (Fig. 10), or are visible as ridges on the root of the tooth (Scheffer, 1950; Payne, 1978). The annual pattern of these layers has been confirmed for some species from recapture of known-age branded (Carrick and Ingham, 1962a) or tagged (Stirling, 1969; Payne, 1978) individuals. The method is normally feasible only for dead animals but the teeth contain a complete record of their growth throughout life. Alternatively, toenails can be extracted from the flippers of living seals and sectioned to show annual layers (Bengtson and Siniff, 1981); a disadvantage of this method is that wear of the nails limits its application to young animals, the ages of older animals being underestimated.

Laws (1953a) as a routine, used polished cross-sections of canine teeth of elephant seals to count dentine layers. He showed that in immatures the layers are variable but a more regular pattern of two layers per year is characteristic of adults; the age at sexual maturity can therefore be estimated. His findings were confirmed by Carrick and Ingham (1962a). McCann (1981b), using thin sections, further developed the method and confirmed that not only can the age at sexual maturity be back-calculated but also that in adult females the presence or absence of a characteristic suckling layer in the pattern indicates the occurrence or absence of pupping in any year (Fig. 10). His interpretation of the structure of the female tooth is different from Laws' (1953a) most of whose three-year old animals at South Georgia were re-assigned to one year older by McCann.

Laws (1957, 1958), Mansfield (1958), Øritsland (1970b) and Tikhomirov (1975) used cross-sections of crabeater, leopard, Weddell and Ross seal canines. Stirling (1969b) etched and stained the polished surface of sectioned Weddell canine teeth to enhance the annual pattern. Payne (1979b) has used layer counts in longitudinal thin sections of canine teeth, combined with counts of external ridges in younger animals, to age fur seals. As in elephant seals characteristic suckling layers can be identified in the dentine of fur seal teeth (Payne, 1978). Laws (1977a) later found that counts of cementum layers in longitudinal thin sections of crabeater seal third post-canine teeth gave best results and an upper age of 39 years has now been determined in this way for this species. As in elephant and fur seal teeth, and the baleen whale ear plug (Chapter 13), the transition between immature and mature patterns (Fig. 10) can be used to estimate the age at which the animal became sexually mature. Attempts are being made to back-calculate body length, and identify pregnancies from the tooth structures (Laws, unpublished).

Having established a method of estimating age, it is then possible to apply it in studies of body growth and population structure.

7.5 Independent growth

The typical postnatal growth pattern in seals is negatively exponential, and is very rapid in the first year, decreasing towards puberty, which is attained at about 80–90% of final length (Laws, 1956c, 1959), subsequently levelling-off as physical maturity is attained. Acceleration or retardation of the growth-rate leads to advancement or deferment of puberty. In the polygynous species which show extreme sexual dimorphism, typified in the Antarctic by the fur and elephant seals, the male shows a secondary growth spurt at about the time of puberty.

7.5.1 Growth in length

In Fig. 11 average growth curves are shown for the two strongly polygynous species. The fur seal female shows a relatively simple negatively exponential

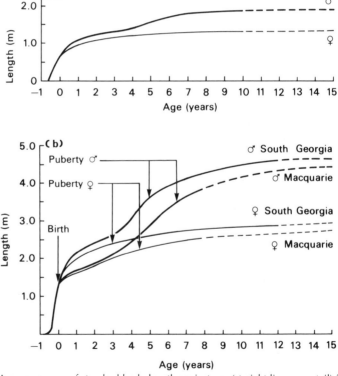

Fig. 11. Average curves of standard body length against age (straight line, nose-tail) for (a) fur seal, South Georgia (after Payne, 1979b) and (b) elephant seal, South Georgia (after Laws, 1953b) and Macquarie Island (after Carrick *et al.*, 1962a). Mean ages at puberty indicated.

growth curve and the male curve shows a growth spurt associated with puberty. In the elephant seal there is a striking acceleration of foetal growth, as already mentioned. Growth then continues up to and beyond 15 years. There is a male growth spurt at puberty (3–7 years) which is most pronounced in the South Georgia population.

Carrick *et al.* (1962b) drew attention to the slower growth-rates at Macquarie Island as compared with South Georgia, which were associated with precocious sexual maturity in the latter population, and suggested that "four factors that might be considered as causes of this difference are variation in food supplies, adequacy of breeding space on the islands, availability of potent bulls, and the effects of sealing operations" at South Georgia (described in Chapter 15). They stated, giving reasons, that "the first three possibilities are readily dismissed". Bryden (1968a), however, proposed that pups on the more crowded beaches at Macquarie failed to achieve their "genetic growth competence" and became permanently stunted, due to disturbance caused by greater male activity interrupting their suckling. However, later work by McCann (1981a and in press) showed that since sealing ended at South Georgia the numbers of bulls on the breeding beaches have increased three- or four-fold, their mean age has increased and harem size has increased (because the older, larger bulls can control larger harems), they haul out earlier and stay ashore longer, so that the length of the breeding season and the social organization are now similar to Macquarie Island. Despite this there is little change in the number of breeding cows, their age structure is still different from the Macquarie Island population, and there has been no significant change in back-calculated age at first pupping since sealing stopped. Pup and adult growth-rates remain as high at South Georgia as in 1951 and it is difficult to escape the conclusion that the principal causative factor is that food availability is better at South Georgia. Other evidence presented by McCann also supports the view that population size, growth-rate and age at maturity are all related to food availability (see also section 7.6).

In Fig. 12 simplified average growth curves are shown for Weddell, leopard and crabeater seals (data for Ross seals are inadequate). As in the elephant seal and baleen whales (Chapter 13) it is likely that growth-rates vary between geographical areas or populations. These curves demonstrate the relatively rapid initial growth, and that there is a sexual dimorphism in favour of the female in these species; in the Ross seal also the females attain greater sizes than the males. The difference is least in the crabeater seal and greatest in the leopard seal; it increases (both absolutely and proportionally) with increasing maximum length. The male final length as a percentage of female final length is 96.7% in the crabeater, 94.3% in the Weddell and 92.1% in the leopard seal. The

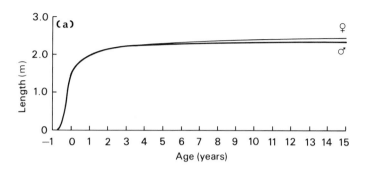

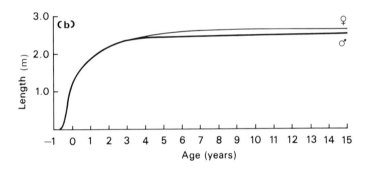

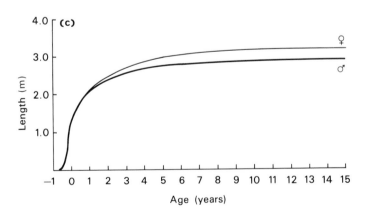

Fig. 12. Average curves of standard body length against age for (a) crabeater seal, Marguerite Bay (Laws and Baird, unpublished); (b) Weddell seal, McMurdo Sound (after Stirling, 1971b); (c) Leopard seal, various localities (after Laws, 1957).

significance of this phenomenon in relation to breeding behaviour was discussed in section 4.

7.5.2 Growth in weight

Payne (1979b) has presented weight growth curves for fur seals collected in November–April; these are similar in shape, though different in scale, to the elephant seal's and do not represent maximal seasonal size. Females show a very regular curve with slight growth beyond five years, reaching 38 kg by age 15 years; males diverge from females in the first few months and the sigmoid curve attains 130 kg by age ten years when it has levelled off. This represents a 3.5 times difference in adult weight. However, Payne calculated that the weight loss of 9–11 year old breeding bulls over 37 days was 1.99 kg day^{-1} and at the beginning of the breeding season their weight might well be such as to represent a 4.5 times weight difference between the sexes.

In Fig. 13 predicted average curves of growth in total body weight for South Georgia and Macquarie Island elephant seals are presented. These were obtained by applying the equations derived by Bryden (1972), for predicting weight from length, to the mean lengths at age represented in Fig. 11. It should be noted that the resulting curves represent animals of average condition; actual weights in any one month would be higher or lower according to the season. The mean ages at puberty (in the female one year less than the mean age at pupping) are also indicated.

The curves indicate that both sexes attain puberty 1½ years earlier at South Georgia at mean weights about 12% greater in the male and 25% greater in the female than at Macquarie Island. South Georgia females' mean weight at 20 years is about 16% greater than at Macquarie. it may be noted that this weight differential (16–25%) closely approximates to the proportionally greater size at birth of South Georgia pups (c.21%; see section 7.2).

The predicted maximum mean weights at age 20 years in the two localities are about 3175 kg and 2550 kg for the male and about 450 kg and 387 kg for the female, suggesting the fully mature male is about seven times the weight of the female. While ashore the male loses weight, as in the fur seal, and at the beginning of the breeding season the male is probably about eight times heavier than the female; this is the greatest sexual dimorphism by weight among mammals.

Extensive body weight data are available for crabeater seals collected in February/March (Laws and Baird, in prep.) and mean weight at age reaches 200 kg at 7 years in both sexes, the male curve levelling off and the female continuing to grow to about 215 kg at 15 years. However, the population mean weight is 193 kg. The average adult female Weddell seal is

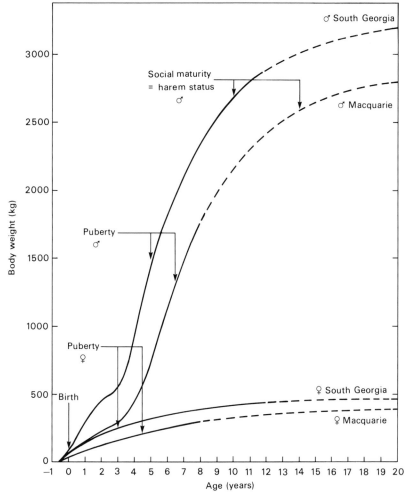

Fig. 13. Predicted curves of average body weight against age for South Georgia and Macquarie Island elephant seals. Mean age at puberty indicated; broken lines are extrapolated curves (see text).

predicted to be about 350 kg if the length/weight relationship is similar to that in the elephant seal.

7.6 Age at sexual maturity

7.6.1 Direct estimation

The age at sexual maturity is defined here as the age of first ovulation in the female and production of sperm by the male (Laws, 1956b). Age at first pupping is about one year later.

In the cow fur seal sexual maturity is attained by about three years (Payne, 1977). Figure 14 shows the percentage pregnant in age classes up to 20 years, increasing from zero at two years, to 55% at three years, to 75% at four years, 85% at five years and 90% by six years. The age at maturity in the male has not been established but males are not socially mature and able to participate fully in the mating activity until eight years.

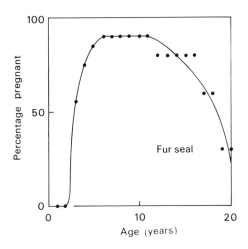

Fig. 14. Fur seal, Bird Island, age-specific pregnancy rates (data from Payne, 1977).

Laws (1956b) concluded that elephant seal females matured at two years in the South Georgia population in 1951, and almost all third year cows were pregnant. Re-examination of some of Laws' 1948–1951 sample by McCann (1981b) showed that there were errors of up to a year in the earlier estimation of ages indicating that maturity was in fact attained at about three years and his South Georgia data from 1978 indicate a mean age at maturity of about three years (range 2–5 years). This is not significantly different from 1951 and, for a recent sample of teeth, back-calculation of the age at maturity (see section 7.4) showed that there had been no signifi-cant change in the age at first pupping of cows born since 1964 when sealing stopped.

At Macquarie Island from 1951–1960 no three-year olds were seen to pup, 33% pupped at four years, only 70% by age six years and 25% pupped for the first time at seven years, indicating a mean age at sexual maturity of about four years (Carrick et al., 1962a).

Male elephant seals at South Georgia attained puberty at about four years in 1951 (Laws, 1956b) and at about six years at Macquarie Island in the 1950s (Carrick et al., 1962a). Social maturity was attained at about eight years (South Georgia, 1951), 10–11 years (South Georgia, 1978) or 14 years (Macquarie, 1950s) (see Laws, 1956b; McCann, 1981a,b; Carrick *et al.*, 1962a).

Possible reasons for these differences were discussed in section 7.5.1, where it was concluded that the most likely factor was food availability. Data for other species are much less extensive, but it is very likely that there are similar population differences, due to food availability or other factors.

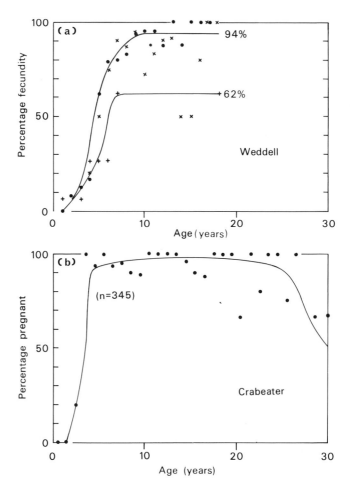

Fig. 15. Age-specific fecundity or pregnancy rates for: (a) Weddell seals: data from Croxall and Hiby (1983) circles; Stirling (1971a) oblique crosses; Siniff *et al.* (1977) upright crosses; and (b) crabeater seals, Marguerite Bay: Laws and Baird (unpublished).

In the Ross seal Øritsland (1970a,b) estimated that females and males achieve sexual maturity at 3–4 and 2–7 years respectively; Tikhomirov (1975) from a larger sample estimated 3–5 years, mostly four years in both sexes. In the leopard seal at various localities it was estimated by different authors at 3–4 years in the female, 4–6 in the male; 3–7 female, 2–6 male; and 3–6 female, 4–6 years male respectively by Laws (1957), Øritsland (1970a,b) and Tikhomirov (1975), the overall average ages probably being about four years in the female and about 4.5 years in the male.

In the Weddell seal the female age at maturity was estimated at three, three, four, six and 3–6 years respectively by Mansfield (1958), Stirling (1971a), Croxall and Hiby (1983), Siniff (1982) and DeMaster (1979) (see Fig. 15a). The male attains sexual maturity at about the same age, but probably does not become socially mature until seven or eight years (DeMaster, 1979).

In the crabeater seal the age of the female at sexual maturity was estimated at 16 months–2 years (Bertram, 1940), two (Laws, 1958), 2–6 (Øritsland, 1970a,b), 3–5 (Tikhomirov, 1975), 2–6, average 3.8 years (Bengtson and Siniff, 1981 and Fig. 15b), and 2–6 years, average 3.8 years (Laws and Baird, in prep.), but the age criteria of the first two authors gave low values. Laws and Baird concluded that the male attains puberty at similar ages; Tikhomirov (1975) gave 4–7 years.

7.6.2 Back-calculation from tooth structure

Laws (1977a), Söderberg (1977) and McCann (1981b) showed for crabeater, grey and ringed, and elephant seals respectively, that an individual seal's age at sexual maturity can be estimated from the teeth and so mean ages at maturity for populations can be back-calculated (see section 7.4). Laws' (1977a) data suggested that in one population of crabeater seals the age at maturity for both sexes had declined from about four years in 1950 to about 2.5 years by 1968, and later work on a larger sample modified but broadly confirmed this (Laws and Baird, in prep.). Figure 16 shows the mean age at maturity for year classes 1940–1975, sexes combined (because there was no significant difference) from Marguerite Bay, Antarctic Peninsula. Up to 1955 the age at maturity was fairly level and above four years and subsequently it appears to have advanced to 2.5 years for the 1974 year class. The onset of the advancement correlated well with the opening in 1955 of the former whaling Sanctuary in this region and Laws (1977a) suggested that it was a result of greater availability of food, krill, consequent on the reduction of the baleen whale stock. Bengtson and Siniff (1981) tentatively suggested that the age at sexual maturity had increased in more recent years following the virtual cessation of Antarctic whaling.

Söderberg (1977) presented data showing a similar advancement of maturity in grey and ringed seals from the Baltic.

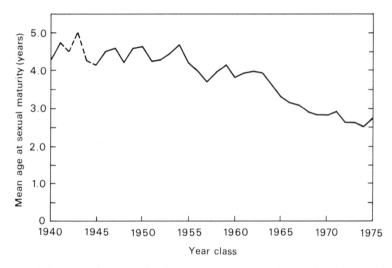

Fig. 16. Crabeater seal, Marguerite Bay, mean age at sexual maturity, for year classes 1940–1975 (Laws and Baird, unpublished).

The interpretation of these data is controversial; it has been suggested that the decline in the age of maturity of the baleen whales may result partly from a statistical artefact (Cooke and De la Mare, 1982). Also, it is possible that faster-growing, early-maturing animals, may be subject to higher natural mortality so that the earlier maturing individuals are under-represented in the older year classes. Bengtson and Laws (in press) concluded that the use of back calculation of the age at maturity from crabeater teeth is dubious. However, they showed, by ovarian studies, that there had been advancement in the age at maturity, followed, from 1963, by its expected deferment as food (krill) availability was expected to become less favourable.

8. The Annual Reproductive Cycle

Section 4 was concerned with behavioural aspects of the annual cycle. Here physiological aspects are reviewed.

8.1 Timing of the breeding season

Like all Southern Hemisphere pinnipeds the Antarctic seals produce their pups in the spring in a short synchronized period which varies according to species and latitude. Figure 4 illustrates the pupping seasons in populations of five species. The Ross seal is probably intermediate between crabeater and leopard. For each population the timing is probably rather constant from year to year. In ten seasons at Signy Island the first Weddell seal pup was seen on average on 19 August (range 10–24) (Smith and Burton, 1970). McCann (1980a, 1981b) showed that in the elephant seal the rate of increase and the date on which the maximum number of cows was ashore was almost identical in three successive seasons; over 80% of the pups were born in the three weeks from 6–26 October. He drew attention to records spanning more than 160 years which also indicate that the timing of the pupping season is rather constant. He showed that the timing of the breeding season, as indicated by the date when the maximum number of cows was hauled out, varied only from 15–25 October for nine breeding grounds ranging in latitude from 46 to 62°S; for four breeding sites south of the Antarctic Convergence the corresponding dates ranged from 18–25 October and for five sites on or north of the convergence the span was only 15–17 October. In the Weddell seal the peak birth date varies with latitude from 7 September at Signy Island (61°S) to 23 October at McMurdo Sound (78°S) (Lindsey, 1937; Mansfield 1958; Stirling, 1969a). For the Ross seal, Tikhomirov (1975) stated that the peak pupping period was 3–18 November, and the observations of Øritsland (1970a,b) and Thomas *et al.* (1980) did not conflict. There are few data on fur seals, other than at South Georgia, or on leopard seals.

Within a population age classes tend to pup or to mate at different times; Laws (1956a) showed that young elephant seal females pupped earlier than old females and this was confirmed by McCann (1980a, 1981b); in the crabeater seal, younger seals ovulated later in the spring than older females did (Bengtson and Siniff, 1981). McCann suggested that the synchrony of pupping was promoted by the probability, first, that very early or late pups would achieve independence at an unfavourable time in terms of food availability and secondly, that there would be a selective pressure for mating with the fittest bulls at the peak of the season. Coulson (1981) suggested that in the grey seal, pupping date is determined by the factors that terminate delayed implantation (see section 8.2.3), which he found to be correlated with sea surface temperature. Griffiths and Bryden (1981) suggested that it was influenced by day length. Like other polar seals the southern elephant seal has a large pineal gland and pineal activity is a function of day length. They suggested that the rapid spring increase in photoperiod inhibits pineal gland function and initiates the breeding season.

8.2 The female cycle

8.2.1 General features

Laws (1956b, 1960) summarized the annual cycle of adult elephant seals at South Georgia. Births peak about mid-October, parturition occurring seven days after cows haul out; oestrus and mating occur about 19 days after parturition (*c.* 3 November), but the blastocyst remains unimplanted for four months (*c.* 120 days) until early March, and embryonic and foetal growth occupies the remaining 7.5 months (*c.* 226 days). Lactation continues for 23 days after parturition, and the unusual moult of the elephant seal has been described in section 5.3. It may be significant that implantation of the blastocyst occurs towards the end of the moulting process.

In the crabeater seal the mean birth date is about 19 October, the mean conception date is about 18 November, implantation is delayed about 2½ months (80 days) until early-mid February, and the remaining 8.5 months (*c.* 255 days) is available for embryonic and foetal growth (Laws and Baird, in prep.). The duration of the lactation period was estimated to be five weeks on the basis of the pattern of growth layers in the teeth (Laws, 1958), but it is likely that it is shorter, perhaps four weeks (Bengtson and Siniff, 1981). The leopard seal was thought to be anomolous, mating several months after the pup is weaned (Hamilton, 1939; Harrison, 1969; Siniff *et al.*, 1980). Siniff and Stone (in press) have shown this is not the case.

Further details of the timing of breeding season events in these and other species were given in section 4 and Figs 4 and 17 (see also Table V).

TABLE V
Approximate duration (days) of stages in the annual cycle of the female

Species	Lactation period	Parturition to conception	Conception to implantation	Parturition to implantation	Implantation to parturition
Fur	110	8	125	133	232
Elephant	23	19	120	139	226
Crabeater	28	30	80	110	255
Weddell	50	48	48	96	269
Leopard	30?	48	48	96	269
Mean	(48)	31	84	115	0
Range	(87)	40	77	43	43
Range as % of mean	(181)	129	92	37	17

8.2.2 Lactation

This lasts about 23 days in the elephant seal, probably about 28 days in the crabeater seal, about 45–50 days in the Weddell seal, and 110–115 days in the fur seal (Table V); these periods are all much longer than in Arctic seals such as the harp seal (nine days) and hooded seal (ten days). Bonner (in press) summarized the duration of lactation in phocids as 9–28 days in pack ice (the crabeater is the upper extreme), 19–46 days on land, 32–68 days on fast ice and in otariids 117–360 days (occasionally to 720 days). Generally in mammals foetal growth is restricted by maternal size (section 7.2) and the milk formed from the mother's fat deposits enables her to remain with the young. Nursing is an important mechanism that allows the young to pass through stages in which it could not process the adult diet; there is usually a rapid weight loss after weaning while successful independent feeding behaviour is being developed (Millar, 1977; Pond, 1977). In the phocid seals the process is telescoped into a short period and the large young build up fat reserves to carry them through the post-weaning period; this is a great strain on the mother who rapidly loses weight. The result is that size at weaning as a proportion of asymptotic adult female weight is 40% in the fur seal, 46% in the elephant seal, 40% in the Weddell and 50% in the crab-eater seal (see data in section 7)—rather higher than the average for terrestrial mammals (Millar, 1977). (Other information related to lactation and suckling is given in sections 4, 5 and 7 and has been reviewed by Bonner (1983)).

The rapid growth of the phocid seals is due to the quantity and quality of the milk produced. In the elephant seal the average non-lactating mammary gland volume is $520 \, cm^3$, in lactating females, $2860 \, cm^3$, though the rate of secretion is not known. Milk analyses for three species are summarized in Table VI.

TABLE VI
Analyses of milk composition in three species

	Fat	Water	Non-fat solids Protein	Sugar	Ash	
Fur seal, *A. gazella*	26.4	51.1	22.4	—	0.6	Bonner (1968)
Elephant seal, *M. leonina*	13–49 *c.* 40		13.8–4.0	0.3–5.1		Bryden (1968b) Peaker and Goode (1978)
Weddell seal, *L. weddellii*	42.2	43.6 (55–27)	14.1			Kooyman (1981d)

As lactation proceeds, the fat content of elephant seal milk increases from c. 12% at birth to over 40% in the second week and the water content decreases correspondingly; this could be necessary to maintain the water balance of the fasting lactating female. Bonner (in press) reviews work suggesting a switch in metabolic processes of the pup as it grows and lays down blubber. The process may be different in the fur seal because lactation is prolonged and the female makes on average 17 trips of 4.3 days to sea to feed, interspersed with 2.1 days suckling bouts (Doidge and Croxall, 1983).

8.2.3 Delayed implantation

This is a widespread phenomenon in mammals and the pinnipeds are a group in which many species exhibit it. The blastocyst arrives in the uterus about six days after successful mating and the subsequent period until implantation varies from five weeks in the leopard seal and Weddell seal to four months in the elephant seal.

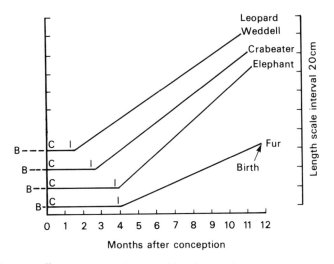

Fig. 17. Diagram to illustrate comparative annual female reproductive cycles and foetal growth, adjusted to a common date of conception. B, birth; C, conception; I, implantation.

In Table V and Fig. 17 the durations of the various stages in the annual cycle are summarized. These conclusions are derived from analysis of observations made by Bengtson and Siniff (1981), Bertram (1940), Hamilton (1939), Harrison (1969), Harrison *et al.* (1952), Laws (1956b, 1964), Mansfield (1958) and Øritsland (1970a,b) and Siniff and Stone (in press). The duration of the period from parturition to conception is inversely proportional to the period from conception to implantation, or parturition to implantation, and directly proportional to the period from implantation to parturition. If conception is considered to be the key event (Fig. 17) and the period of active foetal growth relatively invariable, as indicated in Table V, the complementary relationship is clear, and delayed implantation could be seen as a mechanism that compensates for the varying period from parturition to conception so as to allow for births at the optimum season of the year. Variation in the length of the period from birth to conception is presumably related to the social behaviour and needs of the pup.

8.3 The male cycle

Variations in the diameters of seminiferous tubules and their histological appearance provide an histological indication of sexual activity in the male. Harrison *et al.* (1952) reported on a small sample of Weddell and crabeater seals and Laws (1956b) obtained a larger sample of elephant seals. These confirmed that in these species spermatogenesis peaks seasonally during the breeding season, September–November, when tubule diameter averages 210–230 μm, declining to 110–130 μm during the winter (Fig. 18). Laws and Baird (in prep.) in a larger sample found a mean tubule diameter of 127 μm in February–March, identical with the lower curve in Fig. 18. Epididymal tubule diameters and testis size also show an increase at this time. Unfortunately, Harrison *et al.* (1952) were able to examine only two leopard seals (in late October and mid-February) with tubule diameter only about 160 μm.

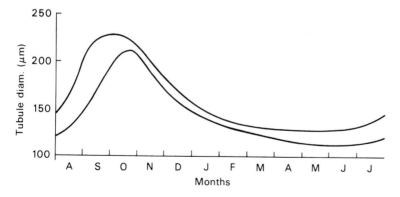

Fig. 18. Seasonal changes in mean diameter of seminiferous tubules of elephant seal (upper curve, after Laws, 1956b) and Weddell and crabeater seals (after Harrison *et al.*, 1952).

9. Population Dynamics

9.1 General considerations

The major problems to be overcome in reaching an understanding of the dynamics of a population are the estimation of the relevant parameters and process rates and their density-dependence. Some are more important than others in affecting abundance and we have only a sketchy idea for Antarctic seals of how any of them vary with population density. In a wide range of species, adult survival appears to be fixed within fairly narrow limits, and does not vary as much as juvenile survival, growth, age at first reproduction and fecundity (Eberhardt and Siniff, 1977). In general, reproductive parameters (age at maturity, percentage pregnant, secondary sex ratio) are easier to quantify than survival, though pup mortality in terrestrial colonies can be determined fairly readily by repeated counts. For an understanding of possible density-dependent effects it is also essential to have a measure of density changes, during the breeding season (for effects on pup survival, mating success, pregnancy rate), and outside the breeding season (effects probably on growth-rate, age at first reproduction and reproductive success generally, through food availability). Absolute population density during the breeding season is difficult and costly to estimate in the pack ice seals, but much easier in land or fast ice breeding species. Conversely, relative non-breeding season densities are more readily estimated in the pack ice seals, though absolute densities are still not known accurately (section 3.1), while the pelagic densities of elephant and fur seals are unknown.

In this section survival rates are approached through age structures (several species), and tag–recapture experiments (fur, elephant and Weddell seals); however, early survival usually has to be inferred to balance the life table because immatures may be under-represented, for obvious reasons, in breeding colonies, and under- or over-represented in collected samples due to geographical segregation. Age-specific pregnancy rates are also reviewed; age at first reproduction was considered in section 7.6. Changes in population size are probably due to concurrent changes in several parameters, rather than to age at first reproduction; changes in the latter may, however, be a useful indication of trends in population size.

9.2 Age structure, fecundity and survival

Laws (1960) constructed probably the first life tables for a pinniped, the southern elephant seal (which were used to formulate new management regulations for the sealing industry, introduced in 1952 (see Chapter 15)), for South Georgia females, exposed only to natural mortality, for males

TABLE VII

Life tables for the southern elephant seal (from McCann, in press)

FEMALE

Age (x)	Survival (lx)	Mortality (dx)	Mortality (qx)
0	1.000	0.400	0.400
1	0.600	0.090	0.150
2	0.510	0.061	0.120
3	0.449	0.054	0.120
4	0.395	0.047	0.120
5	0.348	0.042	0.121
6	0.306	0.037	0.121
7	0.269	0.032	0.119
8	0.237	0.028	0.118
9	0.209	0.025	0.120
10	0.184	0.022	0.120
11	0.162	0.026	0.161
12	0.136	0.030	0.221
13	0.106	0.027	0.255
14	0.079	0.024	0.304
15	0.055	0.019	0.350
16	0.036	0.014	0.389
17	0.022	0.011	0.500
18	0.011	0.007	0.636
19	0.004	0.003	0.750
20	0.001	0.001	1.000

MALE

Age (x)	Survival (lx)	Mortality (dx)	Mortality (qx)
0	1.000	0.400	0.400
1	0.600	0.090	0.150
2	0.510	0.088	0.173
3	0.422	0.072	0.171
4	0.350	0.060	0.171
5	0.290	0.049	0.169
6	0.241	0.048	0.199
7	0.193	0.048	0.249
8	0.145	0.044	0.303
9	0.101	0.030	0.297
10	0.071	0.021	0.296
11	0.050	0.015	0.300
12	0.035	0.011	0.314
13	0.024	0.007	0.292
14	0.017	0.005	0.294
15	0.012	0.004	0.333
16	0.008	0.003	0.375
17	0.005	0.002	0.400
18	0.003	0.001	0.333
19	0.002	0.001	0.500
20	0.001	0.001	1.000

exposed to both natural and hunting mortality, and for males exposed only to natural mortality. The data used were: (a) estimate of pup production based on counts; (b) sex ratio at birth 54% male; (c) age composition of a sample of 74 mature females; (d) pregnancy rate of 82.5% annually from the third year; (e) potential maximum longevity of 18–20 years; (f) the age composition of the male catch. Since Laws' work, commercial operations have stopped (in 1964) and McCann (in press) has derived revised life tables incorporating additional information, including sightings of known-age branded animals which were not available to Laws (Carrick and Ingham, 1962b). The current values for survival (lx), mortality (dx) and mortality rate (qx) indicate higher survival but approximate fairly closely to Laws' values. The current values for male natural mortality indicate a higher survival particularly in the first two years (Table VII). McCann (in press) recalculated Laws' (1960) 82.5% pregnancy rate (to exclude a "senile" individual) as 88%, and for the life table construction assumed pregnancy rates of 2% at three years, 79% at four years, and 85% for five years and over. Sex ratio at birth was estimated at 53% male.

It should be emphasized that these life tables are based on less than adequate information, but added confidence is given by the fact that Laws' predictions about the male catch were remarkably accurate. The catch per unit effort, oil yield and length of the season changed as expected. More importantly the mean age of the catch rose to 7.7 years and stabilized in 1961–1964, indicating that a sustained yield equilibrium had been reached as predicted (see also Laws, 1979; and Chapter 15).

These life tables incorporate 60% female survival to one year and 39.5% survival to first pupping at age four years. Male survival is lower after age two years and diverges progressively from female survival rates. These survival curves are plotted in Fig. 19. Unfortunately they tell us nothing about the operation of density-dependent factors, but some are discussed in section 7 and section 9.3.

Bonner (1968) estimated fur seal survival to first pupping at age three years as 29–56%, decreasing in later years as the population was increasing. Payne (1977) presented an age frequency distribution for 195 lactating fur seals collected in 1971–1973 at Bird Island. He made counts of pups, corrected for density-dependent variation in counting efficiency by a tag–recapture method; he calculated age at recruitment to the breeding population from examination of reproductive tracts, and assumed later pregnancy rates as in the northern fur seal *C. ursinus*; these age-specific rates are shown in Fig. 14. First year survival was estimated from the age structure, corrected for population increase, as 0.645 and adult survival as 0.898, assumed to operate from one year. This schedule estimates survival to first pupping, age three, at 52%, and the survival curve is plotted in Fig. 19. Subsequently a

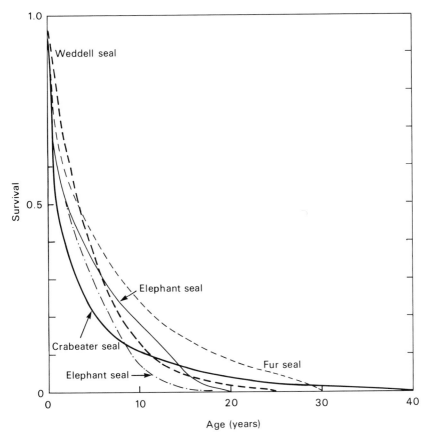

Fig. 19. Equilibrium survival curves (see text) for female Antarctic seals and male elephant seal (lower curve).

project was initiated to investigate density-dependent effects by comparing a high density breeding site (Bird Island; 670 pups at $1.5\,\text{m}^{-2}$) and a low but increasing density site (Schlieper Bay; 415 pups at $0.2\,\text{m}^{-2}$). Pup mortality at Schlieper Bay was only 5% compared with 15–30% at Bird Island. The duration of peri- and post-natal periods of cow attendance on the pup show significant differences and significantly longer feeding trips were made by Bird Island females (Doidge and Croxall, 1983).

Laws and Baird (in prep.) aged a sample of 1304 crabeater seals (Fig. 20). The foetal sex ratio was 55% male:45% female, the sex ratio at birth was 51% male:49% female. The observed later (tertiary) sex ratio of 42% male:58% female indicated a substantially higher male mortality after weaning, and age-specific analysis confirmed an increasing proportion of females, to 63% of animals older than 20 years.

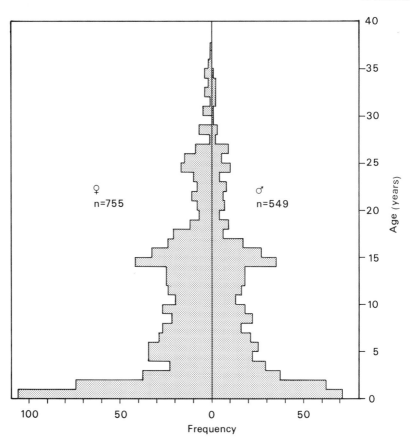

Fig. 20. Age frequency distributions for crabeater seals, Marguerite Bay.

Adult survival was estimated using the minimum variance unbiased esti-
mator derived by Chapman and Robson (1960), on the assumption of an
equilibrium population in which births are equal to deaths. For females this
gives an estimate of 0.89 for annual female adult survival (from eight
years). The survival will be greater if the population is increasing. The
survival will be greater if the population is increasing. The survival curve
was completed by applying the age-specific pregnancy rates, determined for
the sample of females (Fig. 15b) to estimate mortality, and interpolating
intermediate values. The result for females is shown in Fig. 19. It implies a
first year survival of 56% and overall survival to first pupping at, say, four
years, of 25%. The average pregnancy rate for all mature females was 90%;
for ages 3–25 years it was 94%, 97% in the most fertile years, declining at
higher ages. These values compare with overall rates, obtained for much

smaller samples, of 87% (Øritsland, 1970a,b), 83% from 6–24 years (Bengtson and Siniff, 1981), and an implied 94% (Tikhomirov, 1975). Bertram (1940) obtained a pregnancy rate of 79% for this species from the same region as Laws and Baird, suggesting the possibility of an increase in fecundity with time.

The picture for the Weddell seal is more complex, perhaps because more research has been carried out on more populations in time and space (Stirling, 1969a, 1971a; Siniff *et al.* 1977; Croxall and Hiby, 1983) and because of human interference. Croxall and Hiby (1983) used the Jolly–Seber method (Seber, 1973) to estimate annual survival from tag–resighting data at Signy Island. They estimated that the adult female annual survival rate from 1970 to 1977 was constant at 0.80. This is in close agreement with rates for the McMurdo studies of 0.77 (Siniff *et al.*, 1977) and their re-analysis of Stirling's (1971a) data which gave rates of 0.84 and 0.87. Male survival rates were 0.72, 0.75 and 0.88 depending on analytical method (Stirling, 1971a data) and 0.50 (Siniff *et al.*, 1977). There are no data for Signy males.

In Fig. 19 a survival curve for an equilibrium population of Weddell females is plotted, based on a survival rate from birth of 0.815 and Croxall and Hiby's (1983) age-specific fecundity values (shown in Fig. 15a). 94% of females recaptured at age nine years and over were with pups. Stirling (1971a) calculated an overall pregnancy rate of 80.5% to age 17 years, and his data are also presented in Fig. 15a. However, Siniff *et al.* (1977) obtained a fecundity rate of only 62% from 7 to 18 years (Fig. 15a) for 1970–1974; the comparable rate for the same population in 1966–1968 was 83% (Stirling, 1971a) and for Signy, 1960–1977 it was 90%. Siniff *et al.* (1977) and Croxall and Hiby (1983) discuss the reasons for the discrepancy between the two McMurdo studies, reaching different conclusions, the latter attributing it at least partly to biases in techniques.

Siniff *et al.* (1977) suggested that the apparent reproductive success was only 47% over four years, indicating that about one-half the parous females missed pupping each year. The McMurdo Sound population has been the object of an extensive long-term study and pup production has fluctuated between 767 and 250 (Fig. 21). Siniff *et al.* (1977) identified as a critical question the nature of the feedback between population density and recruitment in subsequent years. They proposed several hypotheses for natural population regulation: through a density-dependent effect on survival in the first two years of life, younger animals being forced to the fringes where they experience higher mortality, possibly from predation; the very low birth rate may be due to some mechanism preventing oestrus (which they consider unlikely); females with pups may somehow prevent non-parous females copulating (doubtful). As a working hypothesis they suggested that the prime female reproductive rate is depressed by the stress of weight loss,

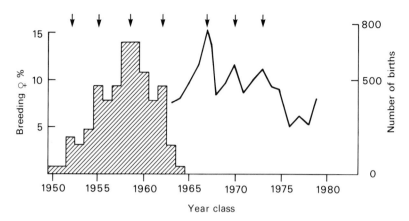

Fig. 21. Frequency distribution of year classes of Weddell seal breeding females at McMurdo Sound: histogram (after Stirling, 1971a); number of births (after Siniff, 1982). Arrows indicate actual or potential peaks in recruitment.

while younger females with little experience are less likely to produce due to social interactions. Understanding is complicated by a small annual harvest, of about 30 from a population of about 1000 adult females. DeMaster's (1981) model suggested that an annual harvest as low as 20 may be critical in causing the decline observed.

Data on leopard seal and Ross seal population dynamics are lacking, apart from some published pregnancy rates. For leopard seals the rates are 85% (Brown, 1957), 93% (Tikhomirov, 1975) and as low as 61% (Øritsland, 1970a,b); the latter recorded a high proportion of abortions, nearly 20%, in his sample. For Ross seal, rates of 88% (Øritsland, 1970a,b) and 90% (Tikhomirov, 1975) have been recorded.

The survival curves presented in Fig. 19 are for equilibrium populations and are necessarily tentative. For increasing populations the survival rate should be increased by the percentage annual increase in population size, and vice versa for decreasing populations. Except for the elephant seal they relate to females, but the lower survival of the male in the elephant seal is true, to a greater or lesser extent, of the other species. The upper limits of 20 years to the longevity of the elephant seal, of 25 years for the Weddell seal, of 30 years for the fur seal and of 40 years for the crabeater seal are probably correct, though they might be extended with larger samples.

Laws (1977a) drew attention to the different shape of the survival curve of crabeater and Weddell seals. His suggestion that these curves are shaped by complementary juvenile and adult mortalities still seems reasonable. The crabeater seal is a solitary breeder in an unstable habitat and clearly suffers from significant predation in the first year of life (section 5.2.2); subsequently it probably has fewer problems and a higher survival rate than the Weddell seal. In contrast the Weddell breeds in low density colonies on a very stable platform, the fast ice, where predation is insignificant; during the early years the young tend to be southerly in distribution and so less at risk from predation than the crabeater seal whose distribution largely overlaps with that of the leopard seal; as an adult the Weddell is subjected to mechanical senescence due to wear of the teeth, which would be expected to cause the observed truncation of the survival curve (section 9.3).

9.3 Causes of death

Laws (1956a) discussed possible causes of death in elephant seal pups. Carrick and Ingham (1962b) estimated 5–10% as the overall rate of pup mortality at Macquarie Island. Of 8107 pups counted on ten beaches at South Georgia in 1951, at least 2.1% died (range 0.8–6.8%). Still births were estimated by Laws to be 0.5%. The highest mortality occurred early in the breeding season when pups melted holes in deep snow and were separated from their parent; in one area 30% of pups died in two weeks in this way. Pups may die if they are separated from their mothers, or are crushed or trampled by bulls. In the marginal ice-breeding populations up to an estimated 80% of pups born on the sea ice may die when it breaks up and Laws (1956a) concluded that this was the major factor preventing increase. Leopard seals occasionally take elephant seal pups. Laws also noted that some 2.6% of weaned pups show stunted growth and their probability of survival is reduced. Bryden (1968a) proposed that elephant seals at Macquarie are permanently stunted, possibly due to density-dependent retarded growth to weaning. Laws (1956a) and Carrick and Ingham (1962b) drew attention to other causes of natural mortality. Adult deaths on land are insignificant; for cows 0.10–0.15%, bulls 1.3–1.5%; predation by killer whales may be significant. Condy (1977a) demonstrated a 5% annual decline in elephant seal numbers at Marion Island over 24 years. He showed a striking seasonal correlation between killer whale and elephant seal numbers there and suggested that predation might be significant.

Bonner (1968), from counts on 15 beaches at Bird Island in 1959 concluded that overall the fur seal pup mortality was about 6% (range 1–13%); it was density-dependent, caused principally by starvation, trampling, bite wounds, drowning. He concluded that in the adult natural mortality was probably mainly at sea and caused by senility and disease. Adult males die ashore behind the breeding beaches, a few each year in the 1950s (but 50 in 1959–1960, when 29 cows were also found dead).

In the crabeater seal the high incidence of predation by leopard seals has already been described (section 5.2.2); it is probably the major cause of death in the first year, and the large fluctuations in recruitment (section 9.4) may possibly be linked with varying predation pressure.

After the first year causes of mortality are not known. However, an unusual occurrence of mass deaths should be mentioned (Laws and Taylor, 1957). In 1955 some 3000 crabeaters wintered, unusually, on sea ice in Prince Gustav Channel, Antarctic Peninsula. They had access to the sea through pools and cracks. The worst affected group, numbering c. 1000 at Cape Lagrelius, were 80 km from the open sea. Deaths were seen first on 4 September; by 21 October 97% were dead and they were still dying on 14 November when the fast ice was breaking up. In other localities deaths ranged from none ($n = 400$), to 10% (200), 50% (50), 90% (500). Overall 68% died and in the main concentrations, over 85%. The outbreak coincided with the breeding season; numerous abortions were seen, some before any sign of disease was noted and there were no live pups. Pathological changes affecting lungs, spleens and kidneys were noted and it was concluded that the deaths were due to disease, probably a virus infection, presumably highly contagious; but Weddell seals in the area were not affected. Deaths were random with respect to age. In the two following years similar but less numerous deaths were observed in this area, but there have been no later reports, although field parties have visited the area.

Another interesting cause of death in crabeaters is starvation due to dispersal inland. Numerous mummified seals were originally reported by the Scott and Shackleton expeditions. Dort (1975) lists the occurrences in the Dry Valley region of South Victoria Land where at least 210 desiccated bodies have been reported, almost all crabeater pups less than six months old (5% of those positively identified were Weddell, leopard or elephant seals). Other occurrences of mummified seal carcasses have been reported from Seymour Island, James Ross Island, Schirmacher Oasis, Sør Rondane, Enderby Land, Vestfold Hills, Haswell Island, Bunger Oasis (British Antarctic Survey, unpublished records; Hiller et al., 1982). They occur to 200 km inland and up to 1400 m above sea level. Radiocarbon dating gives ages of 615–4450 years, but Dort (1975) suggested none is more than 300 years old. Lindsey (1938) suggested that young crabeaters move south when the fast ice breaks up and some wander inland during September–November. Caughley (1960) proposed that these occurrences represent a normal dispersal of young animals trapped in inlets by fast ice formation. Stirling and Kooyman (1971) concluded that crabeaters are more agile and travel further than other species.

Causes of death of the other species are not well known. For the Weddell seal Stirling (1971a) considered pup mortality, predation and wounding, disease, tooth wear, drowning or exposure and starvation. Known pup mortality to weaning was 5% in two years, mostly due to starvation, but some to crushing by adults. Killer whales take some Weddell seals; though they are not scarred like crabeaters, this could mean either that they never escape or are never caught. The fast ice habitat is relatively secure from killer whales so such predation if it occurs would take place almost exclusively in the pack ice. Intraspecific fighting is unlikely to be a significant factor in mortality. Diseases have not been studied in any detail. However, Weddell seals abrade sea ice with their teeth to keep open breathing holes, a behaviour unique to this species. A significant mortality factor, first identified by Bertram (1940), is wear and necrosis of the incisor and canine teeth. Stirling (1969b) assessed this in relation to age and found that tooth wear and necrosis showed little change up to eight or nine years and then increased sharply; as the teeth wear down to the pulp, cavity infection results and abscesses form. Eventually tooth wear "may seriously affect the ability of a seal to abrade ice and maintain breathing holes. If the hole cannot be maintained, a seal in the water may drown and a seal on the surface of the ice may die of starvation or exposure". The McMurdo Sound population is living in probably the most extreme environment occupied by any mammal. It would be interesting to compare age structures from other populations in lower latitudes, particularly the relict population at South Georgia which does not live under fast ice.

Nothing is known about the causes of mortality in Ross and leopard seals.

9.4 Fluctuations in recruitment

Figure 22a shows conspicuous variations in year class strength of Antarctic Peninsula crabeater seals, with rather regular intervals between peak year classes in 1940, 1948, 1953, 1958, 1963, 1967, 1972, 1976, a mean interval of 5.14 years (range 4–8 years). However, the first interval is anomalously long and the accuracy of age determination may be lower in the oldest animals; omitting it reduces the mean interval to 4.67 years (range 4–5 years). These fluctuations in recruitment might be related to annual variations in krill abundance, environmental changes (e.g. pack ice extent or packing, or weather), or to varying predation pressure. There are insufficient data to indicate which if any of these are causative factors and further research is needed. Possibly several factors, including the time from birth to first breeding of the crabeater seal, may operate together or be mutually reinforcing.

Interestingly, there is independent evidence of strikingly similar fluctuations in abundance of juvenile leopard seals at Macquarie Island. Rounsevell and Eberhard (1980) showed that, over 30 years (1949–1979), the annual winter abundance of leopard seals at Macquarie Island regularly oscillated between a few and 100–200 or so (extreme range 0–283) every 4–5 years (Fig. 22b). The seasonal influx occurs mainly between June and December and only non-breeding animals occur, 83% of them 9–38 months old sexually immature seals, with mean age about two years. Peak years are 1949, 1955, 1959, 1963, 1968, 1972, 1977 and the mean interval between peaks is again 4.67 years. This identical periodicity seems unlikely to be due to chance, and these populations might appear to be responding to a common causative factor, or interacting. It may be relevant that Limbert (in British Antarctic Survey, 1980) found a 4–5 year periodicity in the winter start date at Faraday and a periodicity of 4–5 years in mean annual temperatures for coastal Antarctic stations. Rounsevell and Eberhard suggested that "local shortages of both krill and crabeaters may regularly act in concert to produce the observed variation in the numbers of leopard seals in the region of Macquarie Island". The ecologies of the two species are closely related in respect of geographical distribution, habitat preferences, food habits (krill based) and their predator–prey relationship.

Direct comparison between populations several thousand miles apart is difficult to justify unless pan-Antarctic influences operate. Also several age groups are involved in the leopard seal fluctuations, not a single one as is probable in the crabeater, so there would be a smoothing effect. Some possible explanations are:

(1) In crabeater or leopard seal or both, recruitment may be directly correlated with krill abundance, pack ice extent and type, or weather.

(2) Year to year crabeater recruitment may be dependent on leopard seal predation pressures, perhaps influenced by conditions in the pack ice (e.g. packing of floes).

(3) Successful leopard seal conceptions and therefore births may be related to abundance or availability of crabeater pups promoting improved nutritive status of mating leopard seals.

A direct comparison of crabeater and leopard seal populations occupying similar longitudes is desirable. A case can be made for collection and analysis of teeth from crabeaters in pack ice south of Macquarie Island (the simplest approach); or the initiation of a project to study the two species concurrently in one region.

A similar fluctuation might also exist in the krill-eating fur seal at South Georgia. Payne (1977) presented an age frequency which suggests peak year classes at 1949, 1953, 1957, 1961, 1966, mean interval 4.25 years, intriguingly close to the corresponding crabeater peaks and not conflicting with the idea that krill abundance cycles may be the ultimate common feature. Moreover, 1978, a year when krill availability at South Georgia was low, was marked by the highest ever recorded fur seal pup mortality (30%) at Bird Island, Doidge and Croxall (1983); 1978 is a year when crabeater recruitment would have been predictably low. These tentative and speculative explanations will no doubt be testable when more data are available; they raise very fundamental questions about interactions within the ecosystem.

Finally, it may be noted that year class strengths in Weddell seals as measured by a catch curve (Stirling, 1971a) or by pup counts (Siniff, 1982) also appear to fluctuate (Fig. 21).

9.5 Population trends

The increase in the fur seal population at South Georgia has been described in section 3.1, and is shown in Fig. 23. The population was still increasing rapidly in 1982 and so the projected logarithmic curve is not shown as beginning to decelerate until the second half of the decade. Lander (1981), Lander and Kajimura (1982) estimated the current northern fur seal *Callorhinus ursinus* stock at 1.765 million. On this projection the Antarctic fur seal will overtake the northern fur seal in about 1986 as the world's most abundant otariid and as a tentative conclusion it seems not unreasonable to postulate a population of 4 million by the year 2000. However, a number of other species and groups have increased concurrently with the decline of the large baleen whales (birds, other seals, minke whales) and one result of increasing interspecific competition could be to truncate the development of their curves of increase, so that the postulated levels are not attained.

The total elephant seal population is probably fairly stable, although some local populations are increasing, and some are decreasing (McCann, in press). The first serious attempt to estimate crabeater abundance, in 1956/1957, produced an estimate of 5–8 million (Eklund and Atwood (1962)). The censuses on which the crabeater seal population estimates were based relate to the abundance in about 1972 (section 3.1). Beddington and Grenfell (1980) re-analysed Laws' (1977a) data and concluded that the fall in the age at maturity began before 1955. They used an adult annual survival rate of 0.855 (lower than Laws' revised figure of 0.89) and a pregnancy rate of 0.80 (lower than the revised figure of 0.90). They stated that their model implied an increase from 1947 "to the present" (? 1979) of about 2.4 ×; this implies an average annual increase of about 3% over 32 years. They considered that it was probably an underestimate "both in relative terms, since the equilibrium reproductive rate used is the minimal assumption, and in absolute terms because the present figure for total population is probably an underestimate". In fact the "present figure" was for 1972 implying an annual increase of 3.5% and according to the larger data set now available, the pregnancy rate and the adult survival rate are both higher than they assumed, from Laws' (1977a) earlier estimate. It is considered that a maximal annual rate of increase of 7.5% is not unlikely

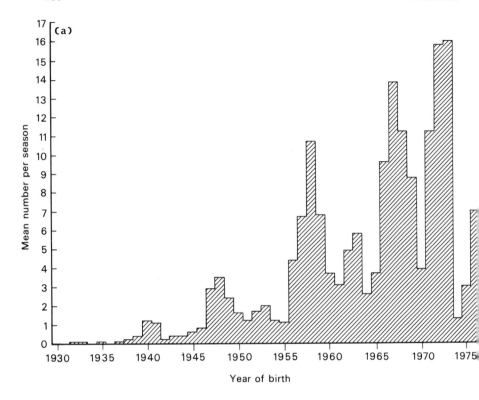

Fig. 22. (a) Crabeater seals. Marguerite Bay, year class strengths derived from age frequency distribution, sexes combined, weighted for number of years covered by sampling. (b) Abundances of leopard seals at Macquarie island (after Rounsevell and Eberhard (1980)).

when compared with the grey seal, *Halichoerus grypus*, which shows a sustained annual increase of 6–11%, the Antarctic fur seal rate of 15–17%, the northern fur seal's sustained 6–8.5% increase (Lander and Kajimura, 1982; Laws, 1979). The curve in Fig. 23 is therefore drawn on these tentative assumptions and the estimate by Eklund and Atwood (1962) of 5–8 millions in 1956/1957. This curve suggests a population of *c.* 5 million up to about 1950 and a projection involving maximal rates of increase in the 1970s and deceleration in the 1980s to reach about 50 million by the end of the century. The 1972 data, although corrected for time of day, omit an unknown proportion of animals in the water and so that point on the curve is likely to be conservative, a conservation that would be balanced if the annual rate of increase has in fact been lower than assumed.

Because of the similarity in distribution, food requirements and the predator–prey relationship of the crabeater and leopard seals, a similar annual increase (7.5%) has been assumed for the leopard seal. Projected

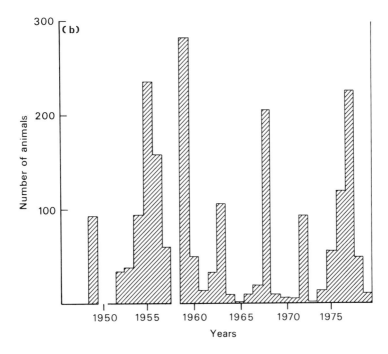

Fig. 22b.

backwards and forwards from 1972 this suggests the total population may have been about 60,000 up to 1955, 440,000 in 1982, and it is projected to reach about 600,000 by the year 2000.

There is no evidence for or against change in the populations of Weddell and Ross seals.

These conclusions on population sizes are summarized in Fig. 23 and Table VIII.

9.5 Biomass, production and ecological efficiencies

Table VIII summarizes the evidence for stock sizes (sections 3.1 and 9.4), mean weights (section 7.5.3), and annual mortality (section 9.4). The latter is taken as female annual mortality averaged over all age classes from data used to construct Fig. 19. The population standing stock biomasses are calculated from estimated stock sizes and population mean weights (Laws, 1977a,b; McCann, in press). Food consumption is estimated by applying the percentage composition by species (section 5.1) and estimates of the annual amounts eaten by species (section 5.5) to the estimated standing stock biomasses.

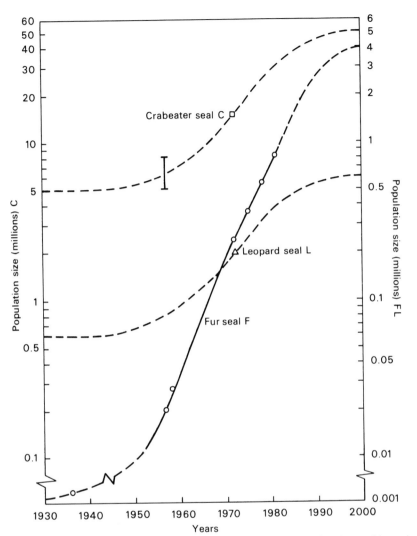

Fig. 23. Curves to show actual (continuous line) or projected trends in abundance of fur seals, crabeater and leopard seals (see text). Vertical bar is crabeater seal population in 1956/1957, estimated by Eklund and Atwood (1962). (Logarithmic scale.)

Applying the annual mortality estimates to stock numerical abundances and to standing stock biomasses gives estimates of total mortality and biomass transfer by death. In an equilibrium population annual biomass transfer should be equivalent to annual production. In increasing populations the survival rate would be higher and so the calculated gross efficiency (production/food consumed ×100) would be lower. A reduction of the

TABLE VIII

Estimates of abundance, biomass, food consumption and ecological efficiency for Antarctic seals

	Crabeater		Leopard		Ross	Weddell	Elephant	Fur		Total	
	1972	1982	1972	1982	1972–1982	1972–1982	1972–1982	1972	1982	1972	1982
1. Stock size (millions)	15	30	0.220	0.440	0.220	0.800	0.750	0.240	0.930	17.23	33.14
2. Mean weight (tonnes)	0.193		0.272	0.272	0.173	0.246	0.500	0.050	0.050	—	—
3. Standing stock (tonnes × 10⁶)	2.895	5.790	0.060	0.120	0.038	0.197	0.375	0.012	0.047	3.577	6.567
4. Food consumption (tonnes × 10⁶)	67	134	1.380	2.760	0.874	4.531	7.500	0.276	1.081	81.56	149.75
5. Annual mortality (%)	0.23	0.23	0.20	0.20	0.20	0.19	0.20	0.15	0.15	—	—
6. Annual mortality (millions) (1 × 5)	3.45	6.90	0.044	0.088	0.044	0.152	0.150	0.036	0.140	3.876	7.474
7. Annual mortality tonnes × 10⁶ (3 × 5) (= annual production (P) if in stable state)	0.67	1.33	0.12	0.024	0.008	0.037	0.075	0.002	0.007	0.804	1.481
8. Gross efficiency (7/4) × 100	1.0	1.0	0.9	0.9	0.9	0.8	1.0	0.7	0.7	0.9	1.0
9. Ecological efficiency (see text)	4.58	4.58	1.86	1.86	4.91	4.11	5.67	2.89	2.59	4.65	4.59

crabeater mortality rate from 0.23 to 0.19 results in a calculated fall in gross efficiency from 1.0 to 0.8. These tentative conclusions suggest that the crabeater, leopard, Ross and elephant seals are more efficient and the Weddell and fur seal less so.

However, ecological efficiency is a more meaningful comparison. The concept of ecological efficiency has been reviewed and discussed by Lavigne *et al.* (1982) where it is defined as energy passed to trophic level n + 1/ingestion at trophic level n × 100. This can be simplified to production/ingestion × 100. They gave comparative values for animals from various trophic levels. The ecological efficiencies of three seals, *Phoca vitulina*, *Pagophilus groenlandicus* and *Phoca hispida*, are 5.9, 3.9 and 3.8 respectively.

For Antarctic seals ecological efficiencies have now been calculated for equilibrium populations, by applying the energetic values of different types of food to the food consumption estimates and converting the seal production estimates by weight to energy (section 5.5, Table VIII). The species appear to fall into several groups of ecological efficiencies: the Weddell, crabeater and Ross at 4.1, 4.6 and 4.9; the elephant seal at 5.7; the leopard seal at the other extreme of 1.9, and the fur seal at 2.6. The values for the first four species are reasonably close to those given above for Arctic seals, and the latter two might in any case not be expected to be comparable. The mean value obtained for all six Antarctic species combined is 4.6, heavily weighted of course by the crabeater seal. This promotes some confidence in the calculations although the figures can only be advanced as a crude approximation.

10. Conclusion

The Antarctic seals are more abundant, in terms of numbers and biomass, than all the other seals in the world combined. Because of their lack of contact with Man they are very approachable and lend themselves to research, both observational and experimental. In this chapter I have tried to review the more important aspects of their ecology and biology, though space has precluded discussion of some aspects of their biology, notably diving physiology.

The areas where most future interest lies concern first, the trophodynamics—food consumption in quality and quantity, the feeding behaviour, energetic and biochemical considerations—and the role of seals in the Southern Ocean ecosystems. Secondly, there is great interest in the implications of this for growth and survival, and the use of growth-rates and reproductive parameters (fecundity, age at maturity) of certain species as indicators of changes in the ecosystem. These are the fields of research with most application in management and conservation, in applying the principles embodied in the Convention for the Conservation of Antarctic Seals and the Convention on the Conservation of Antarctic Marine Living Resources (see Chapter 15). Thirdly, however, there is a wide range of academic questions of basic interest, relating to behaviour, ecology and ecological theory, reproduction and physiology which will continue to attract attention. The Antarctic seals also provide many useful examples of biological principles and scientific method. If this chapter has stimulated interest and leads to the solution of some of the questions it raises, it will have served its purpose.

11. References

Allen, J. A. (1880). "History of North American Pinnipeds: A Monograph of Walruses, Sea Lions, Sea Bears and Seals of North America." *U.S. Geological and Geographical Survey of the Territories. Miscellaneous Publications* No. 12. Government Printing Office, Washington, D.C.

Ashwell-Erickson, S. M., Fay, F. H. and Elsner, R. (1983). Metabolic and nutritional aspects of molting in Bering Sea harbor and spotted seals. *In* "Proceedings of the Fourth Biennial Conference on the Biology of Marine Mammals, San Francisco, December 14–18, 1981".

Barrett-Hamilton, G. E. H. (1902). Southern Cross Collections. *Mammalia*, 1–66.

Bartholomew, G. A. (1970). A model for the evolution of pinniped polygyny. *Evolution* **24**, 546–559.

Beddington, J. R. and Grenfell, B. (1980). The status of major zoological groups in the Southern Ocean. *International Union for the Conservation of Nature*, 85 pp.

Bengtson, J. L. and Laws, R. M. (in press). Trends in crabeater seal age at maturity: an insight into Antarctic marine interactions? *In* "Nutrient Cycles and Food Chains" (W. R. Siegfried, P. R. Condy and R. M. Laws, eds), Proceedings of the 4th SCAR Symposium on Antarctic Biology, Springer-Verlag, Berlin.

Bengtson, J. L. and Siniff, D. B. (1981). Reproductive aspects of female crabeater seals (*Lobodon carcinophagus*) along the Antarctic Peninsula. *Canadian Journal of Zoology* **59**, 92–102.

Bertram, G. C. L. (1940). The biology of the Weddell and crabeater seals. *Scientific Reports of the British Grahamland Expedition, 1934–37* **1**, (1), 1–139.

Best, P. (1971). Stalked barnacles *Conchoderma auritum* on an elephant seal: occurrence of elephant seals on South African coasts. *Zoologica africana* **6**, 181–185.

Bigg, M. A. (1981). Harbour seal. *Phoca vitulina* Linnaeus, 1758 and *Phoca largha* Pallas, 1811. *In* "Handbook of Marine Mammals" (S. H. Ridgway and R. J. Harrison, eds), Vol. 2, Seals, pp. 1–28. Academic Press, London and New York.

Blix, A. S., Iversen, J. A. and Pashe, A. (1973). On the feeding and health of young hooded seals (*Cystophora cristata*) and harp seals (*Pagophilus groenlandicus*) in captivity. *Norwegian Journal of Zoology* **21**, 55–58.

Bonner, W. N. (1958). Exploitation and conservation of seals in South Georgia. *Oryx* **4** (**6**), 373–380.

Bonner, W. N. (1968). The fur seal of South Georgia. *British Antarctic Survey Scientific Reports* No. 56, 1–91.

Bonner, W. N. (1981). Southern fur seals. *Arctocephalus* (Geoffroy Saint-Hilaire and Cuvier, 1826. *In* "Handbook of Marine Mammals" (S. H. Ridgway and R. J. Harrison, eds), Vol. 1, pp. 161–208. Academic Press, London and New York.

Bonner, W. N. (in press). Lactation strategies in Pinnipeds—problems for a marine mammalian group. *Zoological Society of London Symposia* No. 51.

Bonner, W. N. and Hunter, S. (1982). Predatory interactions between Antarctic fur seals, macaroni penguins and giant petrels. *British Antarctic Survey Bulletin* No. 56, 75–79.

Bonner, W. N. and Laws, R. M. (1964). Seals and sealing. *In* "Antarctic Research" (Sir Raymond Priestley, R. J. Adie and G. de Q. Robin, eds), pp. 163–190. Butterworths, London.

Bonner, W. N. and McCann, T. S. (1982). Neck collars on fur seals, *Arctocephalus gazella* at South Georgia. *British Antarctic Survey Bulletin* No. 57, 73–77.

British Antarctic Survey (1980). Annual Report 1979–80. B.A.S., Cambridge.

Brown, K. G. (1957). The leopard seal at Heard Island, 1951–54. *Australian National Antarctic Research Expedition, Interim Report* No. 16, 1–34.

Brown, R. N. R. (1913). The seals of the Weddell Sea: notes on their habits and distribution. *Report of the Scientific Results of the Scottish National Antarctic Expedition* 4, 185–198.

Bruce, W. S. (1913a). Measurements and weights of Antarctic seals. *Report of the Scientific Results of the Scottish National Antarctic Expedition* 4, 163–174.

Bruce, W. S. (1913b). On the skulls of Antarctic seals. *Report of the Scientific Results of the Scottish National Antarctic Expedition* 4, 345–346.

Bryden, M. M. (1968a). Control of growth in two populations of elephant seals. *Nature* (Lond.) 217, 1106–1108.

Bryden, M. M. (1968b). Lactation and suckling in relation to early growth of the southern elephant seal, *Mirounga leonina* (L.). *Australian Journal of Zoology* 16, 739–748.

Bryden, M. M. (1972). Growth and development of marine mammals. *In* "Functional Anatomy of Marine Mammals" (R. J. Harrison, ed.), Vol. 1, 1–80. Academic Press, London and New York.

Burns, J. J. (1981a). Ribbon seal—*Phoca fasciata* Zimmerman, 1783. *In* "Handbook of Marine Mammals" (S. H. Ridgway and R. J. Harrison, eds), Vol. 2, Seals, pp. 1–27. Academic Press, London and New York.

Burns, J. J. (1981b). Bearded seal—*Erignathus barbatus* Erxleben, 1777. *In* "Handbook of Marine Mammals" (S. H. Ridgway and R. J. Harrison, eds), Vol. 2, Seals, pp. 145–170. Academic Press, London and New York.

Calhaem, I. and Christoffel, D. A. (1969). Some observations of the feeding habits of a Weddell seal and measurements of its prey, *Dissostichus mawsoni*, at McMurdo Sound, Antarctica. *New Zealand Journal of Marine and Freshwater Research* 3, 181–190.

Carrick, R. and Ingham, S. E. (1962a). Studies on the southern elephant seal, *Mirounga leonina* (L.). II. Canine tooth structure in relation to function and age determination. *CSIRO Wildlife Research* 7, 102–118.

Carrick, R. and Ingham, S. E. (1962b). Studies on the southern elephant seal, *Mirounga leonina* (L.). V. Population dynamics and utilization. *CSIRO Wildlife Research* 7, 190–206.

Carrick, R., Csordas, S. E. and Ingham, S. E. (1962a). Studies on the southern elephant seal, *Mirounga leonina* (L.). IV. Breeding and development. *CSIRO Wildlife Research* 7, 161–197.

Carrick, R., Csordas, S. E., Ingham, S. E. and Keith, K. (1962b). Studies on the southern elephant seal, *Mirounga leonina* (L.). III. The annual cycle in relation to age and sex. *CSIRO Wildlife Research* **7**, 119–160.

Caughley, G. (1960). Dead seals inland. *Antarctic* **2**, 270–271.

Chapman, D. G. and Robson, D. S. (1960). The analysis of a catch curve. *Biometrics* **16**, 354–386.

Clarke, A. and Prince, P. A. (1980). Chemical composition and calorific value of food fed to mollymauk chicks *Diomedea melanophris* and *D. chrysostoma* at Bird Island, South Georgia. *Ibis* **122**, 488–494.

Clarke, M. R. and Macleod, N. (1982a). Cephalopods in the diet of elephant seals at Signy Island, South Orkney Islands. *British Antarctic Survey Bulletin* No. 57, 27–31.

Clarke, M. R. and Macleod, N. (1982b). Cephalopod remains in the stomachs of eight Weddell seals. *British Antarctic Survey Bulletin* No. 57, 33–40.

Condy, P. R. (1976). Results of the 3rd seal survey in the King-Haakon-VII Sea Antarctica. *South African Journal of Antarctic Research* **6**, 2–8.

Condy, P. R. (1977a). Annual cycle of the elephant seal *Mirounga leonina* (Linn.) at Marion Island. *South African Journal of Zoology* **14**, 95–102.

Condy, P. R. (1977b). Results of the 4th seal survey in the King-Haakon-VII Sea Antarctica. *South African Journal of Research* **7**, 10–13.

Condy, P. R. (1977c). "The ecology of the southern elephant seal *Mirounga leonina* (Linnaeus 1758), at Marion Island." DSc. Thesis, University of Pretoria, South Africa.

Condy, P. R. (1978). Distribution, abundance and annual cycle of fur seals *Arctocephalus* spp. on the Prince-Edward Islands South Africa. *South African Journal of Wildlife Research* **8**, 159–168.

Condy, P. R. (1980). Postnatal development and growth in southern elephant seals (*Mirounga leonina*) at Marion Island. *South African Journal of Wildlife Research* **10**, 118–122.

Condy, P. R., van Aarde, R. J. and Bester, M. N. (1978). The seasonal occurrence and behaviour of killer whales *Orcinus orca* at Marion Island. *Journal of Zoology* (Lond.) **184**, 449–464.

Cooke, J. G. and de la Mare, W. K. (1982). The effects of variability in age data on the estimation of biological parameters of minke whales (*Balaenoptera acutorostrata*). *International Whaling Commission Report* No. SC/34/Mi7, 29 pp.

Corner, R. W. M. (1972). Observations on a small crabeater seal breeding group. *British Antarctic Survey Bulletin* No. 30, 104–106.

Coulson, J. C. (1981). A study of the factors influencing the timing of breeding in the grey seal *Halichoerus grypus*. *Journal of Zoology* (Lond.) **194**, 553–571.

Croxall, J. P. and Hiby, L. (1983). Fecundity, survival and site fidelity in Weddell seals, *Leptonychotes weddelli*. *Journal of Mammalogy*, **20**, 19–32.

Croxall, J. P. and Prince, P. A. (1982). Calorific value of squid (Mollusca: Cephalopoda). *British Antarctic Survey Bulletin* No. 55, 27–31.

Csordas, S. E. (1965). A few facts about the southern elephant seal. *Victorian Naturalist* **82**, 69–74.

Daniel, M. J. (1971). Elephant seal juvenile at Cape Turakirae, Wellington, New Zealand. *New Zealand Journal of Marine and Freshwater Research* **5**, 200–201.

Davies, J. L. (1961). Birth of an elephant seal on the Tasmanian coast. *Journal of Mammalogy* **42**, 113–114.

Dearborn, J. H. (1965). Food of Weddell seals at McMurdo Sound Antarctica. *Journal of Mammalogy* **46**, 37–43.

DeMaster, D. P. (1979). Weddell seal. *In* "Mammals in the Seas", FAO Fisheries series no. 5, Vol. II, pp. 130–134. FAO, Rome.

DeMaster, D. P. (1981). Incorporation of density dependence and harvest into a general population model for seals. *In* "Dynamics of Large Mammal Populations" (C. W. Fowler and T. D. Smith, eds), pp. 389–402. Wiley, New York.

DeMaster, D. P., Thomas, J. A., Stone, S. and Andriashek, D. (1980). Biological studies of seals in pack ice habitat. *Antarctic Journal of the United States* **14**, 179–180.

Dickinson, A. B. (1967). Tagging elephant seals for life-history studies. *Polar Record* **13**, 443–446.

Doidge, D. W. and Croxall, J. P. (1983). Breeding density, pup mortality and mother–pup behaviour in Antarctic fur seals at South Georgia. *In* Proceedings, Fourth Biennial Conference on the Biology of Marine Mammals, San Francisco, December 14–18, 1981".

Dort, W., Jr (1975). Significance and antiquity of mummified seals in southern Victoria Land, Antarctica. *Rapports Procès-Verbaux Conseil Permanent International Exploration du Mer* **169**, 57–69.

Ealey, E. H. M. (1954). Ecological notes on the birds of Heard Island. *Emu* **54**, 91–112.

Eberhardt, L. L. and Siniff, D. B. (1977). Population dynamics and marine mammal management policies. *Journal of the Fisheries Research Board of Canada* **34**, 183–190.

Eklund, C. R. and Atwood, E. L. (1962). A population study of Antarctic Seals. *Journal of Mammalogy* **43**, 229–238.

Erickson, A. W. and Hofman, R. J. (1974). Antarctic seals. *Antarctic Map Folio Series* **18**, 4–12.

Erickson, A. W., Siniff, D. B., Cline, D. R. and Hofman, R. J. (1971). Distributional ecology of Antarctic seals. *In* "Symposium on Antarctic Ice and Water Masses" (G. Deacon, ed.), pp. 55–76. Scientific Committee on Antarctic Research, Cambridge.

Fedak, M. A. and Anderson, S. S. (1982). The energetics of reproduction; accurate measurements from a large wild mammal, the grey seal (*Halichoerus grypus*). *Journal of Zoology* (Lond.) **198**, 473–479.

Frost, K. J. and Lowry, L. F. (1981). Ringed, Baikal and Caspian seals—*Phoca hispida, Phoca sibirica* and *Phoca caspica*. *In* "Handbook of Marine Mammals" (S. H. Ridgway and R. J. Harrison, eds), Vol. 2, Seals, pp. 29–54. Academic Press, London and New York.

Geraci, J. R. (1975). Pinniped nutrition. *Rapports et Procès-Verbaux des Reunions, Conseil International Pour l'Exploration de la Mer* **169**, 312–323.

Gilbert, J. R. and Erickson, A. W. (1977). Distribution and abundance of seals in the pack ice of the Pacific sector of the Southern Ocean. *In* "Adaptations within Antarctic Ecosystems" (G. A. Llano, ed.), pp. 703–748. Smithsonian Institution, Washington, D. C.

Gray, J. E. (1844). The Seals of the Southern Hemisphere. *In* "Zoology of the Voyage of H.M. Erebus and Terror under the command of Captain Sir James Clark Ross" (J. Richardson, ed.) pp. 1–8. London.

Griffiths, D. J. and Bryden, M. M. (1981). The annual cycle of the pineal gland of the elephant seal (*Mirounga leonina*). *In* "Pineal Function" (C. D. Matthews and

R. F. Seamark, eds), pp. 57–65. Elsevier/North Holland Biomedical Press.

Gwynn, A. M. (1953). The status of the leopard seal at Heard Island and Macquarie Island, 1948–1950. *Australian National Antarctic Research Expedition, Interim Report* No. 3, 1–33.

Hamilton, J. E. (1934). The southern sea lion, *Otaria byronia* (de Blainville). *"Discovery" Reports* **8**, 269–318.

Hamilton, J. E. (1939). The Leopard Seal, *Hydrurga leptonyx*. *"Discovery" Reports* **18**, 239–264.

Harrison, R. J. (1969). Reproduction and reproductive organs. *In* "Biology of Marine Mammals" (T. H. Anderson, ed.), pp. 253–348. Academic Press, London and New York.

Harrison, R. J., Matthews, L. H., Roberts, J. M. (1952). Reproduction in some Pinnipedia. *Transactions of the Zoological Society of London* **27**, 437–541.

Hiller, A., Richter, W. and Trettin, R. (1982). Another seal find in the Schirmacher Oasis (Queen Maud Land, Antarctica). *Zentralinstituts für Isotopen und Strahlenforschung* (Leipzig) No. 51, 121–132.

Hofman, R., Reichle, R., Siniff, D. B. and Müller-Schwarze, D. (1977). The leopard seal (*Hydrurga leptonyx*) at Palmer Station, Antarctica. *In* "Adaptations within Antarctic Ecosystems" (G. A. Llano, ed.), pp. 769–782. Proceedings of the 3rd SCAR Symposium on Antarctic Biology. Smithsonian Institution, Washington, D.C.

Hook, O. and Johnels, A. G. (1972). The breeding and distribution of the grey seal (*Halichoerus grypus*, Fab.) in the Baltic Sea, with observations on other seals of the area. *Proceedings of the Royal Society of London* B **182**, 37–58.

Horning, D. S., Jr. and Fenwick, G. D. (1978). Leopard seals at The Snares Islands New Zealand. *New Zealand Journal of Zoology* **5**, 171–172.

Huey, L. M. (1930). Capture of an elephant seal off San Diego, California, with notes on stomach contents. *Journal of Mammalogy* **11**, 229–231.

Huggett, A. St. G. and Widdas, W. R. (1951). The relationship between mammalian foetal weight and conception age. *Journal of Physiology* (Lond.) **114**, 306–317.

Hunt, F. (1973). Observations on the seals of Elephant Island, South Shetland Islands 1970–71. *British Antarctic Survey Bulletin*, No. 36, 99–104.

Ingham, S. E. (1967). Branding elephant seals for life history studies. *Polar Record* **13**, 447–449.

Kaufman, G. W., Siniff, D. B. and Reichle, R. (1975). Colony behaviour of Weddell seals *Leptonychotes weddelli* at Hutton Cliffs, Antarctica. *Rapports et Procès-Verbaux des Reunions, Conseil International Pour l'Exploration de la Mer* **169**, 228–246.

Kettlewell, H. B. D. and Rand, R. (1955). Elephant seal cow and pup on South African coast. *Nature* (Lond.) **175**, 1000–1001.

Keyes, M. C. (1968). The nutrition of pinnipeds. *In* "the Behaviour and Physiology of Pinnipeds" (R. J. Harrison, R. C. Hubbard, R. S. Peterson, C. E. Rice and R. J. Schusterman, eds), pp. 359–395. Appleton-Century-Crofts, New York.

King, J. E. (1957). On a pup of the crabeater seal *Lobodon carcinophagus*. *Annals and Magazine of Natural History* Ser. 12, Vol. 10, 619–624.

King, J. E. (1961). The feeding mechanism and jaws of the crabeater seal (*Lobodon carcinophagus*). *Mammalia* **25**, 462–466.

King, J. E. (1964). "Seals of the World". British Museum (Natural History), Trustees.

King, J. E. (1969). Some aspects of the anatomy of the Ross seal, *Ommatophoca rossi* (Pinnipedia: Phocidae). *British Antarctic Survey Scientific Reports*, No. 63, 1–54.

Kooyman, G. L. (1968). An analysis of some behavioral and physiological characteristics related to diving in the Weddell seal. *In* "Biology of the Antarctic Seas III" (G. A. Llano and W. L. Schmitt, eds). American Geophysical Union, Antarctic Research Series **11**, 227–261.

Kooyman, G. L. (1981a). Crabeater seal—*Lobodon carcinophagus* (Hombron and Jacquinot, 1842). *In* "Handbook of Marine Mammals" (S. H. Ridgway and R. J. Harrison, eds), Vol. 2, Seals, pp. 221–235. Academic Press, London and New York.

Kooyman, G. L. (1981b). Leopard seal—*Hydrurga leptonyx* Blainville, 1820. *In* "Handbook of Marine Mammals" (S. H. Ridgway and R. J. Harrison, eds), Vol. 2, Seals, pp. 261–274. Academic Press, London and New York.

Kooyman, G. L. (1981c). Weddell seal *Leptonychotes weddelli* Lesson, 1826. *In* "Handbook of Marine Mammals" (S. H. Ridgway and R. J. Harrison, eds), Vol. 2, Seals, pp. 275–296. Academic Press, London and New York.

Kooyman, G. L. (1981d). "Weddell Seal, Consummate Diver". Cambridge University Press, Cambridge.

Kooyman, G. L. and Davis, R. W. (1980). Feeding behaviour of female Antarctic fur seals, *Arctocephalus gazella*. *Antarctic Journal of the United States* **15**, 159.

Kooyman, G. L., Davis, R. W., Croxall, J. P. and Costa, D. P. (1982). Diving depths and energy requirements of king penguins. *Science* **217**, 725–727.

Lander, R. H. (1981). A life table and biomass estimate for Alaskan fur seals. *Fisheries Research* **1**, 55–70.

Lander, R. H. and Kajimura, H. (1982). Status of northern fur seals. *In* "Mammals in the Seas", FAO Fisheries Series, No. 5, Vol. IV, pp. 319–345. FAO, Rome.

Lavigne, D. M., Barchard, W., Innes, S. and Øritsland, N. A. (1982). Pinniped bioenergetics. *In* "Mammals in the Seas", FAO Fisheries Series No. 5, Vol. IV, pp. 191–235. FAO, Rome.

Laws, R. M. (1952). A new method of age determination for mammals. *Nature* (Lond.) **169**, 972.

Laws, R. M. (1953a). A new method of age determination in mammals with special reference to the elephant seal (*Mirounga leonina*, Linn.) *Falkland Islands Dependencies Survey, Scientific Reports* **2**, 1–11.

Laws, R. M. (1953b). The elephant seal (*Mirounga leonina* Linn.). I. Growth and age. *Falkland Islands Dependencies Survey, Scientific Reports* No. 8, 1–62.

Laws, R. M. (1956a). The elephant seal (*Mirounga leonina* Linn.). II. General, social and reproductive behaviour. *Falkland Islands Dependencies Survey, Scientific Reports* No. 13, 1–88.

Laws, R. M. (1956b). The elephant seal (*Mirounga leonina* Linn.). III. The physiology of reproduction. *Falkland Islands Dependencies Survey, Scientific Reports* No. 15, 1–66.

Laws, R. M. (1956c). Growth and sexual maturity in aquatic mammals. *Nature* (Lond.) **178**, 193–194.

Laws, R. M. (1957). On the growth rates of the leopard seal, *Hydrurga leptonyx* (De Blainville, 1820). *Saugetierkunde Mitteilungen* **5**, 49–55.

Laws, R. M. (1958). Growth rates and ages of crabeater seals, *Lobodon carcino-*

phagus Jacquinot and Pucheran. *Proceedings of the Zoological Society of London* **130**, 275–288.

Laws, R. M. (1959). Accelerated growth in seals with special reference to the Phocidae. *Norsk Hvalfangst-tidende* **48**, Arg., 425–452.

Laws, R. M. (1960). The Southern elephant seal (*Mirounga leonina* Linn.) at South Georgia. *Norsk Hvalfangst-tidende* **49**, Arg., 466–476, 520–542.

Laws, R. M. (1962). Age determination of pinnipeds with special reference to growth layers in the teeth. *Zeitschrift für Saugetierkunde* **27**, 129–146.

Laws, R. M. (1964). Comparative biology of Antarctic seals. *In* "Biologie Antarctique" (R. Carrick and M. W. Holdgate, eds), pp. 445–454. Hermann, Paris.

Laws, R. M. (1973). Population increases of fur seals at South Georgia. *Polar Record* **16**, 856–858.

Laws, R. M. (1977a). The significance of vertebrates in the Antarctic marine ecosystem. *In* "Adaptations within Antarctic Ecosystems" (G. A. Llano, ed.), pp. 411–438. Proceedings of the 3rd SCAR Symposium on Antarctic Biology. Smithsonian Institution, Washington, D.C.

Laws, R. M. (1977b). Seals and whales in the Southern Ocean. *In* "Scientific Research in Antarctica". Discussion meeting organized by V. E. Fuchs and R. M. Laws. *Philosophical Transactions of the Royal Society of London* **B279**, 81–96.

Laws, R. M. (1979). Monitoring whale and seal populations. *In* "Monitoring the Marine Environment" (D. Nichols, ed.). Symposia of the Institute of Biology, no. 24, pp. 115–140.

Laws, R. M. (ed.) (1980). Estimation of population sizes of seals. *In* "BIOMASS Handbook", no. 2, 21pp. Scientific Committee on Antarctic Research, Cambridge.

Laws, R. M. (1981). Seal surveys, South Orkney Islands, 1971 and 1974. *British Antarctic Survey Bulletin* No. 54, 136–139.

Laws, R. M. and Taylor, R. J. F. (1957). A mass dying of crabeater seals, *Lobodon carcinophagus* (Gray). *Proceedings of the Zoological Society of London* **129**, 315–324.

Le Boeuf, B. J. (1974). Male–male competition and reproductive success in elephant seals. *American Zoologist* **14**, 163–176.

Lindsey, A. A. (1937). The Weddell seal in the Bay of Whales. *Journal of Mammalogy* **18**, 127–144.

Lindsey, A. A. (1938). Notes on the crabeater seal. *Journal of Mammalogy* **19**, 456–461.

Ling, J. K. and Bryden, M. M. (1981). Southern elephant seal—*Mirounga leonina* Linnaeus, 1758. In "Handbook of Marine Mammals" (S. H. Ridgway and R. J. Harrison, eds), vol. 2, Seals, pp. 297–327. Academic Press, London and New York.

Lythgoe, J. N. and Dartnall, H. J. A. (1970). A deep sea rhodopsin in a mammal. *Nature* (Lond.) **227**, 955–956.

McCann, T. S. (1980a). Population structure and social organization of southern elephant seals, *Mirounga leonina* (L.). *Biological Journal of the Linnaean Society* **14**, 133–150.

McCann, T. S. (1980b). Territoriality and breeding behaviour of adult male Antarctic fur seals, *Arctocephalus gazella*. *Journal of Zoology* (Lond.) **192**, 295–310.

McCann, T. S. (1981a). Aggression and sexual activity of male southern elephant seals, *Mirounga leonina*. *Journal of Zoology* (Lond.) **195**, 295–310.

McCann, T. S. (1981b). "The social organization and behaviour of the southern elephant seal, *Mirounga leonina* (L.)". Ph.D. Thesis, University of London.

McCann, T. S. (in press). Size, status and demography of southern elephant seal *Mirounga leonina* populations. *In* "Studies of Sea Mammals in South Latitudes" (J. K. Ling and M. M. Bryden, eds). Proceedings of a Symposium of the 52nd ANZAAS Congress.

Mansfield, A. W. (1958). The breeding behaviour and reproductive cycle of the Weddell seal (*Leptonychotes weddelli* Lesson). *Falkland Islands Dependencies Survey, Scientific Reports* No. 18, 1–41.

Markham, B. J. (1971). Catalogo de los anfibios, reptiles, aves y mamiferos de la Provincia de Magallanes (Chile). Instituto de la Patagonia, Chile.

Matthews, L. (1929). The natural history of the elephant seal. *"Discovery" Reports* **1**, 233–256.

Millar, J. S. (1977). Adaptive features of mammalian reproduction. *Evolution* **31**, 370–386.

Müller-Schwarze, D. and Müller-Schwarze C. (1975). Relations between leopard seals and Adelie penguins. *Rapports et Procès-Verbaux des Reunions Conseil International Pour l'Exploration de la Mer* **169**, 394–404.

Müller-Schwarze, D., Walz, E. C., Trivelpiece, W. and Volkman, N. J. (1978). Breeding status of southern elephant seals at King George Island. *Antarctic Journal of the United States* **13**, 157–158.

Murphy, R. C. (1914). Notes on the sea elephant, *Mirounga leonina* Linne. *Bulletin of the American Museum of Natural History* **33**, 63–79.

Murphy, R. C. (1948). "Logbook for Grace: Whaling brig Daisy, 1912–1913". Robert Hale Ltd., London.

Murray, M. D. (1981). The breeding of the southern elephant seal, *Mirounga leonina* L., on the Antarctic continent. *Polar Record* **20**, 370–371.

Naumov, A. G. and Chekunova, V. I. (1980). Energy requirements of pinnipeds (Pinnipedia). *Oceanology* (Moscow) **20**, 348–350.

Øritsland, T. (1970a). Biology and population dynamics of Antarctic seals. *In* "Antarctic Ecology" (M. W. Holdgate, ed.), Vol. 1, pp. 361–366. Academic Press, London and New York.

Øritsland, T. (1970b). Sealing and seal research in the South-west Atlantic pack ice, September–October, 1964. In "Antarctic Ecology" (M. W. Holdgate, ed.), Vol. 1, pp. 367–376. Academic Press, London and New York.

Øritsland, T. (1977). Food consumption of seals in the Antarctic pack ice. *In* "Adaptations within Antarctic Ecosystems" (G. A. Llano, ed.), pp. 749–768. Proceedings of the 3rd SCAR Symposium on Antarctic biology. Smithsonian Institution, Washington, D.C.

Payne, M. R. (1977). Growth of a fur seal population. *Philosophical Transactions of the Royal Society of London* **B279**, 67–80.

Payne, M. R. (1978). Population size and age determination in the Antarctic fur seal *Arctocephalus gazella*. *Mammal Review* **8**, 67–73.

Payne, M. R. (1979a). Fur seals *Arctocephalus tropicalis* and *Arctocephalus gazella* crossing the Antarctic Convergence at South Georgia, South Atlantic Ocean. *Mammalia* **43**, 93–98.

Payne, M. R. (1979b). Growth in the Antarctic fur seal *Arctocephalus gazella*. *Journal of Zoology* (Lond.) **187**, 1–20.

Peaker, M. and Goode, J. A. (1978). The milk of the fur seal, *Arctocephalus tropicalis gazella*: in particular the composition of the aqueous phase. *Journal of*

Zoology (Lond.) **185,** 469–476. (The species concerned was in fact the elephant seal, *Mirounga leonina.*)

Penney, R. L. and Lowry, G. (1967). Leopard seal predation on Adelie penguins. *Ecology* **48,** 878–882.

Perkins, J. E. (1945). Biology at Little America III, the West Base of the United States Antarctic Service Expedition 1939–1941. *Proceedings of the American Philosophical Society* **89,** 270–284.

Pierard, J. and Bisaillon, A. (1979). Osteology of the Ross seal *Ommatophoca rossi. Antarctic Research Series* **31,** 1–24.

Pond, C. M. (1977). The significance of lactation in the evolution of mammals. *Evolution* **31,** 177–199.

Racovitza, E. G. (1900). La vie des animaux et des plantes dans l'Antarctique. *Bulletin du Societe Royale Belge de Geographie* (Brussels) **24,** 177–230.

Ray, C. (1970). Population ecology of Antarctic seals. *In* "Antarctic Ecology" (M. W. Holdgate, ed.), Vol 1, pp. 398–414. Academic Press, London and New York.

Reeves, R. R. and Ling, J. K. (1981). Hooded seal—*Cystophora cristata* Erxleben 1777. *In* "Handbook of Marine Mammals" (S. H. Ridgway and R. J. Harrison, eds), Vol. 2, Seals, pp. 171–194. Academic Press, London and New York.

Repenning, C. A., Peterson, R. S. and Hubbs, C. L. (1971). Contributions to the systematics of the southern fur seals, with particular reference to the Juan Fernandez and Guadelupe species. *In* "Antarctic Pinnipedia" (W. H. Burt, ed.). *Antarctic Research Series* **18,** 1–34. American Geophysical Union, Washington, D.C.

Roberts, A. (1951). "The Mammals of South Africa". The Mammals of South Africa Book Fund, Johannesburg.

Ronald, K. and Healey, P. J. (1981). Harp seal—*Phoca groenlandica* Erxleben, 1777. *In* "Handbook of Marine Mammals" (S. H. Ridgway and R. J. Harrison, eds), Vol. 2, Seals, pp. 55–87. Academic Press, London and New York.

Rounsevell, D. and Eberhard, I. (1980). Leopard seals, *Hydrurga leptonyx* (Pinnipedia), at Macquarie island from 1949 to 1979. *Australian Wildlife Research* **7,** 403–415.

Scheffer, V. B. (1950). Growth layers on the teeth of Pinnipedia as an indication of age. *Science* (New York) **112,** 309–311.

Scheffer, V. B. (1958). "Seals, Sea Lions and Walruses. A Review of the Pinnipedia". Stanford University Press, California.

Scolaro, J. A. (1976). Censo de elefantes marinos (*Mirounga leonina,* L.) en el territorio continental Argentino. Comission Nacional de Estudios Geo-Heliofisicos, Centro Nacional Patagonico, Informes Tecnicos, 1.4.1, pp. 12.

Seal, U. S., Erickson, A. W., Siniff, D. B. and Cline, D. R. (1971a). Blood chemistry and protein polymorphism in three species of Antarctic seals (*Lobodon carcinophagus, Leptonychotes weddelli* and *Mirounga leonina*). *In* "Antarctic Pinnipedia" (W. H. Burt, ed.). *Antarctic Research Series* **18,** 181–192. American Geophysical Union, Washington, D.C.

Seal, U. S., Erickson, A. W., Siniff, D. B. and Hofman, R. J. (1971b) Biochemical, population genetic, phylogenetic and cytological studies of antarctic seal species. *In* "Symposium on Antarctic Ice an Water Masses" (G. Deacon, ed.), pp. 77–95. Scientific Committee on Antarctic Research, Cambridge.

Seber, G. A. F. (1973). "The Estimation of Animal Abundance". Hafner Press, New York.

Sergeant, D. E. (1973). Feeding, growth and productivity of northwest Atlantic harp seals (*Pagophilus groenlandicus*). *Journal of the Fisheries Research Board of Canada* **30**, 17–29.

Shaughnessy, P. B. (1969). Transferrin polymorphism and population structure of the Weddell seal *Leptonychotes weddelli* (Lesson). *Australian Journal of Biological Sciences* **22**, 1581–1584.

Sinha, A. A. and Erickson, A. W. (1972). Ultrastructure of the placenta of Antarctic seals during the first third of pregnancy. *American Journal of Anatomy*, **141**, 317–327.

Siniff, D. B. (1982). Seal population dynamics and ecology. *Journal of the Royal Society of New Zealand* **11**, 317–327.

Siniff, D. B. and Bengtson, J. L. (1977). Observations and hypotheses concerning the interactions among crabeater seals, leopard seals and killer whales. *Journal of Mammalogy* **58**, 414–416.

Siniff, D. B. and Stone, S. (in press). The role of the leopard seal in the trophodynamics of the Antarctic marine ecosystem. *In* "Nutrient Cycles and Food Chains" (W. R. Siegfried, P. R. Condy and R. M. Laws, eds). Proceedings of the 4th SCAR Symposium on Antarctic Biology. Sprinter-Verlag, Berlin.

Siniff, D. B., Cline, D. R. and Erickson, A. W. (1970). Population densities of seals in the Weddell Sea, Antarctica in 1968. *In* "Antarctic Ecology" (M. W. Holdgate, ed.), Vol. 1, pp. 377–394. Academic Press, New York and London.

Siniff, D. B., Tester, J. R. and Kuechle, V. B. (1971). Some observations on the activity patterns of Weddell seals as recorded by telemetry. In "Antarctic Pinnipedia" (W. H. Burt, ed.), *Antarctic Research Series* **18**, 173–180. American Geophysical Union, Washington, D.C.

Siniff, D. B., DeMaster, D. P., Hofman, R. J. and Eberhardt, L. L. (1977). An analysis of the dynamics of a Weddell seal population. *Ecological Monographs* **47**, 319–335.

Siniff, D. B., Stirling, I., Bengtson, J. L. and Reichle, R. A. (1979). Social and reproductive behaviour of crabeater seals (*Lobodon carcinophagus*) during the austral spring. *Canadian Journal of Zoology* **57**, 2243–2255.

Siniff, D. B., Stone, S., Reichle, D. and Smith, T. (1980). Aspects of leopard seals (*Hydrurga leptonyx*) in the Antarctic Peninsula pack ice. *Antarctic Journal of the United States* **15**, 160.

Smith, E. A. and Burton, R. W. (1970). Weddell seals of Signy Island. *In* "Antarctic Ecology" (M. W. Holdgate, ed.), Vol. 1, pp. 415–428. Academic Press, New York and London.

Smith, T. G. (1973). Population dynamics of the ringed seal in the Canadian eastern Arctic. *Fisheries Research Board of Canada, Bulletin* **181**, pp. 55.

Söderberg, S. (1977). Falling age at sexual maturity in Baltic seals. Proceedings from the Symposium on the Conservation of Baltic Seals, April 26–28, 1977, Haikko, Finland, pp. 27–31.

Solyanik, G. A. (1964). Experiment in marking seals from small ships. *Soviet Antarctic Expedition Bulletin* **5**, 212.

Sorensen, J. H. (1950). Elephant seals of Campbell Island. New Zealand Department of Scientific and Industrial Research, Wellington, Cape Expedition Series, Bulletin 6, pp. 31.

Stewart, R. E. A. and Lavigne, D. M. (1980). Neonatal growth of northwest Atlantic harp seals, *Pagophilus groenlandicus*. *Journal of Mammalogy* **61**, 670–680.

Stirling, I. (1969a). Ecology of the Weddell seal in McMurdo Sound Antarctica. *Ecology* **50**, 573–586.

Stirling, I. (1969b). Tooth wear as a mortality factor in the Weddell seal *Leptonychotes weddelli*. *Journal of Mammalogy* **50**, 559–565.

Stirling, I. (1969c). Distribution and abundance of the Weddell seal in the western Ross Sea, Antarctica. *New Zealand Journal of Marine and Freshwater Research* **3**, 191–200.

Stirling, I. (1971a). Population dynamics of the Weddell seal (*Leptonychotes weddelli*) in McMurdo Sound, Antarctica, 1966–1968. *In* "Antarctic Pinnipedia" (W. H. Burt, ed.), *Antarctic Research Series* **18**, 141–161. American Geophysical Union, Washington, D.C.

Stirling, I. (1971b). Population aspects of Weddell seal harvesting at McMurdo Sound, Antarctica. *Polar Record* **15**, 653–667.

Stirling, I. (1975). Factors affecting the evolution of social behaviour in the pinnipedia. *Rapports Procès-Verbaux des Reunions Conseil International Pour l'Exploration de la mer* **169**, 205–212.

Stirling, I. and Kooyman, G. L. (1971). The crabeater seal *Lobodon carcinophagus* in McMurdo Sound Antarctica and the origin of mummified seals. *Journal of Mammalogy* **52**, 175–180.

Stoddart, D. R. (1972). Pinnipeds or Sirenians at Western Indian Ocean islands. *Journal of Zoology* (Lond.) **167**, 207–217.

Stone, H. S. and Siniff, D. B. (1983). Leopard seal feeding and food consumption in Antarctic spring and summer. Proceedings of the Fourth Biennial Conference on the Biology of Marine Mammals, San Franciso, December 14–18, 1981.

Tedman, R. A. and Bryden, M. M. (1979). Cow-pup behaviour of the Weddell seal, *Leptonychotes weddelli* (Pinnipedia), in McMurdo Sound, Antarctica. *Australian Wildlife Research* **6**, 19–38.

Thomas, J. DeMaster, D., Stone, S. and Andriashek, D. (1980). Observations of a newborn Ross seal pup (*Ommatophoca rossi*) near the Antarctic Peninsula. *Canadian Journal of Zoology* **58**, 2156–2158.

Tikhomirov, E. A. (1975). Biology of the ice forms of seals in the Pacific section of the Antarctic. *Rapports Procès-Verbaux des Reunions Conseil International Pour l'Exploration de la mer* **169**, 409–412.

Trouessart, E. L. (1906). Mammifères pinnipedes. *In* "Expedition Antarctique Française (1903–1905)" (J.B.A.E. Charcot, ed.), pp. 1–27. Masson et Cie, Paris.

Turbott, E. G. (1952). Seals of the Southern Ocean. *In* "The Antarctic Today" (F. A. Simpson, ed.), pp. 195–215. Wellington, New Zealand.

Valette, L. H. (1906). Viaje à las Islas Orcades Australes. Republica Argentina, Anales del Ministerio de Agricultura, Seccion de Zootecuia, Bacteriologi, Veterinaria y Zoologia, Tomo III, 1–68. Buenos Aires.

van Aarde, R. J. and Pascal, M. (1980). Marking southern elephant seals on Îles Kerguelen. *Polar Record* **20**, 62–65.

Whitehead, H. P. (1981). "The behaviour and ecology of the humpback whale in the northwestern Atlantic". Ph.D. Thesis, University of Cambridge.

Wild, F. (1923) "Shackleton's Last Voyage". Appendix II, Natural History. Cassell and Co., London.

Wilson, E. A. (1907). Mammalia (Whales and Seals). In "National Antarctic Expedition, 1901–1904, Natural History". Trustees British Museum, London.

Yaldwyn, J. C. (1958). Decapod crustacea from subantarctic seal and shag stomachs. *Records of the Dominion Museum* **3**, 121–127.

13

Whales

S. G. Brown and C. H. Lockyer

1. Introduction

1.1 The species involved

Seven species or subspecies of Mysticete (baleen or whalebone) whales and eight species or subspecies of Odontocete (toothed) whales occur in waters south of the Antarctic Convergence (Table 1). Six of the baleen whales belong to the family Balaenopteridae (rorquals). There is no evidence that the other southern hemisphere rorqual, Bryde's whale *Balaenoptera edeni-brydei*, occurs in Antarctic waters. There is no confirmed record of the Pygmy right whale *Caperea marginata* south of the Antarctic Convergence, though it has been recorded from the Falkland Islands (Ross *et al.*, 1975).

The eight species or subspecies of toothed whales belong to four cetacean families. In addition to these species, the dusky dolphin *Lagenorhynchus obscurus* has been recorded from Îles Kerguelen, and so may occur south of the Antarctic Convergence. All records of the southern right whale dolphin *Lissodelphis peronii* are north of the Antarctic Convergence except for a single nineteenth century sight record (Fraser, 1955).

All of the baleen whales and the sperm whale are at present, or have been in the recent past, caught by the Antarctic whaling industry, the rorquals and the sperm whale being the mainstay of the industry. The killer whale, the two beaked whales and the pilot whale have also been caught in much smaller numbers. Commerson's dolphin is a small incidental catch of crab fishing in Argentina (Mitchell, 1975).

1.2 Zoogeography

There is no exclusively polar cetacean in the southern hemisphere and all the species occurring south of the Antarctic Convergence are more widely distributed. The five balaenopterid species are found in both southern and northern hemispheres and although they undertake extensive latitudinal migrations, the populations of the two hemispheres are separate, a gap between the two stocks being maintained at all times. There is as yet no evidence for the occurrence of the pygmy blue whale in the northern hemisphere. There are two forms of the minke whale in the southern hemisphere, the main difference between them being that one has the distinct white band on the flipper, which is characteristic of the species in the northern hemisphere, and the other is without the band. This second form has been described as a separate species *Balaenoptera bonaerensis* by some authors (Kasuya and Ichihara, 1965) but the relationship of the two forms is not yet clear (Omura, 1975) and a single species is recognized here.

The southern right whale is the southern hemisphere member of the genus *Eubalaena*. The migrations of this genus are generally similar to those of the *Balaenopteridae*, but less extensive, and its distribution is markedly antitropical with another species in the North Atlantic and North Pacific.

The eight Odontocetes occurring south of the Antarctic Convergence represent a minority of the 42 marine species inhabiting the southern hemisphere (Nishiwaki, 1977). The sperm whale is essentially a tropical and warm temperate species in both hemispheres and most of the females and immature whales of both sexes are found in these waters, with only some of the adult males moving into polar waters. Arnoux's beaked whale and the southern bottlenose whale are restricted to the southern hemisphere. Each has a single additional species, in the North Pacific (Baird's beaked whale *Berardius bairdii*) and North Atlantic (northern bottlenose whale *Hyperoodon ampullatus*) respectively.

The killer whale is world-wide in distribution, with concentrations in the colder waters of both hemispheres. The long-finned pilot whale has a distinct antitropical distribution, with one subspecies in the southern hemisphere and one in the northern hemisphere (*Globicephala melaena melaena*) (Davies, 1960). The hourglass dolphin is one of three species of the genus *Lagenorhynchus* occurring in temperate and colder waters of the southern hemisphere and there are also three northern hemisphere species. Commerson's dolphin has the southernmost distribution of the four species of the genus *Cephalorhynchus* which is confined to the southern hemisphere. The genus *Phocoena* includes four species, two in each hemisphere, and the spectacled porpoise is the only one known to inhabit offshore island waters.

Gaskin (1976) has reviewed the evolution and zoogeography of cetaceans. He suggests that the temperate southern hemisphere may have been a major evolutionary centre for many Odontocete groups. Fordyce (1977) notes that the earliest known fossil Mysticetes (*Mauicetus spp*) occur in the mid-Oligocene of New Zealand; he postulates that rapid changes in productivity,

TABLE I

Cetacean species occurring south of the Antarctic Convergence

Mysticetes

BALAENOPTERIDAE
Blue whale — *Balaenoptera musculus*
Pygmy blue whale — *Balaenoptera musculus brevicauda*
Fin whale — *Balaenoptera physalus*
Sei whale — *Balaenoptera borealis*
Minke whale — *Balaenoptera acutorostrata*
Humpback whale — *Megaptera novaeangliae*

BALAENIDAE
Southern Right whale — *Eubalaena australis*

Odontocetes

PHYSETERIDAE
Sperm whale — *Physeter macrocephalus*

ZIPHIIDAE
Arnoux's beaked whale — *Berardius arnuxii*
Southern bottlenose whale — *Hyperoodon planifrons*

DELPHINIDAE
Killer whale — *Orcinus orca*
Long-finned pilot whale — *Globicephala melaena edwardii*
Hourglass dolphin — *Lagenorhynchus cruciger*
Commerson's dolphin — *Cephalorhynchus commersonii*

PHOCOENIDAE
Spectacled porpoise — *Phocoena dioptrica*

associated with the establishment of the Circum-Antarctic Current at that time, may have led to the New Zealand region being a focal point for Mysticete evolution. Davies (1963) discusses the importance of Pleistocene ocean temperatures in the evolution of the present antitropical distribution of some species.

2. Methods of Study

Whales are elusive animals; many species are inhabitants of the open ocean and access to them is difficult. Their study owes much to the facilities provided by the whaling industry, and it was the rise and spread of modern whaling, especially in Antarctic waters, which gave the opportunity for studies which laid the foundations of our knowledge of the biology of the commercially important species.

Knowledge of the biology of some of the smaller species not hunted by whalers is still fragmentary and dependent upon chance stranded specimens and scattered observations at sea. This applies to all of the Odontocetes in Table 1 except the sperm whale, killer whale and long-finned pilot whale. Information on the biology of the last species is mostly derived from studies of northern hemisphere animals. Similarly, some information is available for the northern bottlenose whale *Hyperoodon ampullatus* and Baird's beaked whale *Berardius bairdii* in the northern hemisphere but not for their southern hemisphere counterparts. Where species are not mentioned, little or no information is available.

The statistics of catches worldwide are a major source of information on the distribution and population abundance of whales. They are published annually by the Bureau of International Whaling Statistics in Norway and include details of species, sex and length; place and date of catch, and information on the catching effort employed.

Biological collections from captured whales examined at shore whaling stations or on pelagic factory ships, provide information on various aspects of the life cycle. Ovaries, testes samples, examination of mammary glands, foetal records and measurements reveal the reproductive cycle; ear plugs and baleen plates from Mysticetes, and teeth from Odontocetes give information on age; stomach contents provide data on food and feeding. Body measurements yield information on growth and, with external characteristics, on racial identity. Studies of blood groups may also provide information on the latter.

Systematic recording of whales seen at sea, from commercial whale scouting vessels or independent research ships, is a source of data on distribution and population abundance. The marking of whales with an internal dart fired into the animal at sea and recovered when it is later killed and processed, has provided information on their movements, migrations, stock identity, population estimates and a means of checking age determination methods (Brown, 1977b, 1978).

In recent years the application to whales of mathematical methods of population analysis developed in fisheries research has led to estimates of population parameters and stock sizes, enabling much improved management of commercial whaling to be introduced (Chapman *et al.*, 1964; Chapman, 1974; Mackintosh, 1965).

3. Basic Biology

3.1 General description

A general account of the attributes of whales is given in Mackintosh (1965) and more detailed accounts of their anatomy, physiology and behaviour in Slijper (1962) and Andersen (1969).

3.1.1 Mysticetes

The approximate lengths at sexual maturity and maximum growth for the six balaenopterids occurring in Antarctic waters are given in Table II. Adult southern hemisphere blue, fin and sei whales are slightly larger than those of the northern hemisphere (Mackintosh, 1965). In Mysticetes it is believed that simple pairing occurs but whether these pairs persist throughout the breeding season or from year to year is unknown. The females are a little larger than the males.

Mysticetes are characterized by the presence of two rows of transverse baleen plates in the mouth, one on each side of the upper jaw. These take the place of teeth and form a filter mechanism to sieve food organisms, small planktonic animals or shoaling fish, from the sea (Mackintosh, 1965). The shape, colour and texture of the baleen plates and fringe of bristles are characteristics for the different species; the number of plates in the baleen row also varies according to the species, ranging from 130 to 480 (Nemoto, 1959). The large right whales have the longest baleen plates and the finest bristles and, in general, the finer the fringe of bristles, the smaller the food organisms eaten.

Associated with the feeding mechanism of the rorquals and the humpback whale, but not the right whale, is a series of parallel ventral grooves running from the chin towards the umbilicus and covering the whole undersurface of the mouth, throat and body between the flippers (see 6.1.1).

3.1.2 Odontocetes

Available measurements for the species occurring in Antarctic waters are included in Table II. All Odontocetes possess teeth though in some of the Ziphiidae functional teeth are absent. The teeth are homodont and are used for capturing prey which is then swallowed whole. Species feeding on squid generally have fewer teeth than those feeding on fish. The sperm whale is the largest of the Odontocetes and is the most strongly dimorphic in size of all cetaceans, a dimorphism which appears to be a corollary of the species' polygynous social behaviour (Best, 1976a). Marked dimorphism also occurs in killer whales. In most other Odontocete species the males are larger than the females. Pilot whales are also polygynous (Sergeant, 1962) and other species may be, though little is known of their social behaviour.

TABLE II

Measurements of species occurring in the Antarctic.
Data from Mackintosh (1972), Mitchell (1975)

		Approximate length at	
		Sexual maturity (m)	Maximum growth (m)
MYSTICETES			
Blue whale		23.0	30.5
Pygmy blue whale		18.9	21.1
Fin whale		19.5	26.0
Sei whale		13.7	18.3
Minke whale		7.5	9.0
Humpback whale		11.9	15.2
Southern right whale		—	18.3
ODONTOCETES			
Sperm whale	♂	11.9	18.3
Sperm whale	♀	8.8	11.6
Arnoux's beaked whale		—	10.0
Southern bottlenose whale		—	7.5
Killer whale[a]	♂	6.7	9.4
Killer whale[a]	♀	4.9	8.2
Long-finned pilot whale	♂	—	6.0
Long-finned pilot whale	♀	—	4.6
Hourglass dolphin		—	1.8
Commerson's dolphin		—	1.4
Spectacled porpoise		—	2.0

[a]Northern hemisphere specimens.

3.2 Annual cycle, distribution and migrations

3.2.1. Mysticetes

As already noted (1.2) the stocks of balaenopterids in northern and southern hemispheres are separate. In all five species there is believed to be an annual cycle of breeding in tropical, subtropical or warm temperate waters in winter and feeding in polar or cold temperate waters in summer, with spring and autumn migrations between the two regions. Gestation lasts nearly a year so that both mating and parturition take place in winter in warm waters. Krill *Euphausia superba* and other planktonic crustaceans forming the staple food of these species are concentrated in Antarctic and cold temperate waters and there is apparently little available food in warmer waters, because blue, fin, humpback and sei whales examined at subtropical whaling stations in winter usually have little or no food in their stomachs compared with animals examined on the Antarctic feeding grounds (Bannister and Baker, 1967; Best, 1967; Chittleborough, 1965; Mackintosh and Wheeler, 1929). There is therefore also an annual cycle of feeding and non-feeding periods, and during the latter the whales live largely on reserves of fat built up in the blubber during the summer feeding period.

Most is known about the seasonal distribution and migrations of humpback whales (Dawbin, 1966). They breed in tropical coastal waters with a temperature of about 25°C and there are at least six southern hemisphere stocks which concentrate in winter in breeding areas on the east and west coasts of South America, Africa and Australia, and among the island groups of the south-west Pacific ocean. Each stock migrates southwards in the spring to Antarctic feeding grounds where they form five areas of concentration situated in the south-east Pacific, South Atlantic, to the south of South Africa, in the south-east Indian ocean, and to the south of New Zealand. Although concentrated in these five separate areas, evidence from whale marking shows that some whales from different breeding areas overlap on the feeding grounds. Nevertheless, most whales return northwards to the same breeding area season after season and there is little interchange of individuals between stocks, but presumably enough to ensure the apparent racial homogeneity of southern hemisphere humpback whales. The speed of migration averages about 15 degrees of latitude per month and there are no consistent differences in the speed of different age or breeding categories.

There is a very clear segregation in time of different classes or categories of humpback whales throughout the seasonal cycle. The southward spring migration is led by the recently pregnant females and the immature males, followed by resting females and mature males, and finally females in early lactation. On the Antarctic feeding grounds the different groups apparently become randomly mixed but on the northward migration they again segregate. Females at the end of lactation accompanied by weaning yearling calves depart northward first, followed in succession by immature animals, mature males with resting females, and finally females in late pregnancy. Pregnant females therefore spend the greatest amount of time on the feeding grounds south of 60°S (about 6.5 months, late November–May), and lactating females accompanied by their calves least (about 4.5 months, late December–April). Dawbin (1966) suggests that the marked decline in day length during their stay in Antarctic waters provides the stimulus initiating different migration times for lactating females and pregnant females and the annual cycle varies with changes in reproductive (hormonal) condition. The phenology of immatures of both sexes and of mature males appears to be relatively constant from season to season.

The southern hemisphere breeding grounds of the other balaenopterids are unknown and it is uncertain whether they assemble in concentrations in breeding areas like humpbacks, or remain widely dispersed in temperate and tropical waters. However, it is likely that there are one or more breeding stocks in each of the South Atlantic, Indian and South Pacific Oceans. Mackintosh (1966) discusses this problem in relation to blue and fin whales and notes that the available evidence is inconsistent. He mentions a record of a concentration of rorquals (including fin whales) far offshore in the central South Atlantic Ocean in 20°S latitude in August, and evidence that some fin whales move towards the continents in warmer latitudes in winter. They follow possible migration routes along continental coasts in deep water, not far beyond the continental slope. As in humpback whales, the migrations of the rorquals are in the form of a procession rather than a mass movement of the whole population. There is a prolonged stream of arrivals on the Antarctic feeding grounds from about September to January and of departure from about March to July (Mackintosh, 1966). Some blue and fin whales are, however, present in the Antarctic during the winter as shown by catches at South Georgia during June–August 1914–1919 (Harmer, 1931). Southward migration by fin whales from subtropical South American waters to the Antarctic feeding grounds, and northward migration from these to South African waters has been demonstrated by whale marking (Brown, 1962a).

In the Antarctic, blue and fin whales are found in all longitudes (Omura, 1973) but they are concentrated in certain sectors. This was recognized from catch statistics in the 1930s (Hjort et al., 1932) and on this basis the whaling grounds south of 50°S latitude were divided into five and later six Antarctic whaling Areas (Mackintosh, 1942):

Area	I	120° –60°W	Area IV	70°E –130°E
Area	II	60°W– 0°	Area V	130°E –170°W
Area	III	0° –70°E	Area VI	170°W–120°W

They have been adopted by the International Whaling Commission for management purposes for all of the commercially important baleen whales in the southern hemisphere. The southern boundary of the areas is the ice edge, but the northern boundary, originally at 50°S latitude, was later changed to 40°S and is now at the Equator.

The areas represent the grouping of blue and humpback whales more closely than that of fin whales. An analysis of the length distribution of fin whale catches (Laws, 1960), shows that the largest whales are distributed in four groups, broadly in Areas I, IV and V, but with one across the boundary of Areas II and III, suggesting that there is no separation here into two stocks. Whale marking has shown that most blue and fin whales return to the same region of the Antarctic after their winter migrations while some may travel hundreds of miles east or west on the feeding grounds within one summer season, often crossing the boundaries of whaling areas (Brown, 1962b).

Budylenko (1978) suggests that there are six southern hemisphere populations of sei whales, two (east and west) in each of the Atlantic, Indian and Pacific Oceans with possible additional populations in the central Indian and central Pacific Oceans. Migration between South American, South African and Australian waters, and the southern feeding grounds has been demonstrated by whale marking (Brown, 1977a). The general pattern of migration is similar to that of blue and fin whales, though the timing is a little later and they do not penetrate into such high latitudes (Budylenko, 1978; Gambell, 1968). On the feeding grounds south of 40°S latitude, catch statistics suggest that there are five concentrations, broadly related to Areas I, II, V and VI, and with one spanning the boundary of Areas III and IV (Omura, 1973). Marking has shown that the movements of sei whales in the Southern Ocean are similar to those of blue and fin whales but that movement within the whaling areas may be more restricted (Brown, 1977a).

There is little definite information on the existence of separate stocks of minke whales in the southern hemisphere. Doroshenko (1979) suggests there are at least four population units—"Brazilian", "Indian", "New Zealand" and "Chile–Peruvian". Few minke whales have been marked in warmer waters and there is as yet no evidence from marking of annual north–south migrations, but Ohsumi (1973) reports the finding of a marlin (*Makaira* sp.) spear in a whale shot in 64°S latitude in January, and this genus is widely distributed in tropical and subtropical waters of the Indian and Pacific Oceans. The occurrence of minke whales in subtropical and tropical waters in winter and spring (Best, 1974a; Williamson, 1975) suggests that they migrate into these waters, though Laws (1977) believes that Antarctic stocks may have a more southerly year-round distribution. In Antarctic waters in summer the species is circumpolar, but sightings densities indicate concentrations in the Atlantic, Indian and south-west Pacific sectors (Arsenev, 1960; Ohsumi *et al.*, 1970). There are relatively few north of the Antarctic Convergence and they are concentrated in high latitudes close to the ice edge, though there is very marked segregation of sexual and age groups, and younger animals do not move so far south. Taylor (1957) records a group overwintering in pools in sea ice; presumably this was an accidental occurrence.

The pygmy blue whale does not penetrate deep into Antarctic waters. The largest numbers have been caught in summer in a restricted zone between approximately 40°S and 55°S latitude, extending from 0 to 80°E, with concentrations around Marion Island, Îles Crozet and Îles Kerguelen (Ichihara, 1966b). The winter distribution is unknown and they may disperse widely in the Indian Ocean, as there are winter and early spring records in subtropical South African and West Australian waters (Gambell, 1964; Chittleborough, 1963). Zemsky and Boronin (1964), however, suggest that the subspecies remains in the same region throughout the year, breeding in the northern part. A specimen marked in 56°S latitude on 1 December 1962 was captured in 44°S on 4 April 1963 (Ichihara, 1966b). Records from 33°S latitude in Chile (Aguayo L., 1974) indicate that pygmy blue whales may have a much wider distribution.

Much of the information on the distribution of the southern right whale comes from records of nineteenth century whaling, during which the species was much reduced in numbers (Townsend, 1935), but the recent recovery of the species is providing additional information (Best, 1970b, 1974a; Cawthorn, 1978; Omura *et al.*, 1969). There is no direct evidence of the existence of separate stocks, but the distribution in coastal waters in winter suggests the possibility of a stock on each side of the South Atlantic, Indian and South Pacific Oceans.

The migrations are apparently less extensive than in balaenopterids. Available evidence from the south-east Atlantic and south-west Indian Oceans suggests that the winter is spent in latitudes around 20°S–30°S, where most of the calving and mating takes place, and that the whales migrate south to arrive on the southern feeding grounds in late summer or early autumn (Best, 1970b).

In the south-west Pacific Ocean the pattern is apparently different, with mating and calving taking place in the New Zealand "stock" at Campbell Island (52°30′S, 169°10′E) in winter, and the whales moving north in the spring and summer, and returning south in the autumn (Cawthorn, 1978). On the feeding grounds in summer the majority appear to be distributed between 40°S and 50°S latitude; some move further south though rarely south of 60°S (Omura et al., 1969). They occur regularly in small numbers around South Georgia in February and March, and some have been caught as far south as the South Shetland Islands.

3.2.2 Odontocetes

There is much less knowledge of the biology of the Odontocetes. Most information is available for the sperm whale and this does not have the pronounced seasonal cycle with the intimate links between reproduction, feeding and migrations found in the Mysticetes (see 5.2).

The northern and southern hemisphere populations of sperm whales are generally assumed to be separate breeding stocks because there is a six-month difference in mean pairing dates between them. The southern hemisphere populations were divided by Best (1974b) into seven, or possibly eight stocks on the basis of density distribution of catches and sightings, and on geographical boundaries and the movements of marked whales. There is, however, little direct evidence of stock identity (Best, 1976a). Nine stocks or Divisions are now recognized by the International Whaling Commission for management purposes, with northern boundaries at the Equator and southern boundaries at the ice edge. The nine Divisions are:

Division 1	West Atlantic	(60°W– 30°W)
Division 2	East Atlantic	(30°W– 20°E)
Division 3	West Indian	(20°E – 60°E)
Division 4	Central Indian	(60°E – 90°E)
Division 5	East Indian	(90°E –130°E)
Division 6	East Australian	(130°E –160°E)
Division 7	New Zealand	(160°E –170°W)
Division 8	Central Pacific	(170°W–100°W)
Division 9	East Pacific	(100°W– 60°W)

The region of the Sub-tropical Convergence (c. 40°S) generally marks the southern limit of distribution of females and young males, though this limit extends to 45–50°S in the Indian and south-west Pacific Oceans (Ohsumi and Nasu, 1970). South of this limit only adult male sperm whales occur. In warmer waters seasonal movements northwards in the autumn and southwards in the spring are recorded (Best, 1969b; Gambell, 1967). Whale marking has provided direct evidence of some extensive north–south movements, and the seasonal appearance of Antarctic diatoms on the skin of medium-sized and large males in south temperate waters (Best, 1974b) indicate northward movements from Antarctic waters, as does the presence of the beaks of Antarctic cephalopods in the stomachs of sperm whales killed off Durban, South Africa (Clarke, 1972). It is, however, not yet certain that these movements are regular annual seasonal migrations comparable with those of Mysticetes.

Brownell (1974) reviews knowledge of the biology of the smaller Odontocetes found in Antarctic waters and plots the records of their occurrence in detail while Nishiwaki (1977) has charted the approximate southern boundaries of their distribution in the Antarctic. Very little is known of the biology of most species.

The southern bottlenose whale and Arnoux's beaked whale are both circumpolar and apparently occur as far south as the ice edge in the southern summer. Taylor (1957) records a specimen of the latter species in pools in the sea ice in Prince Gustav Channel in winter. "Bottlenose whales" (species uncertain) are regularly seen in leads at Halley Bay (75°S) in winter (Laws, personal communication). Both species are recorded from the coasts of Australia, New Zealand, South Africa and from South American waters.

Identification at sea is difficult and some sight records of "bottlenose whales" in the Southern Ocean may relate to either species (Brownell, 1974; Gianuca and Castello, 1976). McCann (1975) suggests that Arnoux's beaked whale makes seasonal north-south migrations but this needs confirmation.

The killer whale occurs throughout Antarctic waters and has been seen in pools within sea ice in winter (Taylor, *op. cit.*). Around sub-Antarctic islands its occurrence appears to be related to the seasonal abundance of southern elephant seals and penguins (Condy *et al.*, 1978; Voisin, 1972, 1976).

The long-finned pilot whale appears to be generally distributed throughout the Southern Ocean (Davies, 1960). There are few published sight records in Antarctic waters but specimens have been collected at Îles Kerguelen. The hourglass dolphin has a circumpolar distribution in temperate and Antarctic waters.

Commerson's dolphin occurs commonly in coastal waters off Argentina and Tierra del Fuego, and around the Falkland Islands, but apparently not on the Pacific coast of South America (Brownell, 1974). In Antarctic waters it is recorded from South Georgia and Îles Kerguelen, and these may be separate populations. However, pelagic sighting records from Drake Passage (Aguayo L., 1975) suggest that the species may be distributed more widely than present records indicate.

There are very few records of the spectacled porpoise. It occurs in South American coastal waters from Uruguay to Tierra del Fuego and at the

TABLE III

Phenology of reproduction in baleen whales

Species	Month of conception	Gestation period (months)	Month and length at birth (m)	Suckling period (months)	Length at weaning (m)	References
Blue	June–July	11	May 7.0	7	12.8	Mackintosh and Wheeler, 1929; Laws, 1959; Lockyer, 1981a
Fin	June–July	11	May 6.4	7	11.5	
Sei	July	11–11.5	June 4.5	6	8.0	Gambell, 1968; Lockyer, 1977a
Minke	August–September	10	May–June 2.8	4	4.5	Williamson, 1975; Ivashin and Mikhalev, 1978; International Whaling Commission, 1979
Humpback	August	11.5	July–August 4.3	10.5–11	8.8	Chittleborough, 1958; Dawbin, 1966; Matthews, 1937
Southern right	August–October	10	May–July			Donnelly, 1969

Falkland Islands. Elsewhere there is one skull from the Auckland Islands (Baker, 1977) and two sight records from the same area (International Whaling Commission, 1978), and in Antarctic waters one specimen from South Georgia. Baker (*op. cit.*) suggests that it may have a circumpolar sub-Antarctic distribution and occur around other oceanic islands.

4. Growth and Age

4.1 Mysticetes

4.1.1 Foetal growth

The timing of conception and hence birth is strongly seasonal in Mysticetes, occurring in the winter months (see Table III). Foetal growth is characterized by gestation periods of 10–12 months, achieved by an exponential growth phase after about the initial five months from conception (Laws, 1959). This fits into the annual migration and feeding cycle, and the exponential growth phase follows the migration south to the polar feeding grounds. Usually a single foetus develops, although rarely multiple foetuses have been found (Kimura, 1957).

4.1.2 Postnatal growth

The calf. The blue, fin and sei whales suckle the calf for about 6–7 months (see Table III). This time period takes the calf into the summer polar feeding areas with its mother, where it is weaned. The evidence for the minke whale is different, however, and indicates a four month suckling period (International Whaling Commission, 1979), weaning occurring whilst still on the more northerly winter grounds.

The humpback whale has a comparatively long suckling period of nearly 11 months (Chittleborough, 1958; Dawbin, 1966) and the calf is weaned after returning to the temperate winter grounds during June and July. This pattern is very different from that of blue, fin, sei and minke whales. During the suckling phase, the calf increases its length by as much as twice the birth size. In terms of body weight, Lockyer (1981a) has predicted that blue, fin and sei whale calves at weaning will have increased their birth weight by 5–6 times.

Age determination. The most reliable and widely used method of age determination for baleen whales is that of counting growth layers in the ear

Fig. 1. Ear plug from a fin whale, cut to expose the growth layers in the core.

plug. This is a cellular structure composed of fats and keratin of epidermal origin. It is situated in the external auditory meatus, and continues to grow from a germinal epithelium at the proximal end nearest the middle ear throughout the life of the whale. The cells are deposited in alternating bands of light fatty cells and dark keratinized cells (Fig. 1). Each pair constitutes a growth layer, and for southern fin and sei whales there is evidence that one growth layer forms annually (Roe, 1967; Lockyer, 1972, 1974). In blue and minke whales also it has been assumed that one growth layer forms annually. In the humpback whale, however, Chittleborough (1959, 1960, 1962) believes that two growth layers form annually, but this is the only Mysticete whale for which there is any evidence that more than one growth layer forms annually.

Another method of determining age employs the ridges on the surface of the baleen plates, structures also of epidermal origin, but it is limited in its application to juvenile whales because the tip of the plate wears away.

In adult female whales, the ovaries can be used for obtaining an indirect estimate of age. The scars representing ovulations, corpora albicantia, persist in the ovaries, and if the ovulation rate is known, the number of corpora gives an estimate of the time since sexual maturity was attained. If the age at sexual maturity is known, the two can be added to give the total age.

In addition to estimates of total age from ear plugs, the age at sexual maturity can be determined from the transition phase between juvenile widely spaced and /or irregular growth layers and more compact and regular ones (Fig. 1). This has been well described for fin and sei whales (Lockyer, 1972, 1974). A similar pattern has also been observed in minke whale ear plugs and is considered to be correlated with age at sexual maturity (Masaki, 1979).

Growth in length.   The postnatal pattern of growth in baleen whales is typically negatively exponential, and in the first year, growth is very rapid. As puberty is reached the growth-rate slows and then continues at a decreasing rate until physical maturity is attained. At about this time, all the vertebral epiphyses have become fused, and further linear growth is not possible (Laws, 1961). This stage is generally not reached until an age of 25 years or more in rorquals. There is a slight difference in the maximum lengths reached by the two sexes, the female being generally about 5% greater.

The growth curve can be described by the von Bertalanffy formula for blue, fin and sei whales, from about the second year of life. This formula is:

$$L_t = L_\infty \left(1 - e^{-k(t+t_0)}\right),$$

where L is body length, t is age in years and ∞ is age when physical maturity is attained, k is a growth velocity constant and t_0 is a time constant (von Bertalanffy, 1938).

In Fig. 2, simplified average growth curves are shown for blue, fin, sei, minke and humpback whales; for each species the average age at sexual maturity is indicated. The criterion used as evidence of sexual maturity in females, is the presence in the ovaries of at least one corpus luteum or albicans. However, in males, histological examination of the testis tissue is the only completely reliable method. Presence of sperm may be seasonal, but usually the presence of open seminiferous tubules of more than a certain average diameter is a good indication of sexual maturity.

There is much variability within populations regarding growth-rate and also age at sexual maturity, and also between populations. Variations in mean maximum length and age at sexual maturity have been observed for the fin whale in different regions of the Antarctic (Ichihara, 1966a; Lockyer, 1977b, 1979, 1981a). The growth parameters of southern fin and sei whales have been observed to change significantly in some areas over the period commencing about 1930. In the southern hemisphere, between 60°W and 70°E (Areas II and III) the pre-pubertal growth-rate has increased. However, the length at sexual maturity appears to have remained constant, at about 90% maximum length, and so the average age at sexual maturity, determined from the ear plug transition phase, has declined from about 10–6 years in fin whales, and from about 11–8 years in sei whales (Lockyer, 1972, 1974) (Fig. 3). There have also been similar but less marked trends of change in other areas of the Antarctic (Lockyer, 1977b, 1979). These changes parallel the history of exploitation of these species, and one of the explanations advanced for this correlation has been the consequential decrease in intra- and inter-specific competition for food between the surviving whales (Gambell, 1973; Lockyer, 1978; Kawamura, 1978). Another factor to be considered is the massive depletion of the blue, humpback and right whale stocks prior to exploitation of fin and sei whales (Kawamura, 1978; Lockyer, 1972).

Interestingly, Masaki (1979) reported a change in mean age at sexual maturity for southern minke whales before they were hunted, based on the transition phase in ear plugs. The mean age fell from about 14 years for pre-1944 year classes to six years in the late 1960 year classes (Fig. 3). These changes in age at maturity cannot be a direct effect of exploitation of this species, because the hunting of minke whales did not commence seriously until after 1970, but they may be linked to the exploitation of sympatric species. The foods taken by all these species overlap to a greater or lesser

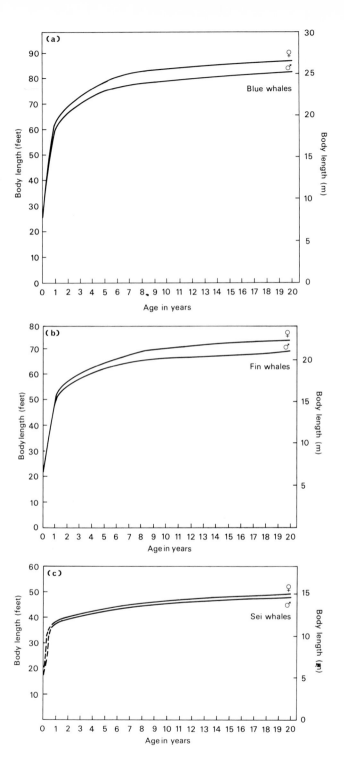

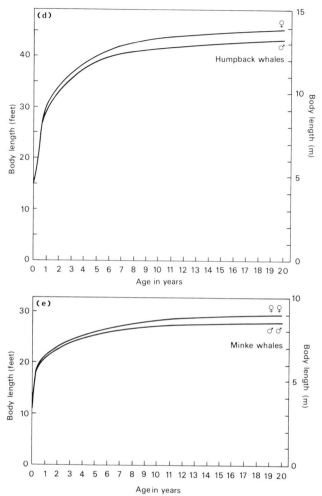

Fig. 2 (a–e). Average curves of body length at age, based mainly on catch data corrected for length bias, for five species of baleen whales.

extent at some period of time in the whales' life cycle and therefore competition is likely.

Growth in weight. The relationship between body length and weight in whales is found to be exponential and can be described by the formula,

$$W = aL^b$$

where W is body weight, L is body length, and a and b are constants. Lockyer (1976) has reviewed literature on this subject, and in Fig. 4, curvilinear relationships of weight and length are shown for different species. The weights used are average total weights at a given size, and incorporate an allowance for blood and fluid. However, they ignore seasonal trends related to changing fatness as well as sexual differences. Clearly, the right whales (assuming that southern and northern right whales have a similar shape and build) are the heaviest per unit length of all the baleen whales and the next heaviest are the humpback whales.

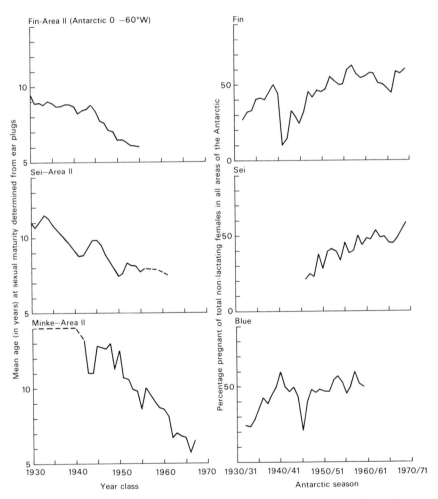

Fig. 3. The apparent decline in mean first age at sexual maturity in fin, sei and minke whales over time, and the apparent increase in percentage of pregnant females in the exploitable population over time in fin, sei and blue whales.

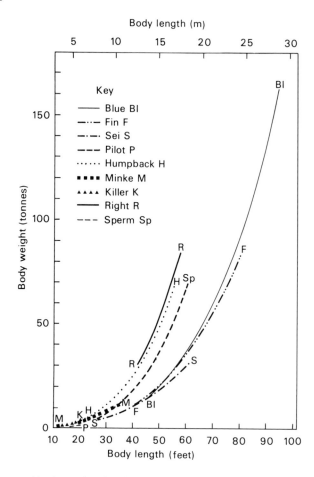

Fig. 4. Average total body weight at length for right, blue, fin, sei, minke, humpback, pilot, killer and sperm whales.

TABLE IV
Proportions by weight of different tissues in the body (after Lockyer, 1976)

Species	% of total body weight			
	Blubber	Muscle	Bone	Viscera
Right (N Pacific)	43	31	13	13
Blue	27	39	17	12
Fin	24	45	17	11
Sei	18	58	12	10
Minke	15	62	14	8
Sperm	33	34	10	9

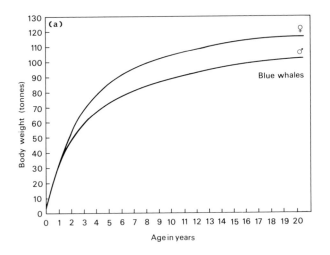

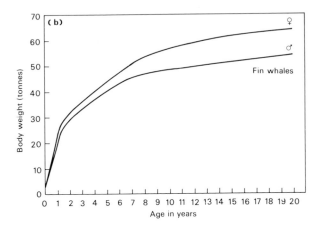

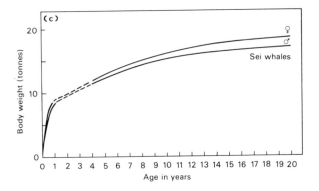

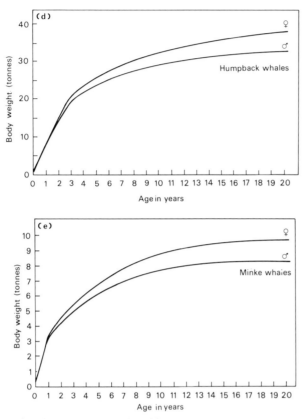

Fig. 5 (a–e). Predicted average curves of total body weight at age for five species of baleen whales.

The muscle and blubber content generally constitute 40–60%, and 15–30% respectively in the rorqual whales, but the right whale carries proportionately more blubber and less muscle than the rorquals. In Table IV the proportions by weight of different body tissues are given for several whale species.

By substituting weight for length, the linear growth curves illustrated in Fig. 2 can easily be converted to mean weight at age curves. In Fig. 5, this has been done for blue, fin, sei, minke and humpback whales. By sexual maturity, approximately 70–75% of the maximum body weight has been reached. The growth in body weight can be described by a formula based on the von Bertalanffy equation, substituting W for L as follows,

$$W_t = W_\infty \left(1 - e^{-k(t+t_0)}\right)^3.$$

This formulation of growth has the same drawback as the linear one, in that it does not fit the growth curve in the early years.

4.2 Odontocetes

4.2.1 Foetal growth

Sperm whales off South Africa are generally conceived during December and birth occurs about 14.5 months later in February or March, when usually a single calf is born (Best, 1968; Gambell, 1972). However, Bannister (1966, 1969) reports that gestation lasts about 16 months off western Australia.

The calf (of either sex) is about 4.05 m in length at birth and weighs just over one tonne. Growth in length is linear with time (Laws, 1959; Best, 1968; Gambell, 1972) and does not have an exponential phase such as that described for Mysticete whales.

Little is known concerning foetal growth in the other southern hemisphere Odontocetes considered here although Sergeant (1962) has provided a growth curve for pilot whales taken off Newfoundland, and there is a growth curve for *Berardius* off coastal Japan (Omura *et al.*, 1955); growth may be comparable for the respective southern species.

4.2.2 Postnatal growth

The calf. The suckling period of sperm whale calves is not definitely established and the most recent evidence is that the calf may continue to be suckled for up to two years (Best, 1974b). At the time of weaning it is about 6.7 m in length (Best, 1974b; Clarke, 1956), and probably weighs about 2800 kg (Lockyer, 1981b). Northern hemisphere pilot whales are born at a length of about 174–178 cm and are suckled up to about 230 cm when teeth are erupting, at an age of 6–9 months. From then on, some solid food is also ingested.

Berardius off coastal Japan is about 4.6 m at birth. The neonatal length of the northern *Hyperoodon* is probably about 3 m and about 4.9 m at weaning (Tomilin, 1967). Newborn killer whale calves measure 2.1–2.5 m (Tomilin, 1967; Jonsgård and Lyshoel, 1970).

Age determination. In Odontocete whales, growth layers in teeth provide the best means of age determination. In all toothed whales, the teeth continue growing throughout life. Occasionally, the pulp cavity closes, as in the maxillary teeth in old sperm whales, but in most species, even when this does occur and dentine deposition stops, growth layers continue to be laid down in the cementum.

In the sperm whale the first mandibular tooth is that most frequently taken for ageing purposes, because it is fairly straight and the crown is usually least worn. Also the pulp cavity remains open. The tooth is bisected and the cut surface is etched in 10% formic acid in order to enhance the growth layers which appear as alternating ridges and troughs (Fig. 6). Current evidence (Best, 1970a; Gambell, 1977) suggests that a ridge and a trough together constitute an annual growth layer, although this is a simplification because the growth pattern is often complicated by accessory ridges.

In the Ziphioid whales, *Berardius* and *Hyperoodon*, teeth can also be used for age determination (Kasuya, 1977). In *Hyperoodon* females they often do not erupt. The dentinal growth layers can be examined in *Hyperoodon* from preparations of thin unstained ground sections. Acid etching or staining of *Berardius* teeth shows cemental growth layers well. The rate of formation of these growth layers is virtually unknown and the relation of body length to age not yet known.

Age can be determined from pilot whale (*Globicephala melaena*) teeth although most knowledge comes from the northern hemisphere pilot whales (Sergeant, 1962). There are growth layers in the dentine of killer whale teeth. However, these dentine layers are very difficult to interpret, and the cementum may be more useful. Here again the rate of layer formation is unknown.

The teeth of small delphinids have to be decalcified and then sectioned and stained for the growth layers to be seen clearly. Usually the dentine is adequate but cementum can also be used for some species of *Lagenorhynchus*. Best (1976b) showed from tetracycline hydrochloride marking experiments that in *L. obscurus* one growth layer is formed annually.

Growth in length. The predicted average curve of growth in body length with age for sperm whales is shown in Fig. 7. It is based on the data of Best (1970a, 1974b) and Gambell (1972), with reference to the work of Nishiwaki *et al.*, (1963), Bannister (1969) and Berzin (1972). There is marked sexual dimorphism, the male growing much larger than the female. Also, in contrast to the simple female growth curve, the male shows a growth spurt at sexual maturity. The female attains sexual maturity at about 7–12 years depending on geographical location, when body length is about 80% of maximum. Physical maturity is reached after about 30 years.

Puberty in males is a prolonged process. It commences at about 9–11 years (depending on geographical location). Sexual maturity at about 18–19 years, and length of about 12 m, corresponds with the movement of these males into

Fig. 6. Bisected sperm whale tooth showing untreated half on the left and acid-etched and pencil-rubbed half on the right. The treated half shows the growth layers clearly.

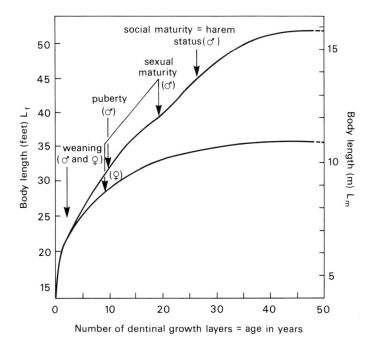

Fig. 7. Average curves of body length at age, based mainly on catch data for sperm whales.

high latitudes for the first time. Functional maturity or social maturity is rather later than sexual maturity; it corresponds to the attainment of harem bull status at a length of about 13.7 m and an age of about 26 years. The final length of the male is about 1.5 times that of the female, and at social maturity the bull has attained well over 85% of its maximum length. The growth pattern of the male sperm whale is comparable with that of the elephant seal which has a social organization and harem system (Laws, 1953 and Chapter 12), similar to sperm whales. In the elephant seal, the male reaches sexual maturity at twice the corresponding age of the female, and by social maturity or harem status, the bull is three times the female's age at sexual maturity.

Sergeant (1962) has described growth curves for the Newfoundland pilot whale, which becomes sexually mature at lengths of 356 cm at age six years in females and 490 cm at age 12 years in males.

Omura *et al.*, (1955) estimate that *Berardius* off Japan matures at lengths of about 10.2 m in females, and 9.9 m in males. Maximum lengths attained are about 12.2 m, and unlike the sperm whale, the female generally grows larger than the male. Kasuya (1977) estimates that maturity occurs at 8–10 years. Maximum longevity is likely to be 70 years.

Growth in weight.   In Fig. 4, the average weight/length relationship is shown for sperm whales, and also for killer whales and pilot whales. Apart from the right and humpback whales, the sperm whale is heavier for its length than any of the baleen whales.

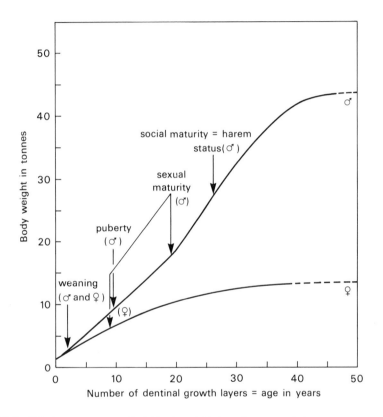

Fig. 8. Predicted average curves of total body weight at age for sperm whales.

As for baleen whales, the Odontocete data do not allow for seasonal variations in body weight although blood and fluid contents are allowed for. The blubber constitutes 33% of total body weight (Table IV), exceeding that of the baleen whales shown except right whales. In Fig. 8 the predicted average growth in weight with age is given for male and female sperm whales. By sexual maturity, the female sperm whale has attained 47% of the final body weight. The male has attained about 22% final body weight at puberty, 41% at sexual maturity and 63% at social maturity.

5. Reproduction

5.1 Timing of breeding season

5.1.1 Mysticetes

As discussed in section 4.1 on foetal growth, the breeding season is well defined, with the majority of conceptions occurring during mid-winter. The breeding grounds for the Mysticetes are in relatively warm waters generally in latitudes of 30–35°S or less (Mackintosh, 1965). Humpbacks are known to extend their range into subtropical waters and the time they spend on the breeding grounds is considered to be relatively short, perhaps one month (Dawbin, 1960; Mackintosh, 1965). Calving also takes place at about this time of year, immediately prior to the mating season.

Sea temperatures in low latitudes are generally 15–20°C or more and provide a less stressful environment for the young calf (whose blubber is relatively thin) than the cold polar waters. Right whales are known to seek sheltered, shallow coastal bays during the breeding season (Donnelly, 1969). The mother remains with the calf for several months in warmer waters, suckling the calf and providing all its nourishment. During the migration south into polar waters, the mother accompanies her calf, generally later than the other whales in the population. On the polar feeding grounds the calf is weaned around mid-summer, about seven months after birth in the case of blue and fin whales.

It has also been shown that the male humpback whale, like the female, has a seasonal sexual cycle (from an analysis of testes weight and spermatogenesis). The testes are smaller in the summer whilst on the Antarctic feeding grounds than during winter on the breeding grounds. Also during the winter the spermatozoa are plentiful in the testis tubules and vasa deferentia (Chittleborough, 1965). Laws (1961) reviewed reproductive data and material for the male fin whale, and found a peak of testicular activity during the winter breeding season. The season is quite protracted, extending from about April to August with a peak in May and June which is close to the usual time of conception for this species in June/July (Table III). Gambell (1968) however, reported a lack of evidence for a seasonal sexual cycle in the male sei whale, and concluded that the distinct breeding season was governed more by the female oestrus cycle.

5.1.2 Odontocetes

The southern hemisphere sperm whale is the only species of toothed whale for which there is a good knowledge of the reproductive cycle. Strictly speaking, the sperm whale is not a truly Antarctic species, except for the large sexually mature bulls; the females but rarely penetrate waters so far south. The female population spends its time in temperate and subtropical waters, with only a slight tendency to seasonal migration.

However, the breeding season of the sperm whale, which extends from August to March, is well defined, and the peak occurs at mid-summer in December in temperate waters (Best, 1968; Gambell, 1972). As discussed in section 4.2 on foetal growth, the gestation period is longer than one year, births occurring during late summer–autumn in about February or later. Unlike the baleen whales which have a marked seasonal migration and feeding season, related to the limited seasonal abundance of their food, thus requiring an adaptation of the gestation period to fit into one year, there appears to be no advantage in a contraction of the gestation period of sperm whales (Laws, 1959).

Neither Best (1969a) nor Gambell (1972) found any seasonal variation in testicular weight, or spermatogenesis; this indicated that there is no seasonal sexual cycle in the male. Best, however, suggested that there was some histological evidence for a seasonal variation in androgenic hormone activity. Nevertheless, there is no clear evidence for a male sexual cycle.

Little can be reported on the timing of breeding of other Odontocetes. Some of these such as pilot whales, and to a lesser extent *Hyperoodon* and *Berardius* have been studied in the northern hemisphere, but timing in the southern hemisphere is likely to be very different and probably six months out of phase.

5.2 Reproductive cycle

5.2.1 Mysticetes

The usual two-year reproductive cycle is closely tied to the annual migratory and feeding cycle. Birth, which occurs in warm waters within a year of conception, is not normally followed immediately by another pregnancy, even if there has been a post-partum ovulation. However, an ovulation at this time results in an incidence of pregnancy of at least 18% in fin whales (Laws, 1961), as judged from the number of whales caught both pregnant and lactating. Gambell (1968) estimated that about 11% of sei whales experience a post-partum ovulation. Chittleborough (1965) mentions that the incidence of post-partum ovulations in humpback whales is probably low, although Matthews (1937) recorded instances of a simultaneously lactating and pregnant humpback cow accompanied by a calf. However, the evidence for minke whales appears different (see below).

With the exception of the minke whale, one ovulation occurs approximately every 1.5 years. Few females become pregnant during the southern summer, a condition which would result from a post-lactation ovulation and put the reproductive cycle out of phase. It would also probably reduce the survival rates of both foetuses and calves. Normally, one calf is produced. This is also the usual pattern for humpback whales (Chittleborough, 1965) and also for right whales (Donnelly, 1969).

The ovulation rate has been determined first by histological examination of the seasonal activity in the ovaries, and by the relative sizes and numbers of Graafian follicles and corpora albicantia and corpora lutea. Secondly, the rate has been determined directly from a correlation of numbers of corpora with the actual age of the whale as determined from ear plugs (Laws, 1961; Gambell, 1968).

Gambell (1973) has reported that the incidence of post-partum and post-lactation ovulations has increased in fin and sei whales, in response to reduction of the whale stocks. He has also reviewed the evidence for increases in the apparent pregnancy rate of the mature non-lactating female blue, fin and sei whales. Because of the present international regulation prohibiting the capture of lactating females, very little is known of the current incidence of simultaneously lactating and pregnant females.

In Fig. 3 there are shown the apparent increases in pregnancy rate for blue, fin and sei whales (from Gambell, 1973). The rate increased from about 25% in both blue and fin in the early 1930s up to 53–54% from about 1952 onwards, and up to 60% in 1969 in fin whales. No data are given by Gambell for sei whales prior to 1945, but the trend after 1945 is similar to that of fin whales, rising from about 25 to 60%. However, it is worth noting that Matthews (1938) observed that for a small sample of sei whales caught off South Georgia between February and April during the seasons 1927–1931, the average pregnancy rate of mature non-lactating females in the catch was 47%, the monthly rates decreasing from about 67 to 14% between February and April. The timing of the catch is undoubtedly important in assessing pregnancy rates because of differential migration by the population. In more recent years, 1960 onwards, most sei whales have been caught in the months December to early March, so a higher average pregnancy rate would be expected.

The minke whale has an ovulation rate of approximately one per 1.15 years (Ohsumi and Masaki, 1975) rather less than for other balaenopterids. There is uncertainty as to whether or not the reproductive cycle is a one-year or two-year one. In the summer period in the Antarctic, catches have shown that nearly 90% of the mature female catch (of which none were lactating) were pregnant. This is a higher incidence than in any other rorqual, although it may in part be due to segregation which will bias the composition of the catch. On the basis that the true pregnancy rate could reach 86% (International Whaling Commission, 1979), it is likely that the minke whale reproduces annually at a minimum interval of 14 months.

As discussed in section 5.1 some male baleen whales have a seasonal sexual cycle, whilst others do not. The cycle of the female is very seasonal, and oestrus is almost certainly independent of male stimulation. The fact that some baleen whale species do show seasonal testicular activity means that when oestrus occurs outside the main breeding season it will almost certainly not result in a pregnancy.

5.2.2 Odontocetes

The reproductive cycle of the female sperm whale usually lasts four years. This comprises 14.5 months gestation and about 24 months lactation, followed by a resting period of about nine months or more. Not all females become pregnant again after this resting period, so that in some, the cycle may be prolonged to five years.

The incidence of post-partum ovulations is approximately 12.5% of females just calved, according to Best (1968). However, Gambell (1972) calculated that post-partum ovulations are very rare, probably less than 1% and all these usually result in pregnancy. Gambell (1972) calculated that approximately 9% of females ovulate during mid-lactation of which 80% conceive, and about 52% ovulate at the end of lactation when 42% conceive. The remaining females ovulate during the main breeding season after a resting phase, so completing the four-year cycle.

A pregnancy rate of 25% is predicted in a population with a four-year cycle, although Gambell found a rate of 19% off Durban, South Africa. This lower value may be explained as the result of a five-year cycle for the majority of females. The average ovulation rate for all females in the population, checked both from direct examination of the ovaries and a comparison of corpora number and tooth dentinal layer counts, indicates one ovulation every 2.2 or 2.3 years, an estimate compatible with a five-year cycle. Best (1968) obtained a value of one ovulation per 1.7 years over a four-year reproductive cycle, but considered only females at the peak of fertility.

Best found that the fertility of newly mature females was approximately half that of females at maximum fertility (between about 3 and 15 corpora) and similarly fertility appeared to decline after 15 corpora had accumulated. This factor almost certainly determines whether or not the female reproductive cycle is four years or more.

As noted in section 5.1, the male sperm whale does not appear to have a seasonal sexual cycle. The male pattern of maturation however, is both prolonged and complex (Best, 1969a). Testis maturation appears to be correlated with body size. Although sexual maturity is normally associated with reproductive development, the sperm whale male also appears to need to attain a social status in the school before he can service a harem. It is these bulls which are important in maintaining fecundity and the reproductive cycle in the females (see section 5.3.2).

From analogy with the northern hemisphere counterparts of some Odontocete species we might conclude that in *Hyperoodon*, the durations of gestation and lactation are respectively less than one year and about 5–7 months (Tomilin, 1967). The breeding season of *Berardius* appears very protracted, estimates of gestation range between ten months (Omura *et al.*, 1955) and 17 months (Kasura, 1977). The length of gestation in the killer whale is probably about one year (Tomilin, 1967). More is known about the pilot whale in which gestation lasts about 15.5 months (Sergeant, 1962). Lactation probably lasts nearly two years, although calves begin to be weaned at 6–9 months. Sergeant estimated that in Newfoundland pilot whales the reproductive cycle in females lasted about 40 months during which time on average 1.3–1.7 ovulations occur (equivalent to a rate of one corpus per 2–2.6 years). Sergeant also found some evidence of seasonal spermatogenic activity in males.

5.3 Social structure

5.3.1 Mysticetes

As discussed in section 3.2, rorquals and humpback whales show segregation of both sexes, sexual classes and ages of whales at different times. This is particularly true during migration. The pregnant females are generally the first to head south on the annual summer feeding migration, followed by adult males and females other than lactating ones, which are generally late in arriving. The immature whales of both sexes, other than unweaned calves, usually arrive later than any of the adults, the peaks for adults and juveniles being separated by up to nearly a month. Returning northwards after the summer, the pregnant females are normally the last to leave. This pattern is well established for blue and fin whales. However, southward migration of juveniles precedes that of adults in the humpback whale.

Whilst on the feeding grounds the whales tend to mingle freely or associate in small groups (Gambell, 1968). On the Antarctic feeding grounds, fin whales have generally been observed in groups of four or less whales. Lockyer (1977c) reported that sei were found in groups of up to ten in the Antarctic, However, Gambell found that whilst off Durban, South Africa between May and September (winter), sei whales were found in even larger groups of up to 30 individuals although group sizes were mainly around 2–6, as well as single animals.

Budylenko (1977) reviewed published data on school structure of sei whales, and concluded that in sub-Antarctic latitudes 40–50°S, schools consisted mainly of juveniles and lactating females with calves. Generally only the mature sei whales penetrate into the Antarctic proper. Lockyer (1977c) found some degree of aggregation by age of sei whales on the southerly feeding grounds. Of mature whales, older whales tend to arrive before younger ones. However, these age classes are not necessarily associated in close groups. Sexual segregation is apparent in the minke whale, the pregnant females, lactating females and males usually remaining in separate areas.

Donnelly (1969) reports that right whales appear around the South African coastal waters from May onwards until departure in October. The earliest arrivals are probably mainly pregnant females, followed in spring by the males and non-pregnant females for mating. At no time are lactating cows and calves seen on the same grounds as the breeding animals. He describes mating in right whales in some detail. Courtship between pairs can occur day long and into the night, with accompanying displays of leaping and vertical head-up postures (spy hopping) or head-down postures and rolling belly to belly.

Breaching, or leaping clear of the water has been observed for all the baleen whales mentioned here. Successive leaps are frequently observed along with tail slapping of the surface water and splashing. Humpback whales are well known for their complex vocalizations (Payne and McVay, 1971). Although it is not known whether or not these are connected with any courtship rituals, the songs have been recorded in the breeding areas and obviously constitute a means of communication between individual whales. Less complex vocalizations have been described or are assumed for other Mysticetes.

Amongst the baleen whales, bonding between individuals of a group does not seem to be especially marked. Attacks on individuals by predators (e.g. killer whales, whaling vessels), usually cause the remaining whales to flee. However, the bond between mother and calf is possibly the strongest (Caldwell and Caldwell, 1966).

5.3.2 Odontocetes

Toothed whales are frequently observed in large schools of animals, sometimes up to several hundred in number. The composition of these schools is variable, consisting in some dolphin species of whole families, and in other species such as the sperm whale, of different sexual classes and age groups.

In the sperm whale, only large mature bulls, often solitary, are found in the Antarctic waters, but in warmer waters well north of the Antarctic Convergence, many kinds of schools are found. Ohsumi (1971) has described at least six categories of school structure: nursery school, harem school, juvenile school, bachelor school, bull school and lone bull. Generally only lone bulls were found south of the Antarctic Convergence and they were sexually mature animals, usually aged over 20 years. In the schools, numbers of whales varied between one and well over 100, averaging 20 whales in coastal waters, and between three and seven whales on the pelagic grounds. Generally, schools in higher latitudes contain larger whales than in lower latitudes.

Ohsumi found evidence for the integrity of certain schools, in that marked female whales were captured from the same school up to ten years after being originally marked. The most closely knit school is the nursery school comprising about 27 whales, composed of mature females and suckling calves, and young juvenile males and females; it is dominated by the mature females.

The harem school is a temporary structure assembled for breeding, when socially mature males join a nursery school. Ohsumi estimated that the average number of females served by such a bull was about 14. Berzin (1972) reviewed information on this subject and gave estimates of between ten and 40 as the usual number of mature females served. However, he concluded that usually it was not more than 12 females. The larger harem sizes quoted in the literature could be due to temporary amalgamation of several harems. Berzin (1972) discusses the possibility that introduction of new genes is achieved by the actual driving out of large old bulls by the females. He cites the occurrence of parallel scars on the heads of bulls as the marks of teeth of females and even of other younger bulls. The testes are frequently found to be lighter in weight and spermatogenically inactive in very old bulls compared with younger ones.

Juvenile schools consist only of immature males and females, and from these the females, once mature, revert to the nursery schools, and the males move to bachelor schools. The males usually leave the nursery schools and juvenile schools before puberty at around the age of ten years. Leadership in the male herds is not usually evident, unlike the matriarchal nursery schools, where it is strong.

The behaviour of schools is generally co-ordinated in that diving is synchronized and consequently surfacing and blowing after diving. This is especially evident during chasing (Lockyer, 1977d).

The degree of co-ordination is variable amongst different schools. Male schools generally break up readily on the approach of danger or threat. However, nursery schools in particular remain close, and tend to reconvene even if temporarily split. The female is well known for her protective attitude to her calf when threatened and will often remain or actively intervene even in the presence of imminent danger. Berzin (1972) reviews many such incidences. Nishiwaki (1962) records that after the shooting of the largest whale in a school of about 20–30, the other whales formed a tight circle around the injured animals, with heads towards the centre and tails outstretched.

Sperm whales have been reported as aggressive when provoked or injured, when the head is frequently used as a ram and the jaws used for biting and snapping. It is possible that the not infrequent cases of broken and damaged jaws and teeth are the results of fighting. They are known to be playful, and have been seen to take various poses, head up, tail up and side up. They have been seen and photographed playing with a baulk of floating timber (Nishiwaki, 1962); this habit and especially that of pushing foreign objects upwards from the surface is one which has been described often for dolphins. Sperm whales, like nearly all cetaceans, are well known to leap clear or breach from the sea surface (Gaskin, 1964).

Sounds are produced usually in the form of rapid sharp clickings, in the frequency range 5–32 kHz. Each click is a series of 1–9 short sound pulses repeated at intervals of about a second or less (Backus and Schevill, 1966). This may be a form of communication and also of echo-ranging. Lockyer (1977d) has recorded much clicking and also creaking produced when separate groups join up to form a single group during diving. Watkins and Schevill (1975) found that sonar "pingers" at short range apparently influenced sperm whale vocalization. Lockyer (1977d) concluded that sperm whales probably need to produce sounds for echo-ranging and communication in the extreme depths to which they normally dive, if only to locate each other.

Killer, pilot, bottlenose whales and *Berardius* are all well known to swim in schools, and in the case of pilot whales these can be large, sometimes containing several hundred animals. Pilot whales have a strongly developed schooling behaviour and do not part company when chased as often seen in some sperm whale schools. In fact, Sergeant (1962) has reported that schools convene more closely when alarmed. For this reason, pilot whales often strand in large numbers and can even be driven ashore en masse.

Sergeant (1962) reported that pilot whales off Newfoundland were generally found in pelagic schools of 20–100 individuals, although stranded schools often exceed 200 whales. He identified breeding schools of mixed composition, including females (mature, pregnant and lactating), adult males, juveniles of both sexes, and calves, and also bachelor schools of adult animals, chiefly male. All schools however, tend to disperse whilst feeding. Males have been caught bearing many heavy scars, and these have been attributed to fighting. Sergeant (1962) mentions that scars on the trailing edge of flippers, dorsal fins and tail flukes are common. He concluded that these injuries were inflicted during the breeding season.

Killer whales have been observed swimming in schools of up to 150 or more (Tomilin, 1967). However, they are more frequently observed in schools of 10–30 individuals. Condy *et al.* (1978) observed an average group size of about 3–4 individuals within schools. Such groups may comprise families, males and females, mature and immature, and calves, and males may also form separate schools. The breeding behaviour involves much breaching, as in other cetaceans, and rolling on one side with ventral surfaces opposed. Most of the social behaviour studies of the killer whale have been in relation to feeding activities, and these will be discussed in the next section.

Hyperoodon is generally found in small schools of about 2–20 individuals although when these amalgamate on the feeding grounds the resulting school may number hundreds. Such schools observed in the northern hemisphere, generally comprise family groups where an adult male usually takes leadership (Tomilin, 1967). Schools consisting of only a few adult males have also been observed.

6. Feeding

6.1 Method of feeding

6.1.1 Mysticetes

Nemoto (1959, 1966, 1970) arbitrarily classified baleen whales into three feeding categories. These are swallowing, skimming, and swallowing and skimming. The baleen whales considered are here classified as follows:

(1)	Skimming	right whale
(2)	Swallowing	blue whale
		pigmy blue whale
		fin whale
		minke whale
		humpback whale
(3)	Swallowing and skimming	sei whale

The fringe of the right whale baleen is extremely fine compared to that of other species, and the baleen fringe of swallowing types is much coarser than that of the sei whale.

The swallowing, and swallowing and skimming types of whales are characterized by ventral grooves in the throat region. The numbers of these vary between about 20 and 90 according to species (Nemoto, 1959). The jaw shapes and feeding apparatus are different in the right whale and rorqual, and the rostral areas of the head are also very different, being very high, arched and narrow in the right whale.

The actual method of feeding used by the right whale is to swim slowly forward with jaws agape, filtering water as it moves. The swallowing method employed by most rorquals is for the whale to gulp a quantity of water and food, so expanding the ventral grooves. The jaws then close, and with the simultaneous expansion and pushing forward of the tongue within the mouth and the contraction of the ventral grooves, and water is filtered upwards out through the baleen plates like a jet, and the food retained for swallowing. Gaskin (1976) gives excellent illustrations of sequences of such feeding in fin whales, based on film footage. The sei whale is believed to feed by a method somewhere between the two just described, according to Nemoto's study of its anatomy. Gill and Hughes (1971) give an account of a sei whale feeding.

Rorquals have been seen swimming on one side when feeding and surfacing obliquely under the prey. The angle of the jaws is actually quite flexible so permitting the mouth to open more than 90°.

Generally, baleen whales feed close to the surface and rarely dive deep. Thus sight is probably important, although echo-locating may also be employed.

6.1.2 Odontocetes

In feeding methods used by Odontocetes, echo-location is very probably employed (Gaskin, 1976) and is almost certainly of extreme importance to sperm whales. Several facts point to this. Sperm whales are known to make deep dives to at least 1200 m (Lockyer, 1977d), where they may remain for periods of up to one hour. Even at 200 m, light is negligible so that prey cannot be located by sight, and the sperm whale must feed in total darkness. Beale (1835) reported a blind whale that was healthy and had evidently been feeding normally, suggesting that sight was not important in feeding. The only methods of locating prey would therefore be by touch or echo-location and touch alone would be haphazard and inefficient, because location of prey would be random.

Assuming that the sperm whale receives detailed information on its environment by means of echo-locating similar to sonar, it must then seize the prey. The mandibular teeth are homodont, number 22–28 per side and the maxillary teeth may be unerupted. They are certainly not used for seizing prey because whales with damaged jaws and broken or worn teeth feed normally (Tomilin, 1967) and in juvenile males and females, the teeth are unerupted, yet their diet is similar to that of toothed individuals. Also the food found in sperm whale stomachs is usually intact with no tooth or bite marks. As yet no one has observed a sperm whale feeding although several theories describing possible methods have been advanced.

Teeth are probably not used directly in feeding by bottlenose and beaked whales. These whales, however, like the sperm whale, are known to dive very deeply and for similar long periods (Tomilin, 1967). As the diet is rather similar to that of sperm whales (Gaskin, 1976), it seems likely that these animals may employ a similar feeding method to this species.

Delphinids are known to actively chase their prey and use their sharp teeth for seizing and grasping (Gaskin, 1976). Phocoenoids have teeth which are generally spade-shaped, and Gaskin considers that these are adapted for cutting and shearing.

The killer whale uses its powerful teeth for grasping, biting and tearing. Unlike other Odontocetes, it will attack large prey such as seals, penguins and even other cetaceans, some of the latter being the large rorquals (Tomilin, 1967; Gaskin, 1976). The killer whale hunts in packs or schools (Condy et al., 1978), and they appear to co-ordinate a group attack on large prey (Tarpy, 1979), which is often preceded by chasing and harassing. The killer whales are neither deep nor lengthy divers, which means that many large toothed whales, even if slow swimming, can easily escape their attentions by diving out of range. Most prey are thus taken near the sea surface, or even off the ice floes and on shore in the surf zone (Condy et al., 1978). Condy et al. give good evidence that sight is very important to the killer whale in locating prey, especially seals on beaches. Despite the presence of powerful teeth, smaller prey do not appear to be chewed before being swallowed by the killer whale. Only large prey are torn or fragmented before ingestion.

6.2 Food preferences

6.2.1 Mysticetes

The chief food of all rorquals, and the humpback whale, when south of the Antarctic Convergence is the large, pelagic swarming euphausiid *Euphausia superba* (Marr, 1962; Mackintosh, 1965; Nemoto, 1959; Gaskin, 1976; see also Chapter 9). These euphausiids are mostly taken in the size range 27–50 mm in body length, although some of sizes down to 15 mm are also consumed (Mackintosh, 1974). Other swarming species consumed locally in the Antarctic are *Euphausia crystallorophias*, *E. vallentini*,

E. spinifera, Thysanoessa macrura and the amphipod *Parathemisto gaudichaudi* (Nemoto, 1959). In the sub-Antarctic, *E. similis* is also taken, and sei, minke and right whales, and also young fin whales, take copepods of the genus *Calanus* (Gaskin, 1976; Kawamura, 1978; Ohsumi *et al.*, 1970). In waters where the density of planktonic organisms is low, shoaling fish are often taken instead. This is especially true in the northern hemisphere, where capelin or herring, pollack, cod, saury and other fish are taken (Nemoto, 1959; Gill and Hughes, 1971).

Generally right whales consume smaller crustaceans, e.g. copepods, than other baleen whales. This is probably possible because of their finer baleen fringe.

The food taken in temperate or subtropical waters during winter is usually more variable than during summer. Suitable food species are less common in these waters and frequently sparse and hence the whales are more opportunistic in habit. Euphausiids, amphipods, copepods, fish and other plankton may all be taken as and when available.

6.2.2 Odontocetes

Squid form the greater part of the diet in sperm whales (Clarke, M. R., 1980), and are also known to be the preferred food of many other Odontocetes such as pilot whales (Sergeant, 1962). The distribution of the latter species has been closely correlated with that of the squid *Illex illecebrosus* on which it feeds off Newfoundland. Bottlenose and beaked whales feed almost exclusively on cephalopods (Tomilin, 1967).

The bottlenose, beaked and sperm whales can all dive very deeply for feeding, so that squid and other cephalopods may be taken from all strata from the sea surface down. Many bathypelagic cephalopods are only known to exist from their presence in sperm whale stomachs, either whole or only as beaks which are characteristic for each species. Clarke (1956), Clarke, M. R. (1980), Tomilin (1967) and Berzin (1972) all give accounts of the varieties of squid and also other items supplementary to the diet such as fish. Clarke (1955) has recorded the presence of a whole giant squid *Architeuthis* in the stomach of a sperm whale taken off the Azores. In capturing prey, the sperm whale frequently meets resistance, as the disc-shaped scars from sucker wounds on the head testify.

In Antarctic waters, Berzin (1972) mentions the squid *Architeuthis, Onychoteuthis banksii* and *Moroteuthis robusta* as components of the diet of sperm whales.[*] Although fish are often included in the diet, they form a less important component in the Antarctic than in other areas (Berzin, 1972).

---

[*] See Clarke, M. R. (1980) for revision of these identifications.

The diet of the killer whale is very catholic. Fish, cephalopods, birds, seals and other cetaceans are all attacked or taken. The diet appears to be greatly influenced by local prey availability. In some localities only capelin or cod are taken, whereas elsewhere seals form the major component of the diet. Condy *et al.* (1978) found that the seasonal arrival and distribution of elephant seals at Marion Island in latitude 46°54'S, was closely paralleled by that of killer whales. However, penguins were also taken.

Delphinids and Phocoenoids both prefer fish, mainly pelagic fish, although small squid are taken if readily available (Gaskin, 1976).

6.3 Ecological separation

As noted in section 6.2.1, all baleen whales appear to be in competition for the same food source, that is krill, when south of the Antarctic Convergence. The whales converging on the polar feeding grounds in the summer tend to have staggered peaks of arrival, so that neither different species nor age classes of the same species are directly in competition all of the time (section 3.2.1).

Lockyer (1981a) mentions that peak arrivals of blue whales in December occur about one month in advance of fin whales. Also, adults arrive up to one month before juveniles in both species.

Sei whale numbers apparently reached a peak later than blue and fin whales (Harmer, 1931; Matthews, 1938), most not arriving until March. However, since the late 1950s Nemoto (1962), Bannister and Gambell (1965) and Gambell (1968) have presented evidence that sei whales have been arriving earlier on the Antarctic feeding grounds, with peak abundances in January. The reduction in blue, fin and humpback whales (through whaling) has led to a drastic reduction in competition for food and may have resulted in their earlier arrival (Nemoto, 1962; Lockyer, 1974). However, cyclical changes in water temperature and climate also may be factors causing an earlier arrival.

The extent of penetration into polar waters is also an important factor reducing interspecies competition. Minke whales are known to penetrate far south into the ice and up to the ice edge (Ohsumi, 1976), and they are generally found to be in greatest abundance further south than other species, judging from whale sightings (Masaki, 1977; Masaki and Yamamura, 1978). The distributions of blue, fin and humpback whales as determined by sightings are variable, but are not as consistently far south as that of minke whales, although the majority of these animals are located south of the Antarctic Convergence.

In contrast, sei and southern right whales tend to be most abundant further north outside the Antarctic Convergence (Masaki, 1977; Masaki and Yamamura, 1978). Adult sei whales are generally found further south than the juveniles (section 5.3.1), and such segregation probably also occurs in other rorquals. Kawamura (1978) considers aspects of competition for food amongst the southern baleen whales. In his opinion, southern right and sei whales are, or were before right whales were greatly depleted, probably in direct competition for copepods. Kawamura presents a model to explain how a decrease in the number of right whales would allow an increase in the sei whale population, where originally the excess of right whales over sei suppressed growth of the latter because of the level of carrying capacity of the environment. As yet there is only slight evidence that the sei whales have increased their original numbers. This evidence based on work of Gambell (1968) and Best (1975), is discussed in the Report of the Special Meeting on southern hemisphere sei whales (International Whaling Commission, 1978).

Very little is known of competition for food and possible ecological separation in Odontocetes in Antarctic waters.

7. Bioenergetics

7.1 Mysticetes

7.1.1 Quantities of food eaten

As explained in section 3.3.1, the baleen whales have a marked seasonality in feeding habits. The feeding season lasts for about four months during the southern summer, when krill, and/or copepods are consumed in the Antarctic.

Mackintosh and Wheeler (1929), Matthews (1937) and Lockyer (1981a) give data on the incidence of feeding in blue, fin and humpback whales in the Antarctic. This varies from about 60–100% of stomachs examined according to the month and year but generally averages well over 85%. Sei whales examined in the Antarctic were found to have a similar incidence of feeding to blue, fin and humpback (Gambell, 1968). However, the incidence of feeding in sub-Antarctic waters, where the bulk of the population are feeding, has been found to be only about 40–55% (Kawamura, 1974). The incidence of feeding for all species while north of the main feeding grounds in winter has been found to be relatively low, averaging less than 20%, although it is higher in juveniles than adults (Matthews, 1937; Dawbin and Falla, 1949; Dall and Dunstan, 1957; Mackintosh and Wheeler, 1929; Bannister and Baker, 1967; Lockyer, 1981a).

The quantities of food consumed are probably maximal south of the Antarctic Convergence, depending on local availability. For example, Brown (1968) found a 14.7 m female sei whale (off South Georgia) to have 305 kg of krill in the stomach. Certainly Mackintosh and Wheeler (1929) found that over 70% of baleen whale stomachs containing food were full or nearly full, whilst off South Africa in low latitudes less than 25% were full, and the remainder were nearly empty. Lockyer (1981a) estimated, from the incidence of feeding and fullness of stomachs, that the daily winter intake was only about 10% of the quantity consumed daily on the southerly feeding grounds in summer.

According to Nemoto (1959), Kawamura (1970, 1974), Ohsumi et al. (1970), Zenkovich (1969) and Ohsumi (1979), baleen whales may feed from twice to four or five times daily when on the feeding grounds, according to species and local food availability (e.g. diurnal vertical plankton migration; ice cover). Whilst feeding maximally, about 3–4% of body weight is consumed daily (Klumov, 1963). This value is similar for many cetaceans, some of which have been observed in captivity (Sergeant, 1969; Gray, 1964). For a single newly-weaned captive gray whale, values up to 13% (Wahrenbrock et al., 1974) have been observed, but over-feeding is always a possibility and feeding rates in calves are likely to be much higher than in adults.

Lockyer (1981a) has calculated that with four months of intensive feeding and eight months of reduced feeding, the daily intake averaged over a year would amount to only 12–16 g food kg^{-1} body weight.

The calorific value of whole *E. superba*, excluding gravid females, is estimated to be about 1000 kCal kg^{-1} wet weight (Lockyer, 1981a; Clarke, A., 1980). Adult krill consists of about 76–80% water, 2.8–4,1% ash, 2.4–6.3% lipid, 0.3–0.7% carbohydrate, 1.9–2.1% chitin and 10.4–10.6% protein (Clarke, A., 1980). The gravid females contain a much higher percentage of lipid than males and hence a higher calorific value. Generally Clarke's findings are similar to data of Heyerdahl (1932), Hirano et al. (1964), Il'ichev (1967) and Vinogradova (1967), although crude protein estimates of these authors are higher, in the range 13.7–19.6%. However, it should be emphasized that Clarke's estimate was based on a direct measure of protein, and not a total nitrogen analysis.

7.1.2 Seasonal fattening

Because the majority of whales feed intensively for one-third of the year and at a very reduced rate (perhaps amounting to periodic starvation) during the remaining two-thirds of the year, much of the food energy must be stored in the body to meet the continuous metabolic requirements. It is generally stored as fat in tissues of the blubber, muscle, viscera and bone (Lockyer, 1981a).

The most obvious and easily measured indicator of fattening is the blubber which increases in thickness during the summer. The extensive literature has been reviewed by Lockyer (1981a) who also gives new data for some rorquals. In general, regardless of season, the blubber thickness appears to be relatively thicker in immature whales than adults, and pregnant females have the thickest blubber of all whales. In contrast, lactating females are extremely thin.

Lockyer (1981a) has estimated that the total increase in body weight during the summer feeding season amounts to 30–100% of lean body weight for rorquals such as fin, blue and humpback. For comparison doubling of body weight is not unusual in hibernating mammals.

The increase in body weight is assumed to be mainly caused by fat accumulation. The distribution of weight increases has been estimated by Lockyer to be in the range of at least 31–71% in the blubber, 30–64% in the muscle and 59–82% in the viscera in blue and fin whales. Reference to Table IV (section 4.1) indicates that total body weight increases are at least 6–13% due to blubber, 11–17% due to muscle and 5–7% due to viscera. Bone normally contains 56–69% oil and 8–13% water; as the oil content, if increased, must replace the water, it is unlikely to exceed 80% of bone tissue and because oil will replace water, little if any weight increase will be detectable.

Lockyer (1981a) has assumed that the calorific value of the fat storage tissue, which probably holds a maximum of 80% lipid, is 7560 kCal kg^{-1}. It is also assumed that all the stored fat is potentially mobile.

7.1.3 Growth energy requirements

In section 4.1, linear growth curves have been presented and a means of translating these into weight growth curves. In rorquals the rate of growth in the suckling period is very great and Lockyer (1981a) has estimated that suckling blue and fin whales gain about 81 kg day^{-1} and 52.5 kg day^{-1} respectively. Tomilin (1946) estimated that such calves consume about 90 kg day^{-1} and 72 kg^{-1} of milk. The calorific value of rorqual milk has been found to be between 3657 and 4305 kCal kg^{-1} (Tomilin, 1946). Lockyer (1981a) used a calculated value of 4137 kCal kg^{-1} from the assumption that average whale milk consists of 36% fat, 13% protein, 1% ash and 49% water.

With the assumption that most growth energy is channelled into muscle and viscera development, calorific value of growth is generally taken to be about 1500 kCal kg^{-1} mammal flesh (Petrides and Swank, 1966; Brody, 1968).

Lockyer (1981a) calculated gross growth efficiencies of about 30% for suckling blue and fin whales. It is expected that such efficiences defined as

$$\frac{\text{Calories of net growth} \times 100}{\text{Calories of food consumed}}$$

are likely to be similar for other baleen whales. Such levels of growth efficiency are usual amongst other suckling animals such as cattle (Brody, 1968). Growth is always defined as net growth, or that which is developmental, and excludes temporary growth due to fat storage. On the assumption that growth in weaned and older whales is channelled into development of tissue in the proportions given in Table IV, section 4.1, Lockyer (1981a) calculated gross growth efficiencies for pubertal and adult (but physically immature) blue and fin whales, of about 4.6% and 0.8% respectively. It is clear that, as in all mammals, relatively more energy is required for growth in juveniles than near-adults which use nearly all consumable energy for maintenance and reproduction, not growth.

7.1.4 Metabolic energy expenditure

Direct measurement of metabolic energy output is extremely difficult in cetaceans, and there are no reliable data for any balaenopterids or right whales. Brodie (1975), Kawamura (1975) and Lockyer (1981a) have presented theoretical estimates of metabolic energy requirements for fin and the latter author also for blue whales. These have been based chiefly on both interpolation and extrapolation of data on metabolic rates of other mammals, and also calculation of energy requirements based on a knowledge of the behavioural habits of the whales, their respiratory rhythms and swimming speeds, their subsistence on stored fat during the winter months, and various anatomical and physiological data.

In comparing the estimates of basal metabolic rate calculated by these authors, equivalent values are mostly in the range $3-8\,\text{kCal}\,\text{kg}^{-1}$ body weight day^{-1}. The problem encountered by all authors was that the lipid store alone could not be calculated to sustain the rorqual throughout the winter months and migratory periods. Although Lockyer (1981a) estimated that only about 10% of the daily summer food intake was likely during winter, it should nevertheless be emphasized that this supplementary food must be important to the whale's survival. Lockyer also pointed out that actual metabolic expenditure would be higher than basal rate because of the whale's necessity to swim and generally maintain itself. The basal rate therefore has no practical significance except to indicate a minimum possible level of energy expenditure necessary to life, such as might arise during extreme starvation.

Lockyer (1981a) gives a range of estimates of basal, resting and active metabolic rates, calculated by several different methods for blue and fin whales. The resting rate is generally up to about 20% higher than basal, and active rate is usually up to ten times basal rate, excluding brief moments of exertion when 20 or more times basal rate can be experienced.

Lockyer (1981a) estimated that the relative amounts of energy required for growth and maintenance metabolism changed with age. Whilst the suckling calf utilized about 68% of consumed energy for metabolism, by puberty 94% was used for this purpose, and by near physical maturity, nearly all was required for metabolism.

Both Kawamura (1975) and Lockyer (1981a) agree that theoretically it is possible for a migrating rorqual to complete its journeys in 15 days, swimming continuously. There is some evidence given by Kawamura that whales do not slow or cease swimming at night, and even more positive evidence from Brown (1971) who recorded that a sei whale marked in the Antarctic was recovered ten days later some 3550 km distant, and thus averaged 14.5 km h^{-1}. Kawamura states that a sustained speed equivalent to 18.5 km h^{-1} is possible, and Lockyer comments that for the largest rorquals such as blue and fin, a speed of 24 km h^{-1} is possible. Although nothing is known of energy expenditure in right whales their swimming speeds and those of humpbacks are undoubtedly much slower than these values.

One aspect of the energy budget which appears not to be problematical is that of regulating heat loss to the environment. The large whales' blubber is sufficiently thick that even with minor exertion, overheating could be a potential problem. However, the flippers, dorsal fin (when present) and tail flukes are all highly vascularized, with retia mirabilia which adjust blood flow effectively to rid the whale of excess heat. Water evaporation in the lungs, excretion and cooling of the buccal cavity when feeding, are other ways of losing heat. However, these are likely to be of minor importance.

7.1.5 Special energy demands of female reproduction

As noted in section 7.1.2, pregnant females are relatively fat and lactating females lean. Lockyer (1981a) observed that the blubber fat of pregnant blue and fin whales was about 25% thicker than that of resting females. This would probably correspond to an increase in the body weight of pregnant females of at least 60–65% during the summer feeding season. The fat so stored is calculated to be barely adequate to meet the demands of pregnancy and especially lactation, which perhaps explains the leanness of lactating whales compared with resting ones. Lockyer (1981a) estimated that in order to accumulate extra fat, pregnant females must remain longer on the southern feeding grounds to consume more food. Dawbin (1966) gave evidence that pregnant humpbacks remain in the Antarctic longer than four months; this probably also applies to other species. In order to accumulate an extra 10–15% fat, the whale would probably need to remain an extra month, making a total stay of five months.

Nearly all of the extra fat stored for reproduction is used in lactation. The energy cost of lactation is calculated to be about 12–15 times the cost of foetal development (Lockyer, 1978). The recovery of the female after lactation must influence fecundity, pregnancy rate and survival of subsequent calves. Lockyer also points out that the relative energy cost of the reproductive cycle is much greater for the newly mature female which is still growing, than for the fully adult female.

7.2 Odontocetes

7.2.1 Quantities of food eaten

The maximum quantity of food in the stomach of sperm whales has been measured at about 200 kg (Betesheva, 1961). Berzin (1972) records the finding in a sperm whale stomach of a 12 m giant squid *Architeuthis*, weighing 200 kg, but Lockyer (1981b) has reviewed information on stomach capacities relative to body size in sperm whales from data of Berzin (1972), and Hosokawa and Kamiya (1971), and 200 kg would amount to only a moderate fullness of the first chamber of the stomach in most sperm whales.

Using Sergeant's (1969) relationship that

$$\text{Heart weight} = 0.11 \times \text{daily food consumption}$$

Lockyer (1981b) calculated that daily food consumption would be 3% of body weight in sperm whales. The total stomach capacity (all three chambers) is about 3–4 times that of the first chamber, and is equivalent to 3–4% body weight. Thus to acquire sufficient food, the whale must replenish the first stomach chamber completely at least 3–4 times daily.

The estimate by Kellogg (1940) that a sperm whale consumes about 1000 kg food daily is probably a good one for a whale of about 14–15 m length. Sergeant (1962) found that an average-sized pilot whale of 396 cm requires 12–14 kg to fill its stomach. He reckoned, from data on captive pilot whales and digestion times, that the stomach would be filled up to three times daily.

Sergeant (1969) calculated daily feeding rates for several toothed cetaceans based on weight of food consumed, and estimates were 5.5–14% body weight for phocoenoids, 4–11% body weight for dolphins, 4–6% body weight for adult pilot whales and 4% body weight for killer whales.

The calorific values of whole food eaten by Odontocetes is variable, but squid are likely to be in the range 800–1000 kCal kg^{-1}, cod about 950 kCal kg^{-1}, oily fish such as herring and mackerel (usually taken by small dolphins) about 1500–2500 kCal kg^{-1}. Items such as birds and seals, taken by killer whales, may have more variable nutritive value.

7.2.2 Growth energy requirements

During the prolonged suckling period of sperm whales, the calf grows from about 4 m to 6 m in length in the first year, and doubles its body weight to about 2 tonnes (see section 4.2). Little is known of the actual milk consumption at this time, but Lockyer (1981b) has calculated that about 20 kg milk is consumed daily at an average calorific value of 3840 kCal kg^{-1}. The estimated gross growth efficiency for the calf is just over 14%. As predicted from other animals, this level of efficiency falls as the whale grows older, and Lockyer has calculated that in females it is about 3.8% at sexual maturity, and at puberty, sexual maturity and harem status in males, it is 4.6%, 2.2% and 2.0% respectively. By the attainment of physical maturity, growth energy requirements are probably minimal, and these are mostly needed for cyclic development of the reproductive organs. Virtually nothing is known about the requirements of other southern hemisphere species of toothed cetaceans.

7.2.3 Metabolic energy expenditure

The problems of determining metabolic rates for large Odontocetes are similar to those for the Mysticetes. However, there is the advantage that dolphins, killer and pilot whales can be maintained in captivity and monitored for metabolic energy output. The majority of estimates of metabolic rate for large cetaceans are extrapolations of data for smaller species as pointed out in section 7.1.4. Lockyer (1981a) has reviewed data on resting metabolic rates for small Odontocetes; these average from about 155 kCal kg^{-1} body weight day^{-1} for small phocoenoids to about 35 kCal kg^{-1} body weight day^{-1} for larger dolphins and even less for small whales. Lockyer (1981a,b) estimated the resting metabolic rates for sperm whales by extrapolation, and gave values equivalent to 5–8.5 kCal kg^{-1} body weight day^{-1}. As assumed for Mysticetes, the basal metabolic rate is about 85% of resting rate, and active metabolic rate is approximately ten times basal rate.

A major difference between Mysticetes and Odontocetes (especially the sperm and bottlenose whales), apart from the more constrained annual cycle in the former, is the capacity for deep, prolonged diving in the latter. This activity must require energy expenditure well above that at the resting level. Lockyer (1977d, 1981b) has pointed out the greater diving ability of the larger sperm whales, especially the mature bulls, and has suggested that there is a proportional increase in the energy expenditure of the activity involved in the deeper and longer diving excursions. However, these matters have only been discussed at a theoretical level, and as yet there is little empirical information of the physiological stress of diving either in sperm whales or other large toothed whales. Lockyer (1981b) has estimated that the proportion of energy required for metabolism relative to that needed for growth increase with size, age and maturity. At birth, 80% of the consumed energy is directed into maintenance, whereas by sexual maturity about 95% is used up in this way, and at physical maturity nearly all is channelled into metabolism.

7.2.4 Special energy demands of female reproduction

The energy demands of pregnancy and lactation are possibly less stressful on the female sperm whale than on the female baleen whale which is dependent on a seasonal food supply. Lockyer (1981b) has calculated that the energy cost of pregnancy in the sperm whale is negligible until the fifth or sixth month of gestation. An increase in daily food consumption of only about 5–10% would suffice to cover the entire energy cost of pregnancy. However, lactation would create a greater energy demand requiring an increased daily food intake of 32–63%, the higher end of the range being for the newly mature and still growing female, the lower for the physically mature female. This increased requirement for food would be satisfied by a replenishment of the stomach (first chamber) 4–5 times daily. As noted in sections 6.3.1 and 7.1.5 pregnant and lactating female Mysticetes usually segregate from the main population for feeding, and this is generally the situation in sperm whales. One of the main reasons for such segregation may be that feeding habits differ from those of the rest of the population.

8. Populations

8.1 Estimation of population size

Estimation of population size is very important for commercially exploited cetaceans in order to manage the resource properly. Nearly all our knowledge of population sizes is for such species, because there has been no pressure for the collection of such information on unexploited species.

Research on the population dynamics of whales is a large, controversial and complicated field and in this section we briefly summarize the methodology and estimates of population sizes. There are several computer models for modelling whale populations, but they will not be described here. Further information on the dynamics and trends can be found in the literature cited. A good general introduction, including details of computer models, can be found in Allen (1980) and Gambell (1976b) gives a useful review.

There are several methods which are used to determine population size, and these are now reviewed briefly. The first two methods rely on direct observations. Other methods of determining population size rely on indirect evidence from catch and effort statistics and biological data.

8.1.1 Whale marking

This method can provide estimates of population size and of fishing mortality (Chapman, 1974). The proportion of marks recovered from the total effectively marked animals provides a factor which relates the associated catch to the total population being exploited.

8.1.2 Sightings

Here, the number of whales sighted within a given area is extrapolated to cover a much larger area occupied by the population. This method depends greatly on a knowledge of the diving and social habits of the species concerned, and also the boundaries of their distribution.

8.1.3 DeLury method

This relies on accurate catch and effort data (DeLury, 1947) from the whale fishery. The catch per unit of effort is plotted against the accumulated catch in successive years. Where the plot is extrapolated to zero catch per unit of effort, the stock size can be determined for the initial year of fishery. This method depends on the catch per unit of effort declining as the fishery progresses. Also, allowances must be made for natural mortality and recruitment, particularly if they are changing during the period investigated (Chapman, 1970).

8.1.4 Mortality coefficient method

If, in addition to catch and effort statistics, the age composition of the catch is known, then mortality coefficients can be calculated from linear logarithmic regression of catch on age class after the initial age at full recruitment. It also requires an assumption that the stock is neither increasing nor decreasing. Such estimates give a total mortality coefficient combining natural and fishing mortalities. However, calculation of the mortality co-efficient at the commencement of the fishery will give an estimate of the natural mortality coefficient, and the fishing mortality coefficient can then be derived by subtraction of this from total mortality. The ratio between the catch and fishing mortality coefficient gives an estimate of population size.

8.1.5 Least squares method

This method (Allen, 1966, 1968) utilizes catch and age composition data. The catches of a year class are compared in one season when it is partially recruited to the exploited stock with those in the consecutive season when it is fully recruited. The proportion of new recruits in a year class fully recruited for the first time can thus be calculated; also by extending back in time, the proportion of new recruits in all the catches can be derived. The population size is then calculated using the recruitment figures thus derived, by finding the value which minimizes the sum of the squares of the differences between the actual catches and those anticipated.

8.1.6 Recruitment curve method

This method depends on the relationship between population size, catch and recruitment which is a theoretical value based on estimates of repro-ductive parameters. The method for calculation of current population size relies on a base-line estimate of original population size which then has deducted from it annual catches adjusted by allowing for recruitment (see Doi *et al.*, 1967).

8.1.7 Cohort analysis

This method requires data on age composition of each season's catch, natural mortality coefficient and estimated annual rate of exploitation. The value for exploitation rate is used to calculate population size in each year class. Thus changes in population size by year class can be followed each season (International Whaling Commission, 1978).

Other procedures are given in the recent Reports of the International Whaling Commission, and some, together with general principles, are sum-marized by Chapman (1974) and Mackintosh (1965).

8.2   Numbers and standing stock biomass

In managing commercially exploited cetaceans, the concept of maximum sustainable yield (MSY) is generally adopted. (Although see Holt (1978) for a critique of this criterion.) In theory, the net recruitment rate (recruitment rate less mortality rate) of an exploited population is anticipated to increase as the population is reduced. At the maximum population size (that permitted by the carrying capacity of the environment), gross recruitment and natural mortality rates balance to maintain the population at that size and in equilibrium. Once the population is reduced by whatever means, parameters associated with fecundity, growth and mortality are expected to alter (Gambell, 1976a). This disturbs the balance between recruitment and natural mortality so that there is effectively a surplus of recruits in order to return the population to maximum size. This surplus or replacement yield can be harvested in a fishery as a sustainable yield, in that after the catch has been taken, the net recruitment rate remains at zero, so maintaining the population at that size.

In the most efficient fishery operations, management strives to reduce the population to a level at or close to the MSY level. This can be determined according to a method of Schaefer (1953), and involves plotting the calculated sustainable yields against population size. The plot takes the form of a dome-shaped curve, with sustainable yields of zero corresponding with population sizes of zero and the maximum supported by the environment. The peak of this curve indicates the MSY and its corresponding population size. In baleen whale species this MSY level of population size is about 50% or higher of the initial maximum size. In sperm whales, however, the males and females need to be analysed separately because of their polygynous social structure.

The MSY can be determined either in terms of numbers or biomass of animals. This matter was discussed by the International Whaling Commission (1976) at a special meeting. It was determined that generally MSY by weight required a higher population level than that of MSY by number, although the difference was small at less than 5% in baleen whales. However, the difference in sperm whales was 7–18%. Some scientists (Holt, 1976) believe that MSY expressed in terms of biomass is a more reliable and conservative approach to species management than MSY by number. Either approach is likely to be acceptable to the whaling industry providing MSY can be predicted accurately, but some conservationists seek an even more conservative measure.

In Table V, estimates of initial, current and MSY population levels in terms of numbers are given for large whale species; these population sizes refer to the entire southern hemisphere. The International Whaling Commission divides the southern hemisphere oceans into six Areas for stock management of baleen whales and nine Divisions for that of sperm whales. Population estimates, stock classification and catch limits are given annually for all Areas and Divisions, e.g. International Whaling Commission (1981). Conservation of whales is discussed in Chapter 15.

9. Summary

Seven species or subspecies of Mysticete whales, including six rorquals, occur in Antarctic waters, together with eight Odontocetes. There is no exclusively polar cetacean in the southern hemisphere and the five rorqual species, and sperm, killer and long-finned pilot whales, also occur in the northern hemisphere. All seven baleen whales and the sperm whale have been subject to whaling, and much of our knowledge of their biology comes from the examination of captured animals and from catch statistics.

Northern and southern hemisphere stocks of rorquals are separate. All five species are believed to have an annual cycle of winter breeding in tropical or warm temperate waters and summer feeding in polar or cold temperate waters, with spring and autumn migrations between the two regions. Gestation lasts nearly a year so that both mating and parturition occur in warm waters. Their staple food is concentrated in Antarctic and cold temperate waters; they therefore also have an annual cycle of feeding and non-feeding periods. On the feeding grounds, all rorqual species form concentrations which are the basis of the International Whaling Commission's six southern hemisphere management Areas. All species are believed to be divided into one or more separate stocks in each of the South Atlantic, Indian and South Pacific Oceans. Southern right whales may also have comparable stock divisions and they undertake similar but less extensive migrations. Segregation of the sexes and of sexual and age classes, especially during migrations occurs in all species.

Sperm whales north and south of the Equator are assumed to be separate breeding stocks. In the southern hemisphere nine management Divisions (stocks) are recognized by the International Whaling Commission. Females and young males are generally confined to waters north of the Sub-tropical Convergence; only adult males occurring further south. Movements take place between polar and warmer waters but it is uncertain whether these are regular annual seasonal migrations comparable to those of Mysticetes. Little is known of the detailed distribution or biology of other Antarctic Odontocetes.

The Mysticetes, with the possible exception of the minke whale, have a two-year reproductive cycle and conception and birth are strongly seasonal.

TABLE V

Estimated exploitable stock sizes in terms of numbers of the large whales ($\times 10^{-3}$), based on Gambell (1976a) with revisions

Species	Initial stock	MSY stock	Present stock (most recent estimate)	MSY
Blue	180 (150–210)	100–125	8[a]	6
Pygmy blue	10	5	5	0.2
Humpback	100	50	3–total population size	2–4,
Fin	400 (375–425); Area VI only—19.4[h](1930 base)	234 (209–248)	85.2[b], Area VI only—8.9[h]	7.7 (6.8–8.6)
Sei	150 (125–150); 63.9–113[i]	54 (47–62)[c]	54[d](52–57)[d]; 11–76.4[i]	4.5 (4.1–5.0)
Minke	172[d] ⎫ 1930 base 225[e] ⎭ No recent estimates by Area	103 based on[d] 135[e]	Area— I—28.6 II—56.4 III—88.2 IV—44.4 V—51.8 VI—54.1 ⎬[j] Total 323.5[j] 173.6[g]	Replacement yields ⎫ ⎬ ⎭

Replacement yields:

	♂	♀
Area— I—	0.6	0.6
II—	0.9	1.1
III—	1.5	1.8
IV—	0.7	0.8
V—	0.9	1.0
VI—	0.8	0.8

}[j]

11.1[g] Replacement yield or 8.1 if combined sexes

				3—total population size		
Right	?(probably >194[f])	78[d]	?		3.8[d]	?
Sperm ♂	170[d]; Division 2—23 3—25.7 4—15.8 $\Big\}$ k 5—15.8 9—48.4 Also Division 9 only[j] 39.2—50.9	78[d]	?	71[d]; Division 2—10.6 3— 6.6 4— 7.6 $\Big\}$ k 5— 4.2 9—16.3 Also Division 9 only[j] 4.5—8.5		
Sperm ♀	160[d]; Division 2—49.1 3—55.0 4—33.9 $\Big\}$ k 5—33.8 9—59.7 Also Division 9 only[j] 52.5—82	125[d]	125[d]; Division 2—41.1 3—42.9 4—32.3 $\Big\}$ k 5—30.8 9—29.9 Also Division 9 only[j] 18.4—36.5		0.85[d]	

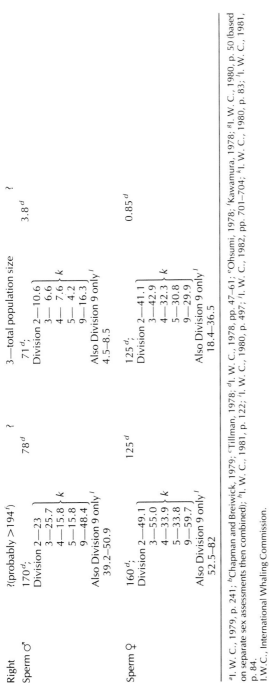

[a]I. W. C., 1979, p. 241; [b]Chapman and Breiwick, 1979; [c]Tillman, 1978; [d]I. W. C., 1978, pp. 47–61; [e]Ohsumi, 1978; [f]Kawamura, 1978; [g]I. W. C., 1980, p. 50 (based on separate sex assessments then combined); [h]I. W. C., 1981, p. 122; [i]I. W. C., 1980, p. 497; [j]I. W. C., 1982, pp. 701–704; [k]I. W. C., 1980, p. 83; [l]I. W. C., 1981, p. 84.
I.W.C., International Whaling Commission.

The gestation period of 10–12 months fits the annual migration and feeding cycle with foetal growth including an exponential phase in the second half of pregnancy. In blue, fin and sei whales, the calf suckles for approximately six months and is weaned on the summer feeding grounds. Minke and humpback whale calves suckle for four and 11 months respectively and are weaned on the northerly winter grounds. In all species growth is rapid in the first year but decreases with increasing age, ceasing with physical maturity at about 25 years old. Females reach maximum lengths about 5% greater than males. In fin, sei and minke whales an increase in pre-pubertal growth rate in recent decades has led to a decline in the average age at sexual maturity. This decline parallels the history of exploitation of fin and sei whales and is believed to result from a reduction in intra- and inter-specific competition for food as their numbers have been reduced by whaling.

Sperm whales are polygynous, with marked sexual dimorphism, and they exhibit complex social behaviour. The female reproductive cycle is usually four years. Gestation lasts from 14.5 to 16 months according to region and an exponential foetal growth phase is absent. The calf may suckle for up to two years. Puberty is prolonged in males and sexual maturity at about 18 years corresponds with their first movement into polar waters. Functional (social) maturity at about 26 years is attained with harem bull status.

The baleen whales feed in surface waters on swarming planktonic crustaceans, especially *Euphausia superba*. Interspecific competition is reduced by differential timing of their arrival on the feeding grounds, and differences in geographical distribution. Intensive feeding, with 3–4% of body weight consumed daily, lasts for four months. Food energy is stored as fat to meet metabolic requirements during the remainder of the year, with increases in body weight of 30–100% in rorquals. Pregnant females probably feed for an additional month to meet the extra energy demands of pregnancy and lactation.

Some Odontocetes, especially sperm whales, feed at depth using echolocation. Unlike baleen whales, these species are not dependent upon a seasonal food supply. Sperm whales, feeding mainly on squid, consume about 3% of their body weight daily. This is increased in pregnant females to meet the energy demands of late pregnancy and lactation.

Several methods are employed to estimate population size in commercially exploited cetaceans and the concept of maximum sustainable yield is used in their management.

10. References

Aguayo L., A. (1974). Baleen whales off continental Chile. *In* "The Whale Problem. A Status Report" (W. E. Schevill, ed.), pp. 209–217. Harvard University Press, Cambridge, Massachusetts.

Aguayo L., A. (1975). Progress report on small cetacean research in Chile. *Journal of the Fisheries Research Board of Canada* **32**, 1123–1143.

Allen, K. R. (1966). Some methods for estimating exploited populations. *Journal of the Fisheries Research Board of Canada* **23**, 1553–1574.

Allen, K. R. (1968). Simplification of a method of computing recruitment rates. *Journal of the Fisheries Research Board of Canada* **25**, 2701–2702.

Allen, K. R. (1980). "Conservation and Management of Whales". University of Washington Press, Seattle.

Andersen, H. T. (ed.) (1969). "The Biology of Marine Mammals". Academic Press, New York and London.

Arsenev, V. K. (1960). Distribution of *Balaenoptera acutorostrata* Lacep. in the Antarctic. *Norwegian Whaling Gazette* **49**, 380–382.

Backus, R. H. and Schevill, W. E. (1966). *Physeter* clicks. *In* "Whales, Dolphins and Porpoises" (K. S. Norris, ed.), pp. 510–528. University of California Press, Berkeley.

Baker, A. N. (1977). Spectacled porpoise, *Phocoena dioptrica*, new to the sub-Antarctic Pacific Ocean. *New Zealand Journal of Marine and Freshwater Research* **11**, 401–406.

Bannister, J. L. (1966). Sperm whales. *Report of Division of Fisheries and Oceanography, CSIRO, Australia* (1965–66), 22–23.

Bannister, J. L. (1969). The biology and status of the sperm whale off Western Australia—an extended summary of results of recent work. *Report of the International Whaling Commission* **19**, 70–76.

Bannister, J. L. and Baker, A. de C. (1967). Observations on food and feeding of baleen whales at Durban. *Norwegian Whaling Gazette* **56**, 78–82.

Bannister, J. L. and Gambell, R. (1965). The succession and abundance of fin, sei and other whales off Durban. *Norwegian Whaling Gazette* **54**, 45–60.

Beale, T. (1835). "A Few Observations on the Natural History of the Sperm Whale". Effingham Wilson, London.

Bertalanffy, L. von (1938). A quantitative theory of organic growth. *Human Biology* **10**, 181–213.

Berzin, A. A. (1972). "The Sperm Whale". [Israel Program for Scientific Translations, Jerusalem.]

Best, P. B. (1967). Distribution and feeding habits of baleen whales off the Cape Province. *Division of Sea Fisheries Investigational Report South Africa* **57**, 1–44.

Best, P. B. (1968). The sperm whale (*Physeter catodon*) off the west coast of South Africa 2. Reproduction in the female. *Division of Sea Fisheries Investigational Report South Africa* **66**, 1–32.

Best, P. B. (1969a). The sperm whale (*Physeter catodon*) off the west coast of South Africa 3. Reproduction in the male. *Division of Sea Fisheries Investigational Report South Africa* **72**, 1–20.

Best, P. B. (1969b). The sperm whale (*Physeter catodon*) off the west coast of South Africa 4. Distribution and movements. *Division of Sea Fisheries Investigational Report South Africa* **78**, 1–12.

Best, P. B. (1970a). The sperm whale (*Physeter catodon*) off the west coast of South

Africa 5. Age, growth and mortality. _Division of Sea Fisheries Investigational Report South Africa_ **79**, 1–27.

Best, P. B. (1970b). Exploitation and recovery of right whales _Eubalaena australis_ off the Cape Province. _Division of Sea Fisheries Investigational Report South Africa_ **80**, 1–20.

Best, P. B. (1974a). Status of the whale populations off the west coast of South Africa, and current research. _In_ "The Whale Problem. A Status Report" (W. E. Schevill, ed.), pp. 53–81. Harvard University Press, Cambridge, Massachusetts.

Best, P. B. (1974b). The biology of the sperm whale as it relates to stock management. _In_ "The Whale Problem. A Status Report" (W. E. Schevill, ed.), pp. 257–293. Harvard University Press, Cambridge, Massachusetts.

Best, P. B. (1975). Status of whale stocks off South Africa, 1973. _Report of the International Whaling Commission_ **25**, 198–207.

Best, P. B. (1976a). A review of world sperm whale stocks. Scientific Consultation on Marine Mammals, Bergen. Paper ACMRR/MM/SC/8 REV.1.

Best, P. B. (1976b). Tetracycline marking and the rate of growth layer formation in the teeth of a dolphin, _Lagenorhynchus obscurus_. _South African Journal of Science_ **72**, 216–218.

Betesheva, E. I. (1961). Feeding of commercial species of whale in the Kuriles Region. _Trudy Instituta Morfologii Zhivotnykh_ **34**, 7–32.

Brodie, P. F. (1975). Cetacean energetics, an overview of intraspecific size variation. _Ecology_ **56**, 152–161.

Brody, S. (1968). "Bioenergetics and Growth". Hafner, New York.

Brown, S. G. (1962a). A note on migration in fin whales. _Norwegian Whaling Gazette_ **51**, 13–16.

Brown, S. G. (1962b). The movements of fin and blue whales within the Antarctic zone. _"Discovery" Reports_ **33**, 1–54.

Brown, S. G. (1968). Feeding of sei whales at South Georgia. _Norwegian Whaling Gazette_ **57**, 118–125.

Brown, S. G. (1971). Whale marking—progress report, 1970. _Report of the International Whaling Commission_ **21**, 51–55.

Brown, S. G. (1977a). Some results of sei whale marking in the southern hemisphere. _Report of the International Whaling Commission, Special Issue_ **1**, 39–43.

Brown, S. G. (1977b). Whale marking: a short review. _In_ "A Voyage of Discovery" (M. Angel, ed.), pp. 569–581. Pergamon Press, Oxford.

Brown, S. G. (1978). Whale marking techniques. _In_ "Animal Marking. Recognition Marking of Animals in Research" (B. Stonehouse, ed.), pp. 71–80. Macmillan, London.

Brownell, R. L. Jr (1974). Small Odontocetes of the Antarctic. _Antarctic Map Folio Series_ **18**, 13–19.

Budylenko, G. A. (1977). Distribution and composition of sei whale schools in the southern hemisphere. _Report of the International Whaling Commission Special Issue_ **1**, 121–123.

Budylenko, G. A. (1978). Distribution and migration of sei whales in the southern hemisphere. _Report of the International Whaling Commission_ **28**, 373–377.

Caldwell, M. C. and Caldwell, D. K. (1966). Epimeletic (care-giving) behavior in Cetacea. _In_ "Whales, Dolphins, and Porpoises" (K. S. Norris, ed.), pp. 755–789. University of California Press, Berkeley.

Cawthorn, M. W. (1978). Whale research in New Zealand. _Report of the International Whaling Commission_ **28**, 109–113.

Chapman, D. G. (1970). Re-analysis of Antarctic fin whale population data. *Report of the International Whaling Commission* **20**, 54–59.

Chapman, D. G. (1974). Estimation of population parameters of Antarctic baleen whales. *In* "The Whale Problem. A Status Report" (W. E. Schevill, ed.), pp. 336–351. Harvard University Press, Cambridge, Massachusetts.

Chapman, D. G. and Breiwick, J. (1979). Updated estimates of fin whale stocks in southern oceans. *Report of the International Whaling Commission* **29**, 86.

Chapman, D. G., Allen, K. R. and Holt, S. J. (1964). Reports of the Committee of Three Scientists on the Special Investigation of the Antarctic Whale Stocks. *Report of the International Whaling Commission* **14**, 32–106.

Chittleborough, R. G. (1958). The breeding cycle of the female humpback whale, *Megaptera nodosa* (Bonnaterre). *Australian Journal of Marine and Freshwater Research* **9**, 1–18.

Chittleborough, R. G. (1959). Determination of age in the humpback whale, *Megaptera nodosa* (Bonnaterre). *Australian Journal of Marine and Freshwater Research* **10**, 125–143.

Chittleborough, R. G. (1960). Marked humpback whale of known age. *Nature* (Lond.) **187**, 164.

Chittleborough, R. G. (1962). Australian catches of humpback whales 1961. *Report of Division of Fisheries and Oceanography, CSIRO, Australia* **34**, 1–13.

Chittleborough, R. G. (1963). Australian catches of humpback whales 1962. *Report of Division of Fisheries and Oceanography, CSIRO, Australia* **35**, 1–5.

Chittleborough, R. G. (1965). Dynamics of two populations of the humpback whale, *Megaptera novaeangliae* (Borowski). *Australian Journal of Marine and Freshwater Research* **16**, 33–128.

Clarke, A. (1980). The biochemical composition of krill, *Euphausia superba* Dana, from South Georgia. *Journal of Experimental Marine Biology and Ecology* **43**, 221–236.

Clarke, M. R. (1972). New technique for the study of sperm whale migration. *Nature* (Lond.) **238**, 405-406.

Clarke, M. R. (1980). Cephalopoda in the diet of sperm whales of the southern hemisphere and their bearing on sperm whale biology. *"Discovery" Reports* **37**, 1–324.

Clarke, R. (1955). A giant squid swallowed by a sperm whale. *Norwegian Whaling Gazette* **44**, 589–593.

Clarke, R. (1956). Sperm whales of the Azores. *"Discovery" Reports* **28**, 237–298.

Condy, P. R., van Aarde, R. J. and Bester, M. N. (1978). The seasonal occurrence and behaviour of killer whales *Orcinus orca*, at Marion Island. *Journal of Zoology* (Lond.) **184**, 449–464.

Dall, W. and Dunstan, D. (1957). *Euphausia superba* Dana from a humpback whale, *Megaptera nodosa* (Bonnaterre), caught off Southern Queensland. *Norwegian Whaling Gazette* **46**, 6–9.

Davies, J. L. (1960). The southern form of the pilot whale. *Journal of Mammalogy* **41**, 29–34.

Davies, J. L. (1963). The antitropical factor in cetacean speciation. *Evolution* **17**, 107–116.

Dawbin, W. H. (1960). An analysis of the New Zealand catches of humpback whales from 1947 to 1958. *Norwegian Whaling Gazette* **49**, 61–75.

Dawbin, W. H. (1966). The seasonal migratory cycle of humpback whales. *In* "Whales, Dolphins and Porpoises" (K. S. Norris, ed.), pp. 145–170. University of California Press, Berkeley.

Dawbin, W. H. and Falla, R. A. (1949). A contribution to the study of the humpback whale based on observations at New Zealand shore stations. *Proceedings of the Seventh Pacific Science Congress* **4**, 373–382.

DeLury, D. B. (1947). On the estimation of biological populations. *Biometrics* **3**, 145–167.

Doi, T., Ohsumi, S. and Nemoto, T. (1967). Population assessment of sei whales in the Antarctic. *Norwegian Whaling Gazette* **56**, 25–41.

Donnelly, B. G. (1969). Further observations on the southern right whale, *Eubalaena australis*, in South African waters. *Journal of Reproduction and Fertility* (Suppl.) **6**, 347–352.

Doroshenko, N. V. (1979). Populations of minke whales in the southern hemisphere. *Report of the International Whaling Commission* **29**, 361–364.

Fordyce, R. E. (1977). The development of the Circum-Antarctic Current and the evolution of the Mysticeti (Mammalia: Cetacea). *Palaeogeography, Palaeoclimatology, Palaeoecology* **21**, 265–271.

Fraser, F. C. (1955). The southern right whale dolphin, *Lissodelphis peroni* (Lacépède), external characters and distribution. *Bulletin of the British Museum (Natural History)*, Zoology **2**, 339–346.

Gambell, R. (1964). A pygmy blue whale at Durban. *Norwegian Whaling Gazette* **53**, 66–68.

Gambell, R. (1967). Seasonal movements of sperm whales. *Symposia of the Zoological Society of London* **19**, 237–254.

Gambell, R. (1968). Seasonal cycles and reproduction in sei whales of the southern hemisphere. *"Discovery" Reports* **35**, 31–134.

Gambell, R. (1972). Sperm whales off Durban. *"Discovery" Reports* **35**, 199–358.

Gambell, R. (1973). Some effects of exploitation on reproduction in whales. *Journal of Reproduction and Fertility* (Suppl.) **19**, 533–553.

Gambell, R. (1976a). World whale stocks. *Mammal Review* **6**, 41–53.

Gambell, R. (1976b). Population biology and the management of whales. *In* "Applied Biology" (T. H. Coaker, ed.), Vol. I, pp. 247–343. Academic Press, New York and London.

Gambell, R. (1977). Dentinal layer formation in sperm whale teeth. *In* "A Voyage of Discovery" (M. Angel, ed.), pp. 583–590. Pergamon Press, Oxford.

Gaskin, D. E. (1964). Recent observations in New Zealand waters on some aspects of behaviour of the sperm whale (*Physeter macrocephalus*). *Tuatara* **12**, 106–114.

Gaskin, D. E. (1976). The evolution, zoogeography and ecology of Cetacea. *Oceanography and Marine Biology Annual Review* **14**, 247–346.

Gianuca, N. M. and Castello, H. P. (1976). First record of the southern bottlenose whale, *Hyperoodon planifrons* from Brazil. *Scientific Reports of the Whales Research Institute* (Tokyo) **28**, 119–126.

Gill, C. D. and Hughes, S. E. (1971). A sei whale, *Balaenoptera borealis* feeding on Pacific saury, *Cololabis saira*. *California Fish and Game* **57**, 218–219.

Gray, W. B. (1964). "Porpoise Tales". Barnes, New York.

Harmer, S. F. (1931). Southern whaling. *Proceedings of the Linnean Society of London* **142**, 85–163.

Heyerdahl, E. F. (1932). Hvalindustrien. I Ramaterialet. *Publikationer Kommander Chr. Christensens Hvalfangstmuseum i Sandefjord* **7**, 23–26.

Hirano, T., Kikuchi, T., Ino, T., Tanone, N., Taguci, T. and Okada, T. (1964). Contents of inorganic substances and vitamin B_{12} in *Euphausia*. *Journal of the Tokyo University of Fisheries* **50**, 65–70.

Hjort, J., Lie, J. and Ruud, J. T. (1932). Norwegian pelagic whaling in the Antarctic. I. Whaling grounds in 1929–1930 and 1930–1931. *Hvalrådets Skrifter* **3**, 1–37.

Holt, S. J. (1976). Criteria for management—weight or numbers? The relevance of whaling effort. *Report of the International Whaling Commission, Scientific Report* **26**, 409–413.

Holt, S. J. (1978). Some implications of Maximum Sustainable Net Yield as a management objective for whaling. *Report of the International Whaling Commission* **28**, 191–193.

Hosokawa, H. and Kamiya, T. (1971). Some observations on the cetacean stomachs, with special considerations on the feeding habits of whales. *Scientific Reports of the Whales Research Institute* (Tokyo) **23**, 91–101.

Ichihara, T. (1966a). Criterion for determining age of fin whale with reference to ear plug and baleen plate. *Scientific Reports of the Whales Research Institute* (Tokyo) **20**, 17–82.

Ichihara, T. (1966b). The pygmy blue whale, *Balaenoptera musculus brevicauda*, a new subspecies from the Antarctic. *In* "Whales, Dolphins, and Porpoises" (K. S. Norris, ed.), pp. 79–113. University of California Press, Berkeley.

Il'ichev, Y. F. (1967).The chemical composition of krill and its use for feed and food purposes. *In* "Soviet Fishery Research on the Antarctic Krill" (R. N. Burukovskiy, ed.), pp. 38–55. Atlantic Scientific Research Institute for Fisheries and Oceanography, Kaliningrad.

International Whaling Commission (1976). *Report of the International Whaling Commission, Scientific Report* **26**, 105–109.

International Whaling Commission (1978). *Report of the International Whaling Commission* **28**.

International Whaling Commission (1979). *Report of the International Whaling Commission* **29**.

International Whaling Commission (1980). *Report of the International Whaling Commission* **30**.

International Whaling Commission (1981). *Report of the International Whaling Commission* **31**.

International Whaling Commission (1982). *Report of the International Whaling Commission* **32**.

Ivashin, M. V. and Mikhalev, Y. A. (1978). To the problem of the prenatal growth of minke whales *Balaenoptera acutorostrata* of the southern hemisphere and of the biology of their reproduction. *Report of the International Whaling Commission* **28**, 201–205.

Jonsgård, Å. and Lyshoel, P. B. (1970). A contribution to the knowledge of the biology of the killer whale *Orcinus orca* (L.) *Nytt Magasin for Zoology* **18**, 41–48.

Kasuya, T. (1977). Age determination and growth of the Baird's beaked whale with a comment on the fetal growth rate. *Scientific Reports of the Whales Research Institute* (Tokyo) **29**, 1–20.

Kasuya, T. and Ichihara, T. (1965). Some informations on minke whales from the Antarctic. *Scientific Reports of the Whales Research Institute* (Tokyo) **19**, 37–43.

Kawamura, A. (1970). Food of sei whale taken by Japanese whaling expeditions in the Antarctic season 1967/68. *Scientific Reports of the Whales Research Institute* (Tokyo) **22**, 127–152.

Kawamura, A. (1974). Food and feeding ecology in the southern sei whale. *Scientific Reports of the Whales Research Institute* (Tokyo) **26**, 25–144.

Kawamura, A. (1975). A consideration on an available source of energy and its cost for locomotion in fin whales with special reference to the seasonal migrations. *Scientific Reports of the Whales Research Institute* (Tokyo) **27**, 61–79.

Kawamura, A. (1978). An interim consideration on a possible interspecific relation in southern baleen whales from the viewpoint of their food habits. *Report of the International Whaling Commission* **28**, 411–420.

Kellogg, R. (1940). Whales, giants of the sea. *National Geographic Magazine* **77**, 35–90.

Kimura, S. (1957). The twinning in southern fin whales. *Scientific Reports of the Whales Research Institute* (Tokyo) **12**, 103–125.

Klumov, S. K. (1963). Food and helminth fauna of whalebone whales (Mystacoceti) in the main whaling regions of the world ocean. *Trudy Instituta Okeanologii* **71**, 94–194.

Laws, R. M. (1953). The elephant seal (*Mirounga leonina* Linn.) I. Growth and age. *Falkland Islands Dependencies Survey Scientific Reports* **8**, 1–62.

Laws, R. M. (1959). The foetal growth rates of whales with special reference to the fin whale, *Balaenoptera physalus* Linn. *"Discovery" Reports* **29**, 281–308.

Laws, R. M. (1960). Problems of whale conservation. *Transactions of the North American Wildlife Conference* **25**, 304–319.

Laws, R. M. (1961). Reproduction, growth and age of southern fin whales. *"Discovery" Reports* **31**, 327–486.

Laws, R. M. (1977). The significance of vertebrates in the Antarctic marine ecosystem. *In* "Adaptations Within Antarctic Ecosystems" (G. A. Llano, ed.), pp. 411–438. Smithsonian Institution, Washington, D.C.

Lockyer, C. (1972). The age at sexual maturity of the southern fin whale (*Balaenoptera physalus*) using annual layer counts in the ear plug. *Journal du Conseil. Conseil Permanent International pour l'Exploration de la Mer* **34**, 276–294.

Lockyer, C. (1974). Investigation of the ear plug of the southern sei whale, *Balaenoptera borealis*, as a valid means of determining age. *Journal du Conseil. Conseil Permanent International pour l'Exploration de la Mer* **36**, 71–81.

Lockyer, C. (1976). Body weights of some species of large whales. *Journal du Conseil. Conseil Permanent International pour l'Exploration de la Mer* **36**, 259–273.

Lockyer, C. (1977a). Some estimates of growth in the sei whale, *Balaenoptera borealis*. *Report of the International Whaling Commission, Special Issue* **1**, 58–62.

Lockyer, C. (1977b). A preliminary study of variations in age at sexual maturity of the fin whale with year class, in six Areas of the southern hemisphere. *Report of the International Whaling Commission* **27**, 141–147.

Lockyer, C. (1977c). Some possible factors affecting age distribution of the catch of sei whales in the Antarctic. *Report of the International Whaling Commission, Special Issue* **1**, 63–70.

Lockyer, C. (1977d). Observations on diving behaviour of the sperm whale *Physeter catodon*. In "A Voyage of Discovery" (M. Angel, ed.), pp. 591–609. Pergamon Press, Oxford.

Lockyer, C. (1978). A theoretical approach to the balance between growth and food consumption in fin and sei whales, with special reference to the female reproductive cycle. *Report of the International Whaling Commission* **28**, 243–249.

Lockyer, C. (1979). Changes in a growth parameter associated with exploitation of southern fin and sei whales. *Report of the International Whaling Commission* **29**, 191–196.

Lockyer, C. (1981a). Growth and energy budgets of large baleen whales from the southern hemisphere. *In* "Mammals in the Seas", pp. 379–487. FAO Fisheries Series No. 5, Vol. III. FAO, Rome.

Lockyer, C. (1981b). Estimates of growth and energy budget for the sperm whale, *Physeter catodon*. *In* "Mammals in the Seas", pp. 489–504. FAO Fisheries Series No. 5, Vol. III. FAO, Rome.

McCann, C. (1975). A study of the genus *Berardius* Duvernoy. *Scientific Reports of the Whales Research Institute* (Tokyo) **27**, 111–137.

Mackintosh, N. A. (1942). The southern stocks of whalebone whales. *"Discovery" Reports* **22**, 197–300.

Mackintosh, N. A. (1965). "The Stocks of Whales". Fishing News (Books) Ltd, London.

Mackintosh, N. A. (1966). The distribution of southern blue and fin whales. *In* "Whales, Dolphins, and Porpoises" (K. S. Norris, ed.), pp. 125–144. University of California Press, Berkeley.

Mackintosh, N. A. (1972). Biology of the populations of large whales. *Science Progress* **60**, 449–464.

Mackintosh, N. A. (1974). Sizes of krill eaten by whales in the Antarctic. *"Discovery" Reports* **36**, 157–178.

Mackintosh, N. A. and Wheeler, J. F. G. (1929). Southern blue and fin whales. *"Discovery" Reports* **1**, 257–540.

Marr, J. (1962). The natural history and geography of the Antarctic krill (*Euphausia superba* Dana). *"Discovery" Reports* **32**, 33–464.

Masaki, Y. (1977). Japanese pelagic whaling and whale sighting in the Antarctic, 1975–76. *Report of the International Whaling Commission* **27**, 148–155.

Masaki, Y. (1979). Yearly change of the biological parameters for the Antarctic minke whale. *Report of the International Whaling Commission* **29**, 375–395.

Masaki, Y. and Yamamura, K. (1978). Japanese pelagic whaling and whale sighting in the 1976/77 Antarctic season. *Report of the International Whaling Commission* **28**, 251–261.

Matthews, L. H. (1937). The humpback whale, *Megaptera nodosa*. *"Discovery" Reports* **17**, 7–92.

Matthews, L. H. (1938). The sei whale, *Balaenoptera borealis*. *"Discovery" Reports* **17**, 183–290.

Mitchell, E. (ed.) (1975). Review of biology and fisheries for smaller cetaceans. *Journal of the Fisheries Research Board of Canada* **32**, 875–1240.

Nemoto, T. (1959). Food of baleen whales with reference to whale movements. *Scientific Reports of the Whales Research Institute* (Tokyo) **14**, 149–290.

Nemoto, T. (1962). Food of baleen whales collected in recent Japanese Antarctic whaling expeditions. *Scientific Reports of the Whales Research Institute* (Tokyo) **16**, 89–103.

Nemoto, T. (1966). Feeding of baleen whales and krill, and the value of krill as a marine resource in the Antarctic. *In* "Symposium on Antarctic Oceanography" (R. I. Currie, ed.) pp. 240–253. Scott Polar Research Institute, Cambridge.

Nemoto, T. (1970). Feeding pattern of baleen whales in the ocean. *In* "Marine Food Chains" (J. H. Steele, ed.), pp. 241–252. Oliver and Boyd, Edinburgh.

Nishiwaki, M. (1962). Aerial photographs show sperm whales' interesting habits. *Norwegian Whaling Gazette* **51**, 395–398.

Nishiwaki, M. (1977). Distribution of toothed whales in the Antarctic Ocean. *In*

"Adaptations Within Antarctic Ecosystems" (G. A. Llano, ed.), pp. 783–791. Smithsonian Institution, Washington, D.C.

Nishiwaki, M., Ohsumi, S. and Maeda, Y. (1963). Change of form in the sperm whale accompanied with growth. *Scientific Reports of the Whales Research Institute* (Tokyo) **17**, 1–14.

Ohsumi, S. (1971). Some investigations on the school structure of sperm whale. *Scientific Reports of the Whales Research Institute* (Tokyo) **23**, 1–25.

Ohsumi, S. (1973). Find of marlin spear from the Antarctic minke whales. *Scientific Reports of the Whales Research Institute* (Tokyo) **25**, 237–239.

Ohsumi, S. (1976). An attempt to standardize fishing efforts as applied to the stock assessment of the minke whale in Antarctic Area IV. *Report of the International Whaling Commission, Scientific Report* **26**, 404–408.

Ohsumi, S. (1978). Assessment of population sizes of the southern hemisphere minke whales adding the catch data in 1976/77. *Report of the International Whaling Commission* **28**, 273–276.

Ohsumi, S. (1979). Feeding habits of the minke whale in the Antarctic. *Report of the International Whaling Commission* **29**, 473–476.

Ohsumi, S. and Masaki, Y. (1975). Biological parameters of the Antarctic minke whale at the virginal population level. *Journal of the Fisheries Research Board of Canada* **32**, 995–1004.

Ohsumi, S. and Nasu, K. (1970). Range of habitat of the female sperm whale with reference to the oceanographic structure. *International Whaling Commission. Paper Sp/7 to Special Meeting on Sperm Whale Biology and Stock Assessments, 1970* (Honolulu).

Ohsumi, S., Masaki, Y. and Kawamura, A. (1970). Stock of the Antarctic minke whale. *Scientific Reports of the Whales Research Institute* (Tokyo) **22**, 75–125.

Omura, H. (1973). A review of pelagic whaling operations in the Antarctic based on the effort and catch data in 10° squares of latitude and longitude. *Scientific Reports of the Whales Research Institute* (Tokyo) **25**, 105–203.

Omura, H. (1975). Osteological study of the minke whale from the Antarctic. *Scientific Reports of the Whales Research Institute* (Tokyo) **27**, 1–36.

Omura, H., Fujino, K. and Kimura, S. (1955). Beaked whale *Berardius bairdi* of Japan, with notes on *Ziphius cavirostris*. *Scientific Reports of the Whales Research Institute* (Tokyo) **10**, 89–132.

Omura, H., Ohsumi, S., Nemoto, T., Nasu, K. and Kasuya, T. (1969). Black right whales in the North Pacific. *Scientific Reports of the Whales Research Institute* (Tokyo) **21**, 1–78.

Payne, R. S. and McVay, S. (1971). Songs of humpback whales. *Science* **173**, 585–597.

Petrides, G. A. and Swank, W. G. (1966). Estimating the productivity and energy relations of an African elephant population. *Proceedings of the IX International Grasslands Congress*, 831–842.

Roe, H. S. J. (1967). Seasonal formation of laminae in the ear plug of the fin whale. *"Discovery" Reports* **35**, 1–30.

Ross, G. J. B., Best, P. B. and Donnelly, B. G. (1975). New records of the pygmy right whale (*Caperea marginata*) from South Africa, with comments on distribution, migration, appearance, and behavior. *Journal of the Fisheries Research Board of Canada* **32**, 1005–1017.

Schaefer, M. B. (1953). Fisheries dynamics and the concept of maximum equilibrium catch. *Proceedings, Gulf and Caribbean Fisheries Institute* 6th Session, 1–11.

Sergeant, D. E. (1962). The biology of the pilot or pothead whale *Globicephala melaena* (Traill) in Newfoundland waters. *Bulletin. Fisheries Research Board of Canada* **132**, 1–84.

Sergeant, D. E. (1969). Feeding rates of Cetacea. *Fiskeridirektoratets Skrifter Serie Havundersøkelser* **15**, 246–258.

Slijper, E. J. (1962). "Whales". Hutchinson, London.

Tarpy, C. (1979). Killer whale attack! *National Geographic Magazine* **155**, 542–545.

Taylor, R. J. F. (1957). An unusual record of three species of whale being restricted to pools in Antarctic sea-ice. *Proceedings of the Zoological Society of London* **129**, 325–331.

Tillman, M. F. (1978). Extrapolated initial and current stock sizes for southern hemisphere sei whales. *Report of the International Whaling Commission* **28**, 313–314.

Tomilin, A. G. (1946). Lactation and nutrition in cetaceans. *Doklady (Proceedings) of the Academy of Sciences of the USSR* **52**, 277–279.

Tomilin, A. G. (1967). "Cetacea. Mammals of the USSR and Adjacent Countries", Vol. 9. [Israel Program for Scientific Translations, Jerusalem.]

Townsend, C. H. (1935). The distribution of certain whales as shown by logbook records of American whaleships. *Zoologica* (New York) **19**, 1–50.

Vinogradova, Z. A. (1967). The biochemical composition of Antarctic plankton. *In* "Biochemistry of Marine Organisms", pp. 7–17. Ukrainian Academy of Sciences, U.S.S.R.

Voisin, J.-F. (1972). Notes on the behaviour of the killer whale, *Orcinus orca* (L.). *Nytt Magasin for Zoology* **20**, 93–96.

Voisin, J.-F. (1976). On the behaviour of the killer whale, *Orcinus orca* (L.). *Nytt Magasin for Zoology* **24**, 69–71.

Wahrenbrock, E. A., Maruschak, G. F., Elsner, R. and Kenney, D. W. (1974). Respiration and metabolism in two baleen whale calves. *Marine Fisheries Review* **36(4)**, 3–9.

Watkins, W. A. and Schevill, W. E. (1975). Sperm whales (*Physeter catodon*) react to pingers. *Deep-Sea Research* **22**, 123–129.

Williamson, G. R. (1975). Minke whales off Brazil. *Scientific Reports of the Whales Research Institute* (Tokyo) **27**, 37–59.

Zemsky, V. A. and Boronin, V. A. (1964). On the question of the pygmy blue whale taxonomic position. *Norwegian Whaling Gazette* **53**, 306–311.

Zenkovich, B. A. (1969). Whales and plankton in Antarctic waters. *In* "Marine Mammals" (V. A. Arsenev, B. A. Zenkovich and K. K. Chapskii, eds), pp. 150–152. Izdatel'stvo Nauka, Moscow.

14

Marine interactions

I. Everson

1. Introduction

Descriptions of the Antarctic ecosystem have been made by several
workers. Hart (1942), Holdgate (1967) and Knox (1970) outlined the major
qualitative relationships in the marine food web and more recently Everson
(1977) discussed the available information on production and biomass in
the marine ecosystem. The extrapolations and, in many cases, almost total
lack of information, highlighted how little was known in quantitative terms
of ecosystem interactions. More recently Beddington and May (1980) have
devised models which attempt to quantify the effects of simultaneous krill
and whale fisheries upon each other. These developments come at a time
when there is a pressing need for information on which to devise plans for
rational management of resources. The need for these studies should not be
restricted simply to exploited or potentially exploitable resources but extended to all elements of the ecosystem, because unexploited components
may themselves be sensitive indicators of change and also for the reason
that insufficient is known or understood about the functioning of
ecosystems in general.

This chapter is therefore divided into three sections. The first deals with
the major food chain relationships so as to highlight the magnitude of
production by different trophic levels. The second discusses the current
models in terms of their database and their predictive application as management tools. This leads into the final section which deals with identifying
local interactions which might provide further insight into ecosystem functioning and greater refinement of the models.

ANTARCTIC ECOLOGY VOL. 2
ISBN 0 12-439502-3

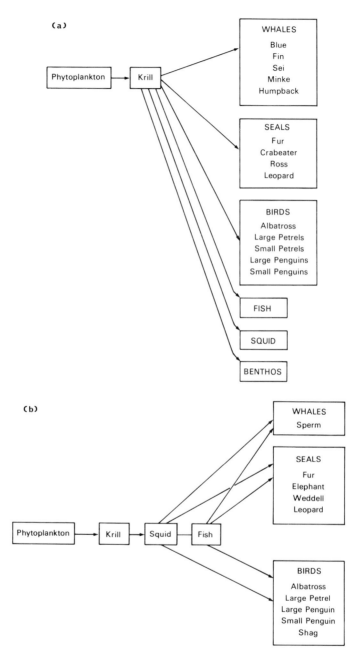

Fig. 1. Food chain relationships. Interactions involving direct consumption (a) and indirect consumption (b) of krill.

2. Food Chain Relationships

Some indications of the major food chain relationships are shown in Fig. 1. This is derived from information provided earlier (Chapters 10–13) and as such is very much a simplification. The main function of the figure is to highlight the already well known fact, that krill is a key food resource both directly and indirectly to the majority of higher trophic levels.

Such diagrams can only present part of the story in that they are purely qualitative. They do however provide a basis for determining predator/prey interactions and hence the quantitative transfer of energy up the food chain. An early study of this type was made by Hardy and Gunther (1935) using the results of the *Discovery* survey around South Georgia in 1926–1927. The chain of relationships they found is summarized below:

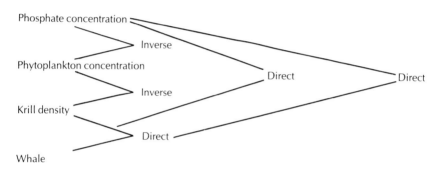

Hardy noted that areas of high phosphate occurrence initially contained little in terms of phytoplankton but the conditions were favourable for primary production. There was in consequence a local "bloom" which reduced the phosphate levels significantly; hence the inverse relationship between the two. The initial increase in phytoplankton occurred at a rate far in excess of the grazing rate of the krill, but as krill accumulated in the area (presumably by remaining in a favourable feeding zone) phytoplankton would be grazed down providing a second inverse relationship. Baleen whales migrating into the Southern Ocean would search out krill concentrations, and so one would expect a direct relationship between krill and whales.

These early conclusions, based on observations during one and in some cases two seasons, probably provide a reasonable indication of what happens in most years. Furthermore, they highlight the need for determining not only standing stock but also rates of change. This concept is not new in ecology but it is worth considering the extent of our knowledge of these two factors in the Southeren Ocean.

Primary production, as we have seen in Chapter 7, is dependent on light, nutrients and the presence of the primary producers in the euphotic zone. The light regime is very seasonal for two reasons, namely the effect of latitude on day length and the presence of sea ice. Day length varies in a predictable manner and can be taken into account in production models. The sea ice distribution is much less predictable, because it is dependent on both atmospheric and oceanic conditions. The overall picture of sea ice distribution does not give a realistic impression of the area over which primary production is limited (in this context the ice-associated primary production is considered to make a minimal contribution to the overall budget), because although at any given time sea ice might cover one to two thirds of the ocean south of the Antarctic Convergence, this ice is not necessarily moving at the same speed or in the same direction as the surface water. As a result, in geographical terms, only about 10% of the ocean surface has sea ice cover throughout the year and as the water itself is moving it may well be true to say that all surface water is ice-free at some time during the productive season. The conclusion from this line of argument must inevitably be that primary production never reaches the maximum levels theoretically possible given the available nutrients and incoming radiation. That the level can be high is well known, although relative to other oceans the Southern Ocean overall is not unusual in this respect.

Nutrients are often said to be non-limiting to primary production. This assumes that all critical nutrients are measured—which is rarely the case. The statement also poses the question: "If nutrients are generally non-limiting, why should upwelling zones be so productive?" The inescapable conclusion is that over much of the ocean nutrients are limiting, but insufficient information is available to identify the limiting factors. Clearly there is a need for more work on this subject.

Much basic information is still missing from the krill story. No unequivocal explanation has yet emerged to explain why krill tend to be found in some regions and not others. Are, for example, krill in the vicinity of the South Shetland Islands a local population or part of a larger "Bellingshausen Stock" or merely a small part of a total Southern Ocean krill stock? Furthermore, growth and natural mortality are largely unquantified, which means that analytical production models cannot be applied. Attempts have been made to estimate annual production conversion efficiency ratios. Chekunova and Rynkova (1974) estimated that an individual krill requires 60 g of phytoplankton to grow to a size of 1.5 g, indicating an efficiency of 2.5%. By comparison with other zooplankters this ratio is very low, although it should be borne in mind that the much higher zooplankton ratios are obtained from copepods which typically complete a generation within a few months. A tentative conversion ratio such as this when used in conjunction with primary production figures that are largely speculative can only result in production estimates of little real value. It should however be stressed that estimates of total krill production are an important pre-requisite for understanding the functioning of the ecosystem as well as for resource management.

Looking at krill from the other end of the food chain we can provide some indication of krill production based on consumption by predators. This can only give a rough indication because the result is obtained by summing most of the parts (i.e. consumption by whales, seals and birds but, ignoring the, as yet, unquantifiable squid) and omitting natural deaths of krill.

Probably the most reliable estimates of krill consumption by predators have been produced for whales. Stock sizes for the large whale species have been estimated for the initial (unexploited) whale stocks and for the present day (Chapter 13). In addition, growth rates are known and energy budgets have been derived (Lockyer, 1981; and Table 1). These results indicate that the initial whale stocks of 43 million tonnes consumed about 190 million tonnes of krill (Laws, 1977a), which with a natural mortality rate of about 5% per annum indicates a conversion efficiency of about 1% for conversion of krill to whale production. This compares very unfavourably with the 10% frequently used for an equivalent conversion by natural fish populations. The low value is largely due to the very slow whale growth rate from about age four years onwards.

TABLE I
Growth efficiencies (%) of large baleen whales

		Blue		Fin		Metabolic energy
		♂	♀	♂	♀	Growth energy
Calves prior to weaning	Gross	32.6		26.5		2.1
	Net	37.8		28.5		
At puberty	Gross	5.0	5.6	4.0	4.0	16.4
	Net	6.3	6.9	5.0	5.2	
Adults	Gross	0.6	0.8	0.7	0.9	98.5
	Net	0.8	1.1	1.1	1.2	

Data from Lockyer, 1976.

The difference between the estimated present-day and initial whale consumption of krill (150 million tonnes) is often referred to as a "krill surplus". This does not mean that this amount is now unutilized in the system, but rather that whales no longer consume it. A proportion (at this stage unquantified) may be cycled directly by decomposition but a significant proportion is now being taken by birds and seals (see Chapters 11 and 12) and has resulted in demographic changes there.

Of the seals the crabeater takes the greatest amount of krill and has a gross efficiency for the conversion of krill to seal of about 1%. Like the larger whales, the seals take several years to reach maturity and thereafter grow very little, resulting in a population containing a large proportion of individuals that have effectively stopped growing. An additional factor, in comparing them with whales, may be that of size, because larger animals need less energy per unit weight than smaller ones. Also, seals of a given size in captivity require very much more food if kept in cold environments than if they are in warm water (Bonner, personal communication). This difference is related to their higher (relative to large whales) surface area to volume ratio and its consequent effect on heat loss. On this basis it is to be expected that the minke whales will also have low conversion efficiencies due to their relatively small size and also because they probably spend more of the year than other species in cold waters (Laws, 1977a and personal communication).

We have seen in Chapter 11 that, although the Southern Ocean avifauna is composed of a moderately diverse assemblage of albatrosses, petrels and penguins, the greatest impact on the ecosystem in terms of krill consumption is caused by one species, the Adélie penguin. The 200,000 tonnes of penguins are thought to take over 33 million tonnes of krill per annum; a figure which suggests that penguins currently take more krill than other avian predators. As is made clear in Chapter 11 these figures are only put forward within the broadest limits but they do serve to indicate the probable level of consumption. In terms of conversion efficiency, the birds appear to be much less efficient than even the seals due to their small size (and hence higher surface area to volume ratio causing increased heat loss problems) and their intrinsically high energy requirements.

In contrast to the whales, seals and birds for which some information is available, the impact of fish and squid on the krill stocks is largely unquantified. No direct information is available on either the standing stock or production of squid, but indirect estimates, based on consumption by predators, suggest that the annual production of squid is in excess of 17 million tons (Everson, 1977). As squid tend to be relatively short-lived and have fast growth rates it is to be expected that they would have a high efficiency of conversion of krill to squid, perhaps even of the order of 30–50%, suggesting food consumption of the order of 34–56 million tonnes.

The total consumption of fish by their predators in the Southern Ocean is estimated to be about 15 million tonnes per annum (Everson, 1977; and Chapter 10), which assuming a 5% conversion efficiency (Everson, 1970) indicates that about 300 million tonnes of food is eaten by the Southern Ocean fish stocks. What proportion krill constitutes of this food is not known but bearing in mind that the diet of some species includes a large proportion of krill, then the total amount eaten must be several tens of millions of tonnes.

Two important points emerge from the foregoing discussion. First, that the annual production of krill is very large and, even using the most conservative estimates of krill consumption, must be over a 100 million tonnes. Secondly, the efficiency of conversion of energy from krill to the next higher trophic level is generally very low—much less than the 10% value often used in deriving preliminary production estimates.

3. Current Models

Ecosystem modelling began with purely descriptive studies of the various components and the recognition that there was a degree of dependence between at least some of these components. Thus, we have already seen that whales are dependent to a very large extent on krill production (Chapter 13) and that krill is dependent on phytoplankton production (Chapter 9). These conceptual models have in recent years been extended to examine these interactions in quantitative terms.

Whilst there is nothing wrong with the statements made above in conceptual terms, they are far from adequate in terms of predictive mathematical models. This is because each of the ecosystem components mentioned is dependent to some extent on some other factors. Thus while krill production depends on phytoplankton production it is also arguably dependent on many other factors such as:

(a) Primary production in previous season   affects overwintering condition of krill ; may influence fecundity and possibly also recruitment and mortality

(b) Physical environment   affects growth rates; influences distribution

(c) Trace elements   affects condition and thus growth, fecundity and mortality

Thus, in order to predict krill production we would need to determine the relationship between krill production and a very wide range of other factors. Ideally, this would involve all variables within the ecosystem. Clearly this is impossible, which means that a given model, whilst on the one hand being realistic for some situations, may well be unreliable or totally misleading in others. It is therefore very important to specify the conditions under which a particular model is valid and keep within them for predictive purposes, for while there may be no logical reason to discredit extrapolation of a particular function, there may be another as yet unquantified variable which only takes effect in the extrapolated part of the function.

Bearing this warning in mind, let us now consider the important questions that models should be addressing and the manner in which they are being answered. To begin with two sweeping generalizations, conservationists are interested in seeing the maintenance of a healthy ecosystem and exploiters are interested in seeing a return on capital investment. Although very often their aims may seem diametrically opposed, their long-term interests should have much in common because both groups would presumably like to know how much of each resource can be taken on a continuing basis. This must be a central question in resource management terms because the understanding of how much of each resource can be taken each year allows the industrialists to invest at a level consistent with maintaining a sustained return on capital.

Having decided on what is an "acceptable" level of exploitation we must also look into possible local effects. For example, if 10% of overall krill Maximum Sustainable Yield (MSY) were taken from 1% of the Southern Ocean this might have a strong adverse effect on local krill consumers and yet minimal unpredicted effect on the krill itself.

In terms of purely ecological studies, there is a wide variety of interactions that could be quantified and these in turn would add a finer tuning to those included above as well as giving insight into the structure and dynamic functioning of the ecosystem as a whole.

Two models describing the relationships between krill and its principal consumers have been presented by Horwood (1981), May *et al.* (1979) and Beddington and May (1980). Both follow essentially the same reasoning. The terminology used here is that of Beddington and May. They use the differential equation (1) below to define the rate of change in the krill population

$$\frac{dN_1}{dt} = r_1 N_1 \left(1 - \frac{N_1}{K} \right) - aN_1 N_2 \tag{1}$$

Where r_1 is the per capita intrinsic growth rate, N_1 krill population size and

K the krill carrying capacity. The predator population (whales) size is N_2 and each predator consumes prey at a rate proportional to density $(\alpha\,N_1)$.

The predator dynamics are described by:

$$\frac{dN_2}{dt} = r_2N_2\left(1 - \frac{N_2}{\alpha N_1}\right)$$

in which r_2 is the per capita intrinsic growth rate for the predator population and the predator carrying capacity is (αN_1), linearly proportional to the prey abundance.

For convenience, Beddington and May rescale equations (1) and (2) into a dimensionless form by defining

$$X_1 = N_1/K, \quad X_2 = N_2/\alpha K$$

and introducing the dimensionless term

$$v = a\alpha K/r_1$$

which defines the rate at which krill are exploited by predators.

If $v = 1$, then $r_1 = a\alpha K$, indicating whales are harvesting krill exactly at its MSY level, whilst if $v > 1$, it represents an exploitation rate of krill above MSY and vice versa.

Equations (1) and (2) refer to the natural situation when no fishing takes place. Harvesting krill to get a yield of Y_1 and whales to get a yield of Y_2 introduces two additional mortality terms, $-Y_1$ and $-Y_2$. Expressing Y_1 and Y_2 in appropriately rescaled form gives modified versions of (1) and (2) as follows:

$$\frac{dX_1}{dt} = r_1X_1\,(1 - X_1 - vX_2) - Y_1 \tag{3}$$

and

$$\frac{dX_2}{dt} = r_2X_2\left(1 - \frac{X_2}{X_1}\right) - Y_2 \tag{4}$$

Beddington and May note that in the particular case where the yields are realized by fishing at constant effort

$$Y_1 = r_1\,F_1\,X_1$$

and $Y_2 = r_2\,F_2\,X_2$

If F_1 and F_2 are rescaled so that $F_i = 1$ corresponds to a fishing rate equal to the population's intrinsic growth rate r_i the dynamics of the whale and krill populations then obey the equations

$$\text{and} \qquad \frac{dX_1}{dt} = r_1 X_1 (1 - F_1 - X_1 v X_2) \qquad (5)$$

$$\frac{dX_2}{dt} = r_2 X_2 \left(1 - F_2 - \frac{X_2}{X_1} \right) \qquad (6)$$

Equations (5) and (6) are further developed by Beddington and May although for our present purposes they are sufficient to provide an adequate description for later analysis. The important point about these equations is that by substitution and rearrangement of terms it is possible to define equilibrium values for Y_1 and Y_2 in terms of F and X. In addition it is possible to maximize Y_1 for given Y_2 and vice versa. The result of such a series of calculations is shown in Fig. 2a where the solid line represents whale MSY for given krill MSY and vice versa. Thus any combination of values below the line (shaded area) is sustainable. The MSY krill for zero Y_2 does not only imply zero yield of whales but that they would be driven to extinction. There is therefore no possible way in which the maximum yield values for both krill and whales could be achieved simultaneously (point marked by a star in Fig. 2a). Furthermore it indicates that for a given krill MSY level there is a whale MSY (or stock size).

This argument can be extended to include other consumers of krill. For an additional unexploited krill predator we would use the equivalent version of (4)

$$\frac{dX_3}{dt} = r_3 X_3 \left(1 - \frac{X_3}{X_1} \right) \qquad (7)$$

This in turn would reduce the krill and whale levels as shown in Fig. 2a.

We know from previous chapters that the annual krill production is utilized by a wide variety of species and that harvesting krill is therefore likely to have some effect on all consumers. Conversely, we would expect that reducing, for example, whales would release more krill for consumption by other predators. It is therefore only sensible to speak of a krill MSY level with respect to given levels of all consumer stocks. Krill MSY in isolation is meaningless.

A further situation discussed by Beddington and May is that of the krill–squid–sperm whale food chain. Using the same terminology they derive the equations

$$\frac{dX_1}{dt} = r_1 X_1 (1 - X_1 - v X_2) - Y_1 \qquad \text{for krill} \quad (8)$$

$$\frac{dX_2}{dt} = r_2 X_2 (1 - \frac{X_2}{X_2} - \eta X_3) \qquad \text{for squid} \quad (9)$$

(The term η defines the rate at which sperm whales exploit squid.)

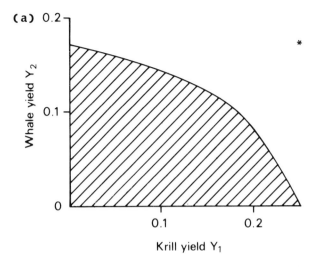

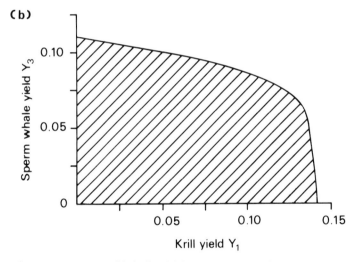

Fig. 2. (a) The maximum sustainable krill yield that is consistent with a prescribed whale yield (or, conversely, the maximum sustainable whale yield consistent with a specified krill yield), for $v = 1$. The star in the top right-hand corner corresponds to krill and whale yields both having their individual MSY values; clearly these yields cannot both be sustained. (b) Similar to Fig. 2(a) except here we are dealing with top (sperm whale) and bottom (krill) species in a system with three trophic levels (krill–squid–sperm whales), described by equations (8)–(10) with $v = 1$ and $\eta = 1$. Again, the boundary of the shaded area gives the maximum sustainable krill yield consistent with a specified sperm whale yield (or, conversely, the maximum value of Y_3 consistent with a fixed value of Y_1). Combinations of yields outside this shaded region are not sustainable; in particular, the star corresponding to krill and sperm whale yields both having their individual MSY values cannot be sustained (Reproduced with permission from Beddington and May, 1980).

$$\frac{\mathrm{d}X_3}{\mathrm{d}t} = r_3 X_3 \left(1 - \frac{X_3}{X_2} \right) - Y_3 \quad \text{for sperm whales} \quad (10)$$

Their model indicates that the greatest yields of krill are achieved in conjunction with low sperm whale yields providing the sperm whale standing stock is higher (Fig. 2b). The reason for this is that a high sperm whale stock, by feeding predominantly on squid, will keep down the squid predation level on krill, thus permitting a higher krill yield.

How effective then, is this model in providing a realistic description of krill and krill predator dynamics in the Southern Ocean? Most importantly the predictions made with the model agree with what we would intuitively expect; in other words, the mathematical model is in agreement with the conceptual model. However, it should be remembered that the terms in each equation are dimensionless, which means that the answers are only indices. To convert these to real values several would need to be expressed in absolute terms. In order for the model to be of much value as a management tool it is necessary to have some information on standing stocks, carrying capacities and conversion factors.

A second point about the model is that it clearly demonstrates the need for considering the major components together rather than as a series of resources whose MSY levels can be determined independently. Thus using this model (with real rather than dimensional values) it should be possible to determine the effects of different harvesting regimes on exploited and unexploited stocks.

The Beddington and May model described above, whilst having some features in its favour, does also have some limitations. First, the model assumes that carrying capacity is stable, whereas one would expect that environmental variations would cause some significant and cyclical phenomena. Such variations may be quite large, although if their periodicity is sufficiently long, the errors introduced in deriving short-term predictions may only be slight. Secondly, the model does not take account of density-dependent effects, which are known to occur. Such effects have been known for a long time and have been quantified (see Chapters 12 and 13), in terms of pregnancy rates and age at first maturity. As an extension of the Beddington and May model, Beddington (1980) has developed a model to describe demographic changes in baleen whale populations resulting from density-dependent changes in reproductive parameters. This model does, however, assume constant krill recruitment and also constant predation rate by other consumers, but neither of these assumptions is valid, and there are very few reliable quantitative data with which to predict the effect of these two variables. The model does however provide some useful insight into the demographic changes which have taken place.

Models of the Beddington and May type, because they consider the major, easily recognizable interactions, are likely to be the most attractive in terms of providing scientific advice for resource management. Although providing some insight into ecosystem functioning, their fundamental shortcomings should not be lost sight of. In addition to those already identified above, it should be remembered that large groups of species are generally lumped into broadly defined compartments. Thus for a krill/predator model it may be justifiable to assume that all seals are crabeater seals and all birds are Adélie penguins, simply because no other species of each group is considered to consume anything like as much krill as these two. This may be true, but it does not necessarily follow that, because a given level of krill fishing will have an acceptably low effect on Adélie penguins, the effect will also be acceptably low for, say, black-browed albatross.

The model also assumes that the major krill consumers are accounted for even though for one group of them, the squids, there are very few data. The 17 million tons of squid consumed by whales, seals and birds each year in the Southern Ocean probably in turn consume a very large amount of krill. With a conversion efficiency of probably 30–50%, but possibly as low as 5%, the squid might be consuming anything from 34 to 340 million tons of krill. The squids should figure in the basic equations but currently this is unrealistic due to the paucity of data.

We therefore have ample justification for investigating these other interactions. Unfortunately, due to the enormous size of the Southern Ocean, realistic assessments are currently not feasible. It has, however, proved possible to model small parts such as the Ross Sea area.

A model of the Ross Sea was devised by Green (Green, 1975; Green Hammond, 1981) whose main objectives were:

(a) To express an hypothesis on the structure of the food web within the Ross Sea ecosystem.
(b) To simulate standing stocks of the major species groups for one year on a weekly basis.
(c) To keep track of carbon flow in the food web on a weekly and an annual total basis.

Starting from a conceptual model, which included environmental variables, Green drew up a matrix of transfer coefficients for the 12 key variables (Fig. 3). Differential equations were then derived so as to describe rates of change of the biomass. The mathematical model thus has 12 simultaneous equations of the form

$$\frac{d}{dt} \text{biomass} = (\text{income rate}) - (\text{loss rate})$$

Using these equations (described in full in Green, 1975), weekly values for the state variables have been derived (Fig. 3).

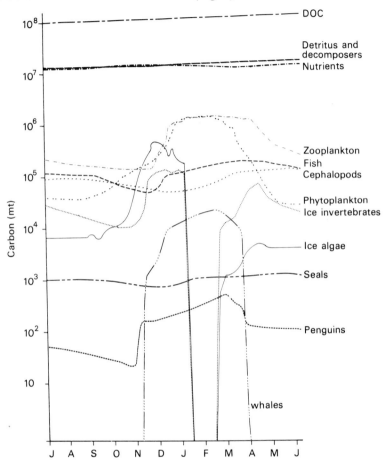

Fig. 3. Variables for Ross Sea model (Reproduced with permission from Green, 1975).

It should be remembered that the data used to calculate these results are largely applicable only to the Ross Sea. This fact probably explains the departures from "typical" Southern Ocean annual variations in, for example, fish and zooplankton biomass. Fish, being relatively long-lived, would be expected to have a more or less stable year-round biomass and not to vary by a factor of about three over the year. Also, zooplankton standing stock is generally considered more or less constant year-round and not to vary by a factor of ten. These differences may well reflect seasonal movements and also highlight the effects of ice cover.

In its present form the Ross Sea model is not intended to be completely realistic, but rather a necessary first step towards providing a greater insight into ecosystem functioning. To satisfy this need it is necessary to increase the complexity of the model. Ideally, this would be done on all fronts, but realistically it should be done by increasing studies on those components important for ecosystem management whilst still continuing to monitor the other variables.

Nor should the Ross Sea model, whilst providing useful insights within its designated area, be used to extrapolate to other areas. The Southern Ocean is a vast area and the Ross Sea cannot be considered as typical in anything but the most general terms. It is better to consider the Southern Ocean as the sum of a series of parts, of which the Ross Sea would be just one. Another such suitable area is that around South Georgia.

4. South Georgia Area

Of all the areas of the Southern Ocean, South Georgia is probably the most intensively studied, partly because of the shore-based whaling activity, but also owing to the *Discovery* Investigations. These have resulted in a large amount of data being available for some of the dominant components in the ecosystem.

4.1 Circulation

South Georgia lies on the northern side of the Scotia Sea. The main circulation pattern of the West Wind Drift brings water to the island from the south and south-west. The presence of the island and its shelf cause considerable turbulence and eddying, the main effects of which are shown in Fig. 4. During the 1920s it was considered that water approaching the island from the south and south-east originated in the Weddell Sea, while water arriving from the west came from the Bellingshausen Sea. The area was therefore also considered one of mixing. More recent research has shown (Bogdanov et al., 1969) that the frontal zone between Weddell and Bellingshausen water now lies somewhat to the south of South Georgia, although the main circulation patterns in the immediate vicinity are broadly the same. Everson (1976) has suggested that this difference may be associated with local climatic change. Thus, the effects of mixing probably vary significantly over the long term and possibly also from year to year.

4.2 Nutrients and phytoplankton

The inverse relationship between phosphate concentration and phyto-plankton abundance noted by Hardy and Gunther (1935) has already been mentioned in this chapter. Their conclusion was largely based on results from the survey which took place in December 1926 and January 1927 and from which they proposed that the phosphate values gave an indication of the production of phytoplankton over "a little time in the past". The time scale involved here must be relatively short, of the order of days or at the most a few weeks.

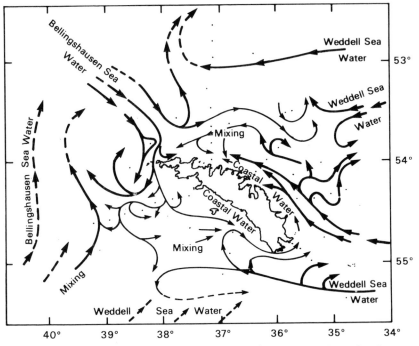

Fig. 4. Chart of surface water movements around South Georgia in December–January 1926/1927 (Reproduced with permission from Hardy and Gunther, 1935, Fig. 6).

One would expect the highest nutrient levels and lowest phytoplankton levels at the very start of the production period. These would change, during a brief period, through a situation when there are moderately high levels of both, to one of high phytoplankton and low nutrient levels (nutrient limiting conditions). After this there is a period of phytoplankton reduction due to grazing and natural deaths, resulting in low phytoplankton and low nutrients before sufficient nutrients are available for a further primary production cycle. This is demonstrated in Fig. 5 and is suggested by Hardy and Gunther (1935). The important point about this relationship is that it is not consistently inverse. We can examine this by analysing the data by months and in terms of location.

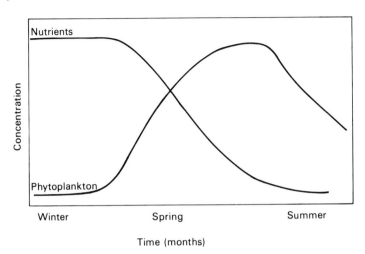

Fig. 5. Nutrient and phytoplankton cycles.

Although Hardy and Gunther only used the results from the December 1926—January 1927 survey in deriving their conclusions, data are also available for surveys in November 1930 and January—February 1930. I have calculated Spearman rank correlation coefficients for phosphate and phytoplankton concentrations for these three surveys and the results are set out in Table II.

TABLE II
Rank correlation coefficients of phytoplankton/phosphate concentrations for the three South Georgia plankton surveys undertaken by R.R.S. *Discovery*

Survey	Spearman's rank correlation coefficients (r_s)	Number of stations	P
November 1930	−0.457	48	>0.01
December 1926–January 1927	−0.190	41	NS
January–February 1930	−0.103	57	NS

Data from Hardy and Grunther, 1935.

During the spring there is a strong inverse correlation between phytoplankton abundance and phosphate concentration, but this is not present later on in the season. Each of the three surveys mentioned above was composed of a series of transects radiating from the island, and in nearly all cases extending into the deep water beyond the continental shelf. The transects from each survey can therefore be considered as representative of a series of zones around the island. I have calculated correlation coefficients for each transect in the same way as those for each survey overall. Of the 21 transects only three had significant correlation coefficients and two of these were positive.

The correlation between phytoplankton and phosphate is therefore not nearly as clear cut as Hardy and Gunther's (1935) analysis would suggest (the 1926/27 survey on which they based their conclusions gives a non-significant correlation coefficient). A combination of factors could account for this. South Georgia is known to be an area of mixing and this could cause very great natural variation in local phytoplankton and phosphate levels. Thus, on any one survey the baseline levels around the island are likely to have very high variances and these would mask any depletion effects for most of the summer. At the start of the season, however, as the bloom is likely to occur more or less simultaneously over the whole region, the negative correlation is likely to be strongest, as is the case.

The two variables are also instantaneous estimates of abundance and these are the results of continuing processes. Thus, although a given level of phosphate would, providing nothing else were limiting, produce a calculable phytoplankton standing stock, the fact that mixing is a continuing process means that neither variable need necessarily be changing in response to the other. In this context, therefore, it is more sensible to consider rates of change rather than absolute levels of abundance as being indicators of the relation between primary production and nutrients.

In Chapter 7 we have seen how nutrient availability affects primary production by controlling either the ultimate standing stock (yield limitation) or the rate of growth. These factors have not yet been quantified, although because we have seen some interesting correlations in the relationships above between phytoplankton and phosphate in relation to time of year and location, this should clearly be a field for much fruitful study in the future.

4.3 Krill and water circulation

Water circulation affects the distribution of krill in a variety of ways, both directly and indirectly. Indirect effects include nutrient supply and regeneration in relation to primary production (discussed in section 4.4), while direct effects include distribution of early life history stages, gross distribution in the Southern Ocean and local effects such as those relating to upwelling and gyres.

South Georgia is an area in which it is generally considered that there is no successful krill spawning (see Everson, 1977 for fuller discussion). The standing stock must therefore be reliant on recruitment from the south. The extent of this recruitment can be gauged by reference to the krill consumption estimates for the dominant predators. The major predators probably consume 10–20 million tonnes of krill during the summer. At its peak this may well be as high as 4 million tonnes a month (In simple terms this would be provided by a belt of water 50 miles wide and 100 m deep, travelling at 0.5 knot and having an average krill density of $1 \, m^{-3}$.) These figures are put forward without any pretence at accuracy, but rather to highlight the extent of this interaction. In the vicinity of South Georgia the krill tend to be concentrated on the lee side (in terms of wind and current) (Elizarov, 1971), and in the boundary region between the north-westerly flowing coastal current and a south-easterly flowing offshore current (Maslennikov, 1972). The dependence of many predators on these local effects (discussed later) indicates a fairly consistent year to year pattern in circulation and thus krill distribution.

Direct information on krill distribution is not currently available, although it can be inferred from the distribution of whale catches. Catch frequencies in ten-mile squares have been determined by Kemp and Bennett (1932) for blue and fin whales around South Georgia for the years 1923–1931. Hardy and Gunther (1935) confirmed that in the few months during which data from net hauls and whale catches were available, the areas where most whales were taken coincided with areas of high krill abundance. Thus, although whale catches are biassed by proximity to shore stations, they are nonetheless useful indicators of localized krill abundance.

To get some idea of average seasonal distribution of krill over the eight seasons for which results are available, I have summed the proportion of the catch taken in each square by months and multiplied by the mean catch for that month. The results are shown in Fig. 6 and these indicate a reasonably consistent pattern of krill distribution, the major concentration being found off the north coast and generally starting about 10–15 miles offshore. This is in an area of mixing (Fig. 4) and largely confirms the statements of Elizarov (1971) and Maslennikov (1972).

Whilst Fig. 6 indicated that the geographical pattern of abundance tended to be reasonably static throughout the season, there is clear evidence of considerable year to year variation and also some changes from month to month. This in indicated in Fig. 7 where contour lines have been drawn to encompass squares where more than ten whales were caught in a month. From Fig. 6 we

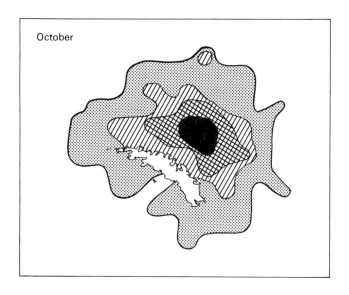

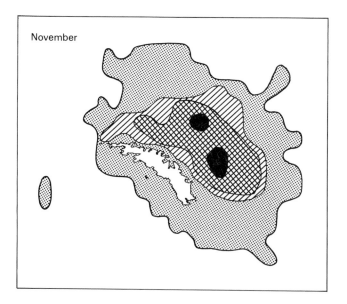

Fig. 6 (a). Blue whale catches by ten-mile squares around South Georgia for October and November. Contours at 1, 10, 20 and 40.

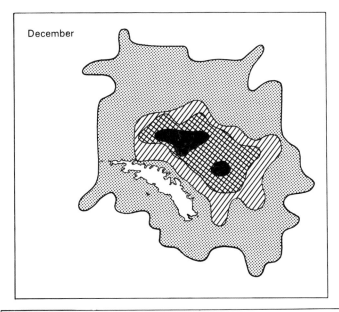

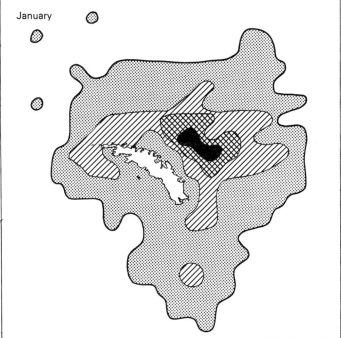

Fig. 6 (a) (*cont.*). Blue whale catches by ten-mile squares around South Georgia for December and January. Contours at 1, 10, 20 and 40.

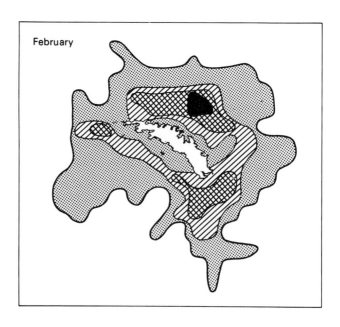

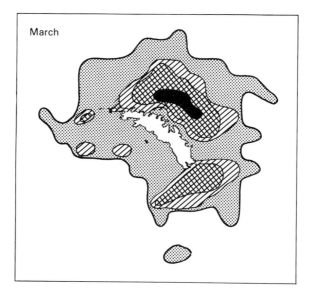

Fig. 6 (a) (*cont.*). Blue whale catches by ten-mile squares around South Georgia for February and March. Contours at 1, 10, 20 and 40.

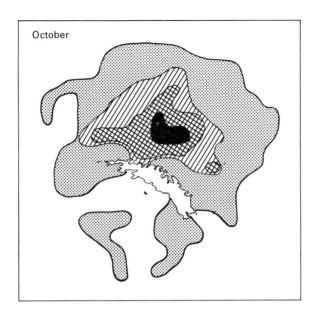

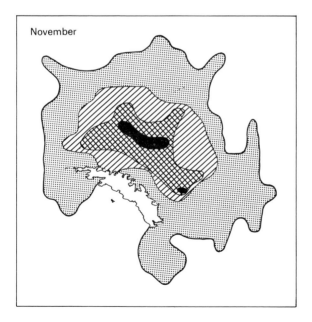

Fig. 6 (b). Fin whale catches by ten-mile squares around South Georgia for October and November. Contours at 1, 10, 20 and 40.

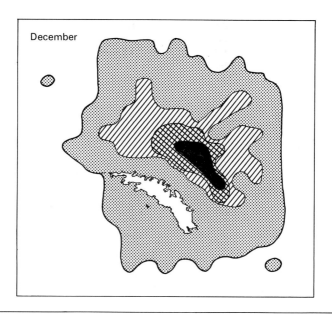

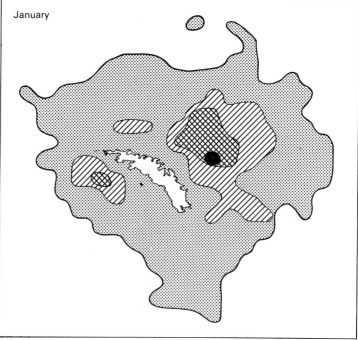

Fig. 6 (b) (*cont.*). Fin whale catches by ten-mile squares around South Georgia for December and January. Contours at 1, 10, 20 and 40.

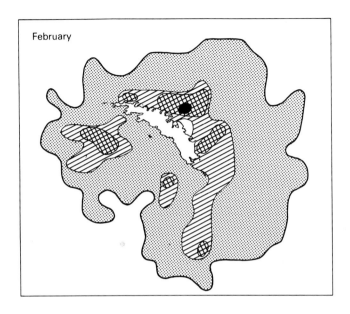

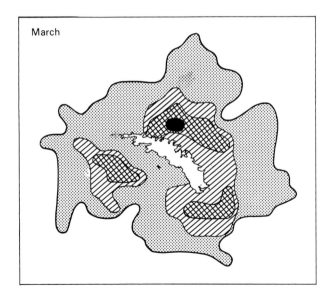

Fig. 6 (b) (*cont.*). Fin whale catches by ten-mile squares around South Georgia for February and March. Contours at 1, 10, 20 and 40.

see, as pointed out by Hardy and Gunther (1935), that whale catches (assumed to indicate krill patches) are often made in more or less the same location for a few months. These then fade, to be replaced by others in different localities. Frequently these localized catches occur close inshore and occasionally some distance offshore. These differences must be related to local water circulation, detailed information on which is unavailable.

4.4 Krill and phytoplankton

The December 1926–January 1927 South Georgia survey also provided data relating krill abundance, as estimated using 1 m diameter nets, to phytoplankton abundance. In their analysis, Hardy and Gunther (1935) concluded that there was an inverse relationship between the abundance of krill and phytoplankton, and this was due either to grazing or else to phytoplankton releasing some substances that discouraged krill from aggregating. They reached this conclusion by considering each station in rank order of phytoplankton concentration and then determining the arithmetic means of the lowest eight stations and five subsequent groups of seven stations. The extremely contagious nature of krill distributions means that the catch frequency distribution is highly skewed. To overcome this, a rank correlation coefficient has therefore been determined for the krill/phytoplankton interaction. For the 43 stations on the 1926–1927 survey this is -0.3499 ($P < 0.05$).

Interactions between phytoplankton and herbivorous zooplankton in temperate waters have been discussed at length by Steele (1974). The generalized picture is one of increased primary production in the spring followed by an increase in copepod biomass; the copepods then graze down the phytoplankton. There is therefore a sequence of cycles of abundance. The copepod biomass, increases in response to an increase in phytoplankton and the difference in timing of peaks, is dependent on herbivore generation time. Thus in the southern North Sea there is a strong positive correlation between copepod numbers and phytoplankton concentration during the year ($r_s = 0.538$, $N = 12$, $P < 0.5$. Data from Colebrook and Robinson, 1961). In the northern North Sea, although the seasonal sequencing is present, the correlation is not as good and is strongest between zooplankton and phytoplankton concentration during the preceding month, ($r = 0.416$, $P < 0.2$) reflecting the longer generation time at higher latitudes.

At South Georgia the situation is somewhat different in that the standing stock of krill, because it can live for several years, theoretically should not vary very much throughout the year. Phytoplankton standing stock, because of the marked seasonal effects, will depend on the balance of production over grazing. In areas where krill are abundant grazing effect will be greatest; thus an inverse correlation is to be expected between krill and phytoplankton abundance, as demonstrated above.

Hardy and Gunther (1935) also give data on the abundance of the euphausiid *Thysanoessa* and the tunicate *Salpa thompsoni*. Both these species have a shorter lifespan than krill and salps are able to reproduce rapidly by asexual budding in favourable conditions (Chapter 9). The rank correlations for each species in relation to phytoplankton are not significant. (*Thysanoessa*/Phytoplankton $r_s = +0.1907$; *Salpa*/Phytoplankton $r_s = -0.00245$). The case of these two species is more nearly analogous to the northern North Sea situation mentioned earlier where there is no significant correlation between phytoplankton and copepod abundances. In this case the grazing effect, whilst dependent on abundance, will also be dependent on the herbivore reproductive rate. Thus, in order to quantify the interactions between phyto- and zooplankton we need information on reproductive rates (for the shorter-lived species) and grazing rates as well as abundance levels.

4.5   Krill and whales

It is clear that during the whaling era there was a strong positive relationship between krill and whale distributions simply because blue and fin whales were entering the area to feed. However, whale foraging ranges extended far beyond the immediate South Georgia area, so that in years of krill-scarcity fewer whales would be found in the region. Furthermore, there is strong evidence to suggest that the time spent by whales in the area was also dependent on the position of the ice edge. In seasons when the ice edge was well north, blue whales tended to delay their southward migration. For a fuller discussion of this the reader is referred to Harmer (1931). In his account Harmer discusses the great variations in whale catches with season and locality and from this it is clear that whale feeding grounds can only be defined in the very broadest terms. To prohibit krill fishing in blue and fin whale feeding areas (as has been proposed by some conservationists) is unrealistic—such a restriction is tantamount to prohibiting krill fishing anywhere.

4.6   Krill and birds

Recent research at Bird Island has highlighted the importance of birds as krill consumers (Chapter 11). They are also of interest because of their dependence on locally abundant krill during the breeding season and as a result breeding success may prove a valuable indicator of local krill abun-

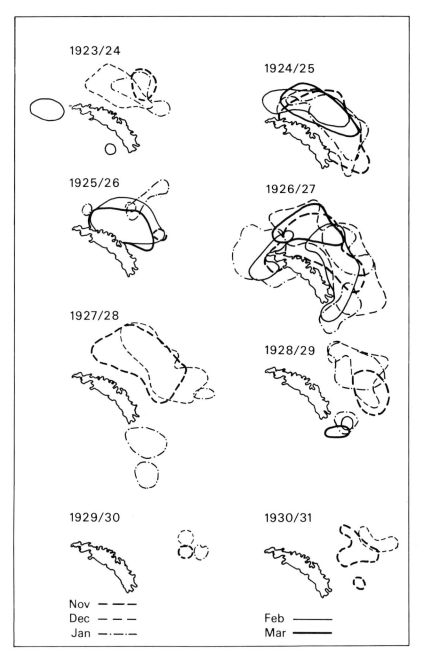

1923/24

1924/25

1925/26

1926/27

1927/28

1928/29

1929/30

1930/31

Nov — — —
Dec – – –
Jan —·—·—

Feb ————
Mar ▬▬▬▬

Fig. 7. "Patches of krill" around South Georgia as indicated by whale catches. Lines encompass grid squares with more than ten whales caught in that month.

TABLE III

Estimated feeding densities of gentoo and macaroni penguins around South Georgia

Species	Location	Foraging range (km)	Coast (km)	Foraging area (km^2)	Breeding population (pairs)	Predation pressure (pairs km^{-2})
Gentoo	South Georgia	31.5	~300	12,567[c]	100,000	8
Macaroni	Willis and Bird I.	115	Small[a]	41,548[a]	5 million	120
Macaroni	Elsewhere on South Georgia	115	~300	55,274[b]	100,000	1.8

From data in Croxall and Prince, 1979, 1980.
[a]Assume circle centred on Willis Island; [b]assume two rectangles 150 × 115 km and semicircle 115 km radius; [c]assume two rectangles 150 × 115 km and circle radius 315 km.

dance (Everson, 1977). The extent of krill predation has been discussed at length in Chapter 11 and by Croxall and Prince (1979, 1980), but of particular interest here is the impact of macaroni and gentoo penguins in the vicinity of South Georgia.

Bearing in mind the average areas of local abundance of krill around South Georgia (Fig. 7), one might expect the main penguin colonies to be located in the middle of the north coast of the island. Although gentoo colonies occur all along the north coast, by far the greater proportion of macaroni penguins nest at the north-west end on Willis Islands and Bird Island. The predation pressure in terms of bird pairs km^{-2} is estimated in Table III and this is illustrated in Fig. 8. To gain an idea of the relative

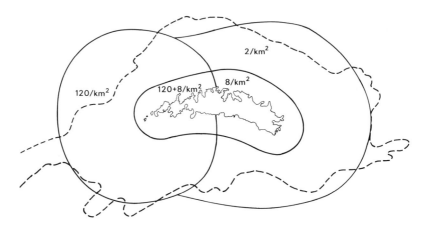

Fig. 8. Penguin feeding densities, South Georgia. Broken line, 1000 fathom contour.

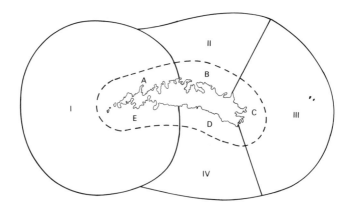

Fig. 9. Penguin feeding areas: I–IV, macaroni penguin; A–E, gentoo penguin.

abundance of krill available within the foraging range of different parts of the island I have divided the surrounding sea into arbitrary areas. Fig. 9, area I, is centred on the main macaroni penguin colonies at Willis and Bird Islands and the other areas divide the remainder more or less equally. Using the whale catch distribution maps in Kemp and Bennett (1932) each area has been given a score for each month of each season from 1923–1924 to 1930–1931. The scoring system used was as follows: fin and blue whales were scored separately and the scores added; 1 point was scored for one or more whales caught and 2 points for ten or more. Each area could thus achieve a maximum score of 4 points. The results are set out in Fig. 10.

Of the macaroni feeding areas, clearly the least favourable is area IV, the remaining areas scoring about the same over the whole season. However, as far as macaroni penguins are concerned, a critical period occurs during January–February when the chicks are being fed. At this time it is essential for food to be available for most of the period. The equivalent period for gentoo penguins is December–January. For the two months combined a maximum score is 8 points and the results are set out in Table IV.

When looked at in this way area IV scores low and on this basis is again the least favourable. The other three macaroni areas produce similar scores but area II has one score of 1 point and two of 4 points, which would have indicated a considerable food shortage in 1927–1928 and possibly some problems in 1929–1930 and 1930–1931. Area I has only one score of less than 5 points (in 1930–1931) and yet in that year it fared at least no worse than the others. Thus, in terms of consistent pattern of food availability, area I is the most favourable, closely followed by III, II and then IV.

Gentoo penguins are somewhat different in that although areas D and E are clearly least favourable, there is little to choose between A, B and C.

The above analysis indicates that there may be some link between the size of breeding colonies and the local abundance of food. The conclusion can be no firmer than this at present, because the assumed krill concentrations relate to the period 1923–1931, whereas the penguin colonies have only recently been assessed. There is, however, every indication that penguin breeding success will prove a useful indicator of local krill abundance during the chick fledging period.

In Chapter 11 we have seen that penguins are not the sole avian consumers of krill at South Georgia. Certain albatrosses and petrels rely quite heavily on krill. As flight is a far more rapid form of movement than swimming, both these groups will have a far wider foraging range than the penguins. They are thus more likely to be able to find krill even in years when it is locally scarce. A high chick mortality of either albatross or petrel species is therefore likely to indicate a widespread scarcity of krill, a situation that would seem most unlikely judging by the 1923–1931 data. Such a situation has been reported

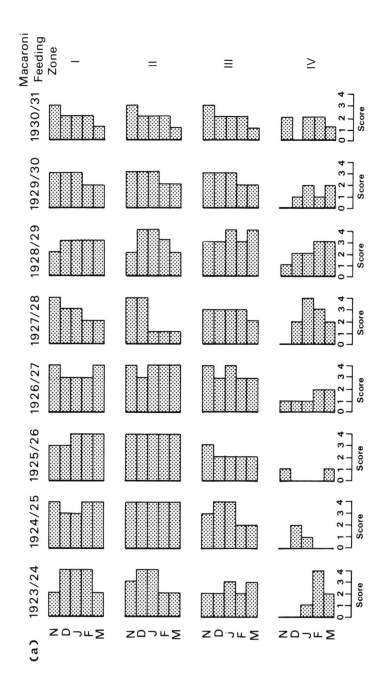

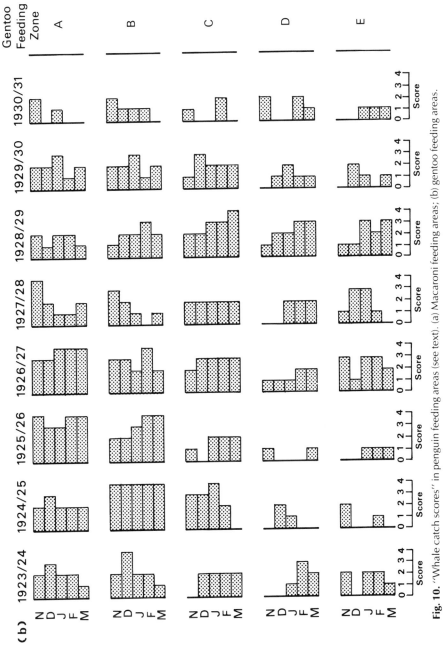

Fig. 10. "Whale catch scores" in penguin feeding areas (see text). (a) Macaroni feeding areas; (b) gentoo feeding areas.

Krill availability scores for penguin foraging areas I–IV and A–E during the months when chicks are being fed. For explanation see text

Season	Macaroni Penguin January and February score				Gentoo Penguin December and January score				
	I	II	III	IV	A	B	C	D	E
1923–1924	8	6	5	5	5	6	3	1	2
1924–1925	7	8	6	1	5	8	7	3	0
1925–1926	8	8	4	0	6	5	2	0	1
1926–1927	6	8	7	3	7	5	6	2	4
1927–1928	5	1	6	7	3	3	4	2	6
1928–1929	6	7	7	5	3	4	5	4	4
1929–1930	5	4	5	3	5	5	5	3	3
1930–1931	4	4	4	4	1	2	0	0	1
Scores <5	1	3	2	5	3	3	4	8	7
Scores <4	0	1	0	4	3	2	3	7	5

(Bonner *et al.*, 1978) during the 1977–1978 season, when it was known that krill were generally scarce in the vicinity of South Georgia. Albatross and petrel breeding failure could also be caused by fewer krill being present in the top metre of the sea; the mere presence of krill in the sea is not sufficient and they must also occur within the diving depth range of the predators (Croxall and Prince, 1980) at some time during each 24 hour period. As yet, no information is available to quantify the magnitude of this effect.

Thus, in spite of being one of the most intensively studied regions of the Southern Ocean, there are clearly many question marks concerning interactions in the South Georgia area. This applies to the physical and chemical environment as well as to all levels of the food chain. In spite of this it is evident that changes occur which with careful scientific planning should be quantifiable. When this has been achieved we will be in a far better position to assess these various components.

5. Conclusions

Studies of interactions in the Southern Ocean can be considered under three broad headings: initial identification of possible interactions (recognition of the components in the food web), followed by quantitative analysis of two kinds—consideration of the Southern Ocean as a single unit, and breaking down this vast ocean area into a large number of small compartments. All three are necessary to a complete understanding of the ecosystem.

Descriptions of ecosystem interactions have frequently been made and it is clear that the dominant relationships are well recognized. The only advances in this field are likely to come either from local studies that indicate atypical behaviour by a species, or by detailed examination of a species or group.

Quantitative studies on the Southern Ocean scale have developed quite rapidly, to the extent that now we are in a position to specify the effects of different levels of predation for some species that are dependent on krill. This is a valuable first step in providing initial figures on which to base management strategy. The preliminary nature of such estimates cannot be over-emphasized, however, because, although results follow intuitive thinking, they are based on a very incomplete database. This is due to the fact that adequate quantitative data are not currently available for key groups such as birds and squid, which are known to be major krill consumers.

Local studies such as those at South Georgia and the Ross Sea further highlight the inadequacies of the database. This is a serious situation as harvesting is likely to be locally intensive and, even though the total catch may be acceptable on a Southern Ocean scale, the effect could be very great and long-lasting locally. There is therefore a pressing need for further research in this field. Two key factors are the determination of levels of abundance and rates of change of abundance; implicit in this are an understanding of water-circulation patterns and the need for year-round observations.

This need has been noted for some time and international recognition of it has led to the formulation of the SCAR programme of Biological Investigations of Marine Antarctic Systems and Stocks (BIOMASS). This programme is now in full swing and, it is hoped, will provide timely answers to the key questions.

6. References

Beddington, J. (1980). Modelling and management of the Southern Ocean. Unpublished report to the International Union for the Conservation of Nature and Natural Resources.

Beddington, J. and May, R. (1980). Maximum sustainable yields in systems subject to harvesting at more than one trophic level. *Mathematical Biosciences* **51**, 261–281.

Bogdanov, M. A., Oradovskiy, S. G., Solyankin, Ye. V., and Khvatskiy, N.V. (1969). On the frontal zone in the Scotia Sea. *Oceanology* **9**, 777–783.

Bonner, W. N., Clarke, A., Everson, I., Heywood, R. B., Whitaker, T. M. and White, M. G. (1978). Research on krill in relation to the Southern Ocean ecosystem by British Antarctic Survey. *International Council for the Exploration of the Sea, Biological Oceanography Committee*, C.M. 1978/L:23, 6 pp.

Chekunova, V. I. and Rynkova, T. I. (1974). Energy requirements of the Antarctic crustacean *Euphausia superba* Dana. *Oceanology* **14**, 434–440.

Colebrook, J. M. and Robinson, G. A. (1961). The seasonal cycle of the plankton in the North Sea and the north-eastern Atlantic. *Journal du Conseil* **26**, 156–165.

Croxall, J. P. and Prince, P. A. (1979). Antarctic seabird and seal monitoring studies. *Polar Record* **19**, 573–595.

Croxall, J. P. and Prince, P. A. (1980). Food, feeding ecology and ecological segregation of seabirds at South Georgia. *Biological Journal of the Linnean Society* **14**, 103–131.

Elizarov, A. A. (1971). Distinctive features of water dynamics in areas of mass krill concentrations. *Trudy VNIRO* **79**, 31–39.

Everson, I. (1970). The population dynamics and energy budget of *Notothenia neglecta* Nybelin at Signy Island, South Orkney Islands. *British Antarctic Survey Bulletin* No. 23, 25–50.

Everson, I. (1976). Antarctic krill: a reappraisal of its distribution. *Polar Record* **18**, 15–23.

Everson, I. (1977). "The Living Resources of the Southern Ocean". Southern Ocean Fisheries Survey Programme GLO/SO/77/1. FAO, Rome.

Green, K. A. (1975). "Simulation of the pelagic ecosystem of the Ross Sea, Antarctica: a time varying compartmental model". PhD thesis. Texas A and M University, College Station.

Green Hammond, K. A. (1981). Modelling of Antarctic ecosystems. *In* "Biological Investigations of Marine Antarctic Systems and Stocks (BIOMASS)" (S. Z. El-Sayed, ed.), Vol. II, pp. 23–29. Scientific Committee on Antarctic Research, Cambridge.

Hardy, A. C. and Gunther, E. R. (1935). The plankton of the South Georgia whaling grounds and adjacent waters 1926–27. *"Discovery" Reports* **11**, 1–456.

Harmer, S. F. (1931). Southern whaling. *Proceedings of the Linnean Society of London* **142**, 85–163.

Hart, T. J. (1942). Phytoplankton periodicity in Antarctic surface waters. *"Discovery" Reports* **21**, 261–356.

Holdgate, M. W. (1967). The Antarctic ecosystem. *Philosophical Transactions of the Royal Society* **B252**, 363–383.

Horwood, J. W. (1981). On the joint exploitation of krill and whales. *In* "Mammals in the Seas", Vol. III, FAO Fisheries Series No. 5, Vol. III, pp. 363–368. FAO, Rome.

Kemp, S. and Bennett, A. G. (1932). On the distribution and movements of whales on the South Georgia and South Shetland whaling grounds. *"Discovery" Reports* **6**, 165–190.

Knox, G. A. (1970). Antarctic marine ecosystems. *In* "Antarctic Ecology" (M. W. Holdgate, ed.), Vol. I, pp. 69–93. Academic Press, London and New York.

Laws, R. M. (1977a). Seals and whales of the Southern Ocean. *Philosophical Transactions of the Royal Society* **B279**, 81–96.

Laws, R. M. (1977b). The significance of vertebrates in the Antarctic marine ecosystem. *In* "Adaptations within Antarctic Ecosystems" (G. A. Llano, ed.), pp. 411–438. Smithsonian Institution, Washington, D.C.

Lockyer, C. (1981). Growth and energy budgets of large baleen whales from the

Southern Hemisphere. *In* "Mammals in the Seas", Vol. III, FAO Fisheries Series No. 5, Vol III, pp. 379–487. FAO, Rome.

Maslennikov, V. V. (1972). On the effect of water dynamics on the distribution of *Euphausia superba* Dana in the area of South Georgia. *Trudy VNIRO* **75,** 107–117.

May, R. M., Beddington, J. R., Clark, C. W., Holt, S. J. and Laws, R. M. (1979). Management of multispecies fisheries. *Science* **205,** 267–277.

Steele, J. H. (1974). "The Structure of Marine Ecosystems". Harvard University Press, Cambridge, Massachusetts.

15

Conservation and the Antarctic

W. N. Bonner

1. Introduction

1.1 The meaning of conservation

Ecology is the study of how plants and animals interact with each other and their environment. Since no biological systems are static, it is the study of change. In recent years Man's activities have acquired the capability of greatly accelerating changes in ecosystems, and because these often occur in directions which are or seem to be immediately or ultimately disadvantageous to Man, other activities are invoked which will reduce, arrest or reverse the changes. These activities constitute the modern concept of conservation.

Although this concept is a comparatively new one it has recently achieved very wide currency and there are few people in developed nations who do not have some idea of what is implied by it. The activities of organizations, both international and national, scientific and popular, have attracted the attention of the public, while the seemingly endless flow of television programmes on conservation topics (some of them sadly commercialized) have stimulated and maintained this interest. However, those who assume an enlightened attitude to conservation should remember that this is not yet universal, nor forget how recently the general approach to natural resources was to assume that they were there to be exploited without regard to the consequences.

Despite the existence of a consensus about what, broadly, is involved in conservation it has remained an elusive term to define. Since effective conservation almost always requires political action on either the national or international scale, its definition is often tailored by opposing sides to serve their individual ends, There would, nevertheless, be general agreement that the concept involves the arresting of irreversible change or maintaining the *status quo*. Most English-speaking biologists would make a distinction between "conservation" and "preservation", but for linguistic reasons alone, this distinction is not possible in many other languages. Few English dictionaries have been revised sufficiently recently to provide an up-to-date definition in a rapidly developing field. Perhaps the most useful is that in Webster's "New Collegiate Dictionary" (1975):

> *Conservation* (1) a careful preservation and protection of something, esp: planned management of a natural resource to prevent exploitation, destruction, or neglect.

Some would raise objections to the use of "preservation" in this definition, but, inescapably, preservation is closely associated with conservation as, for example, in art where one who preserves an artistic heritage is known as a conservator. A more important defect of the definition, considered in a biological sense, is the reference to the *prevention* of exploitation. For most conservation policies to be of practical value they must extend to control, not prevent, the exploitation of those natural resources which for one reason or another will inevitably be subject to exploitation.

Holdgate (1970) made a useful distinction between "resource conservation"—the management of natural resources for the benefit of mankind, so that their available production can be harvested without unnecessary or irreversible harm to the system; "wildlife conservation"—the protection of plant and animal species and of samples of the natural ecosystem they comprise; and "conservation of amenity"—the protection of visually important features of the landscape, for aesthetic reasons. These fields are not mutually exclusive and all are applicable in the Antarctic, and it will be useful to bear them in mind in considering the problems of Antarctic conservation.

1.2 The need for conservation

The need for conservation is usually most clearly appreciated when what is to be conserved is already nearly destroyed. In the Antarctic we can, for example, now see clearly the need that existed, and still exists, for an effective conservation policy for the great whales. But any resource which is potentially capable of being harvested creates the same need for conservation. It seems that Antarctica is one of the few places where this need has been anticipated in advance of destructive exploitation (see below, p. 843). A case can be made for conservation policies for resources for which no exploitative value can currently be seen, on the grounds that future generations may find a use for them. This argument grades imperceptibly into the proposition that the present generation must not squander or abuse the Earth's resources which should remain available to the generations to come. Aesthetic arguments for general conservation, which are not based on any prospect of use or value, but maintain that systems and species have a right to exist without interference by heedless activity from Man, are hard to discuss scientifically. However, they represent a view of a significant segment of society that is often vocal and occasionally influential.

1.3 The special position of the Antarctic

A general need exists for conservation on a world scale, but it can be argued that the need is more pressing in some parts of the world than in others. Antarctica is not pristine, but it has been substantially less affected by man than the other continents, so that conservation policies can start nearer the natural baseline (with some notable exceptions) than they would elsewhere. Further, certain ecosystems are inherently fragile in the sense that they have small capacity to absorb change without being profoundly altered, and hence may need more active management if they are to be conserved. The Antarctic terrestrial and freshwater ecosystems can be included in this category.

The land surface and freshwater pools of the Antarctic continent and its offlying islands are still in the process of colonization (Dunbar, 1977; Heywood, 1977) and are characterized by low species diversity. As such systems evolve and mature, they will change as further species reach them and establish themselves by natural means. These changes can be greatly accelerated by Man's activities, particularly the accidental or deliberate introduction of new colonists. Widespread species, such as the grass *Poa annua*, or the brown rat *Rattus norvegicus*, have found it particularly easy to establish themselves on sub-Antarctic islands because of the lack of competition or predators.

The relation between species diversity, stability and polar conditions has been discussed by several authors (e.g. Dunbar, 1973; Margalef, 1977). Dunbar (1977) concluded that low information content in a system (which is equivalent to low species diversity) is associated in polar regions with a low degree of non-oscillatory stability. In the Arctic there is usually a high degree of oscillatory stability, but this is space-dependent and does not manifest itself in the less extensive Antarctic vegetated areas.

In physical terms the Antarctic terrestrial ecosystem may be very fragile. The fellfield communities of lichens and mosses growing on loose rock fragments or undeveloped soils (Chapter 2) are easily destroyed by trampling. Boot-prints on moss swards may take months or years to disappear and brittle macro-lichens and cushions of moss are easily dislodged from slopes and rocks. Because growth rates are generally low in the severe climatic conditions, recovery is a lengthy process. However, many Antarctic plants are adapted to colonizing the bare ground exposed by the retreat of ice, so the recolonization of areas artifically denuded of vegetation may be expected ultimately to occur. The timescale, however, may be very long. Some individual Antarctic lichen plants, e.g. *Usnea antarctica*, may be up to 600 years old (Hooker, 1980), and cushions of the slow-growing *Azorella selago* may be over 100 years old on Marion Island (Huntley, 1972).

Freshwater ecosystems in the Antarctic are restricted in extent but many contain an important proportion of the total biota, particularly in higher latitudes, though like the terrestrial ecosystem (and for the same reason) they have low species diversity (Heywood, 1977). Antarctic lakes vary greatly in their characteristics and in a sense, each of them is unique. This can be interpreted as making the systems highly vulnerable, because once a lake is altered, another of its type may not be found elsewhere. Because lakes form natural sinks, they are potentially susceptible to pollution, in the Antarctic as elsewhere. Natural eutrophication of maritime Antarctic lakes as a consequence of fouling by birds or seals is a regular occurrence (Heywood, 1978; Parker, 1972). Low temperatures and low light levels for most of the year prevent the plants utilizing the available nutrients and conditions may quickly become anoxic.

The Antarctic marine ecosystem is much more resistant to impact than the terrestrial or freshwater systems. The vast extent of the Southern Ocean (about 36 million km^2) means that there is great buffering capacity and ensures that initially most impacts will be localized. Environmental conditions in the sea are less extreme, more uniform and more continuous than on land, all factors that tend to make for stability. Despite the resilience of the system as a whole, selective exploitation of predators at the top of the food pyramid has wrought a profound change—the biomass of baleen whales has been reduced to about 16% of its initial value (Laws, 1977; Chapter 13).

Dunbar (1973) has drawn attention to the vulnerability of a system when all the energy flow between plants and carnivores is channelled through a single herbivore link. In the Antarctic marine ecosystem krill, *Euphausia superba*, may make up about half the zooplankton biomass (Holdgate, 1967). Though not a sole link, it is a very important one, and substantial exploitation of krill could have very serious consequences for the Antarctic marine ecosystem as a whole. This is discussed further below (p. 844).

1.4 Potential impacts in the Antarctic

1.4.1 Commercial exploitation of living resources

The most immediate threat to natural systems is commercial exploitation. If an exploitable resource for which there is a demand is identified, and the technology for its exploitation exists (or can easily be developed) then in the absence of regulation exploitation will develop and gain momentum. This will continue until either the resource is so severely depleted that it is no longer economically feasible to harvest it (as was the case with the Antarctic fur seal, *Arctocephalus gazella*, in the nineteenth century), or until the demand ceases or is temporarily satiated (as was the case with the whale-oil market in 1930); or until some means of control is applied to the industry to check its expansion, or to reduce the existing effort (as in the case of the more recent regulations applied by the International Whaling Commission to the Antarctic whale hunt). Historically it would seem that the resource will in any case be severely depleted. This has been so in the Antarctic, where seals were the first to be exploited, followed by whales. Currently the major targets for exploitation are fish and krill. Other potential exploitable living resources exist in the Antarctic (for example, birds, particularly penguins, and squid) and these too might be at risk should demand and technology make their exploitation commercially viable.

1.4.2 Casual destruction

Non-commercial destruction, usually in the form of food-gathering, sport-hunting, or pest-control, is a threat to rare species throughout the world, but this is of negligible significance in the Antarctic.

1.4.3 Habitat destruction and mineral exploitation

Throughout the world, many terrestrial ecosystems and the species that comprise them are threatened by habitat destruction as increasing human populations bring more land into intensive cultivation, or clear forests for timber extraction. Habitat destruction in the Antarctic (other than that caused by introduced species, see below 1.4.4), is confined to the neighbourhood of currently or previously occupied scientific stations (which will be considered in greater detail below, 4.3) and a few whaling station sites. Although highly significant locally, this type of impact has relatively little effect on the ecosystem as a whole, though the tendency to occupy sites that are snow- or ice-free during the summer and are readily accessible from the sea means that many such sites have already been affected by Man.

Of much greater potential impact would be the destruction of habitats through the development of extractive industries in Antarctica. Both hard minerals and hydrocarbons have been identified in Antarctica (the latter only as "shows" in one or two research drillings) (SCAR, 1977) but no deposits likely to be of value in the foreseeable future are known. However, increasing economic pressures may lead to exploitation. Technology is at present inadequate to allow the extraction of minerals from beneath the ice sheet, so that the initial impact would be confined to the ice-free coastal regions and islands. Because of the high costs of operating in Antarctica only substantial deposits would be likely to be worked but even this would have severe effects on the local environment. The types of impact associated with scientific stations would occur, almost certainly on a much larger scale, and additionally there would be special problems, for example, dust pollution of remote areas, dispersal of toxic effluents and drilling fluids, etc. Offshore oil exploitation is the prospect likely to attract commercial interest first. A particular hazard here would be the existence of submarine well-heads. These could not be allowed to protrude above the maximum depth of iceberg scour and would need protection if the risk of severe spills were to be reduced to acceptable proportions. Some oil spills will be inevitable if an industry develops. The impact of spills on the marine ecosystem is likely to be localized; birds would be particularly at risk, but effects would probably be insignificant in relation to the total population. These, and associated effects, have been considered by a SCAR group of specialists on the Environmental Impact Assessment of Mineral Resource Exploration and Exploitation in Antarctica (EAMREA), whose report (Zumberge, 1979) emphasizes the essentially local nature of most extractive industry and the vast buffering capacity of the Southern Ocean, though it draws attention to the somewhat less remote possibility of large-scale effects on land, in particular those of airborne pollutants, which might affect the growth of lower plants, or the albedo of the snowfields.

The impact of oil development in the Ross Sea was examined in detail by Holdgate and Tinker (1979). They concluded that impacts would be minimal during the pre-drilling stage. This could start immediately and might last for 2–4 years. At the exploration drilling stage, lasting a further 5–10 years, impact would again be small, providing drilling rigs were serviced from outside the Antarctic. Finally, at the production stage, there would be two main hazards: oil pollution from a major supertanker spill, which might damage krill, seal and seabird populations; and the impact of construction on onshore tanker terminals and base facilities at an ice-free shore location.

1.4.4 Introductions

The introduction of exotic species by Man has modified many of the world's natural habitats. The havoc wrought by introduced animals, particularly rabbits and goats, is often most apparent, but plant species can also have far-reaching, if less obvious, effects. For an introduced alien to have a significant impact in the new ecosystems in which it finds itself it has to establish as a reproducing stock. In this sense the Antarctic proper has been virtually unaffected by introduced species, with the important exception of micro-organisms which are referred to below (4.3). The sub-Antarctic islands, however, have nearly all been affected in this way.

1.4.5 Pollution

Pollution can take many forms; the one of most significance in the context of conservation is the uncontrolled spread of man-made substances which are harmful to life, because this type of pollution may affect the environment at large. Some of the most important substances in this class are organochlorines, and the discovery of DDT residues in Antarctic wildlife (Sladen *et al.*, 1966; George and Frear, 1966) was an early indication of the global nature of this sort of pollution. Another group of industrial chlorinated hydrocarbons, the poly-chlorinated biphenyls (PCB's) have since been found in the Antarctic (Risebrough and Carmignani, 1972). Although some pollutants are introduced as a direct result of human traffic to Antarctica, other transfer processes exist which bring these substances from the northern hemisphere, where industry is concentrated, to the Antarctic. Migrating birds which feed in polluted northern areas may transport pollutants to the Antarctic ecosystem, but the ratio of the various pollutants found caused Risebrough *et al.* (1976) to conclude that atmospheric transport is the most important route. Marine circulation does not appear currently to be an important factor in introducing pollutants but it is possible that pollutants entering the seas in the northern hemisphere in large quantities may eventually (perhaps on a time-scale of 30–50 years hence) appear in Antarctic surface waters. Radio-isotopes form another class of pollutant substances which may readily be detected in low concentrations. Radio-isotopes have been transported to Antarctica for experimental purposes and to fuel nuclear power-plants. These do not account for general background levels in Antarctic snow, which are related to events (largely nuclear testing) outside the Antarctic. Although low levels of man-made substances have been detected in Antarctica, it is important to realize that the concentrations found have not so far been shown to have any effect on Antarctic ecosystems.

2. The Early History of Antarctic Exploitation

2.1 Nineteenth-century fur sealing

The first resource to be exploited in the Antarctic was the Antarctic fur seal. Cook recorded this swarming in great numbers on the beach where he landed in South Georgia in 1775, and in 1778 the first sealing expedition visited South Georgia (Roberts, 1958); by the turn of the century the industry had reached its peak. In 1800–1801 17 vessels were sealing off South Georgia and the total catch was 112,000 skins. Weddell (1825) calculated that by 1822 at least 1,200,000 fur seals had been taken from South Georgia and the species was nearly extinct there. The South Shetlands were another important sealing ground. Sealing started there the same year, 1819, that the group was discovered. In 1820–1821 47 British and American vessels were working the islands and took about 250,000 seals. A further season sufficed to complete the almost total extermination of the seals there. Weddell (1825) wrote:

> The quantity of seals taken off these islands, by vessels from different parts, during the years 1821 and 1822, may be computed at 320,000, and the quantity of sea-elephant oil at 940 tons. This valuable animal, the fur seal, might, by a law similar to that which restrains the fishermen in the size of the mesh of their net, have been spared to render annually 100,000 furs for many years to come. This would have followed from not killing the mothers till the young were able to take the water; and even then, only those which appeared to be old, together with a proportion of the males, thereby diminishing their total number, but in slow progression. This system is practised at the river of Plata. The island of Lobos, in the mouth of that river, contains a quantity of seals, and is farmed by the Governor of Monte Video, under certain restrictions, that the hunters shall not take them but at stated periods, in order to prevent the animals from being exterminated. The system of extermination was practiced, however, at Shetland; for whenever a seal reached the beach, of whatever denomination, he was immediately killed, and his skin taken; and by this means, at the end of the second year, the animals became nearly extinct; the young, having lost their mothers when only three or four days old, of course all died, which at the lowest calculation exceed 100,000.

This first intensive period of sealing, up to about 1825, practically exterminated the Scotia arc stock of the Antarctic fur seals and as a consequence, pressure on the seals relaxed. In the 1870s, however, there was a brief recrudescence of sealing in this region and small and rapidly diminishing catches were made at South Georgia, the South Shetlands, and South Sandwich Islands. The last visit of the old-time sealers to the Antarctic was made in 1907 when an American vessel took 170 furs from South Georgia (Larsen, 1920).

Despite the determined efforts made by the sealers to catch the last survivors of the stock a remnant in fact persisted. In 1908 a British administration was set up for the Falkland Island Dependencies (which included all the breeding grounds of the Antarctic fur seal in the Atlantic sector) and an ordinance protecting fur seals was promulgated. In the absence of further sealing (apart from an isolated catch at the South Sandwich Islands by Norwegians in 1928–1929, Sivertsen, 1954) the fur seal stocks recovered and are now again abundant at South Georgia and are present in smaller numbers at all the previous breeding island groups (Bonner, 1968; Laws 1973; Payne, 1977).

Similar uncontrolled exploitation went on at other Antarctic and sub-Antarctic islands where the Antarctic fur seal and its two relatives, the sub-Antarctic fur seal (*A. tropicalis*) and the New Zealand fur seal (*A. forsteri*) occurred. No species of fur seal was exterminated by the sealers, and with the decay of the industry and protective legislation there has been recovery in all areas. Some fur seal stocks (e.g. that at South Georgia) have reached levels at which rational exploitation on a sustained yield basis could be contemplated. However, there does not appear any likelihood of this taking place.

2.2 Elephant sealing

The nineteenth-century fur sealers combined with the hunting of fur seals the pursuit of the less valuable elephant seals (*Mirounga leonina*). Elephant seals produced an oil equivalent in value and use to whale oil. The history of the exploitation of elephant seals largely paralleled that of the fur seals but because they were a less valuable quarry whose utilization was more labour-intensive, the elephant seals were less relentlessly pursued.

Casual ship-based elephant sealing died out with the disappearance of the South Sea whalers, though not before many elephant seal populations had been severely affected. Recovery was, however, more rapid than in the case of the fur seals, and in South Georgia stocks had recovered sufficiently for the inception of a land-based industry in 1910. This provided one of the best examples of rational management of a natural resource (Laws, 1953a, 1960; Bonner, 1958). Because of its interest to conservationists, as demonstrating what the progress of the sealing industries might have been if proper controls had been exercised from the start, this industry is worth examining briefly.

The biology of the elephant seal makes it particularly well suited to sustain selective exploitation. The males have a strongly polygynous breeding habit, and associated with this is an extreme development of sexual dimorphism (Laws, 1960; and Chapter 12). If follows from this that adult males are readily distinguishable and that when they are removed by sealing from a breeding group their place is taken by other males which have not yet achieved the status of harem masters. The regulations imposed by the administration in South Georgia took account of these features. The total kill in any one season was restricted to 6000 adult bulls. Initially this quota was divided equally between three of the four divisions into which the coastline of the island (with the exception of some reserved areas) was divided, the division not worked being rotated round the island. In the early years of sealing the breeding season of the seals was covered by a closed season, but this regulation was later abandoned, since seals taken at the breeding season produced more oil and the sealing operations had little effect on breeding success.

This system operated reasonably efficiently for nearly 40 years, but an arbitrary decision to increase the quota in 1948 to 7500 bulls had an adverse effect on the stock and evidence of a decline was apparent. Following a study of the biology of this species and the discovery of a method of determining the age by means of incremental layers in the teeth (Laws, 1953b) action was taken to arrest the decline. This included a return to a quota of 6000 in 1952 and the distribution of this quota in proportion to the stock size in the various divisions. Conditions improved and the mean age of the catch stabilized at about 7.7 years, implying a sustained yield situation had been reached and maintained as predicted on the basis of population studies (Laws, 1960, 1979).

Elephant sealing in South Georgia finally ended in 1964 when the whaling company which cropped the seals ceased operations on account of the lack of whales, leaving an elephant seal stock that must have been near its maximum productivity.

3. Antarctic Whaling

The second great impact on the Antarctic marine ecosystem was the whaling industry. This began in the Falkland Island Dependencies in November 1904 when the Norwegian whaler, C. A. Larsen, established an Argentine-financed whaling company at Grytviken in South Georgia. Despite the great operating distance and a poor market for oil, Larsen's venture proved a success, largely because of the great abundance of whales in the immediate neighbourhood of the whaling station. This encouraged the setting up of other whaling companies in the Antarctic. By 1911 eight whaling station leases had been granted at South Georgia and nine shore-based factory ships and a shore station were working at the South Shetlands.

The early whaling installations were all shore-based, hence their activities could be controlled by the country in whose territory or territorial waters they were established. All the Antarctic whaling stations or shore-based factory ships at that time were in the Falkland Islands Dependencies, whose administration was well aware of the risks of uncontrolled hunting. No catch limits were set, but the number of licences issued for whaling expeditions was limited. Right whales were protected and it was forbidden to take whales accompanied by calves. Regulations were made concerning the utilization of all parts of the whale. Additionally, a duty was levied on the oil produced

> so that money should be available to finance scientific investigations in order that any further restrictive legislation which became necessary could be based on sound knowledge. . . . Surely it was a splendid and enlightened policy; from the whales killed money was provided for a proper investigation to prevent overfishing and the destruction of the stock (Hardy, 1967, p. 36).

These restrictions, coupled with the duty, had the effect of causing the whalers to seek some means of avoiding British governmental control. The solution was found in 1925 when the first successful stern-slip floating whale-factory, the h.k. *Lancing* operated in the Antarctic. This development enabled the whole process of whaling, including flensing and cooking out the products, to be carried out on the high seas, beyond the reach of any restrictive legislation.

Ironically, it was in the same year that the scientific expedition financed by the Falkland Island Dependencies whale-oil duty—the *Discovery* Investigations—began work in South Georgia. The work done by the *Discovery* scientists, and their successors, the staff of the Whale Research Unit of the National Institute of Oceanography, now the Sea Mammal Research Unit of the Natural Environment Research Council, provided the much-needed scientific basis for rational control. If authority to impose restrictions based on the scientists' recommendations had remained in the hands of a single, competent administration, the story of the Southern Ocean whales might well have been different. Because of the invention of the stern-slip factory this opportunity was missed and before science could usefully contribute to the control of whaling it was necessary for some international agreement to regulate activities outside territorial waters.

The first effective restriction of pelagic whaling was an economic one. In 1930–31 40,201 whales were killed in the Antarctic and the oil market was saturated. This led to an agreement between the principal whaling companies to refrain from fishing the following season, but in later years the catch quickly built up again (Mackintosh, 1965). The first attempt at international control was an International Convention for the Regulation of

Whaling drawn up in 1931 under the auspices of the League of Nations. This came into force in 1935 and provided for the protection of right whales, calves and whales accompanied by calves, and for the collection of whaling statistics. By this time it was already largely obsolete in its effects on Antarctic whaling, since the companies' production agreements provided better regulations. In 1937 and 1938 further restrictions were agreed governing the length of the catching season, setting the minimum permitted length of whales to be killed, providing some protection for humpback whales, establishing a sanctuary between 70°W and 160°W longitude, where no whaling would be permitted, and making arrangements for national inspectors on each factory-ship. Not all whaling countries, e.g. Japan and Germany, joined in these arrangements.

In 1944 for the first time an internationally-accepted limit was agreed on the number of whales allowed to be killed. Rather than set individual quotas related to the stock of each species an overall quota of 16,000 "Blue Whale Units" was set. One Blue Whale Unit (BWU) was equivalent to 1 blue, 2 fin, 2.5 humpback or 6 sei whales, and the quota could be taken in any combination of these. The concept of Blue Whale Units had been derived from the production agreements drawn up by the whaling industry after the collapse of the market in 1931 (Brown, 1963) and related to the equivalent oil production of these whales. This method of setting catch limits can in retrospect be seen as an unfortunate decision, since it took no account of the varying degree of protection which each stock required and allowed a depleted species to be still further reduced while the industry remained economically viable on another more abundant species (Gambell, 1977). This affected first the most valuable whales, and initially blue whales and then fin whales, were legally hunted long after their stocks had fallen below the levels which were calculated as corresponding to the maximum sustainable yield (Fig. 1). The quota of 16,000 BWU (which was probably not far above the combined maximum sustainable yield for the four species (Gulland, 1976)) operated for the first time in 1945–1946, when Antarctic whaling recommenced after the war.

In December 1946 the representatives of 14 governments, including the current principal whaling nations, signed another International Convention for the Regulation of Whaling. This established the International Whaling Commission (IWC), the body which presently controls most of the world's whaling. A Scientific Sub-Committee (later Committee) was set up in 1949 and its report in 1953 recommended reducing the quota to 14,500 BWU to conserve stocks. In 1956 this reduced quota came into effect, against strong opposition from some whaling nations. Because from the start the quota was international, nations competed with each

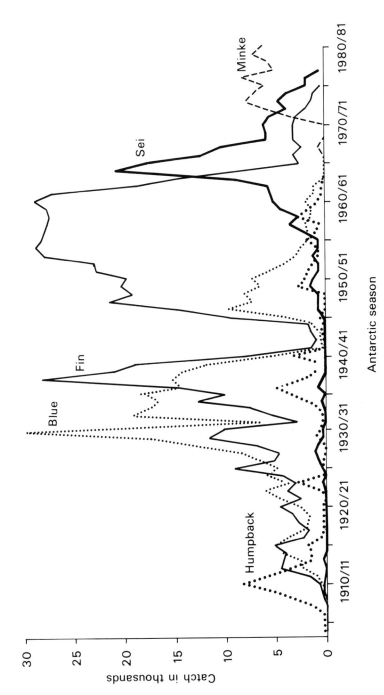

Fig. 1. Antarctic catches of whales 1904/1905–1980/1981 (including land stations, moored factory ships and pelagic whaling). Sources were the relevant tables of International Whaling Statistics (from data supplied by S. G. Brown).

TABLE I

Antarctic pelagic whaling expeditions 1946–1981

Season	Norway	Japan	U.S.S.R.	U.K.	Netherlands	South Africa	Panama	Total expeditions	Total catcher boats	IWC catch limit baleen whales (BWU)
1946/1947	7	2	1	3	1	1	—	15	129	16,000
1951/1952	10	3	1	3	1	1	1	20	268	16,000
1956/1957	9	5	1	3	1	1	—	20	225	14,500
1961/1962	7	7	4	2	1	1	—	21	261	(17,780)[a]
1966/1967	2[b]	4	3	—	—	—	—	9	120	3500
1971/1972	—	2	3	—	—	—	—	7	89[c]	2300
1976/1977	—	2	2	—	—	—	—	4	43	—[d]
1977/1978	—	1	2	—	—	—	—	3	34	—[e]
1978/1979	—	1	2	—	—	—	—	3	30	—[f]
1979/1980	—	1	2	—	—	—	—	3	17	—[g]
1980/1981	—	1	1	—	—	—	—	2	9	—[h]
1981/1982	—	1	1	—	—	—	—	2	9	—[i]

[a] Catch limit suspended by IWC, limit set by whaling countries.
[b] One combined factory/catcher boat operated.
[c] Includes one combined factory/catcher boat.
[d] Catch limit set for 1976/1977 pelagic season and 1977 southern hemisphere coastal season of 1863 sei and 8900 minke whales.
[e] As above, but 771 sei and 5690 minke whales.
[f] As above, but 6221 minke whales.
[g] As above, but 8102 minke whales.
[h] As above, but 7072 minke whales.
[i] As above, but 8102 minke whales.
(Table prepared by S. G. Brown.)

other, leading to over-investment in factory ships and catcher boats. Between the seasons 1946–1947 and 1961–1962 the average gross tonnage of catchers increased from 382 to 657, and their average horsepower from 1233 to 2723 (Brown, 1963).

Ultimate agreement on the allocation of national quotas (though outside the mechanism of the Convention) eventually improved the situation, but at the cost of three seasons (1959–1962) of uncontrolled quotas, Norway and Holland having withdrawn from the Convention on failing to reach agreement on the application of national quotas. Norway rejoined in 1960 and Holland in 1962, but by this time blue and humpback stocks were at very low levels while fin stocks were seriously reduced and declining rapidly. The extent of the reduction, and its rate, were not generally agreed and the IWC set up a Committee of Three (later Four) Scientists in 1960. The report of these scientists, who were experienced in fish population studies but were unprejudiced by previous association with whaling, showed that the catches of fin whales were greatly in excess of current sustainable yield and the stocks were far below optimum level. Blue and humpback stocks were even more depleted, hence catches had to be reduced drastically (Gulland, 1976). Quotas were successively reduced to 2300 BWU in 1971–1972 (blue whales meanwhile having been absolutely protected in the Antarctic in 1967 and humpbacks in 1963) and the Blue Whale Unit was finally abandoned in 1972, after repeated recommendations from the Scientific Committee for separate stock quotas. In 1975 the IWC introduced a fresh concept of regulation — the New Management Procedure (NMP). This divided all whale stocks into Protection stocks, Sustained Management stocks or Initial Management stocks, depending on whether they were below, at, or above maximum sustainable yield (MSY) level. No catching is allowed from Protection stocks; quotas should be set for Sustained Management stocks to keep them near the MSY level; while quotas for Initial Management stocks should be designed to bring them gradually towards MSY level (May, 1978).

The Antarctic whaling grounds were divided into six areas and the total allowable catch of rorquals in all of them in 1981–1982 should not exceed 8102 minke whales (a species which was of no commercial significance in the Antarctic prior to the 1970s). Fin and sei whale stocks, like the remaining blues and humpbacks, were classed as Protection stocks. No pelagic sperm whaling is now permitted, and killer whales (*Orcinus orca*) are also protected, so only minke whales are currently taken in the Antarctic.

The exploitation has been thorough. Whaling continues, though at a tiny fraction of its former intensity. The stocks of Antarctic baleen whales have been reduced to about 35% of their initial numbers, or 16% of their initial biomass (Laws, 1977, Table 2).

Reviews of the role of the IWC in the regulation of whaling are given by McHugh (1974) and Gambell (1977). The membership of the IWC has increased rapidly in recent years, largely by the addition of member nations whose interests are mainly in conservation, rather than exploitation, of whales. Currently there are 34 members, including all those nations engaged in Antarctic whaling, or who have been so engaged in the past.

It can be seen now that the internationally agreed control body under the Whaling Convention, the IWC, was unable to prevent the decline of the whale stocks, though the action it took retarded it, allowing a greater harvest of whales than would otherwise have been the case (Gulland, 1966). The IWC has often been accused of neglecting its duties, but it is difficult to see what more it might have done. It was, and is, a voluntary association; if a signatory nation disagrees with a Commission decision and registers an objection within 90 days, that decision is not binding on the objecting nation. Without this provision, the Convention itself would probably never have been agreed, and it means that effective decisions must be unanimous. That the Commission did not always accept the advice of its Scientific Committee is undeniable. Compromise, or even reversal of a recommendation, was often the price paid to have a powerful whaling nation stay within some limits, rather than register an objection and operate outside control.

From 1930 onwards, the scientifically-based estimates of prudent catches were never sufficient to provide an adequate return on the enormous capital invested. Had the Commission possessed the power to limit the catching equipment—the factory ships and catchers—and allocate species quotas on a national basis from the resumption of whaling after the 1939–1945 war, it is probable that a regulated and economic industry, which would have profited from well-founded scientific advice, would have developed under the guidance of the IWC. In the outcome, the IWC is seen as having failed in its main task. Whether it is now too late for the New Management Procedure to permit the recovery of whale stocks to pre-harvest levels is conjectural.

4. Expeditions in Antarctica

The impact of scientific expeditions on natural systems is rarely as severe as that of commercial exploitation, but it may be by no means negligible and is often conspicuous. Although scientific expeditions are as old as both sealing and whaling in the Antarctic, it was not until this century was well advanced that the pace of exploration and research reached the level at which it had a significant, if local effect on Antarctic ecosystems.

4.1 Impact of specimen collections on scientific observation

Direct scientific activity probably has a negligible effect. The collection of scientific specimens usually represents a very small drain on a large resource. The effect will be more significant where local colonies of birds and seals, particularly those at the limit of their range, or long-lived or immobile organisms (e.g. lichens, some marine benthos) are used for destructive research. Repeated sampling from limited areas of terrestrial vegetation can cause substantial changes or even destruction of the site. At Signy Island a moss-carpet study site had to be abandoned after six years of sample coring. Repeated visits to the site had compacted it and altered its drainage; additional damage was caused by skuas (*Catharacta skua lönnbergi*) which tore away moss from the edge of core-holes.

Non-destructive scientific observation also may have deleterious effects. Close approach may cause penguins to abandon their nests and cease breeding for that year (Muller-Schwarze and Belanger, 1978). Disturbance of seals on land may cause increased activity which might adversely affect energy balance or could cause loss of young through trampling.

Equipment and materials used for science may affect the system. Parker *et al.* (1978) have drawn attention to environmental problems caused by loss of drill fluids in the Dry Valleys Drilling Project. At Lake Fryxell diversity and total number of soil microbes were lower in areas of calcium chloride contamination (derived from spilt drill fluid); at Lake Vida spilled diesel fuel appears to have caused a decrease in the number of detectable microbes.

4.2 Collection for non-scientific purposes

The killing of animals, mostly Adélie or chinstrap penguins (*Pygoscelis adeliae* and *P. antarcticus*) and crabeater and Weddell seals (*Lobodon carcinophagus* and *Leptonychotes weddellii*) to provide food for men and sledge dogs was an accepted feature of all early Antarctic expeditions. Impacts were local and had an insignificant effect on total stocks. Modern expeditions tend not to rely on local food supplies and with the decline in the number of sledge dogs maintained in the Antarctic this type of pressure has shrunk to negligible proportions. Laws and Christie (1976) recorded that between 1970 and 1973, 918 crabeater seals and 1003 Weddell seals were taken in the Antarctic Treaty area as essential food for men and dogs as well as for scientific purposes. The much larger human populations at shore-based whaling stations had a greater effect on local stocks and one species, the wandering albatross (*Diomedea exulans*), may have been significantly affected. Prior to about 1950 the eggs of this slow-breeding bird were collected by whalers at several localities in South Georgia. Matthews (1951) records the collection of over 2000 eggs on one occasion in the 1920s. At one locality much used for egg-collecting because of its easy access Matthews states 288 eggs were taken; in 1946 Rankin (1951) recorded 298 nests. Today there is none. It is probable there has been a similar, but unquantified, decline in the wandering albatross elsewhere in South Georgia and as these birds represent a sizeable proportion of the world population this should be accounted a significant impact.

Sport or trophy hunting has probably been confined to the killing of a few leopard seals (*Hydrurga leptonyx*), which has had no effect on stocks. Casual collection of "souvenir" specimens by base personnel causes more problems to the scientist than to the environment. Parker (1972) records areas of freshly-exposed rock and soil at Palmer station where lichens and mosses had been collected by base members, but in general this form of collection has little environmental effect.

4.3 Impact of base installations

Permanent occupation of Antarctic bases began in 1904 at Laurie Island when the Scottish National Antarctic Expedition handed over operation of the meteorological station there to the Argentine meteorological service. This remained an isolated example for four decades, though there were, of course, many important transitory expeditions which left buildings in the Antarctic. In the 1940s there was a sudden expansion of Antarctic activity, notably in the Antarctic Peninsula sector, when Argentina, Chile and the United Kingdom established permanent bases. Another more wide-spread expansion occurred during or just prior to the International Geophysical Year in 1957–1958, when a large number of permanent or semi-permanent base installations were established in both mainland Antarctica and on the islands.

As noted earlier (p. 826), base sites are often chosen because they are reasonably level, free from permanent snow and ice and have good access to the sea in summer. These features also make such sites likely to support permanent vegetation, or breeding colonies of seabirds, or both, hence bases almost inevitably have some impact. The building of Hallett station eliminated the breeding sites of about 7850 Adélie penguins (Eklund, 1959) and although the buildings have since been removed Muller-Schwarze and Belanger (1978) reported that the birds had not recolonized the area.

The changes caused by the establishment of bases have been reviewed by Lipps (1978) for the Antarctic Peninsula, while Cameron (1972) has drawn attention to conditions associated with some bases and temporary camp sites in continental Antarctica. A chief result of human occupation is the accumulation of waste and the contamination of the environment by it. Large dumps of worn out or abandoned equipment and packaging are a conspicuous feature of many Antarctic bases. While such dumps may be aesthetically unpleasing they may have little biological effect. Human wastes and domestic effluents are more biologically active and could be of greater significance. There is a general revulsion about leaving untreated sewage exposed. Many bases flush such waste out to sea in a relatively untreated form, a practice which may impose a localized biological load on the marine system at the outfall. A waste disposal treatment plant was built at McMurdo, but as Tyler (1972) pointed out, this merely changes the form of the waste to something more acceptable aesthetically, and represents a change for the worse, since more energy and materials have to be imported to build the treatment plant, and more people (producing more waste) are required to run it.

A particular problem is caused by chemical wastes. Some commonly-used chemical solutions are very toxic, for example some colour-film processing solutions, and if these accumulate in sumps during the winter freeze-up, to be released to the sea in a sudden rush when the thaw comes, local pollution may be severe.

A code of conduct drawn up at the Eighth Consultative Meeting of the Antarctic Treaty nations covers the disposal of wastes by expeditions and stations. It enjoins that for coastal stations, with certain exceptions, liquid waste should be macerated and flushed to sea, non-combustibles dumped in the sea, combustibles burnt, but batteries, all plastics, rubber and radio-isotopes should be removed from the Treaty Area.

Introductions pose another problem. Plants can easily be introduced inadvertently when their seeds or propagules arrive in hay or packing material used at an expedition base. In South Georgia, alien plants are most commonly found in the vicinity of the abandoned whaling stations (Greene, 1964), but one species, *Poa annua*, is more widely distributed. None of the introduced plants in the sub-Antarctic islands has made a considerable impact on the native flora except where the indigenous vegetation has been opened up by introduced herbivores (Holdgate and Wace, 1961). Exotic plants can grow in Antarctic conditions (Holdgate, 1964; Edwards and Greene, 1973; Edwards, in press), but with the exception of *Poa annua* and *P. pratensis*, (Longton, 1966) none has established itself there.

Animal introductions have made a more visible impact. The early visits of the sealers introduced brown rats (*Rattus norvegicus*) and house mice (*Mus musculus*). Deliberate introductions which have established them-selves ferally include reindeer (*Rangifer tarandus*) at South Georgia and Kerguelen; rabbits (*Oryctolagus cuniculus*) at Kerguelen and Macquarie Island; and cats at Kerguelen, Macquarie and Marion Island (Holdgate and

Wace, 1961; Imshaug, 1972). Rabbits in particular have caused great vegetative changes by eating out *Poa foliosa* and *Stilbocarpa polaris* at Kerguelen and Macquarie Island (Costin and Moore, 1960; Holdgate and Wace, 1961), while reindeer at South Georgia have been shown to cause significant change by selectively grazing *Acaena magellanica* and destructively cropping *Poa flabellata* during the winter (Kightley and Smith, 1976; Leader-Williams *et al.*, 1981). A potential hazard of a novel kind concerns the projected introduction of Pacific salmon (*Onchyrhyncus* sp.) into inshore waters of South America (Joyner *et al.*, 1974). The intention is that the smolts will cross the Antarctic Convergence to feed on krill in the Southern Ocean, returning for harvest to their release point. It is conceivable that, should the operation develop without adequate controls, a new and unquantified factor would be introduced into the krill-based food pyramid.

4.4 Tourist impact

Although not yet generally recognized as constituting Antarctic expeditions, tourists are becoming of increasing significance in the Antarctic. Any large area of wilderness, particularly a wilderness which is scenically beautiful and inhabited by large populations of animals as striking and seemingly tame as penguins, will inevitably attract tourists. The remoteness of Antarctica and its offlying islands has until recently prevented the development of a tourist traffic, but in recent years several vessels have begun making regular visits to the region. A later development has been the initiation of tours to over-fly the Antarctic Continent. Tourists, by their presence, may destroy the features they have come to see. Repeated visits by tourists arriving in helicopters at the Cape Royds Adélie penguin rookery caused a steep decline in the number of nesting birds which was reversed when the visits were restricted (Thomson, 1977). In general, however, tourist pressure is likely to be localized, since the number of suitable access points is limited, and tourists rarely move far from their transport. These features tend to make it easier to control tourist impact.

5. Legislative Controls

5.1 The Antarctic Treaty and the agreed measures

National societies create codes to control behaviour and provided the codes are adequate and can be publicized and enforced, threats to the environment can be averted and conservation enforced by national law.

Antarctica, however, presents special problems, since uniquely on the Earth's land surface, there is no general agreement on the extent or existence of national sovereignty. Conflicting and unrecognized claims arising from this led to a political confrontation during the 1950s. This situation was partly resolved by the signing of the Antarctic Treaty, which came into force in 1961.

The Treaty, signed by the 12 nations then active in the Antarctic, agreed to freeze the situation with respect to the recognition or non-recognition of territorial claims for purposes of encouraging scientific research. It provided a basis for the development of scientific cooperation without political interferences (Roberts, 1977). The "preservation and conservation of living resources in the Antarctic" was named as one of the matters of common interest about which parties to the Treaty should consult together. Thus the Treaty provided a framework within which conservation agreements could be drawn up by the consultative parties.

The first such agreement was the "Agreed Measures for the Conservation of Antarctic Fauna and Flora", which was drawn up as a recommendation of the Third Antarctic Treaty Consultative Meeting in Brussels in 1964 (Anderson, 1968; SCAR, 1972). Like the Treaty itself, the Agreed Measures applied to all land and ice-shelves south of 60° latitude, and in them is repeated an Article of the Antarctic Treaty (Article VI) which maintains that the traditional rights of nations on the high seas are not affected. Amongst these is the right to fish.

There are four main articles in the Agreed Measures. The first of these, Article VI deals with the protection of native fauna. It prohibits the killing, wounding or capturing of any native mammal (excluding whales) or bird. The larger whales are protected on the high seas by the provisions of the International Whaling Convention, but the position of smaller cetacea, such as southern bottlenose whales (*Hyperoodon planifrons*) or Commerson's dolphins (*Cephalorhynchus commersonii*), is doubtful—ignored by the IWC they are specifically excluded from the Agreed Measures. The general prohibition on killing, etc., native mammals or birds, may be lifted by permit, which can be issued (a) to provide indispensable food for men or dogs; (b) to provide specimens for scientific study or information; or (c) to provide specimens for museums, zoos, etc. The issue of permits, to be done by the "appropriate authority" of each Participating Government, has to be in terms as specific as possible. They must be such that no more animals are taken than can normally be replaced at the following breeding season (a form of sustainable yield regulation), and ensure that the variety of species and the balance of the natural ecological systems are maintained. Certain species can be designated "Specially Protected Species" (currently all species of fur seals of the genus *Arctocephalus* and the Ross seal, *Ommato-*

phoca rossii) and permits relating to them can be issued only for a compelling scientific purpose, and must be drawn so as to ensure the action permitted will not jeopardize the existing natural ecological system or the survival of that species.

Article VII enjoins that Participating Governments take appropriate measures to minimize harmful interference with the normal living conditions of native mammals and birds, and to alleviate pollution of coastal waters. This is a wide-ranging provision and a list of examples of what constitutes harmful interference is given. The Article recognizes that some interference is a necessary concomitant of the presence of a station, and permits some otherwise prohibited activities to the minimum extent required for the establishment, supply or operation of stations.

Article VIII lays down measures for the designation of "Specially Protected Areas" (SPA's), where special protection is given to preserve unique natural ecological systems or those of outstanding scientific interest. Here, in addition to other prohibitions that apply elsewhere in the Treaty Area, entry (except by permit) is prohibited, the collection of any native plant (except by permit) is prohibited and the driving of vehicles is forbidden. The Seventh Consultative Meeting recommended that the existing SPA's should be reviewed and that the following categories should be included in the list of SPA's:

(a) Representative examples of the major Antarctic land and freshwater systems.
(b) Areas with unique complexes of species.
(c) Areas which are the type locality or only known breeding habitat of any plant or invertebrate species.
(d) Areas which contain especially interesting breeding colonies of birds or mammals.
(e) Areas which should be kept inviolate so that in the future they may be used for purposes of comparison with localities that have been disturbed by Man.

A defect in the application of SPA's as the only means of protecting localized areas was that in providing the protection the area was effectively closed to scientific research, since permits having effect in an SPA could be issued only for "a compelling scientific purpose which could not be served elsewhere". A lesser degree of protection was required and at the Seventh Consultative Meeting provision was made for the designation of Sites of Special Scientific Interest (SSSI's). It was recognized that wilful or accidental interference might jeopardize scientific investigations, and that sites, because of continuing scientific investigations, or because they were of non-biological interest, might require protection. Such sites might be designated SSSI's and provided with management plans which would regulate access and the type of activity permitted at the site.

Article IX of the Agreed Measures regulates the introduction of non-indigenous species. The regulation does not apply to food, except in so far as the importation of living poultry is banned.

The Agreed Measures, supplemented by the recommendations from the Consultative Meetings, provide an effective conservation regime within the area of competence of the agreement. The agreement itself, however, does not deal with enforcement, which is left to Participating Governments. Some expeditions interpret regulations, for example those concerning SPA's, in different ways; the Code of Conduct for waste-disposal seems to have had little effect so far.

The islands of the Antarctic and sub-Antarctic north of 60°S are not covered by the Treaty and are all under effective national control. All have some form of conservation legislation associated with them. In some cases (e.g. South Georgia) this is drawn up on similar lines to that under the Antarctic Treaty. In others (e.g. Macquarie Island) the whole island has the quality of a national nature reserve. At all these places there are adequate legal instruments for conservation, though in such sparsely-inhabited regions enforcement is difficult. A special problem which has recently arisen is the increasing number of private yachts now cruising in Antarctic waters which are almost independent of national control.

5.2 The Convention for the Conservation of Antarctic Seals

The Antarctic seals, particularly the vast stocks of crabeater seals, offer a potential resource of great magnitude, though rather surprisingly only one small expedition, the m.v. *Polarhav* in 1964, has attempted to tap this (Øritsland, 1970). Since the right to fish and hunt seals on the high seas was reserved unaffected by the Agreed Measures, a further international agreement was required to give protection to seals in the sea or on floating ice. This was achieved when the Convention for the Conservation of Antarctic seals was signed in London in 1972 and came into force in 1978. this was a unique conservation instrument, in that it provided protection in advance of the heavy exploitation that has preceded the introduction of all similar international conservation measures.

The Convention applies to the sea and floating ice south of 60°S, but there is provision for reporting catches to the north of this. It covers all species of seal that occur in Antarctic waters. In an Annex, Permissible Catch Limits, subject to review, are specified of 175,000 crabeater seals, 12,000 leopard seals and 5000 Weddell seals in any one year. the taking of Ross seals, elephant seals and fur seals of the genus *Arctocephalus* is completely banned. The specified limits are very conservative, and it is likely that if an industry were to develop, they would be adjusted upwards. Special permits can be issued to take seals, as in the Agreed Measures, for food, research or museum specimens, etc. There is a close season of 1 March–31 August and additionally adult Weddell seals are protected from 1 September to 31 January while they are concentrated for breeding on fast-ice, and hence vulnerable to sealing. The Southern Ocean is divided into six zones, one to be rested from sealing each year in rotation, and there are three sealing reserves. If commercial sealing were to begin in the Antarctic, the Convention provides for the establishment of a Commission and Scientific Advisory Committee, but until then information on seals killed and biological data and materials are to be supplied to SCAR, who would be invited to suggest amendments to the Annex to the Convention, and report on any harmful effects that the harvest of seals might have. The Convention provides for a review of operations at five-yearly intervals.

Currently no nation appears to be interested in undertaking Antarctic sealing, but the Convention provides the means to regulate an industry, should one develop.

5.3 The Convention for the Conservation of Antarctic Marine Living Resources

With the catastrophic decline of the whaling industry in the 1960s some nations turned their attention to other possible marine resources in the Antarctic. The obvious one was fish, and substantial catches have been taken (Everson, 1977; Chapter 10). This resource, however, was limited in extent, whereas it was apparent that a much larger harvestable resource existed in the Southern Ocean. This was krill, *Euphausia superba*, the central component of many of the region's food webs. Because of the reduction in biomass of the baleen whales caused by over-harvesting it was argued that a "surplus" of krill existed which could be harvested on a sustainable yield basis at a rate of the same order, or even greater, than the combined total of all existing world fisheries. Technical problems were soon overcome and it was clear that the potential for a large industry existed (see Chapter 9).

While the Agreed Measures provided a framework for conservation on land, and the International Whaling Commission and the Convention for the Conservation of Antarctic Seals potentially provided for the interests of whales and seals respectively on the high seas, there was no international agreement that would regulate a krill fishery. However, because of its key role in the ecosystem, substantial harvesting of krill would certainly have far-reaching effects on other organisms, most conspicuously seabirds, seals and whales.

Recognizing the gap in the conservation legislation, the Antarctic Treaty nations set out to negotiate a new convention on Antarctic marine living resources. This had its origin in 1975, when the Treaty powers recognized the need to promote rational use of these resources. At the Ninth Antarctic Treaty Consultative Meeting in London in 1977, the broad outlines of the Convention were laid down; these were further discussed in Canberra in 1978 when a draft was revised. Following further meetings in Buenos Aires, Washington and Berne the Convention was signed at Canberra in May 1980. The objective of the Convention, which covers all marine living organisms, including birds, is conservation, though included in this term is the concept of rational use. Its aim is to ensure that harvesting shall not deplete populations below the levels which ensure stable recruitment; this implies that they should be maintained near those levels which ensure the greatest net annual increment. The importance of the balance of ecological relationships between harvested, dependent and related populations is recognized, and the restoration of depleted populations is one of the objectives. Changes in population which are not potentially reversible in a few decades are to be prevented.

Although belonging to the Antarctic Treaty family of agreements, the Convention for the Conservation of Marine Living Resources (CAMLR) has extended its area of influence north of 60°S, and has adopted a biological boundary, the Antarctic Convergence, as its northern limit. This, of course, is in line with its ecological approach.

The Convention provides for the setting up of a Commission, advised by a scientific committee (on the lines of the IWC) which would facilitate research, compile and analyse data and recommend conservation measures, including regulations on the quantities of any species which may be harvested in the area as a whole, or any designated sub-areas; protected species; characteristics of a species which may be harvested (e.g. age or size limits); open and closed seasons and areas; and regulation of effort and method of harvesting. It is not proposed that there should be any catch or effort allocation to individual states, though this might have been a useful provision if powers for it had been available. Experience with the whaling industry has shown that if catching effort is allowed to increase by competition between countries, the subsequent regulation of catch becomes difficult.

As with the IWC, implementation of the CAMLR is in the hands of individual contracting parties but a system of observation and inspection is to be established. Conservation measures are binding on all signatory nations unless they have objected within a 90-day period, another parallel with the IWC. Decisions of the Commission are to be taken by consensus, rather than by a majority. It came into force in 1982.

The CAMLR was opened to signature at Canberra by the states participating in the conference, in other words, the Antarctic Treaty states. Additionally, it is open to accession by any state interested in research or harvesting activities in relation to marine living resources in the area to which it applies. However, only nations actively engaged in research or harvesting activities would be entitled to be members of the Commission.

Like all international agreements, CAMLR is a compromise, and hence cannot be entirely satisfactory to all parties. Nevertheless, in its ecosystem approach and its provision for scientific advice through the Commission's scientific committee, it provides a solid basis from which effective conservation can be exercised.

6. Future Prospects

With the conclusion of the convention covering marine living resources, there seems to be an adequate legal framework for conservation in the Antarctic. However, effective conservation will depend on nations enforcing this legislation and taking advantage of the opportunities provided by it for establishing special sites, making regulations, etc. All nations in the Antarctic have the means of controlling the activities of their nationals so as to avoid harmful impacts. Antarctic Treaty nations with the advice of SCAR have already set up a network of SPA's and SSSI's to reserve characteristic areas of the environment. The price of conservation will be continual vigilance. Increasing human populations will inevitably place more demands for resources, minerals from both the land and the shallow sea. High operational costs may make the Antarctic less attractive to industry than some other parts of the Earth's surface, but they will not protect it entirely. A wider understanding of the principles and philosophy of conservation may be the best defence. This may be achieved by education of the public, perhaps particularly by the publishing of accounts of the Antarctic environment and ecosystem through the media of popular books, magazines and films. Increasing tourist traffic can also play a role here. Tourists to Antarctica tend to be those already interested in wilderness and wildlife, and because of the inevitable expense involved in visiting such a remote area, they tend also to be monied, and hence influential, people in their own communities. Such persons, on their return home, can be effective ambassadors for the cause of conservation in the Antarctic.

Even with the best possible education in conservation, there will still be a conflict between the exploiters and the conservationists. In the past in the

Antarctic the balance has been very much in favour of the exploiters. It now seems possible that this balance will change, so that conservation, *including rational use*, will become the accepted approach. If this comes about the conservation strategies adopted will need to be based on sound scientific advice, advice that will depend on a full understanding of the ecology of the Antarctic.

7. References

Anderson, D. (1968). The conservation of wildlife under the Antarctic Treaty. *Polar Record* **14**, 25–31.

Bonner, W. N. (1958). Exploitation and conservation of seals in South Georgia. *Oryx* **4**, 373–380.

Bonner, W. N. (1968). The fur seal of South Georgia. *British Antarctic Survey, Scientific Report* No. 56, 81 pp.

Brown, S. G. (1963). A review of Antarctic whaling. *Polar Record* **11**, 555–566.

Cameron, R. E. (1972). Pollution and conservation of the Antarctic terrestrial ecosystem. *In* "Conservation Problems in Antarctic" (B. C. Parker, ed.), pp. 267–305. Virginia Polytechnic Institute and State University, Blacksburg.

Costin, A. B. and Moore, D. M. (1960). The effects of rabbit grazing on the grasslands of Macquarie Island. *Journal of Ecology* **48**, 729–732.

Dunbar, M. J. (1973). Stability and fragility in arctic ecosystems. *Arctic* **26**, 179–185.

Dunbar, M. J. (1977). The evolution of polar ecosystems. *In* "Adaptations within Antarctic Ecosystems" (G. A. Llano, ed.), pp. 1063–1076. Smithsonian Institution, Washington, D.C.

Edwards, J. A. (in press). An experimental introduction of vascular plants from South Georgia to the maritime Antarctic. *British Antarctic Survey Bulletin*.

Edwards, J. A. and Greene, S. W. (1973). The survival of Falkland Islands transplants at South Georgia and Signy Island, South Orkney Islands. *British Antarctic Survey Bulletin*, Nos. 33 and 34, 33–45.

Eklund, C. R. (1959). Antarctic ornithological studies during the IGY. *Bird Banding* **30**, 114–118.

Everson, I. (1977). The living resources of the Southern Ocean. Food and Agriculture Organisation of the United Nations; United Nations Development Programme, Rome. GLO/SO/77/1, 156 pp.

Gambell, R. (1977). Role of the International Whaling Commission. *Marine Policy* October 1977, 301–310.

George, J. L. and Frear, D. E. H. (1966). Pesticides in the Antarctic. *Journal of Applied Ecology* **3** (suppl.), 155–167.

Greene, S. W. (1964). The vascular flora of South Georgia. *British Antarctic Survey, Scientific Report* No. 45, 58 pp.

Gulland, J. A. (1966). The effect of regulation on Antarctic whale catches. *Journal du Conseil permanent international pour l'Exploration de la Mer* **30**, 308–315.

Gulland, J. A. (1976). Antarctic baleen whales: history and prospects. *Polar Record* **18**, 5–13.

Hardy, A. (1967). "Great Waters". Collins, London.

Heywood, R. B. (1977). Antarctic freshwater ecosystem: review and synthesis. *In* "Adaptations within Antarctic Ecosystems" (G. A. Llano, ed.), pp. 801–828. Smithsonian Institution, Washington, D.C.

Heywood, R. B. (1978). Maritime Antarctic lakes. *Verhandlugen der Internationalen Vereinigung Limnologie* **20,** 1210–1215.

Holdgate, M. W. (1964). An experimental introduction of plants to the Antarctic. *British Antarctic Survey Bulletin* No. 3, 13–16.

Holdgate, M. W. (1967). The Antarctic ecosystem. *Philosophical Transactions of the Royal Society* **B252,** 363–383.

Holdgate, M. W. (1970). Conservation in the Antarctic. *In* "Antarctic Ecology" (M. W. Holdgate, ed.), pp. 942–945. Academic Press, London and New York.

Holdgate, M. W. and Tinker, J. (1979). Oil and other minerals in the Antarctic: The environmental implications of mineral exploration or exploitation in Antarctica. Scientific Committee on Antarctic Research, Cambridge, England.

Holdgate, M. W. and Wace, N. M. (1961). The influence of man on the floras and faunas of Southern Islands. *Polar Record* **10** (68), 475–493.

Hooker, T. N. (1980). Growth and production of *Usnea antarctica* and *U. fasciata* on Signy Island, South Orkney Islands. *British Antarctic Survey Bulletin* No. 50, 35–49.

Huntley, B. J. (1972). Notes on the ecology of *Azorella selago. Journal of South African Botany* **38,** 103–113.

Imshaug, H. A. (1972). Need for the conservation of terrestrial vegetation in the Sub-antarctic. *In* "Conservation Problems in Antarctica" (B. C. Parker, ed.), pp. 229–240. Virginia Polytechnic Institute and State University, Blacksburg.

Joyner, T., Mahnken, C. V. W. and Clark, R. C. (1974). Salmon—future harvest from the Antarctic Ocean? *Marine Fisheries Review* **36,** 20–28.

Kightley, S. P. J. and Smith, R. I. L. (1976). The influence of reindeer on the vegetation of South Georgia: I. Long-term effects of unrestricted grazing and the establishment of exclosure experiments in various plant communities. *British Antarctic Survey Bulletin* No. 44, 57–76.

Larsen, C. A. (1920). "Report of Interdepartmental Committees on Research and Development in the Dependencies of the Falkland Islands". Command 657, H.M.S.O., London.

Laws, R. M. (1953a). The Elephant seal industry at South Georgia. *Polar Record* **6,** 746–754.

Laws, R. M. (1953b). A new method of age determination in mammals, with special reference to the Elephant seal (*Mirounga Leonina,* Linn.). *Falkland Islands Dependencies Survey, Scientific Report* **2.**

Laws, R. M. (1960). The Southern Elephant seal (*Mirounga leonia,* Linn.) at South Georgia. *Norsk Hvalfangsttidende* Nos 10 and 11, 466–476 and 520–542.

Laws, R. M. (1973). Population increase of fur seals at South Georgia. *Polar Record* **16,** 856–858.

Laws, R. M. (1977). Seals and whales of the Southern Ocean *Philosophical Transactions of the Royal Society* **B279,** 81–96.

Laws, R. M. (1979). Monitoring whale and seal populations. *In* "Monitoring the Marine Environment" (D. Nichols, ed.), pp. 115-140. Institute of Biology, London.

Laws, R. M. and Christie, E. C. (1976). Seals and birds killed or captured in the Antarctic Treaty area, 1970–73. SCAR Bulletin No. 54. *Polar Record* **18** (114), 318–320.

Leader-Williams, N., Scott, T. A. and Pratt, R. M. (1981). Forage selection by introduced reindeer on South Georgia, and its consequences for the flora. *Journal of Applied Ecology* **18,** 83–106.

Lipps, J. H. (1978). Man's impact along the Antarctic Peninsula. *In* "Environmental Impact in Antarctica" (B. C. Parker and M. C. Holliman, eds), pp. 333-371. Virginia Polytechnic Institute and State University, Blacksburg.

Longton, R. E. (1966). Alien vascular plants on Deception Island, South Shetland Islands. *British Antarctic Survey Bulletin* No. 9, 55–60.

McHugh, J. L. (1974). The role and history of the International Whaling Commission. *In* "The Whale Problem: A Status Report" (W. E. Schevill, ed.), pp. 305–335. Harvard University Press, Cambridge, Massachusetts.

Mackintosh, N. A. (1965). "The Stocks of Whales". Fishing News (Books) Ltd., London.

Margalef, R. (1977). Ecosystem diversity differences, poles and tropics. *In* "Polar Oceans" (M. J. Dunbar, ed.), pp. 367–389, SCOR/SCAR Polar Oceans Conference, May 1974, Montreal. Arctic Institute of North America, Montreal.

Matthews, L. H. (1951). "Wandering Albatross". Macgibbon and Kee, London.

May, R. M. (1978). Whaling: past, present and future. *Nature* (Lond.) **276,** 319–322.

Muller-Schwarze, D. and Belanger, P. (1978). Man's impact on Antarctic birds. *In* "Environmental Impact in Antarctica" (B. C. Parker and M. C. Holliman, eds), pp. 373–383. Virginia Polytechnic Institute and State University, Blacksburg.

Øritsland, T. (1970). Sealing and seal research in the Southwest Atlantic pack ice, September–October, 1964. *In* "Antarctic Ecology" (M. W. Holdgate, ed.), pp. 367–376. Academic Press, London and New York.

Parker, B. C. (ed.) (1972). Conservation of freshwater habitats on the Antarctic Peninsula. *In* "Conservation Problems in Antarctica", pp. 143–162. Virginia Polytechnic and State University, Blacksburg.

Parker, B. C., Howard, R. V. and Allnutt, F. C. T. (1978). Summary of environmental monitoring and impact assessment of the DVDP. *In* "Environmental Impact in Antarctica" (B. C. Parker and M. C. Holliman, eds), pp. 311–351. Virginia Polytechnic Institute and State University, Blacksburg.

Payne, M. R. (1977). Growth of a fur seal population. *Proceedings of the Royal Society Ser.* **B279,** 67–79.

Rankin, N. (1951). "Antarctic Isle, Wildlife in South Georgia". Collins, London.

Risebrough, R. W. and Carmignani, G. M. (1972). Chlorinated hydrocarbons in Antarctic birds. *In* "Conservation Problems in Antarctica" (B. C. Parker, ed.), pp. 63–78. Virginia Polytechnic Institute and State University, Blacksburg.

Risebrough, R. W., Walker, W. II, Schmidt, T. T., De Lappe, B. W. and Connors, C. W. (1976). Transfer of chlorinated biphenyls to Antarctica. *Nature* (Lond.) **264,** 738–739.

Roberts, B. B. (1958). Chronological list of expeditions. *Polar Record* **59.** 97–134.

Roberts, B. B. (1977). International co-operation for Antarctic development: the test for the Antarctic Treaty. *Polar Record* **119,** 107–120.

SCAR (1972). "SCAR Manual" (2nd edition). Scientific Committee on Antarctic Research, Cambridge, England.

SCAR (1977). Antarctic resources—effects of mineral exploitation. SCAR Bulletin No. 57. *Polar Record* **18,** 631–648.

Silvertsen, E. (1954). A survey of the eared seals (family Otariidae) with remarks on the Antarctic seals collected by m.k. *Norvegia* in 1928–29. *Scientific Results of the Norwegian Antarctic Expedition* **36,** 1–76.

Sladen, W. J. L., Menzie, C. M., Reichel, W. L. (1966). DDT residues in Adélie penguins and a crabeater seal from Antarctica. *Nature* (Lond.) **210**, 670–673.

Thomson, R. B. (1977). Effects of human disturbance on an Adélie penguin rookery and measures of control. *In* "Adaptations within Antarctic Ecosystems" (G. A. Llano, ed.), pp. 1177–1180. Smithsonian Institution, Washington, D.C.

Tyler, P. E. (1972). Sanitation and waste disposal in Antarctica. *In* "Conservation Problems in Antarctica" (B. C. Parker, ed.), pp. 241–246. Virginia Polytechnic Institute and State University, Blacksburg.

Weddell, J. (1825). "A Voyage Towards the South Pole, Performed in the Years 1822–24." Longman, Hurst, Ress, Orme, Brown and Green, London.

Zumberge, J. H. (1979). "Possible Environmental Effects of Mineral Exploration and Exploitation in Antarctic. An Adaptation of a Report by the Group of Specialists on the Environmental Impact of Mineral Resource Exploration and Exploitation in Antarctica". Scientific Committee on Antarctic Research, Cambridge, England.

Subject Index

Individual organisms are listed under vernacular and/or scientific names as used in text; see both.

A

Ablation Point, 281, 313
Acaena magellanica, 21, 28, 68, 91, 94, 99, 100, 107, 113, 122, 123, 124, 126, 128, 132, 253, 264, 266, 840
    A. tenera, 99, 113, 132
Acarina, 174, 192, 195, 197, 211, *see also individual species*
    feeding biology, 197
    physiology, 197–200, 211
Acarospora macrocyclos, 109
Acetylene reduction, 129
Achnanthes austriaca, 291
    A. brevipes, 310
    A. microcephala, 291
Achromobacter, 168
Acremonium, 168
Actiniaria, 423
Actinomycetes, 164
Adamussium colbecki, 441
Adaptation, 133, 134, 136, 164, 423, 644, 662
Adineta grandis, 328
Adinetides, 178
Adenocystis utricularis, 383, 388
Aerial photography, 629
Aerobiology, 164, 165, 167, 168
Agreed Measures for the Conservation of Antarctic Flora and Fauna, 840–843
Agriolimax reticulatus, 182

Agrostis magellanica, 80, 106
Alaskozetes antarcticus, 197–199, 200, 202–206
Albatrosses, 546, 552, 558–560, 564, 568, 570, 572, 581, *see also individual species*
    black-browed, 562, 563, 567, 574, 578, 587–592, 795
    black-footed, 618
    Buller's, 590
    grey-headed, 562, 563, 567, 574, 578, 585, 587, 589–592
    Laysan, 618
    light-mantled sooty, 545, 546, 562, 567, 591
    royal, 561, 562, 567, 590
    shy, 618
    sooty, 546, 562, 582, 588, 590
    wandering, 546, 561, 562, 563, 566, 569, 579, 581, 582, 585, 588–590, 837, 838
    waved, 618
    yellow-nosed, 540
Algae, 109, 112, 119–120, 286, 315, 512, *see also individual organisms*
    benthic, marine, 381–390, 408, 409
    blue-green, 108, 129, 209, 309, 312, 325
    epiphytes, 290, 291, 293, 388, 390
    felts, *see* Lakes, phytobenthos
    freshwater, 171, 290
    ice-associated, 374, 377–381, 393, 396, 400, 408, 409, 633, 786, 796

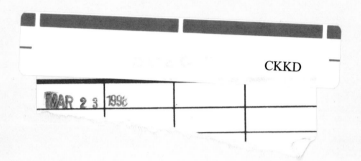